UNITED NATIONS PEACEKEEPING
1946–1967
DOCUMENTS AND COMMENTARY

UNITED NATIONS PEACEKEEPING

1946–1967

DOCUMENTS AND COMMENTARY

II
Asia

ROSALYN HIGGINS

M.A., LL.B. (Cantab.), J.S.D. (Yale)

Issued under the auspices of the
Royal Institute of International Affairs

OXFORD UNIVERSITY PRESS

LONDON   BOMBAY   KARACHI   KUALA LUMPUR

1970

*Oxford University Press, Ely House, London W.*1

GLASGOW NEW YORK TORONTO MELBOURNE WELLINGTON
CAPE TOWN SALISBURY IBADAN NAIROBI LUSAKA ADDIS ABABA
BOMBAY CALCUTTA MADRAS KARACHI LAHORE DACCA
KUALA LUMPUR SINGAPORE HONG KONG TOKYO

JX
1981
P7
H5
vol. 2

58659

PRINTED IN GREAT BRITAIN BY
EBENEZER BAYLIS AND SON, LIMITED
THE TRINITY PRESS, WORCESTER, AND LONDON

CONTENTS

Part 3

UNITED NATIONS ENFORCEMENT ACTION IN KOREA, 1950–3

Part 4

UNITED NATIONS MILITARY OBSERVER GROUP IN INDIA AND PAKISTAN (UNMOGIP), 1949–

Part 5

UNITED NATIONS INDIA–PAKISTAN OBSERVATION MISSION (UNIPOM), 1965–6

MAPS

ABBREVIATIONS

a.i.	Agenda item
ann.	annex
AJIL	*American Journal of International Law*
B.	*Bulletin*
BYIL	*British Yearbook of International Law*
GAOR	*General Assembly Official Records*
GLJ	*Georgetown Law Journal*
GOC	Good Offices Committee
ICJ Rep.	*International Court of Justice Reports*
ICRC	International Committee of the Red Cross
ICLQ	*International and Comparative Law Quarterly*
ILQ (later *ICLQ*)	*International Law Quarterly*
Int. Org.	*International Organization*
J.	*Journal*
ONUC	Organisation des Nations Unies au Congo
plen.	plenary
R.	*Review*
res.	resolution
s.	section
SCOR	*Security Council Official Records*
sess.	session
suppl.	supplement
UNCI	UN Commission for Indonesia
UNCOK	UN Commission on Korea
UNEF	UN Emergency Force
UNIPOM	UN India-Pakistan Observation Mission
UNKRA	UN Korean Reconstruction Agency
UNMOGIP	UN Military Observer Group in India and Pakistan
UNSF	UN Security Force in West Irian
UNTCOK	UN Temporary Commission on Korea
UNTEA	UN Temporary Executive Authority
UNTS	UN Treaty Series
YBUN	*Yearbook of the United Nations*

PREFACE AND ACKNOWLEDGEMENTS

THIS is the second of three volumes of documents and commentary on United Nations peacekeeping operations. The first volume dealt with UN actions in the Middle East: the Palestine Truce Supervision Operation (UNTSO), the Emergency Force in Egypt (UNEF), the observer group in Lebanon (UNOGIL), and the observer mission in the Yemen (UNYOM). This volume is concerned with UN operations in Asia, and covers the UN observers in Indonesia, the observers and security force (UNSF) in West Irian, enforcement action in Korea, and the observer groups in India and Pakistan (UNMOGIP and UNIPOM).

The third, and final, volume will deal with peacekeeping in the Balkans, Cyprus, and the Congo.

The concept of 'peacekeeping' is open to a variety of definitions, and it has been used in several ways by different persons writing on the subject. To some, peacekeeping is a broad concept, referring to the entire role of the UN in maintaining, or restoring, international peace. According to this definition, any book on peacekeeping must refer not only to UN Forces, but to investigation committees, special representatives of the Secretary-General, and diplomacy within the UN system. Others have suggested that peacekeeping is a term which has come to refer to UN Forces and observer groups which are operational on a territory with the consent of its government. Yet others have insisted that the term peacekeeping cannot include UN observers. There is, of course, no one 'correct' definition. All of these definitions, and some others besides, may be permissible according to the purpose of the particular study. In these three volumes UN peacekeeping has been taken to refer to operations in which personnel owing allegiance to the UN are engaged in military or para-military duties; and/or are carrying weapons for their own defence in the pursuit of duties designated by the UN as necessary for the maintenance or restoration of peace. These criteria have been taken as the relevant ones, whether or not the operation depends upon the consent of the government on whose territory it is taking place. Accordingly, this study deals with para-military actions such as ONUC in the Congo and UNEF in Egypt; with military operations such as the UN action against North Korea; and with the military observer groups which have served in the Lebanon, Kashmir, the Middle East, and elsewhere. It does not include separate examination of the diplomatic role of the Secretary-General, or of the various contributions to peace which have been made by his personal representatives or by special fact-finding commissions.

In view of the existing literature on UN peacekeeping, it may be appropriate to set out the reasons why it has been felt necessary to compile these volumes.

The existing literature may roughly be grouped in three categories. First, studies of particular operations—Korea, the Emergency Force in Egypt, the Congo operation—of which the studies by Burns and Heathcote, Poirier, Goodrich, and Gabriella Rosner are excellent examples. Second, studies such as those by Wainhouse or Ruth Russell, which seek to touch on all the UN's peacekeeping activities, if only briefly. And finally, studies by international lawyers such as Bowett and Seyersted drawing attention to the complex legal problems involved. The detailed studies of the first category are, by definition, limited to one or two operations; the broader-ranging studies of the second group are necessarily limited in depth; and the legal studies again either emphasize the better-known operations or concentrate upon a particular cluster of legal problems.

Moreover, though each of these studies is an extremely important contribution to the subject, none of them makes much use of primary source materials. There are references to, and occasionally brief quotations from, UN documents, but these are to support the author's text. There is no one single place to which the student of peacekeeping can turn for ready access to all the documentation. He has been obliged to flounder among the voluminous and unsifted UN documentation—with which he may not be familiar—and has had no guarantee that he has discovered all the relevant materials or that he has fully appreciated their implications. The events of May–June 1967 in the Middle East clearly illustrate the need that is felt for readily available documentation on UN peacekeeping. The public debates of these weeks also show the dangers of familiarity with only isolated documents, rather than the entire range of documentary evidence presented within its proper historical, political, and legal context.

For this reason, my aim in these volumes has been to provide a study of all the UN peacekeeping operations, giving the least known the same close attention as the best known, so that the reader who wishes to study the Balkans in 1949 or Kashmir in 1965 will, I trust, find as much pertinent material as the reader who may seek information on the Middle East or the Congo. I have also tried to ensure that the user of these volumes should be enabled to familiarize himself not only with the details of the UN's role in each country concerned, but also to pursue any interest he might have in, for example, the financing of UN peacekeeping, or the problems of command structure, in all the operations.

The arrangement has been devised to facilitate both comparative analysis and understanding of the significance of particular documents. While the volumes are broadly regional in scope, in each the main order is the order in time at which each operation started. But the documents comprising any one operation are not presented purely chronologically but are divided by categories which are common to all operations, such as the functions of the force, financing, relations between the UN and the host states, etc.

The main aim of the commentaries is to link the documents so as to present the entire story of each operation and to clarify points which are not wholly apparent in the UN texts. I have endeavoured to avoid using the commentaries as a vehicle for editorial opinion: the object is to clarify the differing viewpoints of the protagonists, not to pronounce in favour of any viewpoint. Only in two circumstances does the commentary go beyond this role. The first is in the historical introduction which prefaces each operation, demonstrating how the UN became involved. The second is to analyse points at issue in the case of documents which touch on problems of international law, and to refer the reader to relevant published work.

The materials themselves are limited to official UN documents and records of UN organs. I have been well aware of the dangers of limiting the source materials in this way, but the decision has been dictated by two compelling reasons. In the first place, if the aim were to provide a comprehensive survey of UN documentation on peacekeeping, the size of the endeavour would leave little space for government documents or quotations from books or articles. Second, language is inevitably a limiting factor: translation of documents from, for example, Russian or Arabic, would be a task of considerable magnitude, and would in any event entail an initial process of selection which I am not competent to conduct. However, all nations have the opportunity of presenting their viewpoint within the UN in one of the five major working languages. I have sought to offset any shortcomings of this decision by several means. Great pains have been taken to present all the different arguments raised, though I have relied on statements issued at the UN for this purpose. I have also endeavoured to give information which is relevant to an understanding of the documents, whether Attlee's celebrated flight to Washington in 1950, Eshkol's domestic position in early 1967, or Shastri's death in 1966. Reference is also made in footnotes to some of the more important national documents, and to various secondary sources. Finally, a bibliography of major books and articles is given at the end of each Part.

These bibliographies necessarily refer to particular operations. However, there are certain basic books, which do not fall readily within any one operation, to which any student of UN peacekeeping must refer, and I have made great use of the following: Lincoln Bloomfield and others, *International Military Forces* (1964); Derek Bowett, *United Nations Forces* (1964); Arthur Burns and Nina Heathcote, *Peacekeeping by UN Forces* (1963); Jack Citrin, *United Nations Peacekeeping Activities: a Case Study in Organizational Task Expansion* Denver, Col., 1965, mimeo.); Arthur Cox, *Prospects for Peacekeeping* (1967); Per Frydenberg, *Peacekeeping: Experience and Evaluation* (1964); Ruth Russell, *United Nations Experience with Military Forces: Political and Legal Aspects* (1964); Finn Seyersted, *United Nations Forces in the Law of Peace and War* (1966); John Stoessinger, *Financing the United Nations System* (1964); David Wainhouse, *International Peace Observation* (1966); and Oran Young, *Trends in International Peacekeeping* (Princeton, N.J., 1966).

A word needs to be said about my method of using the documents. Although I have avoided brief quotations, many documents are not reproduced in their entirety. This is because UN documents are frequently repetitive, and once the decision had been taken to present them under subject headings, rather than chronologically, it became apparent that not everything in a document was relevant to the particular heading. I can here only rely on the conventions of scholarship. All omissions are indicated in the customary manner. My selection has been made solely for the purpose of placing materials within the categories to which they logically belong. The reader may at all times confirm this by means of citations which appear at the end of every document and of the check-list of documents which appears in an appendix at the end of each Part. It remains to add that a few documents of major importance, which one has come to think of as an integral whole—such as the Secretary-General's report in 1958 of the experience of UNEF—are reproduced in their entirety, though small extracts from them may also appear under other headings where they naturally belong. Numbered footnotes are those of the Editor; footnotes bearing symbols are quoted from the document concerned. When the printed version of any UN document was not available at the time of writing, it was necessary to rely on the provisional or mimeographed versions, as has been indicated in citing the sources. These versions differ in minor respects from the ultimate, authorized record.

As the Contents page shows, the documents and accompanying commentary are divided throughout into twelve sections. Inevitably, there are certain difficult choices that have had to be made as to the section to which a particular document belongs. The effectiveness of a UN operation may in part depend upon whether satisfactory relations exist between the UN and the host country. Thus sometimes materials seem relevant both to section 9 and section 12. Equally, an operation may be hampered by lack of financial support, and the documentary materials again relate both to section 11 and to section 12. There are many other examples which could be given. I have sought, when faced with these choices, to place documents within those sections where their centre of gravity seems to fall. In each case, the text makes the position clear. In the final analysis, the detailed synopsis at the beginning of each Part, or the index, should lead the reader to them, but I have followed certain guidelines. In each Part section 12 on Implementation covers matters which have not fallen under the previous sections, though cross-references are provided to these where they are relevant. The great bulk of field reports to the UN (Chief of Command reports, etc.) fall within this section, except in so far as they dealt with matters specifically enumerated in sections 5–11. Agreements made between the UN and the nations providing forces or observers will always be found in section 8, as will treatment of claims for compensation for death or injury. Directives and instructions issued by the UN to its observers or forces fall under section 6, as does the question of jurisdiction over offences by UN para-military personnel. Status of Forces Agreements are examined within the framework of section 9.

It remains to explain that throughout I have sought to do more than merely provide the formal documents. Thus the examination of relations between the UN and a host state is by no means confined to a reproduction of the relevant Status of Forces Agreement; other documents and the commentary trace the ups and downs of the relationship. I have attempted to illustrate and explain what really happened, what difficulties arose, and what understandings were reached.

In these endeavours I have been greatly aided by many people, to whom I would here like to express my thanks. This study has been financed by the Carnegie Endowment for International Peace, for whose generosity and patience as this project expanded—and expanded still further—I am most grateful. The support of the Carnegie Endowment has been far more than financial: the great personal interest which Joe Johnson and Anne Winslow have shown in this venture, and their readiness to join in seeking the answers to particularly knotty points, has been a constant source of encouragement to me. Various officials in the UN Secretariat have given me generous assistance. Brian Urquhart has been extraordinarily kind in clarifying matters for me on which the documents were obscure, and in responding to queries to which no answers could be found in London. I am very grateful that he should have found time to help me when he has so many pressing and important duties. George Sherry has also been extremely helpful in answering, from UN headquarters, a stream of queries flowing from my pen. Blaine Sloan, David Ho, and Oscar Schachter have helped me greatly with information relating to legal points which have arisen, and the readiness with which they have answered my questions has been most helpful. And Bruce Turner has patiently explained to me some of the more baffling aspects of UN accounting procedure.

I also wish to record my thanks to Mr H. S. Vahali, of the High Commission of India in London for so readily and efficiently answering questions about the location of UN observer posts in India. Sir Edward Lambert, formerly UK Deputy Consul-General in Batavia, has been most courteous in responding to my request for information on certain matters relating to the UN observers in Indonesia.

Nor can I allow the debt which I owe the London UN Information Centre to go unacknowledged. It is to Margaret McAfee that I have gone with my most intractable problems, with demands for the most recondite documents. I thank her for her efficient and good-humoured assistance, and also William Henson for his help. Sture Linner and George Ivan Smith have each, in turn, greatly facilitated my researches in a variety of ways.

James Knott, of the International Information Center on Peacekeeping Operations, has been a constant source of information on the size, national composition, and logistics of UN Forces. Arthur Hillis, formerly of the United Kingdom Mission to the UN, has advised me on technical questions relating to the financing of certain UN operations. And Donald Watt has cast a historian's critical eye over the historical introduction to each Part.

The entire manuscript has been read by Eli Lauterpacht of Trinity College, Cambridge; Geoffrey Goodwin of the London School of Economics; and Herbert Nicholas of New College, Oxford. The extraordinary care with which they have read this work and their comments and proposals have been invaluable. I have adopted many of their suggestions and am deeply grateful for the care they have taken and the interest they have shown.

In Chatham House many people have lent their labours to this venture. The members of the Library staff under the direction of Dorothy Hamerton have all been immensely helpful, and June Wells and Angela Williams have, successfully, borne the brunt of my insatiable appetite for UN documents. Their efficiency and enthusiasm are much appreciated. I would also like to thank the Press Library, and in particular Elizabeth Campbell and Susan Boyde. Bridget Martyn took the roughest edges off parts of this volume, and to her I extend my thanks. My thanks also go to Rena Fenteman, who has helped me with her knowledgeable comments and editorial advice on some parts of this volume; the overall editing was done by Hermia Oliver, who has brought to it her customary expertise and meticulousness. I have relied on her editorial experience and judgement, and have benefited greatly from her considerable labours. A special expression of appreciation is due to my secretary, Rene Landman: she has coped valiantly with the many secretarial problems that arise in preparing a study of this sort, and has somehow transformed a myriad of instructions, clippings, references, and comments into a coherent manuscript. Above all, she has helped to keep both of our heads (just) above the sea of documents. Nor should the contribution of Maggie Lim be underestimated, for she has, with speed and good humour, done all the photocopying which this volume has entailed.

Finally, I must thank my husband, Terence Higgins, whose tolerance, forbearance, and encouragement has contributed so much to this work.

While I am in the debt of all these persons, none of them is of course in any way responsible for any shortcomings or errors in this book, nor do they necessarily share the views expressed therein.

R.H.

London, June 1969

Part 1

UNITED NATIONS
OBSERVERS IN INDONESIA
1947–50

1. INTRODUCTION (p. 3)
POLITICAL institutions under Japanese occupation; the end of World War II and the establishment of the KNIP; Sukarno and Hatta proclaim Indonesian independence; problems for the British military authorities; negotiations between Sukarno and the Dutch; Britain assailed by Russia in the Security Council; the Linggadjati Agreement signed in March 1947 on the basis of conflicting interpretations; Dutch-Indonesian relations deteriorate and disorders occur; the first Dutch 'police action' of November 1947; the Security Council calls for a cease-fire and establishes a Commission of career consuls in Batavia.

2. ENABLING RESOLUTIONS AND VOTING (p. 9)
Security Council resolutions of August 1947 calling for a cease-fire; establishing the career Consular Commission and tendering good offices; resolution of November 1947 extending the authority of the Good Offices Committee (GOC); resolution of February 1948 on the *Renville* Truce Agreement; resolution of July 1948 on the observation of the *Renville* Agreement; resolutions of December 1948 on the second Dutch 'police action'; resolution of January 1949 reconstituting the GOC as the UN Commission for Indonesia and proposing a political solution; resolutions of September and October 1949 on the financing of UNCI.

3. FUNCTIONS AND MANDATE (p. 20)
Role of military attaché in assisting the career consular representatives; reporting and cease-fire tasks of the Consular Commission; functions of the military observers under the *Renville* Truce Agreement; mandate of the GOC and its use of the observers; UNCI employs the observers to assist in disengagement; tasks under Regulations adopted to govern implementation of cease-fire arrangements.

4. CONSTITUTIONAL BASIS (p. 25)
Absence of specific Charter basis in resolutions; controversy as to the relevance of Chapter VII; Netherlands rests on Article 2(7) and denies applicability of Article 2(4); Australia contends that the Security Council should act under Article 40; other members point to Articles 33 and 36.

5. POLITICAL CONTROL (p. 32)
Ultimate exercise of control by Security Council over the Consular Commission, the GOC, and the UNCI; role of the Secretary-General.

6. ADMINISTRATIVE AND MILITARY CONTROL (p. 33)
Decentralized authority for administrative and military matters; procedures under the Consular Commission; new arrangements made after the *Renville* Truce Agreement; the Military

Executive Board; reduction and relocation of observer teams after the Round Table Conference.

7. COMPOSITION AND SIZE (p. 34)
Nationalities and members in the first phase; and in the second phase.

8. RELATIONS WITH CONTRIBUTING STATES (p. 38)
Dual role of Consular Commission observers as UN agents and government personnel; similar dual role of the GOC; absence of any formal agreements.

9. RELATIONS WITH HOST STATES (p. 39)
Dutch attitudes to Security Council's jurisdiction; disagreement with Consular Commission over van Mook line; the GOC seeks to clarify its relations with the Netherlands and Indonesia; the GOC not invited to Bandung constitutional conference called by the Netherlands; Dutch reaction to US–Australian initiatives on the GOC; Netherlands withdraws co-operation during second 'police action'; predicament of military observers; Security Council calls for the release of political prisoners; permission delayed for return of UN observers to the field; persisting difficulties in 1949 in the relationship between Netherlands and UNCI.

10. RELATIONS WITH OTHER STATES INVOLVED (p. 58)
Attitude of Soviet Union to UN role in Dutch-Indonesian hostilities.

11. FINANCE (p. 60)
Initial converting of expenses of observers by government concerned; Dutch cover most costs of GOC; evolving concept of UN financial responsibility; Secretary-General asks to make funds available for UNCI; Security Council resolutions of September and October 1949; costs for 1949–51.

12. IMPLEMENTATION (p. 61)
Attempts of the Consular Commission to establish a cease-fire; dispute over the Security Council's orders and the drawing of the van Mook Line; the GOC given a role beyond mere reporting and holds the *Renville* Truce Conference in January 1948; the *Renville* Truce Agreement and the GOC's list of suggested principles for a political settlement; military aspects of Truce in hands of GOC Security Committee; Netherlands holds a conference at Bandung and the Indonesian government protests; the Critchley-DuBois proposals and the suspension of political negotiations; the situation deteriorates and the Dutch embark upon the second 'police action'; opposition of the GOC and the Security Council; the UNCI comes into being and plays a central role in securing agreement to a Round Table Conference; the Republican government resumes its functions; progress made in achieving military stability and the transfer of sovereignty to Indonesia; the role of the observers; the repatriation of the Netherlands army.

13. ANNEXES (p. 87)
  A. Checklist of Documents (p. 87)
  B. Bibliography (p. 88)

I

INTRODUCTION

AT the advent of World War II Dutch rule over the Indonesian archipelago, stretching from Sumatra to Western New Guinea, had run for nearly three and a half centuries. During the war Indonesia fell under Japanese occupation. Certain nationalist leaders in Indonesia, including Sukarno, worked with the Japanese during the occupation.[1] On 7 August 1945 the Supreme Commander of the Japanese Expeditionary Force, Southern Regions, had permitted the creation of the Indonesian Independence Preparatory Committee (Panitia Persiapan Kemerdekaan Indonesia) to prepare the transfer of authority from Japanese military rule to an independent Indonesia. Sukarno was chairman of the Committee, and Mohammed Hatta vice-chairman. On 15 August 1945, following the Allied use of atomic bombs on Nagasaki and Hiroshima, Japan capitulated. At the end of August the Preparatory Committee was replaced by the Komité Nasional Indonesia Pusat (Central Indonesian National Committee), known as KNIP, which was composed of 135 prominent nationalists. KNIP later established a Working Committee under the socialist Soetan Sjahrir, who had refused to work with the Japanese. Immediately after Japan's surrender Sukarno and Hatta had proclaimed the independence of Indonesia. They established law and order in Djakarta (Batavia) and other towns, used Indonesian civil servants who had gained administrative experience during the war, and organized an armed force—the Tentara Nasional Indonesia (Indonesian National Army).

From the Allies' point of view, it was essential to decide within whose military jurisdiction Indonesia should lie. It had originally been under that of General MacArthur, who had captured Dutch New Guinea, Morotai in the Northern Moluccas, and certain parts of eastern Borneo. However, at Potsdam, in July 1945, the Netherlands East Indies were transferred to Admiral Mountbatten's South-East Asian Command. The Dutch wartime Cabinet of P. S. Gerbrandy was divided on this: Gerbrandy himself approved the British jurisdiction, feeling that Britain as a colonial power would understand Holland's problems, and agreeing with the view that an Indonesian base (rather than operations from SEAC's headquarters in Ceylon) was needed in order to retake Singapore and the Malay Peninsula. The Foreign Minister, E. van Kleffens, and the Minister for Colonies, H. van Mook, however, regarded American military jurisdiction as

---

[1] See W. H. Elsbree, *Japan's Role in Southeast Asian Nationalist Movements 1940–5* (1953) and M. A. Aziz, *Japan's Colonialism and Indonesia* (1955).

3

preferable, believing that SEAC had neither the personnel nor the equipment to make its military jurisdiction effective.[2]

When Lt-General Sir Philip Christison came out as commander to the Allied Forces in the Netherlands East Indies, he was asked what would happen in areas outside the limited enclaves that his forces were to occupy. He replied that, until the Netherlands Indies Civil Administration arrived, 'things will have to go on as they are'.[3] The Republican leadership took this to mean *de facto* recognition, and the phrase was greatly criticized in the Netherlands, where it was read as a betrayal by an ally. The Dutch also felt that the British military authorities greatly underestimated the urgency with which it was essential for the Netherlands Indies Civil Administration to re-establish control; and the resentment of Dutch internees in Indonesia and Republican nationalists alike was aroused when British commanders authorized the use of Japanese to maintain order in certain areas. Meanwhile, Sukarno protested against the arrival of two companies of Dutch combat troops, and warned that this would jeopardize Republican co-operation with the British military authorities. For their part, the Dutch let it be known that they viewed the Republic as a Japanese puppet, and that while they would talk with certain Indonesian nationalists, they would not talk with those they deemed Japanese collaborators. The British, wishing to avoid a repetition of the Greek situation, found themselves torn between their Dutch allies and the Indonesian nationalists. Mountbatten, and in turn, Ernest Bevin, in consequence urged direct negotiations between the parties.

On 9 November 1945 Sukarno asked Sjahrir to form a Cabinet; and Sjahrir chose persons who had resisted the Japanese invasion. The Netherlands government responded by making certain proposals for a predominantly Indonesian government, with a Council of Ministers under a Governor-General representing the Dutch Crown. As this proposal did not acknowledge the existence of the Republic, it was rejected by the Republican authorities. Subsequent negotiations between van Mook and Sjahrir broke down, with the latter refusing to agree to the return of Dutch troops before the Republic had been recognized. While the Netherlands parliamentary opposition portrayed negotiations as appeasement, Bevin pressed for their continuation. After a meeting with Dutch Cabinet members at Chequers on 28 December, it was announced on 19 January 1946 that the British diplomat Sir Archibald Clark Kerr (now raised to the peerage as Lord Inverchapel) would go to Batavia as a special ambassador to assist in negotiations between the Dutch and Indonesians.

However, Britain found herself assailed in the Security Council by the Ukraine SSR, which accused her of using Japanese forces in military actions against the local Indonesian population. This was widely regarded as a counter-move engineered by the Soviet Union in response to a protest from Iran at the continued

[2] I have throughout this section relied heavily on Part I of Alastair Taylor's admirable study, *Indonesian Independence and the United Nations* (1960). This book is indispensable to any study of the Indonesian question, and the reader will find no better introduction to the UN's role than its first forty pages. The writer wishes to record her indebtedness to Professor Taylor's work.

[3] Taylor, pp. 7–8.

presence of Soviet troops in Persia. Vyshinsky claimed that British and Japanese troops were attempting to suppress the Indonesian nationalist movement, and that a commission composed of China, the Netherlands, the United Kingdom, the USSR, and the United States should carry out an on-the-spot inquiry and report to the Security Council.[4] Britain supported[5] the Dutch view[6] that this was a matter falling essentially within Dutch domestic jurisdiction; and the fact that negotiations were beginning was ample proof that there was no threat to international peace. The United States thought that nothing would be gained by sending a commission,[7] and the French thought that the talks in Batavia represented the proper approach.[8] The Ukrainian draft resolution to establish the commission of inquiry received, on 13 February 1946, only the support of the USSR and Poland. There the matter rested.

Meanwhile the Dutch–Indonesian talks had begun in Batavia, in the presence of Lord Inverchapel. Detailed proposals and counter-proposals were made,[9] but the talks ultimately broke down on three main points. The Netherlands government was now willing to concede the Republic's *de facto* authority in Java and Madura, but not in Sumatra, where it did not believe that Republican control was in fact exercised. The Sjahrir government felt unable to make any concession on this point. The Republicans also insisted that any agreement should be in the form of a treaty, thus testifying to the Republic's status in the creation of the sovereign state of Indonesia; whereas the Dutch argued that under Netherlands law they could conclude treaties only with foreign independent powers. Further, the Indonesians wanted the agreement to provide for international arbitration, but the Netherlands government,[10] seeing this as an opening for international intervention, would consider only a conciliation commission. A moderate and not unsympathetic statement by Professor J. H. Logemann to the Dutch second Chamber on the breakdown of the talks subjected the government to strong attacks from the right wing.

After Dutch general elections held on 17 May 1946, a new coalition Catholic-Labour government was formed, with Dr Louis Beel as Prime Minister and Dr J. A. Jonkman as Minister of Overseas Territories. This new Cabinet was not installed until 2 July, and in the meantime Professor W. Schermerhorn and Dr W. Drees, who headed the government created in 1945, continued to provide a caretaker government. This caretaker government resumed talks with the Indonesian Republicans. In July, following a suggestion of van Mook, the new Dutch government held a conference of representatives from Bangka, Billiton, Borneo, East Indonesia and the Riouw archipelago to discuss a federal United States of Indonesia.[11] The Republicans denounced the participants as puppets. Two further, and similar, conferences were held.

On 2 September 1946 the Dutch government formed a Commission-General

---

[4] *SCOR*, 1st yr, 14th mtg, p. 206. [5] Ibid. 11th mtg, p. 180. [6] Ibid. 15th mtg, p. 219.
[7] Ibid. 16th mtg, pp. 235–7. [8] Ibid. 17th mtg, pp. 242–4. [9] See Taylor, pp. 19–25.
[10] At the time of these negotiations (Feb.–Apr. 1946) Schermerhorn was Prime Minister, Logemann Minister of Overseas Territories, and van Mook Lieutenant Governor-General.
[11] For details of the federal theme, see A. Arthur Schiller, *The Formation of Federal Indonesia 1945–49* (1955).

to prepare a political structure for the Netherlands East Indies. This Commission was under the chairmanship of the former Prime Minister, Schermerhorn, and included van Mook. Talks began with the Republicans on 7 October, under the chairmanship of a British intermediary, Lord Killearn. On 15 November 1946 sufficient progress had been made for the parties to initial the Linggadjati Agreement. The text of the Agreement follows:

Preamble—The Netherlands Government, represented by the Commission-General for the Netherlands Indies, and the Government of the Republic of Indonesia, represented by the Indonesian delegation, moved by a sincere desire to ensure good relations between the peoples of the Netherlands and Indonesia in new forms of voluntary co-operation which offer the best guarantee for sound and strong development of both countries in the future and which make it possible to give a new foundation to the relationship between the two peoples; agreed as follows and will submit this agreement at the shortest possible notice for the approval of the respective parliaments:

Article 1—The Netherlands Government recognizes the Government of the Republic of Indonesia as exercising *de facto* authority over Java, Madura and Sumatra. The areas occupied by Allied or Netherlands forces shall be included gradually, through mutual co-operation, in Republican territory. To this end, the necessary measures shall at once be taken in order that this inclusion shall be completed at the latest on the date mentioned in Article 12.

Article 2—The Netherlands Government and the Government of the Republic shall co-operate in the rapid formation of a sovereign democratic State on a federal basis to be called the United States of Indonesia.

Article 3—The United States of Indonesia shall comprise the entire territory of the Netherlands Indies with the provision, however, that in case the population of any territory, after due consultation with the other territories, should decide by democratic process that they are not, or not yet, willing to join the United States of Indonesia, they can establish a special relationship for such a territory to the United States of Indonesia and to the Kingdom of the Netherlands.

Article 4—The component parts of the United States of Indonesia shall be the Republic of Indonesia, Borneo, and the Great East without prejudice to the right of the population of any territory to decide by democratic process that its position in the United States of Indonesia shall be arranged otherwise.

Without derogation of the provisions of Article 3 and of the first paragraph of this Article, the United States of Indonesia may make special arrangements concerning the territory of its capital.

Article 5—The constitution of the United States of Indonesia shall be determined by a constituent assembly composed of the democratically nominated representatives of the Republic and of the other future partners of the United States of Indonesia to which the following paragraph of this Article shall apply.

Both parties shall consult each other on the method of participation in this constituent assembly by the Republic of Indonesia, by the territories not under the authority of the Republic and by the groups of the population not, or insufficiently, represented with due observance of the responsibility of the Netherlands Government and the Government of the Republic, respectively.

Article 6—To promote the joint interests of the Netherlands and Indonesia, the Netherlands Government and the Government of the Republic of Indonesia shall co-operate in the establishment of a Netherlands Indonesian Union by which the Kingdom of the Netherlands, comprising the Netherlands, the Netherlands Indies, Surinam and Curaçao, shall be converted into the said Union consisting on the one hand of the Kingdom of the Netherlands, comprising the Netherlands, Surinam and Curaçao, and on the other hand the United States of Indonesia.

The foregoing paragraph does not exclude the possibility of a further arrangement of the relations between the Netherlands, Surinam and Curaçao.

Article 7—A. The Netherlands Indonesian Union shall have its own organs to promote the joint interests of the Kingdom of the Netherlands and the United States of Indonesia.

B. These organs shall be formed by the Governments of the Kingdom of the Netherlands and the United States of Indonesia and, if necessary, by the parliaments of those countries.

C. The joint interests shall be considered to be co-operation on foreign relations, defence and, as far as necessary, finance as well as subjects of an economic or cultural nature.

Article 8—The King (Queen) of the Netherlands shall be at the head of the Netherlands Indonesian Union. Decrees and resolutions concerning the joint interests shall be issued by the organs of the Union in the King's (Queen's) name.

Article 9—In order to promote the interests of the United States of Indonesia in the Netherlands and of the Kingdom of the Netherlands in Indonesia, a High Commissioner shall be appointed by the respective Governments.

Article 10—Statutes of the Netherlands Indonesian Union shall, furthermore, contain provisions regarding:

A. Safeguarding of the rights of both parties towards one another and guarantees for the fulfilment of their mutual obligations.

B. Mutual exercise of civil rights by Netherlands and Indonesian citizens.

C. Regulations containing provisions in case no agreement can be reached by the organs of the Union.

D. Regulation of the manner and conditions of the assistance to be given by the services of the Kingdom of the Netherlands to the United States of Indonesia as long as the services of the latter are not, or are insufficiently, organized; and

E. Safeguarding in both parts of the Union of the fundamental human rights and liberties referred to in the Charter of the United Nations Organization.

Article 11—A. The Statutes of the Netherlands Indonesian Union shall be drafted by a conference of representatives of the Kingdom of the Netherlands and the future United States of Indonesia.

B. The statutes shall come into effect after approval by the respective parliaments.

Article 12—The Netherlands Government and the Government of the Republic of Indonesia shall endeavour to establish the United States of Indonesia and the Netherlands Indonesian Union before January 1, 1949.

Article 13—The Netherlands Government shall forthwith take the necessary steps in order to obtain the admission of the United States of Indonesia as a Member of the United Nations Organization immediately after the formation of the Netherlands Indonesian Union.

Article 14—The Government of the Republic of Indonesia recognizes the claims of all non-Indonesians to the restoration of their rights and the restitution of their goods as far as they are exercised or to be found in the territory over which it exercises *de facto* authority. A joint commission will be set up to effect this restoration and restitution.

Article 15—In order to reform the Government of the Indies in such a way that its composition and procedure shall conform as closely as possible to the recognition of the Republic of Indonesia and to its projected constitutional structure, the Netherlands Government, pending the realization of the United States of Indonesia and of the Netherlands Indonesian Union, shall forthwith initiate the necessary legal measures to adjust the constitutional and international position of the Kingdom of the Netherlands to the new situation.

Article 16—Directly after the conclusion of this agreement, both parties shall proceed to reduce their armed forces. They will consult together concerning the extent and rate of this reduction and their co-operation in military matters.

Article 17—A. For the co-operation between the Netherlands Government and the Government of the Republic contemplated in this agreement, an organization shall be called into existence of delegations to be appointed by each of the two Governments with a joint secretariat.

B. The Netherlands Government and the Government of the Republic of Indonesia shall settle by arbitration any dispute which might arise from this agreement and which cannot be solved by joint consultation in conference between those delegations. In that case a chairman of another nationality with a deciding vote shall be appointed by agreement between the delegations or, if such agreement cannot be reached, by the President of the International Court of Justice.

Article 18—This agreement shall be drawn up in the Netherlands and Indonesian languages. Both texts shall have equal authority.   [Taylor, *Indonesian Independence*, p. 464.]

It will be seen that the Agreement was far from precise.[12] It was strongly opposed among conservative circles in the Netherlands. The Commission-General provided an 'Elucidation' for the benefit of the Dutch second Chamber, and the draft Agreement was eventually approved in the light of this Elucidation. The Agreement was in due course signed by the parties on 25 March 1947—but on the basis of different, and irreconcilable, interpretations. Above all, while the Netherlands now recognized the *de facto* authority of the Republic in Java, Madura, and Sumatra, 'where did *de jure* authority reside? As a corollary, what was the status of the Agreement itself? Was it only a "programme of principles", a political instrument to indicate the lines along which the constitutional conversion of the Kingdom should take place; or was it an international accord between two sovereign States?'[13]

The signing of the Agreement was followed by recognition of the Republic's *de facto* status by the United Kingdom, the United States, Australia, China, India, and a number of Arab states. But a fundamental dispute soon emerged between the Netherlands and the Republic over the attempt by the latter to establish foreign relations, which the Dutch regarded as going well beyond the proper bounds of *de facto* status. There were arguments also over the restoration of Dutch property under Article 14. Relations deteriorated still further when a new memorandum of the Commission-General called for the establishment of a joint Directorate of Internal Security to take over policing tasks from the Republican military organizations. The Republic was also, in effect, asked to recognize the separate authority of East Indonesia and West Borneo, which territories should directly participate in discussions on the implementation of the Linggadjati Agreement. These proposals were rejected. Further counter-proposals and exchanges[14] failed.

Sjahrir resigned on 27 June 1947, and the situation worsened: disorders broke out, and the Netherlands demanded, in an ultimatum expiring at midnight on 16 July, an end to the destruction of foreign properties and the food blockade of Dutch-occupied areas. The Republican authorities agreed to order a cease-fire if the Dutch would do likewise, but continued to refuse to accept a mixed police force. On 20 July the Dutch government announced that it no longer regarded itself as bound by the Linggadjati Agreement, though its aim was now to restore order so that the programme of the Agreement could be implemented. That night, a Dutch 'police action' began in Java and Sumatra. In a letter to the Secretary-General (S/426) the Dutch government explained that its action was

[12] For a detailed account of the major ambiguities, see Taylor, pp. 30–3 and Ch. 11.
[13] Ibid. pp. 31–2.   [14] Ibid. pp. 35–8.

undertaken with reluctance, because the Republican government was incapable of maintaining a sufficient degree of law and order for the Linggadjati principles to be put into effect. The Indian government requested that the Security Council should end the military situation by taking action under Chapter VI of the Charter (S/447); and the Australian government went further by invoking Chapter VII of the Charter and asking the Security Council to call upon the parties as a 'provisional measure' to end the 'threat to peace' (S/449). This was the first invocation of the UN.

On 1 August the Security Council called for a cease-fire and the settlement of the dispute by arbitration or other peaceful means. Fighting continued, and the Soviet Union proposed that a Commission of all Security Council members be set up to supervise the cease-fire. China and the United Kingdom abstained on this proposal, the United States supported it—but it was vetoed by France. Instead, a resolution was adopted (S/525(I)) establishing a Commission of those members of the Security Council who had career consuls in Batavia. This Commission at its first meeting requested the Powers concerned to make available their military attachés. The UN thus had its first 'military observers'— albeit with an anomalous and unclear status; and the Organization was to remain intimately involved in the Indonesian question for the next three years.

In the next section are reproduced those resolutions which trace the developing role of the Security Council, the bodies which it established, and the military observers who served them.

2

ENABLING RESOLUTIONS AND VOTING

AT ITS 173rd meeting the Security Council adopted a resolution on the hostilities between the Netherlands and Indonesia.

The Security Council,
Noting with concern the hostilities in progress between the armed forces of the Netherlands and the Republic of Indonesia,
Calls upon the parties:
(*a*) To cease hostilities forthwith, and
(*b*) To settle their dispute by arbitration or by other peaceful means and keep the Security Council informed about the progress of the settlement. [*SC res. S/459, 1 Aug. 1947.*]

This draft resolution was voted on only in parts; no vote was taken on it as a whole. The text was based on a version originally submitted by Australia, the references to Articles 39 and 40 of the Charter and Article 17 of the Linggadjati Agreement having been deleted at the suggestion of the United States.

It rapidly became apparent that it was necessary to supervise the cease-fire.

There was no clear demarcation line, and Dutch 'mopping up' and Indonesian 'people's defence' operations were continuing. Australia called for a commission to report on developments (S/488). The Netherlands indicated that this would be to give the Security Council jurisdiction which it did not possess, and suggested that instead a report could be made by the career consuls in Batavia. An Australian-Chinese draft incorporated this suggestion, and was adopted on 25 August 1947:

Whereas the Security Council on 1 August 1947 called upon the Netherlands and the Republic of Indonesia to cease hostilities forthwith,

Whereas communications have been received from the Governments of the Netherlands and of the Republic of Indonesia advising that orders have been given for the cessation of hostilities,

Whereas it is desirable that steps should be taken to avoid disputes and friction relating to the observance of the cease-fire orders, and to create conditions which will facilitate agreement between the parties,

The Security Council

1. *Notes with satisfaction* the steps taken by the parties to comply with its resolution 27 (1947) of 1 August 1947;

2. *Notes with satisfaction* the statement issued by the Netherlands Government on 11 August 1947, in which it affirms its intention to organize a sovereign, democratic United States of Indonesia in accordance with the purposes of the Linggadjati Agreement;

3. *Notes* that the Netherlands Government intends immediately to request the career consuls stationed in Batavia jointly to report on the present situation in the Republic of Indonesia;

4. *Notes* that the Government of the Republic of Indonesia has requested appointment by the Security Council of a commission of observers;

5. *Requests* the Governments members of the Council which have career consular representatives in Batavia to instruct them to prepare jointly for the information and guidance of the Security Council reports on the situation in the Republic of Indonesia following the resolution of the Council of 1 August 1947, such reports to cover the observance of the cease-fire orders and the conditions prevailing in areas under military occupation or from which armed forces now in occupation may be withdrawn by agreement between the parties;

6. *Requests* the Governments of the Netherlands and of the Republic of Indonesia to grant to the representatives referred to in paragraph 5 all facilities necessary for the effective fulfilment of their mission;

7. *Resolves* to consider the matter further should the situation require. [*SC res. S/525 (I)*, *25 Aug. 1947.*]

VOTING: 7–0, with 4 abstentions.
 In favour: Australia, Belgium, Brazil, China, France, Syria, USA.
  Against: None.
Abstaining: Colombia, Poland, UK, USSR.

The establishment of the career consuls as a commission of observers was strongly opposed by the Soviet Union, which had urged instead the establishment of a commission of all Security Council members. A resolution which Gromyko had advanced to this effect failed, curiously enough, because of the negative vote of France. The United States supported the Soviet proposal, while China and the United Kingdom abstained. Commenting on draft resolution S/525, the Russian representative said:

First of all, let us see whose consuls are in Indonesia. In Indonesia there is a United States, a French, a United Kingdom, a Chinese, and Australian and I think a Swiss consul (Switzerland is not a Member of the United Nations). Among the five eligible so-called 'career' consuls therefore there are United Kingdom, French and United States consuls. We all know —I think that we can speak frankly in discussing this and all other questions—the attitude adopted by the United Kingdom in the Indonesian question. There is no secret about the position of the French Government in this matter. Something is also known about the position of the United States. Thus, out of the five consuls in Indonesia we find three whose opinions and actions, in the view of the USSR delegation, cannot be relied upon or considered to reflect in any way the Security Council's opinion or that of the countries represented on the Security Council. They will reflect the opinion of three countries, namely the United States, the United Kingdom and France and not the opinion of the countries represented on the Security Council. . . .

I need hardly say that this resolution and the Chinese amendments submitted at the one hundred and eighty-seventh meeting of the Security Council contain a series of further unacceptable suggestions. For instance, it is stated in paragraph 2 that the Security Council notes with satisfaction the statement issued by the Netherlands Government on 11 August; in that statement the Security Council is slandered and abused for having undertaken the consideration of the Indonesian question, but in reply the Council notes the statement with satisfaction. The same applies to paragraph 3, which states that the Security Council notes that the Netherlands Government intends to request the career consuls stationed in Batavia to report on the situation in Indonesia. The proposal of the Netherlands Government however was made in order to by-pass the Security Council and the United Nations. [*SCOR, 2nd yr, 193rd mtg,* pp. 2180 and 2181.]

Two further resolutions were passed by the Security Council at this time. S/525(II) provided for the establishment of a Committee of Good Offices (referred to as the GOC), and S/525(III) reiterated the Council's call for a cease-fire:

The Security Council
Resolves to tender its good offices to the parties in order to assist in the pacific settlement of their dispute in accordance with sub-paragraph (*b*) of its resolution 27 (1947) of 1 August 1947. The Council expresses its readiness, if the parties so request, to assist in the settlement through a committee of the Council consisting of three members of the Council, each party selecting one and the third to be designated by the two so selected. [*SC res. S/525* (II), *25 Aug. 1947.*]

VOTING: 8–0.
 In favour: Belgium, Brazil, China, France, UK, USA.
 Against: None.
Abstaining: Poland, Syria, USSR.

The Security Council,
Taking into consideration that military operations are being continued on the territory of the Republic of Indonesia,
 1. *Reminds* the Government of the Netherlands and the Government of the Republic of Indonesia of its resolution 27 (1947) of 1 August 1947 concerning the cease-fire order and peaceful settlement of their dispute;
 2. *Calls upon* the Government of the Netherlands and the Government of the Republic of Indonesia to adhere strictly to the recommendation of the Security Council of 1 August 1947. [*SC res. S/525 (III), 26 Aug. 1947.*]

VOTING: 10–0.
Abstaining: UK.

In November the authority of the GOC was extended, and both the Consular Commission and its military assistants were requested to make their services available to it.

The Security Council,
Having received and taken note of the report of the Consular Commission dated 14 October 1947, indicating that the Council's resolution 27 (1947) of 1 August 1947 relating to the cessation of hostilities has not been fully effective,
Having taken note that, according to the report, no attempt was made by either side to come to an agreement with the other about the means of giving effect to that resolution,
   1. *Calls upon* the parties concerned forthwith to consult with each other, either directly or through the Committee of Good Offices, as to the means to be employed in order to give effect to the cease-fire resolution, and, pending agreement, to cease any activities or incitement to activities which contravene that resolution, and to take appropriate measures for safeguarding life and property;
   2. *Requests* the Committee of Good Offices to assist the parties in reaching agreement on an arrangement which will ensure the observance of the cease-fire resolution;
   3. *Requests* the Consular Commission, together with its military assistants, to make its services available to the Committee of Good Offices;
   4. *Advises* the parties concerned, the Committee of Good Offices and the Consular Commission that its resolution 27 (1947) of 1 August 1947 should be interpreted as meaning that the use of the armed forces of either party by hostile action to extend its control over territory not occupied by it on 4 August 1947 is inconsistent with Council resolution 27 (1947);
   5. *Invites* the parties, should it appear that some withdrawals of armed forces are necessary, to conclude between them as soon as possible the agreements referred to in its resolution 30 (1947) of 25 August 1947.   [*SC res. S/597, 1 Nov. 1947.*]

VOTING: 7–1.
   In favour: Australia, Belgium, Brazil, China, France, UK, USA.
   Against: Poland.
Abstaining: Colombia, Syria, USSR.

The Soviet Union indicated the grounds for her dislike of the resolution:

   The Security Council has already adopted two resolutions regarding the cessation of military operations; neither of these resolutions has been implemented. Why? Because the Netherlands troops have not been withdrawn to their previously held positions and have continued military operations.
   That is why, in the first place, I consider this draft to be entirely unsatisfactory, weak and inadequate. Secondly, the penultimate paragraph of the Sub-Committee's draft contains the words: 'advises the parties concerned . . .', which show that an extension of control over the territories that were not occupied on 4 August is incompatible with the resolution of the Security Council. This means that territories which had been seized by the Netherlands troops prior to 4 August may be considered to be under the legitimate control of the Netherlands authorities.
   In other words, this legalizes in fact the control exercised by the Netherlands authorities and Netherlands High Command over territories that were occupied by Netherlands troops on 4 August 1947. Of course, it may be said that there is no direct mention of this in the paragraph in question. It is true that the paragraph does not say so explicitly, but that is how it may be interpreted. This is another serious defect of the Sub-Committee's resolution. For this reason I cannot agree with the resolution and cannot support it.
   The representative of China, who praised the resolution, pointed out that it was a logical development of the decisions already taken by the Security Council. I must say that the Chinese representative is right to a certain extent in holding that this resolution is a logical

development of the decisions that were previously taken by the Security Council. However, the decisions taken by the Security Council were ineffective, inadequate and weak, practically exonerating the Netherlands authorities and inadequately defending the lawful and essential rights of the Indonesians.

All these previous decisions failed to lead to the slightest improvement of the situation in Indonesia or to the cessation of military operations. What then remains of the arguments of the Chinese representative who tried to show us that this resolution is a step forward and a logical development of the Council's previous decisions? Indeed, if the previous decisions were not effective, then this resolution is scarcely more so, especially if we take into account the last paragraph, included in the resolution apparently for the purpose of providing it with a high-sounding phrase mentioning the withdrawal of troops. There is a high-sounding sentence in the last paragraph, which reads: '*Invites* the parties, should it appear that some withdrawals of armed forces be necessary, to conclude between them as soon as possible the agreements referred to in its resolution of 25 August 1947'.

The resolution leaves the decision on the question regarding a possible withdrawal of troops to the parties concerned, who, it is alleged, can reach an agreement on the subject. But we know that the Netherlands Government will not even hear of proposals concerning the withdrawal of troops. The Security Council has heard repeated official statements to that effect. Therefore this sentence is meaningless, it merely deludes whoever reads this resolution, because the impression is created that agreement is possible between the Netherlands and Indonesian Governments; but since the Netherlands Government ignores any advice of this nature and rejects all proposals concerning the withdrawal of troops, this paragraph is a well-sounding but quite meaningless sentence that imposes no obligation on anyone.

What then remains of this resolution? The resolution provides no grounds for thinking that the situation might radically change if the Security Council should adopt it. For that reason I am unable to support such a resolution. [*SCOR, 2nd yr, 218th mtg*, pp. 2728–9.]

However, it was left to the Polish delegate to cast a negative vote: the Soviet Union did not press her opposition to a veto—presumably because the resolution was acceptable to Indonesia, and because the Soviet Union did not want to be held responsible, in Asian eyes, for having prevented all action by the Security Council.[1]

By early 1948 progress had been made towards the *Renville* Agreement,[2] and a further resolution was adopted. (The composition of the Security Council had changed in 1948.)

The Security Council,
Having considered the report of the Committee of Good Offices informing the Council of the steps taken by the Netherlands Government and the Government of the Republic of Indonesia to comply with the Council's resolution 27 (1947) of 1 August 1947,
   1. *Notes with satisfaction* the signing of the Truce Agreement by both parties and the acceptance by both parties of certain principles as an agreed basis for the conclusion of a political settlement in Indonesia;
   2. *Commends* the members of the Committee of Good Offices for the assistance they have given the two parties in their endeavours to settle their dispute by peaceful means;
   3. *Maintains* its offer of good offices contained in its resolution 31 (1947) of 25 August 1947; and, to this end,
   4. *Requests* both parties and the Committee of Good Offices to keep the Council directly informed about the progress of the political settlement in Indonesia. [*SC res. S/678, 28 Feb. 1948.*]

[1] See Taylor, p. 386.   [2] See below, pp. 65–7.

VOTING: 7–0.
  In favour: Argentina, Canada, Belgium, China, France, UK, USA.
  Against: None.
Abstaining: Colombia, Ukraine SSR, Syria, USSR.

On 6 July 1948 the Council agreed, with two abstentions (Ukraine, USSR) to cable the GOC for an early report on the delay in the implementation of Article 6 of the *Renville* Truce Agreement. The implementation of the Agreement began, in the summer, to run into serious trouble.[3]

> *The Security Council*
> *Having considered* the Committee of Good Offices' report on the Federal Conference opened in Bandung on 27 May 1948, third interim report (S/848/Add. 1), report on standstill in political negotiations (S/918) and report on restrictions on trade in Indonesia (S/919),
> *Calls upon* the Governments of the Netherlands and the Republic of Indonesia, with the assistance of the Council's Committee of Good Offices, to maintain strict observance of both the military and economic articles of the *Renville* political principles and the six additional principles. [*SC res. S/933, 29 July 1948.*]

VOTING: 9–0.
  In favour: Argentina, Belgium, Canada, China, Colombia, Syria, UK, USA.
  Against: None.
Abstaining: Ukraine SSR, USSR.

By December 1948 the situation had completely deteriorated and the second Dutch 'police action' was initiated.[4] It was at this juncture that a loss of British and United States sympathy for the Dutch case could be clearly perceived:

> *The Security Council,*
> *Noting with concern* the resumption of hostilities in Indonesia,
> *Having taken note* of the reports of the Committee of Good Offices,
> 1. *Calls upon* the parties:
> (*a*) To cease hostilities forthwith;
> (*b*) Immediately to release the President of the Republic of Indonesia and other political prisoners arrested since 18 December 1948;
> 2. *Instructs* the Committee of Good Offices to report to the Security Council fully and urgently by telegraph on the events which have transpired in Indonesia since 12 December 1948, and to observe and report to the Security Council on the compliance with sub-paragraphs (*a*) and (*b*) above. [*SC res. S/1150, 24 Dec. 1948.*]

VOTING: 7–0.
  In favour: Argentine, Canada, Colombia, China, Syria, UK, USA.
  Against: None.
Abstaining: Belgium, France, Ukraine SSR, USSR.
  Note: The representative of Ukraine was in fact absent, and the President ruled that he should be counted as having abstained.

Four days later a clear demand came from the Council for the release by the Netherlands of Republican leaders:

> *The Security Council,*
> *Noting* that the Netherlands Government has not so far released the President of the Republic of Indonesia and all other political prisoners, as required by Council resolution 63 (1948) of 24 December 1948,

---

[3] See below, pp. 69–71.   [4] See below, p. 72.

Calls upon the Netherlands Government to set free these political prisoners forthwith and report to the Security Council within twenty-four hours of the adoption of the present resolution. [*SC res. S/1164, 28 Dec. 1948.*]

VOTING: 8–0.
In favour: Argentina, Canada, China, Colombia, Syria, Ukraine SSR, USA, USSR.
Against: None.
Abstaining: Belgium, France, UK.

The consular representatives were again pressed into action, not merely as the eyes and ears of the GOC, but in order to report directly to the Security Council. The Soviet Union continued to show little enthusiasm for their contribution.

The Security Council
Requests the consular representatives in Batavia referred to in paragraph 5 of its resolution 30 (1947), adopted on 25 August 1947, at the 194th meeting of the Council, to send as soon as possible, for the information and guidance of the Security Council, a complete report on the situation in the Republic of Indonesia, covering in such report the observance of the cease-fire orders and the conditions prevailing in areas under military occupation or from which armed forces now in occupation may be withdrawn. [*SC res. S/1165, 28 Dec. 1948.*]

VOTING: 9–0.
In favour: Argentina, Belgium, Canada, China, Colombia, France, Syria, UK, USA.
Against: None.
Abstaining: Ukraine SSR, USSR.

The Security Council now made, for the first time, detailed proposals for a political solution, and reconstituted the GOC as the UN Commission for Indonesia (UNCI):

The Security Council,
Recalling its resolutions 27 (1947) of August, 30 (1947) and 31 (1947) of 25 August, and 36 (1947) of 1 November 1947, with respect to the Indonesian question,
Taking note with approval of the reports submitted to the Security Council by its Committee of Good Offices for Indonesia,
Considering that its resolutions 63 (1948) and 64 (1948) of 24 and 28 December 1948 have not been fully carried out,
Considering that continued occupation of the territory of the Republic of Indonesia by the armed forces of the Netherlands is incompatible with the restoration of good relations between the parties and with the final achievement of a just and lasting settlement of the Indonesian dispute,
Considering that the establishment and maintenance of law and order throughout Indonesia is a necessary condition to the achievement of the expressed objectives and desires of both parties,
Noting with satisfaction that the parties continue to adhere to the principles of the *Renville* Agreement and agree that free and democratic elections should be held throughout Indonesia for the purpose of establishing a constituent assembly at the earliest practicable date, and further agree that the Security Council should arrange for the observation of such elections by an appropriate agency of the United Nations; and that the representative of the Netherlands has expressed his Government's desire to have such elections held not later than 1 October 1949,
Noting also with satisfaction that the Government of the Netherlands plans to transfer sovereignty to the United States of Indonesia by 1 January 1950 if possible, and in any case during the year 1950,
Conscious of its primary responsibility for the maintenance of international peace and

2

security, and in order that the rights, claims and positions of the parties may not be prejudiced by the use of force,

1. *Calls upon* the Government of the Netherlands to ensure the immediate discontinuance of all military operations, calls upon the Government of the Republic simultaneously to order its armed adherents to cease guerrilla warfare, and calls upon both parties to co-operate in the restoration of peace and the maintenance of law and order throughout the area affected;

2. *Calls upon* the Government of the Netherlands to release immediately and unconditionally all political prisoners arrested by it since 17 December 1948 in the Republic of Indonesia, and to facilitate the immediate return of officials of the Government of the Republic of Indonesia to Jogjakarta in order that they may discharge their responsibilities under paragraph 1 above and exercise their appropriate functions in full freedom, including administration of the Jogjakarta area, which shall include the city of Jogjakarta and its immediate environs. The Netherlands authorities shall afford to the Government of the Republic of Indonesia such facilities as may reasonably be required by that Government for its effective functioning in the Jogjakarta area and for communication and consultation with all persons in Indonesia;

3. *Recommends* that, in the interest of carrying out the expressed objectives and desires of both parties to establish a federal, independent and sovereign United States of Indonesia at the earliest possible date, negotiations be undertaken as soon as possible by representatives of the Government of the Netherlands and representatives of the Republic of Indonesia, with the assistance of the Commission referred to in paragraph 4 below, on the basis of the principles set forth in the Linggadjati and *Renville* Agreements, and taking advantage of the extent of agreement reached between the parties regarding the proposals submitted to them by the representative of the United States of America on the Committee of Good Offices on 10 September 1948, and in particular, on the basis that:

(a) The establishment of the interim federal government which is to be granted the powers of internal government in Indonesia during the interim period before the transfer of sovereignty shall be the result of the above negotiations and shall take place not later than 15 March 1949;

(b) The elections which are to be held for the purpose of choosing representatives to an Indonesian constituent assembly should be completed by 1 October 1949;

(c) The transfer of sovereignty over Indonesia by the Government of the Netherlands to the United States of Indonesia should take place at the earliest possible date and in any case not later than 1 July 1950;

provided that, if no agreement is reached by one month prior to the respective dates referred to in sub-paragraphs (a), (b), and (c) above, the Commission referred to in paragraph 4 (a) below, or such other United Nations agency as may be established in accordance with paragraph 4 (c) below, shall immediately report to the Security Council with its recommendations for a solution of the difficulties;

4. *Resolves* that:

(a) The Committee of Good Offices shall henceforth be known as the United Nations Commission for Indonesia. The Commission shall act as the representative of the Security Council in Indonesia and shall have all of the functions assigned to the Committee of Good Offices by the Security Council since 18 December 1948 and the functions conferred on it by the terms of this resolution. The Commission shall act by majority vote, but its reports and recommendations to the Security Council shall present both majority and minority views if there is a difference of opinion among the members of the Commission;

(b) The Consular Commission is requested to facilitate the work of the United Nations Commission for Indonesia by providing military observers and other staff and facilities to enable the Commission to carry out its duties under the Council's resolutions of 24 and 28 December 1948 as well as under the present resolution, and shall temporarily suspend other activities.

(c) The Commission shall assist the parties in the implementation of this resolution, and shall assist the parties in the negotiations to be undertaken under paragraph 3 above and is authorized to make recommendations to them or to the Security Council on matters within its competence. Upon agreement being reached in such negotiations, the Commission shall make recommendations to the Security Council as to the nature, powers, and functions of the United Nations agency which should remain in Indonesia to assist in the implementation of the provisions of such agreement until sovereignty is transferred by the Government of the Netherlands to the United States of Indonesia.

(*d*) The Commission shall have authority to consult with representatives of areas in Indonesia other than the Republic, and to invite representatives of such areas to participate in the negotiations referred to in paragraph 3 above.

(*e*) The Commission or such other United Nations agency as may be established in accordance with its recommendation under paragraph 4 (*c*) above is authorized to observe on behalf of the United Nations the elections to be held throughout Indonesia and is further authorized, in respect of the territories of Java, Madura and Sumatra, to make recommendations regarding the conditions necessary (*a*) to ensure that the elections are free and democratic, and (*b*) to guarantee freedom of assembly, speech and publication at all times, provided that such guarantee is not construed so as to include the advocacy of violence or reprisals.

(*f*) The Commission should assist in achieving the earliest possible restoration of the civil administration of the Republic. To this end it shall, after consultation with the parties, recommend the extent to which, consistent with reasonable requirements of public security and the protection of life and property, areas controlled by the Republic under the Renville Agreement (outside of the Jogjakarta area) should be progressively returned to the administration of the Government of the Republic of Indonesia, and shall supervise such transfers. The recommendations of the Commission may include provision for such economic measures as are required for the proper functioning of the administration and for the economic well-being of the population of the areas involved in such transfers. The Commission shall after consultation with the parties, recommend which if any Netherlands forces shall be retained temporarily in any area (outside of the Jogjakarta area) in order to assist in the maintenance of law and order. If either of the parties fails to accept the recommendations of the Commission mentioned in this paragraph, the Commission shall report immediately to the Security Council with its further recommendations for a solution of the difficulties.

(*g*) The Commission shall render periodic reports to the Council, and special reports whenever the Commission deems necessary.

(*h*) The Commission shall employ such observers, officers and other persons as it deems necessary.

5. *Requests* the Secretary-General to make available to the Commission such staff, funds and other facilities as are required by the Commission for the discharge of its functions.

6. *Calls upon* the Government of the Netherlands and the Republic of Indonesia to cooperate fully in giving effect to the provisions of this resolution. [*SC res. S/1234, 28 Jan. 1949.*]

VOTING: The draft resolution was voted on only in parts: no vote was taken on the text as a whole. The non-permanent membership of the Council changed once again in 1949, and details of the voting on individual clauses may be found in *SCOR*, 4th yr, 406th mtg.

No negative vote was cast on any of the parts of this resolution. France, the Ukraine, and the USSR abstained throughout the voting on the substantive clauses. The representative of the USSR explained his government's attitude:

Paragraph 3 recommends that negotiations should be undertaken by representatives of the Netherlands Government and representatives of the Republic of Indonesia. Under what conditions will these negotiations take place? If they can be undertaken at all, they will take place under the Netherlands occupation regime. It is quite clear that there can be no question of free negotiations on a footing of equality between the representatives of the Netherlands Government and those of the Indonesian Republic. In the past, as was noted in the reports

of the Committee of Good Offices concerning previous negotiations, the Netherlands syste-
matically made new and exorbitant demands and delivered ultimatums to the Government of
the Indonesian Republic even when the Republic was still an independent and sovereign
State. As long as the occupation regime is in force, the Netherlands representatives will certainly not pay any attention to proposals or arguments advanced by the representatives of the
Republic. Secure in the support of their armed troops, they will force their own unilateral
demands and ultimatums on the Republic. In such conditions, the purpose of the proposal to
resume negotiations can also only be to camouflage aggressive acts by the Netherlands and
not to protect the lawful interests of the Indonesian Republic.

As to the proposal to set up a 'United Nations Commission for Indonesia', this primarily
involves only a change of name, as the commission is nothing more than a new name for the
Committee of Good Offices, the composition of which would remain unchanged. Moreover,
any extension of the Committee's terms of reference would give the United States representative, who plays a leading part in that body, still greater opportunities to intervene in the
domestic affairs of Indonesia.

Experience shows that so far the purpose of such intervention has been not to protect the
lawful interest of the Republic and its people but to cover up the policy of Netherlands
aggressors and to protect the interests of the American monopolies, which, as we know, have
profitably invested hundreds of millions of dollars in Indonesia and work hand in glove with
the Netherlands aggressors for the suppression of the freedom and independence of the Indonesian Republic. Experience shows that the Committee of Good Offices has been nothing
more than a screen behind which the Netherlands authorities prepared new acts of aggression
against the Indonesia Republic. This same Committee of Good Offices, given a new title
and wider powers, will again be nothing but a screen enabling the Netherlands authorities to
take advantage of the results of aggression by abolishing the Indonesian Republic altogether
and by continuing their attempts to deprive the people of the Republic of their freedom and
independence and to drive them back into colonial slavery.

For these reasons, the proposal to set up such a commission is unacceptable to the USSR
delegation. Instead of demanding the withdrawal of Netherlands troops as first a step towards
settling the conflict between the Netherlands and the Republic of Indonesia and towards the
restoration of justice and the protection of the legitimate interests of the Republic, the authors
of the draft resolution confine themselves to instructing the commission to submit at some
undefined future date recommendations concerning the extent to which areas controlled by
the Republic under the *Renville* Agreement may be progressively returned to the administration of the Government of the Republic of Indonesia.

Even this nebulous proposal, however, has a number of qualifying statements, the effect of
which is to deprive it of any practical meaning. Among these qualifications is the use of the
word 'progressively'—this word calls for quotation marks—and the statement that the proposed measures ahall be 'consistent . . . with public security'. There is even a solicitous
provision for retaining Netherlands armed forces in any area of the Republic under the pretext that they may 'assist in the maintenance of law and order'.

Thus we see that the draft resolution does not provide for an immediate and unconditional
withdrawal of Netherlands troops from the territory of the Indonesian Republic. It leaves the
question of their withdrawal to the discretion of the commission and to the discretion of the
Netherlands occupation authorities themselves. Such a proposal can therefore be considered
only as an attempt to strengthen and legitimize the forcible occupation of the Republic's
territory by the armed forces of the Netherlands.

The USSR delegation hold that all Netherlands troops must be withdrawn from the territory of the Indonesian Republic immediately and without conditions or exceptions and that
the question of this withdrawal cannot be left to the discretion of the commission and still
less to that of the Netherlands authorities, which have even tried to excuse their aggression
against the Indonesian Republic by references to the 'maintenance of law and order'.

. Law and order in the territory of the Indonesian Republic must be maintained not by the
armed forces of foreign invaders, but by the Government of the Republic itself. Experience

has shown that the Government of the Republic is capable of establishing and maintaining law and order without the intervention of foreign usurpers. Take away the Netherlands troops from the territory of the Indonesian Republic, confer full freedom and sovereign rights on its Government, and, beyond any doubt, law and order will be restored and maintained. [*SCOR, 4th yr, 402nd mtg*, pp. 17–18.]

At its 421st meeting, on 23 March 1949, the Security Council adopted the text of a telegram to be sent to the UNCI:

It is the sense of the Security Council that the United Nations Commission for Indonesia, in accordance with the Council's resolution 67 (1949) of 28 January 1949, and without preju- dicing the rights, claims and positions of the parties, should assist the parties in reaching agreement as to (*a*) the implementation of the Council's resolution of 28 January, and in particular paragraphs 1 and 2 of the operative part thereof, and (*b*) the time and conditions for holding the proposed conference at the Hague, to the end that the negotiations contemplated by the resolution of 28 January may be held as soon as possible. It is further the sense of the Council that, if such an agreement is reached, the holding of such a conference and the par- ticipation by the United Nations Commission for Indonesia in accordance with its terms of reference would be consistent with the purposes and objectives of the Council's resolution of 28 January 1949.

This text was approved by 8—0 with 3 abstentions (France, Ukraine SSR, USSR).

During 1949 other resolutions were adopted concerning the financing of UNCI representatives and UN observers in Indonesia.[5]

The Security Council,
Considering that, in virtue of General Assembly resolution 231 (III) of 8 October 1948, it is a matter for its own decision whether, in the case of commissions of inquiry or investigation instituted by it, the representative of a Member State participating in such a commission needs to be assisted by an alternate,
Considering that, in cases where this need has been found by the Security Council to exist, the Secretary-General is authorized by the same resolution to reimburse Member States retroactively for the travelling and subsistence expenses of the alternates of their representa- tives on the said commissions,
Notes that since the institution of the under-mentioned commissions the representatives of Member States that are participating or have participated have each had to be assisted by an alternate:
    1. The Committee of Good Offices, which has now become the United Nations Commis- sion for Indonesia;
    2. The United Nations Commission for India and Pakistan. [*SC res. S/1401, 27 Sept. 1949.*]

VOTING: 7–1.
 In favour: Argentina, Canada, China, France, Norway, UK, USA.
  Against: Ukraine SSR.
Abstaining: Cuba, Egypt, USSR.

The Security Council,
Having received a cablegram, dated 5 August 1949, from the Consular Commission at Batavia to the President of the Security Council, requesting that the United Nations assume future costs of military observers in Indonesia,

---

[5] For a discussion of these financial matters, see below, pp. 60–1.

Transmits this message to the Secretary-General.   [*SC res. S/1404, 5 Oct. 1949.*]
VOTING: 9–1.
In favour: Argentina, Canada, China, Cuba, Egypt, France, Norway, UK, USA.
   Against: Ukraine SSR.
Abstaining: USSR.

3

FUNCTIONS AND MANDATE

On 1 August 1947 the Security Council had called upon the Netherlands and Indonesia to cease hostilities (S/459). On 25 August 1947, noting that the Netherlands government intended to request the career consuls stationed in Batavia to report on the Indonesian situation, and that Indonesia wished the Security Council itself to establish a panel of observers, the Council:

5. Requests the Governments members of the Council which have career consular representatives in Batavia to instruct them to prepare jointly for the information and guidance of the Security Council reports on the situation in the Republic of Indonesia following the resolution of the Council of 1 August 1947, such reports to cover the observance of the cease-fire orders and the conditions prevailing in areas under military occupation or from which armed forces now in occupation may be withdrawn by agreement between the parties. . . . [*SC res. S/525 (I), 25 Aug. 1947.*]

In Part II of the same resolution, the Security Council offered to establish, should the parties agree, a three-man Good Offices Committee. This was subsequently set up with the following membership: Australia (selected by the Republic of Indonesia); Belgium (selected by the Netherlands); and the United States (designated by Australia and Belgium).

It was the Consular Commission itself, operating under its mandate of 25 August 1947, that decided that the military officers of the Powers represented could assist by fulfilling certain specific functions, i.e. 'to observe any possible violations of the cease-fire orders; to investigate, where possible, allegations of violations of the cease-fire orders; and to gather any other data that might be of value to the Commission and to the Security Council'.[1] When, on 1 November 1947, the Security Council again called for a cease-fire, it requested the GOC to assist in achieving this and asked 'the Consular Commission, together with its military assistants, to make its services available to the Committee of Good Offices.'[2] Thus the military observers now had broad reporting functions, and also the task of helping the GOC achieve an effective cease-fire. The use of both the GOC and the Consular Commission's military observers for these purposes had been suggested by the representative of Brazil:

[1] S/586, 22 Oct. 1947, Report by the Consular Commission at Batavia.
[2] SC res. S/597, 1 Nov. 1947, para. 3.

In my last intervention in this debate, at the two hundred and tenth meeting of the Council, I called the attention of the Council to the advantage of utilizing the services of the Committee of Good Offices to give effect to the cease-fire order. I further stated that we ought to ask the military attachés in Batavia to assist the Committee in supervising the implementation of the cease-fire order.

It has always seemed to me that we should be adopting a completely unrealistic attitude if we did otherwise. I hold it to be impracticable, if not harmful, to try to settle that question here, without any direct contact with the situation as it has developed in Indonesia. Any directive we may give to the parties concerned cannot have a full effect if it is not properly acted upon by some organ on the spot.

After having read the report of the consuls, which seemed to me an objective and realistic appraisal of the situation, I am convinced of the propriety of these considerations. If the members will look at chapter II, paragraph 9 of the report of the Consular Commission at Batavia, where the gist of the situation appears in its full significance, they will see the following:

'Both sides admit that a cease-fire order should normally be followed by contact between the two parties in order to arrange details for the satisfactory observance of the order. No attempt was made by either to make such contact, largely, if not entirely, because of this lack of confidence.'

If that is the situation as seen by the consular authorities, who have investigated it in all its complexities, it is only too clear that any attempt to bring about the complete cessation of hostilities without using the services of an organ on the spot would be futile.

Since the cease-fire order had not been entirely complied with, the Security Council proceeded to the examination of the several resolutions dealing with the withdrawal of troops to a given line, on the assumption that a decision on that subject would eventually bring about the complete cessation of hostilities. I believe, however, in the light of the facts ascertained by the consular authorities, that such a decision would be doomed to the same fate as the cease-fire order. Withdrawal of troops will not be achieved by an order of the Council if we do not provide for the supervision of its implementation. [*SCOR, 2nd yr, 217th mtg*, pp. 2691–2.]

This assignment of the Consular Commission's military observers to the GOC and, indeed, the role of the GOC in the achievement of a cease-fire, as distinct from a political solution was not without its confusions:

It was the intention of the Security Council, or at least it was the intention of the Australian delegation, that the Consular Commission, with its military advisers, should continue to observe and report on the cease-fire order. It seems to us that the Commission has interpreted that order to mean that it was to submit one report and one report only, and then dissolve. We understand that many of the military observers have left and returned to their own countries. The letter we received this morning from the representative of the Republic of Indonesia also seems to imply that there is no body in existence to observe any of the activities in connexion with the cessation of hostilities.

It seems to me that there is extraordinary confusion in the Council about the functions of the Committee of Good Offices and of the Consular Commission. As far as my recollection goes, I think the representative of the USSR was the only one who clearly expressed that difference when, at our two hundred and thirteenth meeting, he indicated that we were proposing to give to the Committee of Good Offices a function which we did not bestow on it nor intend to bestow on it, namely, any action in connexion with the cease-fire order and the cessation of hostilities.

Even this afternoon we have the representative of Brazil saying, in effect, that it is for the Committee of Good Offices to see how the cease-fire order should be observed; that it is for the Committee to bring about the cessation of hostilities; that that is the function of the Committee of Good Offices.

Well, with all respect, we made it very clear that the Committee of Good Offices was to attempt to bring about the settlement of the long-term problem, that is, the problem of peaceful settlement. We appointed the consuls as our instruments—and they still call themselves, in this report, the Consular Commission of the Security Council—as our agents in connexion with the cease-fire order. We still have that confusion in the resolution before us; in other words, we are now asking the Committee of Good Offices to take certain action and even to supervise the carrying into effect of the order which we appointed another to supervise.

It might be argued, of course, that now that it is on the spot, it has more weight and authority. But what more authority can an organ have than to be invested, as is the Consular Commission, with all the authority of the Security Council? It is the agent of the Council. Those consular officials are very good and are experienced men, and for this particular short-term problem I should think they were far more competent than the Committee of Good Offices. It only derogates from the real work of the Committee of Good Offices to have it mixed up in supervising the cease-fire order and the cessation of hostilities, which is not its function at all. [*Per the representative of Australia, ibid.*, pp. 2701–2.]

The GOC itself decided that these two functions—the achievement of a cease-fire and progress with political talks—had a bearing on each other, and had to be tackled in parallel.[3] The GOC assisted the parties in negotiations, which ultimately resulted in the *Renville* Truce Agreement of 17 January 1948.[4]

Further tasks were given to the military observers under the terms of this Agreement,[5] Article 4 of which had provided that the GOC's military assistants would be 'instructed to assume, in the first instance, responsibility for determining whether any incident requires inquiry by the higher authorities of either or both parties'.

In an Annex the following elaboration of this task was offered:

3. As regards paragraph 4 of the foregoing agreement, it is understood that the military assistants of the Committee of Good Offices will have every opportunity in the execution of paragraph 4 of the truce agreement, for determining whether any incid nt requires inquiry by the higher authorities of either or both parties, in which case they will of course at the same time refer the matter to their principal, namely, the Committee of Good Offices, the services of which will be available to assist in adjusting differences between the parties in regard to the truce. [*S/649/Rev. 1, Ann. to App. XI.*]

Further, Article 5 of the *Renville* Truce Agreement provided that:

. . . The Committee's military assistants will be available to advise the appropriate authorities of the parties and to serve in such other proper capacities as may be requested. Among other, they should:

(*a*) Call upon pools of police officers established by each party in its demilitarized zone to accompany the military assistants in their endeavours and activities throughout that demilitarized zone. Police officers of one party will not move into and throughout the demilitarized zone of the other party unless accompanied by a military assistant of the Committee of Good Offices and a police officer of that other party;

(*b*) Promote co-operation between the two police forces.

So far as this was concerned, the clarifying Annex provided: 'The question of an extension of demilitarized zones will, upon the request of either party, be

---

[3] S/649/Rev. 1, 10 Feb. 1948, 1st Interim Report of GOC, para. 15.
[4] For details of the manner in which the GOC implemented its mandate, see below, pp. 64–5.
[5] For full text of the *Renville* Agreement, see below, pp. 65–7.

considered forthwith by the Committee's military assistants who, acting within the intent of paragraph 5, will advise the appropriate authorities.'[6]

For discharging the responsibilities under the *Renville* Truce Agreement, the GOC thus used the services both of the Consular Commission and its military assistants, in accordance with the Security Council resolution of 1 November 1947.[7] The organization of the military assistants for these purposes is described elsewhere.[8] The military phases of the implementation of the *Renville* Agreement were assigned to a Security Committee. A sub-committee, on which senior military assistants of the GOC and military experts of the parties served, was established to deal with particular problems which arose in respect of delineating a *status quo* line in the Pronodjiwo area in East Java.[9] Military assistants also usefully observed the evacuation of Indonesian troops from Dutch-controlled to Indonesian-controlled areas[10] and were given further detailed instructions by the GOC on the handling of alleged violations of the Agreement. Under Article 4 of the Agreement, as we have seen, the military observers were authorized to settle locally certain incidents concerning the demilitarized zones. Elsewhere, the military observers in the region concerned were to report all incidents in the demilitarized zones to the GOC, which would then decide on the action to be taken. Senior military assistants were also authorized to make recommendations to the GOC, in consultation with GOC representatives on the Security Committee, on action to be taken in respect of other alleged infringements.[11]

In addition to these specific functions allotted to the military assistants under the *Renville* Agreement, it may be noted that the organ which they served—the GOC—had its mandate enlarged as a result of two Security Council resolutions in 1948. In resolution S/689 of 28 February 1948 the GOC was requested to pay particular attention to the political developments in western Java and Madura; and in resolution S/842 of 6 July 1948 it was agreed to ask the Committee for an early report on the existing restrictions on the domestic and international trade of Indonesia and the reason for the delay in implementing Article 6 of the Truce Agreement—that is to say, the provisions for self-determination of the Indonesian people and the political principles contained in the *Renville* Truce formula.

During the summer of 1948 relations between the Netherlands and Indonesia deteriorated once more, and in December a second Dutch 'police action' took place. The GOC issued certain instructions to the observers as to their duties in these changed circumstances:

2. The military observers have received from the Committee the following instructions:

(*a*) To observe and report on the extent of compliance with the cease-hostilities resolution of the Security Council;

(*b*) To observe and report on the continuance of military operations, if any, including their scope and mission;

(*c*) To observe and report on the effect of hostilities on the normal pursuits and welfare of

[6] Ibid. annex to app. xi, para. 2.   [7] S/787, 19 May 1948, GOC 2nd Interim Report.
[8] See below, pp. 33–4.   [9] S/787, p. 58.   [10] Ibid. p. 59.   [11] Ibid. p. 62, s. 6, para. (d).
2*

the civilian population, and the nature and effect of relief and rehabilitation activies.   [*S/1193,*
8 Jan. 1949, GOC Report to President of Security Council.]

On 28 January 1949 the Security Council called for an end to military activities, and for the release by the Netherlands of the imprisoned Indonesian political leaders (resolution S/1234). It also recommended progress, through an election, to an independent United States of Indonesia as soon as possible, and decided that the GOC should henceforth be known as the UNCI. Resolution S/1234 also provided that the Consular Commission was to facilitate UNCI's work by providing military observers. The details of the tasks assigned to UNCI, in which the observers were to assist, have been reproduced above at pp. 16–17. On 23 March 1949 the Security Council dispatched a cable to UNCI instructing it to help the parties implement operative paragraphs 1 and 2 of resolution S/1234, and to assist in reaching agreement on the time and conditions for holding a conference at The Hague.

UNCI in fact used the military representatives in a variety of ways. They assisted a sub-committee established under UNCI's auspices, composed of representatives of the two parties and of UNCI, in making preparations for the return of the Republican government to Jogjakarta.[12] The military observers were also requested to lend their assistance in overseeing the evacuation of those who wished to leave Jogjakarta before the return of the Republican authorities.[13] The purposes for which the military observers were to lend their assistance to UNCI and the parties were further elaborated in Regulations which were adopted to govern the implementation of the agreement to cease hostilities.[14]

UNCI successfully contributed to negotiations which led to the Round Table Agreements of November 1949; and on 27 December 1949 sovereignty was transferred to Indonesia (below, p. 74). The observer functions of the UN were largely fulfilled at this time. However, UNCI was given certain duties under the Agreements concerning the repatriation of the Netherlands army and the holding of a plebiscite for the federal territories.[15] In the exercise of its functions

the Commission relied on information submitted to it by the parties, upon its own observation and upon reports received from its military observers. Under revised instructions issued by the Commission, military observers were requested to report on any important development which, in their considered judgment, could affect the implementation of the agreements reached at the Round Table Conference or attained in further discussions between the parties. [*S/2087, 13 Apr. 1951, UNCI Report on Activities since the transfer of sovereignty,* para. 6.]

The UNCI adjourned *sine die* on 3 April 1951; and with that the activities of the UN observers came to an end.

---

[12] S/1373 & Corr. 1, UNCI 1st Interim Report, para. 19.   [13] Ibid. para. 21.
[14] Ibid. app. VIII; for full text, see below, pp. 75–82.
[15] S/1417/Add. 1, app. XVI, Art. 24 and ibid. app. XI, Art. 2.

4

CONSTITUTIONAL BASIS

NONE of the resolutions on the Indonesian question specifically states the Charter basis of the Security Council's authority or decisions. In July 1947 Indonesia was not yet an independent state; but the goal of independence and a substantial measure of self-government (including responsibility for internal law and order) had been conceded to her by the Linggadjati Agreement. Indonesia had been accorded *de facto* recognition by several states.

Could hostilities between the Netherlands and Indonesia—the first Dutch 'police action'—be of legitimate concern to the Security Council? If so, could it make recommendations under Chapter VII of the Charter? Further, was it also entitled by Chapter VI of the Charter to be concerned with the peaceful settlement of the dispute over the implementation of the Linggadjati Agreement, and to offer its assistance? Finally, could it go beyond merely offering its assistance, and make specific recommendations for a political solution?

The majority of members of the Council appeared to feel that, given the existence of major hostilities and the not insignificant status accorded to Indonesia at Linggadjati, the matter could be of international concern and could give rise to a threat to international peace. Certainly the language of the calls which the Security Council made for an end to hostilities was peremptory, and accorded with the tone of Chapter VII. At the same time, the machinery which the Council established was essentially that of inquiry and good offices; the Charter basis of the Consular Commission, the GOC, and the UNCI would seem to lie within Chapter VI. Not until the breakdown of the *Renville* Truce Agreement and the second Dutch 'police action' in December 1948 did the Security Council itself go beyond the provision of good offices and peace observation, and make specific proposals for a settlement. In spite of the silence of the resolutions concerned, it would seem that the Security Council was acting both under Chapter VI and under Chapter VII. The duties of the military observers were concerned with peace observation and with supervising particular truces and cease-fire orders.[1]

From the point of view of the Netherlands, however, the first 'police action' represented an internal security operation against lawless elements by a colonial Power. She believed the matter to be essentially within her domestic juris-

---

[1] 'Truce supervision and peace observation were an integral part of the task of mediation and therefore their combination was helpful' (D. Wainhouse, *International Peace Observation* (1967), p. 322).

diction, entitling her to the benefits of Article 2 (7) of the Charter.[2] She viewed her co-operation with the Security Council as entirely discretionary. Van Kleffens explained the Dutch position to the Security Council, declaring that the 'police action'

is a form of military action with which this Council has no concern. . . . [it] is being taken not only with the full backing of all the political parties and all the trade unions in the Netherlands, with the sole exception of the communists, but also—and this seems to me extremely important—with the full understanding and the publicly-voiced approval of the Governments of the two fellow States, if I may use that expression, of the Republic of Indonesia—namely, Eastern Indonesia and Borneo. This action has been undertaken with the prior knowledge of the two sister States of Indonesia. I am not revealing any secret when I say that the Governments of these two States—and I use the word 'States' in the sense of States to be merged into the federation, not sovereign and independent States—of Eastern Indonesia and Borneo have asked us more than once to take such action earlier, but we were anxious to exhaust every possibility of avoiding a clash before resorting to these measures.

What was it that made us take this action in Java and Sumatra, and what is the true nature of the action? The Council will recall that, in the Linggadjati Agreement, many points were settled about the future nature of the United States of Indonesia and the form in which the United States of Indonesia-to-be would be affiliated with the Kingdom of the Netherlands under the House of Orange. However, although we supposed that it went without saying, the Agreement did not settle such matters as cessation of the loathsome practice of keeping of hostages, or of the Indonesian Republic's acting as if it were a sovereign State, which over its signature in the Linggadjati Agreement it has said it was not. It did not settle then that there would be no more direct agreements with other States; that there would be no more blockade of territories held by Dutch troops in such areas as Batavia and Semarang and Soerabaya and elsewhere; that there would be at last an observance of the truce which was signed at the end of last year and for violations of which we have had innumerable complaints.

. . . I have asked the Government of the Indies for documentary evidence of more than one thousand violations of the armistice which have come to our knowledge. . . . [*SCOR, 2nd yr, 171st mtg.*]

Van Kleffens also referred to a statement made by his government:

'The Netherlands Government, although persisting in its denial of the Council's jurisdiction in this matter, fully understands the Council's desire to see the use of arms come to an end in this as in other cases. Moreover the Netherlands Government welcomes the Council's resolution in this sense that it justifies the hope that, under the pressure of world opinion, the Government of the Republic of Indonesia will now be found disposed to carry out what so far it has failed to do in spite of constant and urgent requests and representations on the part of the Netherlands Government and notwithstanding corresponding friendly advice on the part of other Powers.

'In taking police action the Netherlands Government has had, from the outset, strictly limited objectives in view; reference may be made in this connexion to the communication made on its behalf to the Secretary-General of the United Nations on July 21 in which the limited nature was pointed out of the action aiming at the cessation of a situation the continuation of which could no longer be countenanced in the interest of the people.

'Having taken into serious consideration the views which led the Security Council to address an appeal to both parties, the Netherlands Government has instructed the Lieutenant-

---

[2] Art. 2 (7) provides 'Nothing contained in the present Charter shall authorize the United Nations to intervene in matters which are essentially within the domestic jurisdiction of any state or shall require the members to submit such matters to settlement under the present Charter; but this principle shall not prejudice the application of enforcement measures under Chapter VII'.

Governor-General of the Netherlands Indies to enter into contact with the authorities of the Republic in order to arrive at the cessation, on both sides, of hostile action of any kind.

'The Netherlands Government confidently anticipates that the good offices offered by the Government of the United States of America and gladly accepted by the Netherlands Government, will contribute greatly toward attaining the result aimed at in the resolution of the Security Council.' [*SCOR, 2nd yr, 174th mtg.*]

When faced with resolution S/459 of 1 August 1947, by which the Security Council called for an end to hostilities and the settlement of the dispute by arbitration or other peaceful means, the Netherlands had to consider her position.

All these points the Council looked for in vain in the Linggadjati Agreement. They are not mentioned there. But it goes without saying that if there was to be constructive co-operation on the basis of that Agreement—co-operation in the real sense of the word, of which there was hardly any trace, as everything was promises and disavowals and evasions and words, words, words—if then, there was to be constructive effort, at least the hostages should have been freed. Here I may mention—and these are the latest data that are at my disposal—that by the end of May seven hundred white hostages, and about ten thousand other hostages, were still being held. I ask the Council to realize what that means. These were people almost all of whom had been kept in Japanese concentration camps ever since the islands of Indonesia had been overrun by the enemy, and these concentration camps rank with the most dreadful which this earth has seen in the course of the last fifteen years or so. When V-J day came, these people might rightly have expected that they would at last be set free; but they were not set free. They were kept by the Government of the Republic of Indonesia most of the time in circumstances of great squalor. I submit to the Council that, as *The Times* of London wrote one day, the keeping of hostages is a practice which is inconsistent with the principles of any government that calls itself a civilized government, even if it is only the government of a State in the sense I have described, and not a sovereign and independent State.

As regards foreign relations, there was no cessation of endeavours to make agreements with other States, in spite of the fact that article II of the Linggadjati Agreement provides that the only sovereign State in those parts would be the United States of Indonesia—that is, the Republic plus Eastern Indonesia and Borneo, linked together on the basis of a federation. [*Ibid. 174th mtg.*]

The Dutch position was that a use of force by a colonial authority could not be a breach of Article 2 (4) of the Charter—under which members are prohibited from the use of force 'in their international relations' and 'against the territorial integrity or political independence of any State'. The matter had been brought before the Security Council by Australia, which took a contrary view. Australia had called for provisional measures to be taken under Article 40 of Chapter VII of the Charter. The Australian representative explained the juridical basis of this request:

It is with a deep sense of responsibility that the Australian Government has drawn the attention of the Council under Article 39 of the Charter of the United Nations to the situation in Indonesia. We had certainly hoped that circumstances would never arise which would make it necessary for Chapter VII to be invoked, and we have done so only after making strenuous attempts, in consultation with other Governments, particularly the United Kingdon, the United States and India, to bring about a solution by negotiation and mediation.

However, although the parties to any dispute are bound to seek a solution by mediation and negotiation under Article 33, all attempts to bring the parties together have failed, and it is felt that further delay is not justified because of the loss of life being sustained. The events of the last few days have been most disturbing to the Australian Government. Not only is Indonesia adjacent to our territory, but we are bound by the closest possible economic and commercial ties with this important area. Therefore, we not only share the concern which all Members of the United Nations must have in the restoration of peace and security, but we feel that the interests of Australia are especially affected by the dispute between the Government of the Republic of Indonesia and the Government of the Netherlands, as the result of which hostilities have been in progress in Java and Sumatra during the last ten days.

We feel further that we have a responsibility to bring this situation to the attention of the Council, for it is one of international concern and already has far-reaching repercussions. It affects the well-being and stability of the whole of the South-west Pacific and South-east Asia in which we are directly concerned.

This is the first time a case has been brought before the Council under Chapter VII. Under Article 39, we are alleging a breach of the peace. There are no precedents as to what constitutes a breach of the peace, but we assume that this means a breach of international peace and applies to cases where hostilities are occurring, but where it is not alleged that one particular party is the aggressor or has committed an act of aggression.

That hostilities are in progress is now well established. The Security Council should take cognizance of the substance and reality of what is taking place. There have been large-scale military operations involving the use of naval units, aircraft and tanks, and regular *communiqués* have been issued by the respective commanders. From these *communiqués*, it is apparent that fighting has taken place over a wide area between organized forces, that there have been substantial casualties, and that hostilities are continuing. These are the essential facts of the military situation in Java and Sumatra.

The Council should also note that the hostilities proceeding are not merely police action but are in fact warfare; that is, in international law, armed conflict between two States. It can be clearly established that the Republic of Indonesia does constitute a State.

First, the original Netherlands-Indonesian Draft Agreement of 15 November was negotiated and initialled by representatives of the two Governments, the Netherlands and the Republic of Indonesia.

Secondly, the Government of the Republic of Indonesia has been recognized by the Netherlands Government as exercising *de facto* authority over Java, Madura and Sumatra by the Linggadjati Agreement, article I.

Thirdly, the Republic of Indonesia has been given *de facto* recognition by a number of other Governments including the United Kingdom, United States, India, members of the Arab League and Australia. We understand also that Egypt, Syria, and Iraq have given diplomatic recognition, and that Egypt and Syria have concluded treaties of friendship with the new State. Indeed, the Arab League as far back as 18 November of last year, proposed that the Arab States should consider recognizing the Republic.

Lastly, in the Linggadjati Agreement under article XVII, there is provision for the President of the International Court of Justice to nominate the Chairman of an arbitration body. This is significant. As the members are aware, only States may be parties in cases before that Court. *Ibid. 171st mtg.*]

Eventually, however, Australia accepted an American suggestion that reference to any specific Charter article be deleted; and resolutions S/459 and S/525, though ordering a cease-fire, mention no particular article.[3] The Netherlands representative repeated that the Council had no jurisdiction: the Charter was applicable only to disputes between sovereign states, and this fundamental

---

[3] The US representative was later to say that, in calling on 1 August 1947 for a cease-fire, the Council had adopted a provisional measure under Art. 40 (*SCOR*, 4th yr, 389th mtg, p. 43); the Belgian representative insisted that the whole question of jurisdiction had deliberately been left open (ibid. 402nd mtg, p. 3); while the Chinese representative frankly stated that the juridical issue had been blurred in order to achieve a speedy cease-fire (ibid. 390th mtg, p. 2).

fact was being ignored because the conflict was in this case occurring between peoples of different races. Further, there was no threat to international peace and security, and therefore neither Chapter VI nor Chapter VII was applicable.[4] That being said, the Netherlands government announced that it would show its good faith by approaching the career consuls in Batavia and giving them every opportunity for unbiased investigation.

The President of the Security Council pointed out the problem which the Council faced:

As far as I understand the situation, the Indonesian Republic is a State *de facto* having authority within its territory. If atrocities or irregularities and illegalities are committed by that Government and if that Government is solely responsible for public order within its territory, then it may be considered that these accusations come under domestic jurisdiction.

On the other hand, if the claim of the Netherlands Government that it is still responsible for public order and for the safety of the country and that it is interfering to re-establish order is correct, the matter may be considered differently.

This matter is not very clear to the Council at the present time. The Council considered that under the Linggadjati Agreement, the Indonesian Republic was responsible for internal public order and that it was to maintain it. The Indonesian Republic has its own administration and its own methods of dealing with matters within its territory and we have not heard any proof to the contrary in that respect; we have not heard that the Netherlands Government is responsible for public order within the territory of the Indonesian Republic. [*Ibid. 192nd mtg*, p. 2148.][5]

It is possible, therefore, to view both the call for a cease-fire and the establishment of the Consular Commission as provisional measures under Article 40 of the Charter;[6] or to view the call for a cease-fire as a provisional measure under Chapter VII, but the machinery established as falling under Chapter VI. Certainly the phrase in resolution S/459 which called upon the parties to 'settle their dispute by arbitration or by other peaceful means' would seem an implied reference to Article 33 of Chapter VI, where 'negotiation, enquiry, mediation, conciliation, arbitration, judicial settlement, resort to regional agencies or arrangements' are mentioned. Good offices is not as such mentioned, but Article 33 includes the omnibus phrase 'or other peaceful means of their own choice'. Further, Article 36 gives to the Security Council the authority to 'recommend appropriate procedures or methods of adjustment' in respect of disputes the continuance of which is likely to endanger international peace and security.

Inevitably, each of these two facets of the Security Council's work—the peaceful settlement aspect, and the observance of the cease-fire orders aspect—assumed varying importance during the years 1949–50. With the breakdown of the *Renville* Truce arrangements and the advent of the second Dutch 'police action', the Security Council resolutions of December 1948 and January 1949

[4] Ibid. 2nd yr, 192nd mtg, pp. 2144–5.

[5] For the related question of the basis of the invitation extended to Indonesia to participate in the Security Council's decisions, see ibid. pp. 2148–9; and Higgins, *The Development of International Law through the Political Organs of the United Nations* (1963), p. 50. A good general discussion of the competence of the Security Council in the Indonesian question may be found in Taylor, pp. 336–73.

[6] This is the view taken by Taylor, p. 341.

emphasized the necessity of ending hostilities, while at the same time seeking means to enable the parties to move to an ultimate political solution.

Resolution S/1165 of 28 December 1949 asked the Consular Commission to send a complete report covering the cease-fire orders and the conditions prevailing in the areas under military occupation. Not surprisingly, the Consular Commission found itself in some difficulty:

The text of the Security Council's resolution of 28 December (S/1165) was conveyed to the Chairman of the Consular Commission by the then Acting Principal Secretary of the Committee of Good Offices on 29 December. The Commission called an informal meeting the following day in order to consider what steps could be taken to comply with the Council's resolution. It appeared that the Council's instructions to the Committee of Good Offices and its request to the Consular Commission overlapped to some extent, and it was evident that in order to comply with the Council's request the Commission would need the services of the military observers who were under the jurisdiction of their respective Consuls-General but had been at the disposal of the Committee of Good Offices since its inception.

The Chinese Consul-General, as Chairman of the Commission, was accordingly requested to visit the Chairman of the Committee of Good Offices in order to ascertain the views of the latter as to the best way to give effect to the Council's instructions. It was understood that the Committee, after ascertaining what arrangements could be effected with the Netherlands authorities, would telegraph the Council for elucidation.

On 3 January the head of the Netherlands Far Eastern Office in Batavia sent letters to the Chairman of the Committee and to the Commission announcing that a cease-fire had been ordered on the night of 31 December and promising facilities for both bodies and for the military observers. The Chairman of the Commission thereupon ascertained from the Chairman of the Committee that the Committee considered that the resolution of 24 December and the previous practice of the Committee covered all the points on which the Commission had been requested to report. The Chairman added that the Committee wished to send the military observers into the field at the earliest possible moment and indicated that the Committee would accordingly prefer that the Commission should not make a request for their service at this time. The Committee considered that the Council resolution of 1 November 1947 and subsequent resolutions were still in force.

The Commission met later the same day. In consideration of remarks made by representatives at the Council's meeting on 28 December that the object of the resolution dated that day was to assist the Committee and not in any way to slight or by-pass it, the Commission decided that the military observers should be left provisionally at the disposal of the Committee pending elucidation from the Council, and that a telegraphic explanation of the situation should be sent to the Council before its next meeting for this reason and to avoid duplication of work.

Practical reasons make clarification of the respective positions of the Committee and the Commission urgently necessary especially concerning the disposal of military observers.

(*Signed*) Francis SHEPHERD
Chairman Consular Commission
[*S/1190, 6 Jan. 1949, Report from Chairman of Consular Commission to Security Council.*]

The jurisdictional controversy continued into the later phases of the dispute, though after the second Dutch 'police action' in December 1948 it became clear that both the United States and the United Kingdom now believed—in the face of circumstances and the passage of time—that the Security Council had competence. When reminded by the Belgian representative that the United States representative had said in 1947 that 'my Government would not be prepared . . . to support action by the Council based on the conclusion that it has such jurisdiction'[7] (i.e. to make recommendations for a political solution as well as for a cease-fire), Ambassador Jessup of the United States now declared that recent events made essential firm recommendations by the Security Council. The United Kingdom also now thought that the Council had an 'obligation . . . to do everything possible and permissible to achieve a settlement'.[8] By January 1949 it was effectively left to Belgium to champion, within the Security Council, Dutch objections to jurisdictional competence. Recalling that in 1947 the Security Council had declined to adopt a Belgian proposal (S/517) to submit the question of competence to the International Court, the Belgian representative declared:

> For more than seventeen months it [i.e. the Security Council] has been operating on an ambiguous basis, whereas this ambiguity could have been removed in the period of six to nine weeks necessary to obtain the opinion of the Court. . . .
> While the Security Council may be said to have incurred the risk of overstepping its powers, it cannot rightly, in what it has done hitherto, be accused of complete lack of caution. On the whole it has taken care not to do more than the exercise of good offices. By its resolution of 25 August 1947 [S/525 II] it offered its good offices to the parties concerned, who accepted them. It confirmed this offer by its resolution of 28 February 1948 [S/678]. In remaining within the limits of good offices the Council has shown wisdom. The solutions to which its good offices may lead owe their validity to the fact of acceptance by the parties concerned. This acceptance of solutions proposed, in particular by the Security Council, may to a large extent remedy any defect in respect of lack of competence attached to the measures taken by the Council.
> In my opinion, the Council should not depart from this cautious attitude in its forthcoming attempt to find ways of settling the Indonesian question. In international politics it has mostly been found vain and useless to attempt to act without the good will and collaboration of the responsible Governments. Is the Security Council really in a position to ignore this experience? Would it not evince its wisdom by confining its work to the exercise of good offices?
> The Council should not contemplate other measures before having made sure, by reference to the Court, that it is empowered to take them. . . . [*Per the representative of Belgium, SCOR, 4th yr, 402nd mtg,* p. 4.]

However, by its resolution S/1234 of 29 January 1948, the Security Council showed clearly that it felt that it had the authority not only to call for an end to hostilities, but to make detailed proposals for a political settlement.[9] It did so notwithstanding the protests of the Netherlands that this was a gross intervention.[10]

Finally, it may be noted that in this early use of military observers by the UN, it was never entirely made clear whether they were agents of the Security Council or representatives of their own governments; or both. (For further comment, see s. 8, p. 38 below.)

---

[7] *SCOR*, 4th yr, 402nd mtg, p. 3.

[8] Ibid. 403rd mtg, p. 16.

[9] Taylor (p. 365) makes the point that while this may have been a departure in the direction of intervention, from the Dutch point of view, it was also the first UN resolution unequivocally to recognize that sovereignty *did* still repose with the Netherlands.

[10] *SCOR*, 4th yr, 406th mtg, p. 10.

5

POLITICAL CONTROL

THE Security Council exercised ultimate political control over the Consular Commission, the GOC, and the UNCI by virtue of the mandate which it laid down in its resolutions. The ultimate political goal of independence for Indonesia had already been achieved at Linggadjati. As the GOC's function was that of Good Offices, by definition it was permitted a very broad initiative—of which it fully availed itself—in the making of proposals to the parties. The UNCI came into existence within the framework of certain specific political recommendations by the Security Council itself[1] for a long-term settlement.

So far as the military observers were concerned, we have already seen that although they remained formally a part of the Consular Commission, they performed a variety of functions for each of the UN bodies in Indonesia.[2] They originally came into existence at the suggestion of the Consular Commission itself,[3] and reference to their existence entered the language of subsequent Security Council resolutions. Ultimate political control over them would seem to have rested with their respective governments, in whose employ they remained, and to whom they continued to owe allegiance. They sought to implement tasks assigned to them by the Security Council (and approved by their own governments) and by the terms of the *Renville* and Round Table Agreements, to the conclusion of which the GOC and UNCI had contributed. In terms of freedom of movement they operated, legally and necessarily, within the practical framework of the consent of the Netherlands and Indonesia.

When their numbers were reduced, after the transfer of sovereignty, the UNCI communicated its decisions on the reduction and phasing out to the Secretary-General, requesting him to inform the governments of those nations contributing military observers.[4] The decision of April 1951 to terminate completely the services of the observers was also taken by UNCI, and once again communicated to the Secretary-General for transmission to the five member states concerned.[5]

---

[1] See above, pp. 15–17, and below, p. 74.
[2] See above, pp. 20–4.   [3] S/586, p. 1.
[4] At that stage, five nations—Australia, Belgium, France, UK, USA.
[5] S/2087, 13 Apr. 1951, UNCI Report on Activities, app. II, pp. 33–4.

6

ADMINISTRATIVE AND MILITARY CONTROL

THE Consular Commission, the GOC, and the UNCI retained remarkable administrative freedom, organizing their own meetings and rules of procedure as they thought fit. Equally, the arrangements for the use of the military observers were left to be resolved in the field. This highly decentralized practice —which reflects both the novelty of the experiment and the fact that the military observers remained at all times in the service of their governments—contrasts with later practice whereby instructions are issued directly from the Secretary-General or his nominated Chief of Staff.

The chairmanship of the Consular Commission, under whose jurisdiction the military attachés formally lay, rotated monthly. However, the responsibility for organizing and administering the team of military observers was vested in, and apparently remained with, Colonel Mayer of the United States.[1]

By the end of September 1947 the military observers were 27 in number, and were operating mainly in teams of two. After the *Renville* Truce Agreement, their duties were enlarged beyond mere passive observation to assistance in the implementation of the truce. New administrative arrangements were made:

For discharging the responsibilities in connexion with the implementation of the Truce Agreement, the Committee of Good Offices obtained the services of the Consular Commission, together with its military assistants, in accordance with the resolution of the Security Council of 1 November 1947. The military assistants were formed in a pool under the direction of a Military Executive Board composed of the senior military assistants of the members of the Committee of Good Offices acting as a body and without regard to rank. The senior military assistants of China, France and the United Kingdom, the members of the Consular Commission not represented on the Committee of Good Offices, may attend the meetings of the Military Executive Board and the Security Committee as observers, when they are concerned with technical matters. Orders and directives issued to the officers of these countries are transmitted through the respective senior military assistants and are subject to the approval of the Consul General concerned, since an oath of allegiance taken by these officers precludes their accepting orders from any but military or civilian authorities of their own country. . . .
[S/787, 19 May 1948, GOC 2nd Interim Report, p. 57.]

The Military Executive Board was in fact to prove a very effective administrative unit. There did exist, however, the curious situation whereby the three career consular states which were not represented on the GOC (China, France, and the UK) were not party to major administrative and political decisions involving the

---

[1] The Editor has been unable to discover where and how this decision was taken. It appears, strangely enough, to have occasioned no protest from the Soviet Union.

use of their military attachés, notwithstanding the observer-status arrangements made in the Military Executive Board and Security Committee.

The hazards faced by the observers during the hostilities of December 1948 and January 1949 led to the issuance of further instructions:

88. Following the attack on the Commission's military observers in North Sumatra [*S/1293*] and several incidents of shooting at United Nations vehicles, indicating that the Commission's military observers might be exposed to increased hazards, the Commission decided to adopt additional measures for the safety of its military observers. Accordingly the following measures were put into effect:

(*a*) In certain areas to be designated by the Military Executive Board the Commission's military observers should be permitted to carry arms (either pistol or carbine, at the observer's discretion);

(*b*) Both parties should be advised that their armed personnel should not be carried in United Nations vehicles. When armed escorts accompany United Nations vehicles, they should travel in separate vehicles;

(*c*) United Nations personnel should be permitted to travel in armed vehicles of either party when necessary;

(*d*) United Nations vehicles should in future fly the United Nations flag as an identification, and the Commission's military observers should wear identification armbands;

(*e*) Light automatic weapons should be provided for United Nations vehicles operating in certain areas to be designated by the Military Executive Board.

The necessary side arms and light automatic weapons have been provided on loan by the Netherlands authorities. [*S/1373 & Corr. 1, UNCI 1st Interim Report*, pp. 28–9.]

Certain new decisions on re-deployment and the reduction of overall numbers were made after the successful conclusion of the Round Table Conference and the transfer of sovereignty. The decision to reduce the number of teams and to locate them in 3 places in Sumatra, 3 in Java, 1 in Borneo, 1 in the Riouw Archipelago, and 1 in East Indonesia[2] was taken upon a proposal of UNCI which was approved by the Military Sub-Committee of the Contact Committee established after the Round Table Conference. A decision to reduce the numbers of military observers from 63 to 35 was apparently taken on the authority of the UNCI alone.

[2] See p. 36 below.

7

COMPOSITION AND SIZE

(*a*) **First Phase**
By resolution S/525 (I) the Security Council requested those governments members of the Council and with career consuls in Batavia[1] to instruct them to

[1] It is of interest to note that the Netherlands itself had intended asking for an investigation by the career consuls in Batavia—and this would have included, in addition to the Consuls-General of

prepare reports for the Security Council on the observance of the cease-fire order and the conditions in areas under military occupation or from which armed forces in occupation might be withdrawn by agreement between the parties.

It was these career consuls themselves who urged the assistance of military observers:

And whereas, having received instructions from our respective Governments, we: Charles Eaton, Consul-General of Australia, P. Vanderstichelen, Consul-General of Belgium, Chia-tung Tsiang, Consul-General of China, Etienne Raux, Consul-General of France, Francis M. Shepherd, Consul-General of the United Kingdom and Walter A. Foote, Consul-General of the United States of America duly constituted ourselves the Security Council Consular Commission to give effect to the resolutions of the Security Council. Charles Livengood, Consul-General of the United States, and T. Lambert, Deputy Consul-General of the United Kingdom, participated in the work of the Commission.

At the first meeting, it was unanimously agreed that each of the Powers represented should be requested to furnish military officers to observe any possible violations of the cease-fire orders; to investigate, where possible, allegations of violations of the cease-fire orders; and to gather any other data that might be of value to the Commission and to the Security Council. In compliance with this request, the following observers were attached to the Commission: Australia 4, Belgium 2, China 4, France 3, United Kingdom 4 and the United States 8. In addition, the resident United Kingdom Military Liaison Officer and the United States Naval Aide were attached to the Commission; Mr Glenn A. Abbey, Consul of Career of the United States was appointed Secretary and Mr C. F. MacLaren, Information Officer of the United Kingdom Consulate-General was appointed Press Relations Officer. [*S/586, 22 Oct. 1947, Report by Consular Commission.*]

(*b*) Second Phase

By resolution S/525 (II) the Security Council established a Committee of Good Offices 'consisting of three members of the Council, each party selecting one and a third to be designated by the two so selected'.

Indonesia selected Australia; the Netherlands selected Belgium; and Australia and Belgium selected the United States. At its first meetings in the autumn of 1947 the Australian member was Mr Herbert Evatt; the Belgian member Mr Paul van Zeeland; and the American member Mr Frank Graham.

On 1 November 1947, in resolution S/597, the Security Council requested the Consular Commission, together with its military assistants, to make their services available to the GOC. Their number, however, dwindled to fifteen by the end of the year.[2]

On 17 January 1948 the *Renville* Truce Agreement was signed; and for its implementation the services of the GOC, the Consular Commission, and the

Australia, Belgium, China, France, the UK, and the USA, the Consul-General of Switzerland (*SCOR*, 2nd yr, 192nd mtg, p. 2145). The UN resolution S/525 (I), in operative paragraph 3, merely notes that the Netherlands intends to make this request of 'the career consuls stationed in Batavia', while operative paragraph 5 requests the issuance of appropriate instructions for this purpose by 'the Governments *members of the Council* which have career consular representatives in Batavia'. (Italics mine.)

[2] See Taylor, p. 424 n. 74.

military observers were required. The latter were now re-formed under a Military Executive Board, and their numbers increased:

For discharging the responsibilities in connexion with the implementation of the Truce Agreement, the Committee of Good Offices obtained the services of the Consular Commission, together with its military assistants, in accordance with the resolution of the Security Council of 1 November 1947. The military assistants were formed in a pool under the direction of a Military Executive Board composed of the senior military assistants of the members of the Committee of Good Offices acting as a body and without regard to rank. . . . The number of military assistants was increased to 15 Australians, 4 Belgians, 15 Americans, 5 Chinese, 6 French and 10 British, a total of 55, which has now been reduced to 47 by normal attrition. [*S/787, 19 May 1948, GOC 2nd Interim Report.*]

It was decided, for reasons of continuity and personal competence, that the original three-nation membership of the GOC should continue, even when the 1947 membership of the Security Council changed: 'At its 224th meeting, on 19 December 1947, the Council decided that the membership of the Committee of Good Offices should continue unchanged, in spite of the fact that after 31 December 1947 one of its members (Australia) would cease to be a member of the Council.'[3]

In July 1948 the Security Council granted a request of the GOC to provide eighteen jeeps and spare parts for use by military observers.[4]

Coert duBois, the US member of the GOC, left Indonesia during the summer of 1948 for health reasons; he was replaced by H. Merle Cochran.

Under resolution S/1234 of 28 January 1949 it was resolved that the GOC would henceforth be known as the UNCI. UNCI was to have all of the GOC's functions, and was to act by majority vote. Cease-fire orders were also issued to deal with the military hostilities which marked the breakdown of the *Renville* Agreement. This necessitated a further increase in the numbers of the military observers: 'In view of the added responsibilities of the military observers, resulting from the adoption of a cease-hostilities agreement, the Commission decided, upon the request of its Military Executive Board, that its members would recommend to their Governments an increase in the number of military observers.'[5] In fact, by July 1949 the previous figure of 55 had fallen to 40 (partly due to the recall of the Chinese military observers in May). In August 1949 it was increased to 63.[6]

The number of military observers altered again after the transfer of sovereignty. Both the number of teams and the number of men were reduced, prior to ultimate withdrawal on 6 April 1951.

Prior to the transfer of sovereignty on 27 December 1949, there were 13 military observer teams located in Sumatra, Java and East Indonesia, whose functions were to observe and report on the implementation of the cease-hostilities agreement reached by the parties on 1 August 1949, in the Batavia discussions.

Following the transfer of sovereignty, the military observers were called upon to fulfil a new task—that of observing and reporting on the implementation of the agreements reached at the Round Table Conference, and in particular of the provisions concerning the withdrawal

---

[3] *Resolutions and Decisions of the Security Council,* 1947, p. 10.   [4] S/929, 28 July 1949.
[5] S/1373 & Corr. 1, UNCI 1st Interim Report, p. 29.   [6] Taylor, p. 424 n. 74.

from Indonesia of troops under Netherlands command and the reorganization and demobilization of the Royal Netherlands Indonesian Army (KNIL).

On 6 February 1950, the Military Sub-Committee of the Contact Committee approved the Commission's proposal to reduce the number of teams and to locate them in three places in Sumatra (Medan, Padang and Palembang), three in Java (Bandung, Semarang and Surabaya), one in Borneo (Bandjermasin) one in the Riouw Archipelago (Tandjong Pinang) and one in East Indonesia (Makassar). The Military Executive Board, composed of the Commission's senior military assistants, was maintained in Djakarta.

At the same time, the Commission decided to reduce the number of military observers from sixty-three to thirty-five, apportioned as follows: Australia, Belgium and the United States, nine each; France and the United Kingdom, four each.

The Commission communicated this decision to the Secretary-General of the United Nations, requesting him to inform the Governments of the five Member States concerned.

In view of the satisfactory progress in the withdrawal of the forces under Netherlands command in Indonesia and in the demobilization and reorganization of the KNIL, and following the gradual closing down of assembly areas where these troops had been concentrated, the Commission suggested to the parties on 24 May that, as from 1 August 1950, some teams in Sumatra and Java should be recalled and the total establishment of military observers be reduced from thirty-five to twenty.

The parties approved the proposed reduction and the five Governments concerned were requested to leave at the Commission's disposal twenty-one observers apportioned as follows: Australia, Belgium and the United States, five each; France and the United Kingdom, three each. (In that way the Commission wished to provide one reserve for unforeseen contingencies.)

Following the complete withdrawal of troops under Netherlands authority from Sumatra and Borneo, on 4 September, the Commission approved the Military Executive Board's recommendation to recall the teams stationed there and to allocate their members to teams in Java.

The number of twenty-one military observers was further reduced by normal attrition, and on 29 September the Commission decided not to replace the officers who had already left, or whose departure was imminent. Consequently, the number of observers was reduced to thirteen (Australia, Belgium and the United States, three each; France and the United Kingdom, two each).

Although the contingent of thirteen observers remains officially at the disposal of the Commission, several officers were recalled from Indonesia; however, the Governments concerned undertook the responsibility of replacing them, if so requested. Such replacement was not found necessary.

On 14 March 1951, the Commission decided that, in view of the satisfactory state of the implementation reached in the arrangements made for the withdrawal of the Netherlands troops from Indonesia, the services of the military observers would no longer be required as from 6 April 1951.

The Commission communicated this decision to the Secretary-General of the United Nations, requesting him to inform the Governments of the five Member States concerned. Consequently, all military observers were recalled from Indonesia on or about 6 April 1951.

[S/2087, 13 Apr. 1951, UNCI Report on Activities since transfer of Sovereignty, app. II, pp. 33-4.]

8

RELATIONS WITH CONTRIBUTING STATES

THE observers were formally the Consular Commission's but also gave their services to the GOC and the UNCI. The states from which they were drawn were thus Australia, Belgium, France, China, the United Kingdom, and the United States.

Though their functions were determined by the Security Council, their *modus operandi* was devised entirely in the field, by each of the bodies which they served.[1] It was never entirely clear whether the military observers were acting as agents of the Security Council or as representatives of their governments. Indeed, the status of the bodies which they served was also ambiguous—the Consular Commission would seem to have been a group of government representatives acting *pro tem* as agents for the Security Council; the members of the GOC and the UNCI had a dual role as representatives of their governments and as individuals. Alastair Taylor has noticed the importance of the GOC members as individual persons, and the initiatives they advanced as such; and observes: '. . . In all cases, the actions of these members were apparently personal, yet they reflected the policies and interests of their governments. . . . They were concerned with interpreting their mandate from the Security Council (i.e. its resolutions) on the basis of directives received from their respective capitals'.[2]

In any event, there is nothing in the records which indicates any debate about the allegiance or status of either the Consular Commission and the GOC, or the military assistants whose services they utilized. Any potential conflict between their role as government representatives and agents of the Security Council was minimized by the fact that their governments were, in any event at the outset, members of the Security Council, and in the case of four of the nations providing military attachés (USA, UK, France, and China) possessed the right of veto by which they could prevent the passage of unacceptable directives.[3]

Certainly the military observers did not receive from the Secretary-General instructions comparable to those which later UN observer groups customarily

[1] See above, pp. 20-4.   [2] Taylor, p. 420.
[3] Taylor (p. 420) notes that the position of the US on the GOC was a special one—unlike the other two members, the US had not been nominated by either of the parties to the dispute. This meant that 'the American representative felt free either to mediate between the positions of his colleagues or to approach the parties directly. In the circumstances, the position advocated by the United States was invariably decisive and it also tended to be equated (at least in the State Department's view) with the over-all interests of the Council—or rather with the interests of the majority of its members.'

received—namely, a notification that their allegance was, for the duration of their service, to the UN only, and that they were forbidden to receive instructions from their own governments. None the less, as shown by the reports sent to New York concerning their ability to fulfil their duties during the second Dutch 'police action', they were clearly greatly concerned with carrying out the mandate entrusted to them by the UN. The further instructions issued to the observers by the Military Executive Board at this time also show a progressive identification of their role as that of 'UN personnel'.[4]

[4] See above, p. 34.

9

RELATIONS WITH HOST STATES

FOR the purposes of this section both the Netherlands and the Republic of Indonesia are treated as 'host states', though from one point of view only the Netherlands qualified for this description until sovereignty was formerly transferred to Indonesia on 27 December 1949. However, Indonesia had already attracted a measure of recognition as a *de facto* state by 1947, and the various UN bodies relied on Indonesian, as much as on Dutch, consent for their activities.

Broadly speaking, the UN retained good relations with both the Netherlands and Indonesia throughout this period, though the Netherlands had reservations about the UN's legal authority in this matter, and the UN was outspoken in its criticism of the second Dutch 'police action' at the end of 1948. The Dutch views on the scope of the Security Council's jurisdiction and competence are dealt with in Section 4 (above, pp. 25–7).

Notwithstanding its reservations, the Netherlands promised co-operation: 'The Netherlands Government, although persisting in its denial of the Council's jurisdiction in this matter, fully understands the Council's desire to see the use of arms come to an end in this as in other cases.'[1] When the Netherlands government had announced that it intended to ask the consuls stationed in Batavia to report on the situation, Indonesia was anxious that any such scheme should be harnessed to the Security Council: and it was this formula, whereby the Security Council would also request the career consuls to report to it, that was eventually employed in resolution S/525 (I):

The Indonesian delegation categorically stated at the one hundred and eighty-fourth meeting that the Republic of Indonesia will remain bound by each and every decision of the Security Council to appoint a commission or commissions for supervision of the cease-fire

[1] *SCOR*, 2nd yr, 174th mtg, p. 1716.

order and for arbitration. The Indonesian delegation again signifies its adherence to that pledge, and also wishes to stress at this point how vital it is that the composition of any such commission or commissions should be above suspicion. My delegation therefore asks the Security Council to give the undertaking that all such commissions will be impartial. If there should exist any doubt on the question of impartiality, it must necessarily follow that the decisions arrived at by those commissions will neither command the confidence of the parties concerned nor be conducive to beneficial results.

The Indonesian delegation is prepared to accept any resolution on impartial arbitration, provided that the Security Council is not by-passed. But this delegation must confess to a feeling of disquiet about the other resolution contained in document S/513 and concerning the supervision of the cease-fire, which asks for a commission composed of the career diplo- mats now in Batavia.

Until now, most of these men have looked at the situation in Indonesia through Dutch eyes and they will naturally be considered prejudiced observers. This suspicion is heightened by the action in this Council of the delegations of some countries which those officials repre- sent in Batavia. Openly and clearly and without a shadow of a doubt, these delegations have taken the side of the Netherlands in this Council. Their partiality is patent.

The Indonesian delegation feels that the personnel of any commission appointed by the Security Council should be untainted and free from the slightest breath of suspicion. We again stress the need for impartiality and add that any Security Council commission appointed to supervise the cease-fire and to carry out other investigations will receive the active assistance and co-operation of the Republic of Indonesia in the execution of its duties.   [*SCOR, 2nd yr, 194th mtg*, pp. 2191–2.]

Although individual Security Council members spoke out frankly on the merits of the Indonesian–Netherlands dispute—and from time to time the representatives of Australia and the United States strongly criticized the Netherlands position—the Council itself avoided criticizing any one party and addressed its resolutions to both equally. Thus 'the parties' were called upon to cease hostilities on 1 August 1947 (S/549) and the governments of both the Netherlands and Indonesia were requested 'to grant to the representatives referred to in paragraph 5 [the Consular Commission] all facilities necessary for the effective fulfilment of their mission'.[2] In its report issued on 24 October 1947 the Consular Commission reported that it had 'received every courtesy and assistance from both Netherlands and Republican authorities in executing its task' (S/586). None the less, the Netherlands made some criticisms of the report, feeling that it had been unsympathetic to the establishment of 'the van Mook line'[3] and had not properly appreciated the difficulties which the Dutch faced in implementing the cease-fire order:

Hardly any attempt is made to explain why we could not carry out to the letter the Council's resolutions calling for a cease-fire. On 22 October, at the two hundred and thirteenth meeting, I tried to supply this explanation, which alone places our actions in their true light. Nor did the consuls attempt to go into the question as to whether there was not, perhaps, a very cogent reason why there could be no fruitful consultation between our authorities and those at Jogja- karta concerning the observance of the Council's resolutions calling for a cease-fire. That explanation, too, I endeavoured to supply last week.

Moreover, no attempt was made to ascertain why the Lieutenant Governor-General was

[2] SC res. S/525 (I).
[3] For details of the van Mook line, and the problems flowing from its establishment, see below, p. 64.

constrained to fix his demarcation line; and this is all the more striking since in appendix VIII of the report that compelling reason was stated and reported to the Council by the Commission.

It is clear that neither what have been called our mopping-up operations nor the establishment of the demarcation line were acts initiated by us, but were inevitable consequences of acts of the Jogjakarta Government. Continued mopping up became inevitable because many Republican leaders continually urged their followers to attack us, in spite of the cease-fire resolutions. . . . [*Ibid. 216th mtg*, p. 2672.]

When the GOC was established pursuant to resolution S/525 (II), the Committee sought at an early stage to clarify its relationship to the Netherlands and Indonesia:

5. As regards its reponsibilities under the terms of the Security Council's resolutions, the Committee conveyed its views formally to the parties in a document dated 19 November, the substance of which had been conveyed informally on 7 November, to the committee representing the Netherlands Government. In that document the Committee stated that it would render all assistance possible to the parties in reaching a political settlement. In that connexion, the Committee would assume any and every task devolving upon it as the result of agreements or requests made by the parties from time to time. Nothing the Committee might do would bind either party, except under circumstances where two conditions were fulfilled, namely (1) that both parties asked the Committee to make recommendations, and (2) that both parties stated in advance that they would regard such recommendations as binding. However, under the terms of paragraph 4 of the Security Council resolution S/597 of 1 November 1947 on the Indonesian question, the Committee considered itself directed by the Council to offer its assistance to the parties, in the absence of any direct agreement between the parties, in reaching agreement on an arrangement which would ensure the observance of the cease-fire resolution, without awaiting a request by either party that the Committee offer such assistance.

7. In reply to a question put to the Committee by the delegation of the Republic of Indonesia regarding its procedure for assisting in the pacific settlement of the dispute, the Committee stated the following on 30 October:

'(1) The Committee of Good Offices on the Indonesian question considers it, as among its first duties, to take note of all the wishes of the parties and also to take note of any suggestions either party would wish to make.

'(2) The Committee desires to make it clear that it is ready, for its part, to make suggestions to the parties, if and when the Committee is requested to do so by the parties. In particular, the Committee would be prepared, if and when so requested by the parties, to offer its suggestions to the parties on appropriate procedures or methods of adjustment, as well as on such basic matters as are related to procedures for the settlement and terms of settlement.

'(3) As regards the question raised by the Prime Minister of the Republic of Indonesia at the meeting of the Committee with the Republican Government relating to the choice of a suitable place for conducting discussions on substantive matters, the Committee desires to make clear that it is ready to offer its suggestions, if so requested by the parties.

'(4) Finally, the Committee desires to emphasize that it will welcome and consider any suggestion made at any stage by either party, and will be ready to use its good offices to secure the best consideration of such suggestions as may be made.'

8. On 31 October, the Chairman of the committee representing the Netherlands Government stated the agreement of his committee with the interpretation of the functions of the Committee of Good Offices as stated by it, as set forth in paragraph 7 above, in its reply to a question put to it by the delegation of the Republic of Indonesia. [*S/649/Rev. 1, 22 Sept. 1950, GOC 1st Interim Report, 10 Feb. 1948.*]

During 1948 the GOC had contributed substantially to the successful *Renville* Truce Agreements, and to the attempts to implement these at both a military and political level.[4] However, by the late summer relations between Indonesia and the Netherlands were again deteriorating. The Netherlands government had incurred the suspicion of the Indonesians by calling a conference at Bandung in May 1948, to which a number of groups not associated with the Republic of Indonesia were invited. An invitation was not extended to the GOC.[5] Nor were the Dutch responsive to proposals put forward by the Australian and United States representatives of the GOC:

During latter part May Australian and United States representatives on Committee had become increasingly concerned at failure of parties to make any significant progress regarding major points in dispute particularly as apprehensive state of mind appeared to be developing on the part of the Republic. Accordingly these two representatives began independently to consider means of reconciling positions of parties and several working papers were prepared. Last and most extensive of these drafts was made available to Committee as whole on 4 June.

On same date Lieutenant Governor-General Netherlands Indies, Dr Van Mook, wrote Committee enclosing copy of invitation to Mr Hatta, Republican Prime Minister, to take part in informal discussion with him in Batavia. Invitation expressed concern over fact that 'on number of important points discussions between two delegations had revealed such divergence of views that bridging gap along lines followed so far seems difficult'. It voiced hope that discussion with Hatta might make it possible to obtain clear picture of these differences and possibilities of solving them.

Van Mook's letter to Committee stated 'I may add that Her Majesty's Government attach greatest importance these discussions between Netherlands and Republican authorities. It is evident that anything that might affect these discussions or their outcome in any way should be avoided in present circumstances. I therefore trust that Committee Good Offices will appreciate that greatest reserve and restraint should be shown by all concerned in order avoid anything that might be prejudicial to cause of these discussions.'

To this letter Chairman of Committee sent following reply dated 9 June:

'I been requested by Committee Good Offices state its behalf that Committee while welcoming every effort of parties to reach by themselves settlement of issues in dispute between them feels itself under obligation take such appropriate steps within its competence as it considers might assist in avoiding any possible deterioration in present negotiations toward pacific settlement dispute.

'To this end Committee is now considering further ways and means of assisting parties.'

On 10 June, Australian and United States representatives handed to Hatta and Van Mook respectively and simultaneously copies of joint working paper on an outline of an overall settlement on basis of above-mentioned draft 4 June prepared by two delegations stressing it should be kept confidential time being. Paper was accompanied by covering letter wherein two delegations explained background which led them attempt positive contribution towards agreement. Covering letter explained working paper tentative and subject reconsideration in light of discussions questions or objections which it might provoke. Two representative expressed belief that only by coming forward with such suggestion now that parties appeared unable to make further progress towards agreement could they acquit themselves of their obligation and justify seven and half months Committee spent Indonesia endeavouring assist parties. Letter expressed hope paper might prove useful in any conversation that might take place between Van Mook, Hatta and two delegations of their respective Governments should negotiations continue between them. Belgian representative was unable agree either to substance of paper or to procedure and therefore reserved his position.

On 14 June, Australian and United States representatives received from Van Mook letter stating that in conformity with instruction his Government he regretted inform them neither he nor Netherlands delegation could see their way to take paper into consideration.

---

[4] For details, see below, pp. 69–71.   [5] S/842, pp. 91–118.

Australian and United States representatives replied jointly 17 June to Van Mook expressing regret he had not shared their hope that paper might prove useful. Notwithstanding contrary views of Belgian representative they considered that working paper provided framework of settlement consistent with 'Renville' Principles and fair to both parties and that discussion on basis of paper could pave way to progress towards agreement.

In conclusion, two representatives stated they been puzzled by procedural difficulties which they appeared have encountered and that they were still not clear as to what exactly had made it impossible to consider working paper on its merits.

As Committee learned later contents of working paper had fallen into hands of Press by 15 June. Meanwhile 16 June few minutes before Steering Committee of Conference was scheduled to meet following letter was received from Acting Chairman Netherlands delegation:

'Have honour inform you that in view publication of strictly confidential document handed by du Bois to Van Mook 10 June, Netherlands delegation has requested instruction from Netherlands Government.

'Pending receipt these instructions Netherlands delegation thinks it advisable discontinue for time being discussions between both delegations with exception discussions concerning implementation Truce Agreement.'

Connexion this letter Committee wishes to state that Committee and Secretariat given assurances every precaution was taken avoid any leakage information connexion working paper.

With view clarifying position Committee asked Netherlands delegation in letter 18 June whether in position continue with Conference not only on subjects related to implementation of Truce Agreement but on whole scope of negotiations between delegations under Committee auspices.

Twenty June, Van Mook summoned Herremans, Chairman of week, and assured him that negotiations between delegations were to be resumed. [S/850, 22 June 1948, Cable to Security Council from GOC.]

Negotiations were in fact deadlocked, and the GOC was left with a growing feeling that there was little contribution that it could make.[6] The Netherlands indicated that the United States–Australian initiative merely prejudiced her direct negotiations with the Republic of Indonesia.[7] Meanwhile, a general election was being held in Holland on 7 July 1948, in which the Indonesian question was a central issue. There was growing dissatisfaction with the administration in Indonesia of van Mook, and the new government replaced his post—that of Lieutenant Governor-General—with that of High Representative of the Crown, and called for his resignation as from November 1948. Relations between the Netherlands and the Republic of Indonesia continued to deteriorate. After talks between the parties at the end of November, the Netherlands sent the following summary of its position to the GOC:

(a) The informal discussions have made clear that the Republican Government cannot exercise effective control over its armed forces, and therefore that effective co-operation on the part of the Republic to combat infringements of the truce cannot be expected;

(b) The Republican point of view regarding the powers of the High Representative of the Crown and particularly regarding his control over the armed forces during the interim period is not only fundamentally irreconcilable with the Netherlands sovereignty as formulated in

[6] The difficult position of the GOC during this period is chronicled by Taylor, pp. 125–66.
[7] For an examination of the political reasons underlying the Dutch refusal to discuss the Critchley-duBois proposals (see below, p. 70), see ibid. pp. 132–5.

the first of the six additional *Renville* principles, but would continue 'the present intolerable situation of two opposing armies under separate command';

(*c*) The refusal to recognize Netherlands sovereignty during the interim period nullifies the acceptance by the Republic of the draft agreement submitted by the United States delegation on 10 September 1948 as a basis for negotiations;

(*d*) The Netherlands Government must now proceed to the promulgation of the decree setting up an interim federal government 'drafted on the basis of the results of consultations with the representatives of the Federal Territories'.

The statement concludes that the 'Netherlands Government regrets that negotiations under the auspices of the Committee at this stage are futile' in that the Republican Government does not 'in fact recognize either the truce or the *Renville* principles, and a basis for agreement is fundamentally lacking'. [*S/1117, 12 Dec. 1948, Cablegram from GOC to President of Security Council.*]

On 19 December 1948 hostilities broke out between the Netherlands and Indonesia. Dutch co-operation with the GOC was withdrawn during this 'police action', and it was made particularly difficult for the military observers to fulfil their duties.

2. Despite frequent requests, the Netherlands authorities have not yet provided the United States representative or the deputy Australian representative, who are in Batavia, with any information regarding the welfare of the members of the Committee and their staff, and of the United Nations Secretariat who were in Kaliurang on 19 December 1948; nor have the Netherlands authorities provided means of communication between the two groups. . . .

5. The Committee draws the attention of the Security Council to the following points. . . .

(*a*) In their repudiation of the *Renville* Truce Agreement, the Netherlands government did not comply with the provisions of article 10 of that Agreement.

(*b*) The Committee is not aware of any circumstances connected with the concentration of Republican forces or the manœuvres of the Republican Army which should have given rise to apprehensions and alarm, leading to precipitate action on the part of the Netherlands.

(*c*) The tone of the Netherlands letter of 17 December 1948 to the United States representative (*vide* supplementary report of 18 December 1948) and the requirement of a reply within a time limit which was impossible of fulfilment give to this letter some features of an ultimatum.

(*d*) Military operations of the nature carried out by the Netherlands forces must have involved considerable planning, and it is difficult for the Committee not to conclude that plans for such operations were in progress during the exchange of correspondence referred to in the Committee's special report of 12 December 1948 and the supplementary report thereto of 18 December 1948, and at the time the Netherlands authorities facilitated the transfer of the Committee's headquarters to Kaliurang.

(*e*) Not only have the possibilities of negotiations under the auspices of the Committee not been exhausted, but they have not been adequately explored. There have been no negotiations under the auspices of the Committee since 23 July 1948. The recent direct talks cannot be regarded as negotiations, as they took the form of Netherlands demands for the complete surrender of the Republic to the Netherlands position on all important issues.

(*f*) In commencing military operations on 19 December 1948, the Netherlands Government acted in violation of its obligations under the *Renville* Truce Agreement. [*S/1138, 21 Dec. 1948, Report of GOC.*]

The GOC now reported to the Council on the predicament of its military observers:

1. The Committee desires to inform the Security Council that most of the Committee's military observers in Netherlands-controlled territory are in the course of complying with

orders received from the Netherlands military commanders in their areas to proceed to Batavia.

2. On 12 December, the Netherlands Commander-in-Chief agreed with the Chairman of the Committee's Military Executive Board that the military observers should remain at their regularly assigned stations in Netherlands-controlled territory.

3. On 22 December the Chairman of the Committee's Military Executive Board was officially informed by a representative of the Netherlands Commander-in-Chief that the High Representative of the Crown had issued instructions that all of the Committee's military observers were to be concentrated in Batavia. The Chairman of the Military Executive Board learned the same day that orders to this effect had been issued to the Netherlands commanders in the field as early as 21 December.

4. On 22 December the United States representative made inquiries of the Acting Chairman of the Netherlands delegation regarding these instructions. On 23 December 1948, the Chairman of the Committee received the following letter, No. 3990, from the Acting Chairman of the Netherlands delegation:

'Since the Government of the Netherlands has, in accordance with article 10 of the Truce Agreement, notified the Committee of Good Offices and the Republican delegation that the Truce Agreement is to be considered as no longer binding, the task of the military assistants of the Committee, as set forth in articles 4, 5 and 5b of said agreement, has now come to an end.

'Instructions were therefore issued to all territorial commanders that they suggest all military observers to report to the Board of Senior Military Observers at Batavia as their activities have terminated.

'In this connexion, it is noted that the Chairman of the Board of Senior Military Observers was verbally informed of this step beforehand.

'With regard to suggestions that military observers should remain with the headquarters to which they were attached, I have the honour to draw your attention to the fact that the demarcation lines and demilitarized zones no longer exist and the headquarters to which the various teams of military observers were attached have become mobile. Under the present circumstances it will be clear that the Netherlands military authorities are unable to accept any responsibility for military observers who move with these headquarters or by themselves in operational areas.

'In view of the above it would be sincerely appreciated if the Committee of Good Offices would request the Board of Senior Military Observers to issue orders similar to the suggestion made by the territorial commanders, to the effect that all military observers return to Batavia in order to report to the Board.'

5. After reading the foregoing letter, the Chairman of the Committee's Military Executive Board reaffirmed the facts stated in paragraphs 2 and 3 above.

6. The Truce Agreement of 17 January 1948 confers certain express functions on the military observers. In addition, the resolution of the Security Council of 1 November 1947 requests that the services of military observers, mentioned first in the resolution of 25 August 1947, be made available to the Committee of Good Offices. Therefore, the Committee feels an obligation to report immediately to the Council that this action, taken by the Netherlands Military Command without reference to the Committee, will deprive the Committee and consequently the Security Council of the services of the military observers in the field.

7. Although military observers in the field are obliged to conform with the directions of the Netherlands Military Commanders in their respective areas, the Committee is not complying with the request contained in the final paragraph of the letter quoted above, but is awaiting advice from the Security Council as to the future functions of the Committee's military assistants. [S/1146 & Corr. 1, 23 Dec. 1948, Report of GOC.]

The Security Council in the meantime adopted resolution S/1150 on 24 December 1948, calling upon the parties to cease hostilities and to release the President of the Republic of Indonesia and other political prisoners arrested since 18 December: these demands were addressed to both parties, though manifestly it only lay within the hands of one of them to comply. The GOC was instructed to report fully both on compliance with this resolution and with events in Indonesia since the outbreak of hostilities. The GOC now contacted the Netherlands government and the Republican government:

2. To enable the Committee of Good Offices to carry out the instructions given it by the above resolution, it requests immediate notice from you as to the steps which have been taken by your Government to implement the resolution. It is requested that your Government also keep the Committee immediately, fully and currently informed of further steps taken by your Government in compliance with the resolution and furnish it with copies of the relevant orders issued to the appropriate authorities.

3. It will further be necessary for the Committee's military observers to proceed to the areas where fighting has been in progress, including Jogjakarta. Instructions have been issued to the Committee's Military Executive Board to make arrangements for the despatch of military observers to the field. The Committee trusts that instructions will be issued to the Netherlands Military Command to give full co-operation to the Military Executive Board and to the Committee's observers.

4. The Committee requests that the aircraft at the disposal of the Committee of Good Offices be permitted, as heretofore, to operate freely in Java and Sumatra.

5. The Committee's Military Executive Board will consult with the military officials of your Government on the necessary details.

6. In order that the Republican Government may comply with the resolution, it is requested that the President of the Republic and the members of his Government be given all facilities to issue directions from Jogjakarta, or from such other centres as they may desire, to cease hostilities. [S/1154, 25 Dec. 1948, Cablegram from GOC.]

On 29 December the GOC reported:

7. Notwithstanding the request made to the Netherlands Government in its letter of 25 December (report of 26 December) the Committee's military observers have been concentrated in Batavia. With no authorization from the Netherlands authorities for the observers to return to the field, and with no permission given to operate the aircraft at its disposal, the Committee had no facilities to obtain first-hand information through its own representatives as to the military situation and operations. [S/1166, 29 Dec. 1948.]

All contact between the GOC and the Republican authorities had broken down because of the imprisonment of the latter.

While the Security Council resolutions avoided condemning the Netherlands in so many words, the GOC, in a detailed report, made clear its own assessment of where responsibility lay:

C. ANALYSIS

12. Article 10 of the Truce Agreement of 17 January 1948, cited in the Netherlands note of 18 December 1948, reads as follows:

'This Agreement shall be considered binding unless one party notifies the Committee of Good Offices and the other party that it considers the truce regulations are not being observed by the other party and that this Agreement should therefore be terminated.'

Analysis of the conditions precedent to a termination of the Truce Agreement set forth as applied to the facts of the present case leads to the following conclusions:

(a) The requirement of article 10 that notice be given to the Committee of Good Offices was not fulfilled. The letter dated 18 December 1948, signed by the Acting Chairman of the

Netherlands delegation and addressed to the 'Chairman of the Security Council's Committee of Good Offices on the Indonesian question, Kaliurang', was handed in Batavia to the United States representative at 23.30 hours Batavia time on 18 December. The letter was addressed to the Chairman of the Committee. It was not delivered to him. The Committee's headquarters, as recognized in the address given on the letter, had formally been transferred to Kaliurang for the current period on 15 December. The United States representative, at the time away from the current headquarters of the Committee and not the Chairman of the week, was not authorized, either explicitly or implicitly, to receive notice on behalf of the Committee. Notice was not received by the Committee until approximately 10.30 hours on Wednesday 22 December, when a letter from the United States representative was handed to the members of the Committee while they were in process of removal from Kaliurang to Jogjakarta, *en route* to Batavia. The United States representative had attempted vainly to transmit the notice earlier, but the Netherlands telegraph office refused to receive messages addressed to Republican areas, and Kaliurang was completely isolated. By the time, therefore, notice had been received, the Netherlands forces had been carrying on hostilities on the Republican side of the *status quo* line for more than three days.

(*b*) Similarly, the requirement of article 10 that notice be given to the other party was not fulfilled. Delivery to the Secretary-General of the Republican delegation in Batavia was not the type of notice contemplated in article 10, particularly, as by act of the Netherlands Government communications with the Republican Government and Republican-controlled territory had already been cut off. It was thus physically impossible to convey the contents of the letter to the Republican Government. The Secretary-General himself was arrested shortly after 01.00 hours on 19 December.

(*c*) Even if delivery of the letters in question at 23.30 and 23.45 hours on 18 December, respectively, had been sufficient to constitute notice, military action was instituted before the expiration of a reasonable time thereafter. As article 10 does not expressly specify any period of time that must elapse after giving the required notice before the notifying party can take action to the prejudice of the notified party, it requires by necessary implication a reasonable time. Military action was begun less than half an hour after the delivery of the second of the two notes above.

It is therefore the finding of the Committee of Good Offices that the facts established that:

(*a*) No effective notice of termination of the Truce Agreement of 17 January 1948 was given by the Netherlands Government.

(*b*) The Netherlands forces crossed the *status quo* line and initiated hostile military action against the Republic while the obligations of the Truce Agreement were still fully operative.

It should be noted that even if the Truce Agreement had been terminated in full accordance with the provisions of article 10 of the Truce the initiation of hostilities would none the less have been contrary to the cease-fire resolution of the Security Council of 1 August 1947.

13. The letter dated 17 December 1948 from the United States representative to the Acting Chairman of the Netherlands delegation (supplementary report, S/1129) shows that each of the communications received by the Committee or its members from the Netherlands delegation on 17 December emphasized the element of urgency. The particular requests made in the communications received from time to time during the day differed, and in some cases, conflicted with one another. All indicated, however, that time was of the essence. Finally, the telegram dated 17 December, which transmitted the reply of the Netherlands Government to the letter of the Vice-President of the Republic dated 13 December, emphasized that 'it is absolutely essential that the reply from the Republican Government be received in Batavia before Saturday 18 December 1948, 10 a.m. Batavia time for relay to the Netherlands Government'. The final telegram received late Friday evening re-emphasized the ten o'clock deadline, and stated that, in order to make it possible for the reply to be received in time, arrangements had been made in Batavia to have the plane assigned to the Committee of Good Offices leave there for Jogjakarta at 05.00 hours Batavia time, so that its return flight to Batavia with the reply could be begun at 07.00 hours Batavia time.

The telegram of 17 December, to which this immediate reply was required, called for com-

3

plete acceptance by the Republic, in the form of a binding declaration, of the entire Netherlands position on the basic issues between the parties, including those concerning the implementation of the truce. It also indicated that, whether or not those conditions were accepted, the decree setting up the Interim Federal Government would be promulgated on the basis of the previously prepared text. However, if all basic conditions were accepted by the Republic, the Netherlands Government would 'consult with the Republic and the other federal territories concerning later changes in the decree on less essential points'.

In his reply the United States representative also emphasized that he could not 'consistently with my obligations as a member of the Committee of Good Offices, press Dr Hatta to reply summarily on the conditions imposed by your telegram because it calls for a non-negotiated blanket assent which would preclude the possibility of *bona fide* negotiations, rather than effect their resumption'.

The reply of the United States representative further emphasized the factors which made it virtually physically impossible for the Vice-President of the Republic to prepare any reply of the character required at Kaliurang, not the seat of most Republican officials who would have to be consulted, at less than 18 hours notice, including transmission time.

The Committee finds that, in light of the pattern of events established by the various communications of 17 December, the Netherlands reply to the Vice-President of the Republic, dated 16 December but received on 17 December, constitutes as ultimatum providing a choice only between surrender to the Netherlands position on every basic issue between the parties and an unnamed alternative. On 17 December the Committee, still unwilling to believe that one party would abandon entirely the processes of peaceable negotiations and agreement, was reluctant to believe that the unnamed alternative was submission to armed invasion. The events of 18-19 December have proven otherwise.

14. The Committee draws attention to chapter 1 of the fourth interim report (S/1085) and to the special reports that have been subsequently submitted to the Security Council. These reports make clear that there have been no political negotiations in the Committee of Good Offices for a period of seven months and detail the efforts made by the members of the Committee to induce the parties to resume negotiations. These efforts continued up to the day before the outbreak of hostilities.

The Committee welcomed efforts of the parties to reach an agreement by direct conversations between themselves and hastened to facilitate the bringing together of the parties for that purpose. It was prepared to officiate finally, if called upon to do so, in the formalizing of an agreement, by whatever legitimate procedure it might have been obtained. The Committee cannot accept, however, the view that, where direct talks have failed, either party may thereafter refuse to negotiate further and thus prevent the issues separating the parties from being considered in their context in full negotiations before the Committee of Good Offices. On the contrary, the Committee finds in a failure of direct conversations merely an additional necessity for recourse to the techniques of the Committee for whatever assistance it can provide.

The recent Netherlands notes have put great emphasis on violations of the truce by the Government of the Republic. It is unquestionably the case that there have been large-scale infiltrations and an undue number of incidents and disorders. Many of these have occurred in Netherlands-controlled territory. Which of these can properly be called truce violations will not be considered here, nor will the Committee seek again to emphasize the fundamental principle set forth in the introduction to the fourth interim report, which states that 'the rising number of infringements of the Truce Agreement during this period is testimony to the relationship between the maintenance of the truce and progress in political negotiations'. It is unquestionably true that better implementation of the truce was required. It was for that very reason that the Committee called on the parties to discuss the problems of implementation of the truce in the Security Committee, which had been established for the purpose of supervising the enforcement of the mutual obligations of the parties under the Truce Agreement.

With truce violations as with political negotiations, the Committee finds that its facilities for adjustment and reconciliation have not been exhausted, much less effectively utilized.

It finds no legitimate basis on which a party could here forsake the forum of negotiations for that of armed force.

15. The Committee will exert its utmost efforts to carry out the functions conferred upon it in the resolution of the Security Council of 24 December 1948, namely, to observe and to report on its observance by the parties of the cease-hostilities order. But, if fighting is to give way to negotiations, the Committee as a whole recognizes that certain inevitable difficulties must be overcome. The members of the Committee differ only in the relative weight they give to these difficulties. . . . [*S/1156, 26 Dec. 1948, Report of GOC.*]

Though the initial UN resolution was addressed to both parties, representatives in the Security Council were more outspoken. In a scathing criticism of the Dutch action, Ambassador Jessup of the United States said:

The purpose of the Security Council cease-fire resolution of 24 December was to stop the fighting in Indonesia immediately so that the dispute could be settled not by force but by the processes of peaceful settlement enjoined on Member States by the Charter. Even though members of the Security Council were well aware that it was the Netherlands authorities which had initiated the resumption of military action, the resolution of the Security Council called on both parties to order a cease-fire. In such situations as those which existed at that time, this is an appropriate form of Security Council resolution, since the cessation must be mutual, no matter who is responsible for starting the fighting. It must be assumed that, in ordering a cease-fire, the Security Council could only have intended that such an order would apply equally and simultaneously to both sides. The Council could not have expected one side to comply unilaterally while the other considered itself free to comply at such a time and in such a way as it saw fit. The continuance of military action by the Netherlands forces until all military objectives had been taken cannot be regarded as compliance with the cease-fire order. Certainly the reservation of the right by one side to use its own forces in the territory of the other to eliminate the armed resistance of that other side which may thus far have escaped destruction, cannot be regarded as compliance with the cease-fire resolution.

Taking these factors into account, I am sure that the Security Council has no intention of approving action consolidating military victories which themselves were gained as a result of open defiance of an order of the Security Council.

Probably the most striking and clearest disregard of the orders of the Security Council is to be found in the refusal of the Netherlands authorities to release President Soekarno, Prime Minister Hatta and the other leading officials of the Government of the Republic of Indonesia. Quite aside from the disregard of the Security Council resolution of 28 December (*S/1164*) which required that these prisoners should be released within twenty-four hours, there is the present fact these persons are still not at liberty. The Security Council cannot be expected to accept the view of the Netherlands Government that these prisoners have been released because they are given a certain liberty of movement on the island of Bangka. In an archipelago comprising thousands of islands, liberty of movement which is restricted to a single island and one which, I might add, was under Netherlands control even under the *Renville* Agreement, cannot be regarded as being in conformity with the Security Council resolution of 24 and 28 December.

I have just seen document S/1199 containing a further report from the Committee of Good Offices concerning the question of the detention of President Soekarno, Prime Minister Hatta and other leading officials of the Republic of Indonesia.

It appears from this document that there is some question as to the present whereabouts of these officials, but I find nothing in the text of the letter from the Netherlands delegation of 11 January, which is reproduced in that document, to alter the essential facts and the conclusions from those facts which I have just drawn.

The clear intent of the resolutions of the Security Council on this point was that the high officials of the Republican Government should be restored to a position in which they would be free to exercise their governmental authority. The minimum which would seem to be called for at this moment is that the President and other interned officers of the Republic should be allowed to return to their capital and to exercise their appropriate functions there, free from the constraint of any occupying army. They should be free to establish and maintain contact with other officials of their Government. They should also be free to provide their own forces for the maintenance of law and order in Jogjakarta.

Further, my Government, in considering the Netherlands–Indonesian dispute, cannot but recall a history of non-co-operation on the part of the Netherlands in the work of the Committee of Good Offices in Indonesia. The failure to achieve a political settlement and the protracted negotiations which followed the signing of the *Renville* Agreement in January 1948 brought about in Indonesia an increased tension between the Netherlands and the Republic, with a consequent increase in provocative incidents which sorely strained the truce. The bill of particulars for these acts over a period of months is recorded in the reports of the Committee of Good Offices to the Security Council. From these reports it appears that even prior to the resumption of military action against the Republic, the Netherlands pursued a policy which had the effect of weakening the Republic, working unnecessary hardship on the population, isolating the Republican Government economically and politically, and presenting it with a prefabricated interim administration for Indonesia with which it was to associate itself but which it had no part in forming.

My Government considers these acts and the failure of the Netherlands to enter into *bona fide* negotiations since May of last year to be indicative of a reluctance to utilize the procedure for pacific settlement made available by the United Nations, and to be in conflict with both the spirit and the letter of the Linggadjati and the *Renville* Agreements. From a purely pragmatic point of view, it should be pointed out that the quick military successes of the Netherlands forces will not effect a solution of the Indonesian problem. My Government cannot associate itself with any aspect of the Netherlands military action. The use of force in this situation makes the solution of the problem far more complex and difficult. The problem remains a matter of international concern with which the Security Council must continue to deal. It cannot be solved if we begin on the basis of acceptance of the fruits of the illegal use of force.

The Republic of Indonesia represents the largest single political factor in the projected federation and should therefore have a voice in the formation of the federation. The Republic has a two-fold nature. First, it is a political entity; secondly, it is the heart of Indonesian nationalism. This latter attribute cannot be eliminated by any amount of military force. The Netherlands Government may find that, far from assuring law and order in the Indies, the course upon which it has embarked may instead let loose forces of terror, chaos and sabotage. It may well be that the only victory will be that of the forces of anarchy.

My Government is of the opinion that real peace in Indonesia can be expected only if there is a settlement of the political issues on the basis of the principles and procedures agreed to by the parties in the Linggadjati and *Renville* Agreements (*S/649, Appendices XIII and VIII*) and under the auspices of the United Nations. The responsibility for the future rests in the first instance on the Netherlands authorities. The Security Council has a right to assume that the Netherlands Government will, in accordance with its obligations, bring to an end its defiance of the Security Council and give its full co-operation towards reaching a fair and reasonable solution of the Indonesian question   [*SCOR, 4th yr, 398th mtg.*]

This speech marked a perceptible hardening in the United States position. The Netherlands also lost some of the support she had previously enjoyed from the United Kingdom.[8]

The Netherlands ended her military activities in Java on 31 December 1948 and in Sumatra on 5 January. On 28 December the Security Council had adopted resolution S/1165 under which the consular representatives in Batavia

---

[8] See *SCOR*, 4th yr, 400th mtg, pp. 9–11.

were asked to report on the observance of the cease-fire in areas under military occupation.[9] The Dutch authorities now contended that arrangements for the return of the observers to the field could not proceed because of a confusion over the functions of the GOC and the Consular Commission, and the observers' role in relation thereto. The Consular Commission's military observers had, it will be recalled, earlier been assigned to assist the GOC.[10]

2. On 31 December, the Committee addressed the following letter to the Acting Chairman of the Netherlands delegation:

'Batavia, 31 December 1948

'We have the honour to refer to numbered paragraphs 3, 4 and 5 of our letter dated 25 December 1948, in which we requested that arrangements be made which would make it possible for Committee's military observers to return to the field. This request was made by the Committee in order that it would be in a position to carry out the functions conferred upon it by the resolution of the Security Council of 24 December 1948.

'In your reply of 25 December 1948, you indicated that you would reply to the Committee as soon as instructions had been received from Her Majesty's Government.

'We are as yet in possession of only incomplete and unofficial reports of the recent debates in the Security Council. However, it would appear from these reports that Mr van Roijen expressed himself to the effect that all possible facilities would be granted to the military observers. We are informed that, in the debate of 27 December, Mr van Roijen made the statement that instructions had already been issued that military observers of the Committee of Good Offices be given an opportunity to study events. It seems possible that you may be now in receipt of instructions from your Government.

'We should therefore appreciate immediate notification as to whether your Government will now permit the Committee's military observers to return to suitable posts in the field with full use of transportation and other facilities as heretofore enjoyed.

'The Committee does not wish to press you unduly. You will understand, however, that we are anxious to perform fully and expeditiously the duties entrusted to us by the Security Council. We therefore feel constrained to request a reply no later than noon of 1 January 1949.

(*Signed*) 'H. M. COCHRAN
'*Chairman*'

3. On 1 January, the Committee received the following letter from the Netherlands delegation:

'Batavia, 1 Juanuary 1949

'As a result of your letter of 31 December 1948, I have again asked the Netherlands Government for instructions regarding the arrangements to be made to make it possible for the military observers to return to the field. I regret to say that so far these instructions have not reached me.

(*Signed*) 'T. ELINK SCHUURMAN'

'Batavia, 3 January 1949

. . . 'With reference to my letter of 1 January 1949, No. 1, I am now in a position to state that the Netherlands Government has sent to the Government of Indonesia the necessary instructions to enable the Committee of Good Offices, the Consular Commission and the military observers to carry out the task as formulated in the penultimate paragraph of Mr van Roijen's statement of 27 December 1948 and in numbered paragraph 4 of his statement of

[9] For text, see above, p. 15.
[10] 'This jurisdictional problem would have remained theoretical, had it not been that the Dutch used the jurisdiction confusion as an excuse for preventing the military observers from returning to the field' (Wainhouse, p. 315).

29 December 1948. In this connexion it is observed that the Netherlands authorities, as a result of the shortage of material, will, especially in the beginning, only be able to place at the disposal of the Committee of Good Offices, the Consular Commission and their military observers limited transport facilities. It is therefore suggested that the Committee of Good Offices use as much as possible its own aircraft and other means of transportation. It will be clear that under the present circumstances the visit to some areas might be temporarily restricted as a result of measures taken by Netherlands authorities for reasons of safety and military necessity. Moreover, it is pointed out that the visits to certain areas may entail considerable personal risk for which the Netherlands Government must disclaim responsibility. . . .

(*Signed*) 'T. ELINK SCHUURMAN'

6. On 3 January, the Committee replied as follows to the Netherlands letter of the same date:

'Batavia, 3 January 1949

'I have the honour to acknowledge receipt of your letter of 3 January 1949, received by us at approximately 16.00 hours today. In your letter, you note that you have now the necessary instructions which will enable the Committee's military observers to return to the field for the implementation of the duties conferred on the Committee of Good Offices by the resolution of the Security Council of 24 December 1948.

'With your approval, representatives of the Committee's Military Executive Board will be ready to call on the Chief of Staff of the Netherlands Army or his designated representative to discuss preliminary plans relative to the redeployment of the military observers tomorrow morning. I request that you make the necessary appointment.

'We take this opportunity to express the hope that you are now in a position to furnish the Committee with information requested in the Committee's letter of 28 December 1948. Regarding the order of the Commander-in-Chief of the Royal Netherlands-Indonesian Army, the Committee would appreciate being informed as to the time and date of the issue of this order and the persons to whom it was addressed and the method of its transmission.

'It is the hope of the Committee that all necessary arrangements can be completed on 4 January so that the redeployment can be begun by tomorrow afternoon.

'I should much appreciate, therefore, a reply to this letter with reference to the second and third paragraphs above by 10.00 hours tomorrow, 4 January.

(*Signed*) 'T. K. CRITCHLEY
'*Chairman*'

7. At the same time, the Committee wrote to the Secretary-General of the Republican delegation as follows:

'Batavia, 3 January 1949

'I have the honour to inform you that the Committee has received today a letter from the Acting Chairman of the Netherlands delegation advising that instructions have been received which will permit the Committee's military observers to return to the field.

'In reply the Committee has suggested preliminary arrangements and has instructed its Military Executive Board to consult with the Netherlands Military Command on the details for the redeployment of the military observers.

'The Committee would appreciate your advice as to the manner in which you will be able to facilitate the return of the military observers to the field. It is the hope of the Committee that all necessary arrangements can be completed on 4 January so that the redeployment can be begun by tomorrow afternoon. I should much appreciate, therefore, a reply to this letter by 10.00 hours tomorrow, 4 January 1949.

(*Signed*) 'T. K. CRITCHLEY
'*Chairman*'

8. On 4 January, the Committee received the following replies from the Secretary-General of the Republican delegation and the Acting Chairman of the Netherlands delegation to its letter of 3 January.

LETTER FROM THE SECRETARY-GENERAL OF THE REPUBLICAN DELEGATION TO THE CHAIRMAN OF THE COMMITTEE OF GOOD OFFICES

Jakarta, 4 January 1949

'I have the honour to refer to your letter of 3 January 1949, requesting advice on the manner in which the return of military observers to the field may be facilitated. This letter was delivered to me at 08.55 hours this morning.

'Unfortunately, as I am still unable to contact either the Republican Government or the Republican delegation, I am unable at this stage to assist the Committee in the redeployment of military observers.

'Any assistance which the Committee can render in obtaining the release of Republican political prisoners and facilitating communications between Republican authorities would, of course, be greatly appreciated. It is also assumed that as soon as practicable arrangements will be made for the military observers to consult with Republican authorities and that the latter will be given an equal opportunity with the Netherlands officials in facilitating inquiries by the military observers.

(*Signed*) 'R. SUDJONO
'*Secretary-General of the delegation of the Republic of Indonesia*'

LETTER FROM THE ACTING CHAIRMAN OF THE NETHERLANDS DELEGATION TO THE CHAIRMAN OF THE COMMITTEE OF GOOD OFFICES

'Batavia, 4 January 1949

'With reference to your letter dated 3 January 1949 received yesterday at approximately 20.45 hours and to our conversations by telephone today at 09.50 hours and 11.20 hours, I have the honour to confirm that a representative of the Chief of Staff of the Royal Netherlands-Indonesian Army will be ready to receive representatives of your Committee's military observers today at 17.00 hours at General Headquarters to discuss preliminary plans relative to the redeployment of the military observers.

'It may be noted that, since no reply has as yet been received from the Consular Commission to the letter referred to in the last paragraph of my letter of 3 January 1949 to your Committee, these discussions can only bear a provisional character and cannot prejudice the performance of the task entrusted to the Consular Commission. Obviously it will be necessary to co-ordinate the plans of your Committee and those of the Consular Commission as far as the Netherlands and Indonesian authorities are concerned.

'The remaining information requested in the Committee's letter of 28 December 1948 will be furnished as soon as the consultations with my Government regarding this matter are concluded....

(*Signed*) 'T. ELINK SCHUURMAN
'*Acting Chairman*'

11. In accordance with the arrangement made by the Acting Chairman of the Netherlands delegation, of which the Committee was advised in the latter's letter of 4 January, members of the Committee's Military Executive Board conferred with a representative of the Chief of Staff of the Royal Netherlands-Indonesian Army at 17.00 hours on that date. Unfortunately it was not possible at this meeting to make any concrete progress towards finalizing the arrangements for sending the military observers into the field. The Committee therefore decided to address the following letter to the Acting Chairman of the Netherlands delegation, summarizing the events of the meeting and setting out the Committee's views with reference to the discussion:

'Batavia, 6 January 1949

'I have the honour to refer to your letter of 3 January 1949, in which you advised that you were in receipt of instructions under which the Committee's military observers could return to the field for the implementation of the duties conferred on the Committee of Good Offices by the resolution of the Security Council of 24 December 1948. In your reply dated 4 January to our letter of 3 January, which emphasized the Committee's desire to complete all necessary arrangements immediately, so that redeployment could be begun the afternoon of 4 January, you confirmed that a representative of the Royal Netherlands-Indonesian Army Chief of Staff would receive representatives of the Committee's military assistants at 17.00 hours on 4 January to discuss the plans.

'Our military representatives have advised us that no concrete progress was made in this meeting towards the return of the military observers to the field. The representative of the Chief of Staff had no authority to decide on arrangements and insisted that the matter would have to be referred to the Commander-in-Chief and Chief of the General Staff, neither of whom was in Batavia at the time. The representative of the Chief of Staff undertook to advise the Chairman of the Committee's Military Executive Board when a decision was made by the Commander-in-Chief, so that a further meeting could be held. Up to 16.00 hours today, forty-six hours later, nothing has been received from him.

'The Committee has studied Mr van Roijen's statements in the Security Council on 27 and 29 December appended to your letter of 3 January, the texts of your letters and the transcript of the meeting with the representative of the Chief of your General Staff. It wishes to make sure that no misunderstanding exists as to its position.

'In your letter of 4 January, you state that as no reply had yet been received from the Consular Commission to a letter similar to that of 3 January addressed to the Committee, "discussions can only bear a provisional character and cannot prejudice the performance of the task entrusted to the Consular Commission". You further state that co-ordination of the plans of the Committee and of the Consular Commission will be necessary "as far as the Netherlands and Indonesian authorities are concerned". Similarly, Colonel Thomson, the representative of your Chief of Staff, after querying at some length the status of the military observers in relationship to the Committee of Good Offices and to the Consular Commission, stated: "But still there is this confusion about the existence of two committees; if the Security Council will notify us, or either of the committees, about the exact position, that will then help us greatly in going ahead with our part of the task". Again he stated: "We consider the clarification of the confusion regarding the functions of the Committee of Good Offices and the Consular Commission as very important". This is one of the matters to be referred to the decision of the Commander-in-Chief and the Chief of Staff before arrangements can be begun.

'In the view of the Committee, there is no confusion of a type which should delay it in the performance of its urgent duty to report. Any position on the part of your Government preventing the early return of the military observers to the field until the "confusion" has been clarified, would in effect paralyse both organs of the Security Council at a crucial time.

'What is important is timely resumption by the military observers of their functions, already in suspension over the entire period in which their reporting would have been of greatest value, and not irrelevant debate as to the manner in which their reports will be channelled to the Security Council, whether through the Committee or through the Consular Commission.

'We wish further to correct the tendency seen in the meeting held with the representative of the Chief of Staff, to limit unduly the scope of the work to be done by the military observers. There were many references to the military observers as having only the function of observing the "cessation of hostilities" now that, as Colonel Thomson put it, "there is no longer any truce, there is no longer any (word missing) and there is no longer a long list of truce infringements". The broad scope of the observations to be carried on by the military observers is very clearly expressed in the conclusion of the statement made on 27 December in the Security Council by Mr van Roijen, the Netherlands representative: "In order to enable the Committee . . . to carry out its instructions to report on the situation after 12 December 1948, the Netherlands Government has issued instructions that the military experts at the disposal of the Committee, and their staff, be given opportunity to study the course of events. I am authorized to add that this last provision means in practice that, to use the words of the Committee of Good Offices itself, the military observers can again be dispatched to the field." It is feared that the position of your Government is not fully understood at all levels by those who are charged with the making of arrangements.

'It is obvious, of course, that the military observers can in practice return to the field only if your Government permits them to do so. Further, as they are dependent to a very great extent on the facilities and opportunities provided by your field commanders, they must operate, if at all, in accordance with the limitations you see fit to impose. However, you will appreciate that the Committee must comply with the instructions given to it by the Security Council. It cannot in any way consent to, or tacitly condone by acceptance, any limitation on the activities of the military observers which would prevent them from performing fully the obligations imposed on them.

'Ten days have passed since the statement of Mr van Roijen, quoted above; almost two weeks since the adoption by the Security Council of the resolution of 24 December. Not one military observer is yet in process of returning to the field, from which, as set forth in our letter of 23 December, the military observers were excluded by Netherlands Army officials soon after hostilities were begun. The Committee must emphasize that the passing of time and the progress of military action may well destroy the value to the Committee and to the Security Council of the direct observations of the military observers, by whom alone, in many cases, can the Committee procure the first-hand information needed for the reports called for by the resolution of the Security Council of 24 December.

'The Committee awaits further word from you or other appropriate Netherlands officials as to whether, and under what conditions, the military observers will be permitted to return to the field.

(*Signed*) 'T. K. CRITCHLEY
'*Chairman*'

CONCLUSIONS

15. Despite the statements made to the Security Council by the Netherlands representative on 27 and 29 December, the Committee has not been in a position to make independent investigations of any kind in the field for the purpose of carrying out its functions under the resolution of 24 December. As a result of the failure of Netherlands authorities to authorize or facilitate the return of the Committee's military observers to the field, they are temporarily immobilized in Batavia and Bandung without any opportunities for observation. It has been heard unofficially and informally that certain military and naval liaison officers attached to some of the consular officials in Batavia took advantage of a Netherlands offer to conduct them on a tour of some of the military areas on 5–6 January. These officers are not the military observers of the Committee of Good Offices and their observations are not available to the Committee, even if their tour was the type of field investigation and observation required by the functions of the Committee.

16. If the Committee of Good Offices is to continue to function, it is requested that the Security Council define the respective functions of the Committee and of the Consular Commission under the resolutions of 24 and 28 December 1948. Inability to determine whether the functions of one are at this point exclusive of the other or concurrent, and the problem of to whom the military observers are primarily responsible, has already created some difficulty and has been made an occasion for delay (paragraph 11 above). It is understood that this point has been raised independently in a telegram dated 6 January from the Consular Commission to the Security Council.

17. The Committee invites the attention of the Security Council to the problem of its present and future status.

The functions exercised under the truce by the Committee and its military assistants have disappeared with the truce itself. The Committee was set up under the resolution of the Security Council of 25 August 1947 to aid the parties in reaching a pacific settlement of their dispute. The first of the twelve Renville principles provided that the Committee would assist in the working out and signing of a political agreement to be achieved by negotiation. But negotiations and the methods of pacific settlement have now been rejected in favour of military action.

4*

The Committee feels a deep and abiding concern for the welfare of Indonesia. It does not, however, wish to be put in the position of seeming to approve, by its participation or even its authentication, any settlement based on force rather than true negotiation.

Divested of the broad functions it formerly exercised by the change in circumstances resulting from the military action instituted on 19 December, there remains to the Committee the function of reporting to the Council under the terms of the resolution of 24 December. Sub-paragraphs (*a*) and (*b*) of the resolution have already been the subject of report. The Committee is also called upon in the resolution of 24 December to exercise what may be looked upon as a continuing reporting function, that of reporting to the Council on the 'events which have transpired in Indonesia since 12 December 1948'. The inability of the Committee to carry out effectively this direction as a result of its failure to obtain permission or facilities for the return of its military observers to the field has already been emphasized, as have the inherent difficulties in the way of useful reporting (paragraphs 14 and 15). But even if its military assistants were permitted to move freely everywhere in Indonesia without undue restrictions and were given adequate facilities, it must be emphasized that the Committee itself was designed primarily as an instrument of negotiation.

These considerations inevitably raise the question whether the continuation of the Committee of Good Offices in the present circumstances would serve any useful purpose or could contribute to a peaceful settlement of the Indonesian problem. [*S/1189, 7 Jan. 1949, Report of GOC.*]

In the event, though no precise guidance was given by the Security Council on the division of jurisdictional competence between the GOC and the Consular Commission,[11] the Netherlands allowed the dispatch of military observers to Java and Sumatra on 9 January 1949.[12] The return to full freedom of movement for the UN observers was slow:

The Committee of Good Offices submits the following analysis of the military situation prepared with the assistance of the Committee's Military Executive Board on the basis of reports by the military observers received since that forwarded in the Committee's report of 14 January (S/1212).

1. The Netherlands Commands have extended facilities for military observers to observe occupied areas as far as they could assure normal safety measures. Full reports from all teams have not yet been received.

2. Military observers are able to observe only the localities taken by the Netherlands Army in its occupation of large towns and the main roads connecting them. They are attached to the Netherlands forces and cannot employ Republican military sources in their reports. Furthermore, military observer teams are at present deployed in such a way as to observe only the territories newly occupied by the Netherlands forces. Their positions, determined by various practical considerations, are not necessarily the best for the observation of current activities. In general no observations are being made on happenings inside the areas on the Netherlands side of the former *status quo* line. Therefore, unofficial reports coming to the personal attention of members of the Committee that there have been movements by armed Republican adherents into areas on the Netherlands side of the former *status quo* lines and such reports of conditions in those areas, have not been verified as yet by the military observers.

3. In general the areas away from the main roads have not been under observation by

---

[11] 'It might be pointed out, however, that in discussions held by the Dutch authorities and the GOC and attended by Sir Francis Shepherd, Chairman of the Consular Commission, Sir Francis had declared that there should have been no misunderstanding since, on January 4, the Dutch delegation had been informed of the Consular Commission's position' (Taylor, p. 178 n. 36). See also, to the same effect, the statement by the representative of Australia, *SCOR*, 4th yr, 397th mtg.

[12] S/1193, p. 19.

military observers as these have not been occupied by the Netherlands forces and, consequently, are not considered safe by the commanders or the military observers because of the guerilla activities. [*S/1223, 24 Jan. 1949, Report of GOC.*]

As late as March 1949 the newly formed UNCI, into which the GOC had been transformed by Security Council resolution S/1234 of 28 January 1949,[13] reported:

22. In order to obtain information that would enable the Commission's military observers to discharge more effectively their duties under the 24 December 1948 resolution, as well as that of 28 January 1949, the following questions were put to the Netherlands authorities:
'1. Will it be possible for the Military Executive Board to see the Netherlands army situation map in order to decide the further deployment of the military observers?
'2. Can the Netherlands authorities give the Military Executive Board any information regarding present guerrilla activities in all occupied areas of Java, Sumatra and Madura?
'3. What military action is being taken against such guerrilla activities, if any?
These questions were first presented to the representative of the Commander-in-Chief of the Royal Netherlands Indonesian Army by the Commission's Military Executive Board on 25 January, and subsequently by the Commission to the Netherlands delegation on 29 January. Reminders were given to the Netherlands delegation on 4 and 7 February. No reply has been received.
'4. May the Military Executive Board send military observers to those areas in order to report on these activities and the resulting conditions?
'5. Will the Netherlands authorities keep the Military Executive Board currently informed regarding disposition of forces as it is known and what military action is taking place?'
23. The most recent report of the Commission's Military Executive Board, dated 26 February, prepared on the basis of reports by the military observers in February, draws attention to paragraphs 2 and 3 of the report of 24 January (S/1223) to the Security Council which states the various factors limiting the military observers in their work. The Board emphasizes that the Netherlands policy of refusing information to military observers and of denying them opportunity to observe areas on the Netherlands side of the former *status quo* line in which unrest is said to continue, severely handicaps them in reporting fully on conditions throughout Indonesia. [*S/1270 & Corr. 1, 1 Mar. 1949, Report of UNCI.*]

Difficulties persisted in the relationship between UNCI and the Netherlands, so far as the UN observers were concerned:

87. On 22 April the Commission informed the Council of reports from some teams of military observers which indicated that they were not obtaining full co-operation from some Netherlands military commanders. It also reported that the Commission had contacted the Netherlands delegation with regard to the matter [*S/1314*].
In a letter dated 27 May the Netherlands delegation assured the Commission that the Netherlands Government was fully aware of the importance of close and full co-operation between the Commission's military observers and the military and civil authorities of both parties. The Netherlands Government had therefore instructed its military and civil officials to assist the military observers as much as possible in the performance of their duties. Although the Netherlands Government maintained 'its objection in principle' to the observation of internal security measures, it would permit the Commission's military observers to observe the military situation in the areas of Java and Sumatra which had been under Netherlands control prior to 19 December 1948. With regard to reports that the population in certain areas had been reluctant to give information to military observers, presumably due to pressure from local Netherlands authorities, the Netherlands delegation informed the Commission that an investigation had been conducted by the competent authorities, that the investigation

[13] For text, see above, pp. 15–17.

gave no indication whatsoever of pressure being put on the population by local Netherlands authorities, and that the Netherlands Government would disapprove very strongly of any such practice. Since receipt of the Netherlands letter of 27 May, no further complaints of that nature have been received by the Commission from its military observers. [*S/1373 & Corr. 1, UNCI 1st Interim Report.*]

However, UNCI was able to establish a relationship with the Netherlands which enabled the Commission to contribute substantially to the Round Table Agreements at the end of 1949, under which sovereignty was finally transferred to the Republic of Indonesia.

10

RELATIONS WITH OTHER STATES INVOLVED

REFERENCE has been made to the attitude of the contributing nations in section 8 above, and to their voting patterns in section 2 above.

A special word may be said here, however, about the position of the Soviet Union. The Consular Commission was composed of those Security Council members who had career consuls in Batavia—a decision which had high among its purposes the exclusion of the Soviet Union. For these, and other, reasons the establishment of the Consular Commission was strongly opposed by the Soviet Union.

First of all, let us see whose consuls are in Indonesia. In Indonesia there is a United States, a French, a United Kingdom, a Chinese, and Australian and I think a Swiss consul (Switzerland is not a Member of the United Nations). Among the five eligible so-called 'career' consuls therefore there are United Kingdom, French and United States consuls. We all know—I think that we can speak frankly in discussing this and all other questions—the attitude adopted by the United Kingdom in the Indonesian question. There is no secret about the position of the French Government in this matter. Something is also known about the position of the United States. Thus, out of the five consuls in Indonesia we find three whose opinions and actions, in the view of the USSR delegation, cannot be relied upon or considered to reflect in any way the Security Council's opinion or that of the countries represented on the Security Council. They will reflect the opinion of three countries, namely, the United States, the United Kingdom and France and not the opinion of the countries represented on the Security Council.

One fails to understand on what grounds the representatives of the United Kingdom, the United States and France, without representatives of the other countries which are members of the Security Council, should supervise and ensure the implementation of the Security Council's decision of 1 August. On what grounds are the other countries represented on the Security Council set aside under this resolution? No convincing reasons can be given to justify the proposal that only five consuls, that is to say, five countries, should ensure the implementation of the Council's decision on the cessation of hostilities.

I will deal with the question of arbitration later.

We know that the Governments of the United Kingdom and of France are favourable to the Netherlands; we also know that the attitude of the Government of the United States is on the whole favourable to the Netherlands. If we are to judge this attitude by individual remarks, apparently intended to have an effect on public opinion, or by the content of the statements which have been made by the representative of the United States on this subject, then the USSR delegation and the Government of the USSR cannot consider that the career consuls of the five Powers can act for the Security Council. There is apparently no justification for thinking that they can do this. As far as the USSR delegation is concerned these consuls do not exist. They are the consuls of the United States, France, the United Kingdom, Australia and China. They are not representatives of the Security Council, they are not a commission of the Council.

The resolution submitted jointly by the representatives of Australia and China, contains in substance a proposal which in practice means by-passing the United Nations. That proposal can only be construed in this way. In its present form, it seems to indicate that the Security Council is taking some kind of action, but in substance and in content, it means that the Security Council voluntarily stands aside and accepts the proposal dictated by Mr van Kleffens, the representative of the Netherlands Government, the representative of the guilty party in this conflict, which, as I have already stated, met with such a warm and, in my opinion, unmerited reception in the Security Council. [*Per the representative of the USSR, SCOR, 2nd yr, 193rd mtg, pp.* 2180–1.]

The Soviet Union took the position that the Netherlands was engaged, as a colonial Power, in systematic repression of the principle of self-determination in Indonesia. Whereas the Netherlands regarded herself as under pressure in the Security Council, Russia regarded the Security Council resolutions as proposals virtually involving complicity with the Netherlands. Similarly, while the Netherlands viewed the American role on the GOC as one largely sympathetic to the Republican case, and hostile to the Dutch colonial role, the Soviet Union portrayed the American role as solid support for the Netherlands. The United States had economic interests in the area and 'acted throughout so as to protect the Netherlands . . . and to put the Indonesian Republic in a still worse position'.[1] The *Renville* Agreements were equally unacceptable to the Soviet Union, being attributed to American pressure.

In 1948 Russia faced the difficult problem of continuing to champion Indonesian nationalism, while within Indonesia the Republican leaders effectively opposed attempts mounted by Indonesian Communists to obtain power. The Soviet Union continued at the UN to oppose the Dutch position and to charge UN resolutions with inadequacy or protection of Dutch and colonial interests. However, she did not exercise her veto, nor did she allude to internal developments in the Republic of Indonesia.[2]

---

[1] *SCOR*, 194th mtg, p. 2206.
[2] For a useful survey of the strategy of the Soviet Union, and her attitude to the Hatta–Sukarno government (and its suppression of the Indonesian Communist rebellion of 1948) see Taylor, pp. 386–9.

II

FINANCE

As time went on, the military observers were less and less identified with the interests of their own governments and more and more thought of as 'UN observers'. They were supplied by the Consular Commission, and were on the payroll of their respective governments. In July 1948 there was made what was probably the earliest call for a contribution by the UN for equipment for the observers: the Chairman of the GOC cabled for eighteen jeeps and spare parts.[1] Generally, however, the costs of the GOC, save for the salaries of the military assistants, were met by the Netherlands. The Dutch government paid for the quarters of the GOC at the Hotel des Indes in Batavia, and for meals and transportation. During this phase the UN itself was financially responsible only for the small UN secretariat accompanying the GOC.[2] No further details are available, as at this time expenditures of individual missions were not listed separately within the general budget allocation for 'special missions'.

By the time the UNCI was established, however, the idea had also evolved of UN financial responsibility. In resolution S/1234 of 28 January 1949, under which UNCI was set up, the Secretary-General was requested, in paragraph 5, 'to make available to the Commission such staff, funds and other facilities as are required by the Commission for the discharge of its functions'. Moreover, as has been seen, in September 1949 the Security Council passed the following resolution:

The Security Council,
Considering that, in virtue of General Assembly resolution 231 (III) of 8 October 1948, it is a matter for its own decision whether, in the case of commissions of inquiry or investigation instituted by it, the representative of a Member State participating in such a commission need to be assisted by an alternate,
Considering that, in cases where this need has been found by the Security Council to exist, the Secretary-General is authorized to reimburse Member States retroactively for the travelling and subsistence expenses of the alternates of their representatives on the said commissions,
Notes that since the institution of the under-mentioned commissions the representatives of Member States that are participating or have participated have each had to be assisted by an alternate:
   1. The Committee of Good Offices, which has now become the United Nations Commission for Indonesia;
   2. The United Nations Commission for India and Pakistan. [*SC res. S/1401, 27 Sept. 1949.*]

---

[1] S/929, 28 June 1948.   [2] Wainhouse, p. 304.

Very shortly afterwards the Council adopted a resolution specifically directed at the question of costs of the observers:

The Security Council,
Having received a cablegram dated 5 August 1949, from the Consular Commission at Batavia to the President of the Security Council, requesting that the United Nations assume future costs of military observers in Indonesia.
Transmits this message to the Secretary-General.   [*SC res. S/1404, 5 Oct. 1949.*]

Expenses were henceforth raised on the regular budget, involving the amounts shown in the following tables:

	1949 $	*1950* $	*1951* $
Temporary assistance	65,079	53,767	28,857
Travel and subsistence of members	34,000	41,782	
Travel and subsistence of staff	77,441	47,610	
Communications services	8,979	3,314	1,225
Stationery and office supplies	2,022	630	
Operation and maintenance of transport equipment	3,764	2,517	
Freight, cartage, and express	2,707	2,356	
Insurance	19,385	11,085	
Miscellaneous supplies and services	2,457	2,283	
Travel and subsistence of observers	50,745	143,486	39,873
Office furniture, fixtures and equipment	1,237	185	
Hospitality	200	791	
Rental and maintenance of premises and equipment		58	
Local transportation	12,700	9,391	
Other	3,098	4,298	
	283,814	319,255	74,253
SOURCE:	*A/1267*	*A/1812*	*A/2125*

Note: There is no detailed breakdown of UNCI's actual expenses for 1951 to be derived from A/2125 (*GAOR*, 7th sess, suppl. 5), which gives only the total of $74,253. The figure appearing in this column have therefore been taken from Wainhouse, p. 305.

12

IMPLEMENTATION

IT has been shown in section 3 above that the broad duty of the UN military observers was to lend appropriate assistance to the Consular Commission, the GOC, and UNCI in the pursuit by these bodies of the fulfilment of Security Council resolutions. The tasks assigned to each of these bodies—and thus indirectly to the observers—were concerned with achieving an end to hostilities and rapid progress to Indonesian independence. The UN resolutions developed the role to be played by these bodies, and they in turn specified what assistance they required from the observers.

It has been correctly stated that 'the United Nations was not concerned with establishing a goal of Indonesian independence, since this had already been decided at Linggadjati. It was concerned only with the transition from the existing situation to independence and the maintenance of peace during that transition period.'[1] This section can do no more than point to the contribution of the UN observers to the ultimate, though hard-won, success of these objectives.[2]

On 25 August 1947 the Security Council established the Consular Commission at Batavia to report on the cease-fire and the conditions in areas under military occupation.[3] It was assisted by the military observers of the consular Powers. This was the first cease-fire order ever issued by the UN, and its acceptance by both Indonesia and the Netherlands was noted with satisfaction.[4] However, hostilities continued none the less, to a large extent because of a basic disagreement between the parties as to the meaning of a 'cease-fire':

> The Commission was informed that there is a difference in military practice between the significance of the order 'Cease fire' and the order 'Cease hostilities'. It understands that 'Cease fire' entails only the stopping of military advances and cessation of actual firing while 'Cease hostilities', on the other hand, appears to entail the cessation of all warlike operations, including the use of all military weapons, naval blockade, air reconnaissance, hostile propaganda, and movements of troops into territory occupied by the other side. 'Cease hostilities' accordingly has a considerably wider significance than 'Cease fire.' . . .
>
> Neither side, however, had any real belief that the order would be carried out by the other. The cease-fire order issued by the Netherlands East Indies Government High Command included the following: 'Not expected that Jogjakarta will fulfil the laid down conditions to cease hostilities, propaganda, destruction, inciting of population and troops and dispersed fighting organizations.'
>
> The Republican Government for its part, in paragraph 5 of the statement sent to the Security Council by the Deputy Prime Minister, said:
>
> 'The Government of the Republic of Indonesia, mindful of the experience gained during the past two years, wishes to express its grave concern about the fact that, unless the execution of the cessation of the cease-fire order is fully and continuously supervised by a third neutral party, there is no guarantee that it will not be unilaterally violated by the Netherlands forces.'
>
> There was thus an unfortunate lack of confidence on both sides that the order would be properly carried out.
>
> Both sides admit that a cease-fire order should normally be followed by contact between the two parties in order to arrange details for the satisfactory observance of the order. No attempt was made by either to effect such contact, largely, if not entirely, because of this lack of confidence. . . .

B. REPUBLICAN INTERPRETATION OF 'CEASE FIRE'

The order given by the President of the Republic in his radio speech on 4 August is quoted as follows:

---

[1] Wainhouse, p. 295.

[2] A full and masterly analysis of the whole story is to be found in Alastair Taylor's *Indonesian Independence and the United Nations*.

[3] S/525 (I); for text see above, p. 10.

[4] For these acceptances, see *SCOR*, 2nd yr, 174th mtg, p. 1716; and S/465 & S/466.

'I order . . . the entire armed forces of the Indonesian Republic and the people struggling at the side of our armed forces to remain in the positions which they now occupy and to cease all hostilities.'

While this order may be regarded as complete in itself, we have found that very little attempt has been made by the Republican Army Headquarters to issue exact and detailed orders to all ranks of the Republican Army and it has been found that the interpretations of 'cease fire' have varied slightly with individual military commanders.

The general interpretation on the Republican side is:

(*a*) Do not fire unless fired upon, and do not initiate any offensive action;
(*b*) Consolidate the present defences;
(*c*) Continue patrols outside the foremost defended localities for the purpose of military intelligence;
(*d*) Repel vigorously any attack by the Dutch.

At the same time, in at least two divisions a policy has been adopted which allows harassing attacks on Dutch concentrations believed ready to advance. This is considered by the Divisional Commanders in question to be a justifiable precaution. Reconnaisance patrols into Netherlands-held territory have also been considered justifiable.

Owing to the late arrival of the Security Council's resolution, the radio speech delivered by President Sukarno at midnight on 4–5 August 1947 was, in effect, the order given by him as Supreme Commander of the Republican Armed Forces to cease hostilities.

The first official action through army channels was a clarifying signal sent out at 3.25 p.m. local time on 5 August 1947 by the Commander-in-Chief to all service commanders, including the Commander of the Sumatra Command, and its purport was that whilst offensive action should cease, an active defence should be maintained. The message was sent out by wireless and telephone, and appears to have been duly acknowledged by the recipients. They in turn forwarded the signal down to unit level. At unit level, military observers have reported that forward sentries were fully acquainted with orders forbidding offensive action and that written orders for patrol leaders expressly forbade the use of force except in self-defence. Whilst the orders issued from Army Headquarters to cease hostilities were doubtless received in Central Java and in areas where communications were available and control possible, there is little likelihood that anything but the President's radio speech reached the guerilla bands within the Netherlands-controlled areas and the Republican forces cut off by the Dutch advance.

C. NETHERLANDS INTERPRETATION OF 'CEASE FIRE'

The Netherlands order for the cease fire contained the following relevant sentences:

'Netherlands Government ordered finish operations soonest under pressure resolution Security Council. Therefore all operations must be ceased 4 August—repeat, 4th—24.00 hours, whereby it must be clear this means operations which aim gains new—repeat, new—territory. To safeguard population, our troops and objects within—repeat, within—now occupied territory operations continue without interruption. Administrative geographical description of territory now held by Netherlands forces will be issued soonest. No—repeat, no—actions allowed outside now occupied territory and objects.'

From official statements made to the Commission it is clear that the Netherlands Army's interpretation of the cease-fire order is based on the principle that it is possible to dominate and control an area, without necessarily occupying the whole of it.

When the order to cease operations was received, all the strategic points which had been the first objectives of the police action had been occupied. The Commander-in-Chief accordingly reported to the Lieutenant Governor-General that the area dominated by those strategic points was under his control.

The Netherlands Army view is, therefore, that the location or movement of any Republican forces within this area is a breach of the cease-fire order and that the Dutch forces are at liberty to take any measures to disperse, capture, or destroy such forces. . . . [*S/586, Repor*[t] *by Consular Commission, 22 Oct. 1947.*]

This conflicting interpretation was closely linked with the establishment by the Netherlands, on 29 August 1947, of the so-called 'van Mook line' (named after the Lieutenant Governor-General). By this the Dutch drew a line between their front-line positions, and claimed the right to continue military action behind it, even where no Netherlands administrative control existed. The Consular Commission reported:

There is no doubt that the continuance of hostile action is due to the decision of the Netherlands authorities to impose military and administrative control over the area defined by the van Mook line, to the refusal of the Republic authorities to recognize their right to do so, and to the continued actions of irresponsible bands. . . .

It was further stated that Mr van Mook had given instructions that although Dutch troops were to stand fast after the cease-fire order, they were to mop up any pockets of resistance, and this called forth the reply by an Indonesian general that all Dutch troops moving within this area were to be attacked.

It is our considered opinion that, in view of the present situation regarding the Netherlands demarcation lines and the present positions of both Netherlands and Indonesian troops, the cease-fire order cannot be observed, and that incidents and guerrilla fighting will continue and probably increase. . . . [*Ibid.* pp. 10 & 26.]

It will be noted that at this juncture the Consular Commission's role was merely to report on the observation of the cease-fire, not to assist in implementing it in any direct way, or to supervise it. Having in the meantime established a Good Offices Committee and asked the Consular Commission together with its military assistants, to make its services available to this Committee,[5] the Security Council now

4. *Advises* the parties concerned, the Committee of Good Offices and the Consular Commission that its resolution . . . of 1 August 1947 should be interpreted as meaning that the use of armed forces of either party by hostile action to extend its control over territory not occupied by it on 4 August 1947 is inconsistent with [the] Council resolution. . . . [*SC res. S/597, 1 Nov. 1947.*]

This left open the problem of delineating territory held on 4 August; but the GOC was at least an organ operating in a positive way, with a role beyond that of mere reporting, in the field. The Committee was able to move the parties towards the holding of the *Renville* Truce Conference in January 1948. This three-man Committee initially met separately with each of the parties, and suggested, when faced with problems about a mutually acceptable site for talks, that meetings should take place on the USS *Renville* in Java waters:

6. Far from conceiving its assistance as having a binding character, the Committee considered that its duties could be fulfilled only through agreement between the parties themselves. The Committee stated, however, that, should the parties reject the Committee's assistance, the Committee's responsibility to the Security Council would be acquitted simply by reporting to the Security Council. . . .

15. The Committee decided that its primary duties, namely, assisting in the pacific settlement of the dispute and assisting the parties to reach an agreement on an arrangement which would ensure the observance of the cease-fire resolution, could best be discharged by getting

[5] Resolutions S/525 (I) & S/597; for texts see above, pp. 10–12.

the parties to meet with each other to undertake political discussions, as well as discussions leading to the implementation of the Council's resolution of 1 November. It was the considered opinion of the Committee that the discussions by the parties concerning implementation of the resolutions regarding the cease-fire and the discussions looking toward a political settlement had a bearing on each other. It was further the opinion of the Committee that both discussions should be undertaken with all possible speed, as any measure of agreement reached in either discussion would facilitate the reaching of agreement in the other. It was believed that any insistence that either discussion should have reached a specified stage of agreement before the other discussion was undertaken, might easily result in stalemate as to both. The Committee recognized the urgency of reaching an agreement to implement the cease-fire resolution, and pending such agreement emphasized the importance of ceasing any activities, or incitement to activities, which contravened that resolution, and of taking appropriate measures for safeguarding life and property. This was a matter of days, and in the Committee's view the parties should immediately undertake discussions to that end either directly or through its good offices. Therefore, while the Committee continued its preparations for holding the political discussions between the parties on board the U.S.S. *Renville* as soon as she arrived, the Committee arranged with the parties that they appoint special committees for the implementation of the Council's resolution of 1 November. On 12 November, the Committee appointed six representatives, two from the delegation of each member of the Committee, to assist the special committees of the parties. Three of the six representatives of the Committee comprise senior military officers attached to delegations of the representatives on the Committee. [*S/649/Rev. 1, 22 Sept. 1950, GOC 1st Interim Report, 10 Feb. 1948.*]

The special committees mentioned in paragraph 15 of S/649/Rev. 1 met from 14 November onwards. The GOC suggested the following way forward:

Both parties have repeatedly stated that they still hold to the principles underlying the Linggadjati Agreement. According to the statements and explanations the Committee has received from both parties, the Committee believes that the principles of this Agreement may be summarized as follows:

(1) Independence of the Indonesian peoples.

(2) Co-operation between the peoples of the Netherlands and Indonesia.

(3) A sovereign State on a federal basis, under a constitution which will be arrived at by democratic processes.

(4) A union between the United States of Indonesia and other parts of the Kingdom of the Netherlands under the Crown.

What the Committee thinks desirable is a concrete elaboration of those principles, conceived and drafted by each of the parties, with the desire and the hope to meet half-way the known or putative views of the other. . . . [*Ibid. App. V, para. 4.*]

The GOC produced not only a plan for the implementation of the truce[6] but also a list of suggested principles for a political settlement.[7] On 17 January 1948 agreement was reached between the Netherlands government and the Indonesian government on a Truce Agreement known as the *Renville* Agreement:

The Government of the Kingdom of the Netherlands and the Government of the Republic of Indonesia, referred to in this agreement as the parties, hereby agree as follows:

1. That a stand-fast and cease-fire order be issued separately and simultaneously by both parties immediately upon the signing of this agreement and to be fully effective within forty-eight hours. This order will apply to the troops of both parties along the boundary lines of the areas described in the proclamation of the Netherlands Indies Government on 29 August 1947, which shall be called the *status quo* line, and in the areas specified in the following paragraph.

[6] S/649/Rev. 1, app. V, ann. 1.   [7] Ibid. ann. 2.

2. That in the first instance and for the time being, demilitarized zones be established in general conformity with the above-mentioned *status quo* line; these zones as a rule will comprise the territories between this *status quo* line and, on one side, the line of the Netherlands forward positions and, on the other side, the line of the Republican forward positions, the average width of each of the zones being approximately the same.

3. That the establishment of the demilitarized zones in no way prejudices the rights, claims or position of the parties under the resolutions of the Security Council of 1, 25, and 26 August and 1 November 1947.

4. That, upon acceptance of the foregoing by both parties, the Committee will place at the disposal of both parties its military assistants who will be instructed to assume, in the first instance, responsibility for determining whether any incident requires inquiry by the higher authorities of either or both parties.

5. That, pending a political settlement, the responsibility for the maintenance of law and order and of security of life and property in the demilitarized zones will remain vested in the civil police forces of the respective parties. (The term 'civil police' does not exclude the temporary use of military personnel in the capacity of civil police, it being understood that the police forces will be under civil control.) The Committee's military assistants will be available to advise the appropriate authorities of the parties and to serve in such other proper capacities as may be requested. Among other, they should:

(*a*) Call upon pools of police officers established by each party in its demilitarized zone to accompany the military assistants in their endeavours and activities throughout that demilitarized zone. Police officers of one party will not move into and throughout the demilitarized zone of the other party unless accompanied by a military assistant of the Committee of Good Offices and a police officer of that other party;

(*b*) Promote co-operation between the two police forces.

6. That trade and intercourse between all areas should be permitted as far as possible; such restrictions as may be necessary will be agreed upon by the parties with the assistance of the Committee and its representatives if required.

7. That this agreement shall include all the following points already agreed to in principle by the parties:

(*a*) To prohibit sabotage, intimidation and reprisals and other activities of a similar nature against individuals, groups of individuals, and property, including destruction of property of any kind and by whomsoever owned, and to utilize every means at their command to this end;

(*b*) To refrain from broadcasts or any other form of propaganda aimed at provoking or disturbing troops and civilians;

(*c*) To initiate broadcasts and institute other measures to inform all troops and civilians of the delicate situation and the necessity for strict compliance with the provisions of sub-paragraphs (*a*) and (*b*);

(*d*) Full opportunity for observation by military and civil assistants to be made available to the committee of Good Offices;

(*e*) To cease immediately the publication of a daily operational *communiqué* or any other information about military operations unless by prior mutual agreement in writing, except weekly publication of lists of individuals (giving names, numbers and home addresses) who have been killed or have died as a result of injuries received in action;

(*f*) To accept the principle of the release of prisoners by each party and to commence discussions with a view to the most rapid and convenient implementation thereof, the release in principle to be without regard to the number of prisoners held by either party.

8. That, on the acceptance of the foregoing, the Committee's military assistants will immediately conduct inquiries to establish whether and where, especially in West Java, elements of the Republican military forces continue to offer resistance behind the present forward positions of the Netherlands forces. If the inquiry establishes the existence of such forces, these would withdraw as quickly as practicable, and in any case within twenty-one days, as set out in the following paragraph.

9. That all forces of each party in any area accepted as a demilitarized zone or in any area

on the other party's side of a demilitarized zone, will, under the observation of military assistants of the Committee and with arms and warlike equipment, move peacefully to the territory on the party's own side of the demilitarized zones. Both parties undertake to facilitate a speedy and peaceful evacuation of the forces concerned.

10. This agreement shall be considered binding unless one party notifies the Committee of Good Offices and the other party that it considers the truce regulations are not being observed by the other party and that this agreement should therefore be terminated. . . .

ANNEX TO APPENDIX XI
CLARIFICATION OF THE TRUCE AGREEMENT

1. As regards paragraph 1 of the foregoing agreement, it is understood that the two parties will endeavour to implement the various points of the truce agreement without any delay and with all means at their disposal; it is equally understood that, should one of the parties meet with special difficulties in carrying out fully within a few days any obligation imposed upon it by the truce agreement, upon notification to the other party the time limit of forty-eight hours provided in the first article of the proposals will be extended up to a maximum of twelve days.

2. As regards paragraph 2 of the foregoing agreement, it is understood that if, as expected, the truce agreement is increasingly implemented and the general situation continues to develop favourably, the demilitarized zones will, as a matter of course be further extended. . . . [*Ibid. App. XI & Annex.*][8]

The parties also agreed on an initial twelve Dutch political principles, and six additional principles proposed by the GOC.[9] The series of meetings held between the GOC military advisers and the Dutch military were undoubtedly an important factor in the achievement of an agreement. The GOC now placed, under the terms of the *Renville* Agreement, its military assistants at the disposal of the parties.

For discharging the responsibilities in connexion with the implementation of the Truce Agreement, the Committee of Good Offices obtained the services of the Consular Commission, together with its military assistants, in accordance with the resolution of the Security Council of 1 November 1947. The military assistants were formed in a pool under the direction of a Military Executive Board composed of the senior military assistants of the members of the Committee of Good Offices. . . . [*S/787, 19 May 1948, GOC 2nd Interim Report*, p. 57.]

The implementation of the military aspects of the Agreement was assigned to a Security Committee of the GOC. In March the GOC reported that the Security Committee had been concerned with: (1) the general cease-fire, (2) the delineation of the *status quo* line and demilitarized zones, (3) evacuation of Republican forces from Netherlands-controlled territory, (4) release of persons being held as prisoners of war, (5) evacuation of families of military personnel and their present welfare, (6) alleged violations of the Truce Agreement, and (7) the widening of the demilitarized zones. The GOC reported:

1. *General cease-fire*
On 17 January 1948 at the time of the signing of the Truce Agreement, the parties agreed on the text of a preliminary cease hostilities order which was issued separately and simul-

---

[8] For text of para. 3 of this Annex see above, p. 22.
[9] S/AC. 10 CONF. 2/3 & S/AC. 10/CONF. 2/4. The details of the prolonged drama of the *Renville* negotiations are excellently described in Taylor, pp. 66–97.

taneously by both parties immediately upon the signing of the Truce Agreement. The Committee's military assistants have reported that this order has generally been well observed.

2. *Delineation of the* status quo *line and demilitarized zones*

Shortly after the signing of the Truce Agreement the military assistants arranged meetings between the local commanders of the parties at a number of places along the *status quo* line laid down in the Truce Agreement. At these meetings agreements were reached as to the delineation and marking of the *status quo* line and the demilitarized zones in the field. At the second meeting of the Security Committee on 23 February the parties reported that the *status quo* line and demilitarized zones had been delineated in all areas without major difficulties, except in (1) the Kemit area in Central Java, (2) the Pronodjiwo area in East Java and (3) the Gubug area in Central Java. The difficulties in the first and third cases arose from the fact that the Netherlands authorities maintained that the delineation of the *status quo* line should be carried out on the basis of the map presented by the Netherlands delegation as an annex to the general regulations under the Truce Agreement; the Republican authorities were of the opinion that the delineation should be based primarily on the text of the proclamation of the Lieutenant Governor of 29 August 1947, as stated in the Truce Agreement. The difficulties in the second case were due to an administrative boundary change during the Japanese occupation. The Security Committee appointed a Sub-Committee, consisting of the Military Executive Board and two military experts from each party, to examine the situation in these areas in detail. The report of this Sub-Committee was discussed at the third and fourth meetings of the Security Committee on 26 February and 1 March, and agreement was reached in regard to the delineation of the *status quo* line in these areas.

3. *Evacuation of Republican Forces from Netherlands-controlled territory to Republican-controlled territory*

. . . the Committee's military assistants, in co-operation with the military authorities of both parties, established contact with Republican military personnel on the Netherlands side of the *status quo* line and explained the provisions of the Truce Agreement providing for their evacuation. Several assembly centres were set up to which the TNI troops could report for evacuation and from these centres move to Republican-controlled territory under the observation of the military assistants.

From the start, the work of evacuation was carried out smoothly. When the original 21 days time-limit for evacuation specified in the Truce Agreement expired on 7 February, the Republican delegation requested an extension until the evacuations were completed. Upon receipt of confirmation from its military assistants that the evacuation was not concluded in the time scheduled because of technical difficulties, the Committee transmitted the Republican request to the Netherlands delegation. The Netherlands military authorities then authorized the Netherlands local commanders to extend the period for evacuations beyond 7 February, when and where necessary. However, on 17 February the Committee was informed by its Military Executive Board that the Netherlands Command had stated that it could not continue extending the period indefinitely and considered that by 24.00 hours on 17 February the evacuations should have been carried out; consequently, Republican military personnel who had not reported by that time for evacuation were considered to be unwilling to carry out the orders of their commanders and were therefore not entitled to the same treatment as those who reported before that time. The Committee immediately addressed a letter to the Netherlands delegation expressing its hope that the Netherlands Command would postpone any action which might interrupt the progress of evacuation in areas where the local Republican commanders had not yet stated that these evacuations were completed. Following the discussion of this matter at the first meeting of the Security Committee on 19 February at which the Republican representative stated that the evacuation could be completed by 22 February, the Netherlands delegation informed the Committee on 24 February of the final decision made by the Netherlands Command that TNI troops who reported during the period 17 February 24.00 hours and 22 February 24.00 hours would be evacuated in the same manner as those who reported before 17 February 24.00 hours. At the third meeting of the Security Committee held on 26 February, the parties expressed agreement that the evacuation of Republican forces under the Truce Agreement had been satisfactorily completed. The total number of Republican combatants evacuated was about 35,000. . . . [*Ibid. s. V.*]

The Security Committee began to make progress, in the face of difficulties, with Items 4, 5, 6, and 7 also. So far as alleged violations of the Truce Agreement were concerned, instructions were issued to the military advisers.[10] A subcommittee was set up to report on the possibility of widening the demilitarized zones.[11]

A further report was issued by the GOC in June 1948:

. . . The military provisions of the truce have been carried out as well or better than could reasonably have been hoped although both delegations, especially Netherlands delegation, have been reporting violations of the Truce Agreement, particularly instances of infiltration for purposes of espionage or intimidation. The problem is complicated by rigid controls exercised upon movement of persons across *status quo* line (demarcation line that divides territories controlled by Netherlands from those controlled by Republic) contrary to what Committee had hoped would be developed from Truce Agreement.

General success of truce however was evidenced outstandingly in February by the evacuation of 35,000 Republican combatants to Republican-controlled territory from behind forward positions of Netherlands troops. Another accomplishment under the truce has been the release of considerable proportion of prisoners held as prisoners of war. Evacuation of families of military personnel of one party from territory controlled by the other has been in progress. . . .

. . . The Committee's military assistants have advised against the widening of the zones on the grounds that the zones constitute 'dead areas' economically while the Netherlands Command asserts that continuation of infiltrations and acts of sabotage make such a widening impossible. The same reason is cited by the Netherlands for the retention by military personnel of police duties in demilitarized zones, although the Committee understands that the replacement of military personnel by civil police in the Republican zone is nearly completed. The use of military personnel in the capacity of civil police was permitted under the Truce Agreement. Although the Republic has stated it demobilized 40,000 members of its army (the Committee has no information on degree to which total strength of Netherlands forces has been affected by the demobilization of the volunteer battalion), the Committee learns from its military assistants that local Republican commanders have largely declined to repair bridges in strategic localities blown up last August on the Republic's side of the *status quo* line as encouragement to increased trade owing to fears of resumption of Netherlands police action. All in all, reviewing present situation Committee has impression of two Governments eyeing each other across the *status quo* line with reserve and suspicion. . . . [*S/848/Add. 1, 23 June 1948, GOC 3rd Interim Report.*]

Problems also arose in respect of the *Renville* political principles.[12]

On 1 May the Netherlands government issued invitations to thirteen authorities in non-Republican parts of Indonesia to attend a Conference at Bandung on the proposed United States of Indonesia. The GOC was not invited to participate. The Indonesian government protested that this contravened the spirit of the *Renville* Agreement. The Netherlands government insisted that the Bandung Conference would be purely consultative, but that the *Renville* Agreement had not fettered its freedom to consult whom it chose. The situation also

---

[10] S/787, p. 62.   [11] Ibid. p. 63.
[12] S/848/Add.1, pp. 126–42; and Taylor, pp. 105–36.

began to deteriorate on the military front. The GOC now decided to take the initiative in drafting a working paper for an over-all political settlement. As the consent of the Belgian member on all points could not be obtained, howeveir the Australian and United States members, T. K. Critchley and C. duBos,, advanced the working paper as a private document. This was eventually reported to the Security Council on 18 June 1948, together with the information that van Mook had rejected the Critchley–duBois proposals (S/850). Political negotiations were suspended on 23 July 1948 (S/918). Discussions concerning the implementation of the truce continued. The delineation of the *status quo* line in the Padang area was left to the local military commanders with the co-operation of the UN military observers. It was decided to maintain the *status quo* line in the Medan and Kloeang areas. Prisoners continued to be exchanged, though the question of missing Dutch personnel had not been resolved.[13] The Security Committee established by the GOC was also concerned in this period with the temporary use of military personnel in the capacity of civil police, and with events in the Java and Sumatra areas, where the right to control was disputed as between the Dutch and Indonesian authorities:

71. . . . In response to a request for information from the Committee of Good Offices, the Committee's senior military assistants informed the Committee, in a memorandum dated 27 August, that the Republican authorities had almost completely replaced military by civilian personnel in the demilitarized zones, but that instructions to Republican civil police were issued through military channels. The Committee's senior military assistants recommended to the Committee that, for the present, the Netherlands authorities should continue to use military personnel for police duties in their demilitarized zones but that they should inaugurate a more vigorous and extensive plan to train and replace military police with civil police.

On the basis of this recommendation the Committee, in a letter dated 15 September to the Netherlands delegation, stated that, while appreciating that a shortage of trained civil police made replacement difficult, the Committee hoped that it would be possible for the Netherlands Indies authorities to inaugurate a more extensive programme for the training of civil police to replace as soon as possible military personnel serving in the demilitarized zones. . . .

72. On 4 August, the Committee was informed by its senior military assistants of an increase in the number of incidents along the *status quo* line both in Java and Sumatra which, in their opinion, arose from an unfortunate readiness on both sides to resort to direct action with firearms when action of another kind might have avoided the incidents. . . .

With regard to the possible steps that could be taken to ease the tension in the demilitarized zones, the Committee expressed its opinion that more regular contact between the local representatives of both parties might assist in promoting a better understanding between them and in avoiding incidents. The Committee suggested that the parties might profitably consider ways and means of achieving this end, and pointed out that consideration should be given to a suggestion made to the Committee in Atjeh (Sumatra) that local offices be established on the *status quo* line where representatives of the parties could meet, daily if necessary, to discuss mutual problems. The Committee expressed the hope that, following the procurement of a number of jeeps for the use of its military assistants, the increased mobility of the military assistants might also prove helpful in avoiding and minimizing incidents along the *status quo* line.

In a letter dated 26 August the Netherlands delegation replied to the Committee's letter of 11 August and expressed its opinion that the incidents were caused by Republican elements and were due to lack of discipline or insufficient supervision by Republican authorities. It

[13] S/1085, paras. 63–8.

stated that the institution of local liaison offices could not therefore bring an end to these infringements of the truce. [*S/1085, 15 Nov. 1948, GOC 4th Interim Report.*]

The accelerating deterioration of the military, as well as the political, situation was evidenced by the military observers.

The Committee takes this occasion to point out that, in cases of infringements of the truce, no military action shall be taken by any local commander unless such an infringement causes serious and acute danger to the safety of troops or the civil population. In this connexion, article 31 of the General Regulations under the truce stipulates as follow:

'The Committee has placed its military assistants at the disposal of the parties to determine whether any incident requires inquiry by the higher authorities of either or both parties; therefore, no military action against infringements of the truce by one of the parties will be taken by any local commander(s) of the other party, unless such an infringement causes serious and acute danger to the safety of troops or the civil population, in which case this shall be reported immediately to the respective Chiefs of Staff and to the nearest military assistant(s) of the Committee of Good Offices or to the Committee itself (see paragraph 29).'

The Committee calls attention to the fact that under article 7 of the General Regulations under the Truce Agreement, crossing the *status quo* line by members of the military forces or police units of either party is not permissible except in the following circumstances, as set forth in article 17:

'Police officers of one party will not move into and throughout the demilitarized zone of the other party unless accompanied by a military assistant of the Committee of Good Offices and a police officer of that other party.'

The Committee is greatly concerned with the need for a strict observance of the Truce Agreement and General Regulations thereunder, and does not want to fail in its responsibility to stress to both parties the seriousness with which it views the present situation. The Committee therefore calls on the parties to avoid such crossings. In particular, the Committee considers both parties should impress upon their military and police commanders the necessity for availing themselves of the services of the Committee's military assistants in the field, who are available to advise the appropriate authorities of the parties and to serve in such other proper capacities as may be requested.

The Committee would be glad to receive and consider any suggestions which your delegation may wish to put forward as to the manner in which the Committee and its military assistants can be of greater help in preventing incidents of the type mentioned in this letter.

The Committee considers that such crossings, if continued or increased, are potentially of sufficient seriousness to cause the Committee to give consideration to the possibility of reporting such crossings to the Security Council. As a consequence, the Committee considers it to be its friendly duty to utilize this letter as a means of informing both parties of this possibility. [*Ibid., App. XVI(a).*]

By December 1948 it became apparent that the Netherlands intended to set up an interim federal government by decree. The GOC was of the opinion that this event

will contribute further to the opinion of the Republic that the Netherlands Government has been proceeding unilaterally to establish ultimately a United States of Indonesia on its own terms and without the Republic. The formation of an interim federal government now without the Republic will greatly complicate a negotiated settlement of the Indonesian dispute and could create serious unrest in Indonesia.

In light of the statements made by the Netherlands delegation that 'neogiations under the auspices of the Committee at this stage are futile', and that there are 'irreconcilable' positions of the parties on certain issues, the Committee does not foresee the possibility of its bringing the parties together in *bona fide* negotiations.

The Committee has no confidence that even the presently unsatisfactory level of truce enforcement can be maintained as the possibility of political agreement becomes more remote. The Committee can see in the present situation only intensification of the factors already making for further economic deterioration, general unrest and social upheaval, Widespread hostilities involving the conflict of organized armed groups on a large scale might be the outcome. . . .   [S/1117, 12 Dec. 1948, Cablegram from GOC to President of the Security Council, para. 7.]

The Committee's prognosis was all too correct. Citing Indonesian violations, on 19 December 1948 the Netherlands terminated the *Renville* Truce Agreement and began a second 'police action'. It interned Republican leaders and took Jogjakarta. The limitations imposed upon the UN observers during this period are recounted above (pp. 51–8). The Security Council demanded an end to hostilities and the release of the President of the Republic of Indonesia and other political figures arrested in the 'police action'.[14] This demand was repeated on 28 December 1948 (S/1164), and the Security Council also asked for a complete report from the Consular Commission on the observance of the cease-fire orders and the conditions in the areas under military occupation or from which armed forces in occupation could be withdrawn (S/1165).

In its own analysis of the situation, the GOC found unequivocally against the Dutch position:

It is therefore the finding of the Committee of Good Offices that the facts established that:
(*a*) No effective notice of termination of the Truce Agreement of 17 January 1948 was given by the Netherlands Government.
(*b*) The Netherlands forces crossed the *status quo* line and initiated hostile military action against the Republic while the obligations of the Truce Agreement were still fully operative. . . . [S/1156, 26 Dec. 1948, Report of GOC.]

The difficulties facing the GOC in carrying out its duties were now immense:

(*a*) Negotiations presuppose two parties, each uncoerced by the armed force of the other and each prepared to move toward the reasonable viewpoint of the other.
(*b*) Politically, the people of one party, without whose support any agreement, even if achieved, may well be unenforceable, will be reluctant to accept as *bona fide* any negotiations in which again they start with an area under their control diminished as a result of the resort to armed force by the other.
(*c*) Practically, when a demarcation line no longer exists, it becomes virtually impossible to ascertain the positions of the Republican forces, particularly in view of the capture by the Netherlands forces of the Republican High Command. As a result it may become necessary to observe any events of a military nature throughout the islands of Java, Sumatra and Madura. This would be difficult enough in itself, but the Committee sees no possibility of its observers being able to distinguish reliably between internal security measures by the Netherlands and hostilities between the parties.   [*Ibid.*, p. 315.]

In the Security Council the representative of the United States, Ambassador Jessup, delivered a blistering condemnation of the Dutch position:

I believe it is fair to say that, in a situation of this kind, the Security Council must place reliance on the report of its own agency in the field, particularly if it conflicts with a report from one of the parties to the dispute.

[14] S/1150, 24 Dec. 1948.

The continuance of military action of the Netherlands authorities after the adoption of the Security Council resolution of 24 December was clearly an act of defiance on the part of the Netherlands authorities. No excuses offered by the Netherlands Government can conceal the fact that it has failed to comply with the Security Council demands both in refusing to order a cease-fire immediately and in refusing to release the political prisoners immediately.

In the opinion of the Government of the United States, the representative of the Netherlands has failed to relieve his Government from the serious charge that it has violated the Charter of the United Nations. [*SCOR, 4th yr, 398th mtg, p. 5.*][15]

On 7 January 1949 the GOC reported that although the Dutch Commander-in-Chief had issued orders to territorial commanders in Java and Sumatra noting that hostilities had ceased, he had none the less charged the troops

(to carry out 'action against roving groups, bands or individuals, who attempt to cause unrest or, as was stated by our representative to the Security Council, to action against disturbing elements who, either individually or collectively, endanger public security or interfere with or prevent the supply of food and other essential commodities to the needy population' The orders permit the continuation of the very type of military action that would be required against the guerrilla resistance likely to be offered by regular or irregular Republic forces paragrap hs 5 and 9 above).

(c) As a result of the immobilization of its military observers, the Committee has no first-hand information as to the effect of the orders discussed above.

(d) The Committee is of the opinion that these orders, issued more than a week after the adoption of the resolution of 24 December, and expressed as they were, cannot be looked upon as satisfactory compliance with sub-paragraph (a) of the resolution.

(e) There is no channel available to the Committee for dissemination of the resolution of 24 December to the Government or to the commanders of the Republican Army (paragraph 8 above).

13. Sub-paragraph (b) of the Security Council's resolution of 24 December, calling for the immediate release of the President of the Republic and other political prisoners, has not been implemented. So far as the Committee is aware, President Sukarno, Vice-President Hatta and the other members of the Republican Government who were captured by Netherlands forces on 19 December are still under detention.

The direct questions relating to the present status, welfare and whereabouts of the political prisoners, addressed to the Netherlands delegation in our letter of 25 December (report of 26 December) have not been answered.

14. As pointed out in paragraph 15 of the report of 26 December, the task imposed upon the Committee by the Security Council in its resolution of 24 December, to observe and report upon the implementation by the parties of the earlier portions of the resolution, was from the outset fraught with inherent difficulties. These difficulties include the absence of demarcation lines between the armed forces of the parties, the impossibility of establishing contact with the Republican forces, and the extreme difficulty of distinguishing hostilities between the parties from security measures. [*S/1189, 7 Jan. 1949, Report of GOC.*]

On 24 January 1949 the GOC reported economic confusion in areas formerly controlled by the Republic and immense damage from looting and the Republican scorched-earth policy. Law and order had not been re-established in the former Republican-controlled territories.[16]

In resolution S/1234 of 28 January 1949 the Security Council reiterated its demands and laid down certain steps to be followed in ensuring that the interim

---

[15] For full statement by Ambassador Jessup see *SCOR*, 4th yr, 398th mtg, pp. 3–10.

[16] S/1223, Report of GOC, paras. 10–12.

federal government be chosen as the result of negotiations.[17] At the same time, the GOC was reconstituted as the UNCI.

Progress was slowly achieved, with UNCI playing a central role. President Sukarno informed the Commission on 7 May 1949 that, in conformity with the Security Council's resolution S/1234, he would agree to an order to end guerrilla warfare, co-operation in the restoration of law and order, and participation in a round-table conference at The Hague to accelerate the complete transfer of sovereignty to the United States of Indonesia. In response to this, the Netherlands government agreed to the return of the Republican government to Jogjakarta and the free exercise of its functions.

. . . a joint sub-committee (Sub-Committee 1) under the auspices of the Commission was set up 'to make the necessary investigations and preparations preliminary to the return of the Republican Government to Jogjakarta'. That sub-committee was composed of the representatives of the two parties and representatives of the Commission, assisted by the Commission's military advisors. . . .

21. It was stressed at the outset by the Netherlands representative to working group 1 that opportunity to leave Jogjakarta should be given to everyone who wanted to do so before the administration was handed over to the Republican authorities. The Republican representative agreed that any persons wishing to leave Jogjakarta should be free to do so.

Measures were then adopted to facilitate such evacuations, and the Commission's military observers were requested to render their assistance. On 9 June, the Netherlands authorities declared the evacuations completed, and estimated that some 30,000 people had been evacuated from the Residency of Jogjakarta.

The evacuations took place in good order, without any serious incidents. . . .

23. . . . The preparations for the return of the Republican Government to Jogjakarta have thus proceeded to such an extent that the Netherlands Government will order its troops to start the evacuation of the Residency of Jogjakarta on 24 June. If this evacuation encounters no hindrance, the Republican Government will be able to return to Jogjakarta on or about 1 July 1949.

24. Plans for the withdrawal of the Netherlands forces were worked out between the two parties, with the assistance of the Commission's military advisers.

The withdrawal started on 24 June and progressed according to plan. On 23 June, one day prior to the beginning of the evacuation, the Sultan of Jogjakarta had issued a special order to all Republican forces in the area to avoid contact with Netherlands forces and to cease all hostile acts during the evacuation. The withdrawal was completed at 14.00 hours on 30 June, and as from that moment responsibility for law and order in the Residency of Jogjakarta was taken over by the Sultan of Jogjakarta acting on behalf of the Republic Government.

The Commission is pleased to report that owing to the co-operation between the parties, the withdrawal was carried out satisfactorily without hindrance or any serious incident.

25. During the period of the withdrawal, the United Nations military observers, organized in six teams under the supervision of the Commission's military advisors, took up positions between the Netherlands and Republican forces.

The Commission wishes to pay tribute to the successful efforts of its military observers in helping to co-ordinate plans for the transfer of military authority in the Residency of Jogjakarta and for their efficiency and effectiveness in observing the execution of this transfer in the field. [S/1373 & Corr. 1, UNCI 1st Interim Report.]

Further progress was made in the summer of 1949:

40. As a result of the agreement of 22 June, further informal discussions and consultations were held in Batavia and Jogjakarta, which led to the adoption of three principal documents:

[17] For text see above, pp. 15–17.

(*a*) the cease-hostilities order; (*b*) the joint proclamation; (c) the regulations governing the implementation of the agreement to cease hostilities, and of a Netherlands-Indonesian manual for the implementation of cessation of hostilities (appendix VIII).

41. At the 8th meeting, on 1 August, the Chairman of the Netherlands and the Republican delegations formally confirmed and accepted the three principal documents and formally approved the Netherlands-Indonesian manual; the Chairman of the FCA, on behalf of representatives of areas in Indonesia other than the Republic, fully endorsed the three principal documents and the manual.

42. At the same meeting, the Central Joint Board referred to in paragraph 7 of the regulations governing the implementation of the agreement to cease hostilities was constituted. The Central Joint Board comprised representatives of each party, representatives of territories other than the Republic which were members of the Federal Consultative Assembly as associate members and civil and military representatives of the Commission. The Central Joint Board was to be under the rotating chairmanship of a civil representative of the Commission.

The Board would have the duty to observe the implementation of the cease-hostilities orders, the proclamation, and any other related orders and directives, and to report and make recommendations thereon to the parties and to the Commission.

43. The cease-hostilities orders were issued simultaneously by the Netherlands and the Republican Governments to their respective armed forces on 3 August to be effective respectively in the case of Java as from midnight 10/11 August 1949, and in Sumatra as from midnight 14/15 August 1949.

The joint proclamation was promulgated by both Governments at the time of the issuance of the cease-hostilities orders.

The regulations governing the implementation of the agreement to cease hostilities were effective simultaneously with the orders to cease hostilities (appendix VIII). . . .

APPENDIX VIII

PRINCIPAL DOCUMENTS ON THE CESSATION OF HOSTILITIES AND NETHERLANDS-INDONESIAN MANUAL FOR THE IMPLEMENTATION OF THE CESSATION OF HOSTILITIES

I. *The cease-hostilities orders*

Pursuant to the 'van Roijen-Roem statements' of 7 May 1949, and in order to implement the Security Council's directive of 23 March 1949 and paragraphs 1 and 2 of the operative part of the Security Council's resolution of 28 January 1949 referred to particularly in the above-mentioned directive, the following orders are issued simultaneously:

A. *By the Netherlands Government*

'As from midnight 10/11 August 1949, in the case of Java, 14/15 August 1949, in the case of Sumatra, hostilities between the parties shall cease.

'All measures shall be taken to cease fire and to terminate all acts intended to harm the other party.

'The orders issued by the Commander-in-Chief on 1 and 5 January 1949 are hereby supplemented and it is ordered, as from midnight 10/11/August 1949, in the case of Java, 14/15 August 1949, in the case of Sumatra, that Netherlands armed forces shall discontinue all military operations.

'The ending of military operations throughout Indonesia will render possible the maintenance of peace and order through co-operation between the Netherlands and Republican armed forces. Mutual co-ordination in patrolling, and co-operation in avoiding clashes and in maintaining peace and order, shall be effected between local commanders in accordance with directives to be issued by the parties, with the assistance of the United Nations Commission for Indonesia.

'Directives and pertinent orders for the implementation of the cease-hostilities order shall be issued in the shortest time possible, beginning from today, by the respective commanders-in-chief through the appropriate channels to their forces. These include a proclamation, regulations and a field manual.

'All persons are hereby warned that any act in violation of this order committed after the above-mentioned times and dates shall be punished in accordance with the existing military regulations.'

B. *By the Government of the Republic of Indonesia*

'As from midnight 10/11 August 1949, in the case of Java, 14/15 August 1949, in the case of Sumatra, hostilities between the parties shall cease.

'All measures shall be taken to cease fire and to terminate all acts intended to harm the other party.

'All personnel of the *Tantara Nasional Indonesia* (TNI) and all other armed adherents of the Republic are ordered, as from midnight 10/11 August 1949, in the case of Java, 14/15 August 1949, in the case of Sumatra, to cease guerrilla warfare.

'The cessation of guerrilla warfare throughout Indonesia will render possible the maintenance of peace and order through co-operation between the Netherlands and Republican armed forces. Mutual co-ordination in patrolling, and co-operation in avoiding clashes and in maintaining peace and order, shall be effected between local commanders in accordance with directives to be issued by the parties, with the assistance of the United Nations Commission for Indonesia.

'Directives and pertinent orders for the implementation of the cease-hostilities order shall be issued in the shortest time possible, beginning from today, by the respective commanders-in-chief through the appropriate channels to their forces. These include a proclamation, regulations and a field manual.

'All persons are hereby warned that any act in violation of this order committed after the above mentioned times and dates shall be punished in accordance with the existing military regulations.'

II. *The joint proclamation*

Simultaneously with the issuance of the cease-hostilities orders the following proclamation shall be promulgated jointly by both Governments;

'Orders to cease hostilities have today been issued by the Government of the Kingdom of the Netherlands and the Government of the Republic of Indonesia. This means that an end has come to conflict between the Republic of Indonesia and the Netherlands.

'Henceforth the endeavours of everyone must be dedicated to banishing any thought of enmity or revenge and to removing any vestige of fear or distrust.

'Many problems remain to be solved. This can be achieved through constructive co-operation in an atmosphere of confidence and security. Efforts with this purpose must have the genuine support of all authorities. Co-ordinated measures must be taken to deal with all persons who would continue to disturb peace and order, disregarding the policies adopted by both Governments. To this end both parties shall make use of radio broadcasts and other means in order to inform all troops and civilians as clearly as possible of the contents of the cease-hostilities order and of this proclamation, and at the same time make them realize the necessity of strictly obeying such order and proclamation and any other directives that may be required.

'In the common interest of the peoples of the Netherlands and Indonesia, and with a view to accomplishing steady progress toward early consummation of happy agreement and the transfer of real and complete sovereignty, both Governments have decreed in common agreement:

'1. That there shall be neither prosecution by course of law nor measures of administrative character against anyone who by the sole fact that he, by offering his services, by seeking protection, or by acting in any other way, has taken sides in the dispute which has divided the Republic of Indonesia and the Netherlands.

'2. That those who have been deprived of their freedom, because of political convictions or functions, or because they have carried arms in the fighting organizations of one of the parties, shall be released as soon as possible.

'3. That those who are being prosecuted or have been condemned because of crimes which are clearly a consequence of the political conflict between the Kingdom of the Netherlands and the Republic shall be released from prosecution or reprieved from penalty in accordance with legislative or other measures to be enacted as soon as possible. These measures shall be communicated to the other party and the United Nations Commission for Indonesia. Measures concerning the social rehabilitation of those released shall be worked out in co-operation between the parties.

'4. That everyone concerned is ordered:

'(a) To refrain from radio broadcasts, Press reports, or any other form of propaganda aimed at challenging or alarming the armed forces or the civilians of the other party;

'(b) To refrain from sabotage and terrorism, and from all direct or indirect threats, destruction and other similar acts directed against persons or groups of persons, or against property wherever it may be or of whomsoever it is;

'(c) To refrain from all acts which might be harmful to mutual co-operation;

'(d) To refrain from all acts of reprisal or retaliation; and

'(e) To avoid and to prevent provocations and incidents of any kind.

'All persons are hereby warned that any act in violation of this proclamation shall be severely punished.'

III. *Regulations governing the implementation of the agreement to cease hostilities by the Government of the Kingdom of the Netherlands and the Government of the Republic of Indonesia*

It is agreed by both parties that the following shall constitute the regulations for the implementation of the cease-hostilities orders and the proclamation promulgated jointly by both Governments.

1. The armed forces of the parties ahall not extend their zones of patrolling, to be delineated in accordance with paragraph 6, or otherwise endeavour to improve their respective military positions at the expense of the other.

2. The armed forces of each party may be moved to any location within the zones of patrolling of that party referred to in paragraph 6.

3. Free movement of civilian population and free traffic of goods between zones shall be permitted without hindrance, except for the right of both parties to take such measures as may be required to ensure that there is no illegal carriage of arms, munitions and other materials of an exclusively warlike character, or propaganda material of a subversive nature.

4. Both parties shall co-operate fully in maintaining law and order, in protecting all elements of the population, and in facilitating each other's measures of self-defence.

5. Patrols of each party shall be permitted only in the areas allocated for that purpose to the respective parties in accordance with paragraph 6. All patrols shall be limited to the maintenance of law and order, including protection of all elements of the population.

6. After consultation among themselves, the parties shall delineate and allocate, according to administrative units, zones of patrolling for the maintenance of law and order. The Central Joint Board, referred to in paragraph 7, shall indicate lines of procedure for that purpose. If in any instance the parties fail to reach agreement on such delineation and allocation, the Central Joint Board shall make recommendations thereon to the parties and to the United Nations Commission for Indonesia (UNCI).

7. A Central Joint Board shall be established, consisting of representatives of both parties, of representatives of territories other than the Republic which are members of the Federal Consultative Assembly, participating as an associate member, and of civil and military representatives of the UNCI and under the chairmanship of a representative (rotated) of the Commission. It will be the duty of the Central Joint Board to observe the implementation of the present regulations, as well as the cease-hostilities order, the proclamation, and any other

related orders and directives, and to report and to make recommendations thereon to the parties and to the UNCI. The Central Joint Board shall, as required, establish local joint committees, consisting of representatives of both parties and of the UNCI, which shall be responsible directly to the Central Joint Board. In the local joint committees dealing with territories outside the Republic, representatives of territories other than the Republic which are members of the Federal Consultative Assembly shall participate with the status of at least associate member in the discussion of questions of direct concern to them.

8. In the zones of patrolling allocated to the Republic in accordance with paragraph 6, the Republican Government accepts in addition to the duty and task for maintaining law and order, the responsibility for feeding, clothing, providing medical supplies and medical services, and in general providing all services needed by the population. Should these facilities not be available to the Republican Government, the latter will report any deficiencies to the Government of Indonesia, if desirable through the UNCI, with a view to seeing what arrangements can be worked out, keeping in mind the interests of the population of Indonesia as a whole, and to determining the manner in which the future Government of the United States of Indonesia may be responsible for the expenditures involved.

9. All times quoted by either side shall be stated in both Netherlands and Republican local times.

10. Consultation, communication and supply between responsible civil and military authorities in all areas will be facilitated by both parties.

11. The present regulations shall enter into force simultaneously with the order to cease hostilities.

MANUAL
Preface

This publication shall be known as the 'Netherlands-Indonesian Manual for the Implementation of the Cessation of Hostilities'.

It is mutually agreed that the contents of this Manual shall be binding upon the Governments of both the Netherlands and the Republic of Indonesia and upon their respective instrumentalities and adherents.

The Manual consists of military definitions and of rules to provide for the implementation of agreements between the parties as set forth in three documents designated:

1. The cease-hostilities orders.
2. The joint proclamation.
3. The regulations governing the implementation of the agreement to cease hostilities.

The material contained herein provides the technical details considered necessary to achieve a satisfactory carrying out of the policies in the military field, agreed upon by the parties.

No material is included which contravenes any of the final provisions of the three basic documents listed above.

With the approval of the parties, this Manual may be supplemented and amended to such extent as found necessary in actual practice, so long as the terms of the above-mentioned three basic documents are not contravened thereby.

It must be stressed that it is of utmost importance to the successful implementation of the agreements that differences be solved at the local level. Likewise it is equally important that decisions reached either locally or at higher level be implemented promptly.

Part I. Glossary of Terms

Wherever used in this Manual or in the documents mentioned therein, terms will be construed as shown in the following glossary:

Acts intended to harm the other party include, in addition to the acts mentioned under 'Hostilities' below:

(*a*) The issue and/or dissemination of propaganda or any material of similar nature by Press radio or other means, which might provoke disorder or disturb the amity between the parties;

(*b*) Intimidation by force or any other means, employed by either party against individuals or groups belonging to the other party;

(*c*) Any other act which might reasonably be expected to obstruct attainment of the aims agreed upon between the parties.

Administrative units means areas, of whatever size, which both sides recognize as tradition–ally having that status, such as *dessas*, *margas*, sub-districts, districts, regencies, residencies or provinces.

Armed adherents comprise the armed forces of a party as defined under the term 'Armed forces' below and, in addition, armed individuals or groups fighting for the Republic under the orders of the commanders of the TNI.

Armed forces comprise the navy, the air force and the land forces as defined in section I, chapter I, articles 1, 2 and 3 of the annex to the International Convention concerning the Laws and Customs of War on Land signed at The Hague, 19 October 1907, which reads as follows:

'*Article 1*

'The laws, rights, and duties of war apply not only to the army, but also to militia and volunteer corps fulfilling all the following conditions:

'1. They must be commanded by a person responsible for his subordinates;

'2. They must have a fixed distinctive sign recognizable at a distance;

'3. They must carry arms openly; and

'4. They must conduct their operations in accordance with the laws and customs of war.

'In countries where militia or volunteer corps constitute the army, or form part of it, they are included under the denomination "Army".

'*Article 2*

'The inhabitants of a territory not under occupation who, on the approach of the enemy, spontaneously take up arms to resist the invading troops without having had time to organize themselves in accordance with article 1, shall be regarded as belligerents if they carry arms openly, and if they respect the laws and customs of war.

'*Article 3*

'The armed forces of the belligerents may consist of combatants and non-combatants. In the case of capture by the enemy, both have the right to be treated as prisoners of war.'

Arms, munitions and other materials of an exclusively warlike character shall be considered items for which a satisfactory peaceful purpose is not established.

Cease-fire will be considered as cessation of all acts enumerated in the definition of 'Hostilities' given below.

FCA means the Federal Consultative Assembly, representing the areas in Indonesia other than the Republic, as far as they are members of this organization.

Guerrilla warfare is irregular warfare or 'hostilities', even if independently waged, individually or by small groups of 'armed adherents'.

Hostilities will include:

(*a*) Any warlike act involving the use of armed forces or armed adherents or any movement of such forces or adherents which might reasonably be expected to provoke, directly or indirectly, retaliatory action by the other party;

(*b*) All acts of destruction, sabotage, sniping, placing of mines, obstruction of roads and railroads by any means, and any other such act which might disturb public order;

(*c*) All acts of intimidation and of reprisal or retaliation committed individually or collectively against either persons or property.

Military operations are any of the acts defined under 'Hostilities' above, conducted by organized military forces and directed or authorized by competent authority responsible to its government.

4

Parties will be construed to denote both the Netherlands and Republican Governments and their respective aherents and instrumentalities.

Patrolling means a police activity, not assuming the character of a military operation, carried out by armed personnel, belonging to either the police, guard forces, or, if necessary, armed forces, including military police, with the purpose of maintaining law and order and/or all other legal purposes which may require such activity.

Propaganda material of a subversive nature includes books, pamphlets, posters and other media of dissemination which are detrimental to the maintenance of established law and order or harmful to either party.

Reprisal or retaliation is an act committed by a person or persons against another or others to satisfy a grievance, or to get even, for an act previously performed or alleged to have been performed against their interests, or for any opinion held or alleged to be or to have been held contrary to their opinions or interests. The term shall therefore include any act taken by the supporters of one party against people because of their political affiliation to the other party, such as:

(*a*) Physical violence;

(*b*) Arrest;

(*c*) Expulsion from dwelling places;

(*d*) Discharge from jobs;

(*e*) Seizure, confiscation or destruction of property.

Sabotage includes any act committed by armed forces or adherents or their agents for the purpose of denying the full use of public utilities, or installations of a military, industrial or commercial nature.

Terrorism is systematic intimidation accomplished by the actual use, presence or threat of force or power thereby inducing a willingness to comply with the will of the intimidator(s) when otherwise such compliance would not be freely and willingly given.

Part II. Rules

Part II contains the rules for the implementation of agreements between the parties.

Central Joint Board

1. The Central Joint Board referred to in paragraph 7 of the regulations governing the implementation of the agreement to cease hostilities shall be comprised of the following:

(*a*) An equal number of representatives to be designated by each party;

(*b*) An equal number of representatives to be designated by the FCA as Associate Member;

(*c*) Three civilian and three military representatives designated by the Commission;

(*d*) Such advisory and secretarial assistants as desired by either party, the FCA or the Commission.

2. The functions of the Central Joint Board shall be as prescribed in paragraph 7 of the regulations governing the implementation of the agreement to cease hostilities.

3. (*a*) Matters referred to the Central Joint Board may be submitted by the Board to the representatives of each party and the FCA for informal discussion and study, with the assistance, if desired, of the Commission's Board representatives;

(*b*) When an agreement is reached, the Central Joint Board shall formalize it and shall provide its further assistance for the implementation thereof.

(*c*) If no agreement can be reached, the Board representatives of each party and of the FCA shall submit their views in a formal meeting. It will then be the duty of the Commission's Board representatives to make such recommendations to the parties, the FCA and/or to the Commission as may be required.

4. In its formal meetings the Central Joint Board shall carry out its functions in accordance with the rules of procedure prescribed in annex I.

Local joint committees

5. The local joint committees referred to in paragraph 7 of the regulations governing the

implementation of the agreement to cease hostilities shall each be comprised of the following:

(*a*) Two representatives designated by each party and by the FCA when the latter is concerned;

(*b*) The members of the local military observer team of the Commission and such civilian representatives of the Commission as shall be determined by that body;

(*c*) Such advisory and secretarial assistants as desired by either party, the FCA or the Commission.

6. The functions and procedure of the local joint committees shall correspond, on the local level, to those prescribed for the Central Joint Board (annex 1), except that (1) FCA representatives may have to vote on matters of procedure and (2) for their meetings the chairmanship of the local joint committees shall be held by the Co-ordinator of the Commission's military observer team or his representative. In the event of a civilian representative of the Commission being present, he shall occupy the chair.

7. When agreement is reached on any matter placed before a local joint committee, a full report shall be submitted promptly to the Central Joint Board. If no agreement can be reached on any such matter the representatives of each party and of the FCA shall submit their views in writing to the chairman of the local joint committee. The latter shall forward the above-mentioned views together with the recommendations of the Commission's representatives to the Central Joint Board.

Delineation of zones of patrolling

8. Zones of patrolling shall be delineated as agreed upon by the local joint committee and/or the Central Joint Board on the basis of the following principles. In the territories outside the Residency of Jogjakarta zones of patrolling shall be allocated in such a way that law and order will be maintained by the Netherlands armed forces, or by the Republican armed forces. To this end both armed forces shall perform their duties under the command of their own officers in areas to be decided upon in joint consultation. In allocating the zones of patrolling, the principle of maintaining the *status quo* shall be adhered to. This implies that the military position of one party shall not be improved at the expense of the other party.

In addition, the following practical considerations should be taken into account:

(*a*) Zones should be delineated as much as possible according to administrative units, in the interest of effective administration.

(*b*) The economic situation should meet as little hindrance as possible.

(*c*) Zones should be allocated in such a way as to facilitate as much as possible the supply of troops and police forces responsible for law and order and the maintenance of the population within the zone, it being understood that the use of lines of communication may be granted by one party to the other by mutual arrangement.

(*d*) In order to avoid an undesirable splitting of an area into too many or too small zones, which would be undesirable for the effective maintenance of law and order, zones where either party has in fact been maintaining law and order may for purposes of patrolling be combined or interchanged.

9. The Central Joint Board shall as soon as possible, and utilizing all the facilities which shall be extended by both parties, issue necessary instructions and the local joint committees shall without delay arrange meetings between the local commanders of both parties.

Patrols and patrolling

10. Local commanders shall impress upon their forces that the more sincere and effective the response to the cease-hostilities orders, the sooner the diminution of patrols and other military burdens can be accomplished. Improvement in the situation that permits diminution in patrols should clear the way for the next step of diminution of outposts. As this process develops, the way is prepared for reduction in armed forces, return of members thereof to their homes and to productive pursuits, and the achievement of the desired goal of peace and prosperity.

11. In order to ensure co-operation in the maintenance of law and order, local commanders

shall establish direct lines of communication with each other. They shall exchange information and provide, where practicable, material support at the request of the other party. This particularly applies, if special measures should be necessary.

12. Each party shall limit its patrolling activity to its assigned zones unless the responsible party requests assistance of the other party. If difficulties arise in such circumstances, the matter shall be referred to the local joint committee, which shall arrange the necessary co-ordination in the general scheme of co-operation between the armed forces of the parties.

13. Armed personnel of one party shall not enter the zone of patrolling assigned to the other party except upon request. If armed personnel of one of the parties should enter by mistake the zone of patrolling of the other party, this personnel, immediately upon becoming aware of this crossing, shall discontinue the carrying out of all measures in progress, and shall return immediately by the shortest route to their own zone of patrolling, without taking with them any persons or goods which may have been seized in the zone of patrolling of the other party. Such a crossing shall be reported within forty-eight hours to the other party as well as to the local joint committee.

14. Should a patrol of one party by any chance contact a patrol of the other party the challenge *Siapa* ('Who's there?') shall be used and the following procedure will pertain:

(*a*) By daylight: the leaders of both patrols shall expose themselves and signal by alternately raising one arm to shoulder height and lowering it until signal is returned by the other patrol.

(*b*) By night: the leaders of both patrols shall signal by giving three flashes with a torch and continue the signal until returned by the other patrol.

Following the recognition signals both patrols shall withdraw from contact unless either patrol requests assistance of the other.

Variations in the above practices may be adopted as local circumstances require.

15. The strength, frequency and equipment of patrols shall be limited to that considered reasonable for the accomplishment of their respective missions. Information on these subjects shall be exchanged between local commanders.

Identification of United Nations military observers

16. United Nations military observers shall be in uniform and shall wear white armbands inscribed 'KTN' and 'UN' in blue. Normally vehicles carrying United Nations personnel are painted white with a blue triangle on the motor hood and bear the inscription 'United Nations' and 'KTN'. The vehicles will display a white flag lettered in blue 'KTN' and 'UN'.

Rules in solving violations

17. (*a*) Each party shall refrain from publicizing any act of the other party which it considers a violation of the agreements, unless the alleged violation and its publication have been discussed by the Central Joint Board;

(*b*) Complaints concerning violations in any territory shall be forwarded to the local joint committee without delay. If no solution is reached, the local joint committee shall communicate the matter to the Central Joint Board;

(*c*) Only complaints of a very important nature shall be forwarded directly to the Central Joint Board.

Use of aircraft

18. The offensive or provocative use of aircraft is prohibited.

19. In the event that, owing to bad weather or technical trouble, aircraft are forced to land on an airfield, or to make a forced landing in territory controlled by or allocated for patrol to the other party, the safety of passengers and crew shall be guaranteed and the necessary assistance given to enable them to return to their own base as soon as possible. In these events both parties shall permit personnel and spare parts to be brought in so that the aircraft can be made airworthy again or all usable parts can be salvaged.   [*S/1373 & Corr. 1, App. VIII.*][18]

[18] Annex: Rules of Procedure of Central Joint Board, omitted.

In January 1950 UNCI presented a second Interim Report, covering the implementation of these Agreements[19] and the Security Council's directives. By 9 September 1949 the Central Joint Board had noted that the envisaged local joint committees were all established and functioning. They faced a plethora of difficult problems:

11. At its third meeting, on 20 August, the Central Joint Board directed the local joint committees to proceed forthwith with the allocation of zones of patrolling as provided for in paragraph 8 of part II of the Netherlands-Indonesian Manual for the implementation of the cessation of hostilities. The Board emphasized that the delineation of zones was only for the purpose of maintaining law and order and should not create demarcation lines in economic, social and other respects. In Java, in the residencies where both parties on the basis of the *status quo* were entitled to zones of patrolling, such zones should be delineated so as to constitute, as far as possible, one contiguous area for each party, except where combined patrolling was to take place. In Sumatra, zones of patrolling were to be delineated so as to limit the zones to the least possible number.

12. At the time the cease-hostilities orders came into effect, the armed forces of both parties were closely intermingled, and the Republican armed forces and armed adherents were widely scattered throughout Java and Sumatra. The delineation and allocation of zones of patrolling by local joint committees, therefore, inevitably met with very serious difficulties. The problem was further aggravated by the divergence of views with regard to the definition and interpretation of the *status quo*, the definition of 'armed adherents', and with regard to administrative responsibility. The question of supplies to the Republican authorities was still another factor which had to be taken into consideration. . . .

17. . . . The Chairman . . . said that . . . he would like to make the following general statement: 'The [UNCI] would draw attention to the fact that two months after the Cease-hostilities Agreement came into effect, the parties in their discussions on the local joint committees have in no single case yet reached agreement on the final allocation of the responsibility in the various areas for the maintenance of law and order. Some committees have already referred their disagreements to this Board, and it is apparent that there is no possibility of an early settlement in those committees where discussions are still proceeding.

'The Commission representatives wish to advise the Board that they consider this situation places too great a strain on the Cease-hostilities Agreement and will give rise to instabilities which would seriously endanger the satisfactory implementation of the Agreement. The UNCI representatives consider that this urgent position calls for immediate steps by the Board and to this end they propose the following measure:

'That the Board appoint a military sub-committee of an equal number of Netherlands and Republican senior staff officers, and the UNCI military representatives, to draw up an arrangement for the allocation of military patrolling responsibilities as between the parties, for the maintenance of law and order, in the first place throughout the island of Java, and subsequently throughout the island of Sumatra. This sub-committee shall report back to the Board no later than . . . October in regard to the arrangements for Java'.'

The Chairman emphasized that the Commission's suggestion did not conflict with the question of the specific recommendations to be made, and requested the parties to give due consideration to the Commission's proposal as a step towards an over-all arrangement.

18. In the meantime, the Republican Government had submitted an *aide-mémoire*, dated 13 October, to the High Representative of the Crown in Indonesia (appendix II, document 8). In this *aide-mémoire* the Republican Government stated that the military situation, especially in East Java, filled it with great concern, and it therefore proposed that the military staffs of both parties immediately meet to work out a scheme of co-ordinated action. Under this scheme Netherlands forces would shortly be concentrated in regency and residency capitals, while the TNI, in consultation with the Netherlands commanders, would be permitted to

---

[19] Full texts of Round Table Agreements in 69 UNTS, 3, 202, 392, 386.

make use of the roads of communication outside the concentration areas allocated to the Netherlands troops; outside the capitals and roads of communication mentioned, no patrols should be carried out by the Netherlands troops. The Netherlands Government, however, considered the Republican proposals contrary to the Cease-hostilities Agreement, and contrary to the recommendations of certain of the local joint committees and the Commission's representatives thereon. The Netherlands Government also believed that the Republican proposals would undermine the administration of the *Negaras* of Pasundan and East Java (appendix II, document 9). The parties continued their correspondence on these proposals for some time, but without agreement.

19. At the Board's meeting on 19 October, a compromise was reached on the Netherlands proposal concerning the allocation of military patrolling responsibilities in Central Java, and the proposal as amended was formally adopted (appendix III). At the same meeting, the representatives of the Republic and the Federal Consultative Assembly declared that they were able to accept in principle the Commission's proposal. However, the Netherlands representative suggested a compromise whereby the military representatives could meet informally whenever a decision by the Board was required on the delineation of zones of patrolling in areas covered by several local joint committees. This suggestion was adopted by the Board, and it was subsequently agreed that military representatives were to investigate and make recommendations concerning the situation in Bukit Tinggi, Palembang, Semarang and Surabaya. However, the progress made in local discussions rendered such a course of action unnecessary.

20. As a result of local agreements, by the middle of December, responsibility for the maintenance of law and order in most of the territories of areas of East and Central Java as defined in the *Renville* Agreement* had been entrusted to the Republican armed forces who assumed military control in the areas concerned and undertook to guarantee safety of life and property. Certain other areas throughout parts of Java and Sumatra had also been transferred to the Republican military authorities. Further discussions between the parties in connexion with the preparation for the transfer of sovereignty expedited transitional agreements in both Java and Sumatra, and thus contributed to the orderly inauguration of the new State.

B. Observance of the Agreement

21. In the Cease-hostilities Agreement both parties agreed to adhere to the principle of maintenance of the *status quo* in allocating zones of patrolling and not to extend their zones of patrolling, or otherwise endeavour to improve their respective military positions at the expense of the other (S/1373, appendix VIII).

22. In view of a difference of opinion between the parties as to the date of the *status quo*, the Central Joint Board stipulated that in the area of each local joint committee, the *status quo* had to be considered in accordance with the factual situation at the time of the coming into effect of the cease-hostilities orders; every consideration should also be given as to which party actually maintained law and order in a given area before that time.

23. In view of further disagreements in several local joint committees over the term 'armed forces' as applied to TNI guerrillas, the Board defined the TNI guerrilla after the cease-hostilities orders as follows:

(*a*) He should be commanded by a person responsible for subordinates;

(*b*) He should have a fixed distinctive sign recognizable at a distance;

(*c*) He should be in possession of an identity card signed by:

    (i) TNI army command for officers above the rank of captain;

    (ii) Divisional commanders for subaltern officers;

    (iii) Brigade commanders for non-commissioned officers and privates.

24. After the issuance of the cease-hostilities orders, reports were received from the

* See *Official Records of the Security Council, Third Year, Special Supplement No. 1* (document S/649/Rev. 1).

Netherlands representatives to the effect that there had been movements of Republican forces in East and Central Java both before and immediately after these orders had come into effect. The local joint committees were accordingly instructed to investigate and report on any infringements, as well as the measures taken by the parties for the implementation of the Agreement. Where it was found that the *status quo* had been infringed, the party responsible was to order an immediate withdrawal of its forces involved. Both parties agreed to urge upon their Governments and military commanders the necessity for the strictest implementation of the *status quo* and of the other provisions of the Cease-hostilities Agreement. The local joint committees were also instructed to arrange with the parties for a withdrawal of forces involved in any infringements of the *status quo* without awaiting specific authority from the Central Joint Board. Special instructions along these lines were sent to the local joint committees in East and Central Java. . . .

26. At its meeting of 24 August, the Board again requested the local joint committees in the areas of Central and East Java to investigate immediately the above Netherlands complaint and to report to the Board.

27. Reports received from those committees and the military observers indicated that, in general, difficulties in the observance of the Cease-hostilities Agreement were closely related to the above-mentioned differences of interpretation concerning the *status quo* and the 'armed adherents' (paras. 22 and 23 above), and the divergence of views over the delineation and allocation of zones of patrolling. These reports further indicated that although incidents occurred, they were in most cases settled within the local joint committees. . . .

35. The Commission wishes to pay tribute to the work of its military observers in assisting the parties, in their capacity as chairmen of the local joint committees, to solve differences on a local level, and in keeping the Commission and the Central Joint Board informed of the situation in their areas. [*S/1449, 16 Jan. 1950, UNCI 2nd Interim Report.*]

It remained for UNCI to fulfil the duties assigned to it under the Round Table Agreements in respect of assistance in the repatriation of the Netherlands army. In this the co-operation and advice of the military observers was indispensable:

6. In the exercise of its functions, the Commission relied on information submitted to it by the parties, upon its own observation and upon reports received from its military observers. Under revised instructions issued by the Commission, military observers were requested to report on any important development which, in their considered judgment, could affect the implementation of the agreements reached at the Round Table Conference or attained in further discussions between the parties.

7. The procedure adopted for the conduct of negotiations prior to the transfer of sovereignty could no longer be applied in the new circumstances, and on 23 January 1950, a 'Contact Committee' was established upon the Commission's initiative to facilitate the implementation of article VI of the covering resolution. The Contact Committee comprised the Commission and representatives of the Indonesian and Netherlands Governments, and its rules of procedure provided that its Chairman should be the Chairman of the Commission and that the Committee could establish sub-committees and working groups whenever considered necessary. In accordance with these provisions, a Sub-Committee for Military Affairs was established at the first meeting of the Contact Committee held on 23 January 1950.

8. Although the Contact Committee held only a few formal meetings, its existence proved valuable, as the parties knew that if they were unable to settle their differences in direct discussions, they could resort to the Contact Committee in an effort to find a solution with the assistance of the Commission. . . .

10. At the time of the transfer of sovereignty, there were in Indonesia approximately 80,000 troops of the Royal Netherlands Army (KL) and 65,000 troops of the Royal Netherlands Indonesian Army (KNIL) composed mostly of soldiers of Indonesian origin.

11. The two main questions which the Governments concerned had to face immediately after

the transfer of sovereignty were, therefore (*a*) the withdrawal of Netherlands troops from Indonesia, and (*b*) the dissolution of the Netherlands-Indonesian Army, either by absorption of its members into the armed forces of the Republic of the United States of Indonesia or of the Kingdom of the Netherlands, or by demobilization and repatriation. . . .

13. At the same time, an agreement was reached concerning the establishment of assembly areas (*rayons*) where Netherlands troops were to be gathered following the transfer of sovereignty and pending their withdrawal from Indonesia. In all, seventeen *rayons* were set up in the neighbourhood of ports and in areas offering sufficient accommodation, in various parts of Sumatra, Java, Madura, Riouw, Bangka and Billiton. It was agreed, however, that the location and area of the *rayons* would be reviewed at the beginning of each month, in the light of the reduction in the number of troops under Netherlands command.

14. The Commission's military observers were requested to observe the implementation of these agreements and regulations. Military observer teams were located in places where Territorial Commands were established and team co-ordinators were instructed to maintain close contact with the responsible commanders of both the Netherlands and the Indonesian forces. The military observer teams were of a mobile character, in the sense that they could visit any area where observation was required for any particular purpose. As the *rayons* were closed down, the military observer teams were withdrawn and the number of observers reduced. . . .

15. While the repatriation of Royal Netherlands Army (KL) from Indonesia proceeded satisfactorily, the implemention of the provisions regarding the reorganization of the Royal Netherlands Indonesian Army (KNIL), met with some difficulty. Article 31 of the regulations concerning land fighting forces adopted at The Hague (*S/1417/Add. 1, app. XVI*) specified that the KNIL should cease to exist on the completion of its reorganization, and that this should take place within a period of six months from the date of the publication of the conditions for enlistment in the armed forces of the Republic of the United States of Indonesia. However, the parties had different views concerning the date on which this period of six months should begin. These difficulties were overcome in direct discussions between the Indonesian Minister of Defence and the Netherlands Secretary of State for War, and on 8 May 1950 it was agreed that the reorganization of the KNIL: should be completed by 26 July 1950.

16. In its special report dated 28 July 1950 (*S/1663*) the Commission informed the Security Council of the agreement reached between the two Governments on 15 July regarding the dissolution of the Royal Netherlands Army troops remaining under Netherlands Command at that date, who were to be given the temporary status of Royal Netherlands Army (KL) personnel and, pending demobilization and transportation to their ultimate destination, were to be assembled in camps under Netherlands authority. These camps were located in various places in Java, Borneo and the Celebes. The agreement also provided that the Netherlands Army High Command in Indonesia was to be dissolved on 26 July and a 'Liquidation Command' substituted with purely administrative functions.

17. In accordance with the general principle adopted by the parties, the former members of the KNIL were to be repatriated to and demobilized in their places of origin. However, the agreement signed on 15 July included the provision that 'to those former KNIL military personnel of Indonesian nationality who so expressed the wish, full opportunity shall be given to be discharged outside their places of origin'.

18. By the time of the signing of the agreement, 67,000 KL troops had left Indonesia; of the KNIL, 26,000 had joined the Indonesian Army, 18,750 had been demobilized in Indonesia and 3,250 had departed for the Netherlands. Thus, at the end of July, 13,000 KL troops and 17,000 ex-KNIL troops enjoying KL status, remained in Indonesia under Netherlands Command.

19. Events outside the control of the parties delayed the withdrawal and repatriation operations. As a result of the revolt in the South Moluccas (chapter VI), no further demobilization and repatriation of ex-KNIL troops of Ambonese origin was considered possible or practicable. Consequently, some 12,000 servicemen and dependents were obliged to remain in camps

under Netherlands responsibility. At the beginning of August, tension between the ex-KNIL personnel in camps in Makassar and the local population led to serious incidents . . . it was feared that similar incidents might occur in other places where ex-KNIL troops of Ambonese origin were stationed, should their demobilization be delayed too long.

20. With a view to preventing the occurrence of incidents, the Commission, after consultation with the parties, instructed its senior military observers to visit the assembly areas of troops still under Netherlands authority and to report to the Commission on any circumstances which, in their view, might affect co-operation between the Netherlands and Indonesian authorities. The visits which the senior military observers paid to the camps in East Java, Borneo and The Celebes, and the discussions they had with both the Indonesian and Netherlands authorities on the spot, helped to ease the tension. In the beginning of September, camps in Borneo and the Celebes were closed and all ex-KNIL personnel therein either demobilized or transferred to camps in West, Central and East Java. The members of the Commission visited these camps between 16 and 22 September. Their inspection tour, on which they were accompanied by representatives of the parties, included the camps at Bandung, Semarang, Surabaya and Malang. The Commission paid particular attention to the living conditions of the ex-KNIL personnel; it met spokesmen of troops from Amboina and the neighbouring islands and heard their views on their future disposition. . . . [*S/2087*, *13 Apr. 1951, UNCI Report on Activities since transfer of sovereignty.*]

UNCI made certain recommendations to deal with the specific repatriation problems caused by the revolt in the South Moluccas.[20]

[20] S/2087, paras. 21–8.

13

ANNEXES

A. *Checklist of Documents*

SECURITY COUNCIL

1. RESOLUTIONS

S/459	1 Aug. 1947		S/933	29 July 1948
S/525 (I)	} 25 Aug. 1947		S/1150	24 Dec. 1948
S/525 (II)			S/1164	} 28 Dec. 1948
S/525 (III)	26 Aug. 1947		S/1165	
S/547	3 Oct. 1947		S/1234	28 Jan. 1949
S/597	1 Nov. 1947		S/1401	27 Sept. 1949
S/689	} 28 Feb. 1948		S/1404	5 Oct. 1949
S/678				

2. REPORTS OF CONSULAR COMMISSION

S/586	22 Oct. 1947		S/1190	6 Jan. 1949

3. INTERIM REPORTS OF GOOD OFFICES COMMITTEE

S/649/Rev. 1   22 Sept. 1950   1st   (*SCOR*, 3rd yr, spec. suppl. 1)

4*

S/787	19 May 1948	2nd	(SCOR, 3rd yr, suppl. for June 1948)
S/848/Add. 1	23 June 1948	3rd	
S/1085	15 Nov. 1948	4th	(SCOR, 3rd yr, suppl. for Dec. 1948)

4. OTHER REPORTS AND COMMUNICATIONS OF GOOD OFFICES COMMITTEE

S/850	22 June 1948	S/1189	7 Jan. 1949
S/1117	12 Dec. 1948	S/1193	8 Jan. 1949
S/1146 & Corr. 1	23 Dec. 1948	S/1212	14 Jan. 1949
S/1154	25 Dec. 1948	S/1223	24 Jan. 1949

5. REPORTS OF UN COMMISSION FOR INDONESIA
S/1270 & Corr. 1 1 Mar. 1949 (SCOR, 4th yr, suppl. for Feb. 1949)
S/1373 & Corr. 1 4 Aug. 1949 (SCOR, 4th yr, spec. suppl. 5)
S/1449   16 Jan. 1950 (SCOR, 5th yr, spec. suppl. 1)
S/1417   10 Nov. 1949 (SCOR, 4th yr, spec. suppl. 6)
S/2087   13 Apr. 1951 (SCOR, 6th yr, spec. suppl. 1)

6. DEBATES IN THE SECURITY COUNCIL
SCOR, 1st yr, 1st ser., mtgs 12–18
SCOR, 2nd yr, mtgs 171, 174, 178, 181, 184–5, 187, 192–3, 201, 205–25
SCOR, 3rd yr, mtgs 247–9, 251–2, 256, 259, 316, 322–3, 326, 328–9, 341–2, 387–96
SCOR, 4th yr, mtgs 397–8, 400–6, 410, 416–21, 448–9, 454–6

B. *Bibliography*

1. Netherlands and Netherlands Indies Governments
*Activities of the Republican Indonesians in the Netherlands and Abroad Contrary
to the Truce Agreement and the Eighteen Renville Principles.* Batavia, 1948,
*Three Months of Truce on Java and Sumatra; Documents submitted to the Com-
mittee of Good Offices by the Netherlands.* Batavia, 1948.
*Why Political Negotiations Between the Netherlands and the Indonesian Republic
Failed.* The Hague, 1948.

2. Republic of Indonesia
Documenta Historica, compiled by Osman Raliby. Djakarta, Bulan-Bintang,
1953.
History of Indonesia's National Movement. New York, 1949.
The Republic of Indonesia, a Review. Mimeo. materials containing documents
issued by the Republic of Indonesia, n.d.

3. General
Anderson, Benedict R. *Some Aspects of Indonesian Politics under the Japanese
Occupation 1944/45.* Ithaca, N.Y., Cornell Univ., 1961.
*Asian Relations; Report of the Proceedings and Documentation of the First Asian
Relations Conference, New Delhi, Mar.–Apr. 1947.* Asian Relations Org., 1948.
Aziz, M. A. *Japan's Colonialism and Indonesia.* The Hague, 1955.

Bot, Th. H. *New Relations Between the Netherlands and Indonesia*. The Hague, 1951, mimeo.
Chaudhry, I. *The Indonesian Struggle*. Lahore, 1950.
Coast, John. *Recruit to Revolution: Adventure and Politics in Indonesia*. London, 1952.
Djajadinigrat, Idrus Nasir. *The Beginnings of the Indonesian–Dutch Negotiations and the Hoge Veluwe Talks*. Ithaca, N.Y., Cornell Univ., 1958.
Elsbree, Willard H. *Japan's Role in Southeast Asian Nationalist Movements, 1940–45*. Cambridge, Mass., 1953.
Emerson, Rupert. Reflections on the Indonesian Case. *World Politics*, vol. I, 1948.
—— *Representative Government in Southeast Asia*. London, 1955.
—— Mills, L., and Thompson, V. *Government and Nationalism in Southeast Asia*. New York, 1942.
Furnivall, J. S. *Colonial Policy and Practice; a Comparative Study of Burma and Netherlands India*. London, 1948.
Gerbrandy, P. S. *Indonesia*. London, 1950.
Henderson, William. *Pacific Settlement of Disputes: the Indonesian Question 1946–9*. New York, Woodrow Wilson Foundation, Sept. 1954.
Kahin, George McT. Indirect Rule in East Indonesia. *Pacific Affairs*, vol. 22, 1949.
—— ed. 'Indonesia', in *Major Governments of Asia*. Ithaca, N.Y., Cornell Univ., 1958.
—— *Nationalism and Revolution in Indonesia*. Ithaca, N.Y., Cornell Univ., 1952.
de Kat Angelino, A.D.A. *Colonial Policy*. The Hague, 1931. 2 vols.
Khanh, Tran Bun. *L'Indonésie, introduction à une décolonisation*. Brussels, Centre pour l'étude des problèmes du monde musulman contemporain, 1965.
Leimena, J. *The Dutch-Indonesian Conflict*. Djakarta, 1949.
McVey, Ruth T. *The Soviet View of the Indonesian Revolution*. Ithaca, N.Y., Cornell Univ., 1957.
Mook, H. J. Van. *The Stakes of Democracy in Southeast Asia*. New York, 1950.
Mountbatten, Louis, 1st Earl. *Report to the Combined Chiefs of Staff by the Supreme Allied Commander, Southeast Asia, 1943–45*. London, 1951.
Preger, W. *Dutch Administration in the Netherlands Indies*. Melbourne, 1944.
Sastroamidjojo, Ali and Delson, Robert. *The Status of the Republic of Indonesia in International Law*. Reprinted from *Columbia Law Review*, Mar. 1949.
Sastroamidjojo, Usman. *The Indonesian Struggle for Freedom*. Perth, 1948.
Schiller, A. Arthur. *The Formation of Federal Indonesia 1945–1949*. The Hague, 1955.
Sjahrir, Soetan. *Out of Exile*. New York, 1949.
Talbot, Phillips, ed. *South Asia in the World Today*. Chicago Univ., 1950.
Thayer, Philip W. ed. *Southeast Asia in the Coming World*. Baltimore, 1953.
Ubani, B. A. and others. *The Indonesian Struggle for Independence*. Bombay, 1946.

Vandenbosch, Amry. *The Dutch East Indies.* 3rd ed. Berkeley, Calif. Univ.,
    1941.
—— *Dutch Foreign Policy since 1815.* The Hague, 1959.
Van der Kroef, Justus M. *Indonesia in the Modern World.* New York, 1954–6.
    2 parts.
Wehl, David. *The Birth of Indonesia.* London, 1948.
Wertheim, W. F. *Indonesian Society in Transition.* 2nd ed. New York, 1959.
Wolf, Charles. *The Indonesian Story.* New York, 1948.

Part 2

UNITED NATIONS
OBSERVERS AND SECURITY FORCE (UNSF)
IN WEST IRIAN, 1962-3

1. INTRODUCTION (p. 93)

PROVISIONS for Dutch New Guinea in Round Table Draft Charter of Transfer of Sovereignty, 1949; ambiguities revealed, and Indonesians press for incorporation into Indonesia; Sastro-amidjojo's government takes the matter to the General Assembly in 1954; Assembly encourages bilateral talks; Dutch position under Article 73(e) of UN Charter; Netherlands trusteeship proposals of 1961 rejected by Indonesia as colonialism; military clashes in 1962 occasion diplomatic initiatives by Acting Secretary-General U Thant; the 'Bunker Plan' accepted by the parties in August 1962.

2. ENABLING RESOLUTIONS AND VOTING (p. 110)

General Assembly approves the Indonesia-Netherlands Agreement on 21 September 1962; Related Understandings on cessation of hostilities; voting patterns of Soviet Union and *Communauté française*.

3. FUNCTIONS AND MANDATE (p. 115)

Role assigned to UN military observers; and to UN Security Force under Article VII of Agreement; novelty of UN administration.

4. CONSTITUTIONAL BASIS (p. 118)

The general powers of the Secretary-General and the UN observers; no specific requirement for observers in Memorandum of Understanding on the cessation of hostilities; constitutional basis neither of UNTEA nor of UNSF mentioned in Assembly resolution 1752 (XVII); Articles 99 and 14 of UN Charter; absence of Soviet protest.

5. POLITICAL CONTROL (p. 122)

Military observers under direct control of Sercretary-General; political control over UNSF dependent upon notion of UNSF as an integral part of UNTEA; Dr Abdoh appointed Administrator of UNTEA: role of secretariat officials.

6. ADMINISTRATIVE AND MILITARY CONTROL (p. 124)

Appointment of Brigadier-General Rikhye to organize work of military observers; Major-General Said Uddin Khan made Commander of UNSF; and makes arrangements also for the command of Indonesian forces in West Irian, and the Papuan Volunteer Corps and police.

7. COMPOSITION AND SIZE (p. 125)

Twenty-one military observers provided by six nations; 1,600 troops provided by Pakistan for UNSF; logistical and other support; the use of Papuans.

8. RELATIONS WITH CONTRIBUTING STATES (p. 127)
No formal agreements concluded either in respect of Observers or UNSF.

9. RELATIONS WITH HOST STATES (p. 128)
Liaison arrangements in respect of the military observers; UNSF and Article XXVI of the
Netherlands–Indonesia Agreement; legal problems flowing from UN's status as administering
agency in West Irian; Dutch co-operation in troop repatriation; UNTEA grants amnesty;
Indonesia presses for a shortening of UNTEA's agreed period of authority: dispute over use
of Papuan flag.

10. RELATIONS WITH OTHER STATES INVOLVED (p. 134)
Absence of major interest by other powers in the UNTEA experiment.

11. FINANCE (p. 134)
Agreement by Indonesia and the Netherlands to share costs; Article XXIV of Indonesia–
Netherlands Agreement; costs of UNTEA and status of funds from 1963–5.

12. IMPLEMENTATION (p. 138)
Success of military observers in achieving an effective cease-fire and paving the way for
UNTEA and UNSF; UNSF's contribution to the maintenance of law and order; the risks
of a breakdown in administration and the problems caused by the departure of Dutch personnel; scepticism as to the likelihood of a plebiscite in 1969; the Secretary-General assesses
the performance of UNSF and UNTEA.

13.   ANNEXES (p. 148)

I

INTRODUCTION

THE dispute between Indonesia and the Netherlands over the territory of Dutch New Guinea (West Irian) began almost at the moment that the Netherlands formally recognized the sovereign independence of Indonesia. The UN had been directly and deeply involved in the Indonesian claims of independence,[1] and, after sporadic violence over a period of some four years, agreement was ultimately reached at a Round Table Conference held at The Hague in August–November, 1949. A Draft Charter of Transfer of Sovereignty[2] was accepted by both the parties, Article 1 of which stated: 'The Kingdom of the Netherlands unconditionally and irrevocably transfers complete sovereignty over Indonesia to the Republic of the United States of Indonesia and thereby recognizes said Republic of United States of Indonesia as an independent and sovereign State.'

The Round Table Conference failed to agree, however, on the status of New Guinea. It therefore agreed to a formula suggested by the United Nations Commission for Indonesia[3]—namely, that the *status quo* should be maintained in New Guinea for a year, by which time its future status would be resolved by further negotiations between the parties. Article 2 of the Draft Charter of Transfer of Sovereignty thus stated:

With regard to the residency of New Guinea it is decided:

a in view of the fact that it has not yet been possible to reconcile the views of the parties of New Guinea, which remain, therefore, in dispute,

b in view of the desirability of the Round Table Conference concluding successfully on 2 November 1949,

c in view of the important factors which should be taken in account in settling the question of New Guinea.

d in view of the limited research that has been undertaken and completed with respect to the problems involved in the question of New Guinea,

e in view of the heavy tasks with which the Union partners will initially be confronted, and

f in view of the dedication of the parties to the principle of resolving by peaceful and reasonable means any differences that may hereafter exist or arise between them,

that the status quo of the residency of New Guinea shall be maintained with the stipulation that within a year from the date of transfer of sovereignty to the Republic of the United States of Indonesia the question of the political status of New Guinea be determined through negotiations between the Republic of the United States of Indonesia and the Kingdom of the Netherlands.

This agreement was supplemented in November 1949 by an exchange of letters confirming that 'The clause in article 2 of the Draft Charter of Transfer

[1] See Part 1 above, and for an admirable account, see Alastair Taylor, *Indonesian Independence and the United Nations* (1960).
[2] 69 UNTS, 206. [3] On the establishment of this Commission, see Part 1, pp. 15–17.

of Sovereignty reading: the status quo of the residency of New Guinea shall be maintained, means: through continuing under the Government of the Netherlands'.[4]

The clause was still not without ambiguity, however, and the Indonesians were to argue that the Dutch had a mere right of administration for one year, but no sovereignty, for the term 'sovereignty' had been deliberately omitted. The Dutch, on the other hand, claimed that reference to the continuation of the *status quo* could only be taken to mean that West New Guinea would remain under Netherland's sovereignty.[5] By December of 1950 the Indonesians were demanding the incorporation of New Guinea into Indonesia, with guarantees for Dutch economic and concessionary rights in that territory. The Dutch refused to relinquish sovereignty over Western New Guinea until the population had exercised the right of self-determination. They offered to place the question of West Irian before the International Court of Justice, but the Indonesians declined on the grounds that it was a political question.

It was the new Indonesian government of Ali Sastroamidjojo which in 1954 decided to take the matter to the UN.[6] The First (Political) Committee of the General Assembly adopted a draft resolution hoping that the parties would try to find a solution in conformity with the UN Charter, and asking them to report on their progress.[7] The plenary meeting of the Assembly voted paragraph by paragraph, and as no paragraph obtained a two-thirds majority, the draft resolution was not accepted. By the next year, 1955, the Bandung Conference had indicated its support for Indonesia, and the Harahap government (which had replaced Sastroamidjojo) brought the matter again to the UN,[8] though it was more conservative in its approach. Outside of the UN, a new round of Dutch-Indonesian talks had begun, and the UN contented itself with a unanimous resolution[9] hoping that the negotiations would provide a peaceful solution. The talks failed and the Harahap Cabinet was replaced by Sastroamidjojo, who, with wide backing, brought the issue once more before the eleventh General Assembly.[10] The First Committee adopted a draft resolution asking the Assembly President to appoint a three-man Good Offices team. However, the vote in the Assembly was 40 to 25, with 13 abstentions, and as this was not a two-thirds majority, the resolution was not accepted.[11] Much the same pattern was followed at the twelfth session of the Assembly,[12] when the First Committee suggested that the services of the Secretary-General be offered to assist the parties to a settlement. Once again, the General Assembly, by a vote of 41–29–11, failed to provide the needed two-thirds majority (A/3757). The reluctance of certain members to approve such mildly worded resolutions aimed

[4] This exchange of letters may be found ibid. p. 332.

[5] The Dutch and Indonesian positions are stated in *GAOR*, 9th sess., 1st Cttee, 726th mtg. For some interesting comments on how far the misunderstanding was already present during the Round Table Conference, see Taylor, pp. 440–1 n. 8.

[6] *GAOR*, 9th sess., ann., a.i. 61; and A/2694.

[7] A/2831; and *GAOR*, 9th sess., 1st Cttee, 726th–36th mtgs.

[8] *GAOR*, 10th sess., ann., a.i. 65; and A/2932.   [9] GA res. 915 (X).   [10] See A/3200.

[11] A/3565.   [12] *GAOR*, 12th sess., ann., a.i. 62.

at peaceful solution appears to have stemmed from their belief that it was a matter solely within Holland's domestic jurisdiction.

The dispute was not inscribed upon the Assembly's agenda at the thirteenth, fourteenth, or fifteenth sessions. At the sixteenth session the dispute entered a new phase. The Netherlands, viewing West New Guinea as a colony awaiting self-determination, had continued to regard itself as an Administering Authority under the terms of Chapter XI of the Charter (on non-self-governing territories) and had viewed itself as bound by Article 73(e) to transmit information on the territory to the UN. Thus the question of West Irian remained before the UN in the Fourth Committee. At the fifteenth session of the Assembly the celebrated resolution 1514(XV) had been passed, calling *inter alia* for immediate steps towards independence for all remaining trust and non-self-governing territories. The Netherlands government now saw this resolution as a means of withdrawing from its increasingly burdensome colonial task in West New Guinea, without giving way on the principle of self-determination for the Papuans. Accordingly, it placed before the sixteenth Assembly a draft resolution (A/L.354) under agenda item 88 on 'The situation with regard to the implementation of the Declaration on the Granting of independence to colonial countries and peoples'. This resolution in effect envisaged the transfer of West New Guinea from Dutch sovereignty to the UN, who would administer it as a sort of trusteeship (though the term 'trusteeship' was not explicitly used), until the people of the territory could be prepared for a plebiscite. The proposal merits citation in full:

The General Assembly,

Recalling its resolution 1514 (XV) declaring, *inter alia*, that immediate steps shall be taken in Trust and Non-Self-Governing Territories or all other territories which have not yet obtained independence, to transfer all powers to the peoples of those territories, without any conditions or reservations, in accordance with their freely expressed will and desire, without any distinction as to race, creed or colour, in order to enable them to enjoy complete independence and freedom,

Considering the important role of the United Nations in assisting development towards independence in Trust and Non-Self-Governing Territories,

Noting that Western New Guinea is administered under the terms of Chapter XI of the Charter and that the Administering Authority has declared that self-determination for the people of Western New Guinea in accordance with the principles of the Charter is the sole purpose of its policy,

Recognizing the paramount importance of respect for the principle of self-determination in accordance with the principles of the Charter of the United Nations,

Noting also the statement that the Netherlands is prepared to implement resolution 1514 (XV) as promptly as possible, under the supervision, and with the assistance, of the United Nations, and for this purpose is prepared to transfer sovereignty to the people of the Territory.

Recognizing that the Territory concerned will for some time to come require international technical and economic assistance and guidance,

Noting further that the Netherlands is prepared to agree that its present powers should, to the extent required for the above purpose, be exercised by an international organization or authority, with executive power, established by and operating under the United Nations,

Noting also that the Netherlands is prepared to continue its contribution to the development of the Territory on the basis of its present contribution until such time as may be decided upon the the future,

Recognizing that the future status of the Territory should be determined in accordance with the wishes of the population,

Recognizing the need for a full and impartial report on the present conditions in the Territory and on the possibilities of an early implementation of resolution 1514 (XV) with regard to the Territory,

    1. *Decides* to set up a United Nations commission for Netherlands New Guinea composed of . . . .

    2. *Requests* the commission to investigate the possibilities of an early implementation of resolution 1514 (XV) in respect of Netherlands New Guinea and more specifically to this end to inquire into:

    (*a*) The political, economic, social and educational conditions in the Territory;

    (*b*) The opinion amongst the population as to its present situation and its future;

    (*c*) The possibility of organizing a plebiscite under the supervision of the United Nations in order to register the wishes of the population concerning their future, and the timing of the plebiscite;

    (*d*) The desirability and possibility of bringing the Territory, during the interim period, partially or wholly under the administration of an international development authority, established by, and operating under, the United Nations;

    3. *Requests* the commission to report to the General Assembly at its seventeenth session;

    4. *Requests* the Secretary-General to make available to the commission the necessary staff and administrative facilities. [*A/L. 354, 9 Oct. 1961.*]

It was accompanied by a detailed memorandum which spells out in greater detail what the Netherlands envisaged.[13]

Memorandum on the future and the development of Netherlands New Guinea

    1. On 14 December 1960 the General Assembly approved resolution 1514 (XV), the Declaration on the granting of independence to colonial countries and peoples. The Netherlands supported this resolution and is fully prepared to put it into practice with regard to the sole dependent Territory under its administration, that is, Netherlands New Guinea.

    2. The Netherlands at present administers the Western part of New Guinea as a Non-Self-Governing Territory under Chapter XI of the Charter of the United Nations. In accordance with Article 73 e of the Charter, the Netherlands Government has yearly transmitted reports on its administration, including information on political conditions, to the Secretary-General, and has participated in a constructive way in the work of the Committee on Information from Non-Self-Governing Territories.

    3. As mentioned in those reports, the Netherlands has taken important steps to accelerate the development of the population of Netherlands New Guinea towards self-government, i.e., by the establishment of a New Guinea Council as well as local councils and the training of indigenous cadres to accelerate the Papuanization of the administration. Further steps towards the transfer of power, also in the field of administration, are being taken or are in an advanced stage of preparation. This policy of the Netherlands Government is in conformity with paragraph 5 of the above mentioned Declaration.

    4. In the course of the general debate at the fifteenth session of the General Assembly, the Minister for Foreign Affairs of the Netherlands declared that the Netherlands was prepared to subject its policy and its actions, aimed at the speediest possible attainment of self determination by the Papuan people, to the continuous scrutiny and judgement of the United Nations.

    5. Further to this statement, the Netherlands Government now wishes to place the ques-

---

    [13] See also A/4954, reiterating the Dutch case to date; and the statement of Mr Luns in *GAOR*, 16th sess., 1016th plen. mtg.

tion of the implementation of the above-mentioned Declaration with regard to Netherlands New Guinea before the General Assembly. In doing so the Netherlands Government is led by the following motives:

(a) The sole purpose of the Netherlands in its policy in respect of Netherlands New Guinea is the granting of complete self-determination to the people of New Guinea in accordance with the principles of the Charter of the United Nations;

(b) In conformity with resolution 1514 (XV), the Netherlands is prepared to terminate its sovereignty over Netherlands New Guinea at the earliest possible date, that is, as soon as the right of self-determination of the population is properly safeguarded;

(c) The Netherlands Government, however, is aware that the Territory will still for some time to come require interntaional technical and economic assistance and guidance;

(d) The Netherlands therefore is looking for ways by which resolution 1514 (XV) can be implemented as soon as possible with respect to Netherlands New Guinea and by which at the same time the population may receive the necessary guarantees of assistance and guidance required for the integral development towards self-determination;

(e) In its resolution 1514 (XV) the General Assembly declared that the Administering Powers should take immediate steps to transfer all powers to the peoples of those Territories administered by them at the earliest possible date. In conformity with this expressed desire the Netherlands now requests that the General Assembly assist in attaining that aim.

6. Following are concrete proposals, based on the above-mentioned motives, which, if approved and adopted by the General Assembly, would implement in a practical way resolution 1514 (XV) and lead to a speedy political and educational development of the Territory and to early termination of the present Netherlands administration while at the same time providing a *bona fide* guarantee of the right of self-determination.

(a) The Netherlands is prepared to bring the administration and the development of the Territory under the active supervision of the United Nations and is prepared to accept a decision of the General Assembly which clearly guarantees the right of self-determination of the population;

(b) To this end the Netherlands is prepared to transfer its sovereignty to the people of Netherlands New Guinea;

(c) In this connexion, the Netherlands is prepared to agree that its present powers should, to the extent required for the above purpose, be exercised by an organization or international authority, established by and operating under the United Nations, which would be vested with executive powers and which could gradually take over tasks and responsibilities and thus prepare the population for early self-determination under stable conditions;

(d) The Netherlands is prepared to continue its contribution to the development of the Territory on the basis of the present annual level of about $30 million and until such time as may be decided upon in the future.

7. The above-mentioned proposals (sub-paragraph (c)) would constitute a form of international administration by an international development authority under the supervision of the General Assembly. The United Nations may not be able to provide all the necessary personnel for such an authority. For this reason the Netherlands, and more specifically the Netherlands civil service in New Guinea, could continue to perform such tasks as the General Assembly might deem necessary for the purpose of promoting a smooth transition from national to international administration.

8. This new form of administration could, if required, be established by an agreement to be concluded between the United Nations and the Netherlands.

9. The authority may consist of a governing board to be composed of representatives, appointed by the United Nations, and of an administrator, to be appointed by the Secretary-General on the recommendation of the board, and his staff of experts, each heading a special government department. The Secretary-General might wish to consult the specialized agencies concerned about their possible participation in the administration or in the authority itself.

10. Responsibility for economic, social and educational development should at once be

entrusted to the authority with executive power. International experts could be recruited in accordance with the rules applicable to the United Nations technical assistance personnel.

11. The Netherlands Government is prepared to request its civil servants of Netherlands nationality at present serving in New Guinea and numbering approximately 2,800 to remain in their posts as international civil servants.

12. If and where required, the Netherlands Government is prepared to continue its responsibility under United Nations supervision in those fields of administration where its presence might usefully serve the purpose of the development of New Guinea under international control.

13. As stated above, the Netherlands Government is prepared to continue its financial contribution for the administration and development of the Territory on the basis of its present contribution. The budget of the Territory could be drafted jointly by the Netherlands Government and the Authority.

14. Since these proposals are entirely new and without precedent in the history of the United Nations, the General Assembly might wish to study them more closely. The General Assembly might also wish to acquaint itself with the present conditions in the Territory and the wishes of the population and to have a complete and impartial report thereon.

15. Therefore the Netherlands Government suggests that a United Nations commission be set up which should be requested to investigate the possibilities of an early implementation of resolution 1514 (XV) in respect of Netherlands New Guinea and more specifically to this end to inquire into:

(a) The political, economic, social and educational conditions in the Territory;

(b) The opinion amongst the population as to its present situation and its future;

(c) The possibility for organizing a plebiscite under the supervision of the United Nations in order to register the wishes of the population of the Territory, and the timing of the plebiscite;

(d) The desirability and possibility of bringing the development of the Territory, during the interim period partially or wholly under the administration of an international development authority, established by and operating under the United Nations.

The commission should report together with its recommendations to the General Assembly at its seventeenth session.

16. To this end the Netherlands has submitted a draft resolution (A/L.354) for consideration by the General Assembly. [*A/4915.*]

The Indonesian reply (A/4944) was made by Dr Subandrio, the Foreign Minister, in a speech in Djakarta on United Nations Day. He claimed that the policy 'was not decolonization, but, on the contrary, merely a tactic to strike at Indonesia'. It was said that the Dutch were trying 'to use the right of self-determination as a means to cut off a part of the territory of the Indonesian Republic'. Dr Subandrio claimed that West New Guinea was being suppressed by force of arms, and reserved the right to Indonesia to 'liberate our brothers in West Irian, also by force'.

This reaction to the Dutch proposal was to find fairly substantial support among the non-aligned states. It was felt by many that a solution which sought to ignore Indonesia was no solution at all. Thus Mr Dosomu-Johnson, the Liberian representative, said:

67. If we were ignorant of the situation as it existed three or four years ago in West Irian, we would not question but admire the step taken by the Netherlands Government in the interests of West Irian. Knowing, however, the situation, and the background of the issue here, my delegation is inclined to the opinion that any action taken by this Assembly with regard to West Irian must also consider the long standing claims of Indonesia to this Terri-

tory. Any settlement regarding West Irian, we opine, must be made in consultation with Indonesia. [*GAOR, 16th sess., 1054th plen. mtg.*, p. 640.][14]

While many non-aligned nations indicated that they admired the Dutch initiative but found it inappropriate, the communist nations opposed it as 'another colonialist attempt to continue colonialist domination in a new and disguised form'.[15] Western nations were more sympathetic: Australia, with a special interest in the question because of her control of the trust territory of East New Guinea and of the Papuans, supported the Dutch proposals.[16] (Although Papua was not a trust territory, the Australians had since the war governed Papua and New Guinea as one political unit—a situation which had been formalized by the Papua–New Guinea Act of Union in 1949. The UN had initially strongly opposed the idea of one unit, but the Visiting Mission of 1962, led by Sir Hugh Foot, paved the way for acceptance of the reality.) It has been stated[17] that at no time was a joint trusteeship of Australian and Netherlands New Guinea suggested, and this appears to be true; however, Australia appears to have envisaged the possibility of an ultimate union of the peoples of the trust territory of New Guinea, of Papua, and of West New Guinea after such time as they had each exercised their right of self-determination.[18] In the final event the Netherlands proposal was not pressed to a vote. Other resolutions which were put to the vote failed to obtain a two-thirds majority.[19]

The situation now rapidly deteriorated—so much so that one month later the Acting Secretary-General, U Thant, felt the need to send cables to President Sukarno and the Prime Minister, de Quay, stating his deep concern and urging the two parties to come together to seek a solution. He made a further approach on 15 January 1962, when a naval clash occurred off West New Guinea. The details of the Dutch protest over the Indonesian use of force are to be found in S/5062. At U Thant's suggestion the permanent representatives of the Netherlands and Indonesia at the UN then consulted him. On 29 January 1962 the Acting Secretary-General appealed to the Netherlands to agree to the release of Indonesian prisoners as a humanitarian gesture to ease tensions, and Dr de Quay agreed.[20] U Thant then asked the President of the International Committee of the Red Cross to designate an official to make arrangements for repatriation, and this task was accomplished by 11 March 1962.

Meanwhile, the Secretary-General continued his consultations, and it was agreed that informal talks would take place between the parties and Ambassador Ellsworth Bunker, the latter acting as representative of U Thant. During the period of those talks the Netherlands had further occasion to protest to the

[14] For a similar view by Ghana—which then proposed that a Good Offices Committee of five should be set up—see *GAOR*, 16th sess., 1057th mtg, p. 691; and by Pakistan, ibid. 1061st mtg, p. 764.
[15] Ibid. 1058th mtg, p. 707, para. 75.
[16] During the earlier dispute over Indonesian independence, Australia, it should be noted, had maintained a strong pro-Indonesian line.
[17] Ruth Russell, *UN Experience with Military Forces: Political and Legal Aspects* (1964), p. 127.
[18] *GAOR*, 16th sess., 1055th mtg, pp. 653–4.
[19] See A/L.367 & Rev. 1 (*GAOR*, 16th sess., ann., a.i. 88, p. 26).
[20] UN Press Release WNG/1, 15 Aug. 1962.

UN about armed infiltration, by sea and air, of small numbers of Indonesians into West New Guinea.[21] The Acting Secretary-General responded by urging restraint upon both parties. He declined the Dutch request to send UN observers to the scene: '. . . I could consider such a move only if a request were made by both the Netherlands and Indonesian Governments'.[22] A further series of incidents was reported by the Netherlands;[23] and the Indonesians made it clear that they regarded any claim of aggression as unacceptable, for 'Indonesians who have entered and who in future will continue to enter West Irian, are Indonesian nationals who move into Indonesia's own territory now dominated by the Dutch by force'.[24] It will be noted that this exchange of communications on West Irian appears as Security Council documents—that organ being the appropriate body for questions concerning an alleged illegal use of force—whereas discussions on the *status* of West Irian had always previously occurred in the Assembly.

None the less, in spite of this 'raising of the ante', Ambassador Bunker continued his work and on 29 May 1962 the Acting Secretary-General appealed to the parties to resume negotiations on the basis of his proposals. On 13 July U Thant was able to announce the resumption of talks in the presence of Ambassador Bunker on the basis of the 'Bunker plan'.[25] The negotiations now made rapid progress, and by 31 July the Secretary-General was able to announce that a preliminary agreement had been reached, and that official negotiations were now to take place under his auspices.

The final negotiations took place at UN headquarters, under the Chairmanship of U Thant, with Ambassador Bunker continuing to act as mediator. An Agreement was signed by Indonesia and the Netherlands on 15 August 1962. Under Article XXVII instruments of ratification were to be exchanged at UN headquarters, and this was done on 20 September. Article XXVIII provided that the Agreement would come into effect upon the adoption of an approving resolution by the General Assembly, which resolution was required by Article I of the Agreement.

Accordingly, the Secretary-General requested, pursuant to rule 14 of the Rules of Procedure, the inclusion of this supplementary item upon the agenda of the seventeenth session of the Assembly.[26] The General Committee of the Assembly allocated time for an early hearing, even ahead of the conclusion of the general speeches.

The Agreement provided for the administration of West New Guinea (West Irian) to be transferred by the Netherlands to a UN Temporary Executive Authority (UNTEA), established by and under the jurisdiction of the Secretary-General. The UNTEA, to be headed by a UN Administrator, was in due course, after 1 May 1963, to transfer the administration to Indonesia. The Agreement

---

[21] S/5123, 21 May 1962.   [22] S/5124, 23 May 1962.
[23] S/5126, 24 May 1962; S/5135, 25 June 1962; S/5155, 10 Aug. 1962; S/5157, 14 Aug. 1962.
[24] S/5128, 25 May 1962.
[25] See the preliminary exchange of communications on 29 May, 5, 7, 17, 20, 27 & 28 June and 3 July.
[26] A/5170 & Add. 1 (*GAOR*, 17th sess., ann., a.i. 89).

contained certain guarantees for the population of the territory, including provisions for the exercise of the right of self-determination under arrangements made by Indonesia with the advice, assistance, and participation of the Secretary-General, who was to appoint a UN Representative for that purpose. The act of self-determination was to take place before the end of 1969.

The text of the Agreement follows.

AGREEMENT BETWEEN THE REPUBLIC OF INDONESIA AND THE KINGDOM OF THE NETHERLANDS CONCERNING WEST NEW GUINEA (WEST IRIAN)

The Republic of Indonesia and the Kingdom of the Netherlands,

Having in mind the interests and welfare of the people of the territory of West New Guinea (West Irian) hereinafter referred to as 'the territory',

Desirous of settling their dispute regarding the territory,

Now, therefore, agree as follows:

RATIFICATION OF AGREEMENT AND RESOLUTION OF THE GENERAL ASSEMBLY OF THE UNITED NATIONS

Article I

After the present Agreement between Indonesia and the Netherlands has been signed and ratified by both Contracting Parties, Indonesia and the Netherlands will jointly sponsor a draft resolution in the United Nations under the terms of which the General Assembly of the United Nations takes note of the present Agreement, acknowledges the role conferred upon the Secretary-General of the United Nations therein, and authorizes him to carry out the tasks entrusted to him therein.

TRANSFER OF ADMINISTRATION

Article II

After the adoption of the resolution referred to in article I, the Netherlands will transfer administration of the territory to a United Nations Temporary Executive Authority (UNTEA) established by and under the jurisdiction of the Secretary-General upon the arrival of the United Nations Administrator appointed in accordance with article IV. The UNTEA will in turn transfer the administration to Indonesia in accordance with article XII.

UNITED NATIONS ADMINISTRATION

Article III

In order to facilitate the transfer of administration to the UNTEA after the adoption of the resolution by the General Assembly, the Netherlands will invite the Secretary-General to send a representative to consult briefly with the Netherlands Governor of the territory prior to the latter's departure. The Netherlands Governor will depart prior to the arrival of the United Nations Administrator.

Article IV

A United Nations Administrator, acceptable to Indonesia and the Netherlands, will be appointed by the Secretary-General.

Article V

The United Nations Administrator, as chief executive officer of the UNTEA, will have full authority under the direction of the Secretary-General to administer the territory for the period of the UNTEA administration in accordance with the terms of the present Agreement.

Article VI

1. The United Nations flag will be flown during the period of United Nations administration.

2. With regard to the flying of the Indonesian and Netherlands flags, it is agreed that this matter will be determined by agreement between the Secretary-General and the respective Governments.

Article VII

The Secretary-General will provide the UNTEA with such security forces as the United Nations Administrator deems necessary; such forces will primarily supplement existing Papuan (West Irianese) police in the task of maintaining law and order. The Papuan Volunteer Corps, which on the arrival of the United Nations Administrator will cease being part of the Netherlands armed forces, and the Indonesian armed forces in the territory will be under the authority of, and at the disposal of, the Secretary-General for the same purpose. The United Nations Administrator will, to the extent feasible, use the Papuan (West Irianese) police as a United Nations security force to maintain law and order and, at his discretion, use Indonesian armed forces. The Netherlands armed forces will be repatriated as rapidly as possible and while still in the territory will be under the authority of the UNTEA.

Article VIII

The United Nations Administrator will send periodic reports to the Secretary-General on the principal aspects of the implementation of the present Agreement. The Secretary-General will submit full reports to Indonesia and the Netherlands and may submit, at his discretion, reports to the General Assembly or to all United Nations Members.

FIRST PHASE OF THE UNTEA ADMINISTRATION

Article IX

The United Nations Administrator will replace, as rapidly as possible, top Netherlands officials, as defined in annex A, with non-Netherlands, non-Indonesian officials during the first phase of the UNTEA administration which will be completed on 1 May 1963. The United Nations Administrator will be authorized to employ, on a temporary basis, all Netherlands officials other than top Netherlands officials defined in annex A, who wish to serve the UNTEA, in accordance with such terms and conditions as the Secretary-General may specify. As many Papuans (West Irianese) as possible will be brought into administrative and technical positions. To fill the remaining required posts, the UNTEA will have authority to employ personnel provided by Indonesia. Salary rates prevailing in the territory will be maintained.

Article X

Immediately after the transfer of administration to the UNTEA, the UNTEA will widely publicize and explain the terms of the present Agreement, and will inform the population concerning the transfer of administration to Indonesia and the provisions for the act of self-determination as set out in the present Agreement.

Article XI

To the extent that they are consistent with the letter and spirit of the present Agreement, existing laws and regulations will remain in effect. The UNTEA will have the power to promulgate new laws and regulations or amend them within the spirit and framework of the present Agreement. The representative councils will be consulted prior to the issuance of new laws and regulations or the amendment of existing laws.

Article XII

The United Nations Administrator will have discretion to transfer all or part of the administration to Indonesia at any time after the first phase of the UNTEA administration. The UNTEA'S authority will cease at the moment of transfer of full administrative control to Indonesia.

Article XIII

United Nations security forces will be replaced by Indonesian security forces after the first phase of the UNTEA administration. All United Nations security forces will be withdrawn upon the transfer of administration to Indonesia.

INDONESIAN ADMINISTRATION AND SELF-DETERMINATION

Article XIV

After the transfer of full administrative responsibility to Indonesia, Indonesian national laws and regulations will in principle be applicable in the territory, it being understood that they be consistent with the rights and freedoms guaranteed to the inhabitants under the terms of the present Agreement. New laws and regulations or amendments to the existing ones can be enacted within the spirit of the present Agreement. The representative councils will be consulted as appropriate.

Article XV

After the transfer of full administrative responsibility to Indonesia, the primary task of Indonesia will be further intensification of the education of the people, of the combating of illiteracy, and of the advancement of their social, cultural and economic development. Efforts also will be made, in accordance with present Indonesian practice, to accelerate the participation of the people in local government through periodic elections. Any aspects relating to the act of free choice will be governed by the terms of this Agreement.

Article XVI

At the time of the transfer of full administrative responsibility to Indonesia a number of United Nations experts, as deemed adequate by the Secretary-General after consultation with Indonesia, will be designated to remain, wherever their duties require their presence. Their duties will, prior to the arrival of the United Nations Representative, who will participate at the appropriate time in the arrangements for self-determination, be limited to advising on, and assisting in, preparations for carrying out the provisions for self-determination except in so far as Indonesia and the Secretary-General may agree upon their performing other expert functions. They will be responsible to the Secretary-General for the carrying out of their duties.

Article XVII

Indonesia will invite the Secretary-General to appoint a Representative who, together with a staff made up, *inter alia*, of experts referred to in article XVI, will carry out the Secretary-General's responsibilities to advise, assist and participate in arrangements which are the responsibility of Indonesia for the act of free choice. The Secretary-General will, at the proper time, appoint the United Nations Representative in order that he and his staff may assume their duties in the territory one year prior to the date of self-determination. Such additional staff as the United Nations Representative might feel necessary will be determined by the Secretary-General after consultations with Indonesia. The United Nations Representative and his staff will have the same freedom of movement as provided for the personnel referred to in article XVI.

Article XVIII

Indonesia will make arrangements, with the assistance and participation of the United Nations Representative and his staff, to give the people of the territory the opportunity to exercise freedom of choice. Such arrangements will include:

(*a*) Consultations (*Musjawarah*) with the representative councils on procedures and appropriate methods to be followed for ascertaining the freely expressed will of the population;

(*b*) The determination of the actual date of the exercise of free choice within the period established by the present Agreement;

(*c*) Formulation of the questions in such a way as to permit the inhabitants to decide (*a*) whether they wish to remain with Indonesia; or (*b*) whether they wish to sever their ties with Indonesia;

(*d*) The eligibility of all adults, male and female, not foreign nationals, to participate in the act of self-determination to be carried out in accordance with international practice, who are resident at the time of the signing of the present Agreement and at the time of the act of self-determination, including those residents who departed after 1945 and who return to the territory to resume residence after the termination of Netherlands administration.

Article XIX

The United Nations Representative will report to the Secretary-General on the arrangements arrived at for freedom of choice.

Article XX

The act of self-determination will be completed before the end of 1969.

Article XXI

1. After the exercise of the right of self-determination, Indonesia and the United Nations Representative will submit final reports to the Secretary-General who will report to the General Assembly on the conduct of the act of self-determination and the results thereof.

2. The Parties to the present Agreement will recognize and abide by the results of the act of self-determination.

RIGHTS OF THE INHABITANTS

Article XXII

1. The UNTEA and Indonesia will guarantee fully the rights, including the rights of free speech, freedom of movement and of assembly, of the inhabitants of the area. These rights will include the existing rights of the inhabitants of the territory at the time of the transfer of administration to the UNTEA.

2. The UNTEA will take over existing Netherlands commitments in respect of concessions and property rights.

3. After Indonesia has taken over the administration it will honour those commitments which are not inconsistent with the interests and economic development of the people of the territory. A joint Indonesian-Netherlands commission will be set up after the transfer of administration to Indonesia to study the nature of the above-mentioned concessions and property rights.

4. During the period of the UNTEA administration there will be freedom of movement for civilians of Indonesian and Netherlands nationalities to and from the territory.

Article XXIII

Vacancies in the representative councils caused by the departure of Netherlands nationals, or for other reasons, will be filled as appropriate consistent with existing legislation by elections, or by appointment by the UNTEA. The representative councils will be consulted prior to the appointment of new representatives.

FINANCIAL MATTERS

Article XXIV

1. Deficits in the budget of the territory during the UNTEA administration will be shared equally by Indonesia and the Netherlands.

2. Indonesia and the Netherlands will be consulted by the Secretary-General in the preparation of the UNTEA budget and other financial matters relating to United Nations responsibilities under the present Agreement; however, the Secretary-General will have the final decision.

3. The Parties to the present Agreement will reimburse the Secretary-General for all costs incurred by the United Nations under the present Agreement and will make available suitable funds in advance for the discharge of the Secretary-General's responsibilities. The Parties to the present agreement will share on an equal basis the costs of such reimbursements and advances.

PREVIOUS TREATIES AND AGREEMENTS

Article XXV

The present Agreement will take precedence over any previous agreement on the territory. Previous treaties and agreements regarding the territory may therefore be terminated or adjusted as necessary to conform to the terms of the present Agreement.

PRIVILEGES AND IMMUNITIES

Article XXVI

For the purposes of the present Agreement, Indonesia and the Netherlands will apply to United Nations property, funds, assets and officials the provisions of the Convention on the Privileges and Immunities of the United Nations. In particular, the United Nations Administrator, appointed pursuant to article IV, and the United Nations Representative, appointed pursuant to article XVII, will enjoy the privileges and immunities specified in secton 19 of the Convention on the Privileges and Immunities of the United Nations.

RATIFICATION

Article XXVII

1. The present Agreement will be ratified in accordance with the constitutional procedures of the Contracting Parties.

2. The instruments of ratification will be exchanged as soon as possible at the Headquarters of the United Nations by the accredited representatives of the Contracting Parties.

3. The Secretary-General will draw up a *procès-verbal* of the exchange of the instruments of ratification and will furnish a certified copy thereof to each Contracting Party.

ENTRY INTO FORCE

Article XXVIII

1. The present Agreement will enter into force upon the date of the adoption by the General Assembly of the resolution referred to in article I of the present Agreement.

2. Upon the entry into force of the present Agreement, the Secretary-General of the United Nations will register it in accordance with Article 102 of the Charter.

Article XXIX

The authentic text of the present Agreement is drawn up in the English language. Translations in the Indonesian and Netherlands languages will be exchanged between the Contracting Parties.

IN WITNESS WHEREOF the undersigned plenipotentiaries, being duly authorized for that purpose by their respective Governments, have signed the present Agreement.

DONE at the Headquarters of the United Nations, New York, on this fifteenth day of August 1962, in three identical copies of which one shall be deposited with the Secretary-General and one shall be furnished to the Government of each of the Contracting Parties.

(*Signed*) SUBANDRIO
For the Republic of Indonesia

J. H. VAN ROIJEN
For the Kingdom of the Netherlands

C. SCHURMANN
For the Kingdom of the Netherlands

ANNEX A

Top Netherlands officials to be replaced as rapidly as possible with non-Netherlands, non-Indonesian officials.

I.	*Government*	
	Head, Government Information Bureau	1
	Head, Popular Information Service	1
II.	*Department of Internal Affairs*	
	Director	1
	Divisional Commissioners (*Residenten*):	6
	1—Hollandia	
	2—Biak	
	3—Manokwari	
	4—Fakfak	
	5—Merauke	
	6—Central Highlands	
	Administrative Head of the General Police	1
III.	*Department of Finance*	
	Director	1
IV.	*Department of Social Affairs and Justice*	
	Director	1
V.	*Department of Public Health*	
	Director	1
VI.	*Department of Cultural Affairs* (including Education)	
	Director	1
	Head, Broadcasting System	1
VII.	*Department of Economic Affairs*	
	Director	1
VIII.	*Department of Transport and Power*	
	Director	1
IX.	*Department of Public Works*	
	Director	1
	TOTAL	18

[*A/5170 & Add. 1 (GAOR, 17th sess., ann., a.i. 89); 274 UNTS 6311.*]

In addition, the Assembly was presented with, and approved along with the Agreement itself, (1) a note dated 15 August 1962 from the representative of Indonesia and the representatives of the Netherlands, to the Acting Secretary-General, concerning a cease-fire, with an attached Memorandum of Understanding on cessation of hostilities;[27] (2) a Memorandum of Understanding on certain financial matters; (3) a note dated 15 August 1962 from the representative of Indonesia and the representatives of the Netherlands addressed to the Acting Secretary-General concerning the issue of passports and consular protection, with identical replies of the same date from U Thant to Indonesia and the Netherlands, and further identical replies from Indonesia and the Netherlands to U Thant; and (4), aides-mémoire of 15 August 1962 from the Acting Secretary-General, handed to the representatives of Indonesia and the Netherlands concerning the modalities of transfer of authority over West New Guinea. Items (2), (3), and (4) are here reproduced:

(2)

MEMORANDUM OF UNDERSTANDING CONSTITUTING AN AGREEMENT BETWEEN THE REPUBLIC OF INDONESIA AND THE KINGDOM OF THE NETHERLANDS ON CERTAIN FINANCIAL MATTERS DURING THE PERIOD OF ADMINISTRATION OF WEST NEW GUINEA (WEST IRIAN) BY THE UNITED NATIONS TEMPORARY EXECUTIVE AUTHORITY (UNTEA)

1. With the view to preparing the budget for the period of administration of the territory of West New Guinea (West Irian) by the United Nations Temporary Executive Authority (UNTEA) in accordance with article XXIV of the Agreement between the Republic of Indonesia and the Kingdom of the Netherlands concerning West New Guinea (West Irian), a committee will be set up as soon as possible consisting of representatives of the Secretary-General of the United Nations, the Government of the Republic of Indonesia and the Government of the Kingdom of the Netherlands in order to collect the necessary information and to make appropriate recommendations to the Secretary-General. The committee will make recommendations to the Secretary-General concerning the amount to be placed at the disposal of the United Nations Administrator by the Netherlands and the Indonesian Governments at the beginning of the UNTEA period.

2. In establishing the budget for the UNTEA period, the United Nations Administrator will make his calculations on the basis of a rate of exchange for the New Guinea guilder at US $1.00 = N.G. fl. 3.62.

DONE this fifteenth day of August 1962 in three original copies.

IDENTICAL LETTERS DATED 15 AUGUST 1962 FROM THE ACTING SECRETARY-GENERAL ADDRESSED TO THE REPRESENTATIVE OF INDONESIA AND TO THE REPRESENTATIVES OF THE NETHERLANDS CONCERNING CERTAIN FINANCIAL MATTERS

I have the honour to refer to the discussions that took place on 13 and 14 August 1962 at United Nations Headquarters between representatives of the Government of Indonesia, the Government of the Netherlands and the Secretariat concerning certain financial arrangements which are envisaged in connexion with the United Nations Administration of West New Guinea (West Irian).

In response to the request of the representatives of the two Governments these arrangements are set forth below.

The Secretary-General will prepare, in consultation with the two Governments, a budget covering the total anticipated costs involved in its administration of the Territory, and will request the two Governments to make advances of funds in such currencies and at such time(s) as may be required to cover the anticipated costs.

[27] For texts, see below, pp. 111–13.

The funds made available by the Governments to the Organization will be treated as trust funds in accordance with United Nations financial regulations 6.6 and 6.7 and will be administered in accordance with the established United Nations financial regulations and rules relating to trust funds, reserve and special accounts, and, in particular, United Nations financial regulations 10.1 (*d*), 10.2 and 11.3 relating to the arrangements in respect of (*a*) the maintenance of an internal financial control to provide for an effective current examination and/or, review of financial transactions in order to ensure the regularity of the receipt, custody and disposal of the funds, the conformity of obligations and expenditures with the purposes and rules relating to the trust funds, and the economic use of these resources; (*b*) providing that no obligations shall be incurred until allotments or other appropriate authorizations have been made in writing under the authority of the Secretary-General and (*c*) maintaining a separate special account for all funds received in trust from the Governments.

As soon as possible after the termination of the United Nations responsibility for administration of the Territory an audited statement of the income and expenditures arising from and in connexion with its administration of the Territory will be rendered to the two Governments, and any balance of funds in the trust fund that are not required to cover commitments entered into by the Organization in this connexion will be refunded in equal shares to the two Governments.

If, after preparation of the initial budget, unforeseen developments should occur giving rise to the need for additional funds from the two Governments, the Secretary-General would prepare a supplemental budget in consultation with the two Governments, and request such additional desposits in the trust fund as would be required.

It may be anticipated that the budget estimates would consist of two major parts, the first relating to what may be described as the normal territorial operations and accounts, and the second relating to expenses to be incurred by the United Nations for staff and other costs (salaries, United Nations Joint Staff Pension Fund contributions, insurance, travel expenses, communications costs, etc.) which may not be dealt with appropriately as part of the normal territorial operations. The second part of the budget would also include the costs of any security personnel that might be required and for which no provision has been made in the existing budget for the Territory.

It is my understanding that the representatives of the two Governments participating in the discussions expressed agreement with the arrangements set forth above, but I would be pleased if you would advise me of your Government's concurrence regarding them.

(3)

NOTE DATED 15 AUGUST 1962 FROM THE REPRESENTATIVE OF INDONESIA AND THE REPRESENTATIVES OF THE NETHERLANDS, ADDRESSED TO THE ACTING SECRETARY-GENERAL, CONCERNING THE ISSUE OF PASSPORTS AND CONSULAR PROTECTION DURING THE ADMINISTRATION OF WEST NEW GUINEA (WEST IRIAN) BY THE UNITED NATIONS TEMPORARY EXECUTIVE AUTHORITY (UNTEA)

On behalf of our respective Governments, on the occasion of the signature of the Agreement between the Republic of Indonesia and the Kingdom of the Netherlands concerning West New Guinea (West Irian), we have the honour to bring to your attention the following agreement arrived at between our Governments and hereby placed on record, concerning the issue of passports and consular protection during the period of the administration by the United Nations Temporary Executive Authority (UNTEA) provided for in the aforesaid Agreement:

'1. The UNTEA shall have the authority at its discretion to issue travel documents to Papuans (West Irianese) applying therefor without prejudice to their right to apply for Indonesian passports instead;

'2. The Governments of Indonesia and of the Netherlands shall at the request of the Secretary-General furnish consular assistance and protection abroad to Papuans (West Irianese) carrying the travel documents mentioned in the previous paragraph, it being for the person concerned to determine to which consular authority he should apply.'

Should the above be acceptable to you, we have the honour further to propose that the note and your reply to the above effect shall be regarded as constituting and placing upon record the agreement reached in this matter.

IDENTICAL REPLIES DATED 15 AUGUST 1962 FROM THE ACTING SECRETARY-GENERAL ADDRESSED TO THE REPRESENTATIVE OF INDONESIA AND TO THE REPRESENTATIVES OF THE NETHERLANDS

I have the honour to acknowledge the receipt of the note of today's date addressed to me by the representatives of the Republic of Indonesia and the Kingdom of the Netherlands, concerning the issue of passports and consular protection during the period of the administration by the United Nations Temporary Executive Authority (UNTEA) of the territory of West New Guinea (West Irian), and reading as follows:

(*See text of the preceding note.*)

In reply I have the honour to inform you that I am prepared to instruct the UNTEA, when it is established as provided for in the Agreement between the Republic of Indonesia and the Kingdom of the Netherlands concerning West New Guinea (West Irian), to undertake the function referred to in the note under reference. I would like to take this occasion to request your Government to undertake consular assistance and protection abroad to Papuans (West Irianese) as provided in paragraph 2 of the note under reference.

This note and your note under reference shall be regarded as constituting and placing on record the agreement reached in this matter.

IDENTICAL REPLIES DATED 15 AUGUST 1962 FROM THE REPRESENTATIVE OF INDONESIA AND THE REPRESENTATIVES OF THE NETHERLANDS ADDRESSED TO THE ACTING SECRETARY-GENERAL

I have the honour to acknowledge the receipt of your note of today's date, indicating your willingness to undertake certain functions concerning issue of passports during the period of the administration by the United Nations Temporary Executive Authority (UNTEA) of the territory of West New Guinea (West Irian) and requesting my Government to undertake consular assistance and protection abroad to Papuans (West Irianese) requesting such assistance and protection during the period of the UNTEA Administration. I have the honour to inform you that my Government will undertake such consular assistance and protection.

We have the honour to acknowledge the receipt of your note of today's note, indicating your willingness to undertake certain functions concerning issue of passports during the period of the administration by the United Nations Temporary Executive Authority (UNTEA) of the territory of West New Guinea (West Irian) and requesting my Government to undertake consular assistance and protection abroad to Papuans (West Irianese) requesting such assistance and protection during the period of the UNTEA Administration. We have the honour to inform you that our Government will undertake such consular assistance and protection.

(4)

AIDE-MÉMOIRE DATED 15 AUGUST 1962 FROM THE ACTING SECRETARY-GENERAL, HANDED TO THE REPRESENTATIVE OF INDONESIA, CONCERNING THE MODALITIES OF THE TRANSFER OF AUTHORITY OVER WEST NEW GUINEA (WEST IRIAN)

1. The authority of the Government of the Netherlands over the territory will be terminated when the Special Representative of the Secretary-General takes charge. On the same day the United Nations flag will be hoisted.

2. From the same date the withdrawal and repatriation of the armed forces of the Netherlands will begin under the supervision of the Secretary-General's Special Representative and will be concluded as soon as possible.

3. On 31 December 1962 the Netherlands flag will be struck, and the Indonesian flag be hoisted side by side with the United Nations flag.

4. The transfer of authority to Indonesia will be effected as soon as possible after 1 May 1963.

AIDE-MÉMOIRE DATED 15 AUGUST 1962 FROM THE ACTING SECRETARY-GENERAL, HANDED TO THE REPRESENTATIVES OF THE NETHERLANDS CONCERNING THE MODALITIES OF THE TRANSFER OF AUTHORITY OVER WEST NEW GUINEA (WEST IRIAN)

1. The authority of the Government of the Netherlands over the territory will be terminated when the Special Representative of the Secretary-General takes charge. On the same day the United Nations flag will be hoisted.

2. From the same date the withdrawal and repatriation of the armed forces of the Netherlands will begin under the supervision of the Secretary-General's Special Representative and will be concluded as soon as possible.

3. On the day of the transfer of authority to the United Nations, the Netherlands flag will be hoisted side by side with the United Nations flag, and it will fly until 31 December 1962.

4. The transfer of authority to Indonesia will be effected as soon as possible after 1 May 1963. [*A/5170 & Add. 1*, pp. 6–7.]

The UN thus had a twofold peacekeeping role: the provision of a security force under Article VII of the Agreement, to service UNTEA; and the provision of military observers to implement the cease-fire which was to enter into effect before UNTEA assumed authority. This latter task was provided for in the Memorandum of Understanding on cessation of hostilities which was attached to the Indonesia–Netherlands Agreement.

2

ENABLING RESOLUTIONS AND VOTING

ON 21 September 1962 the General Assembly passed the following resolution approving the Agreement concluded between Indonesia and the Netherlands.

The General Assembly,

Considering that the Government of Indonesia and the Netherlands have resolved their dispute concerning West New Guinea (West Irian),

Noting with appreciation the successful efforts of the Acting Secretary-General to bring about this peaceful settlement,

Having taken cognizance of the Agreement between the Republic of Indonesia and the Kingdom of the Netherlands concerning West New Guinea (West Irian) (A/5170, annex),

1. *Takes note* of the Agreement;

2. *Acknowledges* the role conferred upon the Secretary-General in the Agreement;

3. *Authorizes* the Secretary-General to carry out the tasks entrusted to him in the Agreement. [*GA res. 1752 (XVII)*.]

VOTING: 89–0–14.

In favour: Afghanistan, Albania, Argentina, Australia, Austria, Belgium, Bolivia, Brazil, Bulgaria, Burma, Burundi, Byelorussian Soviet Socialist Republic, Cambodia, Canada, Ceylon, Chile, China, Colombia, Congo (Leopoldville), Costa Rica, Cuba, Cyprus, Czechoslovakia, Denmark, Ecuador, El Salvador, Ethiopia, Federation of Malaya, Finland, Ghana, Greece, Guatemala, Guinea, Honduras, Hungary, Iceland, India, Indonesia, Iran, Iraq, Ireland, Israel, Italy, Jamaica, Japan, Jordan, Laos, Lebanon, Liberia, Libya, Luxembourg, Mali, Mexico, Mongolia, Morocco, Nepal, Netherlands, New Zealand, Nicaragua, Nigeria, Norway, Pakistan, Panama, Paraguay, Peru, Philippines, Poland, Romania, Saudi Arabia, Senegal,* Sierra Leone, Somalia, Spain, Sudan, Sweden, Syria, Tanganyika, Thailand, Tunisia, Turkey, Ukrainian Soviet Socialist Republic, Union of Soviet Socialist Republics, United Arab Republic, United Kingdom of Great Britain and Northern Ireland, United States of America, Uruguay, Venezuela, Yemen, Yugoslavia.

Against: None.

Abstaining: Cameroon, Central African Republic, Chad, Dahomey, France, Gabon, Haiti, Ivory Coast, Madagascar, Mauritania, Niger, Rwanda, Togo, Upper Volta.

The Agreement (p. 101 above) which the Assembly approved included the provision in Article VII that the Secretary-General should provide such security forces as the UN Administration should deem necessary.

It may also be assumed that the approval of the Assembly extended to the Related Understandings which were attached to the main Agreement. The first of these was a Note to the Secretary-General from the Netherlands and Indonesian representatives, transmitting a Memorandum of Understanding on cessation of hostilities.

Related Understandings to the Indonesia–Netherlands Agreement

NOTE TO THE ACTING SECRETARY-GENERAL FROM THE REPRESENTATIVES OF INDONESIA AND THE NETHERLANDS TRANSMITTING MEMORANDUM OF UNDERSTANDING ON CESSATION OF HOSTILITIES, 15 AUGUST 1962

On behalf of our respective Governments, on the occasion of the signature of the Agreement between the Republic of Indonesia and the Kingdom of the Netherlands concerning West New Guinea (West Irian), we have the honour to bring to your attention the Memorandum of Understanding arrived at between our Governments concerning the cessation of hostilities in West New Guinea (West Irian), the signed original of which is contained in Annex A to this note.

In bringing the annexed Memorandum of Understanding to your attention we have the honour to request, on behalf of our respective Governments, that you indicate your willingness to undertake as an extraordinary measure the functions conferred upon the Secretary-General in it in order to give the earliest possible effect to the cessation of hostilities, reserving your right to report to the General Assembly of the United Nations at the appropriate time. Our respective Governments have in mind, in making this request, the urgent necessity for your assistance and that of United Nations personnel in implementing the agreement on cessation of hostilities.

The Memorandum of Understanding sets out the agreement arrived at between our respective Governments that our Governments will, on an equal basis, meet all costs incurred by you in carrying out your responsibilities under the Memorandum. To this end, our Governments have agreed to make available in advance such sums as you may deem necessary.

* In a letter dated 24 September 1962 addressed to the Secretary-General, the representative of Senegal asked that his vote should be recorded as negative.

ANNEX A

Memorandum of Understanding on cessation of hostilities constituting an agreement between the Republic of Indonesia and the Kingdom of the Netherlands

1. Cessation of hostilities in West New Guinea (West Irian), hereinafter referred to as 'the territory', is to take place at 00.01 GMT on Saturday, 18 August 1962. As from that moment the following rules will be observed:

(*a*) Cease-fire by both parties.

(*b*) Indonesia and the Netherlands will not reinforce their military forces in the territory nor resupply them with military matériel.

(*c*) The Secretary-General of the United Nations will assign United Nations personnel (i) to observe the implementation of this Agreement and (ii) in particular to take necessary steps for the prevention of any acts endangering the security of forces of both parties to this Agreement.

(*d*) Any incidents that might occur will be immediately reported by the party concerned to the United Nations personnel in order that they may take the necessary measures to restore the situation in consultation with both parties.

2. The cessation of hostilities will be communicated to the Netherlands and Indonesian armed forces by the following means:

(*a*) Messages transmitted through Indonesian and Netherlands radio-stations and via other means of communication.

(*b*) The dropping of leaflets in the areas concerned in accordance with the provisions of paragraph 3 hereof.

3. In order to overcome the special difficulties in communicating the cease-fire to Indonesian forces in the territory, prearranged flights will be carried out by Indonesian aircraft, with the purpose of dropping leaflets on which a text approved by the Secretary-General will be printed. The Indonesian authorities agree to enable the distribution of this pamphlet to isolated posts as soon as possible and not later than a fortnight from the cessation of hostilities. On these flights United Nations personnel will be on board to report, in advance and after the flight, on the time and the route of the flight and the areas of dropping leaflets.

4. To facilitate resupply of Indonesian troops in the territory and in order that they may be under the authority, and at the disposal of, the Secretary-General at the appropriate time, Indonesia will make the necessary arrangements with regard to their location in selected areas, in agreement with the Secretary-General. The Secretary-General will act in consultation herein with the Netherlands Administrative Authorities.

5. The resupply of non-military matériel of the Indonesian armed forces in the territory will be effected by the United Nations personnel in co-operation with Indonesian and Netherlands authorities. United Nations personnel may use one or two unarmed Indonesian vessels for transport to one or more ports agreeable to the Netherlands authorities. Air supply will be carried out under the direction of the United Nations personnel in United Nations aircraft.

6. With a view to carrying out the arrangements mentioned under paragraphs 3, 4 and 5 hereof, a United Nations liaison and an Indonesian liaison, each consisting of three officers, will be established at a Netherlands force headquarters in the territory. Military liaison officers will be included in the Permanent Missions to the United Nations of the Netherlands and Indonesia for liaison with the Secretary-General's Office.

7. As soon as possible after the adoption by the General Assembly of the United Nations of the resolution referred to in article I of the Agreement between the Republic of Indonesia and the Kingdom of the Netherlands concerning West New Guinea (West Irian), and not later than 1 October 1962, a United Nations security force including an infantry battalion with ancillary arms and services will be placed by the Secretary-General at the disposal of the United Nations Temporary Executive Authority (UNTEA) in the territory primarily to supplement the existing Papuan police in the task of maintaining law and order.

8. The Netherlands will make arrangements through the intermediary of the Secretary-General to repatriate Indonesian prisoners as soon as possible after the signing of the Agree-

ment between the Republic of Indonesia and the Kingdom of the Netherlands concerning West New Guinea (West Irian).

9. Indonesia and the Netherlands will jointly request the Secretary-General to undertake the functions conferred on him in this Agreement.

10. Indonesia and the Netherlands will share on an equal basis all costs incurred by the Secretary-General under this Agreement, and will make available in advance such sums as he deems necessary.

DONE on this fifteenth day of August 1962.

IDENTICAL REPLIES DATED 15 AUGUST 1962 FROM THE ACTING SECRETARY-GENERAL ADDRESSED TO THE REPRESENTATIVE OF INDONESIA AND TO THE REPRESENTATIVES OF THE NETHERLANDS

I have the honour to acknowledge the receipt of the note of today's date addressed to me by the Representative of the Republic of Indonesia and the Representatives of the Kingdom of the Netherlands, concerning the cessation of hostilities in West New Guinea (West Irian), reading as follows:

(*See text of the preceding note.*)

In reply I have the honour to inform you that, subject to the terms and conditions of the note under reference, I am prepared to undertake the responsibilities specified in that note and its related annex.

[*A/5170 & Add. 1, ann. B.*]

It may be noted that of the permanent members of the Security Council, the United States, the USSR, the United Kingdom, and China all voted in favour of the resolution. While the affirmative vote of the United States, the United Kingdom, and China was to be expected, the Soviet vote, and that of the other communist countries, was perhaps a matter of mild surprise, in so far as the Agreement on West Irian gave to the Secretary-General an authority of considerable scope. UNTEA was to be established by, and under the jurisdiction of, the Secretary-General, and not the Security Council. By this time—September 1962—the Soviet Union had already made it abundantly clear that she deplored the tendency to extend the role of the Secretary-General beyond the powers strictly given to him under the Charter. Although Hammarskjöld had by now been succeeded by U Thant, the Soviet opposition to a strengthened Secretariat, manifested especially in the context of the Congo, could not so soon have abated. Moreover, as we shall see, the Secretary-General was under the agreement not only to be responsible for UNTEA, the civil arm of the West Irian operation, but was also to provide UN security forces. These forces were to be under the authority of, and at the disposal of, the Secretary-General himself—a power which one might reasonably have expected the Soviet Union, in the light of the protests she had lodged concerning the Secretary-General's role in the Congo, adamantly to oppose. Nor did the fact that the arrangement was approved by the Assembly give the Soviet Union logical grounds for withholding her opposition, for she had also argued—in the context of UNEF[1]—that the Assembly had no jurisdiction in matters involving 'action'; and that all UN forces, whether their function was 'policing' or 'enforcement', were engaged in 'action'. This right was, the Soviet Union had contended, presented solely to the Security Council under the terms of Article 11 (2) of the Charter. The position of the

[1] See Vol. I of this study, *The Middle East.*

Soviet Union and the Eastern European nations is clearly explained in the Soviet pleadings before the International Court of Justice in the Case of *Certain Expenses of the United Nations*.[2]

In short, the affirmative vote of the Communist nations on the West Irian Agreement of August 1962 runs, to some extent, counter to their strongly argued position on the proper limits to the authority of both the Secretary-General and the General Assembly. Nor is an adequate explanation to be found in the view that the Agreement was acceptable to Indonesia, and therefore had to be supported by the Soviet Union. It may be recalled that when UNEF was established—with the full consent of Egypt, whose cause Russia had unreservedly championed in the Suez dispute—Russia none the less *abstained* on the vote as she objected in principle to the assumption of such powers by the General Assembly.[3]

The group of abstaining states on General Assembly resolution 1752(XVII) is interesting. Other than Rwanda and Haiti, it is comprised entirely of France and states belonging to the *communauté française*. Significantly, some three days after the vote Senegal, another state belonging to the same group, requested that its vote should be now recorded as negative. France had not on Suez, for example, opposed a 'policing' role for the Assembly; but her position has been to seek a limit to the individual discretion allowed to the Secretary-General, and to reserve all major issues to the Security Council. It seems reasonable to suppose, therefore, that she abstained from this vote because she felt that the temporary administration of a territory was a matter too important to be left to the Secretary-General, with the mere prior approval of the Assembly. Indeed, France may have doubted the ability of the UN as an organization to take upon itself this administrative function. France did not seek to make any public explanation of her vote. Two other abstaining states, however, did so—Dahomey and Togo. The representative of Dahomey declared quite frankly a thought that was in the minds of many Western nations, but which they had declined to allow to affect their vote: that the Agreement did not in fact promote self-determination. His statement deserves quotation:

242. The Government of Dahomey recognizes the efforts made by the Secretary-General and by the Governments of the Netherlands and Indonesia to achieve a pacific settlement of the problem of West New Guinea. We have always been in favour of negotiations and of peace. But we have also been, and continue to be, in favour of the absolute right of peoples to self-determination. Despite all its goodwill, my Government cannot endorse arrangements whereby a people of 700,000 is transferred from one Power to another under a bilateral treaty concluded without previous consultation with the party chiefly concerned, the Papuan people.
243. Much has been said on the subject of self-determination; but when we peruse this Agreement, what do we see in the articles dealing with self-determination? Not once—I repeat, not once—do we find in the text any mention of a 'referendum', the most normal, the most usual and the most objective form of public expression of opinion. The most precise formula we find is the vague one of 'the freely expressed will of the population', without any indication of how that will is to be expressed. That is left entirely to the discretion of the councils,

---

[2] See *Pleadings, Certain Expenses of the United Nations 1962*, p. 271 and ICJ *Reports, 1962*, pp. 163–4 & 175–6.
[3] See Vol. I of this work, *The Middle East*, pp. 235–6.

which are described as 'representative' without the slightest definition of the manner in which they are to be appointed.

244. Furthermore, the United Nations presence, which will doubtless be extremely effective during the transitional period in which it will be responsible for the administration of West New Guinea, will subsequently be very limited. It will be confined to advising on and assisting in preparations for carrying out the provisions for self-determination. In other words, the actual public expression of opinion will be organized entirely by the party which has the greatest interest in the yielding of results that are favourable to it.

245. This is the first time in history that plans have been made for a public expression of opinion which is intended to be objective and which is to be organized by the party chiefly concerned in the matter.

246. For all these reasons my Government, although thankful that peace has been safe-guarded in this part of the world, cannot but regret that that should have been achieved to some extent under the threat of war. Nevertheless, we hope that the Agreement, however unsatisfactory it may be, will be executed and fully observed in its letter and in its spirit. We count upon the Secretary-General to see to it that this is done, and we have no doubt of his ability and his objectivity. [*GAOR, 17th sess., 1127th plen. mtg*, pp. 56–7.]

The explanation of Togo's abstention was less convincing—it was stated that the vote had been taken in haste, and should have been left until later in the Assembly. While it is true that the Agreement had only recently been submitted to the Assembly, it had in fact been available for over a month, and there was obviously some urgency in its implementation. If the UN were to complete its tasks in West Irian by the specified date of 1 May 1963, a rapid start was necessary.

It has been in such countries as the United States, Holland, Belgium, and the United Kingdom that criticism of the Agreement has been most widely voiced. Suggestions were heard that the Agreement was in fact no more than a face-saving device whereby West Irian could be handed over to President Sukarno; that the plebiscite would either never take place or would fail to represent a free choice exercised by Papuans; and that the UN was merely lending itself to a dishonourable settlement whereby the right of the Papuans to self-determination would be ignored. However, all these countries voted in favour of the resolution approving the Agreement, and the UN role therein.

3

FUNCTIONS AND MANDATE

THE Agreement between Indonesia and the Netherlands effectively provided for two peacekeeping units to be made available by the UN. For practical reasons it has been thought desirable to cover both of them in one Section.

(a) UN Military Observers in West Irian

Annex A of the Memorandum of Understanding on cessation of hostilities (pp. 112–13 above), attached to the main Indonesia–Netherlands Agreement on West Irian (pp. 101–6 above) specified that the assistance of observers was needed for certain purposes:

1.(c) The Secretary-General of the United Nations will assign United Nations personnel (i) to observe the implementation of this Agreement and (ii) in particular to take necessary steps for the prevention of any acts endangering the security of the forces of both parties to this Agreement.

(d) Any incidents that might occur will be immediately reported by the party concerned to the United Nations personnel in order that they may take the necessary measures to restore the situation in consultation with both parties.

2. The cessation of hostilities will be communicated to the Netherlands and Indonesian armed forces by the following means:

(a) Messages transmitted through Indonesian and Netherlands radio-stations and via other means of communication.

(b) The dropping of leaflets in the areas concerned in accordance with the provisions of paragraph 3 hereof.

3. In order to overcome the special difficulties in communicating the cease-fire to Indonesian forces in the territory, prearranged flights will be carried out by Indonesian aircraft, with the purpose of dropping leaflets on which a text approved by the Secretary-General will be printed. The Indonesian authorities agree to enable the distribution of this pamphlet to isolated posts as soon as possible and not later than a fortnight from the cessation of hostilities. On those flights United Nations personnel will be on board to report, in advance and after the flight, on the time and the route of the flight and the areas of dropping leaflets.

4. To facilitate resupply of Indonesian troops in the territory and in order that they may be under the authority, and at the disposal of, the Secretary-General at the appropriate time, Indonesia will make the necessary arrangements with regard to their location. . . .

5. The resupply of non-military matériel of the Indonesian armed forces in the territory will be effected by the United Nations personnel in co-operation with Indonesian and Netherlands authorities. United Nations personnel may use one or two unarmed Indonesian vessels for transport to one or more ports agreeable to the Netherlands authorities. Air supply will be carried out under the direction of the United Nations personnel in United Nations aircraft. . . . [*A/5170 & Add. 1, ann. B.*]

It will be seen that, while the assistance of UN personnel was required for certain tasks, it was not the Agreement itself which specified that they should be 'military observers'.[1] The tasks may be summarized as observing the cease-fire; protecting the security of Dutch and Indonesian forces; restoring the situation in the event of cease-fire breaches; assisting in informing Indonesian troops in the jungle of the existence of the cease-fire; and providing a non-military supply line to Indonesian troops.

In the event, Brigadier-General Rikhye, who commanded the observers, also performed one additional function: 'He was also responsible for making arrangements for the arrival of the United Nations Security Force'.[2]

(b) UN Security Force in West Irian

The purpose for which the UN Security Force (UNSF) was to be established is clearly enunciated in Article VII of the Indonesian–Netherlands Agreement on West Irian:

The Secretary-General will provide the UNTEA with such security forces as the United

---

[1] See below, p. 119.   [2] A/5501, *GAOR*, 18th sess., suppl. 1, p. 35.

Nations Administrator deems necessary; such forces will primarily supplement existing Papuan (West Irianese) police in the task of maintaining law and order. The Papuan Volunteer Corps, which on the arrival of the United Nations Administrator will cease being part of the Netherlands armed forces, and the Indonesian armed forces in the territory will be under the authority of, and at the disposal of, the Secretary-General for the same purpose. The United Nations Administrator will, to the extent feasible, use the Papuan (West Irianese) police as a United Nations security force to maintain law and order and, at his discretion, use Indonesian armed forces. The Netherlands armed forces will be repatriated as rapidly as possible and while still in the territory will be under the authority of the UNTEA.

The mandate of UNSF was also referred to in the Memorandum of Understanding on cessation of hostilities.[3] Article 7 thereof stipulated that the Secretary-General should, by 1 October 1962, place a UN Security Force at the disposal of UNTEA 'primarily to supplement the existing Papuan police in the task of maintaining law and order'. The Secretary-General was also asked to be the intermediary in the repatriation of Indonesian prisoners of war, though it was not specified that it was UNSF which should take upon itself this role (Art. 8).

The UNSF was therefore an internal law and security force. Its functions related directly to those of UNTEA itself, for UNSF was to be the 'police' arm of UNTEA, with the task of allowing the quasi-governmental functions of UNTEA to proceed smoothly. UNTEA[4] was to 'administer the territory' (Art. V); to appoint governmental officials and members of representative councils (Arts IX & XXIII); to legislate for the territory, subject to certain qualifications (Art. XI); and to guarantee civil liberties and property rights (Art. XXII).

One may ask at this juncture if this is not an example of a UN force operating in a purely internal situation; and the answer is both yes and no. It is 'yes' in so far as the task of UNSF was not to separate combatants or even supervise the withdrawal of opposing forces, but to maintain law and order. It is 'no' in so far as the situation arose because of a history of conflict between two nations, and further, UNSF was not facilitating a state government to maintain purely internal law and order. Rather, UNSF was supporting a UN subsidiary organ which had assumed, under a treaty, exclusive powers of government.

Incidents involving breach of law and order were comparatively minor and few.[5]

Undoubtedly, one of the purposes of the creation of UNSF was to facilitate a 'phasing-in' of Papuan and Indonesian personnel into the Irianese police-force; details of this process will be found below. Indeed, in the cable sent to the Commander of UNSF upon his arrival in West Irian, U Thant offered the instruction that 'Your main duty is to supplement the existing Papuan police and the Papuan Volunteer Corps in the task of maintaining law and order'.[6] Article 7 of the Memorandum of Understanding on cessation of

---

[3] See above, pp. 112–13.   [4] See above, p. 101.
[5] One such incident appears to have involved a small group of Indonesian troops in Sorong Doom, a small island west of Hollandia, on 12 Dec. 1962. Order was restored by UNSF (UN Press Release WNG/68, 15 Dec. 1962).
[6] UN Press Release WNG/20, 19 Sept. 1962.

hostilities also states: ' . . . a United Nations security force . . . will be placed by the Secretary-General at the disposal of the United Nations Temporary Executive Authority (UNTEA) in the territory primarily to supplement the existing Papuan police in the task of maintaining law and order.' Equally, although this too was not explicitly stated in the Agreement between Indonesia and Holland, UNSF was concerned with preventing a vacuum upon the withdrawal of Dutch troops: 'The withdrawal of the Netherlands naval and land forces from the territory was effected in stages in accordance with a time-table agreed upon by the Temporary Administrator, the Commander of UNSF and the Commander-in-Chief of the Netherlands forces in the territory. By 15 November 1962 this process had been completed without incident.'[7] The repatriation of Dutch troops was provided for in Article VII of the Agreement, and some 9,600 personnel withdrew under its terms.

It is of some historical interest to compare the role of UNSF within UNTEA with previous suggestions for internal forces to support an international administration. Indeed, it is instructive to compare UNTEA generally with the plans envisaged in the Permanent Statute of the Free Territory of Trieste and in the Special Régime for the City of Jerusalem. The arrangements for both Trieste and Jerusalem were meant to have been permanent, and in both cases the recruitment of police forces was anticipated[8]—though the provisions for maintaining law and order in Jerusalem were the more international in character. But the first UN Force supporting a UN governmental authority was in the event to be a temporary and not a permanent one, and in a Pacific island rather than in Europe or the Middle East.

The UNSF was to commence its duties as soon as possible after the adoption of the approving resolution of the General Assembly (21 Sept. 1963) and not later than 1 October. (This provision is contained in Annex A, s. 7 of the Memorandum of Understanding on cessation of hostilities.) However, the Commander arrived some time before the General Assembly enabling resolution was passed[9] to prepare the ground.

[7] A/5501, Annual Report of Secretary-General (*GAOR*, 18th sess., suppl. 1, p. 36).
[8] See GA res. 181 (II), Arts IB.9 & III C.3 (*c*); also Art. 28 of the Permanent Statute for the Free Territory of Trieste, 1946–7 (*YBUN, 1946–7*, p. 388).
[9] See UN Press Release WNG/13, 6 Sept. 1962.

4

CONSTITUTIONAL BASIS

(*a*) UN military observers in West Irian

THE constitutional basis of the observers must presumably be looked for in the general powers of the Secretary-General. Article 97 of the Charter states: 'The

Secretariat shall comprise a Secretary-General and such staff as the Organization may require. . . .' The Memorandum of Understanding on cessation of hostilities (p. 111 above) provided not that the UN should offer the services of military observers as such, but rather that 'The Secretary-General of the United Nations will assign United Nations personnel' to perform certain tasks. From the point of view of Indonesia and the Netherlands, as expressed in this Memorandum, presumably regular Secretariat personnel would have been satisfactory. It appears to have been the Secretary-General who decided that the enumerated tasks required the UN personnel to be military observers. This would seem to be the only example of military observers being established other than upon the prior authorization or directive of the Assembly or Security Council.

The Indonesia–Netherlands Agreement, and the Related Understandings, were approved by the General Assembly on 22 September 1962. But the Secretary-General had in fact already replied on 15 August, in respect of the duties enumerated for UN personnel under the Memorandum of Understanding on cessation of hostilities, that 'I am prepared to undertake the responsibilities specified in that note and its related annex'. This he felt able to do without waiting for Assembly approval. Article 97 of the Charter also declares that the Secretary-General 'shall be the chief administrative officer of the Organization', while Article 98 requires him to perform 'such other functions as are entrusted to him' by the major organs of the UN. From these fairly narrow provisions the Secretary-General's power of diplomatic initiative has grown up, and it is arguable that the provision of observers—even provided on a temporary basis by governments—falls within his general powers, so long as their duties are compatible with the general purposes of the Organization. But at the same time, it must be admitted that these are implied powers and no express authority can be found for them.

What is surprising is the complete absence of protest that the Secretary-General should have agreed, prior to any approval by the Assembly or Security Council, to provide UN personnel; and that he should have decided, in respect of an operation which was completed before the Assembly gave its authorization, that the UN personnel should in fact be military observers. One may compare the total lack of protest by the Sovet Union here with the protests made by that country when, in much fuller consultation with the Security Council, the Secretary-General decided to establish the UN India–Pakistan Observation Mission as a unit distinct from the UN Military Observer Group in India and Pakistan in the Indian subcontinent (below, p. 426).

A final point which further highlights the anomalous constitutional basis of the UN peacekeeping role in West Irian, and the inconsistent national responses thereto: mention of the UN Security Force, with a law and order maintenance role, was also made in the Memorandum concerning the cessation of hostilities. And the Secretary-General's agreement to undertake 'the responsibilities specified in that note' (which, as we have already indicated, was given as early as 15 August, i.e. a month before Assembly approval) presumably related to the provision of a Security Force as well as UN personnel for military-observer
5*

duties. This, too, raised no objection from those nations which usually insist upon the tightest control over the Secretary-General's authority.

(b) The UN Security Force in West Irian

Neither the Indonesia–Netherlands Agreement on West Irian nor General Assembly resolution 1752 (XVII), approving the Agreement, made any specific reference to the constitutional basis of either UNTEA or UNSF. Nor did the Secretary-General in his subsequent report on the operations of UNTEA (UNSF).

The question of West Irian had, of course, long been before the General Assembly, and in 1962 the Security Council had received protests from the Netherlands and responses from Indonesia concerning the use of force. The Security Council had, however, never passed a resolution on the subject of West Irian.

U Thant's offer to the parties of the services of Ambassador Bunker as mediator, representing the Secretary-General, finds no clear Charter authority. The Secretary-General is required under the Charter to act as chief administrative officer and to 'perform such other functions as are entrusted to him by [the main] organs' (Art. 98). He may also 'bring to the attention of the Security Council any matter which in his opinion may threaten the maintenance of international peace and security' (Art. 99). The Secretary-General presumably felt that his authority to approach the parties and to appoint Ambassador Bunker stemmed from the broad authority of his position as chief administrative officer of an organization dedicated to maintaining international peace: a Hammarskjöldian point of view. Moreover, a simple majority of the Assembly (though not the legally required two-thirds majority) had in the past urged him to assist the parties in a settlement.[1]

So far as UNTEA is concerned—and UNSF too—it seems reasonable to trace its constitutional basis to Article 14 of the Charter. This article (which the International Court of Justice found an appropriate basis for UNEF)[2] permits the General Assembly to 'recommend measures for the peaceful adjustment of any situation, regardless of origin, which it deems likely to impair the general welfare or friendly relations among nations. . . .' There seems no reason why the Assembly should not, under Article 14, recommend measures which in fact give a substantial role to the Secretary-General, especially when the parties concerned have already indicated their approval of such a role.

A little more needs to be said, however. The International Court of Justice indicated—*obiter*—that the measures which the Assembly may recommend under Article 14 include the establishment of a peacekeeping force operating with the consent of the government on whose territory it is to be stationed. The ability of the Assembly to set up a force as a subsidiary body is confirmed in Article 22 of the Charter. It is generally assumed that UNTEA is also a subsidiary body of the General Assembly. It is surprising, however, that the authority of the UN to assume an administrative, quasi-governmental role—

[1] See above, p. 94.   [2] See Vol. I of this work, *The Middle East*, pp. 267–8.

especially by a subsidiary organ of the Assembly—was not challenged. Those nations which explained the reason for the abstention from the vote in favour of the Agreement (pp. 114–15 above) explained their case largely in terms of fears that the Agreement did not sufficiently provide for self-determination by the Papuans. France, who abstained, did not voice any objection to the effect that the General Assembly was unable to authorize the UN to participate in a governmental venture. And as has been said, the Soviet Union, who might also have been expected to object, voted for the resolution. This general assumption of the authority of the Assembly to approve such a role for the UN was in sharp contrast to the profound doubts that had been expressed about the authority of the Security Council to assume an international administration role in the case of Trieste and Palestine. Although the responsibilities which were proposed for the Security Council in respect of Trieste would have been of long duration, they were of more limited scope than those which UNTEA exercised in West Irian. The Secretary-General informed the Security Council that he believed that such powers could be implied from Article 24 of the Charter. In the case of Palestine it was the General Assembly which assigned responsibilities to the Security Council in respect of the implementation of the Partition Plan. The Secretary-General again indicated that Article 24 was sufficient authority for the assumption of these new responsibilities, on condition that they related to the maintenance of international peace and that the Security Council acted in accordance with the purposes and principles of the Charter as specified in Articles 1 and 2 of the Charter.[3]

The establishment of UNTEA now requires that the powers of Article 14 should be construed in similar terms, remembering that the executive authority of the Assembly is more limited, and that its role in the maintenance of peace is a secondary one. It is not surprising that such an interpretation should have been approved: what is surprising is the lack of debate which surrounded its approval. No doubt the total agreement of the parties, the limited duration stipulated, and the knowledge that the costs were not to be borne by the UN, served here to foster a feeling that any discussion on the constitutional ability of the UN to administer an entire territory was unnecessary.

The Soviet Union had indicated with regard to UNEF that it regarded the Assembly as incapable of establishing a UN Force. It apparently did not do so in the case of West Irian. There is nothing in the records to show whether the Soviet Union found telling, in this case, the fact that the costs would not be borne by UN members generally, or the fact that this was not a buffer force, situated on a frontier between two hostile nations. In the case of the UN Yemen Operations Mission, where costs were borne by the parties directly involved, the Soviet Union had none the less insisted that the matter be handled by the Security Council.[4]

Finally, it must be remembered that the setting up of UNSF was approved

---

[3] For a succinct analysis of the issues, see Oscar Schachter, 'The Development of International Law through the United Nations Secretariat', 25 *BYIL* (1948), pp. 96–101.
[4] See Vol. I of this work, *The Middle East*, p. 628.

at a time when the argument over the Congo operation was at its height—a fact which makes the smooth operation of UNSF all the more surprising. The Soviet Union in particular had bitterly opposed the assumption by the Secretary-General of the right to select the contingents participating in a UN peace-keeping action, claiming that that right was reserved to the Security Council. Yet she now voted for the Indonesia–Netherlands Agreement, Article II of which provided that UNTEA was to be 'established by and under the juris-diction of the Secretary-General'. Further, the UN Administrator was to 'be appointed by the Secretary-General' (Art. IV); and it was the Secretary-General who was to 'provide the UNTEA with such security forces' as it deemed necessary. The scope of his authority was further underlined by Article VIII, which provided that the Secretary-General would make full reports to Indonesia and the Netherlands 'and may submit, at his discretion, reports to the General Assembly or to all United Nations members'. In fact, after approving the Agreement, the Assembly played no further role, and full discretion was left to the Secretary-General, operating in consultation with Indonesia and the Netherlands.

5

POLITICAL CONTROL

(a) The UN military observers in West Irian

THE military observers, whose task it was to assist in the securing of a cease-fire before UNTEA established itself in West Irian, was under the direct political control of the Secretary-General. Having agreed to the tasks specified for UN personnel by the Netherlands and Indonesia in their Memorandum of Under-standing on cessation of hostilities, the Secretary-General was responsible to these countries for the fulfilment of these duties. At the time at which they were in fact carried out (18 August–21 September 1962) no authorization had yet been given by the General Assembly. Accordingly, in respect of the military observers, the Secretary-General's responsibility to the Assembly was only a retroactive one, though obviously he retained at all times the general responsi-bility to act as the chief administrative officer of the Organization.

The Secretary-General chose, to head the military group, Brigadier-General Rikhye. Brigadier Rikhye was at that time a regular member of the UN Secretariat, being the Secretary-General's Military Adviser.

(b) The UN Security Force in West Irian

UNSF was an integral part of the UNTEA in West Irian. The line of political control over UNSF may therefore be traced in the provision in the Indonesia–Netherlands Agreement with respect to UNTEA.

Article II
(UNTEA) established by and under the jurisdiction of the Secretary-General . . .
Article III
In order to facilitate the transfer of administration to the UNTEA after the adoption of the resolution by the General Assembly, the Netherlands will invite the Secretary-General to send a representative to consult briefly with the Netherlands Governor of the territory prior to the latter's departure . . .
Article IV
A United Nations Administrator acceptable to Indonesia and the Netherlands, will be appointed by the Secretary-General.
Article V
The United Nations Administrator, as chief executive officer of the UNTEA, will have full authority under the direction of the Secretary-General to administer the territory for the period of the UNTEA administration in accordance with the terms of the present Agreement.
Article VII
The Secretary-General will provide the UNTEA with such security forces as the United Nations Administrator deems necessary; . . . [*A/5170 & Add. 1.*]

In accordance with the terms of Article III of the Agreement, the Secretary-General, on 7 September 1962, appointed José Rolz-Bennett, Deputy Chef de Cabinet, as his representative in West New Guinea to make preliminary arrangements for the transfer of administration to UNTEA.[1] Dr Djalal Abdoh of Iran was on 22 October 1962 appointed Administrator of UNTEA, and Dr Sodin Sen his deputy. At the beginning of November Dr Abdoh visited The Hague and Djakarta for consultations, and he took up his appointment in West Irian on 15 November.[2]

Major-General Said Uddin Khan was appointed Commander of UNSF not by Dr Abdoh but by the Secretary-General. UNSF was responsible to Dr Abdoh, who was directly responsible to the Secretary-General as his personal representative. The Secretary-General was guided in his commands by the specific terms of the Indonesia–Netherlands Agreement and collateral understandings. He had no occasion to go back to the General Assembly—or the parties—for clarification or extension of his mandate; and no need arose for an 'advisory committee', of the sort utilized in the UNEF and ONUC operations.

On his Secretariat the Secretary-General was aided not only by Dr Rolz-Bennett in the pre-UNTEA phase, but also by C. V. Narasimhan, the Chef de Cabinet, in certain consultations at a later stage with the Administrator of UNTEA and the Indonesian government (below, pp. 146–7).

[1] UN Press Release WNG/15, 7 Sept. 1962 & A/5501, *GAOR*, 18th sess., suppl. 1, p. 36.
[2] A/5501, p. 36.

6

ADMINISTRATIVE AND MILITARY CONTROL

(a) The UN military observers in West Irian

THE observers were under the sole military and administrative control of Brigadier-General Rikhye. The organization of the observers' work was left to Brigadier Rikhye's discretion, working in consultation with the Dutch and Indonesian governments. He also made the necessary advance administrative arrangements for the arrival of UNSF.

(b) The UN Security Force in West Irian

Article VII of the Indonesia–Netherlands Agreement stipulated that:

> The Secretary-General will provide the UNTEA with such security forces as the United Nations Administrator deems necessary. . . . The Papuan Volunteer Corps . . . and the Indonesian armed forces in the territory will be under the authority of and at the disposal of, the Secretary-General for the same purpose. . . . The Netherlands armed forces . . . whilst still in the territory will be under the authority of the UNTEA.

The wording of this article seems to suggest that the UNSF as such would be under the authority of the Secretary-General himself, together with the Papuan Volunteer Corps and the Indonesian troops in West Irian, while the Dutch armed forces would be under the authority of UNTEA. The distinction in fact merely reflects the intention that the Dutch forces were not to be used for law-and-order functions, and should merely come under the general authority of the Administrator of UNTEA, and through him the Secretary-General; while the other forces might have a law-and-order role to play, and were thus to come under the direction of a military commander, who in turn was responsible to the Secretary-General.

Major-General Said Uddin Khan of Pakistan was appointed by the Secretary-General as Commander of UNSF. He was responsible directly to the Secretary-General, with a duty to provide law and order for the effective running of the UNTEA, headed by Dr Adboh. UNSF was an integral part of UNTEA, and to that extent General Khan was also responsible to Dr Adboh.

General Khan was also in command of the Indonesian forces in West Irian, as well as the Papuan Volunteer Corps and Police. Lt-Colonel Seotarto was nominated as head of the Indonesian group at the headquarters of UNSF.[1] The police force in the territory was headed by a United Kingdom national, J. Robertson, who was directly responsible to General Khan.

Although the Indonesian forces were not actually used in law-and-order actions, they did participate in some joint patrols with the Pakistani units of

[1] Note no. 2680, 10 Oct. 1962, p. 6.

UNSF. It was also decided to help train the Papuan Volunteer Corps, and to that end several of the original Dutch officers were retained, together with Indonesian officers (A/5501).

The Commander of UNSF co-operated closely before and after the arrival of the full complement of UNSF, with Brigadier Rikhye. Brigadier Said Uddin Khan was accompanied in West Irian by his aide-de-camp, Major Muzaffar Khan Malik. In addition, Pakistan appointed a liaison officer, stationed at UN headquarters in New York—Lt-Colonel Shirin Dil Khan Niaz.[2]

No Regulations have been published containing directions from the Secretary-General to UNSF on the conduct of that Force and the manner in which it was to carry out its duties. There is, however, reason to believe that an internal general directive was issued concerning UNSF.

[2] UN Press Release WNG/10, 30 Aug. 1962.

7

COMPOSITION AND SIZE

(a) The UN military observers in West Irian
TWENTY-ONE observers participated in the task of implementing the cease-fire. They were provided by six member states—Brazil, Ceylon, India, Ireland, Nigeria, and Sweden[1]—and were drawn from troops of these nations already serving either in UNEF or ONUC.[2]

(b) The UN Security Force in West Irian
Virtually all the troops for UNSF were provided by Pakistan, while the governments of Canada and the United States provided supporting aircraft and crews.

STRENGTH OF TROOP CONTINGENTS AND OTHER UNITS
TOTAL STRENGTH AS OF 7 FEBRUARY 1963

Countries	Staff Personnel		Troops		Air Force		Navy		TOTAL
	Offs.	Men	Offs.	Men	Offs.	Men	Offs.	Men	
Canada	1				3	8			12
Pakistan	9	10	37	1,371			10*	100	1,537
United States					15	44			59
Total	10	10	37	1,371	18	52	10*	100	1,608

Total strength as of 7 February 1963: 1,608
* Three Naval Staff Officers and one Liaison Officer at the Hqrs.
[*UN Press Release WNG/87, 7 Feb. 1963*]

[1] A/5501, p. 34.   [2] UN, *The United Nations in West New Guinea* (1963), p. 6.

The Commander of UNSF was a Pakistani—Major-General Said Uddin Khan—and all the troop contingents in UNSF were Pakistani. Each unit was self-sufficient in personnel and services. The Dutch troops, who were to be repatriated as soon as possible were, according to the terms of Article VII of the Indonesia–Netherlands Agreement, to be under the authority of the UNTEA while they were still in the territory.

The UN had, for the first time in its history, its own navy, in the form of five naval vessels manned by sailors of the Pakistan navy, under the command of Pakistani officers.[3] (These vessels were among nine taken over from the Netherlands navy.) The general role of the vessels was to provide transport facilities for UNSF, as well as to carry out patrol duties. They also played a role in the quarantine measures imposed to contain a cholera outbreak by checking unauthorized movements of local craft.

Logistical support was provided by air transport units of the United States and Royal Canadian air forces. The detachment from the USAF made available to UNSF some 6 helicopters and 4 DC-3s, while the RCAF detachment provided 2 amphibious Otters.[4] This side of UNSF covered troop transport and communications. The UN also used the US troop carrier *General Blatchford* (which it had under charter for the rotation of UN troops in the Congo) to help bring the Pakistan contingent from Karachi to West Irian.[5]

The UNSF was primarily to supplement existing Papuan civil police in maintaining law and order. In addition to these units, however, under Article VII of the Agreement, the Administrator of UNTEA had at his disposal the Papuan Volunteer Corps, the Indonesian armed forces in West Irian, and the Dutch forces remaining until their repatriation. These totalled approximately 1,500 men.

Before the transfer of administration to UNTEA, all the officers in the police corps were Dutch, there being no qualified Papuans. By the time UNTEA had assumed responsibility for the territory, almost all officers of Dutch nationality had left, being temporarily replaced by officers from the Philippines who, in turn, were later replaced by Indonesians. By the end of March 1963, the entire corps was officered by Indonesians. However, in accordance with the provisions of Article IX of the Agreement, the chief of police continued to be an international recruit. [*A/5501, Annual Report of Secretary-General, 1962–3*, p. 36.]

The Papuan Volunteer Corps (which under Article VII of the Agreement ceased to be part of the Netherlands armed forces upon the transfer of administration to UNTEA) was a militia type of military unit. It is of interest that Brigadier Rikhye, Head of the UN military observer team in West Irian, reported on 10 October that 'in case of need, the Papuan Volunteer Corps would be the first to be used to support civil authority'.[6] This may be contrasted with the Secretary-General's subsequent report that: 'The [Volunteer] Corps . . . was not assigned any duties in connexion with the maintenance of law and order'.[7] What was clear, however, was that the Indonesian troops were the last

---

[3] See UN Press Release WNG/60.
[4] UN Note No. 2680, 10 Oct. 1962 (Press Services), and A/5501, p. 36.
[5] UN Press Release WNG/13.   [6] Note No. 2680 (Press Services) 10 Oct. 1962.   [7] A/5501, p. 36.

to be intended for use by the UN. Article VII of the Agreement (an article so poorly drafted that only the fortuitous calmness of the political situation prevented its ambiguities from being exposed) stated that the Papuan police force would be used 'to the extent feasible', while the Indonesian forces were to be used 'at his discretion'. Dr Abdoh, the Administrator of UNTEA, was later to state that the Indonesian troops would only be used 'as a last resort'.[8]

On 1 October, when authority was transferred to UNTEA, the Indonesian troops in the territory consisted of those who had been brought in by parachute during the Dutch-Indonesian conflict and those who had infiltrated the territory. Agreement was reached with the Indonesian authorities to replace a large number of these troops with fresh territorial troops from Indonesia. It was also agreed that the number of Indonesian troops in the territory would not exceed the strength of the Pakistan contingent of UNSF, except with the prior consent of the UNTEA administration. [*A/5501*, p. 36.]

Finally, we may note that although the Indonesia–Netherlands Agreement did not specify any size for UNSF, paragraph 7 of the related Memorandum of Understanding on cessation of hostilities (above, pp. 111–13) placed a minimum by stipulating that '. . . a United Nations security force *including an infantry battalion with ancillary arms and services* will be placed by the Secretary-General at the disposal of the UNTEA' . . . (Italics mine.)

[8] UN Press Release WNG/63, 30 Nov. 1962.

8

RELATIONS WITH CONTRIBUTING STATES

(a) The UN military observers in West Irian
No formal agreements appear to have been concluded between those six nations which agreed to the temporary secondment of their military personnel to West Irian from UN service in the Middle East or Congo.

(b) The UN Security Force in West Irian
Relations between the UN and the contributing states to UNSF (Pakistan, the United States, and Canada) are extremely poorly documented. No public records appear to exist of any agreements reached between Pakistan and the UN concerning the provision of troops.

Relations between the contributing nations and the UN appear to have been cordial throughout. No particular problems were encountered. A UN Force of predominantly one nationality runs the risk of being classified as not really international, especially if the contributing state has a direct interest in the question to hand (as in the case of the United States in Korea). However, for a comparatively limited operation in a political situation in which the contributing state has no direct interest, a force coming largely from one nationality is obviously able to avoid many of the frictions which inevitably occur between contingents of different countries.

9

RELATIONS WITH HOST STATES

RELATIONS between the UN and the country in which a UN Force is to be stationed obviously depend upon a variety of factors. The precedents of UNEF and, to a considerably greater degree, ONUC, show that there may be difficulties even in operations based on the 'consent' of the host state in resolving the duty of the UN to carry out its mandate and the right of the host government to demand respect for its sovereignty. Again, where the mandate is ambiguous, or where political circumstances change after the initial agreement upon a mandate, the government and the UN Secretariat may develop divergent views as to the proper functions of the UN Force.

Such factors were mercifully absent in West Irian. The basis upon which the UN acted was not a mere brief resolution by a UN organ, but a detailed agreement (the result of long negotiations) between the interested parties. Both Indonesia and the Netherlands were anxious to facilitate the observers' task of securing a cease-fire. Moreover, the UN presence in West Irian was not primarily military at all; it was administrative, and the function of UNSF was the maintenance of law and order within a fairly stable quasi-governmental framework.

(a) The UN military observers in West Irian

No formal agreement was entered into concerning the status of the observers. However, cordial relations with both the Dutch and Indonesian authorities were soon established, and full co-operation ensured that the terms of Articles 1–5 of the Memorandum of Understanding on cessation of hostilities (above, p. 111) were rapidly carried out. Article 6 of this Memorandum had provided that

With a view to carrying out the arrangements mentioned under paragraphs 3, 4 and 5 hereof, a United Nations liaison and an Indonesian liaison, each consisting of three officers, will be established at a Netherlands force headquarters in the territory. Military liaison officers will be included in the Permanent Missions to the United Nations of the Netherlands and Indonesia for liaison with the Secretary-General's office. [*A/5170 & Add. 1, ann. B.*]

Liaison was also established for non-military purposes:

On 1 October 1962, the Governments of Indonesia and the Netherlands established liaison missions to UNTEA in Hollandia/Kotabaru. They were headed respectively by Dr Sudjarwo Tjondronegoro and Mr L. J. Goedhart. Close and effective co-operation between the missions and UNTEA contributed to the speedy and satisfactory solution of the many questions which were of concern to either party. An Australian liaison mission replaced one which had formerly served in Hollandia/Kotabaru as an administrative liaison between the authorities of the territory of Papua/New Guinea and West New Guinea, and now provided effective liaison with UNTEA on matters of mutual interest. [*A/5501*, p. 36.]

(b) The UN Security Force in West Irian

By the time the UN Force was established, the UN itself was administering the territory by means of UNTEA set up by, and under the jurisdiction of, the Secretary-General. During this period, therefore, the territorial 'host' was the UN itself; and the question of a status-of-forces agreement therefore did not arise.

None the less, one may note that Article XXVI of the Indonesia–Netherlands Agreement provided:

For the purposes of the present Agreement, Indonesia and the Netherlands will apply to United Nations property, funds, assets and officials the provisions of the Convention on the Privileges and Immunities of the United Nations. In particular, the United Nations Administrator, appointed pursuant to article IV, and the United Nations Representative, appointed pursuant to article XVII, will enjoy the privileges and immunities specified in section 19 of the Convention on the Privileges and Immunities of the United Nations. [*A/5170*.]

This was of practical relevance in West Irian not during the period of UNTEA's own jurisdiction there, but rather prior to 1 October 1962 and after 1 May 1963. It was also of legal significance in relation to the conduct of UN business in Indonesia or the Netherlands.

To observe, therefore, that Article XXVI of the Agreement fails to make clear whether it applies to UNSF, as well as to UNTEA, is largely academic. However, one may pursue this academic point by reporting that Dr Bowett, in *United Nations Forces* (p. 260), suggests that UNSF troops are not 'officials' as mentioned in Article XXVI, and therefore its terms cannot extend to that body. A contrary view is taken by Seyersted, in *United Nations Forces in the Law of Peace and War* (at p. 79). It is believed that this latter view is the one taken by the UN for it was arguable that UNSF was an integral part of UNTEA, and not separate from it, and that its personnel must thus be considered 'officials' in the present context. It is perhaps at least reasonable to suppose that General Said Uddin Khan, the Commander of UNSF, was an 'official' of the UN. Certainly the wording is far from precise. Again, Section 19 of the Convention on the Privileges and Immunities of the UN refers to rights to be accorded to 'the Secretary-General and all Assistant Secretaries-General in respect of themselves, their spouses and minor children'. The post of Administrator falls into none of these categories, but presumably under this Agreement Dr Abdoh was nevertheless accorded the rights specified in Section 19 of the Convention, namely 'the privileges and immunities, exemptions and facilities accorded to diplomatic envoys, in accordance with International Law'. These privileges and immunities are declared in Section 19 to be 'in addition to the immunities and privileges specified in Section 18'; it is not clear from Article XXVI of the Indonesia–Netherlands Agreement whether these too are to be accorded to

UNSF (assuming that Article XXVI applies at all to UNSF), or only those rights specifically named within Section 19 itself.[1] Finally, it is of interest to learn that in spite of the reference in Article XXVI of the Agreement to the Convention on the Privileges and Immunities, Indonesia is one of the comparatively few nations never to have legally adhered to the Convention.

With regard to the privileges and immunities enjoyed by members of UNSF during the UNTEA period, the position was that they were granted immunity for official acts performed in the course of their duties. In all other respects they were subject to the exclusive criminal jurisdiction of their national authorities. They were subject to local civil jurisdiction for acts performed outside the course of their duties. They were also subject to the rules and regulations of the contingents of which they formed a part without derogating from their responsibilities as part of UNSF.

Broadly speaking, the UN maintained excellent relations with both the Netherlands and Indonesia, though it came under some pressure from the latter to terminate UNTEA's authority earlier than provided for in the Agreement. The Netherlands co-operated fully with the UN over such matters as the repatriation of its troops as required by Article VII of the Agreement. The timetable for this process was agreed upon jointly by the UN Temporary Administrator (José Rolz-Bennett), the Commander of UNSF, and the Commander-in-Chief of the Netherlands forces in the territory.[2] The Netherlands also promptly carried out the intention specified in Article 8 of the Memorandum of Understanding on cessation of hostilities, namely, provision through the representative of the Secretary-General for the repatriation of all Indonesian prisoners held in the territory. (By Amnesty Acts signed on 7 and 11 October 1962, UNTEA granted amnesty to all political prisoners sentenced before 1 October 1962.) It may be noted that Article IX of the Indonesia–Netherlands Agreement also specified that the Netherlands was, during the first phase of UNTEA's administration, to facilitate its tasks by allowing such Netherlands officials as were required to serve UNTEA. In the event about one-quarter of the Dutch staff stayed on for such duties.[3]

Although relations with the government of Indonesia were equally cordial, the UN was subjected to certain efforts, from which the Indonesian government cannot be dissociated, to shorten the agreed period of UNTEA's authority.

---

[1] S. 19 of the Convention on the Privileges and Immunities of the UN provides for immunity from legal process in respect of acts and words in the course of official duty; exemption from tax on salaries, from national service obligations, and from immigration restrictions; and guarantees the same facilities accorded to diplomatic envoys of the same rank in respect of exchange facilities, the right of repatriation in time of international crisis, and the right to import freely personal furniture and effects (1 UNTS 15).

[2] A/5501, p. 36.

[3] One of the areas where the departure of the Dutch was felt most acutely was in the judicial organs of the territory. The UN responded with speed to this challenge, and by 30 November 1962 the UNTEA Administrator had invested a Court of Justice, using qualified Indonesian judicial officers. Great emphasis was laid in the investiture upon the responsibility for preserving the rights of the inhabitants of the territory, and the necessity for all laws to conform with the letter and spirit of the Indonesia–Netherlands Agreement. See A/5501, p. 37, and UN Press Release WNG/62, 30 Nov. 1962.

Such pressures began fairly early in the day, for the UNTEA Administrator was obliged to announce on 8 November 1962—while saying that no formal request for shortening the period had been received—that the transfer of authority to Indonesia could not be advanced.[4] The requests to shorten the period of UN administration were later made explicit, but formally came from Papuan leaders and various groups in the territory rather than from the Indonesian government itself. On 21 November a joint declaration by the representatives of the New Guinea Council was transferred to the Secretary-General, and in January 1963 further demonstrations took place:

PAPUANS PRESENT PETITION TO UNITED NATIONS ADMINISTRATOR
(The following was received from a United Nations Information Officer in Hollandia.)

Papuan demonstrators, numbering about 1,000, marched to the residence of United Nations Administrator, Djalal Abdoh, today, carrying Indonesian flags and banners, and asked a delegation of four to present him with series of requests concerning the future of West New Guinea (West Irian).

The demonstration was orderly and had been authorized by the United Nations Temporary Executive Authority (UNTEA).

The delegates received by Mr Abdoh asked for a shortening of the UNTEA period of administration and for unification with Indonesia 'in the shortest possible time'. They also declared themselves 'faithful to the proclamation of the Republic of Indonesia of 17 August 1945'. Finally, they asked that the Territory be given 'broad autonomy within the Republic of Indonesia'.

The delegates presented their requests in the form of a petition signed by 18 political leaders from the area of Hollandia (Kotabaru).

The Administrator took note of the petition and informed the delegates that he would forward it to the Secretary-General of the United Nations.

The four delegates also delivered the text of their petition to Max Maramis, acting Chief of the Indonesian Liaison Mission to UNTEA. [*UN Press Release WNG/80, 14 Jan. 1963.*]

The Secretary-General resisted these attempts:

These requests were brought to the attention of the Secretary-General in January 1963 by Dr Sudjarwo Tjondronegoro, Deputy to the Foreign Minister of the Republic of Indonesia and head of the Indonesian Liaison Mission to UNTEA. After consultation with the representatives of the Netherlands, the Secretary-General came to the conclusion that, in the circumstances, any shortening of UNTEA was not feasible. However, the Secretary-General sent his Chef de Cabinet, Mr C. V. Narasimhan, to consult with the United Nations Administrator and the Government of Indonesia, with a view to facilitating the entry of Indonesian officials into the administration of West New Guinea (West Irian) in order to ensure the continuity and expansion of all essential services. . . . [*A/5501, p. 39.*]

As a result of these discussions it was agreed that although the period of administration could not be shortened, the replacement of Netherlands officials by Indonesian officials would be accelerated. C. V. Narasimhan was appointed to handle this aspect of matters.

4. During the transitional period of UNTEA, two stages were envisaged: (*a*) the phasing out of the Netherlands civilian and military officials, which would take place substantially from 1 October to 31 December 1962; and (*b*) the phasing in of Indonesian administrative personnel, which was to be accelerated after the latter date.

5. With a view to facilitating in all possible ways the induction into the administration of

---

[4] UN Press Release WNG/52, 8 Nov. 1962.

West New Guinea (West Irian) of Indonesian officials and to ensure continuity and expansion of all essential services, especially those which concern the welfare of the people, and to help as may be possible to accelerate the plans for development of the Territory, the Secretary-General has decided to depute C. V. Narasimhan, Chef de Cabinet, to consult with the Indonesian Government and with Dr Djalal Abdoh, UNTEA Administrator, and to give assistance, within the terms of the Agreement, in carrying out the tasks mentioned above. [*UN Press Release SG/1425, WNG/84, 24 Jan. 1963.*]

Further, Narasimhan announced an acceleration of progressive replacing of UNSF troops by Indonesian troops. By mid-April this process was almost complete, and by 1 May, when the UN handed the administration over to West Irian, UNSF was concentrated in Biak with units departing for Pakistan being replaced by incoming Indonesian forces.[5] Narasimhan indicated that requests for the termination of Pakistani participation in law-and-order functions before 1 May was unacceptable: Article 7 of the Memorandum of Understanding on cessation of hostilities expressly provided for 'a United Nations security force including an infantry battalion with ancillary arms and services'. These provisions could only be altered by the common consent of Indonesia, the Netherlands, and the UN. This decision was accepted without difficulties by Indonesia. As well as pointing to the demonstrations by Papuans, Indonesia had indicated that the presence of UNTEA, though appreciated, was holding up her own development plans for West Irian. It was generally felt that her main objective in encouraging requests for the shortening of the period of UN administration had been to escape the financial liabilities therefor which she was incurring jointly with Holland.

Article VI of the Indonesia–Netherlands Agreement had provided:

1. The United Nations flag will be flown during the period of United Nations administration.

2. With regard to the flying of the Indonesian and Netherlands flags, it is agreed that this matter will be determined by agreement between the Secretary-General and the respective governments.

Accordingly, the Acting Secretary-General exchanged the following two aides-mémoire with Indonesia and the Netherlands respectively.

TWO AIDES-MÉMOIRE CONCERNING THE MODALITIES OF THE TRANSFER OF AUTHORITY OVER WEST NEW GUINEA (WEST IRIAN)

(a) From the Acting Secretary-General to the Representative of Indonesia

1. The authority of the Government of the Netherlands over the territory will be terminated when the Special Representative of the Secretary-General takes charge. On the same day the United Nations flag will be hoisted.

2. From the same date the withdrawal and repatriation of the armed forces of the Netherlands will begin under the supervision of the Secretary-General's Special Representative and will be concluded as soon as possible.

3. On 31 December 1962 the Netherlands flag will be struck, and the Indonesian flag will be hoisted side by side with the United Nations flag.

[5] UN Press Release WNG/90, 13 Feb. 1963 and A/5501, p. 39.

4. The transfer of authority to Indonesia will be effected as soon as possible after 1 May 1963.

15 August 1962

(*b*) From the Acting Secretary-General to the Representatives of the Netherlands

1. The authority of the Government of the Netherlands over the territory will be terminated when the Special Representative of the Secretary-General takes charge. On the same day the United Nations flag will be hoisted.

2. From the same date the withdrawal and repatriation of the armed forces of the Netherlands will begin under the supervision of the Secretary-General's Special Representative and will be concluded as soon as possible.

3. On the day of the transfer of authority to the United Nations, the Netherlands flag will be hoisted side by side with the United Nations flag, and it will fly until 31 December 1962.

4. The transfer of authority to Indonesia will be effected as soon as possible after 1 May 1963.

15 August 1962

[*437 UNTS, 310.*]

On 1 October 1962 a ceremony took place in Hollandia, capital of West Irian, at which the UN and Dutch flags were jointly hoisted. There arose some feeling among Papuan leaders, however, that the Papuan flag should also fly. As the Agreement had made no mention of this, it was decided that only the Dutch and UN flags (and later, the Indonesian and UN flags) could fly from official buildings; but at the same time it was announced that no action would be taken against persons flying the Papuan flag as a 'party' flag on their own private property, though UNTEA could not regard it as official.[6]

UNTEA was at pains to maintain friendly relations with the native Papuans. The New Guinea Council was called, and formally pledged its support to UNTEA:

. . . The Administration attached great importance to that part of the Agreement which dealt with the rights of the inhabitants. The New Guinea Council or its Board of Delegates was consulted by the Administrator on major issues and on new legislation or amendments to existing laws. Its membership was increased by the appointment of two new members to fill existing vacancies. The United Nations Administrator opened the sessions of the New Guinea Council and of some of the Regional Councils, always stressing the close co-operation between the representatives of the population and UNTEA. . . . [*A/5501*, p. 40.]

The UN also played an overt role in urging the resumption of diplomatic relations between Indonesia and the Netherlands, indicating that it would facilitate its own work.[7] The smooth implementation of UNTEA in turn undoubtedly facilitated the amelioration of relations between these two countries, and diplomatic relations were ultimately resumed on 13 March 1963.

---

[6] UN Press Releases WNG/31 & 43, 1 & 24 Oct. respectively.
[7] UN Press Release WNG/43, 23 Nov. 1962. This press release appears to be incorrectly numbered, though correctly dated.

10

RELATIONS WITH OTHER STATES INVOLVED

No nations other than Indonesia and the Netherlands regarded themselves as having a major interest in West Irian after the settlement of 1962. No problems arose between the UN and its general membership in respect of the role of the UN observers or the Security Force.

11

FINANCE

(*a*) **The UN military observers in West Irian**
ARTICLE 10 of the Memorandum of Understanding on cessation of hostilities provided that 'Indonesia and the Netherlands will share on an equal basis all costs incurred by the Secretary-General under this Agreement, and will make available in advance such sums as he deems necessary.'[1] From a budgeting point of view the costs of the military observers were joined with the costs of UNSF, as in both cases they were to be borne equally by the parties.

(*b*) **The UN Security Force in West Irian**
In October 1962, when UNTEA became operational, the UN was already deadlocked in its quarrel over assessment of peacekeeping dues. This, together with the fact that the Agreement for a solution to the West Irian problem involving 'peacekeeping', *stricto sensu*, only to a small degree, encouraged an understanding that all costs would be borne by Indonesia and the Netherlands, and not levied upon the UN.

Article XXIV of the Indonesia–Netherlands Agreement provided that:

1. Deficits in the budget of the territory during the UNTEA administration will be shared equally by Indonesia and the Netherlands.
2. Indonesia and the Netherlands will be consulted by the Secretary-General in the preparation of the UNTEA budget and other financial matters relating to United Nations responsibilities under the present Agreement; however, the Secretary-General will have the final decision.

[1] A/5170 & Add. 1, ann. B.

3. The Parties to the present Agreement will reimburse the Secretary-General for all costs incurred by the United Nations under the present Agreement and will make available suitable funds in advance for the discharge of the Secretary-General's responsibilities. The Parties to the present Agreement will share on an equal basis the costs of such reimbursements and advances.

This was supplemented by attached Memoranda exchanged between the Netherlands, Indonesia, and the Secretary-General. These were annexed to the Indonesia–Netherlands Agreement and were formally approved by the General Assembly on the same occasion (see above, pp. 107–8).

In his Annual Report of 16 June 1962–15 June 1963 the Secretary-General noted that: 'The cost of the operation was underwritten by the Governments of Indonesia and the Netherlands. Both Governments have now paid the full costs in equal part.'[2] This must be interpreted as meaning 'the full estimated costs', because at that moment of time, while contributions were equally divided, Indonesia was reimbursed a larger sum than the Netherlands in cash and kind:

UNITED NATIONS TEMPORARY EXECUTIVE AUTHORITY FOR THE ADMINISTRATION OF WEST NEW GUINEA (WEST IRIAN)

1. *Status of funds as at 31 December 1963*

	$	$
Payments received from:		
Indonesia		13,000,000
Netherlands		13,672,330
Income earned on investments	159,849	
Less:		
Loss on exchange	16,122	143,727
		26,816,057

	Liquidated by disbursements	Unliqui-dated	Total
Less:			
Obligations incurred as recorded under chapter XI—Maintenance and operation of the Security Force, chapter XII—United Nations Costs, and United Nations Costs prior to 1 October 1962 in connexion with cease-fire and cessation of hostilities	3,999,347	361,578	4,360,925
Remitted for expenditures (net) under chapters I through X and related cash on hand, advances and accounts receivable (net)		18,440,909	22,801,834
			4,014,223

[2] A/5501, p. 40.

Represented by:		$	$
Cash at banks and on hand			520,556
Investments			3,859,849
Accounts receivable, advances and other debits			447,867
			4,828,272
Less:			
Reserve for unliquidated obligations		361,578	
Accounts payable and sundry credit balances		1,714	
Due to United Nations General Fund		450,757	814,049
			4,014,223

[*A/5806, GAOR 19th sess., Suppl. 6.*]

2. *Status of funds as at 31 December 1964*

	Indonesia $	*Netherlands* $	*Total* $
For the period through 15 October 1964			
Contributions received			
In cash	13,000,000	10,000,000	23,000,000
In kind	—	3,000,000	3,000,000
	13,000,000	13,000,000	26,000,000
Interest earned	151,147	151,147	302,294
Territorial income	3,142,632	3,142,632	6,285,264
	16,293,779	16,293,779	32,587,558
Less:			
Obligations incurred			
Pre-United Nations Temporary Executive Authority costs	45,358	45,358	90,716
Territorial budget and Papuan Volunteer Corps	10,243,303	10,243,303	20,486,606
Territorial balance of payments deficits	572,613	572,613	1,145,226
Maintenance and operation of the United Nations Security Force	1,722,618	1,722,618	3,445,236
Other United Nations costs	637,503	637,503	1,275,006
	13,221,395	13,221,395	26,442,790
Refunds in cash and kind	3,118,027	2,825,603	5,943,630
	16,339,422	16,046,998	32,386,420
Balance as at 15 October 1964	(45,643)	246,781	201,138
Add:			
Interest earned during the fourth quarter 1964	234	3,112	3,346
Balance as at 31 December 1964	(45,409)	249,893	204,484

	$	$	$
Represented by:			
Cash at bank			17,041
Interest bearing account with bank			327,352
			344,393
Less:			
Reserve for unliquidated obligations		136,841	
Accounts payable		3,068	139,909
			204,484

[A/6006, GAOR, 20th sess., Suppl. 6.]

3. *Status of Funds as at 31 December 1965*

	Indonesia	Netherlands	Total
	$	$	$
Balance as at 31 Dec. 1964	(45,409)	249,893	204,484
For the period 1 Jan.–31 Dec. 1965	—	200,000	200,000
Deduct:			
Payment made to Netherlands	(45,409)	49,893	4,484
Add:			
Savings effected in liquidating prior years' obligations	7	6	13
Refund of prior years' expenditures	2,440	2,440	4,880
Interest income earned and accrued	748	9,376	10,124
	(42,214)	61,715	19,501
Represented by:			
Investments-Interest bearing bank account			137,095
Less:			
Reserve for unliquidated obligations		116,307	
Due to UN General Fund		1,287	117,594
			19,501

[A/6306, GAOR, 21st sess., Suppl. 6.]

Further adjustments were made during the twenty-second session:

4. *Status of funds as at 31 December 1966*

	Indonesia	Netherlands	Total
	$	$	$
Balance as at 1 January 1966	(42,214)	61,715	19,501
Adjustment of earlier erroneous charge to Government of Netherlands	—	23,481	23,481
	(42,214)	85,196	42,982
Deduct:			
Payment due to Government of Netherlands	—	130,978	130,978
	(42,214)	(45,782)	(87,996)

	$	$	$
Add:			
Savings effected in liquidating prior years' obligations	41,609	41,609	83,218
Interest income earned and accrued	605	4,173	4,778
	—	—	—
Represented by:			
Due from United Nations General Fund			138,925
Less:			
Reserve for contingencies		7,947	
Due to Government of Netherlands		130,978	138,925
			—

[*A/6706, GAOR, 22nd sess., Suppl. No. 6.*]

12

IMPLEMENTATION

(*a*) The tasks of the military observers

THE military observers' main tasks were, as we have seen, to secure an effective cease-fire in West Irian and to prepare the way for the arrival of UNTEA and UNSF.

This mandate was rapidly accomplished. At the time of the Agreement there were some 12,000 Netherlands Army troops in West New Guinea, while Indonesian forces comprised 1,500 men who had been parachuted into the jungle or had landed by submarine. Special arrangements had to be made to inform these forces of the cease-fire.[1]

Upon their arrival in the territory, the observers were informed that the Netherlands military command had proclaimed a cease-fire as at 00.01 GMT on 18 August 1962, and had ordered their troops to be concentrated in the main garrison towns. After a visit to Djakarta by Brigadier-General Rikhye, contacts were established with the Indonesian troops, and they were informed of the end of hostilities by radio broadcasts and by pamphlets dropped from the air in the areas where they were located. [*A/5501*, p. 35.]

While the Netherlands ground forces were concentrated in the main garrison town, their air and naval forces continued to patrol the skies and seas of the territory, and it was primarily these which the UN observers used in establishing contact with the Indonesian forces in the jungle, dropping printed leaflets conveying the cease-fire message. The UN observers also re-supplied these troops with food and medicines and helped them regroup in selected places.[2]

---

[1] UN, *The United Nations in West New Guinea* (1963), p. 6.   [2] Ibid. p. 8.

Aerial support was given by the 13th US Task Force for the Far East and the Royal Canadian Air Force. Throughout the entire period the Indonesian radio and the Netherlands-owned radio stations continued to broadcast announcements about the cease-fire. Most of the emergency supplies were provided by the Netherlands military command, who also treated any Indonesian troops that were seriously ill. United Nations aircraft landed supplies in four staging areas: Sorong, Fakfak, Kaimana and Merauke. [UN, *The United Nations in West New Guinea* (1963), p. 8.]

In just over a month, the UN observers had fulfilled their mandate:

On 21 September, Brigadier-General Rikhye was able to report that all actions concerning the cessation of hostilities, including the concentration of the Indonesian forces, in four main areas, the provision to them of emergency supplies, and the repatriation of over 500 Indonesian detainees had been completed without incident. [*A/5501*, p. 35.]

(b) The tasks of the UN Security Force

UNSF was to maintain law and order in the territory. This entailed not only contributing to continuing good relations between the Dutch and Indonesians in West Irian, but ensuring that any vacuum caused by the withdrawal of the Dutch was adequately filled by the UN Force. Further, UNSF saw its law-and-order role as requiring it to build up a viable police force capable of taking over these duties upon UNTEA's departure.

While there has been some criticism by Dutch writers of the way in which UNTEA administered the territory,[3] there can be no doubt that UNSF succeeded fully in implementing the tasks assigned to it under Article VII of the Indonesia–Netherlands Agreement. The Secretary-General's Annual Report for 1962–3 described how Article VII of the Agreement was carried out by the 1,500 Pakistanis serving in UNSF, supported by Canadian and American aircraft and crews:

Major-General Said Uddin Khan of Pakistan, appointed by the Secretary-General as Commander of UNSF, arrived in Hollandia on 4 September for preliminary discussions with the Netherlands authorities and for a survey of future requirements.

By 3 October an advance party of 340 men of UNSF had arrived in the territory. On 5 October the balance of the Pakistan contingent took up its positions. Also included in UNSF were some sixteen officers and men of the Royal Canadian Air Force with two Otter aircraft, and a detachment of approximately sixty United States Air Force personnel with an average of three DC-3's. These provided troop transport and communications. The Administrator also had under his authority the Papuan Volunteer Corps, the civil police and the Netherlands forces remaining until their repatriation, as well as Indonesian troops, totalling approximately 1,500.

In accordance with the terms of article VII, the Papuan Volunteer Corps ceased to be part of the Netherlands armed forces upon the transfer of administration to UNTEA. The Corps, consisting of some 350 officers and men, was concentrated at Manokwari and was not assigned any duties in connexion with the maintenance of law and order. As Dutch officers and non-commissioned officers left the area, they were replaced by Indonesian officers. This process was completed on 21 January, when the command of the Corps was formally transferred to an Indonesian officer and the last Dutch officers left the territory.

During the period of UNTEA administration, the Papuan police were generally responsible for the maintenance of law and order in the territory. Before the transfer of administration to UNTEA, all the officers of the police corps were Dutch, there being no qualified Papuans.

---

[3] See below, p. 141–2.

By the time UNTEA had assumed responsibility for the territory, almost all officers of Dutch nationality had left, being temporarily replaced by officers from the Philippines who, in turn, were later replaced by Indonesians. By the end of March, 1963, the entire corps was officered by Indonesians. However, in accordance with the provisions of article IX of the Agreement, the chief of police continued to be an international recruit.

On 1 October, when authority was transferred to UNTEA, the Indonesian troops in the territory consisted of those who had been brought in by parachute during the Dutch-Indonesian conflict and those who had infiltrated the territory. Agreement was reached with the Indonesian authorities to replace a large number of these troops with fresh territorial troops from Indonesia. It was also agreed that the number of Indonesian troops in the territory would not exceed the strength of the Pakistan contingent of UNSF, except with the prior consent of the UNTEA administration.

The withdrawal of the Netherlands naval and land forces from the territory was effected in stages in accordance with a time-table agreed upon by the Temporary Administrator, the Commander of UNSF and the Commander-in-Chief of the Netherlands forces in the territory. By 15 November 1962, this process had been completed without incident.

The situation was generally calm throughout the period of UNTEA. On 15 December 1962, however, two incidents involving the police and a small group of Indonesian troops occurred in Sorong and Doom. One police constable was killed and four wounded. Order was immediately restored by units of UNSF while the civil administration continued to perform its normal functions. The area remained quiet for the rest of the temporary administration. In general, the inhabitants of the territory were law-abiding and the task of maintaining peace and security in the territory presented no problems. The United Nations Administrator had no occasion to call on the Indonesian armed forces in connexion with the maintenance of law and order but only for the purpose of occasional joint patrols with elements of the Pakistan contingent. [*A/5501*, pp. 36–37.]

The law-and-order duties of UNSF cannot, of course, be viewed in isolation. The immediate task of avoiding any breakdown in administration was necessarily coincidental with maintenance of security. José Rolz-Bennett, the Secretary-General's personal representative and the Temporary Administrator, took over responsibility for the administration immediately upon the departure of the Dutch Governor, Dr Plateel. Under the terms of the Agreement neither Dutch nor Indonesian officials were to hold any major administrative post during the seven-month transition period. Further, while about one-quarter of the Dutch personnel stayed on to work under UN authority, UNTEA was unable to persuade the remainder not to leave the territory before the date set for the transfer of authority from the UN to Indonesia. Rolz-Bennett thus acted with all speed, drawing upon thirty-two nationalities (including Holland and Indonesia) to set up UNTEA as a task force. Communications presented a major problem, both generally, and for UNSF in particular:

. . . the communications were so poor that one had to make a very detailed study and a good deal of thinking to decide whether to spread the troops too much in smaller groups, or relocate them centrally in the administrative towns, then arrange some system of information and transport so that when needed they could rush and be of use. We decided to keep the infantry concentrated in six places and have a system of information and transport that, if they were needed somewhere else, we could rush them from their normal stations to the place of trouble. [*Per General Khan*, quoted in UN, *The United Nations in West New Guinea*, p. 8.]

In the event, UNSF did succeed in achieving adequate mobility for its needs, and also contributed to the orderly change-over in personnel:

The transfer of authority implied a need to adapt existing institutions from the Dutch pattern to an Indonesian pattern. The Chief of Police, Mr J. C. Robertson, was quick to appreciate the tasks involved in this institutional transfer and the need for early implementation. In his view, the first problem was to rebuild the officer and inspection cadres which had almost completely disappeared with the exodus of Dutch officers, and to reinstate a sense of loyalty and discipline in the rank and file, at the same time keeping the police service to the public going and maintaining law and order. The second problem was to reorient the entire service, substituting the Indonesian language and procedures for those of the Dutch so that there would be no upheaval when UNTEA handed over the reins of Government to the Republic of Indonesia. All correspondence had to be changed to the Indonesian language, words of command had to be changed, followed by change of uniforms, insignia, titles. And it had to be done quickly and thoroughly. [*Ibid.*, p. 11.]

It is beyond the scope of this Part to attempt to evaluate UNTEA's (as distinct from UNSF's) success in West Irian. So far as the Editor is aware, only one private study on the UN administration has been published. In this the author, Paul van der Veur, was not uncritical of UNTEA, though he had sympathy for the problems which the UN had to face. He notes that the UNTEA administration began on 1 October, only six weeks after the conclusion of the Agreement; and that the Agreement was only approved by the Assembly on 21 September, the day after Dutch and Indonesian ratification had been secured: 'This hardly left sufficient time to recruit and train personnel'.[4] While the time available was indeed all too short, the Secretary-General's recruitment activities did not, in fact, wait until 21 September; they began, provisionally, on 18 August, as did his organization of the military observers. Dr van der Veur also criticizes the fact that the Administrator, Dr Abdoh, did not arrive until 13 November, though he concedes that the position was in the meantime 'ably occupied' by Temporary Administrator, Rolz-Bennett. He does not specify how Rolz-Bennett's presence, rather than that of Abdoh (who was receiving briefings during this period), impeded UNTEA's work. Dr van der Veur also condemns the use of Indonesian troops under the terms of Article VII of the Agreement: 'This article may have created a novum not only by condoning the presence of Indonesian battle units dropped into the territory but also by authorizing their use in the maintenance of law and order.' This, of course, is a criticism of the terms of a freely concluded Agreement, not of UNTEA. Moreover, as the Secretary-General's report makes clear: 'The United Nations Administrator had no occasion to call on the Indonesian armed forces in connexion with the maintenance of law and order. . . .'[5] More significantly, Dr van der Veur charges that UNTEA failed to fulfil the terms of Article X of the Agreement, under which it was to 'inform the population . . . [of] the provisions for the act of self-determination as set out in the present Agreement': but the evidence he adduces is merely the evidence of the Indonesian campaign to foreclose the UN administration, and to undermine the agreement for a plebiscite.[6] It is also Dr van der Veur's judgement that, in refusing permission for certain Papuan demonstrations, UNTEA was in fact suppressing freedom of expression. He

[4] Paul van der Veur, 'The United Nations in West Irian: a Critique', *Int. Org.* (1964), p. 58.
[5] A/5501, p. 37.   [6] Van der Veur, *Int. Org.* (1964), pp. 62–7.

claims in addition that pressure was brought to bear on Papuans who wished to include in their speeches in the New Guinea Council remarks which might offend the Indonesians. His criticisms concerning language difficulties and the movement of goods to black markets would seem to be valid.[7]

A widespread scepticism that the plebiscite would ever take place was very understandable. Indonesia had withdrawn from the UN,[8] and was floating the suggestion that this released her from her obligations to the UN.[9] Ambiguous remarks were made by President Sukarno's successors. The Foreign Minister, Adam Malik, stated that a plebiscite would be held—though he gave warning that the West Irianese themselves might reject the idea.[10] And four months later, in December 1966, the Home Affairs Minister indicated there would be no plebiscite because the Irianese people did not want one.[11] But in the face of inquiries by the Secretary-General and a protest by the Netherlands, Malik affirmed that a plebiscite would be held 'if the people of West Irian want it'.[12] In September 1966 Indonesia returned to full participation in the UN. In mid-1967 U Thant appointed Fernando Ortiz-Sanz of Bolivia as his special representative, to advise and assist in arrangements for the exercise of the right of self-determination. He reported that the people of West Irian were suffering from a 'complete lack of information' about the decision they would be required to make.[13] In early 1969 there was evidence of Papuan nationalist resistance to Indonesian rule and of personal and political repression by Indonesia. And it was now suggested that the peoples were too primitive to exercise universal adult suffrage, and that only certain designated persons, including tribal leaders, would take part in the plebiscite. Also, many recalled that President Suharto had stated that 'free choice' in the area 'does not mean that we shall abandon the fruits of our struggle for the liberation of West Irian'.[14]

The Secretary-General's own view of UNTEA's implementation of its duties, over and above the role played by UNSF, is reproduced below:

ORGANIZATION OF THE CIVILIAN ADMINISTRATION (ARTICLES V AND IX)

As required under article IX of the Agreement of 15 August, the eighteen top officials in the administration, namely, the nine directors, the six divisional commissioners, the head of police, the head of the government information bureau and the popular information service, and the head of the broadcasting services were gradually replaced by personnel appointed by the United Nations who were neither from Indonesia nor from the Netherlands. Fifteen posts were filled by the end of October, and the remaining three before the end of the year.

As regards the personnel below the top echelon officials, the departure of large numbers of Dutch civil servants after the transfer of administration created a vacuum which had to be filled rapidly in order to prevent the disruption of essential functions and services. In a few instances, this was accomplished by promoting Papuan officials to the vacant posts. There was, however, a great shortage of Papuans adequately trained for the higher posts. In the

[7] Ibid. p. 61.   [8] In January 1965.
[9] *Guardian*, 24 June 1963; *Japan Times*, 25 June 1963; *Straits Times*, 26 Aug. 1963. Certainly the Indonesian government made statements denying that a plebiscite would be held.
[10] See *Dawn*, 20 Aug. 1966.   [11] *The Times*, 8 Dec. 1966.
[12] *Daily Telegraph*, 10 Dec. 1966; *The Times*, 15 Dec. 1966.   [13] *New York Times*, 20 Oct. 1968.
[14] Ibid.

circumstances, a skeleton staff required to maintain essential administrative services and functions was organized, consisting of Netherlands officials, who agreed to work for UNTEA, Papuan personnel, and internationally recruited staff. The Indonesian Government was requested to provide urgently a group of civil servants to fill certain high-priority posts. This request covered several administrative departments and prepared the ground for a gradual phasing-in of Indonesian officials whose presence thus facilitated the subsequent transfer of administrative responsibilities to Indonesia.

The Netherlands Governor of the territory and his senior officials assisted greatly in assembling this emergency staff. These efforts were supported by measures taken by the Netherlands Government to induce Dutch officials to remain in the territory to serve UNTEA. The Government of Indonesia also responded with speed to the United Nations request for staff so that the initial group of Indonesian officials arrived only a few hours after UNTEA had taken over the administration.

The influx of Indonesian personnel was accelerated towards the end of February 1963 and increased with the approaching date of transfer of administration to Indonesia. By the beginning of April, fewer than a dozen Netherlands nationals remained while the total number of Indonesians in the service of UNTEA had reached 1,600. As regards Papuan officials, at the time of transfer of administration to Indonesia on 1 May 1963, they numbered some 7,600, an increase of approximately 600 for the entire period of UNTEA, thus meeting the requirements of article IX of the Agreement.

The pattern of administration that existed prior to 1 October 1962 was continued during UNTEA with certain minor changes required for greater efficiency.

With the sudden departure of the Netherlands personnel from various judiciary organs and until UNTEA took over the administration of the territory, the administration of justice at almost all levels came to a standstill. One of the first concerns of UNTEA was, therefore, to reactivate the entire judiciary. With this end in view, all the vacant positions in the judicial offices were filled by the recruitment of qualified judicial officers from Indonesia. When inducting them into their respective offices, the administrator stressed their responsibility for preserving and safeguarding the rights and liberties of the peoples of the territory.

RIGHTS OF THE INHABITANTS (ARTICLE XXII)

The Administration insured, without let or hindrance, the free exercise by the population of the rights referred to in article XXII, paragraph 1, of the Agreement. Moreover, UNTEA courts were to act as guarantors of these rights. In November 1962, on the occasion of the investiture of certain high members of the judiciary in their respective offices, the United Nations Administrator emphasized that 'in administering justice within the terms of the Agreement, the UNTEA courts will be constantly called upon to uphold the rule of law and the principles of the Charter of the United Nations, to ensure respect for human rights, and to preserve intact, as a public trust, the rights and liberties of the people of the Territory'.

In order to ensure the free movement of the inhabitants of West Irian to and from West New Guinea, as contemplated in the Agreement, UNTEA liberally issued travel documents to all who requested them. At the instance of the United Nations, several Governments agreed to recognize these travel documents and to provide normal facilities to their holders.

No restrictions were imposed during the Administration on the movement of civilians of Indonesian and Netherlands nationalities to and from the territory.

REPRESENTATIVE COUNCILS (ARTICLE XXIII)

At the time of the transfer of authority to UNTEA on 1 October, the New Guinea Council was in session and, in accordance with existing laws, it could be closed only by the Governor and, after 1 October, by the Administrator who replaced the Governor as the Chief Executive.

On 4 December, the members of the New Guinea Council met in the presence of the Administrator and took their new oath of office. The Council's Chairman, Mr. Th. Meset,

6

and all members pledged loyally to support the provisions of the Agreement and swore allegiance to UNTEA. As it seemed desirable that the members should return to their constituencies in order to explain personally to their constituents the new political situation of the territory, the session was closed on 5 December after consultation with the Chairman of the Council. The United Nations Administration took the opportunity of addressing the Council personally, thus demonstrating the Administration's recognition of the Council's role. A Board of Delegates was left in charge after the end of the session.

During the period of UNTEA administration, a number of vacancies in the membership of the New Guinea Council occurred because of the resignation, departure or absence of members from the territory. On the request of the Chairman of the Council to fill some of these vacancies by nomination or election, the United Nations Administrator, in conformity with Article XXIII, signed appropriate decrees appointing two new members to the New Guinea Council. However, no consultation could take place with representative councils since none existed in those districts from which the two members were appointed.

On the request of the Chairman of the Council, the United Nations Administrator opened a special session of the Council on 23 April. The Administrator made a statement to the Council outlining the achievements of UNTEA. The Council remained in session until 30 April when it dissolved itself on 1 May, at 12.31 p.m.

In addition to the New Guinea Council, there were eleven representative councils, known as regional councils, in the various districts. On 14 February, the Administrator opened the new regional council at Ransiki, Manokwari, elections to which had been held in December 1962. In his address, he referred to the political changes which had been brought about by the conclusion of the Agreement of 15 August 1962, and gave a brief outline of the Administration's efforts to ensure the welfare of the population.

The divisional commissioners were specially requested by UNTEA to consult the representative councils in their respective divisions on all important matters, and the Department of Internal Affairs maintained constant liaison with the New Guinea Council, or its Board of Delegates, and consulted it when necessary.

Public information activity of UNTEA (article X)

The responsibilities of the Administration under this article were largely carried out by the Department of Information and its two main branches, the Popular Information Service and the Broadcasting System. In addition to news releases on the activities of the Administration, the publication of two periodicals and daily broadcasts in English, Malay and Dutch, the Department of Information initiated a special informational campaign to explain the terms of the Agreement by broadcasting special features, publishing texts of broadcasts, displaying posters, organizing discussion groups throughout the territory, and so on.

The United Nations Administrator also toured the territory extensively and took part in all public functions in order to gain first-hand information regarding the situation in the island and in order to have the opportunity of explaining personally those parts of the Agreement which related to the United Nations presence in the territory and the changes that would take place on 1 May. These efforts helped to prepare the population for the transfer of administration to Indonesia, and to inform them regarding the provisions of the Agreement on the question of self-determination.

The civilian administration

(a) The budget (article XXIV)

In compliance with the provisions of article XXIV, paragraph 2, and pursuant to the arrangements proposed in identical letters dated 15 August 1962 from the Acting Secretary-General to the representatives of the two governments concerning the financial aspects of the administration of the territory by the United Nations, consultations took place between the Secretariat and the representatives of the two governments regarding the preparation of the

UNTEA budget. At Hollandia/Kotabaru, a committee composed of the representatives of the two sides met under the chairmanship of the Deputy Controller of the United Nations, and agreed on a UNTEA budget for the period 1 October 1962 to 30 April 1963, which was later approved by the Secretary-General. The entire cost of the operation was borne equally by the two governments through funds made available in advance by them to the Secretary-General and treated as a 'Fund in trust'.

As the UNTEA budget committee doubted that UNTEA would be able to collect any revenue, no estimates of income were prepared. The Department of Finance was able to collect, however, by the end of the UNTEA period a total of approximately 15 million New Guinea florins (NGf) in revenues from taxes, custom duties, etc. This was credited to the final budget figure.

(b) *Public Health*

In the sphere of public health, UNTEA had to deal with an epidemic of cholera which had begun to spread on the south west coast of the island. In this it received invaluable assistance from the WHO, which provided the personnel of a health team and the necessary medical supplies. The Administration was able not only to contain the epidemic within a short period, but also to declare the whole territory free of cholera. The Administration also pursued energetically plans for establishing hospitals and clinics in various parts of the territory. For example, a large hospital at Biak and another one at Wamena, in the central highlands, were completed and put in operation by UNTEA.

(c) *Education*

In January 1963, UNTEA established an Advisory Council on Education and gave it the task of assessing the educational needs of the territory arising out of the introduction of the Indonesian language and system of education after 1 May and of drawing up a plan for 1963–1964. The Advisory Council discussed its report in the presence of the Administrator and made various recommendations. Since the Advisory Council included the representatives of the Indonesian Government, in addition to representatives of religious foundations and of UNTEA, the results of its work were expected to prove of great value to the succeeding administration. While the Indonesian language was made the medium of instruction throughout the territory as of November 1962, the Dutch language was also to be used simultaneously until the end of the UNTEA administration.

(d) *Economy*

In the economic sphere, the Administration was mainly concerned with maintaining stability and dealing with a serious unemployment problem, by completing many projects of importance for the economy of the territory, by keeping in check the general price level of commodities and by ensuring adequate supplies for the population. The amount of currency in circulation at the end of the UNTEA administration compared very favourably with the amount at the time of the transfer of authority to UNTEA. It can be generally said that the economic stability of the territory was maintained during the UNTEA administration.

Of the eighty public works projects included in the budget of UNTEA, forty-five were completed at an estimated cost of NGf 18.6 million. At the end of the UNTEA, thirty-two other projects were under construction. The Administration spent over NGf 3 million on these projects and provided all the necessary materials for their completion. It was considered that the continuation of these thirty-two projects would ensure an adequate level of employment in the territory immediately after the termination of UNTEA. With a view to preventing the rise of unemployment upon the completion of these projects, UNTEA, in co-operation with the Indonesian authorities, drew up plans for other similar projects which would be useful for the development of the territory and the welfare of the population. The Indonesian authorities expressed their appreciation to UNTEA, and it was the hope that these plans would facilitate the implementation of future development projects in the territory.

The more important public works projects completed by UNTEA included the ocean wharf and a large hospital at Biak and buildings for the New Guinea Council and the Court of Justice; the extension and improvement of the Sentani airport at Hollandia/Kotabaru and the building of an airstrip at Wamena in the central highlands; and also the rehabilitation and extension of the water supply system at Hollandia/Kotabaru, Biak, Seroei, Fak Fak and Merauke. The Agricultural Research Station at Manokwari, financed by the European Economic Community, was also completed during the UNTEA period.

In a territory where practically all consumer goods have to be imported from the outside, UNTEA maintained a constant watch on the supply situation, with a view to maintaining adequate stocks. To this end, shipping services were maintained by agreement first with a Netherlands shipping company and later with an Indonesian company. Foreign exchange was provided to import buffer stocks of essential commodities and an agreement was concluded to take over and distribute the existing stocks between Indonesian importers and the outgoing Dutch firms.

In addition to dealing with immediate day-to-day problems, much attention was given to the longer-term problems of the territory. Basic data and records were collected for drawing up a plan for the over-all development of the territory.

POLITICAL QUESTIONS

On 31 December 1962, the Netherlands flag was replaced by the Indonesian flag, which was raised side by side with the United Nations flag, as contemplated in the *aide-mémoire* attached to the Agreement.

In the latter part of 1962 and the beginning of 1963, a number of communications from Papuan leaders and various groups in the territory were addressed to the Secretary-General and the United Nations Administrator requesting that the period of UNTEA administration in West New Guinea (West Irian) be shortened and the administration transferred to Indonesia before 1 May 1963.

On 21 November 1962, a joint declaration by the representatives of the New Guinea Council was transmitted to the Secretary-General asking for an early transfer of the administration to Indonesia. A demonstration to the same effect took place on 15 January 1963, when a petition was presented to the Administrator by eighteen political leaders from the area of Hollandia/Kotabaru.

These requests were brought to the attention of the Secretary-General in January 1963 by Dr. Sudjarwo Tjondronegoro, Deputy to the Foreign Minister of the Republic of Indonesia and head of the Indonesian Liaison Mission to UNTEA. After consultation with the representative of the Netherlands, the Secretary-General came to the conclusion that, in the circumstances, any shortening of UNTEA was not feasible.

However, the Secretary-General sent his Chef de Cabinet, Mr. C. V. Narasimhan, to consult with the United Nations Administrator and the Government of Indonesia, with a view to facilitating the entry of Indonesian officials into the administration of West New Guinea (West Irian) in order to ensure the continuity and expansion of all essential services, especially those concerning the welfare of the people, and also to help as far as possible to accelerate plans for development of the territory. Following these consultations, Mr. Narasimhan announced in Djakarta that the transfer of administration would take place on 1 May 1963, and that the replacement of Netherlands officials by Indonesian officials would be accelerated. He foresaw the establishment of a United Nations Development Fund for Irian Barat to be used for development projects and the welfare of the population. Contributions to the Fund would be on a voluntary basis by States Members of the United Nations and members of the specialized agencies. (The Government of the Netherlands had already made public its offer of a contribution of $10 million a year for three years.)

Shortly after Mr. Narasimhan's visit, the Government of Indonesia informed the Secretary-General that it had decided to reopen diplomatic relations with the Kingdom of the Netherlands at the ambassadorial level beginning with an exchange of *chargés d'affaires*. On 13 March

1963, the Secretary-General announced that the two Governments had agreed to resume normal relations and to exchange diplomatic respresentatives.

TRANSFER OF AUTHORITY TO INDONESIA

In accordance with article XII of the Agreement, the Administrator of UNTEA, Dr. Djalal Abdoh, transferred full administrative control to the representative of the Republic of Indonesia on 1 May, and on that date the United Nations flag was taken down. The Secretary-General designated Mr. C. V. Narasimhan, Chef de Cabinet, as his personal representative at the ceremony. By that date UNSF had been concentrated in Biak preparatory to leaving for Pakistan. The various UNSF garrisons were replaced by incoming Indonesian troops. At the end of April the phasing-in of Indonesian personnel was completed according to agreed plans; 1,564 Indonesian officials were working in the administration and the remaining Dutch officials had left. Each department was taken over by an Indonesian official who had previously worked as deputy to the head of the department.

CONCLUSION

In carrying out the task entrusted to him, the Secretary-General was guided solely by the terms of the Agreement of 15 August 1962. The transfer of the administration from the Netherlands to UNTEA and later from the UNTEA to Indonesia was achieved peacefully and without incident. The population was gradually prepared for the changes brought about under the Agreement. Disruption of essential public services and utilities was avoided, and continuity in employment was maintained.

The cost of the operation was underwritten by the Governments of Indonesia and the Netherlands. Both Governments have now paid the full costs in equal amounts.

Furthermore, the smooth implementation of the Agreement hastened the resumption of diplomatic relations between Indonesia and the Netherlands, and the improvement of relations between the two Governments.

The Administration attached great importance to that part of the Agreement which dealt with the rights of the inhabitants. The New Guinea Council or its Board of Delegates was consulted by the Administrator on major issues and on new legislation or amendments to existing laws. Its membership was increased by the appointment of two new members to fill existing vacancies. The United Nations Administrator opened the sessions of the New Guinea Council and of some of the Regional Councils, always stressing the close co-operation between the representatives of the population and UNTEA.

On the completion of UNTEA, the Secretary-General declared that UNTEA had been a unique experience, which had once again proved the capacity of the United Nations to undertake a variety of functions provided it receives adequate support from the States Members of the Organization. Throughout the period of UNTEA, he had been impressed and gratified by the spirit of accommodation shown by the Governments of the Republic of Indonesia and the Kingdom of the Netherlands.

Looking into the future the Secretary-General stated that he was confident that the Republic of Indonesia would scrupulously observe the terms of the Agreement concluded on 15 August 1962 and would ensure the exercise by the population of the territory of their right to express their wishes as to their future. The United Nations stood ready to give the Government of Indonesia all assistance in the implementation of this and the remaining parts of the Agreement.

The Secretary-General also announced that, in consultation with the Government of Indonesia, he had decided in principle to designate a few United Nations experts, serving at Headquarters and elsewhere, to perform the functions envisaged in article XVI of the Agreement. These experts would visit West Irian (West New Guinea) as often as might be necessary and spend such time as might be required to enable them to report fully to him. Before the arrival of the United Nations Representative to be designated under article XVII, their duties would be limited to advising on and assisting in preparations for carrying out the provisions for self-determination, except in so far as the Government of Indonesia and the Secretary-General might agree upon their performing other specialized functions.

In conclusion, the Secretary-General announced that, in consultation with the Governments concerned, he had decided to establish a United Nations Development Fund for Irian Barat (West New Guinea) as a 'Fund in trust', and open to contributions from Member States of the United Nations and the specialized agencies. The Fund would be used to finance pre-investment and investment projects in West Irian, acceptable to the Government of Indonesia, and in co-operation with the United Nations technical assistance to Indonesia. Finally, the Secretary-General expressed the hope that many Governments would contribute liberally to this Fund.   [*A/5501*, & Add. 1 pp. 36–40.]

13

ANNEXES

A. *Checklist of Documents*

INTERNATIONAL AGREEMENTS

69 UNTS 206: Draft Charter of Transfer of Sovereignty of Indonesia
69 UNTS 332: Exchanges of letters
A/5170 & Add. 1, GAOR, 17th sess., ann., a.i.89: Agreement between Netherlands and Indonesia concerning West Irian, and Related Understandings

GENERAL ASSEMBLY

1. DEBATES
   GAOR, 9th sess., 1st Cttee, mtgs 726–36
   GAOR, 16th sess., plen. mtgs 1016, 1054–8
   GAOR, 15th sess., 1st Cttee, mtg 1115
   GAOR, 17th sess., plen. mtgs 1125–9, 1147–53, 1155

2. DOCUMENTS

A/2932	10 Aug. 1955	10th sess., ann., a.i. 65
A/3200	9 Oct. 1956	11th sess., ann., a.i.63
A/L.354	9 Oct. 1961 ⎫	
A/4944	27 Oct. 1961 ⎬	16th sess., ann., a.i. 88 & 22a
A/4954	2 Nov. 1961 ⎭	
A/5501	1963	Ann. Rep. of Secretary-General, 1962–3, 18th sess., suppl. 1.

3. RESOLUTIONS

915(X)	16 Dec. 1955		S/5135	25 June 1962
S/5123	21 May 1962		S/5155	10 Aug. 1962
S/5124	23 May 1962		S/5157	14 Aug. 1962
S/5126	24 May 1962		1752(XVII)	21 Sept. 1962

B. *Bibliography*

Bowett, D. W. *United Nations Forces*. London, 1964. Ch. 7.

Citrin, Jack. *United Nations Peacekeeping Activities: a case study in organizational task expansion*. Denver, Col., 1965. Ch. 4.

Jaspan, M. A. West Irian: the first two years. *Australian Quarterly*, June 1965.

Leyser, Johannes. Dispute and Agreement on West New Guinea. *Archiv des Völkerrechts*, 1963.

Russell, Ruth. *United Nations Experience with Forces: political and legal aspects*. Brookings Staff Paper, Aug. 1964.

Seyersted, Finn. *United Nations Forces in the Law of Peace and War*. Leyden, 1966.

Taylor, Alastair. *Indonesian Independence and the United Nations*. London, 1960.

UN. *The United Nations in West New Guinea*. New York, 1963.

Van der. Kroef, Justus The West New Guinea Settlement: its origins and implications. *Orbis*, 1963.

—— West New Guinea in the Crucible. *Political Science Quarterly*, 1960.

—— Nasution, Sukarno and the West New Guinea Dispute. *Asian Survey*, 1961.

—— Towards 'Papua Barat'. *Australian Quarterly*, Mar. 1962.

—— Dutch Opinion on the West New Guinea Problem. *Australian Outlook*, Dec. 1960.

Veur, Paul van der. The United Nations in West Irian: a critique. *Int. Org.*, 1964.

—— Political Awakening in West New Guinea. *Pacific Affairs*, Spring 1963.

—— West Irian: a new era. *Asian Survey*, Oct. 1962.

Wainhouse, David W. and others. *International Peace Observation*. Baltimore, 1966. Ch. 10.

Part 3

UNITED NATIONS ENFORCEMENT ACTION IN KOREA, 1950-3

6*

concerning claims for utilities by contributing states; controversy between Unified Command and Syngman Rhee.

I

INTRODUCTION

FROM 1910 till 1942 Korea was a Japanese colony. During this occupation an underground independence movement was led by militant Communists in the north-east; outside a so-called provisional government, located in China, was headed by Dr Syngman Rhee and unsuccessfully sought Allied diplomatic recognition. The Allies were reluctant to commit themselves to any one group, thus compromising 'the right of the Korean people to choose the ultimate form and personnel of the government which they may wish to establish'.[1]

Allied policy on Korea was first announced at the Cairo Conference in November 1943 in a joint statement by the United States, the United Kingdom, and China, affirming that 'the aforesaid three great powers, mindful of the enslavement of the people of Korea, are determined that in due course Korea shall become free and independent'.[2] The Potsdam declaration of 26 July 1945 reaffirmed this, and Article 8 of this declaration stated that 'Japanese sovereignty shall be limited to the islands of Honshu, Hokkaido, Kyushu, Shikoku and such minor islands as we determine'.[3] As the Allies were also endeavouring at this stage to bring the Soviet Union into the war against Japan, talks were held with Russian officials to co-ordinate strategy. It was agreed that following Russia's entry into the war, there should be a demarcation line between American and Russian air and sea (but not ground) operations because it was not then expected that American or Russian troops would enter Korea in the immediate future.[4] However, the American service chiefs at Potsdam considered landing in Korea if the Japanese surrendered prior to Soviet occupation,[5] and decided on the 38th parallel, which ran just north of Seoul, as a dividing line between American and Soviet forces, though they did not discuss this with the Russians. On 10 August the Russians began large-scale attacks on Korea. The United States then proposed that for the purposes of accepting the Japanese surrender, the 38th parallel should be the dividing line between American and Russian zones of responsibility. This was agreed by Stalin.[6] It was intended to be a purely temporary demarcation line.

[1] Statement by Joseph C. Grew, Acting Sec. of State, US press release, 8 June 1945 (cited G. M. McCune, *Korea Today* (1950), p. 42).

[2] US Dept of State, *Foreign Relations of the United States: Diplomatic Papers, The Conferences at Cairo and Tehran, 1943* (1961), pp. 448–9.

[3] Id., *The Conference of Berlin, the Potsdam Conference, 1945* (1960), ii. 1475.

[4] Soon Sung Cho, *Korea in World Politics 1940–50* (1967), pp. 42, 51.

[5] S. Truman, *Truman Memoirs*, i: *Year of Decisions*, p. 383 (cited ibid).

[6] A. L. Grey, Jr, 'The Thirty-Eighth Parallel', *Foreign Affairs*, Apr. 1951, pp. 483–4; Cho, pp. 52–54.

On 18 August 1945 Japan surrendered. On 6 September, two days before the arrival of American troops in South Korea, many prominent Korean leaders formed a 'People's Republic' in Seoul with connections throughout the country, including the Russian zone. The President of this Republic was Lyuh Woonhyung, a veteran nationalist who had been one of the organizers of the 'provisional government'. Local committees were set up to preserve order, and in the north these were assisted by the Russian forces. When the American forces arrived, the People's Republic offered its services, but the Americans decided to treat it as merely one political party pending the organization of nation-wide elections. American military government was established in the South in October but left-wing groups continued to support the People's Republic while right-wing groups rallied to the 'provisional government' on the return to Korea of Syngman Rhee. Elections were held for an Interim Legislative Assembly in November 1946, but on a limited franchise, which resulted in a victory for the conservatives. However, half the Assembly was appointed by the military government, and 'in order to give the Assembly as representative a character as possible, many of the appointed members were chosen from the moderate and non-Communist left-wing parties'.[7]

Meanwhile in the North no military government was set up. Instead, Soviet advisers helped to set up a Korean administration of 'People's Committees' with the 'Provisional People's Committee' as the central governing organ. In the summer of 1946 the groundwork was laid for the establishment of a Soviet-style 'democratic' government by the creation of a Democratic Front, represented in the central government by a central committee. In November the first elections were held for membership in the People's Committees on the basis of one list of candidates, all members of the Front. The Soviet Union reported that the Front had secured 97 per cent of the votes. In February 1947 a Convention of People's Committees met in Pyongyang and among other things decided to establish the People's Assembly of North Korea.

In fact a further Allied agreement had taken place after the occupation of Korea with the object of overcoming the division of the country. In December 1945, at the Moscow Foreign Ministers' Meeting, the United States, the Soviet Union, the United Kingdom, and subsequently China, agreed to establish an American–Soviet Joint Commission to assist in the formation of a provisional Korean government, to work out an agreement for a four-power trusteeship for a period up to five years.

Virtually all the Korean political parties, including the Communist Party, objected to the trusteeship proposal, and the right-wing parties in the south united in an Anti-Trusteeship Committee to try to prevent the implementation of the Moscow agreement. This gave the Russians a pretext for demanding that all members of that Committee should be excluded from consultation. The United States found this completely unacceptable, and on 8 May 1946 the Joint Commission was adjourned because negotiations had broken down on this issue. In April 1947 the United States formally proposed that the Commission

[7] Cmd 8078, p. 5.

should be reconvened, and it met again on 22 May. It was agreed that groups of Koreans were to be invited to submit applications for participation in consultations about Korea's future in Seoul and Pyongyang, but in July negotiations again broke down after the Russians had proposed drastic cuts in the number of groups to be consulted in the South.

After a further exchange of correspondence, the United States proposed on 26 August 1967 that elections on a basis of universal suffrage should be held throughout the country for provisional legislatures for each zone, the zonal legislatures then to choose, on a numerical proportional basis, representatives to constitute a national provisional legislature, which would establish a provisional government for a united Korea. This government would then meet representatives of the four signatories of the Moscow agreement to discuss the economic and political future of Korea.[8] Vyacheslav Molotov, the Russian Foreign Minister, rejected these proposals and refused to attend a conference to discuss them. He asserted that under the terms of the Moscow Agreement it was for the Joint Commission to frame measures leading to a provisional government, and that the Commission could still do so.

The United States now resolved to place the matter before the UN. On 23 September the General Assembly placed the matter on its agenda, in the face of objections from the Russians that such a decision would be contrary both to the Moscow agreement and to Article 107 of the Charter.[9] Once defeated on this, however, the Soviet Union now made a new proposal—that both American and Russian forces should be withdrawn by the beginning of 1948, leaving the Koreans free to choose a national government. The United States, aware of the very great discrepancy between the heavily-armed and well-organized North Korean army and the small South Korean army, equipped with light defensive weapons only, asserted that withdrawal could only come about after, and not before, the establishment of an independent government for the whole of Korea. Dr Rhee insisted that such a Russian–American withdrawal could only take place if North Korea were disarmed, or if a large and effective South Korean army were first trained.

The Soviet Union also proposed that Korean representatives should be invited to take part in the UN deliberations. Secretary Dulles said that while such a proposal was unobjectionable in principle, it would again mean endless dispute as to who were the appropriate Korean representatives to be heard.

On 14 November 1947 the General Assembly adopted an American proposal for the establishment of a UN Temporary Commission on Korea (UNTCOK).

Inasmuch as the Korean question which is before the General Assembly is primarily a matter for the Korean people itself and concerns its freedom and independence, and
Recognising that this question cannot be correctly and fairly resolved without the participation of representatives of the indigenous population,

[8] See US Dept of State, *Korea's Independence* (1947).
[9] Art. 107 provides: 'Nothing in the present Charter shall invalidate or preclude action, in relation to any state which during the Second World War has been an enemy of any signatory to the present Charter, taken or authorized as a result of that war by the Governments having responsibility for such action.'

THE GENERAL ASSEMBLY,

1. *Resolves* that elected representatives of the Korean people be invited to take part in the consideration of the question;

2. *Further resolves* that in order to facilitate and expedite such participation and to observe that the Korean representatives are in fact duly elected by the Korean people and not mere appointees by military authorities in Korea, there be forthwith established a United Nations Temporary Commission on Korea, to be present in Korea, with right to travel, observe and consult throughout Korea.

II

THE GENERAL ASSEMBLY,

Recognising the urgent and rightful claims to independence of the people of Korea;

Believing that the national independence of Korea should be re-established and all occupying forces then withdrawn at the earliest practicable date;

Recalling its previous conclusion that the freedom and independence of the Korean people cannot be correctly or fairly resolved without the participation of representatives of the Korean people, and its decision to establish a United Nations Temporary Commission on Korea (hereinafter called the 'Commission') for the purpose of facilitating and expediting such participation by elected representatives of the Korean people:

1. *Decides* that the Commission shall consist of representatives of Australia, Canada, China, El Salvador, France, India, Philippines, Syria, Ukrainian Soviet Socialist Republic;

2. *Recommends* that the elections be held not later than 31st March, 1948, on the basis of adult suffrage and by secret ballot to choose representatives with whom the Commission may consult regarding the prompt attainment of the freedom and independence of the Korean people and which representatives, constituting a National Assembly, may establish a National Government of Korea. The number of representatives from each voting area or zone should be proportionate to the population, and the elections should be under the observation of the Commission;

3. *Further recommends* that, as soon as possible after the elections, the National Assembly should convene and form a National Government and notify the Commission of its formation;

4. *Further recommends* that immediately upon the establishment of a National Government, that Government should, in consultation with the Commission: (*a*) constitute its own national security forces and dissolve all military or semi-military formations not included therein; (*b*) take over the functions of government from the military commands and civilian authorities of North and South Korea, and (*c*) arrange with the occupying Powers for the complete withdrawal from Korea of their armed forces as early as practicable and if possible within ninety days;

5. *Resolves* that the Commission shall facilitate and expedite the fulfilment of the foregoing programme for the attainment of the national independence of Korea and withdrawal of occupying forces, taking into account its observations and consultations in Korea. The Commission shall report with its conclusions to the General Assembly and may consult with the Interim Committee (if one be established) with respect to the application of this resolution in the light of developments;

6. *Calls upon* the Member States concerned to afford every assistance and facility to the Commission in the fulfilment of its responsibilities;

7. *Calls upon* all Members of the United Nations to refrain from interfering in the affairs of the Korean people during the interim period preparatory to the establishment of Korean independence, except in pursuance of the decisions of the General Assembly; and thereafter, to refrain completely from any and all acts derogatory to the independence and sovereignty of Korea. [*GA res. 112 (11)*.]

This resolution was adopted by 43 votes to 0 with 6 abstentions. The countries which did not participate in the voting were Byelorussia, Czechoslovakia,

Poland, the Ukraine, the USSR, and Yugoslavia. The Ukraine refused to serve on the commission.

When the Temporary Commission arrived in Seoul in January 1948 it became immediately embroiled in South Korean politics. The North denounced it as an American tool, and refused to co-operate in any way. And in the South the rightists, Dr Rhee's party, the Society for the Rapid Realization of Korean Independence, and Kim Song-soo's Korean Democratic Party were agitating for immediate separate elections in spite of sharp reproofs by the United States.[10] The Commission was refused entry into or contact with North Korea because the USSR contended that it was an illegal body—a view confirmed in Russian eyes when it reported back to the Assembly's Interim Committee, the establishment of which had been bitterly opposed by Russia.

The Interim Committee now advised the Temporary Commission 'to proceed with the observance of elections in all Korea and, if that is impossible, in as much of Korea as is accessible to it'. Although this suggestion met with the approval of Dr Rhee, other South Korean political groups—the leftists, Dr Kim Kiu-sic's moderates, and Kim Koo's right-wing Korean Independence Party—were all opposed, arguing that they could not now be held in a free atmosphere and that the voting would delay and make more difficult the achievement of unity.[11] Pincered between this possibility and the fear that the rejection of the Interim Committee's suggestions would lead to communist domination over all Korea, the United States supported the plan for election in the South. While a majority of the members of the Temporary Commission were in favour of the holding of such elections, Australia and Canada were opposed to the idea, and Syria was doubtful.

In April 1949 the North Korean leaders invited the leaders of those South Korean parties which had not supported the election plan to attend a coalition conference at Pyongyang, to discuss the formation of an all-Korea government. The conference was attended by some 545 delegates, including 240 from the South, and it called for a unified government and the withdrawal of foreign troops and bases. Dr Rhee denounced the South Korean participants as 'stooges of the communists'.[12]

There was violence and terrorism during the election campaign, but some 95 per cent of the registered voters were reported to have voted. While there was undoubtedly intimidation and bribery, the Temporary Commission endeavoured to scrutinize the conduct of the election wherever possible. A conservative Assembly was elected, consisting largely of the followers of Dr Syngman Rhee and Kim Song-soo. The Temporary Commission reported that the results of the election were a valid expression of the free will of the electorate in those parts of Korea which were accessible to it. At the inauguration of this government General MacArthur declared '. . . an artificial barrier has divided

[10] RIIA, *Survey of International Affairs, 1947–8*, p. 318.

[11] L. M. Goodrich, *Korea: a Study of US Policy in the United Nations* (1956), p. 44.

[12] G. M. McCune: 'The Korean situation', *Far Eastern Survey*, 18 Sept. 1948, p. 201 (cited RIIA, *Survey 1947–8*, p. 320).

your land. This barrier must and shall be torn down'.[13] American military government was now ended.

In the North Tass[14] reported that an extraordinary session of the People's Assembly of North Korea had been held, with forty representatives from the South attending. An ensuing conference was said to have denounced the 'fake' elections in the South, and decided instead to hold elections in August for a 'Supreme People's Assembly of Korea'. Russia claimed not only that elections were held on 25 August, 77 per cent of the votes being in favour of the 360 sponsored candidates, but that they had also taken place in South Korea. This fiction was persisted in. However, it is clear that a convention of over 1,000 professed delegates of the South Koreans met on 22 and 24 August at Haeju, just north of the 38th parallel, and these picked some 360 of their number to represent South Korea in the Supreme People's Assembly.[15] This Assembly formed the People's Democratic Republic under Kim Il-sung. The Minister for Foreign Affairs was a South Korean.

The Soviet Union announced in September 1948 that she was withdrawing her troops, and, together with other members of the Communist bloc, accorded recognition to Kim Il-sung's government. The United States said that she would delay troop withdrawal until the third session of the Assembly had considered the situation.

Dr Rhee, in the meantime, was having to deal with local riots, the quelling of which had caused considerable loss of life. In September 1948 he secured an agreement by the United States to train a Korean force and to supply it with small arms. It has been suggested that the bellicosity of the South, as much as of the North, made the United States reluctant to supply Dr Rhee with tanks and heavy artillery.[16]

The third session of the General Assembly had before it a report of the Temporary Commission[17] which had been presented in October. This attested to the fairness of the elections held under the supervision of the Commission, but also spoke of the harsh methods of the Korean interim government towards its enemies. The United States indicated that there had, in this regard, been some improvement since October; and in reply to Soviet denunciations reminded the Assembly that no observation of the situation in the North had been possible. A Russian resolution to disband UNTCOK was rejected, and the following resolution was accepted by 48 votes to 6, with 1 abstention:

The General Assembly,

Having regard to its resolution 112 (II) of 14 November 1947, concerning the problem of the independence of Korea.

Having considered the report of the United Nations Temporary Commission on Korea (hereinafter referred to as the 'Temporary Commission'), and the report of the interim Committee of the General Assembly regarding its consultation with the Temporary Commission,

Mindful of the fact that, due to difficulties referred to in the report of the Temporary Com-

[13] *NY Times*, 18 Aug. 1948 (cited ibid. p. 321).
[14] *Soviet News*, 5 May 1948 (cited ibid. p. 322).
[15] RIIA, *Survey, 1947–8*, p. 322.   [16] Ibid. p. 324.   [17] A/575/Add. 3 & 4.

mission, the objectives set forth in the resolution of 14 November 1947, have not been fully accomplished, and in particularly that unification of Korea has not yet been achieved,

1. *Approves* the conclusions of the reports of the Temporary Commission;

2. *Declares* that there has been established a lawful government (the Government of the Republic of Korea) having effective control and jurisdiction over that part of Korea where the Temporary Commission was able to observe and consult and in which the great majority of the people of all Korea reside; that this Government is based on elections which were a valid expression of the free will of the electorate of that part of Korea and which were observed by the Temporary Commission; and that this is the only such Government in Korea;

3. *Recommends* that the occupying Powers withdraw their occupation forces from Korea as early as practicable:

4. *Resolves* that, as a means to the full accomplishment of the objectives set forth in the resolution of 14 November 1947, a Commission on Korea consisting of Australia, China, El Salvador, France, India, the Philippines and Syria, shall be established to continue the work of the Temporary Commission and carry out the provisions of the present resolution, having in mind the status of the Government of the Republic of Korea as herein defined, and in particular to:

(*a*) Lend its good offices to bring about the unification of Korea and the integration of all Korean security forces in accordance with the principles laid down by the General Assembly in the resolution of 14 November 1947;

(*b*) Seek to facilitate the removal of barriers to economic, social and other friendly inter-course caused by the division of Korea;

(*c*) Be available for observation and consultation in the further development of representative government based on the freely-expressed will of the people;

(*d*) Observe the actual withdrawal of the occupying forces and verify the fact of withdrawal when such has occurred; and for this purpose, if it so desires, request the assistance of military experts of the two occupying Powers;

5. *Decides* that the Commission:

(*a*) Shall within thirty days of the adoption of this resolution, proceed to Korea, where it shall maintain its seat;

(*b*) Shall be regarded as having superseded the Temporary Commission established by the resolution of 14 November 1947. . . . [*GA res. 195(III), 12 Dec. 1948.*]

The United States now formally recognized the Seoul government. The UN Commission on Korea (UNCOK) then went to Korea and held its first meeting in Seoul in February 1949.

When the Russian and American occupation forces withdrew, the two mutually antagonistic Korean governments were left, facing each other across the 38th parallel. In October 1949 UNCOK was renewed to assist in the reunification of Korea, and also 'to observe and report any developments which might lead to or otherwise involve military conflict in Korea'.[18] Considerable guerrilla activity appears to have been occurring in the South during this period.[19]

In May 1950 elections for a new National Assembly were held in the South; 130 seats were won by Independents, 49 by parties supporting Dr Rhee, and 44 by other parties. The North denounced these elections and called for the withdrawal of UNCOK.

On 25 June 1950 UNCOK cabled to the UN Secretary-General to report

[18] General Assembly res. 293 (IV), 21 Oct. 1949.
[19] A/936 & Add. 1, Report of UN Commission on Korea for period 30 Jan.–28 July 1949.

that South Korea was being invaded. The response of the UN is described in
the following section.[20]

[20] Further details of the events recountered here and of some of the issues dealt with in the ensuing
pages may be found in Goodrich's study of Korea (n. II above).

2

ENABLING RESOLUTIONS AND VOTING

The Security Council,
Recalling the finding of the General Assembly in its resolution of 21 October 1949 that the
Government of the Republic of Korea is a lawfully established government 'having effective
control and jurisdiction over that part of Korea where the United Nations Temporary Commission in Korea was able to observe and consult and in which the great majority of the
people of Korea reside; and that this Government is based on elections which were a valid
expression of the free will of the electorate of that part of Korea and which were observed by
the Temporary Commission; and that this is the only such government in Korea';
Mindful of the concern expressed by the General Assembly in its resolutions of 12 December 1948 and 21 October 1949 of the consequences which might follow unless Member States
refrained from acts derogatory to the results sought to be achieved by the United Nations in
bringing about the complete independence and unity of Korea; and the concern expressed
that the situation described by the United Nations Commission on Korea in its report
menaces the safety and well being of the Republic of Korea and of the people of Korea and
might lead to open military conflict there;
Noting with grave concern the armed attack upon the Republic of Korea by forces from
North Korea,
Determines that this action constitutes a breach of the peace,
I. *Calls for* the immediate cessation of hostilities; and *calls upon* the authorities of North
Korea to withdraw forthwith their armed forces to the 38th parallel;
II. *Requests* the United Nations Commission on Korea
(*a*) To communicate in fully considered recommendations on the situation with the least
possible delay,
(*b*) To observe the withdrawal of the North Korean forces to the 38th parallel, and
(*c*) To keep the Security Council informed on the execution of this resolution;
III. *Calls upon* all Members to render every assistance to the United Nations in the
execution of this resolution and to refrain from giving assistance to the North Korea authorities.   [*SC res. S/1501, 25 June 1950.*]

VOTING: 9–0, with one abstention, one absence.
  In favour: China, Cuba, Ecuador, Egypt, France, India, Norway, UK, USA.
    Against: None.
  Abstaining: Yugoslavia.
      Absent: USSR.

The representative of Yugoslavia, Djuro Nincic, explained his country's vote:

An act of aggression, by whomever it is perpetrated, is an extremely serious matter, upon
which the Security Council should always take the most determined, the most radical, and the
most resolution action. However, we do not feel that the picture we have been able to obtain

so far from the various dispatches that have come in, some of which are contradictory, and from the statements we have heard here, is sufficiently complete and balanced, nor one which would enable us to pass judgment on the merits of the case or assess the final and definitive responsibility and guilt of either of the parties involved.

My delegation is, therefore, of the opinion that, before passing any such final judgment, the Security Council should do everything in its power to adquire all the factual knowledge which would make that final judgment and the action taken in pursuance of it incontrovertible and absolutely beyond any shadow of reproach from any side. That is why we think that, before passing such final judgment, the Security Council should hear a representative of the other party concerned. I am voicing absolutely no opinion upon the merits of the case, but we have heard the representative of South Korea and I feel that we should grant an opportunity for a representative of the Government of North Korea, which has now been accused of aggression, to receive a hearing. That is why my delegation will move a formal proposal to make it possible for a representative of the North Korean Government to state the position of that Government before the Security Council.

This does not mean, however, that we feel that, in the meantime, the Security Council should remain inactive or should fail to take the action which the conditions warrant, but we believe that this action should not be of a nature exceeding the bounds of the evidence . . . which has so far been made available to us . . .   [*SCOR, 5th yr, 473rd mtg*, p. 14.]

The Yugoslav delegate then went on to propose a resolution (S/1500) which would have called for an immediate cessation of hostilities, and invited the government of North Korea to state its case before the General Assembly. Only Yugoslavia voted in favour of this, with Egypt, India, and Norway abstaining. It was therefore not adopted.

A paragraph-by-paragraph vote was taken on resolution S/1501. The first, second, and third paragraphs were adopted by 9 votes to nil, with Yugoslavia abstaining and the USSR absent. The first clause of operative paragraph 1 was adopted by 10 votes to nil (with the USSR absent). The second clause of operative paragraph I, and operative paragraphs II and III were adopted by 9 to nil, with Yugoslavia abstaining and the USSR absent.

The representative of the USSR had withdrawn from the Council on 13 January 1950, stating that he would not participate in the Council's work until 'the representative of the Kuomintang group had been removed', and that the USSR would not recognize as legal any decision of the Council, adopted with the participation of that representative and would not deem herself bound by such decisions.[1]

On 27 June 1950 the Security Council adopted a further resolution (S/1511). The Council now had before it three cablegrams from the Temporary Commission.[2] The Commission reported that the information coming from its military observers indicated that massive preparations had been occurring along the northern side of the 38th parallel in the forty-eight hours before hostilities began, and that the invasion was premeditated and fully planned.

The Temporary Commission thought that there was no hope of getting both sides to accept a cease-fire *simpliciter*—instead the Security Council might try to get them to accept a neutral mediator.

The United States representative now informed the Security Council that

[1] This is not, of course, an attitude which the Soviet Union has maintained.
[2] S/1503, S/1515/Rev. 1, & S/1507.

the President of the United States, in order to give effect to paragraph III of S/1501, had ordered air and sea forces to give cover and support to South Korean troops. The Seventh Fleet had also been instructed to prevent any attack on Formosa.[3] The Council now adopted the United States draft resolution:

The Security Council,
Having determined that the armed attack upon the Republic of Korea by forces from North Korea constitutes a breach of the peace,
Having called for an immediate cessation of hostilities, and
Having called upon the authorities of North Korea to withdraw forthwith their armed forces to the 38th parallel, and
Having noted from the report of the United Nations Commission for Korea that the authorities in North Korea have neither ceased hostilities nor withdrawn their armed forces to the 38th parallel and that urgent military measures are required to restore international peace and security, and
Having noted the appeal from the Republic of Korea to the United Nations for immediate and effective steps to secure peace and security,
Recommends that the Members of the United Nations furnish such assistance to the Republic of Korea as may be necessary to repel the armed attack and to restore international peace and security in the area.   [*SC res. S/1511, 27 June 1950.*]

VOTING: 7 votes to 1, with 1 absence and two members not participating.
In favour: China, Cuba, Ecuador, France, Norway, UK, USA.
  Against: Yugoslavia.
  Absent: USSR.

Not participating: Egypt, India.

The Yugoslav delegate explained his vote:

Korea and the Korean people are another victim of the policy of spheres of influence, a term which, unfortunately, has always been taken to mean spheres of interference as well. In the case of Korea, however, that policy . . . has created a vicious circle from which we cannot emerge on to the broad highway of the strengthening of peace. Indeed it may well lead us straight into a new world war.
  What must the Security Council do in these circumstances? In our opinion the Security Council should act in a direction opposite to the trends followed so far in international relations. It should assist the Korean people to find its own path towards independence and unity.
  We must not and we cannot, after only two days of fighting, abandon all hope that the two parties involved will at last understand the interests of their own people and of international peace; we cannot be sure that they will continue to refuse to enter into negotiations at this fateful hour. That is why we believe that they should be helped to find a common language. We can do this by addressing to them an appeal, more pressing than the first, to cease hostilities, and by suggesting to them a procedure of mediation with the help of the good offices of the Security Council. . . .   [*SCOR, 5th yr, 474th mtg,* p. 6.]

The Egyptian delegate indicated that he did not, at that moment, have instructions from his government, and would not wish that fact to hold up the voting. He wished the Council to recall that he had 'spoken in favour of the adoption of a vigorous attitude by the Council'.[4] However, once Mahmoud Fawzi had been properly instructed by his government, he returned to the Council to

---

[3] *SCOR,* 5th yr, 474th mtg, p. 5.   [4] Ibid. p. 14.

make a rather different speech. He indicated that voting for the resolution of 25 June did not necessarily entail going 'as far as the action stipulated in the resolution of 27 June'. It was necessary to note 'the previous laxities and delays in the action of the Security Council on several aggressions, including the premeditated and savage attack and aggression of political world Zionism on the still bleeding innocent people of Palestine'.[5] Other Arab nations subsequently followed this line of declining to participate in the UN action, giving as the reason the failure of the Security Council to check 'the aggression of Zionism.'[6]

The Indian delegate, who had also been unable to vote due to lack of instructions, told the Security Council on 30 June:

They [the Indian Government] are opposed to any attempt to settle international disputes by resort to aggression. For this reason Sir Benegal N. Rau, on behalf of the Government of India, voted in favour of the first resolution of the Security Council. The halting of aggression and the quick restoration of peaceful conditions are essential preludes to a satisfactory settlement. The Government of India therefore also accept the second resolution of the Security Council. This decision of the Government of India does not, however, involve any modification of their foreign policy. This policy is based on the promotion of world peace and the development of friendly relations with all countries. . . .   [SCOR, 5th yr, 475th mtg, pp. 2–3.]

This approval did not, however, lead to Indian participation in the UN forces. Later, India was to play a prominent mediatory role between North Korea and China on the one hand and the UN on the other over the matter of exchanging prisoners of war.

At the 476th meeting of the Security Council on 7 July, the United Kingdom presented a joint UK–France draft resolution, which provided for a Unified Command over Korean operations, under the direction of the United States:

The Security Council,
Having determined that the armed attack upon the Republic of Korea by forces from North Korea constitutes a breach of the peace,
Having recommended that Members of the United Nations furnish such assistance to the Republic of Korea as may be necessary to repel the armed attack and to restore international peace and security in the area,
1. Welcomes the prompt and vigorous support which governments and peoples of the United Nations have given to its resolutions of 25 and 27 June 1950 to assist the Republic of Korea in defending itself against armed attack and thus to restore international peace and security in the area;
2. Notes that Members of the United Nations have transmitted to the United Nations offers of assistance for the Republic of Korea;
3. Recommends that all Members providing military forces and other assistance pursuant to the aforesaid Security Council resolutions make such forces and other assistance available to a unified command under the United States;
4. Requests the United States to designate the commander of such forces;

[5] Ibid. 475th mtg, p. 13.
[6] For further details see below p. 198 As a historical note, it may also be recalled that this was the first time that Sir Gladwyn Jebb sat as the UK representative on the Security Council. He expressed his disappointment at Egypt's decision and the reasons given for it, though he conceded that as the resolution was only a recommendation, Egypt was free to make this decision if she so chose.

5. *Authorizes* the unified command at its discretion to use the United Nations flag in the course of operations against North Korean forces concurrently with the flags of the various nations participating;

6. *Requests* the United States to provide the Security Council with reports as appropriate on the course of action taken under the unified command.   [*SC res. S/1588.*]

VOTING: 7–0 with 3 abstentions and 1 absence.
In favour: China, Cuba, Ecuador, France, Norway, UK, USA.
Against: None.
Abstaining: Egypt, India, Yugoslavia.
Absent: USSR.

No formal explanation of their votes was given by Egypt, India, or Yugoslavia.

On 27 July 1950 the permanent representative of the USSR, who had been absent from the meetings of the Security Council since 13 January, announced that, in accordance with the established procedure of the alphabetical rotation of the Security Council presidency each month, he was assuming the Council presidency in August. He called a meeting for 1 August. At the 480th meeting on 1 August the President, the representative of the USSR, ruled that 'the representative of the Kuomintang group present at the Council table' was not the representative of China, and could therefore not participate. India and Yugoslavia indicated their support for such a ruling, though the United Kingdom, France, Egypt, Cuba, and Ecuador all insisted that such a ruling went beyond the President's competence. A proposal to overrule the President's ruling was adopted by 8 to 3 (India, USSR, Yugoslavia).

From the beginning of August to 7 September three new draft resolutions were considered by the Council: S/1653, proposed by the United States, would have condemned the North Korean authorities and called upon states to refrain from assistance to North Korea, and from any action which might cause the conflict to spread; S/1668, submitted by the USSR, would have the Security Council end hostilities and call for the withdrawal from Korea of all foreign troops; and S/1679, also submitted by the USSR, would support North Korean charges of wanton bombing of North Korean villages by the United States. None of these resolutions was accepted, the USSR cast a negative vote in the case of S/1653, and the Soviet resolutions failed to command a majority. A further Soviet draft resolution on 26 September, S/1812, also failed to be adopted. It alleged mass exterminations of civilians by the USA, and would have designated such actions a flagrant violation of international law.[7] Later in the year the USSR also complained that the United States had been violating Chinese air space, but vetoed an American proposal for a commission of investigation.[8]

It had thus become clear, during the autumn of 1950, that the Security Council was incapable, because of deadlock between the permanent members, of fulfilling its responsibility for the maintenance of peace. On 3 November 1950 the controversial 'Uniting for Peace' resolution was passed by the General Assembly. The constitutional aspects of this are beyond the immediate scope of

---

[7] For details of these charges, see below, pp. 187–9.   [8] See below, p. 188.

this study;[9] we shall here merely note that its effect was to transfer to the Assembly authority to make certain recommendations when the Security Council was unable to carry out its responsibilities. It was through this resolution (377 (V)) that the initiative passed to the General Assembly—though the Unified Command had already been established by the Security Council. The relevant sections of the 'Uniting for Peace' resolution are reproduced below:

The General Assembly, . . .

A

1. *Resolves* that if the Security Council, because of lack of unanimity of the permanent members, fails to exercise its primary responsibility for the maintenance of international peace and security in any case where there appears to be a threat to the peace, breach of the peace, or act of aggression, the General Assembly shall consider the matter immediately with a view to making appropriate recommendations to Members for collective measures, including in the case of a breach of the peace or act of aggression the use of armed force when necessary, to maintain or restore international peace and security. If not in session at the time, the General Assembly may meet in emergency special session within twenty-four hours of the request therefor. Such emergency special session shall be called if requested by the Security Council on the vote of any seven members, or by a majority of the Members of the United Nations;

2. *Adopts* for this purpose the amendments to its rules of procedure set forth in the annex to the present resolution. . . . [*GA res. 377 (V), 3 Nov. 1950.*]

The Assembly had, of course, long been seized of the overall problem of Korean independence and on 7 October 1950, it passed a major resolution on certain aspects of the Korean situation:

The General Assembly,

Having regard to its resolutions of 14 November 1947 (112 (II)), of 12 December 1948 (195(III)) and of 21 October 1949 (293 (IV)),

Having received and considered the report of the United Nations Commission on Korea,

Mindful of the fact that the objectives set forth in the resolutions referred to above have not been fully accomplished and, in particular, that the unification of Korea has not yet been achieved, and that an attempt has been made by an armed attack from North Korea to extinguish by force the Government of the Republic of Korea,

Recalling the General Assembly declaration of 12 December 1948 that there has been established a lawful government (the Government of the Republic of Korea) having effective control and jurisdiction over that part of Korea where the United Nations Temporary Commission on Korea was able to observe and consult and in which the great majority of the people of Korea reside; that this government is based on elections which were a valid expression of the free will of the electorate of that part of Korea and which were observed by the Temporary Commission; and that this is the only such government in Korea.

Having in mind that United Nations armed forces are at present operating in Korea in accordance with the recommendations of the Security Council of 27 June 1950, subsequent to its resolution of 25 June 1950, that Members of the United Nations furnish such assistance to the Republic of Korea as may be necessary to repel the armed attack and to restore international peace and security in the area,

---

[9] But see, e.g. Andrassy, 'Uniting for Peace', 50 *AJIL* (1956), 574; H. Kelsen, *Recent Trends in the Law of the United Nations* (1951), pp. 978 ff; Goodrich, 'Development of the General Assembly', *Int. Conciliation* Pamphlet 471 (1951); F. Seyersted, *United Nations Forces in the Law of War and Peace* (1966), pp. 440–41; J. Stone, *Aggression and World Order* (1958), p. 193; D. W. Bowett, *United Nations Forces* (1964), pp. 290–8.

Recalling that the essential objective of the resolutions of the General Assembly referred to above was the establishment of a unified, independent and democratic Government of Korea,

1. *Recommends that*

(*a*) All appropriate steps be taken to ensure conditions of stability throughout Korea;

(*b*) All constituent acts be taken, including the holding of elections, under the auspices of the United Nations, for the establishment of a unified, independent and democratic government in the sovereign State of Korea;

(*c*) All sections and representative bodies of the population of Korea, South and North, be invited to co-operate with the organs of the United Nations in the restoration of peace, in the holding of elections and in the establishment of a unified government;

(*d*) United Nations forces should not remain in any part of Korea otherwise than so far as necessary for achieving the objectives specified in sub-paragraphs (*a*) and (*b*) above;

(*e*) All necessary measures be taken to accomplish the economic rehabilitation of Korea;

2. *Resolves* that

(*a*) A Commission consisting of Australia, Chile, Netherlands, Pakistan, Philippines, Thailand and Turkey, to be known as the United Nations Commission for the Unification and Rehabilitation of Korea, be established to (i) assume the functions hitherto exercised by the present United Nations Commission on Korea; (ii) represent the United Nations in bringing about the establishment of a unified, independent and democratic government of all Korea; (iii) exercise such responsibilities in connexion with relief and rehabilitation in Korea as may be determined by the General Assembly after receiving the recommendations of the Economic and Social Council. The United Nations Commission for the Unification and Rehabilitation of Korea should proceed to Korea and begin to carry out its functions as soon as possible;

(*b*) Pending the arrival in Korea of the United Nations Commission for the Unification and Rehabilitation of Korea, the governments of the States represented on the Commission should form an Interim Committee composed of representatives meeting at the seat of the United Nations to consult with and advise the United Nations Unified Command in the light of the above recommendations; the Interim Committee should begun to function immediately upon the approval of the present resolution by the General Assembly;

(*c*) The Commission shall render a report to the next regular session of the General Assembly and to any prior special session which might be called to consider the subject-matter of the present resolution, and shall render such interim reports as it may deem appropriate to the Secretary-General for transmission to Members;

The General Assembly furthermore,

Mindful of the fact that at the end of the present hostilities the task of rehabilitating the Korean economy will be of great magnitude,

3. *Requests* the Economic and Social Countil, in consultation with the specialized agencies, to develop plans for relief and rehabilitation on the termination of hostilities and to report to the General Assembly within three weeks of the adoption of the present resolution by the General Assembly;

4. *Also recommends* the Economic and Social Council to expedite the study of long-term measures to promote the economic development and social progress of Korea, and meanwhile to draw the attention of the authorities which decide requests for technical assistance to the urgent and special necessity of affording such assistance to Korea;

5. *Expresses* its appreciation of the services rendered by the members of the United Nations Commission on Korea in the performance of their important and difficult task;

6. *Requests* the Secretary-General to provide the United Nations Commission for the Unification and Rehabilitation of Korea with adequate staff and facilities, including technical advisers as required; and authorizes the Secretary-General to pay the expenses and *per diem* of a representative and alternate from each of the States members of the Commission.

[*GA res. 376 (V), GAOR, 5th sess., suppl. 20.*]

VOTING: 47–5, with 7 abstentions.
 In favour: 47.
  Against: 5.
Abstaining: 7.
  (*Note:* The Assembly records do not identify those states abstaining.)

By the beginning of December it was necessary for the Assembly to consider the problems raised by China's entry into the war in support of North Korea. The First Committee of the Assembly produced an Interim Report (A/1717) containing the text of a resolution which had been approved after lengthy debate. This was then adopted by the General Assembly:

The General Assembly,

Viewing with grave concern the situation in the Far East,

Anxious that immediate steps should be taken to prevent the conflict in Korea spreading to other areas and to put an end to the fighting in Korea itself, and that further steps should then be taken for a peaceful settlement of existing issues in accordance with the Purposes and Principles of the United Nations,

Requests the President of the General Assembly to constitute a group of three persons, including himself, to determine the basis on which a satisfactory cease-fire in Korea can be arranged and to make recommendations to the General Assembly as soon as possible. [*GA res. 384 (V), 14 Dec. 1950.*]

VOTING: 52–5, with 1 abstention.
 In favour: Afghanistan, Argentina, Australia, Belgium, Bolivia, Brazil, Burma, Canada, Chile, Colombia, Costa Rica, Cuba, Denmark, Dominican Republic, Ecuador, Egypt, El Salvador, Ethiopia, France, Greece, Guatemala, Haiti, Honduras, Iceland, India, Indonesia, Iran, Iraq, Israel, Lebanon, Liberia, Luxembourg, Mexico, Netherlands, New Zealand, Norway, Pakistan, Panama, Paraguay, Philippines, Saudi Arabia, Sweden, Syria, Thailand, Turkey, Union of South Africa, UK, USA, Uruguay, Venezuela, Yemen, Yugoslavia.
  Against: Byelorussia, Czechoslovakia, Poland, Ukraine, USSR.
Abstaining: China.

The President of the Assembly constituted the Group on Cease Fire of the following persons: Lester Pearson (Canada); Sir Benegal Rau (India); and N. Entezam (Iran).

The Assembly also passed resolution 410 (v), 1 December 1950, dealing with relief and rehabilitation in Korea. It was this resolution which established UNKRA—the United Nations Korean Reconstruction Agency.

In February 1951, after further lengthy discussions on the report of the Group on Cease Fire and recent developments, the Assembly passed the following resolution, in which it pronounced directly upon matters relating to peace and security (and not just the independence of Korea and relief work). Clearly, it had in mind the authority bestowed upon it by the Uniting for Peace resolution of the previous November:

The General Assembly,

Noting that the Security Council, because of lack of unanimity of the permanent members, has failed to exercise its primary responsibility for the maintenance of international peace and security in regard to Chinese Communist intervention in Korea,

Noting that the Central People's Government of the People's Republic of China has not accepted United Nations proposals to bring about a cessation of hostilities in Korea with a view to peaceful settlement, and that its armed forces continue their invasion of Korea and their large-scale attacks upon United Nations forces there.

1. *Finds* that the Central People's Government of the People's Republic of China, by giving direct aid and assistance to those who were already committing aggression in Korea and by engaging in hostilities against United Nations forces there has itself engaged in aggression in Korea;

2. *Calls* upon the Central People's Government of the People's Republic of China to cause its forces and nationals in Korea to cease hostilities against the United Nations forces and to withdraw from Korea;

3. *Affirms* the determination of the United Nations to continue its action in Korea to meet the aggression;

4. *Calls upon* all States and authorities to continue to lend every assistance to the United Nations action in Korea;

5. *Calls upon* all States and authorities to refrain from giving any assistance to the aggressors in Korea;

6. *Requests* a Committee composed of the members of the Collective Measures Committee as a matter of urgency to consider additional measures to be employed to meet this aggression and to report thereon to the General Assembly, it being understood that the Committee is authorized to defer its report if the Good Offices Committee referred to in the following paragraph reports satisfactory progress in its efforts;

7. *Affirms* that it continues to be the policy of the United Nations to bring about a cessation of hostilities in Korea and the achievement of United Nations objectives in Korea by peaceful means, and requests the President of the General Assembly to designate forthwith two persons who would meet with him at any suitable opportunity to use their good offices to this end.   [*GA res. 498 (V), 1 Feb. 1951.*]

VOTING: 44-7, with 9 abstentions.
> *In favour:* Argentina, Australia, Belgium, Bolivia, Brazil, Canada, Chile, China, Colombia, Costa Rica, Cuba, Denmark, Dominican Republic, Ecuador, El Salvador, Ethiopia, France, Greece, Guatemala, Haiti, Honduras, Iceland, Iran, Iraq, Israel, Lebanon, Liberia, Luxembourg, Mexico, Netherlands, New Zealand, Nicaragua, Norway, Paraguay, Peru, Philippines, Thailand, Turkey, Union of South Africa, United Kingdom, United States, Uruguay, and Venezuela.
> *Against:* Burma, Byelorussian SSR, Czechoslovakia, India, Poland, Ukrainian SSR and the USSR.
> *Abstaining:* Afghanistan, Egypt, Indonesia, Pakistan, Saudi Arabia, Sweden, Syria, Yemen and Yugoslavia.

The Committee established under paragraph 6 became known as the Additional Measures Committee. After its report had been examined the Assembly adopted a further resolution:

The General Assembly,

Noting the report of the Additional Measures Committee dated 14 May 1951,
Recalling its resolution 498(V) of 1 February 1951,
Noting that:

(*a*) The Additional Measures Committee established by that resolution has considered additional measures to be employed to meet the aggression in Korea,

(*b*) The Additional Measures Committee has reported that a number of States have already taken measures designed to deny contributions to the military strength of the forces opposing the United Nations in Korea,

(*c*) The Additional Measures Committee has also reported that certain economic measures designed further to deny such contributions would support and supplement the military action of the United Nations in Korea and would assist in putting an end to the aggression,

1. *Recommends* that every State:

(*a*) Apply an embargo on the shipment to areas under the control of the Central People's Government of the People's Republic of China and of the North Korean authorities of arms, ammunition and implements of war, atomic energy materials, petroleum, transportation materials of strategic value, and items useful in the production of arms, ammunition and implements of war;

(*b*) Determine which commodities exported from its territory fall within the embargo, and apply controls to give effect to the embargo;

(*c*) Prevent by all means within its jurisdiction the circumvention of controls on shipments applied by other States pursuant to the present resolution;

(*d*) Co-operate with other States in carrying out the purposes of this embargo;

(*e*) Report to the Additional Measures Committee, within thirty days and thereafter at the request of the Committee, on the measures taken in accordance with the present resolution;

2. *Requests* the Additional Measures Committee:

(*a*) To report to the General Assembly, with recommendations as appropriate, on the general effectiveness of the embargo and the desirability of continuing, extending or relaxing it;

(*b*) To continue its consideration of additional measures to be employed to meet the aggression in Korea, and to report thereon further to the General Assembly, it being understood that the Committee is authorized to defer its report if the Good Offices Committee reports satisfactory progress in its efforts;

3. *Reaffirms* that it continues to be the policy of the United Nations to bring about a cessation of hostilities in Korea, and the achievement of United Nations objectives in Korea by peaceful means, and requests the Good Offices Committee to continue its good offices. [*GA res. 500 (V), 18 May 1951.*]

VOTING: 47–0, with 8 abstentions, and 5 not participating in the vote.

In favour: Argentina, Australia, Belgium, Bolivia, Brazil, Canada, Chile, China, Colombia, Costa Rica, Cuba, Denmark, Dominican Republic, Ecuador, El Salvador, Ethiopia, France, Greece, Guatemala, Haiti, Honduras, Iceland, Iran, Iraq, Israel, Lebanon, Liberia, Luxembourg, Mexico, Netherlands, New Zealand, Nicaragua, Norway, Panama, Paraguay, Peru, Philippines, Saudi Arabia, Thailand, Turkey, Union of South Africa, United Kingdom, United States, Uruguay, Venezuela, Yemen and Yugoslavia.

Against: None.

Abstaining: Afghanistan, Burma, Egypt, India, Indonesia, Pakistan, Sweden and Syria.

The Byelorussian SSR, Czechoslovakia, Poland, and Ukrainian SSR and the USSR did not participate in the voting.

The Assembly also indicated its approval of the possibility of armistice negotiations, and envisaged—not knowing how long these would drag on—the holding of a special session to consider their successful conclusion:

The General Assembly,

Desiring to facilitate to the greatest possible extent the negotiations in Panmunjon and the conclusion of an armistice in Korea, and

Wishing to avoid premature consideration of items 17 and 27 of the agenda of the present session,

I

Decides that:

(*a*) Upon notification by the Unified Command to the Security Council of the conclusion of an armistice in Korea, the Secretary-General shall convene a special session of the General Assembly at the Headquarters of the United Nations to consider the above-mentioned items; or (*b*) When other developments in Korea make desirable consideration of the above-mentioned items, the Secretary-General, acting in accordance with Article 20 of the Charter and with the rules of procedure of the General Assembly, shall convene a special session or an emergency special session of the General Assembly at the Headquarters of the United Nations;

II

Requests the Negotiating Committee for Extra-Budgetary Funds established by General Assembly resolution 571 B (VI) of 7 December 1951 to undertake negotiations regarding voluntary contributions to the programme of the United Nations Korean Reconstruction Agency for the relief and rehabilitation of Korea. [*GA res. 507 (VI), 7 Feb. 1952.*]

VOTING: 51–5, with 2 abstentions.
In favour: Afghanistan, Argentina, Australia, Belgium, Bolivia, Brazil, Burma, Canada, China, Colombia, Costa Rica, Cuba, Denmark, Dominican Republic, Ecuador, Egypt, El Salvador, Ethiopia, France, Greece, Guatemala, Haiti, Honduras, Iceland, India, Indonesia, Iran, Iraq, Israel, Lebanon, Liberia, Luxembourg, Mexico, Netherlands, New Zealand, Nicaragua, Norway, Pakistan, Panama, Paraguay, Philippines, Saudi Arabia, Sweden, Syria, Thailand, Turkey, United Kingdom, United States, Uruguay, Venezuela and Yugoslavia.
Against: Byelorussian SSR, Czechoslovakia, Poland, Ukrainian SSR, and USSR.
Abstaining: Chile and Yemen.

The Assembly also made detailed proposals in 1952 and 1953 in its resolutions on the armistice terms, and particularly on the problem of the exchange of prisoners of war. The relevant texts are reproduced in Section 12 below, which deals with the implementation of the UN's purposes in Korea. For the moment, it is sufficient to note that resolution 610 (VII) of 3 December 1952—under which the Assembly made detailed proposals for a Repatriation Commission to handle the prisoner-of-war impasse—was adopted by 54 votes to 5 (Byelorussia, Czechoslovakia, Poland, Ukraine, USSR) with 1 abstention (China). The Chinese representative indicated that his government could not approve the proposed membership of Czechoslovakia and Poland on the Repatriation Commission, as they could not be expected to carry out the terms of a resolution which they had denounced in the Assembly. The Assembly's proposals were, however, rejected.

On 11 March 1953 the Assembly adopted another resolution on relief and rehabilitation, which had been proposed by its First Committee. This resolution, 701 (VII, was approved by 55 votes to 5.

On 23 August 1953, by a vote of 51 to 5 with 4 abstentions, the Assembly passed resolution 706 (VII) which recommended the establishment of a commission to investigate charges that the UN Command was using bacteriological warfare.[10]

On 22 July 1953 came the long-awaited announcement that an Armistice Agreement had been signed in Korea.[11] A month later, the Assembly passed the following resolutions:

[10] See below, pp. 188–9.
[11] See below, p. 290.

A

IMPLEMENTATION OF PARAGRAPH 60 OF THE KOREAN ARMISTICE AGREEMENT

The General Assembly:

1. *Notes with approval* the Armistice Agreement concluded in Korea on 27 July 1953, the fact that the fighting has ceased, and that a major step has thus been taken towards the full restoration of international peace and security in the area;

2. *Reaffirms* that the objectives of the United Nations remain the achievement by peaceful means of a unified, independent and democratic Korea under a representative form of government and the full restoration of international peace and security in the area;

3. *Notes* the recommendation contained in the Armistice Agreement that 'In order to ensure the peaceful settlement of the Korean question, the military Commanders of both sides hereby recommend to the governments of the countries concerned on both sides that, within three (3) months after the Armistice Agreement is signed and becomes effective, a political conference of a higher level of both sides be held by representatives appointed respectively to settle through negotiation the questions of the withdrawal of all foreign forces from Korea, the peaceful settlement of the Korean question, etc.';

4. *Welcomes* the holding of such a conference;

5. *Recommends* that:

(*a*) The side contributing armed forces under the Unified Command in Korea shall have as participants in the conference those among the Member States contributing armed forces pursuant to the call of the United Nations which desire to be represented, together with the Republic of Korea. The participating governments shall act independently at the conference with full freedom of action and shall be bound only by decisions or agreements to which they adhere;

(*b*) The United States Government, after consultation with the other participating countries referred to in sub-paragraph (*a*) above, shall arrange with the other side for the political conference to be held as soon as possible, but not later than 28 October 1953, at a place and on a date satisfactory to both sides;

(*c*) The Secretary-General of the United Nations shall, if this is agreeable to both sides, provide the political conference with such services and facilities as may be feasible;

(*d*) The Member States participating pursuant to sub-paragraph (*a*) above shall inform the United Nations when agreement is reached at the conference and keep the United Nations informed at other appropriate times;

6. *Reaffirms* its intention to carry out its programme for relief and rehabilitation in Korea, and appeals to the governments of all Member States to contribute to this task

B

The General Assembly,

Having adopted the resolution entitled 'Implementation of paragraph 60 of the Korean Armistice Agreement',[12]

Recommends that the Union of Soviet Socialist Republics participate in the Korean political conference provided the other side desires it.

C

The General Assembly,

Requests the Secretary-General to communicate the proposals on the Korean question submitted to the resumed meetings of the seventh session and recommended by the Assembly, together with the records of the relevant proceedings of the General Assembly, to the Central People's Government of the People's Republic of China and to the Government of the

[12] i.e. 'A' above.

People's Democratic Republic of Korea and to report as appropriate. [*GA res. 711 (VII)* *28 Aug. 1953.*]

VOTING:
Resolution 711(VII) A: 43–5, with 10 abstentions; resolution 711(VII) B: 55–1, with 1 abstention; resolution 711(VII) C: 54–3, with 1 abstention.

The Assembly also adopted resolution 712 (VII):

The General Assembly,

Recalling the resolutions of the Security Council of 25 June, 27 June and 7 July 1950 and the resolutions of the General Assembly of 7 October 1950, 1 December 1950, 1 February 1951, 18 May 1951 and 3 December 1952,
   Having received the report of the Unified Command dated 7 August 1953,
   Noting with profound satisfaction that fighting has now ceased in Korea on the basis of an honourable armistice,
   1. *Salutes* the heroic soldiers of the Republic of Korea and of all those countries which sent armed forces to its assistance;
   2. *Pays tribute* to all those who died in resisting aggression and thus in upholding the cause of freedom and peace;
   3. *Expresses its satisfaction* that the first efforts pursuant to the call of the United Nations to repel armed aggression by collective military measures have been successful, and expresses its firm conviction that this proof of the effectiveness of collective security under the United Nations Charter will contribute to the maintenance of international peace and security. [*GA res. 712(VII), 28 Aug. 1953.*]

VOTING: 54–5.

3

FUNCTIONS AND MANDATE

THE FIRST resolution which the Security Council passed,[1] spoke of the need for an immediate cessation of hostilities and a withdrawal of North Korean forces to the 38th parallel. Resolution S/1511 of 27 June recommended 'that the Members of the United Nations furnish such assistance to the Republic of Korea as may be necessary to repel the armed attack and to restore international peace and security in the area.' This purpose was confirmed in paragraph 1 of resolution S/1588 of 7 July 1950, which established the Unified Command.

   While the mandate of the UN Forces was thus clear enough, some controversy did arise as to whether it envisaged the achievement of the objective of reunification by military means. The UN was, in principle, committed to the notion of a unified Korea;[2] and General MacArthur clearly thought that the

---

[1] S/1501, 25 June 1950.   [2] See above, p. 159.

UN Forces should not forfeit the military opportunity of reuniting the country. This controversy arose sharply in the context of whether he should cross the Yalu river, in order to destroy the sources of Chinese support for North Korea, and enter North Korea itself.[3] The majority view in the Assembly came to be, especially in the light of military hardship, that the purpose of the UN action was limited to repulsing the attack against South Korea and securing an honourable peace. Ultimate reunification, however, certainly remained a UN political objective, as the resolution which the Assembly passed upon the signing of the armistice treaties shows.[4]

[3] See below, pp. 178–9, where these controversies are dealt with more fully.
[4] For text, see below, pp. 290–308.

4

CONSTITUTIONAL BASIS

THE constitutional basis of the UN action in Korea has been the subject of much controversy. Argument has centred on two major factors: first, the absence of the Soviet Union from the Security Council when the three crucial resolutions of that organ were passed; and, second, the fact that the UN was in fact engaging in an enforcement action without Article 43 ever having been implemented. Both of these merit separate comment.

(a) The absence of the Soviet Union

The representative of the USSR had left the Security Council on 13 January 1950, in protest at the Chinese representation on that organ. He had announced that no decision of Council in which the Nationalist Chinese representative participated would be regarded by him as valid. He did not return to the Security Council until 1 August 1950, when under the alphabetical rotation system, the Presidency of the Security Council fell to the USSR. During this period of absence three Security Council resolutions, which were the basis of the UN action in Korea, were passed.[1]

Article 27(3) of the UN Charter states: 'Decisions of the Security Council on all other matters shall be made by an affirmative vote of seven members including the concurring votes of the permanent members. . . .' The question therefore arose as to whether the Soviet Union's absence meant that the resolutions had been illegally adopted in the absence of the concurring vote of a permanent member, within the meaning of Article 27(3). The Soviet Union stated her legal objections in the following manner:

[1] S/1501, 25 June 1950; S/1511, 27 June 1950; and S/1588, 7 July 1950. For text, see pp. 160–4.

The Soviet Union Government has received from you the text of the Security Council resolution of 27 June 1950 (*S/1511*) calling the attention of Members of the United Nations to the necessity of intervening in Korean affairs in the interests of the South Korean authorities. The Soviet Union Government notes that this resolution was adopted by six votes. the seventh vote being that of the Kuomintang representative Mr. Tingfu F. Tsiang who has no legal right to represent China, whereas the United Nations Charter requires that a Security Council resolution must be adopted by seven votes including those of the five permanent members of the Council namely the United States, the United Kingdom, France, the Union of Soviet Socialist Republics and China. As is known, moreover, the above resolution was passed in the absence of two permanent members of the Security Council, the Union of Soviet Socialist Republics and China, whereas under the United Nations Charter a decision of the Security Council on an important matter can only be made with the concurring votes of all five permanent members of the Council, viz. the United States, the United Kingdom, France, the Union of Soviet Socialist Republics and China. . . . [*S/1517, 29 June 1950, Cablegram to Secretary-General from Soviet Deputy Minister for Foreign Affairs.*]

This view received the support of the other Communist members of the UN:

Only after the announcement of its decision to intervene, the United States, abusing the authority of the United Nations, endeavoured to find a legal justification of its aggression through the approval of the United States position by the United Nations. The United States wished to receive legal cover and a justification of its actions through the resolution of the Security Council. It is well known, however, that the Security Council does not function at the present moment because, in accordance with Articles 23 and 27 of the Charter, the Security Council is constituted of eleven members, five permanent members among them. All resolutions on non-procedural matters must have the unanimous approval of the five permanent members. The so-called resolution which was communicated to the Government of Poland by the Secretary-General of the United Nations was adopted in the absence of two permanent members of the Security Council, namely, in the absence of the Union of Soviet Socialist Republics and China. [*S/1546, 30 June 1950, Letter to Secretary-General from Acting Chief of the Polish delegation.*]

Even if one believes that the Soviet Union's participation in the Security Council from 1945–50 legally prevented her from claiming in January 1950 that she would not be bound by any decisions on which the Kuomintang representative voted, or that decisions in 'China's' absence were invalid, there still does remain the very real point about compliance with Article 27(3) in Russia's own absence.

The practice had already grown up by 1950 whereby the *abstention* of a permanent member from voting was deemed still to be a 'concurring' vote within the meaning of Article 27(3); that is to say, a decision which received the support of at least seven members was not rendered legally ineffective by the abstention (as opposed to negative vote) of a permanent member. The Soviet Union herself had clearly favoured this interpretation of the legal effects on abstention, and the practice had found favour with all of the permanent members.[2]

The question now, therefore, was whether a permanent member could negate a resolution which was otherwise valid, not by abstaining when present, but by being absent from the vote. The view prevailed—and it is one with which this

[2] For examples (which have greatly grown in number since 1950) see *Repertory of Practice of the Security Council, 1946–51* (1954), pp. 170–5; *Suppl. for 1952–5* (1957), pp. 67–68; *Suppl. for 1956–8* (1959), p. 64; *Suppl. for 1959–63* (1965), p. 96.

Editor concurs—that absence must be regarded as a deliberate abstention from voting, and thus as incapable of preventing the passage of a resolution within the terms of Article 27(3). The opportunity of exercising the veto exists, and if a permanent member declines to exercise it, he cannot seek to achieve the same legal effect by absence. This is perhaps the more so, as Article 28 of the Charter prescribes that: 'The Security Council shall be so organized as to be able to function continuously. Each member of the Security Council shall, for this purpose, be represented at all times at the seat of the Organization.' A permanent member should not be able, as a result of being in breach of its duties under Article 28, to impede the work of the Council.[3]

(b) The Korean action and Chapter VII of the Charter

1. On 3 August 1950 the Soviet Union offered many legal objections to the UN action, among them the argument that the fighting in Korea was a civil war in which the UN was not entitled to intervene:

As regards the war between the North and South Koreans, it is a civil war and therefore does not come under the definition of aggression, since it is a war, not between two States, but between two parts of the Korean people temporarily split into two camps under two separate authorities.

The conflict in Korea is thus an internal conflict. Consequently rules relating to aggression are just as inapplicable to the North and South Koreans as the concept of aggression was inapplicable to the northern and southern states of America, when they were fighting a civil war for the unification of their country. [*SCOR, 5th yr, 482nd mtg*, p. 7.]

Andrei Gromyko had also said:

It is also known that the United Nations Charter envisages the intervention of the Security Council only in those cases where the matter concerns events of an international order and not of an internal character. Moreover, the Charter directly forbids the intervention of the United Nations in the domestic affairs of any State, when it is a matter of conflict between two groups of one State. Thus the Security Council, by its decision of 27 June, violated also this most important principle of the United Nations.

It follows from the aforesaid that this resolution, which the United States Government is using as a cover for its armed intervention in Korea, was illegally put through the Security Council with a gross violation of the United Nations Charter. This only became possible because the gross pressure of the United States Government on the members of the Security Council converted the United Nations into a kind of branch of the United States Department of State, into an obedient tool of the policy of the American ruling circles who acted as violators of the peace. [*S/1603, 14 July 1950.*]

The same point had been made in a Polish note of 30 June 1950 (S/1545).

Article 39 gives the Security Council the authority to determine 'a breach

---

[3] These arguments are clearly explained by the British in Cmd 8078, pp. 14–16, where the proposition is also advanced that the Soviet Union could not challenge Mr Tsiang's presence, as the validity of his credentials as the representative of China had been approved by a simple majority—the majority required under Art. 27 for procedural matters. For further legal views, see also Gross, 'Voting in the Security Council', 60 *Yale LJ* (1951), 210; M. McDougal and Gardner, 'The Veto and the Charter: an interpretation for survival', ibid. p. 258; Stone, *Legal Control of Internat. Conflict* (1954), ch. 8; L. C. Green, 'Korea and the United Nations', 4 *World Affairs* (1950), p. 427; G. D. Attia, *Les forces armées des Nations Unies en Corée et au Moyen Orient* (1963), pp. 124–32; P. Brugière, *Droit de veto* (1952), pp. 107–45; G. Day, *Le droit de veto dans l'ONU* (1952), pp. 136–8.

of the peace', but within the context of Chapter VII, it is clear that what is referred to is a breach of international peace. While a breach of international peace is perhaps most likely to flow from international hostilities, there is no inherent reason why, in particular circumstances, international peace may not be threatened by a civil war. Be that as it may, the Soviet view that Korea at that stage was one legal entity was untenable—there was a clearly defined *de facto* frontier, and two different authorities. What was at issue was an external attack by one authority upon the territory under the control of the other. It is, however, fair to observe that the Assembly, in resolution 195(III), had by implication recognized the South Korean government as the only government of Korea; but rather than dealing with the North Korean invasion of the South as a civil rebellion, it acknowledged this as an external attack. The first resolution, S/1501 of 25 June, spoke of 'the armed attack upon the Republic of Korea by forces from North Korea', but determined that 'this action constitutes a breach of the peace'. The resolution of 27 June (S/1511), while again referring to 'a breach of the peace', clearly stated that the objective was 'to restore international peace and security in the area'. This phrase was reiterated in S/1588 of 7 July 1950.

There is nothing in Chapter VII of the Charter which requires enforcement action to be taken only against recognized states or governments, or indeed only against members of the UN. The non-recognition and non-membership of North Korea was thus no legal impediment to UN action.

2. Article 43 of the Charter provides that all UN members shall make available to the Security Council 'in accordance with a special agreement or agreements' armed forces, 'in order to contribute to the maintenance of international peace and security'. This article has never been implemented, and no agreements have been concluded. Did the fact prohibit the taking of enforcement action by the Security Council? The Soviet Union and her allies have constantly argued that UN enforcement action is dependent upon the prior conclusion of Article 43.[4] However, the majority of nations have preferred the view that the other articles of the Charter which are relevant to enforcement action—Articles 39, 41, and 42—are not legally dependent on the fulfilment of Article 43. Once a finding of a threat to the peace, breach of the peace, or act of aggression has been made under Article 39, the Security Council may recommend the taking of measures mentioned in Article 41 (economic and diplomatic) and in Article 42 (military). Indeed, the wording of Article 42 is broad, leaving open the method of recruitment of UN Forces. It nowhere stipulates that the forces to be used are only those to be recruited under the method in Article 43. The legal relevance of the non-fulfilment of the agreements envisaged in Article 43 is that the Security Council cannot compel the participation of national contingents in a UN enforcement action without prior conclusion of the special agreements

[4] See e.g. *Expenses case, ICJ Rep., Pleadings, 1962*, pp. 270–2; and Conference of the 18-nation Committee on Disarmament in 1962, ENDC/PV. 55, pp. 55–56. The USSR had occasionally gone further and argued that Security Council 'police' action also requires the prior fulfilment of Art. 43, but has been much less consistent in promoting this view. For details see Bowett, *UN Forces* pp. 276–7 n. 36.

anticipated.[5] The better legal view, therefore, is that action under Articles 42 does not require the prior fulfilment of Article 43, except in so far as the Council purports to make such action obligatory on all members.

Although this is the view taken by the great majority of Western international lawyers, it was not the one advanced at the time by Sir Gladwyn Jebb on behalf of the United Kingdom. He appeared to believe that action under Article 42— even on a recommendatory basis—was not possible in the absence of Article 43 being fulfilled:

Had the Charter come fully into force and had the agreement provided for in Article 43 of the Charter been concluded, we should, of course, have proceeded differently, and the action to be taken by the Security Council to repel the armed attack would no doubt have been founded on Article 42. As it is, however, the Council can naturally act only under Article 39, which enables the Security Council to recommend what measures should be taken to restore international peace and security. [*SCOR, 5th yr, 476th mtg*, p. 3.]

This ignore the fact that those measures taken under Article 39 were in fact the very measures enumerated in Article 42. Article 39 is a legal basis for the taking of measures under Article 42, whether by recommendation or obligation (and it will be only the former so long as Article 43 is not implemented),[6] or measures under Chapter VI.

3. If one accepts that, for political reasons, and because of the non-implementation of Article 43, the Security Council could only recommend action, could such recommendations entail enforcement action? Certain lawyers, including eminent jurists in the West, are of the opinion that 'recommendations' under Article 39 are limited to those pacific measures to settle disputes enumerated in Chapter VI, because enforcement measures in Chapter VII were meant to be the result of binding 'decisions'.[7] But there is nothing in the wording of Article 39 which insists that 'recommendations' are to be limited to Chapter VI measures. Moreover, in the Advisory Opinion on *Certain Expenses of the United Nations*[8] the criteria adopted for enforcement action by the Court are that it should be directed *against* a state, and not based on its consent. The Court did not make the concept turn on whether it was authorized by a decision or recommendation.[9] Given that the action was directed *against* North Korea, it may thus be deemed enforcement action, even though taken by means of recommendation. It is also the view of this writer, for reasons given above, that it was enforcement action taken under Articles 39 and 42, although the latter is not specifically mentioned in the resolutions.

4. The Soviet Union and her allies clearly regarded this—at least in the

[5] See L. Sohn, 'The Authority of the United Nations to Establish and Maintain a Permanent Force', 52 *AJIL* (1958), 1230. Also Seyersted, 'United Nations Forces, Some Legal Problems', 37 *BYIL* (1961), 439.

[6] It is even arguable that all the non-fulfilment of Art. 43 leads to is the inability to compel *national contingents* to participate in a UN action, and that the Security Council could still make a decision under Art. 39 to set up a Force under Art. 42 by means of direct individual recruitment (Bowett, p. 278).

[7] e.g. Kelsen, pp. 932–3; Stone, p. 230.

[8] *ICJ Rep. 1962*, pp. 164–5, 167.

[9] Bowett, *UN Forces*, pp. 33–4.

earlier phases—not as UN action at all, but as action by the United States which was seeking to secure a cloak of legality. The view has found some support in the Western world[10] that the UN was not legally entitled to authorize the use of its flag, establish a UN command, or designate the United States its agent. This opinion is based on the belief that nothing is lawful unless expressly authorized by the Charter; whereas the majority of Western lawyers have preferred the view that implied powers are lawful so long as they are consistent with the general and express powers conferred upon particular organs by the Charter.[11] The International Court appears to have supported this latter perspective.[12]

Suggestions have been made, by those who do not believe that the UN was competent to authorize this action, that it was either voluntary action by members which Article 2(4) did not prohibit[13] or collective self-defence under Article 51.[14] There is obviously room for debate here, but in spite of the predominance of the American role, the participating nations did regard their action as falling within an authorization by the Security Council, and not as mere individual action or self-defence. This Editor therefore believes that, while the action in Korea was undoubtedly *sui generis*, it may properly be described as enforcement action recommended by the Security Council under Articles 39 and 42, the command of which was delegated to the United States as agent of the UN.

5

POLITICAL CONTROL

THE Unified Command was established at the request of the Security Council, and may thus be seen as the agent of the UN. So far as military and strategic authority was concerned, control lay virtually exclusively with the United States, under whom the Unified Command had been formed (see below, pp. 195–7). Even in political matters the Unified Command retained a very considerable latitude, though here there was a somewhat greater interplay with the UN Secretariat, Security Council, and General Assembly. In the military

[10] e.g. Kelsen, pp. 936–8.

[11] Bowett, *UN Forces*, p. 33.

[12] '. . . when the Organization takes action which warrants the assertion that it was inappropriate for the fulfilment of one of the stated purposes of the United Nations, the presumption is that such action is not *ultra vires* the Organization' (*Expenses Case, ICJ Rep. 1962*, p. 168).

[13] Art. 2 (4) provides that members 'shall refrain in their international relations from the threat or use of force against the territorial integrity or political independence of any state, or in any other manner inconsistent with the Purposes of the United Nations'.

[14] Bowett, who believes that collective self-defence may be exercised only by those sharing a genuine geographic or economic community of interest, does not accept this: see Bowett, *UN Forces*, p. 34 and his *Self-Defence in International Law* (1958), pp. 215–18.

field, the control of the United States government was complete; in the political field consultations with the UN and some contributing members were more frequent. On occasion the UN made various recommendations. In the final analysis, however, a large range of political decisions was taken by the United States government, as the Unified Command.

The Secretary-General had proposed, on 3 July 1950, a Committee on Co-ordination for the Assistance of Korea, to be composed of the Republic of Korea and the contributing states. This suggestion—which apparently found favour with the United Kingdom, France, and Norway—was rejected by the United States.[1] General MacArthur clearly took the view that the Unified Command had been given a mandate by the UN to run the campaign, and that it was not subject to day-to-day direction from the UN. He subsequently stated: 'my encounter with the United Nations was largely nominal . . . I had no direct connection with the United Nations whatsoever.'[2]

Once it was established that a subsidiary committee was unacceptable to the United States, it became inevitable that political control would effectively lie with the United States government, because there was no other UN organ suitable for the task of political directives. This situation necessarily flowed from the Charter intention that collective UN action against a particular state be taken by the joint consent of the permanent members. Once the Soviet Union returned to the Security Council, that organ became clearly incapable of discussing 'even those broad policy questions which presupposed an intimate knowledge of the military situation and advance military planning'.[3] The Assembly contained representatives of all the Communist states, and was in any event too cumbersome a body for such a task.

The Secretary-General appointed a liaison officer to the UN Command; and the United States made regular reports to the Security Council in accordance with paragraph 6 of Security Council resolution S/1588 of 7 July 1950.[4] The United States used this practice to provide information, rather than to seek political guidance. Indeed, it has been observed that the Secretary-General had difficulty in ensuring that the Security Council received these reports before they were released to the press.[5] They were also subject to censorship in Washington before they reached the Security Council.[6]

It is possible to identify some five major political issues. In each of these the balance struck between the UN and the United States differed.

1. The broad political aims of the war

The initial Security Council resolution (S/1501) called for 'the authorities of North Korea to withdraw forthwith their armed forces to the 38th parallel'.

---

[1] Trygve Lie, *In the Cause of Peace* (1954), p. 334.

[2] *Military Situation in the Far East*, Hearings before the Senate Committee on Armed Services and Foreign Relations, US Senate, 82nd Cong., 1st sess. (1951), pt. 3, p. 1937.

[3] Bowett, *UN Forces*, p. 41.

[4] See above, p. 163–4.

[5] Bowett, p. 42 n. 59, citing Lie, p. 334.

[6] *Military Situation in the Far East*, pt. 1, p. 11.

In resolution S/1511 it then recommended that assistance be given 'to repel the armed attack and to restore international peace and security in the area'. However, on 7 October 1950 the General Assembly passed resolution 376(V), recommending that 'all constituent acts be taken, including the holding of elections, under the auspices of the United Nations, for the establishment of a unified, independent and democratic government in the sovereign State of Korea'. This uncovered a basic dilemma: was the aim of the UN action in Korea limited to the restoration of the *status quo* on 23 June 1950; or was it to be used to achieve the original objectives of the UN in 1947—namely, a united, democratic Korea?[7] The general view appears to be that the Assembly's resolution was an oblique endorsement of the decision already taken by the Unified Command, on 1 September 1950, to cross the 38th parallel.[8]

2. The Chinese intervention in the war

By 5 November 1950 the Unified Command reported the participation in battle of Chinese Communist military units. During the preceding period China had made claims of bombing raids upon her territory, and had made it clear that she regarded this as a major threat to her security.[9] The entry of the Chinese military—originally described as volunteers—into the conflict presented a series of acute political problems, including whether to engage in hot pursuit of aircraft across the Manchurian border, whether to bomb the bridges on the Yalu, and whether to impose an economic and military blockade on China. The General Assembly, on 1 February 1951, adopted resolution 498(V), under which it found that the People's Republic of China had 'engaged in aggression in Korea'. The resolution also established a committee composed of the members of the Collective Measures Committee[10] to consider additional measures necessary to meet the aggression; and requested the President of the Assembly to appoint two persons to meet with him to use their good offices to bring about a cessation of hostilities. Sven Grafstrom (Sweden) and Dr Padilla Nervo (Mexico) joined the President in this political task.[11]

A five-member sub-committee of the Additional Measures Committee was set up on 8 March 1951, consisting of the United States, the United Kingdom, France, Australia, and Venezuela. The draft resolution which it presented to the Assembly was one which had been presented by the United States. On 18 May 1951 the General Assembly noted the report of the Additional Measures Committee, and recommended that every state:

---

[7] For a more detailed discussion see s. 3 above.

[8] This interpretation of the significance of the Assembly's resolution (which does not, of course, necessarily entail the view that the decision to cross the 38th parallel was a wise one) is shared by Lie, p. 345; Goodrich, *Korea*, pp. 142–3; and MacArthur, *Military Situation in the Far East*, pt. 1, p. 245.

[9] For details, see below, s. 10, pp. 226–30.

[10] Australia, Belgium, Brazil, Burma, Canada, Egypt, France, Mexico, Philippines, Turkey, UK, USA, Venezuela, and Yugoslavia. The Collective Measures Committee had been established under the Uniting for Peace resolution. When the Additional Measures Committee held its first meeting on 16 Feb. 1951, Burma and Yugoslavia declined to participate in its work.

[11] A/1779, 19 Feb. 1951. This group followed upon the three-man group set up by General Assembly res. 384 (V), 14 Dec. 1950, to explore the possibility of a cease-fire. See below, pp. 166–7.

(*a*) Apply an embargo on the shipment to areas under the control of the Central People's Government of the People's Republic of China and of the North Korean authorities of arms, ammunition and implements of war, atomic energy materials, petroleum, transportation materials of strategic value, and items useful in the production of arms, ammunition and implements of war;

(*b*) Determine which commodities exported from its territory fall within the embargo, and apply controls to give effect to the embargo;

(*c*) Prevent by all means within its jurisdiction the circumvention of controls on shipments applied by other states pursuant to the present resolution;

(*d*) Co-operate with other States in carrying out the purposes of this embargo;

(*e*) Report to the Additional Measures Committee, within thirty days and thereafter at the request of the Committee, on the measures taken in accordance with the present resolution. . . . [*GA res. 500 (V), 18 May 1951.*]

The operative part of the resolution was adopted by 46 votes to nil, with eight abstentions. With the exception of Yugoslavia (which voted in favour) the Communist countries did not participate in the voting, stating that proposals for an embargo clearly fell within Chapter VII, and as such were reserved solely to the Security Council.

The Assembly did not, however, pass upon the question of hot pursuit across the Manchurian border: it would seem that discussions on the political implications of this were held between the United States and six of the contributing states.[12] The negative response of the six nations consulted was accepted by the United States.

The determination that General MacArthur had, verbally at least, gone beyond his authority, and the decision to relieve him of his post in April 1951, was taken by President Truman alone, without reference to the General Assembly.

3. Cease-fire and Armistice negotiations

Under General Assembly resolution 384(V), a three-man Group on Cease-Fire was established. It consisted of Lester Pearson of Canada, N. Entezam of Iran, and Sir Benegal Rau of India. Its task was 'to determine the basis on which a satisfactory cease-fire in Korea can be arranged and to make recommendations to the General Assembly'. This Group decided to associate the Secretary-General directly with its work. It was, however, able to achieve little, as its report of 2 January 1951 revealed:

The report stated that, as a first step, it had consulted the representatives of the Unified Command as to what they considered to be a satisfactory basis for a cease-fire. The suggestions which had emerged from this consultation could be summarized as follows:

(1) All Governments and authorities concerned, including the Central People's Government of the People's Republic of China and the North Korean authorities, should order and enforce a cessation of all acts of armed force in Korea. The cease-fire should apply to all of Korea.

(2) There should be established across Korea a demilitarized area of approximately twenty miles in depth, with the southern limit following generally the line of the 38th parallel.

(3) The cease-fire should be supervised by a United Nations commission, whose members and designated observers should have free and unlimited access to the whole of Korea.

(4) All Governments and authorities should cease promptly the introduction into Korea of

---

[12] *Military Situation in the Far East*, pt. 3, p. 1723; and Bowett, *UN Forces*, p. 43 n. 64.

any reinforcement or replacement units or personnel, including volunteers, and additional war equipment and material.

(5) Appropriate provision should be made in the cease-fire arrangements in regard to steps to ensure the security of the forces, the movement of refugees, and the handling of other specific problems arising out of the cease-fire.

(6) The General Assembly should be asked to confirm the cease-fire arrangements, which should continue in effect until superseded by further steps approved by the United Nations.

The Group then had attempted to consult the Central People's Government of the People's Republic of China and, for that purpose, had sent a message to that Government's representative in New York and repeated it by cable to the Minister for Foreign Affairs in Peking. The message stressed that, in the interests of stopping the fighting in Korea and of facilitating a just settlement of the issues there in accordance with the principles of the Charter, the Group was prepared to discuss cease-fire arrangements with the Government of the People's Republic of China or its representatives either in New York or elsewhere, as would be mutually convenient.

On 16 December, the Group requested the Central People's Government to instruct its representative in New York to stay there and to discuss with the Group the possibility of arranging a cease-fire. In its reply, on 21 December, the Government of the People's Republic of China had recalled that its representative had neither participated in or agreed to the adoption of the General Assembly resolution establishing the Group. The Central People's Government had repeatedly declared that it would regard as illegal and null and void all resolutions on major problems, especially regarding Asia, which might be adopted by the United Nations without the participation and approval of duly appointed representatives of the People's Republic of China. After the Security Council had unreasonably voted against the question 'Complaint of armed invasion of Taiwan (Formosa)' raised by the Government of the People's Republic of China, that Government had instructed its representatives to remain in New York for participation in the discussion of the question 'Complaint by the Union of Soviet Socialist Republics regarding aggression against China by the United States of America'. However, he had still not been given the opportunity to speak. Under those circumstances, the Central People's Government deemed that there was no further necessity for its representatives to remain in New York.

On 19 December, acting on a recommendation from the sponsors of the twelve-Power draft resolution, the Group had sent another message to the Minister for Foreign Affairs of the People's Republic of China, which was intended to remove any possible misunderstandings which might have arisen out of the separation of the twelve-Power draft resolution from the thirteen-Power resolution adopted by the Assembly on 14 December. The message stressed that the Group's clear understanding and also that of the twelve Asian sponsors was that, once a cease-fire arrangement had been achieved, the negotiations envisaged in the twelve-Power draft resolution should be proceeded with at once, and that the Government of the People's Republic of China should be included in the Negotiating Committee referred to in that draft resolution.

On 23 December, the President of the General Assembly, in his capacity as such, had received from the Minister for Foreign Affairs of the People's Republic of China the text of a statement issued by the Government in Peking on 22 December, in which it was noted that that Government, from the very beginning of hostilities in Korea, had stood for the peaceful settlement and localization of the Korean problem. However, the United States Government had not only rejected the proposals made by his Government and by the USSR for the peaceful settlement of the problem, but had rejected negotiations on the question. The statement then reiterated the basic views on the problems involved, as set forth in the Security Council by the representative of the People's Republic of China and in that organ, as well as in the General Assembly, by the representative of the USSR. In conclusion, the statement held that if the Asian and Arab nations wished to achieve genuine peace, they must free themselves from United States pressure, no longer make use of the Group on Cease Fire and give up the idea of achieving a cease-fire first and negotiations afterwards. The Central People's Government of the People's Republic of China insisted that, as a basis for negotiating a peaceful settlement of the Korean problem, all foreign troops must be withdrawn from the peninsula, Korea's domestic affairs must be settled by the Korean people themselves, the American aggression forces must be withdrawn from Taiwan and the representative of the People's Republic of China must obtain a legitimate status in the United Nations.

The Group concluded its report by stating that, in those circumstances, it regretted that it had been unable to pursue the discussion of a satisfactory cease-fire arrangement and, therefore, felt that it could not usefully make any recommendation in regard to a cease-fire for the time being. [*YBUN, 1950*, pp. 250–1.][13]

In June of the next year, however, moves were made by both sides towards truce negotiations, and the conduct of these was left very much in the hands of the Unified Command. On 23 June the Soviet representative to the UN had suggested that a start could be made by discussions for a cease-fire and armistice providing for mutual withdrawal to the 38th parallel.[14] The Commander-in-Chief reported to the Assembly that 'the United Nations Command repeatedly broadcast to the Commander-in-Chief of the Communist forces in Korea a a proposal that accredited representatives of each command meet on the Danish hospital ship *Jutlandia* off the coast of Wonsan for the purpose of negotiating a cease-fire agreement'.[15]

The decision to approach the North Koreans and Chinese with proposals for talks was taken by the United States, which acted after consultations with the contributing states, but under no directive from the General Assembly. It appears that the scope of her authority in this matter was examined in an unpublished legal memorandum prepared for Secretary-General Lie by his Legal Adviser.[16] The United States regarded it as appropriate to refer the matter to the Assembly for discussion and approval, after truce negotiations were complete.[17]

After some further exchanges between the military a meeting at Kaesong was arranged for 10 July. After various setbacks—including the breaking off of the talks for a period—agreement was reached at the end of November on a demilitarized zone.[18] This agreement was regarded as a purely military one, and was not submitted to the Assembly for confirmation. The negotiations now proceeded to the ensuing items on the agenda—concrete arrangements for an armistice, and arrangements relating to prisoners of war. The negotiations were

---

[13] Group on Cease-Fire, *Report*, A/C.1/643; and *Suppl. Report*, A/C.1/645.

[14] For further details of the negotiations, see below, pp. 263–73.

[15] S/2265, 28 July 1951, 24th Report of UN Command in Korea.

[16] Goodrich (*Korea*, pp. 183–4) says that the memorandum made the following points: '(1) that the United States had the right to conclude a cease-fire or armistice without any additional authorization or instruction from the Security Council or the General Assembly; (2) that this right was restricted to military matters, negotiations on political questions requiring further decisions by the Security Council or the General Assembly; (3) that any cease-fire or armistice must be reported to the Security Council which vested the Unified Command in the United States; and (4) that the "Committee of 16" in Washington, consisting of the United States and fifteen other Members having armed forces in Korea, had a consultative status vis-à-vis the United States but not the status of a United Nations Organ.'

[17] Ibid. p. 184, drawn from a report in the *NY Times*, 30 June, 1951.

[18] For details of the negotiations including the text of the Agreement, see below, s. 12, pp. 281–308.

7*

carried out, on the UN side, by Vice-Admiral Joy, US Navy; Major-General Craigie, US Air Force; Major-General Hodes, US Eighth Army; Rear-Admiral Burke, US Navy; and Major-General Park San Yup, Republic of Korea Army. The UN was not represented by any Secretariat personnel; nor were the fifteen other contributing nations consulted on instructions to be given to the delegation. Responsibility for final decisions regarding positions to be taken in the course of cease-fire negotiations rested with the US government. The UN delegation received its instructions from General Ridgway (and reported to him), and he in turn was responsible to the Joint Chiefs of Staff in Washington.[19]

4. The prisoners-of-war issue in the Armistice negotiations

In one particular matter, however, the General Assembly did contribute its clear views. The question of the return of prisoners of war was one of three matters which held up progress, for months on end, towards an armistice.[20] The Communist side insisted that all prisoners of war should be returned, while the Unified Command rested on the principle that repatriation must be voluntary:

. . . the United Nations Command delegation has stated that all prisoners of war must be released, but that only those should be repatriated or turned over to the other side who can be delivered without the application of force. Your side has opposed this principle, and has instead insisted that certain prisoners of war must be repatriated even if physical force is necessary, asserting that to accord respect to the feelings of the individual prisoner is unprecedented and deprives a prisoner of war of his rights. Your current attitude on this question is inconsistent with the historical facts that during the Korean War your side has followed the practice of inducing captured personnel into your armed forces, and that you have in this and other ways disposed of approximately four-fifths of the military personnel of our side who fell into your custody.

The United Nations Command holds as prisoners of war 116,000 North Koreans and Chinese People's Volunteers; 59,000 or more than 50 per cent of this number held by our side, will return to your side without being forced. In addition, some 11,000 citizens of the Republic of Korea, now in our custody, have elected to go to your side under the principle of free choice. This is in marked contrast to the 12,000 captured personnel of our side whom you have stated you will repatriate, a figure which is less than 20 per cent of those who have admitted having taken into your custody.

The foregoing figures are now a basic factor in the prisoner-of-war question. It was with the full concurrence of your side that the prisoners of war in our custody were screened to determine their attitude as regards repatriation. Once screened, prisoners of war had to be segregated in accordance with their individual determination. No action can now be taken by either side to alter materially this situation. It is an accomplished fact. For you to pretend otherwise would be completely unrealistic.

Moreover, our side has indicated our willingness to send to your side any prisoners of war who may change their views on repatriation between the time of the initial determination and the completion of the exchange of prisoners of war. We have also informed you that, if you wish, you may verify the results of our screening processes after the armistice is signed. Your side can at that time interview those persons held by the United Nations Command who have indicated that they would violently oppose being returned to your side. If any indicate that they are not still so opposed, the United Nations Command will return them promptly to your side. [S/2715, 23 July 1952, 45th Report of UN Command in Korea, p. 16.]

[19] Goodrich, Korea, p. 185.
[20] For the other matters see s. 12 below, pp. 270–1.

It was made clear that prisoners were screened privately, by skilled persons, and were warned against discussing their decision. The screening process, the UN Command explained, was aimed at persuading prisoners to return to North Korea or China, and not to remain in Korea. Only if a prisoner insisted that he would forcibly resist repatriation, by fighting or committing suicide, was he not designated for repatriation. The Soviet Union, presenting in the UN the views of China and North Korea, insisted that the UN stand was contrary to the Geneva Convention of 1949, Article 118 of which provided that prisoners of war should be released and repatriated without delay after the cessation of hostilities.

The retort of the UN Command was that this provision was intended to protect the prisoners of war and was based on the assumption that they would wish to be repatriated. It was also pointed out that Article 118 envisaged the 'release' of prisoners before their repatriation, and that forcible repatriation would run counter to this. The Communist nations pointed in turn to Article 7 of the Geneva Convention which declared that 'prisoners of war may in no circumstances renounce in part or in entirety the rights secured to them by the present convention and by the special agreements referred to in the foregoing Article, if such there be'. The Unified Command insisted that the purpose of this article was to prevent undue pressure by the detaining state, not to compel an unwilling prisoner to return to his own country.

The Soviet Union pointed to incidents and riots in various prisoner-of-war camps as evidence of the appalling conditions there, and claimed that no real choice could be exercised by prisoners who found themselves in these conditions. The United States replied that the incidents had been deliberately fomented by Communist agents to divert attention from the fact that vast numbers of prisoners did not wish to be repatriated to the North.

A very detailed debate took place in the Assembly on this issue.[21] The United States then joined with twenty-one Powers in presenting a resolution on this subject, which would have the Assembly confirm the principle of non-forcible repatriation.[22]

The Assembly accordingly adopted the following resolution:

The General Assembly,

Having received the special report of the United Nations Command of 18 October 1952 on 'the present status of the military action and the armistice negotiations in Korea' and other relevant reports relating to Korea,

Noting with approval the considerable progress towards an armistice made by negotiation at Panmunjom and the tentative agreements to end the fighting in Korea and to reach a settlement of the Korean question,

Noting further that disagreement between the parties on one remaining issue, alone, prevents the conclusion of an armistice and that a considerable measure of agreement already exists on the principles on which this remaining issue can be resolved,

[21] *GAOR*, 7th sess., 1st Cttee, mtgs 510–36.
[22] The issue was before the Assembly in concrete terms, as Art. 51 of the draft armistice agreement was open to interpretation. See below, pp. 298–9.

Mindful of the continuing and vast loss of life, devastation and suffering resulting from and accompanying the continuance of the fighting,

Deeply conscious of the need to bring hostilities to a speedy end and of the need for a peaceful settlement of the Korean question,

Anxious to expedite and facilitate the convening of the political conference as provided in article 60 of the draft armistice agreement,

1. *Affirms* that the release and repatriation of prisoners of war shall be effected in accordance with the Geneva Convention relative to the Treatment of Prisoners of War, dated 12 August 1949, the well-established principles and practice of international law and the relevant provisions of the draft armistice agreement;

2. *Affirms* that force shall not be used against prisoners of war to prevent or effect their return to their homelands, and that they shall at all time be treated humanely in accordance with the specific provisions of the Geneva Convention and with the general spirit of the Convention;

3. *Accordingly requests* the President of the General Assembly to communicate the following proposals to the Central People's Government of the People's Republic of China and to the North Korean authorities as forming a just and reasonable basis for an agreement so that an immediate cease-fire would result and be effected; to invite their acceptance of these proposals and to make a report to the General Assembly during its present session and as soon as appropriate:

PROPOSALS

I. In order to facilitate the return to their homelands of all prisoners of war, there shall be established a Repatriation Commission consisting of representatives of Czechoslovakia, Poland, Sweden and Switzerland, that is, the four States agreed to for the constitution of the Neutral Nations Supervisory Commission and referred to in paragraph 37 of the draft armistice agreement, or constituted, alternatively, of representatives of four States not participating in hostilities, two nominated by each side, but excluding representatives of States that are permanent members of the Security Council.

II. The release and repatriation of prisoners of war shall be effected in accordance with the Geneva Convention relative to the Treatment of Prisoners of War, dated 12 August 1949, the well-established principles and practice of International Law and the relevant provisions of the draft armistice agreement.

III. Force shall not be used against the prisoners of war to prevent or effect their return to their homelands and no violence to their persons or affront to their dignity or self-respect shall be permitted in any manner or for any purpose whatsoever. This duty is enjoined on and entrusted to the Repatriation Commission and each of its members. Prisoners of war shall at all times be treated humanely in accordance with the specific provisions of the Geneva Convention and with the general spirit of that Convention.

IV. All prisoners of war shall be released to the Repatriation Commission from military control and from the custody of the detaining side in agreed numbers and at agreed exchange points in agreed demilitarized zones.

V. Classification of prisoners of war according to nationality and domicile as proposed in the letter of 16 October 1952 from General Kim Il Sung, Supreme Commander of the Korean People's Army, and General Peng Teh-huai, Commander of the Chinese People's Volunteers, to General Mark W. Clark, Commander-in-Chief, United Nations Command, shall then be carried out immediately,

VI. After classification, prisoners of war shall be free to return to their homelands forthwith, and their speedy return shall be facilitated by all parties concerned.

VII. In accordance with arrangements prescribed for the purpose by the Repatriation Commission, each party to the conflict shall have freedom and facilities to explain to the prisoners of war 'depending upon them' their rights and to inform the prisoners of war on any matter relating to their return to their homelands and particularly their full freedom to return.

VIII. Red Cross teams of both sides shall assist the Repatriation Commission in its work and shall have access, in accordance with the terms of the draft armistice agreement, to prisoners of war while they are under the temporary jurisdiction of the Repatriation Commission.

IX. Prisoners of war shall have freedom and facilities to make representations and communications to the Repatriation Commission and to bodies and agencies working under the Repatriation Commission, and to inform any or all such bodies of their desires on any matter concerning themselves, in accordance with arrangements made for the purpose by the Commission.

X. Notwithstanding the provisions of paragraph III above, nothing in this Repatriation Agreement shall be construed as derogating from the authority of the Repatriation Commission (or its authorized representatives) to exercise its legitimate functions and responsibilities for the control of the prisoners under its temporary jurisdiction.

XI. The terms of this Repatriation Agreement and the arrangements arising therefrom shall be made known to all prisoners of war.

XII. The Repatriation Commission is entitled to call upon parties to the conflict, its own member governments, or the Member States of the United Nations for such legitimate assistance as it may require in the carrying out of its duties and tasks and in accordance with the decisions of the Commission in this respect.

XIII. When the two sides have made an agreement for repatriation based on these proposals, the interpretation of that agreement shall rest with the Repatriation Commission. In the event of disagreement in the Commission, majority decisions shall prevail. When no majority decision is possible, an umpire agreed upon in accordance with the succeeding paragraph and with article 132 of the Geneva Convention of 1949 shall have the deciding vote.

XIV. The Repatriation Commission shall at its first meeting and prior to an armistice proceed to agree upon and appoint the umpire who shall at all times be available to the Commission and shall act as its Chairman unless otherwise agreed. If agreement on the appointment of the umpire cannot be reached by the Commission within the period of three weeks after the date of the first meeting this matter should be referred to the General Assembly.

XV. The Repatriation Commission shall also arrange after the armistice for officials to function as umpires with inspecting teams or other bodies to which functions are delegated or assigned by the Commission or under the provisions of the draft armistice agreement, so that the completion of the return of prisoners of war to their homelands shall be expedited.

XVI. When the Repatriation Agreement is acceded to by the parties concerned and when an umpire has been appointed under paragraph 14 above, the draft armistice agreement, unless otherwise altered by agreement between the parties, shall be deemed to have been accepted by them. The provisions of the draft armistice agreement shall apply except in so far as they are modified by the Repatriation Agreement. Arrangements for repatriation under this agreement will begin when the armistice agreement is thus concluded.

XVII. At the end of ninety days, after the Armistice Agreement has been signed, the disposition of any prisoners of war whose return to their homelands may not have been effected in accordance with the procedure set out in these proposals or as otherwise agreed, shall be referred with recommendations for their disposition, including a target date for the termination of their detention to the political conference to be called as provided under article 60 of the draft armistice agreement. If at the end of a further thirty days there are any prisoners of war whose return to their homelands has not been effected under the above procedures or whose future has not been provided for by the political conference, the responsibility for their care and maintenance and for their subsequent disposition shall be transferred to the United Nations, which in all matters relating to them shall act strictly in accordance with international law. [GA res. 610 (VII), 3 Dec. 1952 (YBUN 1962, pp. 201–2).]

5. Claims that the United Nations Command was committing major violations of the international laws of war

The General Assembly and Security Council played a more important political role in discussions of Communist claims that the UN Command was engaged in the deliberate bombing of civilians, the ill treatment of prisoners of war, and in bacteriological warfare.

In August 1950 the Soviet Union submitted to the Security Council a draft resolution[23] which would have condemned the United States for the 'inhuman, barbarous bombing of the peaceful population and of peaceful towns and population areas'. This draft was supported by a protest by North Korea.[24] On 7 September the representative of the USSR submitted new charges to the effect that, under the pretext of fighting guerrillas, the United States had burned to the ground dozens of Korean villages and towns, and carried out mass deportation and executions.

In reply, the representative of the United States quoted a statement by the United States Secretary of State on 6 September, in which it was stressed that the activity of the United States forces in Korea had been and was directed solely at military targets of the invader, but that the communist command had compelled civilians to work at those sites, had used peaceful villages to cover its tanks and used civilian dress to disguise its soldiers. The United Nations Command, however, had exerted every effort, by use of warning leaflets and radio broadcasts, to minimize, to the fullest extent possible, damage and injury to peaceful civilians and property. Alleged violations to the Hague Conventions, he said, should be investigated by the Interna-- tional Red Cross. [*YBUN 1950*, p. 23.]

The Soviet draft resolution was defeated by 9 votes to 1 (USSR) with 1 abstention (Yugoslavia). Further complaints were made by North Korea in cables of 7 and 18 September 1951,[25] and a renewed attempt was made by the Soviet Union to get a resolution passed condemning the alleged civilian bombing as contrary to international law.[26] The resolution was again rejected by the same number of votes. In 1951 new, and different, North Korean charges were made:

The Government of the Peoples' Democratic Republic of Korea sends a vigorous protest to the United Nations against a further monstrous crime which is being committed by the American interventionists by the use of bacteriological weapons in the war against the Korean people.

It is widely known that the United States Far East Command has long been preparing for this criminal act. By MacArthur's orders the mass production of bacteriological weapons was developed in Japan. As reported in the Press, MacArthur's staff spent 1,500,000 yen on the preparation of bacteriological weapons, using the Japanese Government as agents for the placing of orders. From documents of the secret archives of the Syngman Rhee Government captured in the liberation of Seoul by the People's Army and published by the Ministry for Foreign Affairs of the People's Democratic Republic of Korea in a collection of documents and material revealing the instigators of the civil war in Korea, it appears beyond all dispute that the staff of Syngman Rhee's army, created and directed by American military advisers, had planned long before the open attack on North Korea to carry on secret bacteriological warfare against the North and had taken measures to carry out these plans. Thus, according to plan A of intelligence work for 1950, prepared by Section 3 of the Intelligence Bureau of the Staff of the South Korean Army, the task laid down was to infect with bacteria:

[23] S/1679, 8 Aug. 1950.   [24] S/1674, 7 Aug. 1950.
[25] S/1172/Rev. 1 and S/1800.   [26] S/1812, 26 Sept. 1950.

1. Army kitchens;
2. Police mess-rooms;
3. Premises for banquets arranged by the Army, the Government, the Party, etc.;
4. City reservoirs, rivers;
5. Houses of Army, Government and Party leaders. (See document 18 of the aforementioned collection.)

Plan B of the intelligence work of the staff of the South Korean Army gives concrete details of the aforementioned plan A providing for the use of bacteria in diversionary work on the territory of North Korea: in the towns of Chinnampo, Najin, Wonsan, Sinuiju, Ongjin, Dhenjian, Hamhung, Chongjin, Chorwon, Kaeju, Hungnam, Songjin, as well as in units of the People's Army. (See document 19 of the aforementioned collection.)

Of course these criminal plans were drawn up with the knowledge and under the directions of the Americans, who provided Syngman Rhee's followers with the relevant bacteriological means. The United States representatives have repeatedly threatened to use the atomic bomb and bacteriological weapons against the Korean people who are heroically resisting American aggression. Following in the path of the defeated and universally condemned Japanese war criminals, MacArthur, Ridgway and their abettors carried out this threat in the middle of December 1950 and January 1951. Several areas were simultaneously infected with small-pox sicknesses seven to eight days after their liberation from American occupation. Sicknesses broke out in the town of Pyongyang and in the provinces: Pyongan-pukto, Pyongan-namdo, Kangwon-do, Hamgyong-namdo, Hwanghae-do. The number of persons suffering from small-pox mounted rapidly and by April there were more than 3,500 cases, 10 per cent of which were fatal. Small-pox sickness is particularly widespread in the following provinces: Kwangwon-do, 1,126 cases, Hamgyong-namdo, 817 cases, Hwanghae-do, 192 cases.

In the places which were liberated later than the others from American occupation no small-pox sickness has been discovered. Nor has a single case of small-pox sickness been discovered among the combatants of the People's Army and the Chinese volunteer units who, thanks to timely measures, were protected against the small-pox epidemic. The origin of the small-pox infection is indicated in particular by the fact that, according to information received from Japan, a number of small-pox cases were also noted there in the month of January, the infection having been brought in by American army men, who had taken part in the battles in North Korea and had been infected with small-pox as a result of the use of bacteriological weapons by their units. Thus the small-pox epidemic in North Korea is a result of the premeditated crime of the American interventionists, perpetrated in violation of the Geneva Protocol of 17 June 1925 on the prohibition of the use in warfare of asphyxiating, poisonous and other similar gases and bacteriological means, to which the United States is a signatory. . . . [S/2142/Rev. 1, 18 May 1951.]

The UN Command categorically denied these allegations. It stated that there was indeed widespread disease in North Korea, but this was due to the lack of basic preventive and curative measures. The United States herself requested the Assembly to look into these charges (A/2231), and invited an impartial investigation by the International Red Cross.

These controversies concerning heed for the laws of warfare lead to a broader question: to what extent were the parties—and in particular the Unified Command—legally bound by these laws? Quite clearly, the Unified Command was engaging in major hostilities, whether or not one classified the Korean conflict as 'war'.[27] The problems therefore arise: are UN Forces bound, or exempt, from

[27] Any hesitation in classifying the UN action in Korea as 'war' stems from two main factors: first, the UN Charter, except in its preambular reference to 'the scourge of war', refers neither to war nor to the rights and duties of belligerency. Second, it is widely felt that UN 'collective measures' or

the laws of war; and what was the position in the Korean conflict? The UN is not formally a party to the major conventions on the conduct of warfare, most of which contain terms declaring them open to 'states'. It is a matter of some controversy whether the UN could legally accede to these conventions if it wished to do so.[28] But there are strong arguments for suggesting that the customary rules of war conduct remain directly relevant to UN action. The majority view is that the UN is indeed bound by those laws of war which are customary; and the fact that its opponent is fighting an illegal aggressive action does not release either party from their duties under customary international law. This is not the place to recount in full the arguments leading to this conclusion: they have been well presented elsewhere.[29] Certainly the underlying humanitarian aim of these laws would favour, in an admittedly ambiguous situation, an interpretation which acknowledged their binding nature in a UN enforcement action.[30] Equally, there is strength in the view that the customary rules apply not only to states, but also to an entity such as the UN, which possesses a considerable measure of international personality.[31] Much of the content of The Hague Conventions of 1907—and above all, the Fourth Convention to which are annexed Regulations concerning the Laws and Customs of War on Land—are today widely regarded as having become part of general

---

'enforcement action' (which terms *are* used in the Charter) must be sharply differentiated from the traditional, pre-Charter right of individual nations to wage war. This view, which is shared by the Editor, does not of course mean that it is thereby irrelevant to consider the applicability of customary and conventional standards of warfare to UN action.

That the distinction between traditional 'war' and UN enforcement action is not merely academic is shown by the large number of cases (many of them concerning claims on insurance policies containing a 'war' exemption clause) which were decided as a result of the Korean hostilities. There was a marked lack of uniformity in these cases as to whether there was 'war' in Korea. For an affirmative decision, see e.g. *Western Reserve Life Ins. Co.* v. *Meadows*, 152 Tex. 559 (1953); *Christiansen* v. *Sterling Ins. Co.*, US Supreme Court of Washington (1955), *ILR*, 1955, p. 893; *Weissman* v. *Metro Life Ins. Co.*, 112 Fed. Suppl. 420 (SD Cal. 1953). For decisions holding that there was no 'war', see *Beley* v. *Pa. Mut. Life Ins. Co.*, 373 Pa. 231 (1953); *Harding* v. *Pa. Mutual Life Ins. Co.*, 373 Pa. 270 (1953); *Burns* v. *The King* (1953), *ILR* 596; *Australian Communist Party* v. *The Commonwealth*, ibid. p. 594. For articles on these cases and the legal points at issue see Pye, 'The Legal Status of the Korean Hostilities', *GLJ* (1956), p. 45; Green, 'The Nature of the "War" in Korea', 4 *ILQ* (1951) 462. The Attorney-General in the British House of Commons stated that the Korean action was not 'war' (HC Deb., vol. 481, col. 13); see also M. Brandon, 'Is the Korean Conflict "War"?', 11 *ILQ* (1953), 316–19.

[28] For a discussion of this problem see Bowett, *UN Forces*, p. 489, and Seyersted, *UN Forces*, pp. 344–61.

[29] H. Lauterpacht, 'The Limits of the Operation of the Law of War', 30 *BYIL* (1953), 206; Taubenfeld, *AJIL* (1951), pp. 671–9; Attia, pp. 252–71; Bowett, pp. 492–516; Seyersted, pp. 178–210; and M. Greenspan, *The Modern Law of Land Warfare* (1959), p. 25. For a different view see G. Draper, 'The Legal Limitations upon the Employment of Weapons by the United Nations Force in the Congo', 12 *ICLQ* (1963) 387–413; G. Schwarzenberger, 'Legal Effects of Illegal War', *Völkerrecht und Rechtliches Weltbild, Festschrift für Alfred Verdross* (1960), pp. 244 ff.

[30] Thus Lauterpacht, addressing himself to the fact that UN enforcement actions are only permitted against an aggressor, has written: 'Accordingly, any application to the actual conduct of war of the principle *ex injuria jus non oritur* would transform the contest into a struggle which may be subject to no regulation at all. The result would be the abandonment of most rules of warfare, including those which are of a humanitarian character' (30 *BYIL* (1953), 212).

[31] See F. Grob, *The Relativity of War and Peace* (1949).

rules of international warfare, binding not only the parties to the original Conventions, but all the subjects of international law.[32] In principle, therefore, these could be regarded as binding upon the UN.

Immediately the hostilities broke out in Korea, the International Committee of the Red Cross requested both North and South Korea to apply, *de facto*, the humanitarian principles protecting war victims, especially Article 3 of each of the 1949 Geneva Conventions. On 4 July 1950 South Korea signed all four of the 1949 Geneva Conventions, while on 15 July 1950 North Korea replied that it was 'strictly abiding by the principles of Geneva Conventions in respect to Prisoners of War'.[33] It may be recalled that at the time hostilities commenced, the four Geneva Conventions had been signed, but not yet ratified by any of the parties to the conflict.[34]

The United States also let it be known that she would be 'guided by humanitarian principles of Conventions, particularly Article 3 of the Geneva Convention 1949'.[35] The UN Command did not, as such, make any formal pronouncements, but it instructed the forces under its command to observe all the provisions of the Geneva Convention of 1949 relative to the treatment of prisoners of war:

United Nations personnel in charge of prisoners of war camps continue to observe scrupulously all the provisions of the Geneva Convention of 12 August 1949 relative to the treatment of prisoners of war. Prisoners of war are provided with the standard Republic of Korea Army ration and with a gratuitous tobacco issue. At each camp there is a permanently assigned staff of United States and Republic of Korea medical officers, nurses, and medical attendants. More serious cases are treated in hospitals on the same basis as wounded United Nations troops. The geographic co-ordinates of United Nations prisoner of war camps have been furnished to the United States Government for transmission to the International Committee

[32] On the detailed content of those rules which are, or are not, to be considered as falling within the category of 'customary' see Seyersted, p. 181; P. Guggenheim, *Lehrbuch des Völkerrechts*, i (1948), p. 783, and Röed in *Nordisk Tidsskrift for international Ret og Jus gentium* (1955), p. 31.

[33] ICRC, *Le comité international de la Croix-Rouge et le conflit de Corée, Recueil de documents*, ii (1952), p. 9. Seyersted (*UN Forces*, p. 183) makes the point that North Korea's agreement to abide by the principles of the Convention fell short of an undertaking to apply the full provisions of the Conventions: in other words, the North Korean authorities had confirmed only that they were upholding those elements of the 1949 Conventions which were already customary international law. For a broader interpretation of the North Korean response, see Bowett, *UN Forces*, p. 500; Green, in 6 *Archiv des Völkerrechts* (1956–7), p. 419; Attia, pp. 261–2.

[34] The Geneva Conventions of 1929 had, by contrast, been ratified by all the participants save for South and North Korea: and the great part of The Hague Regulations of 1907 had become, as we have stated above, part of general international law by 1950.

[35] *Recueil de documents*, i. 13. Art. 3 was common to each of the four Conventions and provided a minimum humanitarian standard to be applied even when the armed conflict was not of an international character. At the time of the Korean conflict the Geneva Conventions had been ratified by none of the participants. During the course of the conflict it was ratified (among states providing contingents) only by the Philippines, France, and South Africa. The US ratified in 1955, the People's Republic of China in 1956, and the Korean People's Democratic Republic in 1957. The Republic of Korea has still not ratified. When answering questions by the ICRC, many states (e.g. the Netherlands and Luxemburg) replied—as did the US—that they would none the less be guided by the 'humanitarian principles' of the Conventions; others undertook to fulfil their existing obligations under the 1929 Conventions and to abide by the spirit of the 1949 Conventions (e.g. Canada, Australia, and New Zealand), while others said they would apply the later Conventions on a *de facto* basis (e.g. Turkey and the Philippines). See ICRC, *Recueil de documents*, i. 8–11 and Seyersted, *UN Forces*, p. 183 nn. 28–33.

of the Red Cross in accordance with article 23 of the 1949 Geneva Convention. [*S/1834, 5 Oct. 1950, 5th Report of UN Command in Korea*, p. 75.]

In 1951 the United States reiterated:

The United Nations Forces in Korea have been and are under instructions to observe at all times the Geneva Conventions of 1949 on:
1. the amelioration of the condition of the wounded and sick in armed forces in the field;
2. the amelioration of the condition of the wounded, sick and ship-wrecked members of armed forces at sea;
3. the treatment of prisoners of war;
4. the protection of civilian persons in time of war.

In addition, they have been instructed to observe the applicable portions of the Hague Convention IV of 1907 as well as other pertinent principles of international law. These Conventions and principles have been observed by the United Nations forces.

There exists a legitimate, impartial organization of recognized international standing, one of whose functions is to investigate *bona fide* charges of the conduct of military operations not conforming to international law. The International Committee of the Red Cross is that organization. Its representatives are in a position to observe the conduct of United Nations Forces and have been given access to all information they may desire in order that they may submit a factual and impartial report.

The representatives of the International Committee of the Red Cross, however, as well as the United Nations Commission for the Unification and Rehabilitation of Korea, have constantly been denied access to that part of Korea under Communist control. [*S/2232, 6 July 1951*.]

Again, the UN Commander reported that he had permitted the accredited delegate of the ICRC to purchase books and pamphlets for North Korean prisoners of war, and

In accordance with the terms of the Geneva Convention, the material provided is not censored by the United Nations Commander. Furthermore, Mr. Bieri has been informed that prisoners of war are permitted to receive individual parcels or collective shipments containing food-stuffs, clothing, medical supplies and articles of a religious, educational or recreational character which will enable them to pursue studies or cultural activities. The only limitations placed on such shipments are those deemed necessary by the International Committee of the Red Cross. [*S/1860, 21 Oct. 1950, 6th Report of UN Command in Korea*, p. 90.]

This insistence upon endeavours to meet the standards of the Geneva Conventions should not, however, be taken to mean that the Unified Command regarded itself as legally bound by the four Conventions,[36] or even as voluntarily accepting the terms of the Prisoner-of-War Convention, and the humanitarian objectives common to all four:

My present instructions are to abide by the humanitarian principles of the 1949 Geneva Conventions, particularly the common article three. In addition I have directed the forces under my command to abide by the detailed provisions of the prisoner of war convention, since I have means at my disposal to assure compliance with this convention by all concerned; and have fully accredited the ICRC delegates accordingly. I do not have the authority to accept, nor the means to assure the accomplishment of, responsibilities incumbent on sovereign nations as contained in the detailed provisions of the other Geneva Conventions, and hence I am unable to accredit the delegates to the UNC for the purposes outlined in those Con-

[36] On this point, see Seyersted, *UN Forces*, pp. 184–5. He perhaps makes too much of it, especially in the light of S/2232.

ventions. All categories of non-combatants in custody of or under control of military forces under my comd, however, will continue to be accorded treatment prescribed by the humanitarian principles of the Geneva Conventions. [*Telegram of 5 Dec. 1951 from UN C-in-C to ICRC, Recueil de documents, i.87.*]

Certainly it was quite usual for the various parties to the Korean conflict and other UN members to invoke the relevant conventions. Thus in August 1950 Bulgaria formally complained to the Secretary-General that alleged bombings of civil populations, hospitals, and cultural establishments were contrary to 'the formal provisions of article 3 of the Geneva Convention for the protection of civil populations'.[37] The Indian government had declared 'we should be justified in taking all possible steps to be sure that the military operations by this Security Council are conducted in accordance with the laws of civilized warfare'.[38] Equally, when the prolonged debate was occurring on the question of forcible repatriation of prisoners of war (above pp. 184-7) both sides invoked the Prisoners-of-War Convention in support of their case. Later, the Assembly solemnly declared that 'the release and repatriation of prisoners of war shall be effected in accordance with the Geneva Convention relative to the Treatment of Prisoners of War, dated 12 August 1949, the well-established principles and practice of international law and the relevant provisions of the draft armistice agreement'.[39]

Although the Korean People's Democratic Republic had notified both the Secretary-General[40] and the ICRC of her intention to abide by the principles of the Prisoners-of-War Convention, her practice fell short of the promise. Thus the ICRC reports that it was not allowed to visit North Korean prisoner-of-war camps, as Articles 10 and 124 of the 1949 Convention would have allowed.[41]

China did not acknowledge the legal relevance of any of the Geneva Conventions until 16 July 1952, when much of the major fighting had already occurred. She then 'recognized' the four Conventions, subject to certain reservations, but did not ratify until 1956.[42]

The Central People's Government of the People's Republic of China has decided to recognize the 'Protocol for the Prohibition of the Use in War of Asphyxiating, Poisonous or other Gases, and of Bacteriological Methods of Warfare', concluded at Geneva on 17 June 1925, and acceded to in the name of China on 7 August 1929, and has also authorized me to issue a statement relative thereto. Having notified the Government of the Republic of France in accordance with the provisions of the said Protocol, I hereby cable you the text of that statement.

Chou EN-LAI
Minister for Foreign Affairs of the
Central People's Government of
the People's Republic of China

[37] S/1725, 29 Aug. 1950.
[38] *SCOR*, 6th yr, 497th mtg, p. 15.
[39] General Assembly res. 610 (VII).
[40] S/1676, 8th mtg, 1950.
[41] ICRC, *Recueil de documents*, ii. 5; Seyersted, *UN Forces*, p. 186.
[42] Seyersted, p. 186; Attia, p. 262.

Statement of Chou En-lai, Minister for Foreign Affairs of the Central People's Government, on the recognition of the 'Protocol for the Prohibition of the Use in War of Asphyxiating, Poisonous or other Gases, and of Bacteriological Methods of Warfare' of 1925

Chou En-lai, Minister for Foreign Affairs of the Central People's Government of the People's Republic of China, was authorized, on 13 July 1952, to make the following statement:

In accordance with article 55 of the common programme of the Chinese People's political. Consultative Conference, which provides that 'the Central People's Government of the People's Republic of China shall examine the treaties and agreements concluded between the Kuomintang and foreign Governments, and shall, in accordance with their contents, recognize, abrogate, revise, or reconclude them respectively', the Central People's Government of the People's Republic of China has examined the 'Protocol for the Prohibition of the Use in War of Asphyxiating, Poisonous or other Gases, and of Bacteriological Methods of Warfare', concluded on 17 June 1925, and acceded to in the name of China on 7 August 1929. The Central People's Government considers that the said Protocol is conducive to the strengthening of international peace and security and is in conformity with humanitarian principles, and therefore has decided to recognize the accession to the Protocol. The Central People's Government shall undertake to implement strictly the provisions of the Protocol, provided that all the other contracting and acceding Powers observe them reciprocally.

Peking, 13 July 1952

[S/2707, Cable of 16 July 1952.]

This prompted the following observations from Nationalist China:

I have the honour to request that the following statement, issued by the Chinese Minister of Foreign Affairs on 17 July 1952, be circulated as a Security Council document:

The Geneva Convention for the Amelioration of the Condition of the Wounded and Sick in Armed Forces in the Field, the Geneva Convention relative to the Treatment of Prisoners of War, the Geneva Convention relative to the Protection of Civilian Persons in Time of War, and the Geneva Convention for the Amelioration of the Condition of Wounded, Sick and Shipwrecked Members of Armed Forces at Sea, adopted by the Diplomatic Conference at Geneva in August 1949, were all signed on 10 December 1949 on behalf of China by Mr. Wu Nan-ju, Chinese Plenipotentiary duly appointed by the Government of the Republic of China. The puppet Communist régime in Peiping has no right whatever to accede to these conventions in the name of China.

China also signed the Protocol for the Prohibition of the Use in War of Asphyxiating, Poisonous or other Gases, and of Bacteriological Methods of Warfare on 20 September 1926 and ratified it on 26 March 1927. It is equally ridiculous for the same puppet régime to claim accession to the said protocol in the name of China. *[S/2710, Letter of 18 July 1952.]*

It remains relevant to inquire—especially in a case when the UN Command is effectively delegated to one particular country, whether it is not the legal obligations of the contributing states, rather than of the UN itself, which are relevant? In the Korean conflict, where the United States was charged with the establishment of the UN Command, all contributing nations remained bound, individually, by the general (customary) laws of war, and by whatever conventional obligations they had undertaken. They were not released from these obligations by the fact that the UN Command itself may have agreed to be bound by a more limited number of obligations under the Geneva Conventions.

The practice rapidly evolved, however, whereby the contributing states regarded themselves as bound by any commitments entered into by the UN

Commander-in-Chief in respect of the humane treatment of prisoners of war [43] and the sick and wounded.

[43] See statement to this effect by the UK, South Africa, Greece, Australia, New Zealand, and Canada (ICRC, *Recueil de documents*, pp. 25–9). Seyersted also notes (*UN Forces*, pp. 187, 188 n. 54) that in the early phases the Communist nations regarded the Unified Command merely as a coalition of individual states, though in the later states they accepted that they were 'United Nations Forces'.

6

ADMINISTRATIVE AND MILITARY CONTROL

ALL operational control for the action in Korea lay with the United States, acting in her capacity of UN Command.

The proposal for a Unified Command was made in a joint United Kingdom–France draft resolution. The resolution, which was adopted by 7 votes to nil, with 3 abstentions and one member absent,[1] provided:

The Security Council,
Having determined that the armed attack upon the Republic of Korea by forces from North Korea constitutes a breach of the peace,
Having recommenced that Members of the United Nations furnish such assistance to the Republic of Korea as may be necessary to repel the armed attack and to restore international peace and security in the area,
    1. *Welcomes* the prompt and vigorous support which governments and peoples of the United Nations have given to its Resolutions of 25 and 27 June 1950 to assist the Republic of Korea in defending itself against armed attack and thus to restore international peace and security in the area;
    2. *Notes* that Members of the United Nations have transmitted to the United Nations offers of assistance for the Republic of Korea;
    3. *Recommends* that all Members providing military forces and other assistance pursuant to the aforesaid Security Council resolutions make such forces and other assistance available to a unified command under the United States;
    4. *Requests* the United States to designate the commander of such forces;
    5. *Authorizes* the unified command at its discretion to use the United Nations flag in the course of operations against North Korean forces concurrently with the flags of the various nations participating;
    6. *Requests* the United States to provide the Security Council with reports as appropriate on the course of action taken under the unified command. [*SC res. S/1588, 7 July 1950.*]

In accordance with this resolution, the United States designated General MacArthur as Commander-in-Chief of UN Forces in Korea. He was presented with the UN flag which had been used in Palestine.[2] The United States issued a communiqué[3] announcing the establishment of a UN Command. This Unified

    [1] For details of voting, see above, p. 164.
    [2] *YBUN, 1950*, p. 230.
    [3] S/1629, 25 July 1950.

Command was, from an operational point of view, essentially the United States Far East Command in Tokyo. It was composed exclusively of United States officers, though they were later joined by a British Commonwealth Deputy Chief of Staff.[4] The appointment of General MacArthur was, under paragraph 4 of resolution S/1588, within the prerogative of the United States and not subject to subsequent confirmation by any organ of the UN. Subsequently, when President Truman relieved General MacArthur of his command, the decision was taken without reference to the UN—as was the ensuing appointment of General Mark Clark. At no time was it the habit of the United States to do other than inform the UN of changes in command which had been decided upon.[5]

The military chain of command ran from the UN Command to the US Army Chief of Staff, to the Joint Chiefs of Staff, to the US Secretary of Defence, and thence to the President of the United States. Some fifteen members of the UN placed their troops under the operational control of the UN Command.

Detailed arrangements for the utilization of assistance offered were made as a result of bilateral discussions between the Unified Command and the contributing State. These discussions were carried out first between the Unified Command and diplomatic and military representatives of the contributing State in Washington, followed by formal military staff conferences both at Washington and in the theatre of operations. . . .

The general framework for integration of military assistance was provided in the agreements between the contributing State and the Unified Command.[6] The implementation of the plans was assisted by contacts between the contributing State and United States advisory groups, missions, military attachés, or other United States agencies stationed in the contributing State. After the arrival of the contingent in the contact zone, the contingent came under the full operational control of the Unified Command. . . .

One of the most important problems in connexion with the integration of national units concerned command relationships in the theatre. In Korea, all units provided to the Unified Command were attached to one of the major organizations previously designated as components of the Command: Army, Navy or Air Force. National ground forces of divisional size became components of United States Army corps, and units smaller than divisions were incorporated within the appropriate *échelon* of United States divisions. The same principles were followed with respect to Naval and Air Forces. The senior military representative of each State contributing military forces had the right of direct access to the Commander-in-Chief of the United Nations Command 'on matters of major policy affecting the operational capabilities of the forces concerned'. Likewise, the senior military representative in the theatre of each State contributing military forces was given the right of direct communication with his government on administrative matters affecting the forces of his government. [*A/1891, ann. 4, Report of Collective Measures Cttee (GAOR, 6th sess., suppl. 13, pp. 45–46).*]

The ground forces of the various contributing members of the UN were thus incorporated as units into divisions of the US Eighth Army and were under the command of a US officer, except that after 27 July 1951 all units of the British Commonwealth were combined into one division of their own under the Eighth

[4] Seyersted, *UN Forces*, p. 35. Before 25 July 1950 the US had, of course, already placed in Korea combat units under their Far Eastern Command; and the first British Commonwealth units similarly were originally under the control of the US Far Eastern Command (ibid. p. 34).

[5] See, e.g., S/2246, 17 July 1951, p. 15 & S/2617. For details of the dates of the various appointments, see below, p. 202.

[6] See below, pp. 203–6.

Army. All naval and air units were similarly attached to the Seventh Fleet and to the Far Eastern Air Force, respectively.[7] It may also be noted that the forces of South Korea—a non-member of the UN—were incorporated (before the establishment of the UN Command) into United States units.[8]

The channel used by the United States for keeping contributing member states informed of military developments was the Committee of Sixteen in Washington. This Committee was composed of the Washington-based diplomatic representatives of the countries concerned, and South Korea was not included in the membership.[9] The Committee was used to relay information and not for prior consultation or decision-making.

It will be seen, therefore, that in military and operational terms, control was firmly in the hands of the United States. However, the parties involved clearly regarded the United States as the agent of the UN and the action in which they were engaged as a UN action. The contributing governments used the term 'United Nations Command' when communicating with it; the agreements between them and the United States employed the same term; and UN resolutions referred either to UN Forces or to the UN Command.

[7] Seyersted, *UN Forces*, pp. 35–6.
[8] See below, pp. 211–12.
[9] Goodrich, 'Korea: Collective Measures against Aggression', *Int. Conciliation* (1951), p. 167.

7

COMPOSITION AND SIZE

SECURITY Council resolution S/1501 had recommended that member states give aid and assistance to the Republic of Korea. The composition of the Force was thus open in principle to all members. Unlike UN police actions, such as the UN Emergency Force, the UN operation in the Congo, or the UN Forces in Cyprus, the selection of the nations to participate was not in the hands of the Secretary-General. This responsibility was assigned to the United States as head of the Unified Command. It seems, however, that the then Secretary-General, Trygve Lie, suggested informally to the United States that she should use all capable volunteers, including individuals offering their services, perhaps by forming an international brigade; and that this suggestion was rejected.[1]

Not all of the offers of assistance were accepted, either for practical or for political reasons. The United States stipulated that only national contingents were acceptable, and that these had to be of at least battalion strength. Even so, the decision was taken not to accept the offer made by Nationalist China of three infantry divisions.

[1] Lie, p.379.

The international character of the UN Forces was built up slowly: between the end of June and the beginning of August the only UN Forces in Korea were those of the United States. United Kingdom forces, followed by others, arrived in August.

The response to the Secretary-General's request for offers of assistance was very favourable, though many states indicated that they could offer only non-military assistance.[2] The Communist nations were, of course, implacably opposed to the UN action. A distinctive position was taken by the Arab nations, who pointed to their dispute with Israel as a reason for refusing to participate in the UN action:

> In reply to your cablegrams of 25 and 27 June 1950, I have the honour to transmit to you the following statement by the Syrian Government:
>
>> The Syrian Government notes the Security Council resolution dated 25 June 1959 (*S/1501*). Desirous of conforming to the principles and provisions of the United Nations Charter, it will always refrain from giving any assistance to any aggressor. It also declares that because of the obligations of fraternal solidarity existing between Arab countries, it takes the greatest interest in the problems that affect the other Arab States. In this con-nexion the Syrian Government feels obliged to point out that the tolerant attitude shown in the execution of certain United Nations resolutions has been one of the factors contri-buting to the development of the state of affairs which has resulted in the present situation. While affirming its attachment to peace and its anxiety to support any action for its main-tenance in the world within the framework of the United Nations Charter, the Syrian Government expresses its profound wish that any decision tending to rectify injustices and guarantee the freedom of peoples should be carried out in a spirit of law and equity. [*S/1591, 8 July 1950, Cable to Secretary-General from President of Council of Minorities of Syria.*]

A reply in similar vein was received from the Iraq government.[3]

Some countries felt that they were not in a position to send forces—even though supporting the UN action—because they were needed at home for self-defence. Yet others—such as Japan—which played a major part in providing facilities through the US Far Eastern Command in Tokyo—faced constitutional problems about sending forces abroad. Still others were engaged in limited military operations elsewhere, and hence could spare only comparatively slight military support for Korea. It will be recalled that France was tied down in Indochina, while the United Kingdom was faced with military operations in Malaya.

However, some thirty governments made concrete offers of assistance; and eventually military aid was given by some seventeen nations. In January 1953 the Commander summarized the position:

> The United Nations Command in Korea contains fighting forces of the following countries: Australia, Belgium, Canada, Colombia, Ethiopia, France, Greece, Luxembourg, the Nether-

---

[2] e.g. S/1521, 29 June 1950 (Nationalist China); S/1522, 29 June (New Zealand); S/1543, 30 June (South Africa); S/1544, 30 June (Bolivia, Costa Rica, Guatemala, Nicaragua, and Israel); S/1547, 1 July (Thailand); S/1549, 1 July (Luxembourg); S/1550, 1 July (Haiti); S/1582, 6 July (Paraguay); S/1584, 7 July (Philippines); S/1675, 8 Aug. 1950 (Chile); S/1680, 10 Aug. (Liberia); S/1595, 11 July 1950 (Venezuela).

[3] S/1593, 9 July 1950.

lands, New Zealand, the Philippines, Republic of Korea, Thailand, Turkey, Union of South Africa, United Kingdom and United States. There are medical units from Denmark, India, Italy, Norway and Sweden. The following countries have provided transportation, medical supplies, food, funds and other miscellaneous supplies for the relief of the unfortunate people who are the victims of your aggression: Argentina, Austria, Australia, Belgium, Brazil, Burma, Cambodia, Canada, Italy, China, Costa Rica, Cuba, Denmark, Ecuador, El Salvador, Ethiopia, France, Greece, Iceland, New Zealand, Nicaragua, Norway, Pakistan, Panama, Paraguay, Peru, the Philippines, Saudi Arabia, Sweden, Syria, Thailand, Turkey, Union of South Africa, United Kingdom, United States, Uruguay, Vietnam, and Venezuela. [*S/2897, 6 Jan. 1953, 54th Report of UN Command in Korea, p. 2.*]

Of these forces, early contributions were made to augment the United States naval presence by Britain, France, the Netherlands, Canada, and New Zealand.[4] These were later enlarged by naval assistance from Colombia, Thailand, and Australia.

The following table provides more detailed information:

SUMMARIES OF MILITARY ASSISTANCE FOR KOREA (AS OF 15 JANUARY 1952)

GROUND FORCES

Country	Date	Details of Offer	Status
Australia	3 Aug. 1950	Ground forces from Australian Infantry Force in Japan	In action
		Additional battalion of Australian troops	,, ,,
Belgium	13 Sept. 1950	Infantry battalion	,, ,,
	3 May 1951	Reinforcements	,, ,,
Bolivia	15 July 1950	30 Officers	Acceptance deferred
Canada	14 Aug. 1950	Brigade group, including three infantry battalions, one field regiment of artillery, one squadron of self-propelled anti-tank guns, together with engineer, signal, medical, ordnance and other services with appropriate reinforcements	In action
China	3 July 1950	Three infantry divisions	Acceptance deferred
Colombia	14 Nov. 1950	One infantry battalion	In action
Costa Rica	27 July 1950	Volunteers	Acceptance deferred
Cuba	30 Nov. 1950	One infantry company	Accepted
El Salvador	15 Aug. 1950	Volunteers	Acceptance deferred
Ethiopia	2 Nov. 1950	1,069 officers and men	In action
France	20 Aug. 1950	Infantry battalion	,, ,,
Greece	1 Sept. 1950	Unit of land forces	,, ,,
	2 July 1951	Additional unit of land forces	Transmitted to Unified Command
Luxembourg	15 Mar. 1951	Infantry company integrated into the Belgian forces	In action
Netherlands	8 Sept. 1950	One infantry battalion	,, ,,
New Zealand	26 July 1950	One combat unit	,, ,,
Panama	3 Aug. 1950	Contingent of volunteers } Bases for training	Acceptance deferred
Philippines	10 Aug. 1950	Regimental combat team consisting of approximately 5,000 officers and men	In action

[4] S/1694, 17 Aug. 1950, 2nd Report of UN Command in Korea, pp. 128–9.

Country	Date	Details of Offer	Status
Thailand	23 July 1950	Infantry combat team of about 4,000 officers and men	In action
Turkey	25 July 1950	Infantry combat force of 4,500 men, later increased to 6,086 men	,, ,,
United Kingdom	21 Aug. 1950	Ground forces	,, ,,
	Official information communicated on 12 June 1951	Two brigades composed of brigade headquarters	,, ,,
		Five infantry battalions	,, ,,
		One field regiment	,, ,,
		One armoured regiment	,, ,,
United States of America	Official information communicated on 8 June 1951	Three Army Corps One Marine Division } With supporting elements	,, ,,

NAVAL FORCES

Country	Date	Details of Offer	Status
Australia	28 July 1950	Two destroyers	,, ,,
	29 July 1950	One aircraft carrier	,, ,,
		One frigate	,, ,,
Canada	12 July 1950	Three destroyers	,, ,,
Colombia	16 Oct. 1950	One frigate—*Almirante Padilla*	,, ,,
France	19 July 1950	Patrol gun boat	Withdrawn
Netherlands	5 July 1950	One destroyer—*Evertsen*	In action
New Zealand	1 July 1950	Two frigates—HMNZ *Tutira* and HMNZ *Pukaki*	,, ,,
Thailand	3 Oct. 1950	Two corvettes—*Prasae* and *Bangpakong**	,, ,,
United Kingdom	28 June 1950	Naval forces in Japanese waters diverted to Korea	,, ,,
	Official information communicated on 12 June 1951	One aircraft carrier	,, ,,
		Two cruisers	,, ,,
		Eight destroyers	,, ,,
		One Survey ship	,, ,,
United States of America	Official information communicated on 8 June 1951	A fast carrier task group with a blockade and escort force, an amphibious force, reconnaissance and anti-submarine warfare units	,, ,,

AIR FORCES

Country	Date	Details of Offer	Status
Australia	30 June 1950	One RAAF Fighter Squadron	,, ,,
		One air communication unit	,, ,,
		Base and maintenance personnel	,, ,,
Canada	21 July 1950	One RCAF Squadron	,, ,,
Union of South Africa	4 Aug. 1950	One fighter squadron, including ground personnel	,, ,,
United Kingdom	Official information communicated on 12 June 1951	Elements of the Air Force	,, ,,
United States of America	Official information communicated on 8 June 1951	One Tactical Air Force, one Bombardment Command, and one Combat Cargo Command, all with supporting elements	,, ,,

* Destroyed on grounding.

MATERIAL

Country	Date	Details of Offer	Status
Philippines	3 Aug. 1950	17 Sherman tanks and one tank destroyer	In action

TRANSPORT

Country	Date	Details of Offer	Status
Belgium	28 Sept. 1950	Air transport	,, ,,
Canada	11 Aug. 1950	Facilities of Canadian Pacific Airlines between Vancouver and Tokyo	,, ,,
		Dry Cargo Vessels (10,000 tons)	,, ,,
China	3 July 1950	Twenty C-47s	Acceptance deferred
Denmark	22 July 1950	Motor ship *Bella Dan*	Withdrawn
Greece	20 July 1950 } 13 Oct. 1950 }	Eight Dakota transport planes	In action
Norway	18 July 1950	Merchant ship tonnage	,, ,,
Panama	3 Aug. 1950	Use of merchant marine for transportation of troops and supplies	,, ,,
Thailand	3 Oct. 1950	Transport *Sichang* to be attached to Thai troops	,, ,,
		Air transport	,, ,,
United Kingdom	Official information communicated on 12 June 1951	Seven supply vessels	,, ,,
United States of America		(No details available. The Unified Command has, however, arranged for transport of United States troops and material, as well as for the transport of some of the forces and materials listed in the present summary.)	

MEDICAL

Country	Date	Details of Offer	Status
Denmark	18 Aug. 1950	Hospital ship *Jutlandia*	,, ,,
India	29 July 1950	Field Ambulance Unit	,, ,,
Italy	27 Sept. 1950	Field Hospital Unit	,, ,,
Norway	6 Mar. 1951	Surgical Hospital Unit	,, ,,
Sweden	20 July 1950	Field Hospital Unit	,, ,,
United Kingdom	Official information communicated on 12 June 1951	Hospital Ship	,, ,,
United States of America		(No details available. The Unified Command has, however, provided full medical facilities not only for United States troops, but also for the troops of participating governments.)	

MISCELLANEOUS

Country	Date	Details of Offer	Status
Costa Rica	27 July 1950	Sea and air bases	Accepted
Panama	3 Aug. 1950	Bases for training	Acceptance deferred
		Free use of highways	Accepted
		Farm lands to supply troops	Pending
Thailand	2 Feb. 1951	Treatment for frost-bite	,,

[*YBUN 1950, ann. I*, pp. 255–8]

None the less, the United States role and contribution predominated. By the end of 1951, by which time a measure of stability had been achieved owing to the truce negotiations, nearly two-thirds of the total of the UN Forces were American.[5] In terms of services, the United States contribution was 50·32 per cent of the ground forces, 85·89 per cent of the naval forces, and 93·38 per cent of the air forces. The Republic of Korea contributed 40·10 per cent of the ground forces, 7·45 per cent of the naval forces, and 5·65 per cent of the air forces.[6] At their highest, UN Forces were to number some 740,000.

The UN action in Korea fell under the command of three men: General Douglas MacArthur was Commander-in-Chief from 8 July 1950 to 11 April 1951; Lt-General (later General) Matthew Ridgway was Commander-in-Chief from 11 April 1951 until 12 May 1952; and he was succeeded by General Mark Clark.[7]

General MacArthur's dismissal by President Truman on 11 April 1951 was the result not of one controversy, but of a series of disagreements between himself and the Joint Chiefs of Staff in Washington.[8] But it was the issue of how to respond to the Chinese intervention in the war at the end of 1950 which brought matters to a head. MacArthur believed that it was essential to cross the Yalu river and to carry counter-measures to Chinese territory. He was convinced that it was damaging and indeed impossible for the United States to 'fight in this accordion fashion—up and down—which means that your cumulative losses are going to be staggering'.[9] Physical hardship by December 1950 had reached appalling levels, and the Eighth Army was in a state of moral collapse, faced with the Chinese entry, the winter conditions, and widespread fever. MacArthur insisted that the pressure must be relieved by blockading the Chinese coast, bombarding China's industrial capacity to wage war, and reinforcing the UN Forces by bringing the Nationalist Chinese into the war.[10] The United States rejected these proposals on 9 January 1951, and permitted him to evacuate the Eighth Army if necessary. MacArthur now made it clear, in a series of exchanges with Washington, that he would not accept any responsibility for the destruction of the Eighth Army unless his plan were adopted.[11] Meanwhile Truman began by-passing MacArthur by increasingly using Lt-General Ridgway, who had been posted to Korea about a month earlier. MacArthur's proposals found considerable favour in Congress, and Truman was faced with a domestic, as well as foreign, crisis.[12] MacArthur made a series of public statements showing his disapproval of Truman's 'containment' policy, while Ridgway sought to counter this by suggesting that the advance of his

[5] US President, Report to Congress, and *US Participation in the United Nations* (1951), p. 288.
[6] Goodrich, *Korea*, p. 117.
[7] For listings of all the senior commanders of the Eighth Army, the I, IX, and X Corps, the Far East Air Forces, the Fifth Air Force, the Naval Forces, the Seventh Fleet Task Force, and the Republic of Korea Army, see David Rees, *Korea: the Limited War* (1964), pp. 458–9.
[8] Ibid. pp. 178–97.
[9] *Military Situation in the Far East*, pt 1, p. 30.
[10] Ibid. pt 3, pp. 2180–1.
[11] For an excellent summary, see Rees, pp. 182 ff.
[12] Ibid. pp. 197–205.

troops to the 38th parallel would be a tremendous victory. When on 20 March MacArthur was told that Truman would propose a cease-fire when the enemy had been pushed back beyond the 38th parallel, he issued a direct challenge to such a policy, which would not restore Korea to a unified, democratic government. MacArthur followed this public insubordination by a letter to Congressman Joe Martin, which was read on the floor of the House on 5 April. It reiterated that this was the time and place for a military confrontation with the Communist Powers. Truman then took the decision to recall General MacArthur: and this was announced on 11 April.

8

RELATIONS WITH CONTRIBUTING STATES

ON 29 June 1950 the Secretary-General sent to all UN members the text of Security Council resolution S/1511 of 27 June, and asked what help they could give. The details of the replies are dealt with in Section 7 above. All offers were then communicated to the United States government. After 7 July, when the Unified Command was established, the Secretary-General communicated offers to the United States permanent representative at the UN.[1] Informal discussions were often held at UN Headquarters to discuss the matching of potential offers with UN needs.[2]

The Secretary-General informed states making offers that the United States would enter into 'direct consultations with Governments with regard to the co-ordination of assistance' and all offers should be communicated to the Secretary-General, though 'leaving detailed arrangements for . . . an agreement between the Government and the Unified Command'.[3] It was thus left to the discretion of the United States which nations' offers to accept. The United States made the decision according to the needs of the situation, and also established the general principle that a national contingent must be offered at at least battalion strength. It was also required that such units should have supporting artillery, that engineers or ordnance units should be able to function as independent units, and that the contributing states should provide reinforcements to maintain the initial strength.[4]

The United States concluded formal agreements with only a very few of those nations who were contributing to the UN action in Korea.[5] It concluded these

[1] Bowett, *UN Forces*, p. 37.
[2] W. R. Frye, *A United Nations Peace Force* (1957), p. 187; G. Weissberg, *International Status of the United Nations* (1961), pp. 82–83. Bowett, p. 37 n. 38, says that some states, such as Colombia and Argentina, made their offers direct to the Unified Command.
[3] S/1619, 21 July 1950.
[4] Bowett, p. 57.
[5] For full listing, see pp. 198–9.

as 'the executive agent of the United Nations Forces in Korea', and registered them in the UN Treaty Series. Although there were minor variations between the agreements, they were built around a standard form. So far as the participation of armed forces was concerned, the agreement between the United States and the Netherlands given below was the standard form employed:

This agreement between the Government of the United States of America (the executive agent of the United Nations Forces in Korea) and the Government of the Netherlands shall govern relationships in matters specified herein for forces furnished by the Government of the Netherlands for the operations under the Commanding General of the Armed Forces of the Member States of the United Nations in Korea (hereinafter referred to as 'Commander') designated by the Government of the United States of America pursuant to resolutions of United Nations Security Council of June 25, 1950, June 27, 1950 and July 7, 1950.

Article 1. The Government of the United States of America agrees to furnish the Netherlands Forces with available materials, supplies, services, and facilities which the Netherlands Forces will require for these operations, and which the Government of the Netherlands is unable to furnish. The Government of the United States of America and the Government of the Netherlands will maintain accounts of materials, supplies, services, and facilities furnished by the Government of the United States of America to the Government of the Netherlands, its forces or agencies. Reimbursement for such materials, supplies, services, and facilities will be accomplished by the Government of the Netherlands upon presentation of statements of account by the Government of the United States of America. Such payment will be effected by the Government of the Netherlands in United States dollars. Issues of materials and supplies to the Netherlands Forces will not operate to transfer title to the Government of the Netherlands in advance of reimbursement.

Article 2. Pursuant to Article 1, appropriate technical and administrative arrangements will be concluded between authorized representatives of the Government of the United States of America and authorized representatives of the Government of the Netherlands.

Article 3. Classified items, specialized items, or items in short supply furnished to the Government of the Netherlands by the Government of the United States of America will be returned to the Government of the United States of America upon request, as a credit against the cost of materials, supplies, and services previously furnished. If the Government of the Netherlands determines at the time of redeployment of its forces that materials or supplies received from the Government of the United States of America hereunder are not desired for retention, such materials or supplies may be offered to the Government of the United States of America and if accepted, their residual value as determined by the Government of the United States of America will be used as a credit against reimbursement for materials, supplies, and services previously furnished.

Article 4. Each of the parties to this agreement agrees not to assert any claim against the other party for injury or death of members of its armed forces or for loss, damage, or destruction of its property or property of members of its armed forces caused in Korea by members of the armed forces of the other party. Claims of any other Government or its nationals against the Government or nationals of the Government of the Netherlands or vice versa shall be a matter for disposition between the Government of the Netherlands and such third government or its nationals.

Article 5. The Government of the Netherlands will maintain accounts of materials, supplies, services, and facilities furnished by other governments to personnel or agencies of the Government of the Netherlands, either directly or through the Commander. Settlement of any claims arising as a result of the furnishing of such materials, supplies, services, and facilities to the Government of the Netherlands by such third governments, whether direct or through the Commander, shall be a matter for consideration between such third governments and the Government of the Netherlands.

Article 6. The requirements of the Netherlands Forces for Korean currency will be supplied under arrangements approved by the Commander; provided, however, that settlement of any obligation of the Government of the Netherlands for use of such currency will be a matter of consideration between the Government of the Netherlands and the competent authorities of Korea. If, with the approval of the Commander, personnel and agencies of the Government of the Netherlands use media of exchange other than Korean currency in Korea, obligations arising therefrom will be a matter for consideration and settlement between the Government of the Netherlands and the other concerned governments.

Article 7. The Government of the Netherlands agrees that all orders, directives, and policies of the Commander issued to the Netherlands Forces or its personnel shall be accepted and carried out by them as given and that in the event of disagreement with such orders, directives, or policies, formal protest may be presented subsequently.

Article 8. Nothing in this agreement shall be construed to affect existing agreements or arrangements between the parties for the furnishing of materials, supplies, services, or facilities.

Article 9. This agreement shall come into force upon the date of signature thereof, and shall apply to all materials, supplies, services, and facilities furnished or rendered before, on, or after that date, to all claims referred to in Article 4 arising before, on, or after that date, and to all technical and administrative arrangements concluded pursuant to Article 2 before, on, or after that date.

IN WITNESS WHEREOF, the undersigned, being duly authorized by their respective governments, have signed this agreement.

DONE at Washington, in duplicate, this fifteenth day of May, 1952.

For the Government of the United States of America:
Dean ACHESON
For the Government of the Netherlands:
J. H. VAN ROIJEN

[*Agreement between the US and the Netherlands concerning participation of Netherlands Forces, 18 May 1952, 177 UNTS 234.*]

This agreement was identical with that concluded with Belgium (223 UNTS 3), and differed only in small respects from that concluded with South Africa (177 UNTS 241). The only differences in this latter were that in Article 1 the final sentence which appears in the Belgian and Netherlands agreements ('issues of materials and supplies to the Netherland forces will not operate to transfer title to the Government of the Netherlands in advance of reimbursement') is missing: no comparable clause was inserted; and the first sentence of Article 5 replaces the word 'facilities' with the word 'equipment'.

It will thus be seen that the main purpose of these agreements was to arrange for the United States to furnish materials and supplies which the contributing state was unable to supply against reimbursement for dollars, with certain provisions for returning specified items in short supply. This arrangement flowed, of course, from the fact that there was to be no charge upon the budget of the UN itself for the operation in Korea.[6] In the case of Belgium, however, a supplementary agreement was entered into concerning financial arrangements for logistical support furnished by the US to the Belgian units:

The Government of Belgium and the Government of the United States of America, in accordance with Article 2 of the Agreement between the Government of Belgium and the Government of the United States of America Concerning Participation of the Belgian Forces in United Nations Operations in Korea, dated July 15, 1955,[7] agree that the financial arrange-

[6] For details of the financing of the UN operation, see below, pp. 245–50.
[7] 223 UNTS 3; identical with text of Netherlands agreement.

KOREA

ments for materials, supplies, services and facilities furnished by the United States Department of the Army, its forces, or agencies, to the Belgian Forces participating in the Korean Operation, will be as follows:

Article 1

The payment due for the equipment, supplies, services, and facilities furnished to the Belgian Forces by the United States Department of the Army, its Forces or its Agencies, shall be based on:
  (*a*) A sum representing the cost price covering initial supplies of equipment and services furnished to the Belgian Forces;
  (*b*) A fixed sum per man and per day for maintenance of personnel and equipment from date of arrival in Korea.
  (*c*) A fixed sum for ammunition;
  (*d*) A sum representing the cost price covering pieces of heavy equipment having a minimum unit value of 1,000 dollars and supplies subsequent to initial delivery, as well as hospitalization services;
  (*e*) A sum representing the cost, real or estimated, of transportation services.
The cost price to be paid for the pieces of heavy equipment shall be confirmed by a receipt signed by a representative of the Belgian Forces, or by any other form of proof of transfer of the article to the Belgian Forces. The initial payment of these sums by the Belgian Government shall be made on presentations of a bill by the United States Department of the Army. Subsequent payments ahall be made every 3 months as long as the assistance and maintenance are provided by the Government of the United States of America.

Article 2

The fixed sum per man and per day for maintenance of personnel and equipment shall be noted on the financial statements furnished for the Belgian Government and shall be subject to change in case of a charge in the amount and prices of the supplies and services or in other factors affecting the cost of maintenance. The same shall apply for the fixed sum for ammunition.

Article 3

Payment for redeployment costs will be made by the Government of Belgium after the Belgian Forces have returned to Belgium.

Article 4

This agreement shall come into force upon the date of signature thereof and shall apply to all materials, supplies, services and facilities furnished or rendered on, before or after that date. . . . [*Agreement between Belgium and the United States concerning financial arrangements for logistical support, 31 Aug. 1955, 223 UNTS 13.*]

The basic agreements between the United States and the contributing states stipulated—in Article 6—that any claims in respect of currency transferred were not to lie against the United States, but were to be settled between the country concerned and Korea. By means of an exchange of notes between Korea and the United Kingdom, New Zealand, and Australia, forms were devised to settle the advances of Korean currency to meet the local needs of these Commonwealth forces.[8]

The agreements which Holland, Belgium, and South Africa made with the

[8] For text, see below, pp. 248–9.

United States also served to prohibit claims by the former against the latter for injury or death of personnel, or loss or destruction of property.

Arrangements were also entered into between the United States (acting as the Unified Command) and Germany and Sweden respectively, with regard to the participation of Red Cross hospitals from these countries:

Whereas the Government of the United States of America, acting as the Unified Command pursuant to the United Nations Security Council resolution of July 7, 1950, has designated the Commander of the United Nations forces in Korea (hereinafter referred to as the 'Commander');

Whereas the Government of the Federal Republic of Germany desires to lend humanitarian assistance in Korea and therefore proposes the dispatch of a Red Cross hospital (hereinafter referred to as the 'Hospital') and its staff of civilian personnel to Korea;

Whereas Article 27 of the Geneva Convention for the Amelioration of the Condition of the Wounded and Sick in Armed Forces in the Field of August 12, 1949 sets out procedures which the two Governments are willing to employ for the accomplishment of the humanitarian proposal of the Federal Republic of Germany;

The Government of the United States of America and the Government of the Federal Republic of Germany have entered into the present agreement:

Article I

1. The German Red Cross in the Federal Republic of Germany as a recognized national aid society shall, on the instructions and with the consent of the Government of the Federal Republic of Germany, furnish a Hospital for use in connection with the United Nations operations in Korea. The Hospital will devote its facilities to the care of civilians to the extent found feasible by the Commander.

2. The Government of the United States of America, acting as the Unified Command, gives its authorization to the rendering of assistance by the Hospital and shall request the Secretary-General of the United Nations to give the notification to the adverse Party provided for in the second sentence of paragraph 2, Article 27 of the above-mentioned Geneva Convention.

Article II

1. The Hospital shall be placed under the control of the Commander. Its internal operations, administration, and disciplinary control shall be vested in the Head of the Hospital subject to all orders, directives, and policies of the Commander. In the event of disagreement with such orders, directives, or policies, they shall be accepted and carried out as given, but formal protest may be presented subsequently.

2. The German personnel of the Hospital shall wear the uniform of the German Red Cross.

Article III

1. The Government of the United States of America shall assist the Hospital in the discharge of its functions.

2. The Government of the United States of America shall furnish the Hospital with available materials, supplies, services, and facilities, including transportation to and from Korea and such local services as are normally supplied by the Commander to like units, which the Hospital requires for its operations and which it is not feasible for the Government of the Federal Republic of Germany to furnish.

3. In protecting and caring for the Hospital, the Commander shall apply the same standards as he applies to like units under his jurisdiction, taking into account its humanitarian mission as a medical unit of a recognized national aid society.

8

4. The Commander, in so far as possible, will provide for unimpeded communications between the Hospital and the competent German authorities.

Article IV

1. The Government of the United States of America and the Government of the Federal Republic of Germany will maintain accounts of the materials, supplies, services, and facilities furnished by the Government of the United States of America to the Hospital.

2. The Government of the Federal Republic of Germany shall reimburse the Government of the United States of America in United States dollars, upon the presentation of statements of account by the Government of the United States of America, for such materials, supplies, services, and facilities. Issues of materials and supplies to the Hospital will not operate to transfer title in advance of reimbursement.

3. The Governments of the United States of America and the Federal Republic of Germany shall make technical and administrative arrangements regarding the furnishing of materials, supplies, services, and facilities, and the accounting and reimbursement therefor.

4. Classified, specialized, or scarce items furnished to the Hospital by the Government of the United States of America will be returned upon request, at the termination of the activities of the Hospital under this agreement, as a credit to the account of the Hospital. If the Government of the Federal Republic of Germany determines that materials or supplies furnished by the Government of the United States of America are not desired for retention, such materials or supplies may be offered to the Government of the United States of America, and if accepted, their residual value as determined by the Government of the United States of America will be credited to the account of the Hospital.

5. Settlement of obligations for materials, supplies, services, and facilities received by the Hospital from other governments, whether directly or through the Commander, shall be a matter for consideration between the Government of the Federal Republic of Germany and such other governments.

Article V

The requirements of the Hospital for Korean currency will be supplied under arrangements approved by the Commander; provided, however, that settlement of any obligation of the Government of the Federal Republic of Germany for the use of such currency will be a matter for consideration between the Government of the Federal Republic of Germany and the competent authorities of Korea.

Article VI

1. Each of the parties to this agreement agrees not to assert any claim against the other party for injury or death of its personnel, or for loss, damage, or destruction of its property or property of its personnel caused in Korea by personnel of the other party. For the purposes of this paragraph, personnel of the Government of the Federal Republic of Germany shall be defined as personnel of the Hospital and property of the Government of the Federal Republic of Germany shall include the property of the German Red Cross.

2. Claims of any other government or its nationals against the Government or nationals of the Federal Republic of Germany or vice versa shall be a matter for disposition between the Government of the Federal Republic of Germany and such other government or its nationals.

Article VII

The Government of the United States of America shall render to the Hospital such available assistance as may be necessary in connection with the termination of its activities and its redeployment.

Article VIII

This agreement shall come into force upon the date of signature thereof, and shall apply to all materials, supplies, services, and facilities furnished or rendered before, on, or after that date, to all claims referred to in Article VI arising before, on, or after that date, and to all technical and administrative arrangements concluded pursuant to Article IV before, on, or after that date.

IN WITNESS WHEREOF, the undersigned, being duly authorized by their respective Governments have signed this agreement.

DONE at Washington, this twelfth day of February 1954, in duplicate in the English and German languages, each text being equally authentic.

> For the Government of the United States of America:
> Walter BEDELL SMITH

> For the Government of the Federal Republic of Germany:
> D. Heinz L. KREKELER

[Agreement between the United States and the Federal Republic of Germany concerning assistance to be rendered by a German Red Cross Hospital in Korea, 12 Feb. 1954, 223 UNTS 154.]

The following agreement, with a non-member of the UN, was of a somewhat different form from those entered into by the United States in respect of the participation of a Norwegian mobile surgical unit, and the participation of a Swedish Red Cross field hospital:

This Agreement between the Government of the United States of America (the executive agent of the United Nations Forces in Korea) and the Government of the Kingdom of Norway shall govern relationships in matters specified herein for the Mobile Surgical Hospital (hereinafter referred to as Surgical Hospital) furnished by the Government of the Kingdom of Norway for the operations under the Commanding General of the Armed Forces of the Member States of the United Nations in Korea (hereinafter referred to as Commander) designated by the Government of the United States of America pursuant to resolutions of United Nations Security Council of June 25, 1950, June 27, 1950, and July 7, 1950.

Article I

The Government of the United States of America agrees to furnish the Surgical Hospital with available materials, supplies, services, and facilities which the Surgical Hospital will require for these operations, and which the Government of the Kingdom of Norway is unable to furnish. The Government of the United States of America and the Government of the Kingdom of Norway will maintain accounts of materials, supplies, services, and facilities furnished by the Government of the United States of America to the Surgical Hospital. Reimbursement for such materials, supplies, services, and facilities will be accomplished by the Government of the Kingdom of Norway upon presentation of statements of account by the Government of the United States of America. Such payment will be effected by the Government of the Kingdom of Norway in United States dollars. Issues of materials and supplies to the Surgical Hospital will not operate to transfer title to the Government of the Kingdom of Norway in advance of reimbursement.

Article 2

Pursuant to Article 1, appropriate technical and administrative arrangements will be concluded between authorized representatives of the Government of the United States of America and authorized representatives of the Government of the Kingdom of Norway.

Article 3

Classified items, specialized items, or items in short supply furnished to the Surgical Hospital by the Government of the United States of America will be returned to the Government of the United States of America upon request, upon the withdrawal of the Surgical Hospital from Korea, as a credit against the cost of materials, supplies, and services previously furnished. If the Government of the Kingdom of Norway determines at the time of redeployment of its Surgical Hospital that materials or supplies received from the Government of the United States of America hereunder are not desired for retention, such materials or supplies may be offered to the Government of the United States of America and if accepted, their residual value as determined by the Government of the United States of America will be used as a credit against reimbursement for materials supplies, and services previously furnished.

Article 4

Each of the parties to this Agreement agrees not to assert any claim against the other party for injury or death of its personnel, or for loss, damage, or destruction of its property or property of its personnel caused in Korea by personnel of the other party. Claims of any other government or its nationals against the Government or nationals of the Government of the Kingdom of Norway or vice versa shall be a matter for disposition between the Government of the Kingdom of Norway and such third government or its nationals.

Article 5

The Government of the Kingdom of Norway will maintain accounts of materials, supplies, services, and facilities furnished by other governments to personnel or agencies of the Government of the Kingdom of Norway, either directly or through the Commander. Settlement of any claims arising as a result of the furnishing of such materials, supplies, services, and facilities to the Government of the Kingdom of Norway by such third governments, whether directly or through the Commander, shall be a matter for consideration between such third governments and the Government of the Kingdom of Norway.

Article 6

The requirements of the Surgical Hospital for Korean currency will be supplied under arrangements approved by the Commander; provided, however, that settlement of any obligation of the Government of the Kingdom of Norway for use of such currency will be a matter of consideration between the Government of the Kingdom of Norway and the competent authorities of Korea. If, with the approval of the Commander, the Surgical Hospital uses media of exchange other than Korean currency in Korea, obligations arising therefrom will be a matter for consideration and settlement between the Government of the Kingdom of Norway and the other concerned governments.

Article 7

The Government of the Kingdom of Norway agrees that all orders, directives, and policies of the Commander issued to the Surgical Hospital or its personnel shall be accepted and carried out by them as given and that in the event of disagreement with such orders, directives, or policies, formal protest may be presented subsequently.

Article 8

Nothing in this Agreement shall be construed to affect existing agreements or arrangements between the parties for the furnishing of materials, supplies, services, or facilities.

Article 9

This Agreement shall come into force upon the date of signature thereof, and shall apply to all materials, supplies, services, and facilities furnished or rendered on, before, or after that date, to all claims referred to in Article 4 arising on, before, or after that date, and to all technical and administrative arrangements concluded pursuant to Article 2, before, on, or after that date.

IN WITNESS WHEREOF, the undersigned, being duly authorized by their respective Governments, have signed this Agreement.

DONE at Washington in duplicate this seventeenth day of September, 1951.

For the Government of the United States of America:
James W. WEBB
Acting Secretary of State
of the United States of America
For the Government of the Kingdom of Norway:
Eigil NYGAARD
Chargé d'Affaires ad interim of the
Kingdom of Norway at Washington

[*Agreement between the United States and Norway concerning participation of a Norwegian Surgical Hospital, 17 Sept. 1951 140 UNTS 314.*]

The Swedish agreement, which had been signed on 27 June, was in identical terms, save that the final sentence of Article 1 is missing (148 UNTS 77).

9

RELATIONS WITH THE HOST STATE

ALTHOUGH the UN was engaged in enforcement action against North Korea, with its main military command centre in Tokyo, it is none the less still reasonable for our purpose to designate the Republic of Korea as the 'host state'. UN Forces were present in that country at the request of her government.

Relations between the UN and Korea were very much left to the United States to deal with. No formal status-of-forces agreement was entered into.[1] On 25 July 1950 the United States disclosed the text of an agreement under which all military forces of the Republic of Korea were assigned to General MacArthur's command.

LETTER FROM PRESIDENT RHEE TO GENERAL MACARTHUR,
15 July 1950

In view of the joint military effort of the United Nations on behalf of the Republic of Korea, in which all military forces, land, sea, and air, of all the Members of the United Nations fighting in or near Korea had been placed under your operational command, and of

---

[1] There was, however, a status-of-forces agreement with Japan. See s. 10, p. 232.

which you have been designated Supreme Commander of United Nations Forces, I am happy to assign to your command authority over all land, sea, and air forces of the Republic of Korea during the period of the continuation of the present state of hostilities; such command to be exercised either by you personally or by such military commander or commanders to whom you may delegate the exercise of this authority within Korea or in adjacent seas.

The Korean Army will be proud to serve under your command, and the Korean people and Government will be equally proud and encouraged to have the over-all direction of our combined combat effort in the hands of so famous and distinguished a soldier, who also in his person possesses the delegated military authority of all the Members of the United Nations which have joined together to resist the infamous Communist assault on the independence and integrity of our beloved land.

With continued highest and warmest feelings of personal regard,

(*Signed* Syngman RHEE.

REPLY OF GENERAL MACARTHUR TO PRESIDENT RHEE,
18 July 1950

Please express to President Rhee my thanks and deepest appreciation for the action taken in his letter of 15 July. It cannot fail to increase the co-ordinated power of the United Nations forces operating in Korea. I am proud indeed to have the gallant Republic of Korea's forces under my command. Tell him I am grateful for his generous references to me personally, and how sincerely I reciprocate his sentiments of regard. Tell him also not to lose heart, that the way may be long and hard, but the ultimate result cannot fail to be victory.

(*Signed*) Douglas MACARTHUR.

[*S/1627, cited in SCOR, 477th mtg, 25 July 1950, p. 2.*]

The UN did enter into an agreement with the Republic of Korea to regularize the privileges and immunities of the Organization and its organs, representatives of member states and officials, and experts and locally recruited personnel (104 UNTS 323). But this agreement did not cover UN Forces. It was directed to the legal status of the UN Commission for the Unification and Rehabilitation of Korea, established by General Assembly resolution 376 (V), and the UN Korean Reconstruction Agency, established by General Assembly resolution 410 (V).[2] Nor can the 1952 Mutual Security Agreement between Korea and the United States be regarded as a status-of-forces agreement. It merely contained a broad undertaking by Korea 'to take appropriate steps to insure the effective utilization of the economic and military assistance provided by the United States'.[3]

Rather more specific arrangements were made to deal with the problem of currency. The texts of these arrangements are reproduced in Section 11, which covers the financing of the Korean operation.[4] The extent of the authority of the Unified Command in the Republic of Korea, and its penetration into the economic life of that country, is illustrated by the 1952 Agreement on Economic Co-ordination between the Unified Command and the Republic of Korea. This

---

[2] Indeed, pt B, para. 16 (4) of this last resolution had specifically provided that personnel of the UN should be accorded, within Korea, the privileges, immunities, and facilities necessary for the fulfilment of their functions.

[3] Art. 2 (E), 179 UNTS 108.

[4] S/1860 & 140 UNTS 62. See also the arrangements on crediting and finance between the US and contributing states, above, pp. 204–9; and between Korea and Commonwealth states, pp. 248–250.

agreement was obviously aimed at securing for the Unified Command effective control over equipment, services, and supplies:

AGREEMENT ON ECONOMIC CO-ORDINATION BETWEEN THE REPUBLIC OF KOREA AND THE UNIFIED COMMAND

24 May 1952

Whereas by the aggression of communist forces the Republic of Korea became in need of assistance from the United Nations,

And whereas the United Nations by the resolution of the Security Council of 27 June 1950, (*S/1511*), recommended that Members of the United Nations furnish such assistance to the Republic of Korea as may be necessary to repel the armed attack and to restore international peace and security in the area,

And whereas the United Nations by the resolution of the Security Council of 7 July 1950, (*S/1588*), recommended that Members furnishing military forces and other assistance to the Republic of Korea make such forces and other assistance available to a unified command under the United States,

And whereas the United Nations, by the resolution of the Security Council of 31 July 1950, (*S/1657*), requested the Unified Command to exercise responsibility for determining the requirements for the relief and support of the civilian population of Korea and for establishing in the field the procedures for providing such relief and support,

And whereas it became necessary to carry out collective action against aggression on Korean soil,

And whereas, pursuant to the 7 July 1950 resolution of the Security Council of the United Nations, the Unified Command has designated the Commander-in-Chief, United Nations Command, to exercise command responsibilities in Korea,

And whereas the Unified Command has already furnished and is furnishing substantial assastistance to the Republic of Korea,

And whereas it is desirable to co-ordinate economic matters between the Unified Command and the Republic of Korea, in order to ensure effective support of the military forces of the United Nations Command, to relieve the hardships of the people of Korea, and to establish and maintain a stable economy in the Republic of Korea; all without infringing upon the sovereign rights of the Republic of Korea,

Therefore, the Republic of Korea and the United States of America acting pursuant to the resolutions of the Security Council of the United Nations of 7 and 31 July 1950 (hereinafter referred to as the Unified Command) have entered into this agreement in terms as set forth below:

Article I

THE BOARD

1. There shall be established a Combined Economic Board, hereafter referred to as the Board.

2. The Board shall be composed of one representative from the Republic of Korea and one representative of the Commander-in-Chief, United Nations Command (CINCUNC). Before appointing its representative each party shall ascertain that such appointment is agreeable to the other party. The Board shall establish such subordinate organization as may be necessary to perform its functions and shall determine its own procedures. It shall meet regularly at an appropriate location in the Republic of Korea.

3. The primary function of the Board shall be to promote effective economic co-ordination between the Republic of Korea and the Unified Command. The Board shall be the principal means for consultation between the parties on economic matters and shall make appropriate and timely recommendations to the parties concerning the implementation of this Agreement. Such recommendations shall be made only upon mutual agreement of both representatives. The Board shall be a co-ordinating and advisory body; it shall not be an operating body.

4. The Board and the parties hereto shall be guided by the following general principles:

(*a*) The Board will consider all economic aspects of the Unified Command programmes for assistance to the Republic of Korea and all pertinent aspects of the economy and programmes of the Republic of Korea, in order that each of the Board's recommendations may be a part of a consistent over-all programme designed to provide maximum support to the military effort of the United Nations Command in Korea, relieve the hardships of the people of Korea, and develop a stable Korean economy.

(*b*) It is an objective of the parties to increase the capabilities of the Republic of Korea for economic self-support so far as is possible within the limits of available resources and consistent with the attainment of fiscal and monetary stability.

(*c*) Successful conduct of military operations against the aggression of the Communists is the primary consideration of the parties. Accordingly, the command prerogatives of the Commander-in-Chief, United Nations Command, are recognized; and the Commander-in-Chief, United Nations Command, shall continue to retain all authority deemed necessary by him for the successful conduct of such operations and the authority to withdraw and to distribute supplies and services furnished under this Agreement in order to meet emergencies arising during the course of military operations or in the execution of civil assistance programmes. On the other hand, the prerogatives of the Government of the Republic of Korea are recognized, and the Government of the Republic of Korea shall continue to retain all the authority of a sovereign and independent State.

5. The Board shall make recommendations necessary to ensure (*a*) that the expenses of the Board, and the expenses (i.e., local currency (won) expenses and expenses paid from assistance funds) of all operating agencies established by the Unified Command or the Republic to Korea to carry out assistance programmes under this Agreement, shall be kept to the minimum amounts reasonably necessary, and (*b*) that personnel funds, equipment, supplies and services provided for assistance purposes are not diverted to other purposes.

Article II

THE UNIFIED COMMAND

The Unified Command undertakes:

1. To support the recommendations of the Board to the extent of the resources made available to the Unified Command.

2. To require the Commander-in-Chief, United Nations Command, to designate his representative on the Board and to furnish to the Board such personnel and other necessary administrative support from the United Nations Command as the Board may recommend.

3. To furnish to the Board timely information on all civil assistance programmes of the Unified Command and on the status of such programmes.

4. Within the limitations of the resources made available by governments or organizations to the Unified Command, to assist the Republic of Korea in providing for the basic necessities of food, clothing and shelter for the population of Korea; for measures to prevent epidemics, disease, and unrest; and for projects which will yield early results in the indigenous production of necessities. Such measures and projects may include the reconstruction and replacement of facilities necessary for relief and support of the civilian population.

5. To ascertain, in consultation with the appropriate authorities of the Government of the Republic of Korea, the requirement for equipment, supplies and services for assisting the Republic of Korea.

6. To provide for the procurement and shipment of equipment, supplies, and other assistance furnished by the Unified Command; to supervise the distribution and utilization of this assistance; and to administer such assistance in accordance with the above-cited resolutions of the United Nations.

7. To consult with and to utilize the services of the appropriate authorities of the Government of the Republic of Korea, to the greatest extent feasible, in drawing up and implementing plans and programmes for assisting the Republic of Korea, including the employment of

Korean personnel and the procurement, allocation, distribution and sale of equipment, supplies and services.

8. To carry out the Unified Command programme of assistance to the Republic of Korea in such a way as to facilitate the conduct of military operations, relieve hardship and contribute to the stabilization of the Korean economy.

9. To make available in Korea to authorized representatives of the Government of the Republic, of Korea appropriate documents relating to the civil assistance programmes of the Unified Command.

Article III

THE REPUBLIC OF KOREA

The Republic of Korea undertakes:

1. To support the recommendations of the Board.

2. To designate the representative of the Republic of Korea on the Board and to furnish to the Board such personnel and other necessary administrative support from the Republic of Korea as the Board may recommend.

3. To furnish to the Board timely information on the economy of Korea and on those activities and plans of the Government of the Republic of Korea pertinent to the functions of the Board.

4. While continuing those measures which the Government of the Republic of Korea has endeavoured heretofore to make effective, to take further measures to combat inflation, hoarding, and harmful speculative activities; to apply sound, comprehensive, and adequate budgetary, fiscal, and monetary policies, including maximum collection of revenue; to maintain adequate controls over the extension of public and private credit; to provide requisite and feasible pricing, rationing and allocation controls; to promote wage and price stability; to make most efficient use of all foreign exchange resources; to maximize the anti-inflationary effect that can be derived from relief and other imported essential commodities through effective programming, distribution and sales; to provide the maximum efficiency in utilization of available production facilities; and to maximize production for export.

5. With reference to assistance furnished under this Agreement:

(a) To provide operating agencies which will develop and execute, in consultation with operating agencies of the United Nations Command, programmes relating to requirements, allocations, distribution, sale, use and accounting for equipment, supplies and services furnished under this Agreement; to submit to the Board budget estimates of the expenses of such Republic of Korea agencies; to include such estimates in the national budget; to defray those expenses from the resources available to the Government of the Republic of Korea, including, where the Board so recommends, such funds as may be made available under clause 7 (d) (2) of this article; and to ensure that such expenses are kept at a minimum. It is intended that such expenses will be defrayed from the general account revenues of the Republic of Korea when the economy of the Republic of Korea so permits.

(b) To permit the Commander-in-Chief, United Nations Command, to exercise such control over assistance furnished hereunder as may be necessary to enable him to exercise his responsibilities under the above cited resolutions of the United Nations.

(c) To achieve maximum sales consistent with relief needs and to be guided by the recommendations of the Board in determining what equipment, supplies and services are to be distributed free of charge and what are to be sold.

(d) To require Republic of Korea agencies handling equipment and supplies furnished under this Agreement to make and maintain such records and reports as the Commander-in-Chief, United Nations Command, or the Board may consider to be necessary in order to show the import, distribution, sale and utilization of such equipment and supplies.

(e) To impose import duties or charges, or internal taxes or charges, on goods and services furnished by the United Nations Command only as recommended by the Board.

8*

(*f*) To permit and to assist the authorized representatives of the Commander-in-Chief, United Nations Command, freely to inspect the distribution and use of equipment, supplies, or services provided under this Agreement, including all storage and distribution facilities and all pertinent records.

(*g*) To ensure (1) that the people of Korea are informed of the sources and purposes of contributions of funds, equipment, supplies and services and (2) that all equipment and supplies (and the containers thereof) made available by the Unified Command to the civilian economy of the Republic of Korea, to the extent practicable, as determined by the Commander-in-Chief, United Nations Command, are marked, stamped, branded, or labelled in a conspicuous place as legibly, indelibly, and permanently as the nature of such equipment and supplies will permit and in such manner as to indicate to the people of the Republic of Korea the sources and purposes of such supplies.

6. With reference to the assistance furnished under this Agreement which is to be distributed free of charge for the relief of the people of Korea, to ensure that the special needs of refugees and other distressed groups of the population are alleviated without discrimination through appropriate public welfare programmes.

7. With reference to assistance furnished under this Agreement which is to be sold:

(*a*) To sell equipment and supplies at prices recommended by the Board, such prices to be those designed to yield the maximum feasible proceeds.

(*b*) To sell equipment and supplies furnished under this Agreement for cash, unless otherwise recommended by the Board. If the Board should recommend that any such equipment and supplies may be sold to intermediate parties or ultimate users on a credit basis, the amount and duration of such credit shall be no more liberal than that recommended by the Board.

(*c*) To establish and maintain a special account in the Bank of Korea to which will be transferred the balance now in the 'Special United Nations Aid Goods Deposit Account' at the Bank of Korea and to which will be deposited the gross won proceeds of sales of all equipment and supplies (1) furnished under this Agreement, or (2) locally procured by expenditure of won funds previously deposited.

(*d*) To use the special account established in (*c*) above to the maximum extent possible as a stabilizing device and as an offset to harmful monetary expansion. To this end withdrawals from this account shall be made only upon the recommendation of the Board, only for the following purposes, and only in the following order of priority:

(1) For defraying reasonable local currency costs involved in carrying out the responsibilities of the Unified Command for relief and support of the civilian population of Korea, provided, however that such local currency expenses shall not include won advances to the United Nations Command for its *bona fide* military expenses or for sale to personnel of the United Nations Command;

(2) For defraying such proportion of the reasonable operating expenses of operating agencies of the Government of the Republic of Korea provided under clause 5 (*a*) above as may be recommended by the Board.

(3) The balance remaining in this special account, after withdrawals for the above purposes have been made and after provision has been made for an operating reserve, shall periodically upon the recommendation of the Board be applied against any then existing indebtedness of the Government of the Republic of Korea to the Bank of Korea or to any other financial institution organized under the laws of the Republic of Korea.

8. To prevent the export from the Republic of Korea of any of the equipment or supplies furnished by the Unified Command or any items of the same or similar character produced locally or otherwise procured, except upon the recommendation of the Board.

9. To make prudent use of its foreign exchange and foreign credit resources and to utilize these resources to the extent necessary first toward stabilization (by prompt importation into Korea of salable essential commodities) and then toward revitalization and reconstruction of the economy of Korea. The use of such foreign exchange and foreign credit resources shall be controlled or co-ordinated as follows:

(*a*) All foreign exchange (both public and private) of the Republic of Korea accruing hereafter from indigenous exports, visible and invisible, except as described in (*b*) below, shall be controlled solely by the Government of the Republic of Korea.

(*b*) All foreign exchange (both public and private, and from whatever source acquired) now held by the Republic of Korea and that foreign exchange which, subsequent to the effective date of this Agreement, is derived by the Republic of Korea from any settlement for advances of Korean currency to the United Nations Command shall be used only as recommended by the Board.

(*c*) All foreign exchange described in (*a*) and (*b*) above shall be co-ordinated by the Board, in order to integrate the use made of such foreign exchange with the imports included in the Unified Command assistance programmes.

10. In order properly to adapt the assistance programmes of the Unified Command to the needs of the economy of Korea, and in order to co-ordinate imports under those programmes with imports purchased with foreign exchange, to support the recommendations of the Board in the making of periodic plans for the import and export of commodities and to use such plans as a basis for the issuance of export and import licences.

11. In order to make most effective use of the foreign exchange resources of the Government of the Republic of Korea in stabilizing the Korean economy:

(*a*) To maximize the won proceeds from the sale of such exchange or from the sale of imports derived from such exchange.

(*b*) To apply such proceeds first against any existing overdrafts of the Government of the Republic of Korea upon the Bank of Korea, except as otherwise recommended by the Board.

(*c*) To hold or spend the balance of such won proceeds with due regard to the effect of such action on the total money supply.

12. To provide logistic support to the armed forces of the Republic of Korea to the maximum extent feasible and to furnish to the United Nations Command timely information concerning the details of this support in order to permit co-ordinated budgetary planning.

13. To grant to individuals and agencies of the Unified Command, except Korean nationals, such privileges, immunities and facilities as are necessary for the fulfilment of their function within the Republic of Korea under the above-cited resolutions of the United Nations, or as have been heretofore granted by agreement, arrangement or understanding or as may be agreed upon formally or informally hereafter by the parties or their agencies.

14. To ensure that funds, equipment, supplies and services provided by the Unified Command or derived therefrom shall not be subject to garnishment, attachment, seizure, or other legal process by any person, firm, agency, corporation, organization or government, except upon recommendation of the Board.

Article IV

TRANSFER

1. The parties recognize that all or any portion of the responsibilities of the Unified Command may be assumed from time to time by another agency or agencies of the United Nations. Prior to such transfer, the parties shall consult together concerning any modification in this Agreement which may be required thereby.

2. It is the current expectation of the parties that the United Nations Korean Reconstruction Agency (UNKRA), established by resolution of the General Assembly of the United Nations of 1 December 1950, (410 (V)) will assume responsibility for all United Nations relief and rehabilitation activities for Korea at the termination of a period of one hundred and eighty days following the cessation of hostilities in Korea, as determined by the Unified Command, in consultation with the Agent General of the United Nations Korean Reconstruction Agency, that military operations do not so permit at that time, or unless an earlier transfer of responsibility is agreed upon.

218	KOREA

Article V

EXISTING AGREEMENTS

This Agreement does not supersede in whole or in part any existing agreement between the parties hereto.

Article VI

REGISTRATION, EFFECTIVE DATE, AND TERMINATION

1. This Agreement shall be registered with the Secretary-General of the United Nations in compliance with the provisions of Article 102 of the Charter of the United Nations.

2. This Agreement shall enter into operation and effect immediately upon signature hereto. This Agreement shall remain in force so long as the Unified Command continues in existence and retains responsibilities hereunder, unless earlier terminated by agreement between the parties.

DONE in duplicate in the English and Korean languages, at Pusan, Korea, on this . . . day of May 1952. The English and Korean texts shall have equal force, but in case of divergence, the English text shall prevail.

IN WITNESS WHEREOF, the respective representatives, duly authorized for the purpose, have signed the present Agreement.

For the Government of the   *For the Government of the*
Republic of Korea   *United States of America*

[S/2768, 9 Sept. 1952, pp. 40–7.]

So far as claims for utilities were concerned, the United States, acting both as Unified Command and on her own behalf, and also on behalf of the states furnishing military or medical assistance, signed an agreement with Korea at Seoul and on 18 December 1958:

Whereas the United Nations by the resolution of the Security Council of 27 June 1950, recommended that members of the United Nations furnish such assistance to the Republic of Korea as may be necessary to repel the armed attack and to restore international peace and security in the area;

And whereas the United Nations by the resolution of the Security Council of 7 July 1950, recommended that members furnishing military forces and other assistance to the Republic of Korea make such forces and other assistance available to a Unified Command under the United States;

And whereas the United States of America, acting in its capacity as the Unified Command, employed the military forces contributed by members of the United Nations and by the Republic of Korea in repelling the armed attack and restoring international peace and security in the area;

And whereas the United States of America, acting in its capacity as the Unified Command, and the Republic of Korea provided facilities, materials, supplies, equipment, utilities, services, and monies, for the support of the military forces employed against Communist aggression in Korea;

And whereas the United States of America, acting in its capacity as the Unified Command, and the Republic of Korea consider it desirable to negotiate a settlement of claims and counter claims arising from the rendition of utilities services,

Therefore, the Government of the United States of America, on the one hand, in its capacity as the Unified Command and on its own behalf, and the governments of those nations furnishing military forces or field hospitals to the Unified Command: namely, Australia, Belgium, Canada, Colombia, Denmark, Ethiopia, France, Germany, Greece, India, Italy, Luxembourg, the Netherlands, New Zealand, Norway, the Republic of the Philippines, Sweden, Thailand, Turkey, the Union of South Africa, the United Kingdom of Great Britain and Northern Ireland; and the Government of the Republic of Korea, on the other hand; have agreed as follows:

Article I

1. 'Claims and counterclaims' means any demands or requests for, or asserion of right to, payment of money or restoration, replacement, rehabilitation, or removal of property in settlement of any obligation, charge, or account, expressed or implied, including counterclaims and offsets, arising from rendition of utilities services, including claims arising from use, alteration, loss, or destruction of, or damage to property in connection with transmission, use or consumption of any utilities, and includes claims and counterclaims arising from the rendition of personal services required in the establishment, maintenance, and operation of utilities, and those claims and counterlclaims for reimbursement for improvements to personal property, but excludes claims arising out of formal written contacts for utilities services between the Republic of Korea and the Unified Command, between any one of the nations in the United Nations Command, and the Republic of Korea, between the Unified Command or any one of the nations in the United Nations Command and the nationals of the Republic of Korea or other persons residing or owning property in the Republic of Korea, or claims arising out of private commercial contracts.

2. 'Utilities services' includes but is not limitated to the operation and use of transportation and communications facilities and systems, and the operation and use or consumption of electricity, gas, water, steam, heat, light, and power, however produced, and sewage disposal.

Article II

1. This agreement is limited to claims and counterclaims arising from the rendition of utilities services as defined in Article I hereof.

2. This agreement shall not apply to claims arising out of the economic assistance programs and out of the furnishing to the Republic of Korea military forces of material and common use items.

Article III

1. The Republic of Korea forever releases and agrees to hold harmless the United States of America, in its capacity as the Unified Command and on its own behalf, and the governments of those nations furnishing military forces or field hospitals to the Unified Command, and their nationals, from any and all claims arising from the rendition of utilities services in Korea, incident to the action to repel aggression in Korea, during the period from 25 June 1950 to and including 30 September 1955, against the Unified Command, the governments of those nations furnishing military forces or field hospitals to the Unified Command, or their nationals, by the Republic of Korea, nationals of the Republic of Korea, or other persons owning property, rendering services, or residing in Korea.

2. The United States of America, in its capacity as the Unified Command and on its own behalf, and the governments of those nations furnishing military forces or field hospitals to the Unified Command forever release and agree to hold harmless the Republic of Korea and its nationals from any and all claims arising from the rendition of utilities services in Korea, incident to the action to repel aggression in Korea, during the period 25 June 1950 to and including 30 September 1955 against the Republic of Korea, or its nationals by the United States of America, in its capacity as the Unified Command and on its own behalf or the governments of those nations furnishing military forces or field hospitals to the Unified Command, and their nationals.

3. The United States of America, in its capacity as the Unified Command and on its own behalf, and the governments of those nations furnishing military forces or field hospitals to the Unified Command, and the Republic of Korea agree to the settlement of all claims and counterclaims arising from the rendition of utilities services in Korea for the period 1 October 1955 to and including 30 June 1957 by payment of $7,250,000 which will be made by the

respective responsible governments to the Republic of Korea. The obligation to reimburse the Republic of Korea will be the responsibility of the respective responsible governments, who will settle on terms and in currencies to be agreed upon.

4. In consideration of the settlement of utilities claims as provided in paragraph 3, article III:

A. The Republic of Korea forever releases and agrees to hold harmless the United States of America, in its capacity as the Unified Command and on its own behalf, and the governments of those nations furnishing military forces or field hospitals to the Unified Command, and their nationals, from any and all claims arising from the rendition of utilities services in Korea during the period from 1 October 1955 to and including 30 June 1957.

B. The United States of America, in its capacity as the Unified Command and on its own behalf, and the governments of those nations furnishing military forces or field hospitals to the Unified Command, forever release and agree to hold harmless the Republic of Korea and its nationals from any and all claims arising from the rendition of utilities services in Korea during the period from 1 October 1955 to and including 30 June 1957.

Article IV

1. The United States of America, in its capacity as the Unified Command and on its own behalf, and the governments of those nations furnishing military forces or field hospitals to the Unified Command undertake to negotiate arrangements relating to the provision of utilities services and supplies to it by the Republic of Korea or by its nations on and after the effective date of this agreement.

2. The expenditures, activities, and property of the United States of America, in its capacity as the Unified Command and on its own behalf, or of the governments of those nations furnishing military forces or field hospitals to the Unified Command, shall be relieved of all customs, duties, taxes, interest, imposts, and fees or charges of any description levied or authorized by the Republic of Korea, its agencies, or political subdivisions, in the field of utilities services.

Article V

The United States of America, in its capacity as the Unified Command and on its own behalf, and the governments of those nations furnishing military forces or field hospitals to the Unified Command, and the Republic of Korea agree to make available, each to the other, for inspection for a period of 2 years from the date of the signing of this agreement any record or documentary evidence, reasonably available, which may be required by either party to enable it to defend, answer, or establish any claim arising from the rendition of utilities services asserted against it during the period 25 June 1950 to and including 30 June 1957.

Article VI

It is agreed that the value of the Korean currency to be used in computing the value of utilities services rendered, supplies furnished or damages incurred, shall be the military conversion rate or the official rate used for United Nations Command expenditures at the time the supplies were furnished, the utilities services were rendered, or the damages were incurred.

Article VII

This agreement supersedes, in whole and in part, any agreement, expressed or implied, between the parties, relating to the settlement of claims and counterclaims arising from the rendition of utilities services between the dates 25 June 1950 to and including 30 June 1957.

Article VIII

1. This agreement shall be registered with the Secretary General of the United Nations in compliance with the provisions of Article 102 of the Charter of the United Nations.

2. This agreement shall be deemed to have entered into operation and effect on 1 July 1957.

IN WITNESS WHEREOF, the respective representatives, duly authorized for the purpose, have signed the present agreement.

DONE at Seoul in duplicate, in the English and Korea languages, this 18th day of December 1958. The English and Korean texts shall have equal force, but in case of difference, the English text shall prevail.

> For the Government of the United States of America, in its capacity as the Unified Command and on its own behalf and on behalf of the governments of those nations furnishing military forces or field hospitals to the Unified Command:
> George H. DECKER, General U.S. Army
> Commander in Chief, U.N. Command

> For the Government of the Republic of Korea:
> HYUN CHUL KIM

EXCHANGE OF LETTERS

I

18 December 1958

Dear Mr Minister:

I refer to the agreement, signed today, which settles claims for utilities services furnished the United Nations Forces in Korea.

On behalf of the Swedish Government, I hereby state that its acceptance of this agreement is made with the exception of Article VI concerning the value of the Korean currency to be used in computing the value of utilities services rendered, supplies furnished or damage incurred.

Furthermore, since the amount to be paid by the Government of Sweden under this agreement has not been determined on an exact accounting basis but is a negotiated amount, I am also asked to state, that the regulations given in Article VI shall in no way prejudice the settling of other Swedish debts to the Republic of Korea.

> G. H. DECKER
>
> General, United States Army
> Commander in Chief

The Honorable Kim Hyun Chul
Minister of Finance
Republic of Korea
Seoul, Korea

II

MINISTRY OF FINANCE
REPUBLIC OF KOREA
SEOUL

18 December 1958

Dear General Decker:

Reference is made to the 'Utilities Claims Settlement Agreement Between the Unified Command and the Republic of Korea' signed today, and your letter also of this date as to the desires of the Government of Sweden in reference to this Agreement.

The terms of this agreement are solely applicable to the Utilities Claims Settlement and therefore the provisions of Article VI shall in no way prejudice the settling of other Swedish debts to the Republic of Korea.

Accordingly, this letter confirms acceptance by the Government of Republic of Korea of the reservations on the part of Government of Sweden relative to Article VI of the Agreement. Sincerely,

HYUN CHUL KIM
Minister of Finance
Republic of Korea

G. H. Decker
General, United States Army
Commander in Chief
United Nations Command

[*325 UNTS 240*.]

In spite of these limited and piecemeal arrangements, it remains that the only status-of-forces agreement relevant to the Korean hostilities was made with Japan.[5] This was concluded by the United States acting as Unified Command, and by the governments of Canada, New Zealand, United Kingdom, South Africa, Australia, Philippines, France, and Italy. The arrangements employed, while hardly satisfactory from the legal point of view, seemed effective enough in practice; though the diverging objectives of President Rhee and the UN as a whole put a strain upon them, especially in the 1952–3 period. Korea's influence upon the decisions taken by the Unified Command during the armistice negotiations was informal rather than overt. The Republic was represented only by an officer in the Unified Command armistice delegation.

Controversy between the Unified Command and Syngman Rhee came into the open after the conclusion, on 8 June 1953, of the Prisoners-of-War Convention.[6] Although the UN had firmly retained the principle that forcible repatriation of prisoners was unacceptable,[7] the arrangements made on 8 June were still apparently unsatisfactory to Syngman Rhee. The UN Command reported that on 18 June:

officials of the Republic of Korea brought about a break-out from the prisoner-of-war camps of some 27,000 Korean prisoners of war who had previously indicated that they would resist repatriation to North Korea. This action . . . was inconsistent with the Agreement of 8 June on prisoners of war and the United Nations Command at once protested to the Republic of Korea Government. It also informed the Chinese–North Korean Command of the event and told them that, while efforts would be made to recover as many of the escapees as possible, there was not much hope that many of these could be recaptured since they had melted into the South Korean population. This incident, it was reported, led to immediate conversations with the Republic of Korea by the representatives of the Unified Command. After prolonged discussions, it was stated, the Republic of Korea gave assurances that it would not obstruct the implementation of the terms of the Armistice Agreement.

The conclusion of an armistice was, however, further delayed, the United Nations Command stated, since the Chinese–North Korean side demanded assurances that the United Nations Command could 'live up' to the terms of the Armistice Agreement. While giving these assurances, the United Nations Command made it clear that it would not use force

[5] 207 UNTS 237. For text, see below, pp. 233–45.
[6] For text, see incorporated sections of Armistice Agreement, below, pp. 298–302.
[7] For details of this argument, see above, pp. 184–7, and below, pp. 277–81.

against the Republic of Korea forces to ensure compliance with the armistice by the Republic of Korea. [*YBUN, 1953*, pp. 112–13.]

The dismay of the UN at Syngman Rhee's attitude and action was further expressed by a cable which Lester Pearson, the Assembly's President, sent to President Syngman Rhee on 23 June 1953:

Dear Mr President,

As President of the General Assembly of the United Nations I have been shocked to hear of the unilateral action which you have sanctioned in bringing about the release of non-repatriable North Korean prisoners from the United Nations prisoner-of-war camps in Korea.

I take this occasion to recall the decisive action taken by the United Nations when aggression was initiated in June nineteen fifty and the satisfaction which you expressed in the response of the United Nations to the urgent appeals made by you for military and other assistance. That collaboration, aimed at the repelling of aggression and the restoration of your country to a condition of peace and economic well-being, has been marked by three years of effective effort on the part of members of the United Nations, and of your government and people, under the direction of the United Nations command. In view of what this collaboration has meant to your people, it is most regrettable that you have taken action which threatens the results already achieved and the prospect of a peaceful solution of remaining problems.

This release of North Korean prisoners from United Nations prisoner of war camps in Korea is particularly shocking in view of the progress made by the Armistice negotiators in Panmunjom, which has resulted in the acceptance of principles laid down in the United Nations General Assembly's resolution of three December nineteen fifty-two endorsed by fifty-four member nations. The acceptance of the principles underlying this resolution, expecially that of no forcible repatriation of prisoners, which has been the basis of your position as well as that of the United Nations, has only been obtained after two years of patient and persistent negotiation by the United Nations command.

The action taken with your consent, in releasing the North Korean prisoners, violates the agreement reached by the two sides on June eighth nineteen fifty-three embodying these principles, and it occurs at a time when hostilities are about to cease, andwhen the questions of the unification of Korea and related Korean problems can be dealt with by a political conference involving the parties concerned.

In July nineteen fifty, as a means of assuring necessary military solidarity with the United Nations effort in repelling Aggression, you undertook to place the land, sea and air forces of the republic of Korea under the subquote command authority unsubquote of the United Nations command. Your action referred to above violates that undertaking.

As President of the General Assembly of the United Nations I feel it my duty to bring to your attention the gravity of this situation. I hope and trust that you will co-operate with the United Nations command in its continuing and determined efforts to obtain an early and honourable armistice.

I should like to take this occasion to express, as President of the United Nations General Assembly, my profound sympathy for the sufferings of the people of Korea during the past three years, and my admiration for the valiant efforts of the ROK army in its co-operation with the forces of the United Nations. It is my earnest hope that this co-operation will continue, not only in the immediate task of obtaining the armistice but in assuring that the armistice is thereafter faithfully observed, in order that we may jointly proceed toward our common objective of the unification of Korea by peaceful means. If this co-operation were ended, it would be the Korean people who would suffer first and suffer most.—Lester B. Pearson, President of the United Nations General Assembly. [*A/2398, Message from President of General Assembly to President of Republic of Korea, 23 June 1953.*]

10

RELATIONS WITH OTHER STATES INVOLVED

(a) The Korean People's Democratic Republic

THE UN's action was for the purpose of repelling the aggression against South Korea from North Korea. Obviously, the relationship between the UN and North Korea was one of belligerency. North Korea in the early stages attempted to draw a distinction between the UN as such, and the alleged illegal use of the UN machinery by the United States and her allies. The North Korean authorities thus continued to address complaints to the Security Council, and to respond to queries from, e.g., the Group on Cease-Fire of the General Assembly.[1] This attitude may be contrasted with the contemporary Chinese policy of ignoring the UN. It was through the records of the UN that North Korea was able to present her case to the non-Communist world:

On 27 June, the President of the United States, Mr Truman, declared that he had ordered the air and naval forces of the United States to intervene in the military operations in Korea on the side of the South Korean puppet régime, which has unleashed civil war in our country at the behest of the American imperialists. On 30 June Mr Truman announced that American land forces had been sent to South Korea, American aircraft are brutally bombing our peaceful population and flying over Pyongyang and other points in North Korea and the liberated cities of South Korea, attacking units of the People's Army with the purpose of hindering their victorious advance southwards.

The policy pursued by the American imperialists of enslaving the Korean people and turning Korea into a colony of the United States has now developed into open armed intervention against the Korean People's Democratic Republic. American imperialists have long dreamed of establishing their domination in the Fear East. Previously, however, they had to reckon with the imperialist interests of Great Britain, Japan and other Powers and expand their position in the Far East by making deals with those Powers at the cost of enslaving the peoples of Asia. The Korean people will not forget in particular the fact that in 1905 the United States, with a view to reinforcing its domination over the Philippines, negotiated a treacherous deal with Japan and joined in setting up a Japanese protectorate over Korea.

After the Second World War, which resulted in the defeat of Japan and the weakening of Great Britain, American imperialists decided to occupy their place in the countries of the Far East, endeavouring to transform the Pacific Ocean into an American sea and the peoples of the Pacific Ocean countries into the slaves of American monopoly. However, the strengthening of the forces of the democratic camp, the advance of the national liberation movement in the countries of Asia, and particularly the great victory won by the Chinese people, utterly destroyed the base designs of the American imperialists. The Korean people has personally experienced the whole weight of the colonialist policy of American imperialists. Having rid itself of the hateful yoke of the Japanese, it again finds itself threatened with enslavement.

The American imperialists, in their anxiety to keep a grip on South Korea, stubbornly resisted the unification of the Korean people. They disrupted the formation of a single demo-

[1] See above, p. 166.

cratic government based on the Moscow Decision of the Foreign Ministers of the Union of Soviet Socialist Republics, the United States of America, and the United Kingdom. They refused to remove their troops from Korea before they had transformed southern Korea into their own colony with the assistance of the pupper Government of Syngman Rhee created by them.

It is now clear to every Korean that, even after the withdrawal of American troops, South Korea was governed by the American imperialists. It is they who, together with the Syngman Rhee clique, bear full responsibility for the crimes of the military police régime which they have set up in South Korea, for the executions and murders of tens of thousands of the sons of the Korean people destroyed by the Syngman Rhee clique on the orders of their American masters, for the tortures inflicted on hundreds of thousands of patriots thrown into prison and brutally tortured, for all the sufferings of the people of South Korea. The hands of the American imperialists are stained with the blood of the Korean people.

But they did not succeed in enslaving the Korea people, the main hindrance to this being the democratic régime established in North Korea. North Korea has become a powerful base for the fight of the Korean people for unity, independence, and freedom. Its successes in peaceful reconstruction, which have shown the superiority of democracy as compared with the anti-popular military and police régime of South Korea, have inspired the Korean people to fight against the efforts of American imperialists to reduce Korea to a colony, have convinced the people of ultimate victory. That is why the American imperialists and their South Korean lackeys, in their hatred of the Korean People's Democratic Republic, have long been cherishing plans to throttle it by military force. They obstructed the realisation of the proposals for the peaceful unification of Korea, which were frequently put forward by the democratic parties and social organizations and also by the Government of the People's Democratic Republic. With the support of the United States the Government of Syngman Rhee has for two years past openly prepared for an attack on the North, boasting that its army could occupy Pyongyang in a single day and that it was merely awaiting the order to advance, having secured the promise of military support from the United States of America.

At the behest of its American masters, the Syngman Rhee Government on 25 June began civil war in Korea. In provoking this war the American imperialists intended by means of armed intervention to destroy the Korean Democratic Republic and take possession of all Korea. Civil war in Korea was also necessary to the American imperialists in order to create a pretext for aggression against China and Vietnam also, to throttle the national liberation movement of the peoples of the Orient. The United States is trying to cover its intervention in Korea with the name of the United Nations, but everyone knows that the American imperialists have placed the United Nations before a *fait accompli* by undertaking armed intervention; it calculates that it will succeed by means of the votes of countries dependent on the United States of America, using the name of the United Nations to cover any unlawful action whatsoever, even after it has been perpetrated.

The American-dictated resolution of the Security Council based on one-sided, fabricated information is invalid and contrary to the United Nations Charter, since it was adopted without the participation of representatives of the Government of the Korean People's Democratic Republic and also without the participation of representatives of two great Powers, permanent members of the Security Council, the Union of Soviet Socialist Republics and the Chinese People's Republic. Members of the Security Council who voted in favour of this resolution have once again shown that they are prepared to put their signatures to any document dictated to them by the United States, regardless of the rights and interests of the peoples.

In this connexion it is worthy of remark that the pro-American majority in the United Nations which has now shown such a feverish readiness to rescue the bankrupt Syngman Rhee régime ignored the repeated applications of the Korean People's Democratic Republic and social organizations of Korea made in United Nations organs regarding the atrocities and military provocation committed by the Syngman Rhee régime. It also ignored numerous requests made by Korean social organizations, with concrete proposals for the peaceful unification of Korea, thus encouraging the adventurist actions of the United States of America and their South Korean vassals to stir up civil war in Korea. The American imperialists and their South Korean protégés committed a desperate mistake in unleashing civil war in Korea. The troops of Syngman Rhee have met with fitting resistance and, under the blows of the People's Army, which has counterattacked, are fleeing in disorder to the South. The gallant People's Army, in defence of the freedom and independence of the Korean people, is continuing to pursue the enemy.

In the military operations of the past week the People's Army cleared the enemy out of a large area of the southern half of the Republic and liberated Seoul, the national capital. The population is everywhere welcoming its army, which has liberated it from the terrors of the Syngman Rhee régime, and is giving it active assistance in the liberation of the country. The heroic partisans in South Korea have carried out military operations on the enemy's communications and have cut the main railway line from the harbour of Pusan; in collaboration with the insurgent population they have freed a number of towns in South Korea. The flight of the Syngman Rhee army and the popular rising in its rear are further evidence of the rottenness and failure of the anti-popular régime of the South Korean puppets of the United States. The complete bankruptcy of the Syngman Rhee régime has today become obvious.

Seeing the collapse of their plans for the colonization of Korea, the American imperialists are reinforcing their armed intervention against the Korean People. They want to drown the freedom of Korea in the blood of its patriots, but they will not frighten the freedom-loving Korean people. In reply to the bare-faced aggression of the United States, the Korean people will gather even more closely under the banner of the Korean People's Democratic Republic and strengthen their holy war for the freedom, unity and independence of their native land. The Government of the Korean People's Democratic Republic and the whole Korean nation resolutely protest against American armed intervention in Korea, against the barbarous bombardments of Korean towns and villages, against the inhuman slaughter of peaceful citizens. We are convinced that all honourable people in the world will indignantly condemn the aggression of the American imperialists against the freedom-loving people of Korea. We are certain that our just cause will meet with warm sympathy in the hearts of all people. [*S/1554, 3 July 1950, Cablegram of 2 July 1950 to the Secretary-General from the Minister for Foreign Affairs of the Korean People's Democratic Republic.*]

The North Korean authorities also notified the Secretary-General (as well as the ICRC) of their intention to adhere to the principles of the 1949 Geneva Convention on Prisoners of War.[2] The records of the UN were also used by the North Korean Government to make its allegations of bacteriological warfare against the Unified Command.[3]

The difficulties of UN–North Korean relations in the context of the armistice negotiations—and especially on the issue of the forcible return of prisoners of war—are recounted elsewhere.[4]

(b) China

It was clear from the earliest stages of the war that China viewed the hostilities in Korea as a matter of the utmost concern to her own security. The UN action was denounced as illegal, and China on many occasions complained of United States intrusion into her air space, and bombing of her territory. Her entry into the war—through so-called volunteers—was therefore not unexpected.

---

[2] S/1676, 8 Aug. 1950. See also above, pp. 190–3.
[3] S/2142/Rev. 1, 10 May, 1951.
[4] See above, pp. 184–7.

The resolution adopted by the Security Council on 27 June (S/1511) under the instigation and manipulation of the United States Government calling upon the members of the United Nations to assist the South Korean authorities, is in support of United States armed aggression and constitutes an intervention in the internal affairs of Korea and a violation of world peace. This resolution, being adopted moreover in the absence of two permanent members of the Security Council, the People's Republic of China and the Union of Soviet Socialist Republics, is obviously illegal. The United Nations Charter stipulates that the United Nations shall not be authorized to intervene in matters which are essentially within the internal jurisdiction of any State, while the resolution of the Security Council of 27 June exactly violates this important principle of the United Nations Charter. Therefore the resolution of the Security Council with regard to the Korean question is not only destitute of any legal validity, but greatly damages the United Nations Charter. The action taken by Mr Trygve Lie, Secretary-General of the United Nations, on the Korean question serves exactly to aggravate this damage.

Meanwhile, the statement by the United States President Truman on 27 June, of the beginning of armed prevention of Taiwan's liberation by the People's Republic of China, together with the action of the United States Navy in invading the Chinese territorial waters around Taiwan, forms an act of open aggression which thoroughly violates the principle of the United Nations Charter forbidding any Member to use force against the territorial integrity or political independence of any other State. Taiwan is an inseparable part of the territory of China. This is not only a historical fact recognized by the entire world, but is also confirmed by the Cairo Declaration, the Potsdam Declaration and the situation since the surrender of Japan. By keeping silent on this act of open aggression of the United States Government, the Security Council and the Secretary-General of the United Nations have forgone their functions and duties of upholding world peace, and thereby become pliant instruments to the policy of the United States Government. Now, in the name of the Central People's Government of the People's Republic of China I declare: Despite any military steps of obstruction taken by the United States Government, the Chinese people are irrevocably determined to liberate Taiwan without fail. [*S/1583, 6 July 1950, Cablegram to Secretary-General from Chou En-lai.*]

According to the report of the People's Government of Northeast China, on 27 August military airplanes of the United States aggression forces in Korea invaded the air of the People's Republic of China, flying along the right bank of the Yalu river, and strafed our buildings, railway stations, railway carriages and people, killing and wounding a number of them. The situation is extremely serious.

The details are as follows. At 10.04 on 27 August two United States B-29 bombers flew to the sky above the City of Chi-An and its vicinity to the right of the middle stretch of the Yalu River, circling and reconnoitring for more than ten minutes. At 10.05 the same day, four United States airplanes consisting of three P-51's and one 'Mosquito' flew to the sky above the area of Lin-Chiang City and the nearby railway station of Ta-Li-Tzu to the right of the upper stretch of the Yalu River, strafing the station building at Ta-Li-Tzu for two minutes, and along the railway lines for another two minutes, damaging one locomotive. At 11.04 another four United States airplanes came to the same area and machine-gunned the district around the bridge on the river for eleven minutes, damaging two locomotives, one passenger carriage and one guard carriage, and wounding one locomotive engineer and one inhabitant. At 14.30 the same day, a United States B-29 Bomber circled and reconnoitred over the city of An-Tung to the right of the lower stretch of the Yalu River. At 16.40, two United States P-51 planes came over the An-Tung airfield and strafed for two minutes, wounding nineteen and killing three workers, and damaging two trucks.

These provocative and atrocious acts of invading the air of China on the part of the United States aggression forces in Korea are a serious criminal action of encroaching upon China's sovereignty, killing Chinese people, and attempting to extend the war and violate peace, a criminal action which the Chinese people can by no means tolerate. Apart from lodging a serious protest and raising demands to Mr Dean Acheson, the United States Secretary of State, I hereby raise, on behalf of the Central People's Government of the People's Republic of China, this accusation before the United Nations Security Council, and propose that for the sake of peace and security of Asia and the world, the United Nations Security Council is obliged by its inalienable duties to condemn the United States aggression forces in Korea for their provocative and atrocious action of invading China's air, and to take immediate measures to bring about the complete withdrawal of all the United States aggression forces from Korea, so that the situation will not be aggravated and the peaceful regulation of the Korean question by the United Nations will be facilitated. [*S/1722, 28 Aug. 1950, Cablegram to Secretary-General from Chou En-lai.*]

There has been circulated to members of the Security Council a paper (*S/1722*) which charges that military aircraft, operating under the Unified Command which is resisting the aggression upon the Republic of Korea, under the authority of the United Nations Security Council, have overflown and strafed Chinese territory in Manchuria.

The instructions under which aircraft are operating under the Unified Command in Korea strictly prohibit them from crossing the Korean frontier into adjacent territory. No evidence has been received to indicate that these instructions have been violated. The United States, for its part, would welcome an investigation on the spot by a Commission appointed by the Security Council.

With reference to certain statements made in the paper in question, it is hardly necessary to point out that the forces of aggression now breaching the peace in Korea are those which invaded the Republic of Korea from the North and that these forces are being resisted by the United Nations. The action now being taken by the United States and other loyal Members of the United Nations in Korea is being conducted in accordance with and under the mandate of the United Nations.

I request that this letter be circulated to the members of the Security Council. [*S/1727, Letter to Secretary-General from Permanent Representative of United States, 29 Aug. 1950.*]

I have the honor to refer to document S/1808 which charges that aircraft, operating under the United Command, have overflown and bombed Chinese territory in Manchuria.

When somewhat similar charges were made in the Security Council relating to an alleged aerial attack on Chinese territory on 27 August by United Nations forces combating aggression in Korea (*S/1722*) the United States, after looking into the charges, frankly admitted the possibility that an unfortunate mistake had been made (*493rd meeting*) and stated that it stood ready to make payment to the Secretary-General of the United Nations for appropriate transmission to the injured party of compensation for such damages as might be ajudged fair and equitable as a result of an appropriate investigation. We also undertook to see that appropriate disciplinary action was taken. The United States proposed that the Security Council established a Commission to investigate the allegations (*S/1752*). This proposal was vetoed by the Soviet Union representative (*501st meeting*).

I am in receipt of a report from the United States Air Force which indicates that one of its planes in the service of the United Nations may have inadvertently violated Chinese territory and dropped bombs in the vicinity of Antung on the night of 22 September.

My Government deeply regrets any violation of Chinese territory and any damage which may have occurred. Every effort has been and is being taken to avoid unfortunate incidents of the nature charged.

The United States representative has already advised the United Nations Security Council that aircraft operating under the Unified Command in Korea are under instructions which strictly prohibit them from crossing the Korean frontier into adjacent territory (*S/1727*).

My Government remains willing in the case of the present charges, as well as the past charges, to assume responsibility for a pay compensation through the United Nations, for damages which an impartial, on-the-spot investigation might show to have been caused by United Nations planes. My Government considers such an investigation wholly reasonable and an essential prerequisite to ascertaining responsibility and assessing damages. I request that this letter be circulated to the members of the Security Council. [*S/1813, 26 Sept. 1950, Letter to Secretary-General from the Deputy Permanent Representative of United States.*][5]

While rejecting all offers of an impartial investigation, China continued to complain of strafing of its territory by American planes.[6] On 11 November 1950 the Foreign Minister of the People's Republic of China made the following statement about Chinese participation in hostilities:

The MacArthur report (*S/1884*) and Austin's statement (*519th meeting*) are from beginning to end a perversion of the facts and completely contrary to the truth; they also constitute a blustering attempt to intimidate China. The real facts are that the United States of America has invaded Chinese territory, violated Chinese sovereignty and is threatening Chinese security. The Chinese people is fully entitled to charge the United States Government with its provocation and aggression against China, which are becoming daily more and more brutal. Filled with righteous indignation, the Chinese people is voluntarily helping the Korean people to repulse United States aggression and its acts are completely natural and just.

The Central People's Government of the Chinese People's Republic continues as before to demand a peaceful settlement of the Korean question, but the Chinese people has no fear of the threats of any aggressors.

Immediately after the beginning of its aggressive war in Korea, the United States sent its fleet into the waters of Taiwan (Formosa), which belongs to China. It then sent its air forces to invade the air space of North-East China and carried out bombings. The United Nations took under consideration a charge brought by the Chinese Government (*S/1583, S/1715*) that the United States fleet had invaded the waters of Taiwan and is ready to discuss this charge. In the last three months numerous cases have been noted of United States aircraft violating the air borders of China, bombing Chinese territory, killing Chinese civilians and destroying Chinese property. The full tale of the crimes committed in North-East China by the United States air forces which have invaded Korea is given below. Recently the number of air attacks has been increased daily. These crimes committed by the United States armed forces, which are violating the territorial sovereignty of China and threatening its security, have alarmed the whole Chinese people. Righteously indignant, many Chinese citizens are expressing a desire to help the Korean people and resist American aggression. Facts have shown that the aim of United States aggression in Korea is not only Korea itself but also the extension of aggression to China. The question of the independent existence or the downfall of Korea has always been closely linked with the security of China. To help Korea and repel United States aggression means to protect our own homes and our own country. It is, therefore, completely natural for the Chinese people to be ready to help Korea and offer resistance to United States aggression. This natural desire of the Chinese people to help Korea and offer resistance to United States aggression has a whole series of precedents in world history, a fact which no one can deny. Everyone knows that in the eighteenth century the progressive people of France, led and inspired by Lafayette, gave similar voluntary assistance to the American people in their War of Independence. Before the Second World War democrats from all countries of the world, including Britishers and Americans, also helped by similar volunteer action the Spanish people in its civil war against Franco. The whole world admitted that these acts were lawful.

The spontaneous assistance of the Chinese people in Korea and their resistance to United States aggression has a firm moral foundation. The Chinese people will never forget how the Korean people magnanimously gave the Chinese people voluntary assistance in its revolutionary struggle. The Korean people took part not only in the Chinese war of national liberation, but also in the northern march of the Chinese people in 1925 to 1927, in the agrarian

[5] See also A/1415, 24 Sept. 1950, for a complaint made by China to the General Assembly of the bombing of Chinese territory.

[6] S/1876, 30 Oct. 1950.

revolutionary war of 1927 to 1937, and in the war against Japan from 1937 to 1945. Throughout the four stages of the Chinese people's revolution the Korean people always fought shoulder to shoulder with the Chinese people to overthrow imperialism and feudalism. Now that the blood-thirsty United States aggressors are exterminating Koreans, the Chinese are sharing their sufferings and, as must be perfectly obvious, cannot remain indifferent.

The sincere desire of the Chinese to assist the Koreans against United States aggression is absolutely natural, just, magnanimous and lawful. The Chinese People's Government considers that there are no grounds for hindering the despatch to Korea of volunteers wishing to take part, under the command of the Government of the Korean People's Democratic Republic, in the great liberation struggle of the Korean people against United States aggression. As a result of the invasion of Korea and of Chinese Taiwan by American imperialists, and as a result of the bombing raids on North-East China, the security of China has been placed in peril. And now they dare to describe as 'foreign intervention' the rightful action of the Chinese people in rendering voluntary help to the Korean people who are resisting the United States. The American imperialists have forgotten that they themselves are interveners and aggressors. The voluntary action of the Chinese people who are helping Korea to resist the United States has been undertaken for the purpose of repelling American intervention and aggression against China and Korea. [*S/1902, 15 Nov. 1950.*]

In a reply to a communication from the First Committee of the General Assembly[7] the People's Republic of China made it clear that a cease-fire agreed ahead of negotiations would be unacceptable. China proposed:

A. Negotiations should be held among the countries concerned on the basis of agreement to the withdrawal of all foreign troops from Korea and the settlement of Korean domestic affairs by the Korean people themselves, in order to put an end to the hostilities in Korea at an early date;

B. The subject matter of the negotiations must include the withdrawal of United States armed forces from Taiwan and the Taiwan Straits and Far Eastern related problems;

C. The countries to participate in the negotiations should be the following seven countries: The People's Republic of China, the Soviet Union, the United Kingdom, the United States of America, France, India and Egypt, and the rightful place of the central People's Government of the People's Republic of China in the United Nations should be established, as from the beginning of the seven-nation conference.

D. The seven-nation conference should be held in China at a place to be selected. [*YBUN, 1951*, pp. 212–13, *summarizing A/C.1/653, 17 Jan. 1951.*]

When pressed by the First Committee for certain clarifications, the Chinese government stated:

I. If the principle that all foreign troops should be withdrawn from Korea were accepted and put into practice, the Central People's Government of the People's Republic of China would assume the responsibility of advising the Chinese volunteers to return to China.

II. Measures for the conclusion of the war in Korea and the peaceful solution of the Korean problem could be carried out in two stages:

First: A cease-fire for a limited period could be agreed upon at the first meeting of the Seven-Nation Conference and put into effect so that negotiations could proceed further.

Second: In order that the war in Korea might be brought to an end completely and peace in the Far East assured, all conditions for the conclusion of hostilities would have to be discussed in connexion with the political problems, in order to reach agreement on the following points:

Steps and measures for the withdrawal of all foreign troops from Korea; proposals to the Korean people on the steps and measures to effect the settlement of the internal affairs of

[7] A/C.1/650, 13 Jan. 1951.

Korea by the Korean people themselves; withdrawal of United States armed forces from Taiwan and the Straits of Taiwan in accordance with the Cairo and Potsdam declarations; other Far Eastern problems.

III. The definite affirmation of the legitimate status of the People's Republic of China in the United Nations had to be ensured. [*Ibid.*, p. 213.]

A majority of members of the Assembly's First Committee felt that these proposals were unreasonable, because:

Paragraph II conveyed the impression that a temporary cease-fire would come into force only after the proposed seven-nations conference had been convened. Yet, when that paragraph was examined in the light of paragraph I, the impression was that a cease-fire for a limited time would be accepted only after the United Nations had begun the withdrawal of its armed forces. Only then, would the Peking Government agree to advise its volunteers to return home. With regard to the last paragraph, it was argued, its aim was not merely to secure the undertaking that the question of China's representation would be discussed in the United Nations but also to secure agreement on the principle of the admission of the Peking régime. Since the seven-nations conference would be unable to give such an assurance, Peking Government's proposal amounted, in fact, to a demand for admission even before the negotiations had begun. [*Ibid.*, pp. 213–14.]

The First Committee now examined, from the 433rd to the 438th meetings, a variety of draft resolutions. It ultimately passed a draft resolution which was subsequently adopted by the Assembly as resolution 498 (V) on 1 February 1951. It contained the following paragraphs:[8]

Noting that the Central People's Government of the People's Republic of China has not accepted United Nations proposals to bring about a cessation of hostilities in Korea with a view to peaceful settlement, and that its armed forces continue their invasion of Korea and their large-scale attacks upon United Nations forces there,

1. *Finds* that the Central People's Government of the People's Republic of China, by giving direct aid and assistance to those who were already committing aggression in Korea and by engaging in hostilities against United Nations forces there has itself engaged in aggression in Korea. . . . [*GA res. 498 (V)*.]

In the lengthy negotiations of 1952 and 1953 the UN dealt with a Chinese–North Korean delegation. However, in spite of considerable divisions of opinion on this, the UN did not engage in military activities directly against the territory of China; indeed, it was General MacArthur's stated desire to pursue the war across the Yalu which had led to his dismissal. In 1952 the UN was engaged in major controversy with China—as it was with North Korea—over the question of the repatriation of prisoners of war.[9]

China was a party to the final Armistice Agreement[10] in so far as it was signed by the 'Commander of the Chinese People's Volunteers'.

(c) The Soviet Union

Throughout the Korean war the Soviet Union gave full support to the North Korean and Chinese authorities, supporting their positions in the organs of the

[8] For full text, see above, pp. 167–8.
[9] See above, pp. 184–7.
[10] For details, see below, pp. 000–000. See also the Chinese and Korean allegations of mass murder of their PoWs on the island of Pongam, A/2355, A/2358, A/2356.

UN. The details of the Soviet Union's views on the legality of the UN action, on the peace proposals, and on the armistice negotiations, are all recounted in other sections of this chapter.

(d) Japan

The seat of the UN Command was in Tokyo and it was felt necessary to make certain detailed financial and legal arrangements. The financial arrangements are referred to, and reproduced, in Section 11 (pp. 245–50). On 26 October 1953 a protocol was agreed by Australia, Canada, New Zealand, the UK, and the USA, on the one hand, and Japan on the other, dealing with criminal jurisdiction over UN Forces. On 19 February 1954 the same parties entered into an Agreement (with agreed official minutes) regarding the status of UN Forces, together with a protocol for its provisional implementation. The entire texts of these agreements are here reproduced, in the belief that they are of considerable interest as a status-of-forces model, providing important information on many practical and legal problems involved in the establishment and protection of UN Forces:

PROTOCOL ON CRIMINAL JURISDICTION

Whereas the Protocol to amend article XVII, pertaining to the exercise of criminal jurisdiction over the United States forces in Japan, of the Administrative Agreement between the Governments of Japan and the United States of America is to come into force on October 29, 1953; and

Whereas the Government of Japan is ready to meet the desire of the Governments concerned for similar provisions governing the exercise of criminal jurisdiction over their United Nations forces in Japan;

Therefore, the Parties to this Protocol have agreed as follows:—

1. The exercise of criminal jurisdiction (including disciplinary jurisdiction) over the United Nations forces in Japan shall be governed by the provisions set forth in the annex to this Protocol.

The provisions set forth in the annex shall be integrated into a general agreement regarding the status of the United Nations forces in Japan when such agreement is concluded.

2. This Protocol shall be signed by the Governments of Japan, the United States of America acting as the Unified Command, and any State which has sent forces to Korea pursuant to the United Nations Security Council resolutions of June 25, June 27 and July 7, 1950, and the United Nations General Assembly resolution of February 1, 1951, and shall come into force on October 29, 1953, with respect to these signatory States.

After the first coming into force of this Protocol, it shall be open, subject to the consent of the Government of Japan, for signature by the Government of any other State which has sent or may hereafter send forces to Korea pursuant to the aforesaid resolutions, and it shall come into force with respect to such sending State as of the date of its signature unless otherwise agreed.

In WITNESS WHEREOF the representatives of the Governments of the Parties hereto, duly authorised for the purpose, have signed this Protocol.

DONE in Tokyo this 26th day of October, 1953, in the Japanese and English languages, both texts being equally authoritative, in a single copy, which shall be deposited in the Archives of the Government of Japan. Certified copies shall be transmitted by that Government of Japan. Certified copies shall be transmitted by that Government to each of the signatory Governments.

For the Government of Japan:

> Katsuo OKAZAKI
> Takeru INUKAI

For the Government of the United States of America acting as the Unified Command:

> John M. ALLISON

For the Government of the Commonwealth of Australia:

> E. Ronald WALKER

For the Government of Canada:

> R. W. MAYHEW

For the Government of New Zealand:

> R. K. G. CHALLIS

For the Government of the United Kingdom of Great Britain and Northern Ireland:

> Esler DENING

[*Protocol between Australia, Canada, New Zealand, UK, USA, and Japan on the exercise of criminal jurisdiction over UN Forces in Japan, 207 UNTS 260.*]

AGREEMENT ON STATUS OF UN FORCES

WHEREAS it is stated in the notes exchanged by Mr. Shigeru Yoshida, Prime Minister of Japan, and Mr. Dean Acheson, Secretary of State of the United States of America, on September 8, 1951, that upon the coming into force of the Treaty of Peace with Japan signed at the city of San Francisco on the same day Japan will assume obligations expressed in Article 2 of the Charter of the United Nations which requires the giving to the United Nations of every assistance in any action it takes in accordance with the Charter;

WHEREAS in the above-mentioned notes the Government of Japan confirmed that if and when the forces of a member or members of the United Nations are engaged in any United Nations action in the Fear East after the Treaty of Peace comes into force, Japan will permit and facilitate the support in and about Japan, by the member or members, of the forces engaged in such United Nations action;

WHEREAS the United Nations forces still continue to be engaged in action pursuant to the Security Council Resolutions of June 25, June 27 and July 7, 1950, and the General Assembly Resolution of February 1, 1951, which called upon all States and authorities to lend every assistance to the United Nations action; and

WHEREAS Japan has been and is rendering important assistance in the form of facilities and services to the forces which are participating in the United Nations action in Korea;

Now, THEREFORE, in order to define the status of, and treatment to be accorded to, such forces in Japan pending their withdrawal from its territory, the Parties to this Agreement have agreed as follows:

Article I

Except as otherwise provided in this Agreement, the following definitions of terms shall be adopted for the purpose of this Agreement:

(*a*) "United Nations Resolutions" means the United Nations Security Council Resolutions of June 25, June 27 and July 7, 1950, and the United Nations General Assembly Resolution of February 1, 1951.

(*b*) "Parties to this Agreement" means the Government of Japan, the Government of the United States of America, acting as the Unified Command, and each Government which signs, or signs "subject to acceptance" and accepts, or accedes to, this Agreement, as the Government of a State sending forces to Korea pursuant to the United Nations Resolutions.

(*c*) "Sending State" means any State which has sent or may hereafter send forces to Korea pursuant to the United Nations Resolutions and whose Government is a Party to this Agreement as the Government of a State sending forces to Korea pursuant to the United Nations Resolutions.

(*d*) "United Nations forces" means those forces of the land, sea or air armed services of the sending States which are sent to engage in action pursuant to the United Nations Resolutions.

(*e*) "Members of the United Nations forces" means personnel on active duty belonging to the United Nations forces when such persons are in Japan.

(*f*) "Civilian component" means the civilian persons of the nationality of any sending State who are in the employ of, serving with, or accompanying the United Nations forces when such persons are in Japan, but excludes persons who are ordinarily resident in Japan.

(*g*) "Dependents" means the following persons, when such persons are in Japan:

(i) Spouse, and children under 21, of members of the United Nations forces or of the civilian components;

(ii) Parents, and children over 21, of members of the United Nations forces or of the civilian components, if dependent for over half their support upon such members.

Article II

It is the duty of the United Nations forces as well as members of such forces and of the civilian components, and their dependents to respect the law of Japan and to abstain from any activity inconsistent with the spirit of this Agreement, and, in particular, from any political activity in Japan. The authorities of the sending States and the Commander-in-Chief, United Nations Command, shall take appropriate measures to this end.

Article III

1. Subject to the provisions of this Article, the Government of Japan grants permission to members of the United Nations forces and of the civilian components, and their dependents to enter into and depart from Japan for the purpose of this Agreement. The United Nations Command shall appropriately notify the Government of Japan of the number of persons entering and departing, the date of entry and departure, the object of entry, and the expected duration of stay.

2. Members of the United Nations forces shall be exempt from Japanese laws and regulations on passports and visas. Members of the United Nations forces and of the civilian components, and their dependents shall be exempt from Japanese laws and regulations on registration and control of aliens, but shall not be considered as acquiring any right to permanent residence or domicile in the territory of Japan.

3. Upon entry into and departure from Japan members of the United Nations forces shall be in possession of the following documents;

(*a*) personal identity card showing name, date of birth, rank and number, service, and photograph; and

(*b*) individual or collective travel order certifying to the status of the individual or group as a member or members of the United Nations forces and to the travel ordered.

4. For purposes of their identification while in Japan, members of the United Nations forces shall be in possession of the foregoing personal identity card, which must be presented on demand of the appropriate Japanese authorities.

5. Members of the civilian components shall have their status and the organization to which they belong described in their passports. Dependents shall have their status described in their passports.

6. For purposes of their identification while in Japan, members of the civilian components and dependents shall, on demand of the appropriate Japanese authorities. present their passports within a reasonable time.

7. If the status of any person brought into Japan under this Article is altered so that he would no longer be entitled to such admission, the authorities of the sending State shall notify the Japanese authorities, and shall cause such person to leave Japan without cost to the Government of Japan as promptly as possible, unless such person be permitted to remain in Japan in accordance with the Japanese laws and regulations concerned.

8. If Japan, for good cause, has requested the removal from its territory of a member of the United Nations forces or of the civilian components, or a dependent, the authorities of the

sending State concerned shall be responsible for causing the said person to leave Japan without delay.

Article IV

1. Vessels and aircraft operated by, for or under the control of the United Nations forces for the purpose of this Agreement shall be accorded access to such ports or airports as may be agreed upon by the Joint Board provided for in Article XX, free from toll or landing charges. When cargo or passengers not accorded the exemptions of this Agreement are carried on such vessels and aircraft, notification shall be given to the appropriate Japanese authorities, and such cargo or passengers shall be entered according to the laws and regulations of Japan.

2. The vessels and aircraft mentioned in the preceding paragraph, official vehicles of the United Nations forces and of the civilian components, and members of such forces and of the civilian components, and their dependents, and vehicles of such persons shall be accorded access to and movement between facilities and areas in use by such forces in accordance with Article V and between such facilities and areas, and the ports or airports mentioned in the preceding paragraph.

3. When the vessels mentioned in paragraph 1 enter Japanese ports, appropriate notification shall be made to the proper Japanese authorities. Such vessels shall have freedom from compulsory pilotage, but if a pilot is taken pilotage shall be paid for at appropriate rates.

Article V

1. The United Nations forces may use such facilities in Japan, inclusive of existing furnishings, equipment and fixtures necessary for the operation of such facilities, as may be agreed upon through the Joint Board.

2. The United Nations forces may, with the agreement of the Government of Japan through the Joint Board, use those facilities and areas the use of which is provided to the United States of America under the Security Treaty between Japan and the United States of America.

3. Within the facilities the United Nations forces shall have the rights which are necessary and appropriate for the purpose of this Agreement. All questions relating to frequencies, power and similar matters used by electric radiation apparatus employed by the United Nations forces shall be settled by mutual agreement through the Joint Board.

4. The facilities used by the United Nations forces under the terms of paragraph 1 shall be promptly returned to Japan whenever they are no longer needed, without any obligation to restore such facilities to their original condition and without compensation to or by either Party. The Parties to this Agreement may agree, through the Joint Board, on other arrangements with respect to construction or major alteration.

Article VI

The United Nations forces, members of such forces and of the civilian components, and their dependents may use public utilities and services belonging to, or controlled or regulated by the Government of Japan. In the use of such utilities and services the United Nations forces shall be accorded treatment no less favourable than that given from time to time to the ministries and agencies of the Government of Japan.

Article VII

1. Japan shall accept as valid, without a driving test or fee, the driving permit or license or military driving permit issued by the sending State to a member of the United Nations forces or of the civilian components, or a dependent.

2. Official vehicles of the United Nations forces and of the civilian components shall carry a distinctive nationality mark and number.

3. Privately-owned vehicles of members of the United Nations forces and of the civilian

components, and their dependents shall carry Japanese number plates to be acquired under the same conditions as those applicable to Japanese nationals.

Article VIII

The United Nations forces shall have the right to establish and operate, within the facilities in use by them, military post offices for the use of members of the United Nations forces and of the civilian components, and their dependents for the transmission of mail between such military post offices in Japan and between such military post offices and other post offices established and operated outside Japan by the sending States.

Article IX

1. Non-appropriated fund organizations authorized and regulated by the United Nations forces, may be established in the facilities in use by the United Nations forces for the use of members of such forces and of the civilian components, and their dependents. Except as otherwise provided in this Agreement, such organizations shall not be subject to Japanese regulations, license, fees, taxes or similar controls.

2. No Japanese tax shall be imposed on sales of merchandise and services by such organizations, but purchases within Japan of merchandise and supplies by such organizations shall be subject to Japanese taxes.

3. Except as such disposal may be authorized by the Japanese authorities and the United Nations forces in accordance with mutually agreed conditions, goods which are sold by such organizations shall not be disposed of in Japan to persons not authorized to make purchases from such organizations.

4. The obligations for the withholding and payment of income tax, local inhabitant tax and social security contributions, and, except as may otherwise be mutually agreed, the conditions of employment and work, such as those relating to wages and supplementary payments, the conditions for the protection of workers, and the rights of workers concerning labour relations shall be those laid down by the legislation of Japan.

5. The organizations provided for in paragraph 1 shall provide such information to the Japanese authorities as is required by Japanese tax legislation.

6. Such organizations may use military payment scrip in their transactions with persons who are authorized to use military payment scrip as provided for in Article XI. Such organizations may not hold deposit accounts in foreign currency with foreign exchange banks in Japan unless otherwise agreed through the Joint Board.

Article X

1. Members of the United Nations forces and of the civilian components, and their dependents shall be subject to the foreign exchange controls of the Government of Japan.

2. The preceding paragraph shall not be construed to preclude the transmission into or outside of Japan of foreign exchange instruments representing the official funds of the Governments of the sending States or realized as a result of service or employment in connection with this Agreement by members of the United Nations forces and of the civilian components, or realized by such persons and their dependents from sources outside Japan.

3. The authorities of the United Nations forces and the Governments of the sending States shall take suitable measures to preclude the abuse of the privileges stipulated in the preceding paragraph or circumvention of the Japanese foreign exchange controls.

Article XI

1. Military payment scrip may be used by persons authorized by the sending States for internal transactions within facilities in use by the sending States in accordance with the regulations of the States which issued the scrip and in whose currency it is denominated. The United Nations forces shall take appropriate action to ensure that authorized persons are

prohibited from engaging in transactions involving military payment scrip except as authorized by appropriate regulations of the State which issued the military payment scrip. The Government of Japan shall take necessary action to prohibit unauthorized persons from engaging in transactions involving military payment scrip and, with the aid of the United Nations forces if necessary, shall apprehend and punish any person or persons under its jurisdiction involved in the counterfeiting or uttering of counterfeit military payment scrip.

2. The United Nations forces shall apprehend and punish by due process of law members of the United Nations forces or of the civilian components, or their dependents who tender military payment scrip to unauthorized persons and no obligation shall be due to such unauthorized persons or to the Government of Japan or its agencies from the United Nations forces as a result of any unauthorized use of military payment scrip within Japan.

Article XII

1. The United Nations forces shall not be subject to taxes or similar charges on property held, used or transferred by such forces in Japan.

2. Members of the United Nations forces and of the civilian components, and their dependents shall not be liable to pay any Japanese taxes to the Government of Japan or to any other taxing agency in Japan on income received as a result of their service with or employment by such forces or by the organizations provided for in Article IX. The provisions of this Article do not exempt such persons from payment of Japanese taxes on income derived from Japanese sources, nor do they exempt citizens of the sending State who for purposes of income tax of that State claim Japanese residence from payment of Japanese taxes on income.

3. Periods during which the persons referred to in the preceding paragraph are in Japan solely by reason of being members of the United Nations forces or of the civilian components, or their dependents shall not be considered as periods of residence or domicile in Japan for the purpose of Japanese taxation.

4. Members of the United Nations forces and of the civilian components, and their dependents shall be exempt from taxation in Japan on the holding, use, transfer *inter se*, or transfer by death of movable property, tangible or intangible, the presence of which in Japan is due solely to the temporary presence of these persons in Japan, provided that such exemption shall not apply to property held for the purpose of investment or the conduct of business in Japan or to any intangible property registered in Japan. There is no obligation under this Article to grant exemption from taxes payable in respect of the use of roads by private vehicles.

Article XIII

1. Except as otherwise provided in this Agreement, the United Nations forces, members of such forces and of the civilian components, and their dependents, as well as the organizations provided for in Article IX, shall be subject to the laws and regulations administered by the customs authorities of Japan.

2. All materials, supplies and equipment imported by the United Nations forces or by the organizations provided for in Article IX exclusively for the official use of the United Nations forces or those organizations or for the use of members of the United Nations forces and of the civilian components, and their dependents shall be permitted entry into Japan free from customs duties and other such charges.

3. When the goods mentioned in the preceding paragraph are imported, a certificate signed by a person authorized for the purpose, in the form to be determined by the Joint Board, and certifying that they are being imported for the purposes stated in the preceding paragraph, shall be submitted by the United Nations forces to the customs authorities of Japan.

4. Property consigned to and for the personal use of members of the United Nations forces and of the civilian components, and their dependents shall be subject to customs duties and other such charges except that no such duties or charges shall be paid with respect to:

(*a*) Furniture and household goods for their private use imported by members of the

United Nations forces or of the civilian components when they first arrive to serve in Japan or by their dependents when they first arrive for reunion with members of such forces or of the civilian components, and personal effects for private use brought by the said persons upon entrance.

(*b*) Motor vehicles and spare parts imported by a member of the United Nations forces or of the civilian components for the private use of himself or his dependents.

(*c*) Reasonable quantities of clothing and household goods which are mailed into Japan through military post offices for the private use of members of the United Nations forces and of the civilian components, and their dependents, provided that such clothing and household goods are those of a type which would ordinarily be purchased in the sending State to which such persons belong for everyday use.

5. The exemptions granted in paragraphs 2 and 4 shall apply only to cases of importation of goods and shall not be interpreted as refunding customs duties and domestic excises collected by the customs authorities at the time of entry in cases of purchases of goods on which such duties and excises have already been collected.

6. Customs examination shall not be made in the following cases:

(*a*) Units and members of the United Nations forces under orders entering or leaving Japan;

(*b*) Official documents under official seal;

(*c*) Military cargo shipped on a government bill of lading, and mail in military postal channels.

7. Except as authorized by the authorities of Japan and of the United Nations forces in accordance with mutually agreed conditions, goods imported into Japan free from customs duties and other such charges under this Agreement shall not be disposed of in Japan to persons not entitled to import such goods free from customs duties and other such charges under this Agreement.

8. Goods imported into Japan free from customs duties and other such charges pursuant to paragraphs 2 and 4, may be re-exported free from customs duties and other such charges.

9. The United Nations forces, in co-operation with the Japanese authorities, shall take such steps as are necessary to prevent abuse of privileges granted to the United Nations forces, members of such forces and of the civilian components, and their dependents in accordance with this Article.

10. (*a*) In order to prevent offences against laws and regulations administered by the Japanese customs authorities, the Japanese authorities and the United Nations forces shall assist each other in the conduct of inquiries and the collection of evidence.

(*b*) The United Nations forces shall render all assistance within their power to ensure that articles liable to seizure by, or on behalf of, the Japanese customs authorities are handed to those authorities.

(*c*) The United Nations forces shall render all assistance within their power to ensure the payment of duties, taxes and penalties payable by members of such forces or of the civilian components, or their dependents.

(*d*) Any property belonging to the United Nations forces seized by the Japanese customs authorities in connection with an offence against its customs or fiscal laws or regulations shall be handed over to the appropriate authorities of the forces to which such property belongs.

Article XIV

1. Materials, supplies, equipment and services which are required from local sources for the support of the United Nations forces and the procurement of which may have an adverse effect on the economy of Japan shall be procured in co-ordination with, and, when desirable, through or with the assistance of, the competent authorities of Japan.

2. Disputes arising out of contracts concerning the procurement of materials, supplies, equipment, services and labour by or for the United Nations forces, which are not resolved by the parties to the contract concerned, may be submitted to the Joint Board for conciliation,

provided that the provisions of this paragraph shall not prejudice any right which the parties to the contract may have to file a suit.

3. Materials, supplies, equipment and services procured for official purposes in Japan by the United Nations forces, or by authorized procurement agencies of the United Nations forces upon appropriate certification by the authorities of such forces shall be exempt from the following Japanese taxes:

(*a*) Commodity tax

(*b*) Travelling tax

(*c*) Gasoline tax

(*d*) Electricity and gas tax

Materials, supplies, equipment and services procured for ultimate use by the United Nations forces shall be exempt from commodity and gasoline taxes upon appropriate certification by the United Nations forces. With respect to any present or future Japanese taxes not specifically referred to in this Article which might be found to constitute a significant and readily identifiable part of the gross purchase price of materials, supplies, equipment and services procured by the United Nations forces, Japan and the United Nations forces will agree upon a procedure for granting such exemption or relief therefrom as is consistent with the purposes of this Article.

4. Except as such disposal may be authorized by the Japanese authorities and the United Nations forces in accordance with mutually agreed conditions, goods purchased in Japan exempt from taxes referred to in the preceding paragraph shall not be disposed of in Japan to persons not entitled to purchase such goods exempt from such taxes.

5. Neither members of the United Nations forces or of the civilian components nor their dependents shall by reason of this Article enjoy any exemption from taxes or similar charges relating to personal purchases of goods and services in Japan chargeable under Japanese legislation.

6. Local labour requirements of the United Nations forces shall be satisfied with the assistance of the Japanese authorities.

7. The obligations for the withholding and payment of income tax, local inhabitant tax and social security contributions, and, except as may otherwise be mutually agreed, the conditions of employment and work, such as those relating to wages and supplementary payments, the conditions for the protection of workers, and the rights of workers concerning labour relations shall be those laid down by the legislation of Japan.

Article XV

The United Nations forces shall bear for the duration of this Agreement without cost to Japan all expenditures incident to the maintenance of such forces in Japan except that facilities, owned by the Government of Japan, the use of which is made available to such forces by the Government of Japan, shall be furnished by Japan free from rentals and other such charges.

Article XVI

1. Subject to the provisions of this Article,

(*a*) the military authorities of the sending State shall have the right to exercise within Japan all criminal and disciplinary jurisdiction conferred on them by the law of the sending State over all persons subject to the military law of that State;

(*b*) the authorities of Japan shall have jurisdiction over members of the United Nations forces or of the civilian components, and their dependents with respect to offences committed within the territory of Japan and punishable by the law of Japan.

2. (*a*) The military authorities of the sending State shall have the right to exercise exclusive jurisdiction over persons subject to the military law of that State with respect to offences, including offences relating to its security, punishable by the law of that sending State, but not by the law of Japan.

(*b*) The authorities of Japan shall have the right to exercise exclusive jurisdiction over

9

members of the United Nations forces or of the civilian components, and their dependents with respect to offences, including offences relating to the security of Japan, punishable by its law but not by the law of the sending State concerned.

(*c*) For the purposes of this paragraph and of paragraph 3 of this Article a security offence against a State shall include

(i) treason against the State;

(ii) sabotage, espionage or violation of any law relating to official secrets of that State, or secrets relating to the national defence of that State.

3. In cases where the right to exercise jurisdiction is concurrent the following rules shall apply:

(*a*) The military authorities of the sending State shall have the primary right to exercise jurisdiction over a member of the United Nations forces or of the civilian component in relation to:

(i) offences solely against the property or security of that State, or offences solely against the person or property of another member of the force of that State or of the civilian component, or a dependent;

(ii) offences arising out of any act or omission done in the performance of official duty.

(*b*) In the case of any other offence the authorities of Japan shall have the primary right to exercise jurisdiction.

(*c*) If the State having the primary right decides not to exercise jurisdiction, it shall notify the authorities of the other State as soon as practicable. The authorities of the State having the primary right shall give sympathetic consideration to a request from the authorities of the other State for a waiver of its right in cases where that other State considers such waiver to be of particular importance.

4. The foregoing provisions of this Article shall not imply any right for the military authorities of the sending State to exercise jurisdiction over persons who are nationals of or ordinarily resident in Japan, unless they are members of the force of that sending State.

5. (*a*) The authorities of Japan and the military authorities of the sending States shall assist each other in the arrest of members of the United Nations forces or of the civilian components, or their dependents in the territory of Japan and in handing them over to the authority which is to exercise jurisdiction in accordance with the above provisions.

(*b*) The authorities of Japan shall notify promptly the military authorities of the sending State of the arrest of any member of the force of that sending State or of the civilian component, of a dependent.

(*c*) The custody of an accused member of the force of a sending State or of the civilian component over whom Japan is to exercise jurisdiction shall, if he is in the hands of that sending State, remain with that State until he is charged by Japan.

6. (*a*) The authorities of Japan and the military authorities of the sending States shall assist each other in the carrying out of all necessary investigations into offences, and in the collection and production of evidence, including the seizure and, in proper cases, the handing over of objects connected with an offence. The handing over of such objects may, however, be made subject to their return within the time specified by the authority delivering them.

(*b*) The authorities of Japan and the military authorities of the sending State shall notify each other of the disposition of all cases in which there are concurrent rights to exercise jurisdiction.

7. (*a*) A death sentence shall not be carried out in Japan by the military authorities of the sending State if the legislation of Japan does not provide for such punishment in a similar case.

(*b*) The authorities of Japan shall give sympathetic consideration to a request from the military authorities of the sending State for assistance in carrying out a sentence of imprisonment pronounced by the military authorities of the sending State under the provisions of this Article within the territory of Japan.

8. Where an accused has been tried in accordance with the provisions of this Article either by the authorities of Japan or by the military authorities of a sending State and has been

acquitted, or has been convicted and is serving, or has served, his sentence or has been pardoned, he may not be tried again for the same offence within the territory of Japan by the authorities of another State the Government of which is a Party to this Agreement. However, nothing in this paragraph shall prevent the military authorities of the sending State from trying a member of its force for any violation of rules of discipline arising from an act or omission which constituted an offence for which he was tried by the authorities of Japan.

9. Whenever a member of the United Nations forces or of the civilian components, or a dependent is prosecuted under the jurisdiction of Japan he shall be entitled:

(*a*) to a prompt and speedy trial;

(*b*) to be informed, in advance of trial, of the specific charge or charges made against him;

(*c*) to be confronted with the witnesses against him;

(*d*) to have compulsory process for obtaining witnesses in his favour, if they are within the jurisdiction of Japan;

(*e*) to have legal representation of his own choice for his defence or to have free or assisted legal representation under the conditions prevailing for the time being in Japan;

(*f*) if he considers it necessary, to have the services of a competent interpreter: and

(*g*) to communicate with a representative of the Government of the sending State and to have such a representative present at his trial.

10. (*a*) Regularly constituted military units or formations of the United Nations forces shall have the right to police any United Nations forces facilities. The military police of such forces may take all appropriate measures to ensure the maintenance of order and security within such facilities.

(*b*) Outside these facilities, such military police shall be employed only subject to arrangements with the authorities of Japan and in liaison with those authorities, and in so far as such employment is necessary to maintain discipline and order among the members of the United Nations forces.

11. If the provisions of Article XVII of the Administrative Agreement between the Government of Japan and the Government of the United States of America, signed at Tokyo on February 28, 1952, as amended by the Protocol signed at Tokyo on September 29, 1953, are further amended, Parties to this Agreement shall, after consultation, make similar amendments to the corresponding provisions of this Article, provided the forces of the sending State concerned are under circumstances similar to those giving rise to such further amendment.

12. The Protocol on the Exercise of Criminal Jurisdiction over United Nations Forces in Japan, signed at Tokyo on October 26, 1953, and the Annex thereto shall cease to be in force between the Government of Japan and any other Party to this Agreement which has signed the said Protocol as of the date of the entry into force of this Agreement with respect to such Party.

Article XVII

The Parties to this Agreement will co-operate in taking such steps as may from time to time be necessary to ensure the security of the United Nations forces, members of such forces and of the civilian components, their dependents, and their property. The Government of Japan shall seek such legislation and take such other action as it deems necessary to ensure the adequate security and protection within the territory of Japan of installations, equipment, property, records and official information of the United Nations forces, and for the punishment of offenders under the applicable laws of Japan.

Article XVIII

1. Each Party to this Agreement waives all its claims against any other Party to this Agreement for injury or death suffered in Japan by a member of the forces of, or a civilian governmental employee of the former Party, while such member or employee was engaged in the performance of his official duties, in cases where such injury or death was caused by a member of the forces of, or a civilian governmental employee of the other Party in the performance of his official duties.

2. Each Party to this Agreement waives all its claims against any other Party to this Agreement for damage to any property in Japan owed by it, if such damage was caused by a member of the forces of, or a civilian governmental employee of the other Party in the performance of his official duties.

3. Claims, other than contractual, arising out of acts or omissions of members or employees of the United Nations forces done in the performance of their official duties, or out of any other act, omission or occurrence for which the United Nations forces are legally responsible, arising incident to non-combat activities and causing injury, death or property damage in Japan to third parties shall be dealt with by Japan in accordance with the following provisions:

(*a*) Claims shall be filed within one year from the date on which they arise, and shall be considered and settled or adjudicated in accordance with the laws and regulations of Japan with respect to claims arising from the activities of its own employees.

(*b*) Japan may settle any such claims, and payment of the amount agreed upon or determined by adjudication shall be made by Japan in yen.

(*c*) Such payment, whether made pursuant to a settlement or to adjudication of the case by a competent tribunal of Japan, or the final adjudication by such a tribunal denying payment, shall be binding and conclusive.

(*d*) The cost incurred in satisfying claims pursuant to the preceding sub-paragraphs shall be shared by the Parties to this Agreement as follows:

(i) Where one sending State alone is responsible, the amount agreed upon or adjudged shall be shared in the proportion of 75% chargeable to the sending State and 25% chargeable to Japan.

(ii) Where more than one sending State is jointly responsible, the amount agreed upon or adjudged shall be shared in such proportion that the shares of the sending States concerned shall be equal among themselves and the share of Japan shall be one half of that of one of such sending States.

(iii) Where the injury, death or property damage was caused by the United Nations forces of more than one sending State and it is not possible to attribute it specifically to any of the United Nations forces, all of the sending States concerned shall be regarded as responsible for the cause of such injury, death or property damage and the provisions of item (ii) above shall apply thereto.

(*e*) In accordance with procedures to be established, a statement of all claims approved or disapproved by Japan pursuant to this paragraph, the findings in each case, and a statement of the sums paid by Japan, shall be sent periodically to the sending State concerned, together with a request for reimbursement of the share to be paid by such sending State. Such reimbursement shall be made in yen within the shortest possible period of time.

4. Each Party to this Agreement shall have the primary right, in the execution of the foregoing paragraphs, to determine whether its personnel were engaged in the performance of official duty. Such determination shall be made as soon as possible after the arising of the claim concerned. When any other Party concerned disagrees with the results of such determination, that Party may bring the matter before the Joint Board for consultation.

5. Claims against members or employees of the United Nations forces arising out of tortious acts or omissions in Japan not done in the performance of their official duties shall be dealt with in the following manner:

(*a*) The Japanese authorities shall consider the claim and assess compensation to the claimant in a fair and just manner, taking into account all the circumstances of the case, including the conduct of the injured person, and shall prepare a report on the matter.

(*b*) The report shall be delivered to the authorities of the sending State concerned, who shall then decide without delay whether they will offer an *ex gratia* payment, and if so, of what amount.

(*c*) If an offer of *ex gratia* payment is made, and accepted by the claimant in full satisfaction of his claim, the authorities of the sending State shall make the payment themselves and inform the Japanese authorities of their decision and of the sum paid.

(*d*) Nothing in this paragraph shall affect the jurisdiction of the courts of Japan to entertain an action against a member or employee of the United Nations forces unless and until there has been payment in full satisfaction of the claim.

6. (*a*) Members and employees of the United Nations forces, excluding those employees who have only Japanese nationality, shall not be subject to suit in Japan with respect to claims specified in paragraph 3, but shall be subject to the civil jurisdiction of Japanese courts with respect to all other types of cases.

(*b*) In case any private movable property, excluding that in use by the United Nations forces, which is subject to compulsory execution under Japanese law, is within the facilities in use by the United Nations forces, the authorities of the sending State concerned shall, upon the request of Japanese courts, possess and turn over such property to the Japanese authorities. In the case of a sending State the forces of which have no legal authority to take such action, the authorities of that State shall allow the appropriate Japanese authorities to take possession of such property in accordance with Japanese law.

(*c*) The authorities of every sending State shall co-operate with the Japanese authorities in making available witnesses and evidence for a fair hearing and disposal of claims under the provisions of this Article.

Article XIX

The Parties to this Agreement shall as promptly as possible take legislative, budgetary and other measures necessary for the implementation of this Agreement.

Article XX

1. A Joint Board shall be established in Tokyo as the means for consultation and agreement between the Government of Japan and the other Parties to this Agreement on matters relating to the interpretation and implementation of this Agreement.

2. The Joint Board shall be composed of two representatives, one representing the Government of Japan and the other representing the other Parties to this Agreement, each of whom shall have one or more deputies and a staff. The Joint Board shall determine its own procedures, and arrange for such auxiliary organs and administrative services as may be required. The Joint Board shall be so organized that it may meet at any time at the request of either representative.

3. If the Joint Board is unable to reach agreement on any matter, it shall be settled through inter-governmental negotiations.

Article XXI

1. This Agreement shall be signed by the Government of Japan and the Government of the United States of America acting as the Unified Command, and may be signed by the Government of any State which has sent or may hereafter send forces to Korea pursuant to the United Nations Resolutions. After its first signature and until its first entry into force this Agreement shall be open, subject to the consent of the Government of Japan, for signature by the Government of any other such State.

2. Ten days after the date on which the Government of Japan accepts this Agreement, it shall enter into force for the Government of Japan and for each other Government which, on or before the date of acceptance by the Government of Japan, signs, or signs "subject to acceptance" and accepts, this Agreement. For each Government which signs, or accepts, or signs "subject to acceptance" and accepts, this Agreement after the date of acceptance by the Government of Japan, it shall enter into force ten days after the date on which that Government signs, or having signed "subject to acceptance" accepts, this Agreement.

3. The acceptance of this Agreement shall be made by depositing an instrument of acceptance with the Government of Japan. The Government of Japan shall notify each Government which is a Party to this Agreement, of the date of each signature and of deposit of each instrument of acceptance, if any.

4. The provisions of this Agreement, except those of Article XVI and those which are *per se* incapable of retroaction, shall be operative retroactively to April 28, 1952, for the Government of Japan and for each other Government which, on or within six months after the date of first signature of this Agreement, signs, or signs "subject to acceptance" and accepts, this Agreement.

Article XXII

1. After the first entry into force of this Agreement in accordance with paragraph 2 of Article XXI, the Government of any State no signatory to this Agreement which has sent or may hereafter send forces to Korea pursuant to the United Nations Resolution, may, subject to the consent of the Government of Japan, accede to this Agreement by depositing its instrument of accession with the Government of Japan.

2. The Government of Japan shall notify each Government which is a Party to this Agreement, of the date of deposit of each instrument of accession.

3. This Agreement shall enter into force for each acceding Government ten days after the date of deposit of its instrument of accession.

4. The provisions of this Agreement, except those of Article XVI and which are *per se* incapable of retroaction, shall be operative retroactively to April 28, 1952 for each acceding Government which deposits its instrument of accession within six months after the date of first signature of this Agreement.

Article XXIII

1. Any Party to this Agreement may at any time request a revision of any Article. Upon such request the Government of Japan and the Government of the United States of America acting as the Unified Command, in consultation with and on behalf of the sending States concerned, shall enter into negotiations.

2. If any provisions of the Administrative Agreement between the Government of Japan and the Government of the United States of America, signed at Tokyo on February 28, 1952, as amended by the Protocol signed at Tokyo on September 29, 1953, are revised, the Government of Japan and the Government of the United States of America acting as the Unified Command, in consultation with and on behalf of the sending States, shall, except as provided in paragraph 11 of Article XVI, enter into negotiations with a view to agreeing on similar revision of the corresponding provisions of this Agreement.

Article XXIV

All the United Nations forces shall be withdrawn from Japan within ninety days after the date by which all the United Nations forces shall have been withdrawn from Korea. The Parties to this Agreement may agree upon an earlier date by which all the United Nations forces shall be withdrawn from Japan.

Article XXV

This Agreement and agreed revisions thereof shall terminate on the date by which all the United Nations forces shall be withdrawn from Japan in accordance with the provisions of Article XXIV. In case all the United Nations forces have been withdrawn from Japan earlier than such date, this Agreement and agreed revisions thereof shall terminate on the date when the withdrawal has been completed.

IN WITNESS WHEREOF the undersigned, being duly authorized by their respective Governments for the purpose, have signed this Agreement.

DONE at Tokyo this nineteenth day of February, 1954, in the Japanese and English languages, both texts being equally authoritative, in a single original which shall be deposited in the archives of the Government of Japan. The Government of Japan shall transmit certified copies thereof to all the signatory and acceding Governments.

For the Government of Japan:
    Katsuo OKAZAKI
    Subject to acceptance
For the Government of the United States of America acting as the Unified Command:
    J. Graham PARSONS

GOVERNMENTS OF STATES SENDING FORCES TO KOREA
PURSUANT TO THE UNITED NATIONS RESOLUTIONS

For the Goverment of Canada:
    R. W. MAYHEW
    Subject to acceptance
For the Government of New Zealand:
    R. M. MILLER
    Subject to acceptance
For the Government of the United Kingdom of Great Britain and Northern Ireland:
    Esler DENING
For the Government of the Union of South Africa:
    Esler DENING
    Subject to acceptance
For the Government of the Commonwealth of Australia:
    E. Ronald WALKER
For the Government of the Republic of the Philippines:
    José F. IMPERIAL
For the Government of the Republic of France:
    Daniel LÉVI
    12 avril 1954
For the Government of Italy:
    B. L. D'AJETA
    May 19th 54

[*214 UNTS 51.*][11]

[11] For UN agreed official minutes relating to the Agreement regarding the status of the forces in Japan, see 214 UNTS 186.

II

FINANCE

THE financing of the Korean operation very much reflected the *sui generis* nature of that undertaking. The recommendation by the Security Council that members should assist Korea, the particular historical circumstances which made such a vote possible, and the establishment of a Unified Command under the United States, all emphasized the unique aspects of the venture. The voluntary nature of the operation was a reminder both of constitutional difficulties[1] and of implacable opposition by the Communist members of the UN. Clearly, it would

[1] See above, pp. 173–8.

have been legally difficult, and practically impossible, to charge the operations as a cost on the UN budget.

No part of the military operations was thus charged to the UN budget.[2] We have already seen (pp. 203–9), in the agreements made between the United States and the contributing states, that complex bilateral arrangements were made by which the United States provided materials, services, supplies and facilities against reimbursement in dollars. In the case of Belgium,[3] a further supplementary arrangement was made covering financial arrangements for logistical support furnished by the US Department of Army.

The United States and Korea entered into a basic agreement on expenditures by UN Forces, under which Korea provided local currency to the Commander-in-Chief, who was responsible for any transfers made to the forces of countries participating in the UN action.[4] Any claims in respect of the currency transfers were to be settled directly between Korea and the government in question. This point was confirmed by an article in each of the basic agreements made between the United States and the contributing countries.

AGREEMENT BETWEEN THE GOVERNMENT OF THE UNITED STATES OF AMERICA AND THE GOVERNMENT OF THE REPUBLIC OF KOREA REGARDING EXPENDITURES BY FORCES UNDER COMMAND OF THE COMMANDING GENERAL OF THE ARMED FORCES OF THE MEMBER STATES OF THE UNITED NATIONS

Preamble (Object)

This agreement between the Government of the United States of America and the Government of the Republic of Korea shall govern the relationships with respect to provision and use of currency and credits between the Government and people of the Republic of Korea and forces operating in Korea under the Unified Command of the Commanding General of the Armed Forces of Member States of the United Nations designated by the United States pursuant to the resolutions of the United Nations Security Council of June 25, 1950, June 7, 1950, and July 7, 1950 (*S/1501, S/1511, S/1588*).

1. Local currency provided by the Republic of Korea:

The Government of the Republic of Korea shall provide the Commanding General of the Armed Forces of the Member States of the United Nations (hereinafter referred to as the Commanding General), with currency of the Republic of Korea and credits in such currency (hereinafter referred to as local currency and credits) in such amounts, of such types and at such times and places as he may request, for expenditures arising out of operations and activities in Korea and Korean territorial waters involving participation of forces under his command.

2. Return of local currency and cancellation of credits:

The Commanding General may, at any time, return to the Government of the Republic of Korea all or any part of the local currency provided under paragraph 1 above, and request the cancellation of all or any part of any credits in such currency which may have been opened in his favor. Upon the termination of this agreement, the Commanding General shall return to the Government of the Republic of Korea all local currency provided under paragraph 1 above remaining in his possession, and the unused portion of any credits which may have been opened in his favor shall be cancelled.

[2] Though the cost of the UN cemetery and UN medals were so charged, and met with heated opposition.

[3] See Bowett, *UN Forces,* pp. 38–9.

[4] See above, pp. 211–12.

3. Use of other currencies

If it should become desirable to use currency other than the local currency agreed to be provided under paragraph 1 above, the Commanding General may cause such currency to be used to the extent deemed appropriate.

4. Reports to the Republic of Korea:

If the Commanding General transfers local currency and credits to the forces of other countries participating under his command, the Government of the Republic of Korea shall be advised from time to time of such transfers.

5. Deferment of settlement:

Settlement of any claims arising from the provision and use of currency and credits under the agreement, including currency caused to be used under paragraph 3 above, shall take place directly between the Governments of the forces concerned and the Government of the Republic of Korea. Such negotiations shall be deferred to a time or times mutually satisfactory to the respective governments and the Government of the Republic of Korea. Where currency of the United States or of a third country has been transferred by the Commander-in-Chief to the forces of third governments, the right of the Government of the United States to make arrangements for reimbursement for such transfers directly with the recipient government shall not be prejudiced in any manner.

6. Maintenance of records:

Records shall be maintained reflecting the amounts of currency and credits received and transferred under this agreement, including the amounts of currency received and transferred under paragraph 3 above.

7. Effective date and termination:

This agreement shall enter into operation and effect immediately upon the signature hereof and shall continue in effect until it is mutually agreed that the need therefor has ceased.

8. Registration with the Secretary-General of the United Nations:

This agreement shall be registered with the Secretary-General of the United Nations in compliance with the provisions of Article 102 of the Charter of the United Nations.

9. Superseding of agreement of July 6, 1950:

This agreement shall supersede the agreement of July 6, 1950, between the United States Armed Forces in Korea and the Republic of Korea pursuant to which the Bank of Korea agreed to advance currency of the Republic of Korea to the Finance Officer, United States Forces in Korea, against reimbursement at the rate of exchange in effect on the date such currency is expended. Any currency advanced under the agreement of July 6, 1950, shall be deemed to have been provided under this agreement. The agreement of July 6, 1950, is hereby abrogated.

Done in duplicate, in the English and Korean languages, at Taegu, Korea, on this 28th day of July, 1950. The English and Korean texts shall have equal force, but in case of divergence, the English text shall prevail.

In witness whereof, the respective representatives, duly authorized for the purpose, have signed the present agreement.

For the Government of the United States of America:
(*Signed*) John J. MUCCIO
For the Government of the Republic of Korea:
(*Signed*) Soon Ju CHEY

[*S/1860, 21 Oct. 1950, app. & 140 UNTS 56.*]

9*

Korea also entered into a more general economic agreement (S/2768) with the United States, the text of which is reproduced above (pp. 213–22).

Thus it was that a detailed arrangement was entered into as between Korea on the one hand, and the United Kingdom, Australia, and New Zealand on the other, in September 1954:

I

Her Majesty's Minister at Seoul to the Korean Minister of Finance

BRITISH LEGATION

Seoul, September 28, 1954

Monsieur le Ministre,

I refer to the recent discussions concerning the settlement by British Commonwealth Forces, Korea, of the advances in Korean currency made by the Government of the Republic of Korea from July 1950, under the Agreement between the Governments of the Republic of Korea and of the United States of America of July 28, 1950, and about the arrangements of future advances made under that Agreement.

I now have the honour to propose on behalf of Her Majesty's Governments in the United Kingdom of Great Britain and Northern Ireland, the Commonwealth of Australia and New Zealand, an agreement in the following terms:—

(1) The United Kingdom Government shall, immediately upon signature of this letter, make a lump-sum payment of £1·8 million sterling in part payment of the liabilities of the Australian and New Zealand Governments and of the liabilities of the United Kingdom Government in respect of hwan advanced by the Government of the Republic of Korea up to May 31, 1954, and within one calendar month of the date of this letter make a further lump-sum payment in sterling in respect of the balance of the liabilities for advances to the Australian and New Zealand Governments as well as in respect of the balance of the United Kingdom Government's own liability up to May 31, 1954. These liabilities shall be calculated—

  (*a*) For the period up to February 23, 1953, at the military conversion rate prevailing at the time the local currency was actually expended; and

  (*b*) Thereafter at the military conversion rate prevailing at the time the local currency was advanced.

(2) Subject to the provisions of point (9) below, settlements for advances after May 31, 1954, less any sum returned under article 2 of the Agreement between the Governments of the Republic of Korea and the United States of America of July 28, 1950, will be effected monthly in sterling at the military exchange rate in force on the date or dates when advances are made and the middle market rate in London for the United States dollar on the date of the advance. In the event of a devaluation of the hwan affecting hwan advanced, the Government of the Republic of Korea will allow six days' grace after devaluation for the return of hwan balances under article 2 of the aforesaid Agreement. In the event of any changes being made in the spread within which the middle market rate can at present fluctuate (*i.e.*, $2·78–$2·82 to the £, as now officially recognised by the International Monetary Fund) or of any changes occurring in the United Kingdom Exchange Control Regulations which materially affect the Republic of Korea, the methods of calculation and payment for hwan advances after the effective date of the changes shall be reviewed.

(3) Unless on or before December 31, 1954, the United States Government repay to the Government of the Republic of Korea a sum equivalent to that allowed to the United States Government as a 10 per cent. rebate in respect of official expenditure under the terms of the settlement of hwan advances to the United States Forces in Korea, the Government of the Republic of Korea shall—

(i) Within one month of December 31, 1954, repay to the United Kingdom Government an amount equivalent to 5 per cent. of all past drawings made up to and including December 31, 1954, in respect of official expenditure by the United Kingdom, Australian and New Zealand components of the British Commonwealth Forces, Korea;

(ii) Subject to the provisions of point (4) below, allow the United Kingdom Government a rebate of 5 per cent. of drawings made after December 31, 1954, in respect of official expenditure by the United Kingdom, Australian and New Zealand components of the British Commonwealth Forces, Korea.

(4) If before December 31, 1954, the United States Government waive for the future the rebate allowed to them as aforesaid, but without making any repayment in respect of the rebate in the past, the United Kingdom Government shall also waive the rebate as from the date of effective waiver by the United States Government, and the Government of the Republic of Korea shall within one month of December 31, 1954, repay to the United Kingdom Government an amount equal to 5 per cent. of all drawings in respect of official expenditure by the United Kingdom, Australian and New Zealand components of the British Commonwealth Forces, Korea, up to and including the date of the waiver.

(5) If after December 31, 1954, but on or before December 31, 1955, the United States Government repay to the Government of the Republic of Korea a sum equivalent to that allowed the United States Government as a rebate, the United Kingdom Government shall repay to the Government of the Republic of Korea:

(i) The sum repaid by the Government of the Republic of Korea under point (3) (i) above;

(ii) The sum represented by any rebate allowed by the Government of the Republic of Korea under point 3 (ii) above.

(6) If at any time after that date the United States Government waive for the future the rebate allowed to them aforesaid, but without making any repayment in respect of the rebate in the past, the United Kingdom Government shall do likewise.

(7) After December 31, 1955, no retroactive adjustment will be made between the Government of the Republic of Korea and the United Kingdom Government in respect of—

(i) Any rebate allowed;

(ii) Payment made in respect of a rebate by the Government of the Republic of Korea under point (3) (i) and (ii) above.

(8) As to currency advances made to the Canadian Armed Forces, it is understood that the Government of the Republic of Korea will offer to the Government of Canada similar terms on the calculation of the liability as in point (2) above and similar terms on the rebate as in points (3) to (7) above.

(9) The Government of the Republic of Korea agree to grant retrospectively and for the future to the Governments of the United Kingdom, Australia, New Zealand and Canada terms not less favourable than those which may be granted after May 31, 1954, to the Government of the United States in respect of the rate of exchange and the methods of obtaining Korean currency.

2. If the foregoing proposal is acceptable to the Government of the Republic of Korea, I have the honour to suggest that the present note and your Excellency's reply in that sense should be regarded as constituting an agreement between Her Majesty's Governments in the United Kingdom, Australia and New Zealand on the one part and the Government of the Republic of Korea on the other part in this matter which shall enter into force immediately and shall remain in force until such time as it is mutually agreed that the need therefor has ceased.

I have, &c.

W. G. GRAHAM

II

The Korean Minister of Finance to Her Majesty's Minister at Seoul

Seoul, Korea, 28 September, 1954

Sir,

I have the honour to acknowledge receipt of your note of today's date which reads as follows:—

(See note I)

In reply I have the honour to inform you that the above-mentioned terms are also acceptable to the Government of the Republic of Korea, and that they therefore agree with your proposal that your note and this reply should be regarded as constituting the formal agreement between the two Governments in this matter which shall enter into force immediately and shall remain in force until such time as it is mutually agreed that the need therefor has ceased.

I have, &c.

LEE, JOONG CHAI

[*207 UNTS 294.*]

Some mention must also be made of the expenses involved in the use of facilities in Japan. Upon the entry into force of the US–Japan Peace Treaty, there occurred an exchange of Notes relating to the facilities that Japan had provided the Unified Command in its action against Korea. The exchange provided that, if the need for such services should recur,

the expenses involved in the use of Japanese facilities and services to be borne as at present or as otherwise mutually agreed between Japan and the United Nations Member concerned. In so far as the United States is concerned, the use of facilities and services, over and above those provided to the United States pursuant to the Administrative Agreement which will be implemented the Security Treaty between the United States and Japan, would be at United States expense, as at present.   [*136 UNTS 206.*]

This was later modified by the Agreement on the status of UN Forces in Japan of 19 February 1954, the complete text of which is reproduced above (pp. 233–245). Article XV of this stipulated: 'The United Nations forces shall bear for the duration of this Agreement without cost to Japan all expenditures incident to the maintenance of such forces in Japan except that facilities, owned by the Government of Japan, the use of which is made available to such forces by the Government of Japan, shall be furnished by Japan free from rentals and other such charges.'[5]

[5] 214 UNTS 186.

I2

IMPLEMENTATION

THE preponderant role of the United States makes it particularly difficult to assess, through the published UN documentation, the effectiveness of the UN action in Korea. Many of the major decisions were taken outside of the UN framework; much of the political debate and argument is only hinted at in the records of the General Assembly and Security Council; and the formal reports of the Commander are clearly inadequate as a historical record of the changing military situation. The sweeping mood of McCarthyism in America, the turbulent relationship of MacArthur and Truman, culminating in the former's dismissal and return as a national hero to the Congressional Hearings, all find no place in the UN documentation. Yet they are a vital part of the story, and anyone relying solely on the UN records will receive—to a degree far greater than in any other UN operation—an impression that is distorted. Yet the reasons for limiting this study to an examination of UN source materials are still compelling.[1] The most that can be done here is to indicate further source materials to which any student of the Korean war should refer,[2] and to outline the events summarized, referred to—and sometimes ignored—in the UN documents.

Under the terms of Security Council resolution S/1588 of 7 July 1950,[3] the United States was requested to provide the Security Council with reports on the course of action taken by the UN Command. The stated objective of this first resolution, it will be recalled, was to defend South Korea against the attack from North Korea; and in the first few months of the war it looked as if this task was going to be easily accomplished.

I herewith submit the fifth report of the United Nations Command operations in Korea for the period 1 to 14 September, inclusive. Eighth Army *communiqués* Nos. 66 through 89 and Korean releases Nos. 353 through 437 provide detailed accounts of these operations.

Ground operations

On 1 September the North Korean high command employing thirteen infantry divisions, two new tank regiments, and elements of a previously identified command division, launched their strongest offensive to date against the United Nations position in Korea. This comprehensive attack, which constituted one of the enemy's major efforts to date, initially struck hard at the United Nations positions south of Tuksong and, within two days, had extended over the entire United Nations perimeter.

His initial effort, in the south, was unsuccessful. At the southern end of the front the enemy

[1] See Preface, p. xv above.
[2] See bibliography, pp. 311–12 below.
[3] For text, see pp. 163–4.

6th and 7th Divisions had been driven back 3,000 yards to their original positions by 3 September, through determined counter-attacks of the United States 25th Division supported by other United Nations forces. Thereafter, despite constant attacks, North Korean forces made no advances in this sector.

Farther north, in the Naktong River area between Hyonpung and the Nam River, the 10th, 2nd, 4th and 9th enemy Divisions, plus armored elements, began a general offensive eastward over the Naktong which scored initial advances of 6,000 to 8,000 yards against bitter resistance by the United Nations forces. By 5 September, however, the enemy had lost the initiative, and was forced to give ground under heavy United Nations forces' pressure. By the end of the period, the enemy retained only a two to three mile strip east of the Naktong River.

The enemy 3rd and 13th Divisions achieved gains of similar magnitude (6,000-8,000 yards) along the Taegu salient, from 4 to 11 September, in some of the heaviest fighting of the war. By that date, United Nations forces had absorbed the drive on Taegu, and began to register slow progress against strong enemy resistance. In the Simyong sector, the Republic of Korea 8th Division had gained about 3,000 yards by 4 September. During the series of heavy but indecisive engagements which followed, United Nations forces blocked further enemy advances.

The British 27th Infantry Brigade joined the United Nations forces in the defense of the Naktong River line on 7 September. This unit has assumed its proportionate share of the United Nations operations in that sector and is engaged in defensive operations and systematic police action to eliminate small enemy parties in the rear areas.

In the Haeson–Angang sector near the eastern flank of the United Nations perimeter, the North Korean 15th and 12th Divisions posed a most serious threat temporarily. Initiating heavy attacks near Kigye on 3 September, enemy forces penetrated to within four miles of Kyongju by 5 September, though the threat to Kyongju was vitiated by United Nations counter-attacks the next day. On 8 September, the enemy occupied the important town of Yongchon, but was driven out almost immediately by prompt aggressive action of Republic of Korea Army units. At his farthest advance the enemy had seized an area almost ten miles deep and fifteen miles wide in this sector, seriously threatening United Nations communications. However, beginning on 11 September, Republic of Korea and United States Army units conducted vigorous counter-attacks and advanced up to six miles on the west flank of the pocket, relieved pressure on Yongchon and Kyonju, and threatened the North Korean forces in turn with encirclement.

On the east coast the North Korean 5th Division, after yielding some ground to United Nations attacks, resumed the offensive on 4 September. This offensive, co-ordinated with the North Korean 12th and 15th Divisions' penetration on the west of Pohang-dong, necessitated a withdrawal of the Republic of Korea Army units holding Pohang-dong. Following their withdrawal these same Republic of Korean Army units counter-attacked and established a firm line two miles south of Pohang-dong.

During the period, the most significant gains were made initially along the north and west flanks, where enemy forces drove to within seven miles of Taegu, penetrated the lateral road net between Yongchon and Kyongju, and seized Pohang-dong. By 12 September, however, the momentum of the attacks was largely spent and the enemy was forced to fall back in the face of counter-attacking United Nations forces. This abortive effort had cost the enemy an estimated 10,000 casualties without any significant losses to the United Nations forces either in territory or in combat effectiveness. At the end of the period, the United Nations perimeter ran northward from Yulchi on the south coast, to the confluence of the Nam and Naktong Rivers, thence north, parallel with, and two miles east of the Naktong River to Hyonpung, thence along the river for fifteen miles, thence, northeast through Sindong in a broad arc extending eastward below Haeson and Angang to the east coast at a point two miles south of Pohang-dong.

Naval operations

United Nations naval forces during the period of this report continued to demonstrate their versatility of application by sustaining with undiminished intensity all operational tasks undertaken. During the enemy's major attack across the Naktong River, commencing early in the period, naval aircraft were almost entirely engaged in an all-out effort in close support of the ground troops for several days until the attack was effectively reduced. Thereafter, naval aircraft resumed their missions against North Korean targets in addition. A concentrated effort was made especially against transportation facilities, arsenals, military warehouses and supply dumps, and troop concentrations wherever located.

Naval surface forces continued coastal bombardment missions on an increasing scale until continuous day and night firing on the east coast military targets became habitual.

At sea along the Korean coasts a very large number of enemy small craft have been destroyed, including small transports and freighters, trawlers, junks and barges carrying North Korean military personnel and supplies. Difficulty of identification of water-borne craft engaged in military operations continues to be a problem. In some cases the enemy has forced native fishing operations to his use, and it is reported crews are shot if seen conversing with United Nations ships conducting investigations. Nevertheless, every effort is being made to confine destruction of small craft to those conducting military operations.

Enemy opposition to United Nations naval forces was insufficient to hamper United Nations naval operations.

Air operations

Hostile aircraft have been observed on several occasions during the current period but have exerted no influence on the course of operations. It is a certainty that many difficulties will be experienced with the North Korean Air Force unless it procures planes from sources outside North Korea. Any future significant air action by North Korea will be a measure of the assistance given to it in open contravention of the actions and intent of the United Nations. Anti-aircraft artillery fire is increasing somewhat both in volume and in accuracy.

A review of the accomplishments of the United Nations air effort from 25 June through 15 September reveals that, while sustaining losses of approximately 100 aircraft, over 28,000 combat missions have been flown. The greater part of these have been in direct support of United Nations ground forces. More than 10,000 non-combat missions have been flown in support of the United Nations effort. The bomb tonnage delivered to strategic and tactical military targets by the United States Far East Air Forces medium bombers exceeds 17,000 tons.

The previous report of the United Nations Command emphasized the pronouncement made to the civilian communities that military targets would be attacked by air and the warning to civilians to vacate the immediately zone of such targets. There has been and there remains the capability of the United Nations air forces to completely devastate the urban areas of North Korea, but with assiduous care destruction of the civilian population has been avoided and only targets of military significance have been attacked.

Among the targets are the following: Pyongyang arsenal, the largest in North Korea, producing over half the arms and ammunition (exclusive of that from outside sources) employed by the enemy, is about 70 per cent destroyed. The ports and naval bases of Chinnampo and Wonsan have received attacks in force. The largest integrated chemical combine in the Far East, contributing explosives, aluminium and magnesium has been reduced by 80 per cent. Specific targets in this combine have been the Hungnam nitrogen fertilizer plant, the Hungnam chemical plant and the Hungnam explosive plant. The oil refinery at Wonsan is about 95 per cent destroyed. Iron works at Chongjin and steel plants at Songjin and Kyomipo have been attacked with percentage destruction varying from 30 to 90 per cent.

Operations of the Chinnampo smelter, largest producer in North Korea of copper, lead, and zinc, have been sharply curtailed. In addition, at Chinnampo, an aluminium plant and one of the few North Korean magnesium producers have sustained 50 to 80 per cent destruction. Other similar targets have been and are being attacked.

Along the highway and railroad nets some 250 bridges have been rendered unusable by the dropping of at least one span of each. Important marshalling yards and railroad repair facilities in North Korea are from 25 to 80 per cent destroyed.

Total daily sorties have at one time during this period exceeded 700. The smooth co-ordination of the total United Nations air effort with the over-all ground effort continued exemplary.

Prisoners of war

Since my last report (*S/1796*) many additional North Korean prisoners were captured by United Nations forces. This brings the total number of prisoners in United Nations custody to over 4,000. . . . [*S/1834, 5 Oct. 1950, 5th Report of UN Command in Korea.*]

On 15 September 1950 there began operation CHROMITE—the celebrated amphibious landings at Inchon[4] which led to a spectacular, but bloody, victory. There ensued the liberation of Seoul, at the cost of nearly 20,000 North Korean troops and an appalling number of civilian lives.[5]

I herewith submit the sixth report of the United Nations Command operations in Korea for the period 15 to 30 September, inclusive. Eighth Army *communiqués* Nos 90 through 117, 10th Corps *communiqués* Nos 1 through 9, Korean releases Nos. 438 through 509, and United Nations Command *communiqués* Nos 6 through 10 provide detailed accounts of these operations.

Introduction

Events of the past two weeks have been decisive. The strategic concepts designed to win the war are rapidly proving their soundness through aggressive application by our ground, sea and air forces.

The seizure of the heart of the enemy's distributing system in the Seoul area has completely dislocated his logistical supply to his forces in South Korea and has quickly resulted in their disintegration. Caught between our northern and our southern forces, both of which were completely self-sustaining because of our absolute air and naval supremacy, the enemy is thoroughly shattered through disruption of his logistical support and our combined combat activities.

The prompt junction of our two forces is dramatically symbolic of this collapse.

Continuing operations will take full advantage of our initiative and unified strength to provide for the complete destruction of the enemy and his early capitulation.

Ground operations

(*a*) *The envelopment*

At dawn 15 September, the United States X Corps made an amphibious assault on the Inchon area. The first phase in this wide envelopment was seizure of Wolmi-do, a small island which dominates Inchon harbor. The 3rd Battalion of the 5th United States Marine Division surprised the North Koreans with a perfectly co-ordinated attack that secured the island in two hours fighting.

The second phase of this operation involved the securing of the Inchon peninsula. The 1st United States Marine Division and four Republic of Korea Marine battalions accomplished this feat with lightning-like blows that kept the North Korean 18th Division and garrison units off-balance and unable to collect their forces for co-ordinated action. Kimpo airfield, the largest in Korea, was cleared on 17 September and opened for United Nations operations on 18 September. Elements of the 7th United States Division augmented by Republic of Korea Army forces were next brought into Inchon and rapidly took over the southern flank, advancing speedily ten miles to the south and securing Suwon.

The liberation of Seoul and the denying to the North Koreans of road and rail lines in this

[4] See Rees, ch. 5, for a detailed military analysis of Inchon.
[5] Commentators observed that the close support tactics of the US brought massive destruction in their wake. 'At the heart of the West's military thought lies the belief that machines must be used to save its men's lives; Korea would progressively become a horrific illustration of the effects of a limited war where one side possessed the firepower and the other the manpower' (ibid. p. 90).

communication hub comprised the third phase of this operation. On 19 September, the 1st United States Marine Division and two Republic of Korea Marine battalions crossed the Han River and started the attack on Seoul from the north. The remainder of the 1st United States Marine Division and the United States 7th Division enveloped Seoul from the south and west. The 17th Republic of Korea Regiment attacked through the center. By this time the North Korean forces had been able to bring in reinforcements from the 9th North Korean Division that was on the Eighth Army front and from scattered garrison and training units. The North Korean defense of Seoul was co-ordinated and fanatic, requiring the X Corps Commander to direct actual fighting with its hardships on civilian life and property. The liberation of the city was conducted in such a manner as to cause the least possible damage to civil installations. The third phase was completed on 28 September with only mop-up fighting continuing in the area. The President of Korea moved the Government of the Republic of Korea into Seoul on 29 September.

The obstacles to this wide envelopment were not only the enemy opposition, but also the natural obstacles of poor beaches fronted by miles of mud flats, a narrow channel, and an extraordinary tidal range of over twenty-nine feet. The success demonstrated a complete mastery of the technique of amphibious warfare, clockwork co-ordination and co-operation between the units and services participating. There was nothing noteworthy about the North Korean opposition, but there could have been. The potential was there. The North Koreans were proceeding with the construction of coastal fortifications, dug-in tanks and guns of all calibers, beach defenses and mining operations. Had this development been delayed for as much as a month, the enemy would have been ready and the assault, if possible, would have been more costly to United Nations assault forces.

(b) The main attack

In co-ordination with the landing of X Corps at Inchon on 15 September, the Eighth Army launched its main attack on 16 September. After reports of the successful landings at Inchon, the forces of Korean, British, and United States Army troops attacked along their actual front against strong enemy resistance. Some of the most severe fighting of the entire war resulted. The North Korean forces had a tight ring around the United Nations forces in the Eighth Army area and were pressing their attacks. United Nations forces had inflicted severe punishment to the attacking enemy. This ring around the United Nations forces, though strong, was by this time lacking in depth. The first few days of the main attack were replete with attacks and counterattacks meeting head on.

By 18 September, the North Koreans began to give ground slowly around the entire Eighth Army front. By 20 September, the United Nations forces were punching holes in the North Korean ring. The port of Pohang-dong on the east coast was retaken by the 3rd Republic of Korea Division on 20 September.

The IX Corps in the south with the United States 2nd Infantry Division, United States 25th Division and attached Republic of Korea units, got its attack rolling rapidly. In the Masan area, on the south coast, the enemy 6th and 7th Divisions had begun to yield ground by 19 September. Within four days our forces had driven westward almost to Chinju, and during the next week, enemy forces had been displaced almost to Hadong, a distance of thirty five miles.

The I United States Corps to the north with the 1st United States Cavalry Division, 24th United States Infantry Division, the 1st Republic of Korea Division and the 27th British Brigade, crossed the Naktong River on 19 September, built up a firm bridgehead on the 20th, and then sprang from this bridgehead in a furious driving attack up the main Kumchon–Taejon axis, pushing back the North Korean 1st, 3rd, 10th, and 13th Divisions about thirty-five miles west of their 15 September line.

On the northern and western fronts, the enemy 8th, 12th, 5th and 15th Divisions resisted fiercely until 22 September, when a series of precipitous withdrawals carried them more than seventy miles northward within six days.

The I and II Republic of Korea Corps on this front are responsible for this rapid progress.

To keep the enemy continually on the move, these Republic of Korea units developed a leap-frog system, with one regiment resting while one was driving. The enemy losses in personnel and equipment in this area were particularly heavy. At Uisong, over one hundred tons of rice and supplies and most of the equipment of a division were captured.

In large, the enemy has relinquished effective tactical control of nearly all Republic of Korea territory south of the 37th parallel, while United Nations forces now control a territory four times greater than at the commencement of the Inchon landings. In his general retreat, the enemy has suffered thousands of casualties and was forced to abandon large quantities of arms, ammunition, and equipment on all parts of the front. The loss of this material which includes field guns, tanks, trucks, and aircraft, will further reduce the North Korean fighting potential.

United Nations advanced positions on the north mark a general line from Nakpung on the east coast, westward through Panwanggok, and Chungju, and north through Ansong, to the east of Seoul, and west to Kumpo on the coast. On the southwest, United Nations advanced positions follow a line from the vicinity of Hadong northwest through Tamyang, Kumje, to Iri and north through Nonsan and Chochiwon to Paranjang, on the west coast. . . . [*S/1860, 21 Oct. 1950, 6th Report of UN Command in Korea.*]

The events recounted in this report led to widespread optimism that troops of the UN would be 'home by Christmas'; but three major military victories faced the Unified Command with new political problems. It had now become necessary to decide whether the UN's role was to be limited to pushing back the North Korean forces to north of the 38th parallel or whether the objective was to be the reunification of Korea. The Security Council resolution of 27 June had spoken of restoring 'international peace and security in the area'; possibly it could have been interpreted to authorize an advance into North Korea, but Truman decided to seek another resolution. There was comparatively little opposition either within the United States, or among the allies, to Truman's belief that it was necessary to push north to the Yalu.[6] The required draft resolution was introduced into the Assembly by the United Kingdom (Russia had by now rejoined the Security Council) and was adopted, as General Assembly resolution 376 (V), on 7 October 1950. The voting was 47 votes to 5, with 7 abstentions, the five negative votes being those of the USSR, Ukraine, Byelorussia, Poland, and Czechoslovakia, and the seven abstentions Egypt, Lebanon, Syria, Yemen, Saudi Arabia, Yugoslavia, and India. It will be recalled that this resolution[7] recommended that

(*a*) All appropriate steps to be taken to ensure conditions of stability throughout Korea.

(*b*) All constituent acts be taken, including the holding of elections, under the auspices of the United Nations, for the establishment of a unified, independent and democratic government in the sovereign State of Korea.

Here, effectively, was the authorization to cross the 38th parallel and advance to the Yalu[8]—though the wording of the resolution had deliberately been left

---

[6] In the US George Kennan opposed an advance to the Yalu, but was overruled. 'There were also pressing domestic political reasons why Korean unification should be attempted. There were mid-term elections in November and even before the end of September, Senator Knowland had announced that a failure to cross the parallel would constitute appeasement of Russia' (Rees, p. 100).

[7] For full text, see above, pp. 165–6.

[8] Though Rees (p. 103) notes that the decision had already been taken by the Joint Chiefs of Staff on 20 Sept.

imprecise, both as a concession to the non-aligned nations, and to leave some room for manœuvre if China and Russia were, contrary to expectations, to enter the war.

It was now that MacArthur issued his call for an unconditional surrender:

Official messages offering the North Korean forces an opportunity to bring to an end the hostilities were transmitted by radio and leaflets throughout Korea on 1 October and again on 9 October.

. . . Eighty-five million leaflets have been air-dropped over Korea by United Nations Forces. One million five hundred thousand special leaflets were dropped with a large reproduction of the United Nations flag and a short statement of United Nations efforts towards establishment of a free, unified and democratic Korea. Radio Seoul has been restored to operation and is now being used for United Nations and Republic of Korea broadcasts. . . .

APPENDIX

TEXT OF GENERAL MACARTHUR'S MESSAGE OF 9 OCTOBER 1950

In order that the decisions of the United Nations may be carried out with a minimum of further loss of life and destruction of property, I, as the United Nations Commander-in-Chief, for the last time call upon you and the forces under your command in whatever part of Korea situated, to lay down your arms and cease hostilities. And I call upon all North Koreans to co-operate fully with the United Nations in establishing a unified, independent and democratic government of Korea, assured that they will be treated justly and that the United Nations will act to relieve and rehabilitate all parts of a unified Korea. Unless immediate response is made by you in the name of the North Korean Government, I shall at once proceed to take such military actions as may be necessary to enforce the decrees of the United Nations. [*S/1883, 3 Nov. 1950, 7th Report of UN Command in Korea.*]

The Chinese, in a series of statements and broadcasts, now made it clear that they would regard their vital interests as threatened if the UN advanced towards the Yalu. The Peking government was not assuaged by the assurances of the General Assembly that the UN sought no wider war. Two weeks earlier MacArthur had reported

for the first time in the Korean war, Chinese soldiers of the Chinese communist forces were captured in combat in Korea. They wore North Korean uniforms, and may have been volunteers. There is no positive evidence that Chinese Communist units, as such, have entered Korea, although incomplete interrogation of these prisoners of war indicates that possibility. [*S/1885, 6 Nov. 1950, 8th Report of UN Command in Korea.*]

None the less, it seems that the advice given to President Truman was that China would not, in any significant way—her own warnings notwithstanding— enter the war;[9] and that even if she did, MacArthur's instructions permitted him sufficient freedom of manœuvre. The incorrectness of these assumptions was to change the whole course of the war. Hundreds of thousands of Chinese now began to enter Korea, undetected, over the great frontier bridges at Antung and Manpojin.[10]

[9] See 'Substance of Statements made at Wake Island', reprinted in R. H. Rovere and A. M. Schlesinger, *The General and the President* (1952), pp. 253–62.
[10] See A. S. Whiting, *China Crosses the Yalu* (1960), pp. 116–24; and Rees, p. 110.

By the middle of October 1950, the United Nations forces had in prisoner of war enclosures over 130,000 North Korean military personnel and had killed or wounded over 200,000 more. Thus, the personnel of the North Korean forces were eliminated, their equipment was captured or destroyed, and all but the northern borders of Korea was held by United Nations forces. For all practical purposes, the conflict with the armed forces of the former North Korean régime had been terminated.

Beginning in October 1950, Chinese Communists started moving into Korea and attempted to cover their moves by statements that it was individual volunteer participation. It is perfectly clear that the Chinese started moving the mass of their forces to position for the invasion by the middle of September. The Chinese Communist forces are now invading Korea and attacking United Nations forces in great and ever increasing strength. No pretext of minor support under the guise of volunteerism or other subterfuge now has the slightest validity. These irrefutable facts prove that the Chinese Communist régime has directed an invasion of Korea and an assault against the United Nations forces.

During the first half of the period there were extensive operations by United Nations air forces of all types in sustained attacks on enemy lines of communications, supplies and troop concentrations, in conjunction with a regrouping and re-supply of United Nations Army forces. On 24 November a general attack was launched by all available United Nations forces. The attack progressed satisfactorily for two days, at which time strong attacks, principally by Chinese Communist forces, required readjustment of United Nations forces and resuming defensive operations. The United Nations offensive successfully developed and revealed the strength and intentions of the Chinese Communists.

Ground operations

The enemy forces now opposing United Nations operations in Korea demonstrated considerable strategic and tactical skill during the period of this report. These forces, now predominantly Chinese Communist, surrendered very extensive areas in the east coastal sector in the zone of operations of the X United States Corps.

In the west sector, on a line arching northward between Kasan and Tokchon, the enemy displayed little interest in combat from 16 to 25 November, inclusive. In many instances, United Nations units advanced several miles without contacting the enemy, and United Nations patrols ranging northward five to eight miles met only occasional resistance in the eastern part of the sector. On 26 and 27 November, the enemy, apparently reinforced by several fresh Chinese Communist armies (corps) from Manchuria, attacked all along the line, devoting his major effort to the United Nations Eighth Army right flank in the Tokchon area. These strong, sustained attacks, characterized by the usual Communist infiltration and flanking tactics, forced advanced United Nations units on the United Nations Eighth Army left flank and center to displace ten to twelve miles to a main line of resistance extending between Pakchon and Won-Ni. Powerful Communist thrusts north of Tokchon forced United Nations units back about twenty-five miles to the vicinity of Taepyong on the Taedong river. During the intense fighting in these actions, the enemy suffered heavy personnel losses as a result of maximum United Nations air and ground efforts. However, such losses are no longer of crucial military importance, in view of the enemy's tremendous capacity for troop reinforcement from secure bases in Manchuria.

The enemy opposition on the right flank of the Eighth Army is now accepted as a major Chinese Communist force thrust which clashed with United Nations forces, and which involved elements of approximately eight Chinese Communist divisions, while holding operations on the remainder of the Eighth Army position involved approximately six additional Chinese Communist divisions. As part of this general Chinese Communist offensive, savage attacks were directed against United Nations forces in the general vicinity of the Chosin Reservoir with a Chinese force estimated at six to eight divisions.

During the period 24 November to 1 December, the Chinese Communist forces are credited with having taken over direct responsibility for the entire front in North Korea, except for a short line of contact north of Chongjin on the east coast. The Chinese Communists reportedly have transferred most of the North Korean forces to Manchuria for retraining and re-equipping. At present, the only significant military power now confronting United Nations Forces in Korea is Communist China.

Identified and accepted Chinese Communist units are as follows:

38th Chinese Communist Forces Army (Corps)
    112th Chinese Communist Forces Division;
    113th Chinese Communist Forces Division;
    114th Chinese Communist Forces Division;
39th Chinese Communist Forces Army (Corps)
    115th Chinese Communist Forces Division;
    116th Chinese Communist Forces Division;
    117th Chinese Communist Forces Division;
40th Chinese Communist Forces Army (Corps)
    118th Chinese Communist Forces Division;
    119th Chinese Communist Forces Division;
    120th Chinese Communist Forces Division;
42nd Chinese Communist Forces Army Corps)
    124th Chinese Communist Forces Division;
    125th Chinese Communist Forces Division;
    126th Chinese Communist Forces Division;
50th Chinese Communist Forces Army (Corps)
    148th Chinese Communist Forces Division;
    149th Chinese Communist Forces Division;
    150th Chinese Communist Forces Division;
66th Chinese Communist Forces Army (Corps)
    196th Chinese Communist Forces Division;
    197th Chinese Communist Forces Division;
    198th Chinese Communist Forces Division;
20th Chinese Communist Forces Army (Corps)
    59th Chinese Communist Forces Division;
    60th Chinese Communist Forces Division;
    89th Chinese Communist Forces Division.

This undoubtedly represents a total strength of about 200,000.

Units other than those listed above which have been identified, reported, and tentatively accepted are the 70th Chinese Communist Forces Division of the 24th Chinese Communist Forces Army (Corps) and the 79th and 80th Chinese Communist Forces Divisions of the 27th Chinese Communist Forces Army (Corps). In addition is the doubtful and unaccepted presence of the 94th Chinese Communist Forces Division of the 32nd Chinese Communist Forces Army (Corps).

Judging from experience of the past, it is considered that there is a strong possibility that both the 24th and the 27th Chinese Communist Forces Armies (Corps) are in the area of operations. . . .

The enemy aircraft could appear in much greater numbers and become increasingly aggressive. Should this occur, and in the strength believed available to the Chinese Communist air forces, it is believed that the enemy air force would be capable of:

1. Diverting a considerable portion of the United Nations air effort from the direct support of ground action;

2. Hindering the United Nations air lift in Korea;

3. Striking United Nations vessels and installations of Korea; and

4. Providing possibly effective support of enemy ground action.

The readily accessible sanctuary in Manchuria has provided the enemy with an advantage that is almost impossible for our airmen to overcome, despite our superiority in other respects.

A significant development in the United Nations air operations has been the increased number of attacks mounted at night against the enemy, whose major movements are attempted under cover of darkness.   [*S/1953, 28 Dec. 1950, 10th Report of UN Command in Korea.*]

During the period of November to the end of December, the United States had sought to reassure China that she had no hostile intent. MacArthur had continued in the attempt to push north, but the feeling began to grow—in the capitals of the Allies[11] as much as in Washington—that American policy was now based on a vast misjudgement, and that great dangers lay in following MacArthur unreservedly.

From 1 to 9 December 1950 the UN Forces were engaged in a massive retreat from Chosin, with appalling losses. By Christmas Day, the advance to the Yalu had been completely reversed, and North Korea was once again under Communist control.[12]

In the new year the Communists made a series of offensives into South Korea. Relations between MacArthur and Washington were now deteriorating rapidly. The General believed China should be bombed and blockaded and that full use should be made of Chinese Nationalist forces based on Formosa. He felt that his hands were being tied, and that the ignominy of the retreat was unfairly falling on him. When refused permission to blockade and bomb China, he let it be publicly known that the Eighth Army was demoralized by the lack of political support. A series of messages now flew between Washington and Tokyo. Meanwhile Truman and the Joint Chiefs of Staff, were seeking through Ridgway to change gear to a war of containment.[13] It was hoped that if the Communists could be forced back to the 38th parallel, negotiations could open on the basis of the *status quo ante*. Under Ridgway's direction the UN Forces, by 10 February 1951, had retaken Inchon and neutralized Seoul.

In his 13th Report, covering the period 1–15 January 1951, MacArthur had stated:

13th Report
. . . As United Nations forces withdraw, Communist forces extend their supply lines farther and farther to the South, thereby increasing the difficulties of supplying their forces as these lines are under repeated air attack.

The most significant event during the period was the enemy's carrying his attack below the 38th parallel. . . .

14th Report
I herewith submit the fourteenth report of the United Nations Command operations in Korea for the period 16 to 31 January, inclusive.

Having been unable to continue his general offensive, the enemy during the period of this report has been, in the main, on the defensive. Aggressive United Nations reconnaissance in force on the western part of the front during the period 16 to 31 January met only light to

---

[11] For British reactions, see HC Deb., vol. 481, cols. 1161–440. It was on 3 Dec. that the Prime Minister, Clement Attlee, announced that he was flying to Washington. Great anxiety had been expressed in England about becoming involved in a war with China.

[12] 'After a brief flirtation with the terrifying potentialities of a policy of liberation, a chastened, uncertain, but still stubborn Democratic Administration was returning to its true love—containment' (Trumbull Higgins, *Korea and the Fall of MacArthur* (1960), p. 88).

[13] For details of this period, see Rees, chs. 10–12.

moderate resistance as far north as Suwon and Kumyangjang, and indicated that the enemy has apparently abandoned Ichon. At the same time, air sightings and other reports indicated numerous small-scale displacements on enemy forces northward in the area south of the Han River. The pattern of enemy resistance became slightly more uniform by 29 January as the United Nations offensive advanced to a general line three to five miles north of Suwon, Kumyangjang, and Ichon.

North Korean forces continued to defend stubbornly in the Wonju area until 24 January; however, United Nations patrols advanced ten miles northward into Hoengsong and, by 28 January, the enemy had withdrawn to positions about three miles north of that town. North Korean forces also offered only moderate resistance in the east coast sector, as United Nations forces advanced eight to ten miles in the Yongwol and Samchok area.

In the deep re-entrant on the Yongwol–Andong–Uisong axis, the North Korean troops withdrew from positions to which they had earlier infiltrated, leaving about one division in the mountainous area east of Tanyang, and another astride the road between Andong and Yongju. These two divisions materially augmented a force of about 5,000 guerrillas who were operating in the area east of Uisong. These two enemy regular units and the guerrilla forces were relatively active throughout the period, but broke contact and dispersed whenever they met superior United Nations forces. The guerrilla elements south and east of Uisong on one occasion extended their activities to the Yongdok area on the east coast, and some elements displaced southward into the Pohyan-San Mountain area, about 20 miles northwest of Pohang.

Front lines ran generally eastward from Suwon, near the west coast, to Yoju, thence northeast to Hoengsong, south-east to Yongwol, and northeast to Nakpong on the east coast. [*S/2021, 24 Feb. 1951, 13th & 14th Reports of UN Command in Korea.*]

Hard-driving United Nations forces scored advances of twelve to twenty-five miles along the entire front against stubbornly resisting enemy forces. Some of the most intensive fighting of the war took place in the Anyang and Yangpyong areas south and east of Seoul, Chinese Communist and North Korean forces, comprising the North Korean I Corps and the Chinese Communist 50th and 38th Armies, in an aggregate of eight divisions, fought tenaciously in the Anyang, Kyongan, Yangpyong areas to protect the main route of approach to Seoul, but United Nations forces took Anyang on 7 February and advanced three miles north of the town on the following day. By 10 February the battered enemy in this area had been driven north across the Han River, and United Nations forces had taken possession of the Port of Inchon, Kimpo Airfield, and the south bank of the Han, to the south and west of Seoul. Enemy attempts to re-cross the river were repelled on 12 February.

Heavy fighting continued throughout the period in the area south of Yangpyong. The Chinese Communist forces of the 38th Army were forced back five to six miles on both sides of the Yoju-Yangpyong axis, and sustained heavy casualties. However, enemy resistance remains firm to the south and east of Yangpyong, and intensive action continues. Meanwhile, the enemy is maintaining his Han River bridgehead between Seoul and Yangpyong.

In the central portion of the front against light to moderate resistance United Nations forces took Hoengsong on 2 February and advanced nine miles to the north by 11 February. On the night of 11–12 February the enemy launched a heavy counter-offensive north of Hoengsong with two Chinese Communist armies on a ten-mile front, the 40th and 66th Armies in conjunction with the North Korean V Corps in an aggregate of five to eight divisions. In this effort, the enemy penetrated our positions in several places, principally against the Republic of Korea 3rd and 8th Divisions, achieved extensive infiltrations, and forced United Nations units to withdraw several thousand yards to a new defensive line south of the town. Our forces evacuated Hoengsong on 13 February and withdrew to the vicinity of Wonju for further operations.

In eastern Korea, enemy resistance was spotty as United Nations forces advanced up to twenty-five miles. By 7 February Kangnung on the east coast was taken, and Chumunjin fell on the following day. By 10 February, United Nations forces had advanced several miles northward towards the 38th parallel.

In the Uihong area, almost 100 miles south of the main front, United Nations forces continued vigorous action to suppress relatively strong North Korean remnants and guerrilla forces. In repeated engagements of battalion and regimental size, the enemy forces invariably withdrew after a few hours of fighting. Guerrilla forces in this area are now almost constantly on the defensive and have lost the initiative.

Front lines at the end of the period ran generally from Inchon on the west coast to Seoul, southeast to Kwanju, east to the Han River below Yangpyong, east to Wonju or north thereof, northeast to Kanpyong, and thence to Chumunjin on the east coast. [*S/2053, 26 Mar. 1951 15th & 16th Reports of UN Command in Korea.*]

At the end of March 1951 the Republic of Korea's 1st Corps crossed the 38th parallel, taking the North Korean town of Yangyang. Ridgway now ordered a tentative advance across the parallel, on grounds of tactical security only, to tackle the supply and communications zone of the so-called Iron Triangle north of the parallel at Chorwon-Kumhwa-Pyonggang, where fresh Chinese armies were massing. By the second week in April six US divisions had crossed the parallel. The report for the second half of March 1951 noted:

During this period the enemy has been driven northward about 15 miles over the entire front, except in the Seoul area, where United Nations forces advanced 25 miles. The heaviest fighting occurred from 23 to 25 March near Uijongbu, Naegang and Hyon, on the western front, and at Chaun-ni on the central front. Enemy resistance appeared to be stiffening toward the end of the period, especially along the central front in the Kapyong and Chunchon area. In his withdrawal the enemy has made increasing use of mortars and landmines.

Front lines at the close of the period ran generally from Munsan east through Chunchon to the vicinity of Hyon-ni, and thence northeast to Yangyang, which fell to United Nations forces on 27 March. [*S/2107, 26 Apr. 1951, 18th Report of UN Command in Korea.*]

During this same period, while Ridgway's divisions strove first to hold, then to push back the Chinese, the rift between MacArthur and President Truman was approaching the point of crisis when MacArthur's letter to Congressman Joe Martin was read from the floor of the House. In it MacArthur agreed with Martin's suggestion that Chinese Nationalist troops should land on the Chinese mainland, and he went on, in broader terms, to criticize the political conduct of the war. President Truman was now confirmed in his resolve to dismiss MacArthur. On 11 April Ridgway heard of MacArthur's recall and learned that he had succeeded him as Commander of the UN Forces in Korea. The domestic repercussions of this decision have been well recounted elsewhere.[14]

In the spring, the Communists launched new military offensives. These were, after heavy losses on both sides, repulsed, and between May and June 1951 the UN Forces were able to push forward to the Iron Triangle.[15] On 18 May the General Assembly passed resolution 500 (V) calling on members to place an embargo on trade with China.[16] With these limited military and diplomatic victories secured, with unity among the Allies restored after MacArthur's removal, it was now felt that the time was ripe to seek to obtain an armistice. Reporting on the period 16 to 30 June 1951, the Commander noted:

[14] See Trumbull Higgins, *Korea and the Fall of MacArthur*; Samuel Huntingdon, *The Soldier and the State* (1957); John Spanier, *The Truman-MacArthur Controversy and the Korean War* (1959).

[15] See S/2204, 20 June 1951, 21st Report of UN Command in Korea for period 1–15 May 1951.

[16] For text, see s. 2, pp. 168–9.

On the last day of this period, the United Nations Command repeatedly broadcast to the Commander-in-Chief of the Communist forces in Korea a proposal that accredited representatives of each command meet on the Danish hospital ship *Jutlandia* off the coast of Wonsan for the purpose of negotiating a cease-fire agreement. No reply had been made to the proposal by midnight of 30 June. The full text of the radio message follows:

'As Commander-in-Chief of the United Nations Command, I have been instructed to communicate to you the following: I am informed that you may wish a meeting to discuss an armistice providing for the cessation of hostilities and all acts of armed forces in Korea, with adequate guarantees for the maintenance of such armistice.

'Upon the receipt of word from you that such a meeting is desired, I shall be prepared to name my representative. I would also at that time suggest a date at which he could meet with your representative. I propose that such a meeting could take place aboard a Danish hospital ship in Wonsan Harbour.' [*S/2265, 28 July 1951, 24th Report of UN Command in Korea.*]

In July cease-fire negotiations began at Kaesong (nominally no-man's land, but in fact controlled by the Communists). A new phase had begun.

MESSAGE FROM GENERAL RIDGWAY BROADCAST TO THE COMMUNISTS ON 13 JULY 1951

To General Kim Il Sung and General Peng Teh-Huai:

In my initial message to you on 30 June I proposed that representatives meet aboard a Danish hospital ship. I suggested that site since it would have afforded equal freedom of access to both parties, including any elements such as newsmen associated with the party. It would have provided a completely neutral atmosphere free of the menacing presence of armed troops of either side. It would have provided adequate communications facilities of all kinds.

Your reply to my message made no reference to my proposed meeting place. Instead you proposed Kaesong. In the interest of expediting the end of bloodshed and to demonstrate the good faith under which the United Nations Command was proceeding, I accepted Kaesong as the site for our discussion.

In so doing I expected that the condition referred to above, vital to the success of any such discussions, would be afforded at Kaesong. In order to provide further assurances that such conditions would in fact exist at the conference site, my liaison officers in the initial meeting with yours on 8 July proposed that a 10-mile-wide corridor centered on the Kumchong–Kaesong-Munsan road and limited by Kumchon on the north and Munsan on the south be established a neutral zone free of any hostile action by either party.

They further recommended that United Nations forces within this corridor remain south of an east-west line to the south edge of Kaesong while your forces within this corridor remained north of an east-west line to the north edge of Kaesong, leaving the town of Kaesong restricted to entry only by those individuals in the delegation party.

Agreement on this proposal would have insured freedom of movement to both delegations, to and from the meetings and within the town of Kaesong. However, your liaison officers declined to agree to this proposal, stating that it was not needed to insure satisfactory conditions at the conference site for both delegations.

To show good faith and to avoid delay I accepted your assurances instead of my proposal to establish a neutral zone. Since the opening of the conference it has been evident that the equality of treatment so essential to the conduct of armistice negotiations is lacking. Since the first meeting at Kaesong your delegation has placed restrictions on the movement of our delegation. It has subjected our personnel to the close proximity of your armed guard, it has delayed and blocked passage of our couriers. It has withheld its co-operation in establishment of two-way communications with our base even though it agreed to do so immediately. It has refused admittance to the conference area to certain personnel in our convoy which I desire and for whose conduct I stated I assumed full responsibility.

Extension of the present recess and the delay in resuming the conference of our delegation is solely due to those unnecessary and unreasonable restrictions against which my representatives have repeatedly protested.

As pointed out to your representatives by Vice Admiral Joy, my personal representative in the first meeting of 10 July, the hope for success of these discussions rested upon the good faith of both sides. With good faith, mutual confidence might be established, an atmosphere of truth created and the attainment of an honourable and enduring settlement brought measurably nearer.

The record of the United Nations Command delegation to date is open for world inspection. It establishes beyond any shadow of doubt their honourable intentions and good faith at every stage of the proceedings. With full and solemn realization of the vital importance of our conferences to all the people of the world, the United Nations Command delegation is prepared to continue our discussions in the same spirit of good faith at any time that we receive assurance that your delegation will proceed in like spirit.

The assurances which I require are simple and few. They include as primary prerequisites the establishment of an agreed conference area of suitable extent completely free of armed personnel of either side. Each delegation must have complete reciprocity of treatment to include complete and equal freedom of movement to, from and within the agreed conference area and complete and equal freedom at all times, in the selection of the personnel in its delegation party, to include representatives of the Press.

I therefore now propose that a circular area with its center approximately at the center of Kaesong and with a 5-mile radius be agreed upon as a neutral zone. The eastern limit of the neutral zone shall be the present point of contact of our forces at Panmunjom. I propose that we both agree to refrain from any hostile acts within this zone during the entire period of our conference. I propose that we agree that the area of the conference site and the roads leading thereto used by personnel of both delegation parties be completely free of armed personnel.

I further propose we both agree that the total personnel of each delegation within the neutral area at any time be limited to a maximum of 150. I propose that we agree that the composition of each delegation be at the discretion of its commander. It is understood that personnel to be admitted to the actual conference chamber should be limited to these agreed upon by your representatives and mine.

If you agree to these proposals the present recess can be terminated and conference resumed without delay and with some expectation of progress. Radio telephone is available to you for communication to me of your reply. If you prefer to send your reply by liaison officer I guarantee his safety within my lines during daylight, providing you inform me of the time and route by which he will travel and the manner by which he may be identified. Should you continue to insist that restrictions are necessary for our personal safety or for any other reason, I propose that the conference site be moved to a locality which will afford the few simple assurances I have specified herein.

> (*Signed*) M. B. RIDGWAY,
> *General, United States Army*
> *Commander in Chief, United Nations Command*

ENGLISH TRANSLATION OF CHINESE VERSION OF MESSAGE DELIVERED TO GENERAL RIDGWAY'S LIAISON OFFICER AT 06.40 KOREAN TIME 15 JULY 1951

To General Ridgway:

Received your letter dated 13 July. In order to clear away misunderstanding and arguments over various procedural problems and so that peace negotiation activities may progress smoothly, we agree with your proposal that during the conference period the Kaesong area is to be marked as a nuetral zone; that both sides suspend any form of hostile action; and that all armed personnel be removed from the conference site area and from the passage leading thereto used by your and my delegation groups.

As regards the size of this zone and other concrete problems related thereto, we suggest that settlement be made by the delegations of both sides at one meeting.

With reference to the newsmen's problem which has caused the suspension of conference this time, it has no bearing upon the problem of the neutral zone. Other than the one occasion when the latter problem was raised by your Liaison Officer on 8 July, it had not been brought up again by your delegation. Furthermore, the duty of a liaison officer is to discuss problems of minor details and he has no authority to discuss a problem, the nature of which concerns such establishment of a neutral zone. The newsmen problem that has caused the suspension of conference this time is a minor problem; it is not worth stopping the conference because of this problem; it is less worth letting the conference break up on account of this problem.

Your delegation did raise this question at the meeting. At the time, our delegation felt that before the meeting has taken any shape and even when an agenda has not been passed, it is not appropriate for newsmen of the various countries to come to Kaesong. Therefore no agreement was reached on this problem.

We insist on the principle that all problems must be agreed upon by both sides before being carried out. We believe that this is a fair principle and may not be disputed. Since no agreement was reached on the newsmen problem, your side should not by yourself force any action (on the matter).

In order that the conference may not be buried in prolonged suspension or break up as a result of such a minor question, we now agree to your suggestion that your twenty newsmen will be considered as part of the working personnel of your delegation. We have already instructed out delegation to provide facility to your side over this problem.

(*Signed*) KIM IL SUNG
Supreme Commander, Korean People's Army
(*Signed*) PENG TEH-HUAI
Commander, Chinese People's Volunteer Army

ENGLISH TRANSLATION OF NORTH KOREAN VERSION OF MESSAGE DELIVERED TO GENERAL RIDGWAY'S LIAISON OFFICER AT 06.40 KOREAN TIME 15 JULY 1951

To General Ridgway:
We have received your letter of 13 July.

In order to carry out the peace conference smoothly we agreed to the proposals that the misunderstandings and arguments on some minor details will be eliminated, that the Kaesong area will be a neutral zone during the conference period, that hostilities of both groups will be suspended, and that the roads to the conference site which are used by both delegates, and the area of the conference site, will be cleared of all armed personnel.

However, we propose that the limits of the conference area, and other concrete problems in connexion with this should be left to and settled by a meeting of the delegates of both sides.

The current problem of newspapermen which was the reason for this recess has no connexion with the problem of establishment of a neutral zone. In regard to the question of a neutral zone, aside from the raising on the question once by your liaison officers at the meeting of 8 July, your delegates never raised this question.

The mission of the liaison officers was to discuss minor details, but not problems such as the establishment of a neutral zone.

The problem of the newspaper reporters, which was the reason for this recess, is a minor one. This is not a sufficient reason to cause a recess and, even more, it is not a sufficient reason to bring about a break in the conference.

At the time when your delegation raised this question at the conference table, our delegates were of the opinion that as there were yet no results in the meeting, and even more, as the agenda had not even been determined, they did not feel that it was appropriate for newspapermen of various countries to come to Kaesong. It was for this reason that agreement could not be obtained. We maintain the principle that all matters will be carried out with the agreement of both sides. We believe that such a principle is the most impartial, and leaves no room for argument or opposition.

Inasmuch as we have not reached agreement on the question of newspapermen, it should not be put into effect forcefully by your side alone.

In order to avoid a long recess for a breakup of this conference because of such a small question, we agree to your proposal, namely, we agree to twenty news representatives of your side being part of the working personnel of your delegation.

We have already issued the order that out delegates shall provide convenience for your delegates.

(*Signed*) KIM IL SUNG . . .
(*Signed*) PENG TEH-HUAI . . .

COMMUNIQUÉ AND SUPPLEMENTARY ANNOUNCEMENT ISSUED 15 JULY BY THE UNITED NATIONS COMMAND AFTER THE THIRD SESSION OF CEASE-FIRE NEGOTIATIORS IN KAESONG

Communiqué

The third meeting of the Korean armistice negotiators convened at 2.09 p.m. today, Sunday, 15 July 1951, at the same conference site that has been used for the two previous meetings.

When the helicopters carrying the members of the United Nations Command delegation landed near the conference site, no North Korean or Chinese on guard were apparent.

Admiral Joy, who had traveled to Kaesong by jeep, took the initiative and opened the meeting. He extended his regrets for being nine minutes late, but stated that the delay was occasioned by actions of sentries in holding up two one-quarter ton trucks (jeeps) of his convoy. The Admiral's jeep and one other had gone ahead of the convoy in order to arrive at the conference at the scheduled time. Sentries delayed the Admiral until the convoy closed. He further stated that he expected no repetition of such an event on the part of the Communist forces.

The senior members of the United Nations Command delegation then elaborated on certain details previously advanced in General Ridgway's message of 13 July and proposed that:

1. The road leading to the conference site of Kaesong shall be open to unrestricted use by vehicles of the United Nations Command delegation. No notice will be required for such movement.

2. The neutral area, five miles in radius, with the traffic circle in Kaesong as its center, would contain no armed personnel except the minimum needed for military police purposes. Such personnel could be armed with small arms.

3. Any personnel required for security at the conference site would be unarmed. The conference site would be defined as an area having a radius of one-half mile centered on the conference house.

At 2.22 p.m., General Nam Il, senior Communist delegate, requested a fifteen-minute recess to discuss with his delegation Admiral Joy's proposals.

At the end of the recess General Nam Il agreed in principle and accepted the United Nations Command proposals. It was suggested and agreed upon that it would be appropriate for the liaison officers of the two delegations to work out the minute details of establishing the neutral area of the conference.

Significant of the desires of both delegations to get on with the main work of the conference was the complete absence of any controversy over the arrangement for neutrality of the site. The delegation then proceeded for the remainder of the meeting to discuss agenda items.

Announcement

During a meeting of the liaison officers, which immediately followed the negotiation session held between the United Nations Command delegation and the North Korean Chinese delegation this afternoon at Kaesong, all of the proposals made by Vice Admiral Charles Turner Joy relating to the neutrality of the zone for the discussion were reviewed.

No particular problems in implementing the provisions are anticipated and, for the most part, the proposals have already been placed into effect.

Colonel Chang, senior Communist Liaison Officer, appeared to be very anxious to resolve any future difficulties on a liaison officer level in order that the delegates might not be diverted

COMMUNIQUÉ ISSUED 16 JULY BY THE UNITED NATIONS COMMAND AFTER THE FOURTH SESSION OF CEASE-FIRE NEGOTIATIORS IN KAESONG

Convening for the fourth time, the armistice negotiations continued at 10.00 hours today, Monday, 16 July 1951.

The senior United Nations Command delegate opened the meeting, presenting further arguments in favour of the items on the agenda proposed by the United Nations Command. All procedural matters having been previously agreed upon, only agenda items were open for discussion.

After Admiral Joy spent the best part of the morning presenting the view of the United Nations Command delegation, General Nam Il requested a two-hour recess to enable him to discuss these views with his delegation. Upon reconvening, General Nam Il presented the reaction of his delegation to the views of the United Nations Command.

The conference adjourned at 13.50 hours after having agreed to reconvene at 11.00 hours tomorrow, Tuesday, 17 July.

The United Nations Command delegation reports that some progress was made toward the formation of a mutually agreed upon agenda.

The Communists have fulfilled their agreement with respect to the neutrality of the conference site in that no armed personnel were observed.

The United Nations Command delegation posed for United Nations photographers during the two-hour recess and the Chinese–North Korean delegation posed after the conference was over.

COMMUNIQUÉ ISSUED 17 JULY BY THE UNITED NATIONS COMMAND AFTER THE FIFTH SESSION OF CEASE-FIRE NEGOTIATORS IN KAESONG

Convening at 11.00 hours Seoul time today, the fifth session of the Korean armistice negotiations was opened by the North Korean and Chinese senior delegate.

Most of the time of the morning session was taken up by discussion of the items of the agenda proposed by the United Nations Command, with both senior delegates participating. In addition, clarification of definitions and translations took considerable time.

The afternoon session of the conference was more formal, with the North Koreans' senior delegate elucidating and explaining details of his proposed agenda. Both the English and Chinese translations appear to have been prepared in advance.

The United Nations Command delegation felt that some progress may be recorded in the conference discussions.

The fifth session adjourned at 14.35 hours until 10.00 hours Seoul time, 18 July 1951.

COMMUNIQUÉ ISSUED 18 JULY BY THE UNITED NATIONS COMMAND AFTER THE SIXTH SESSION OF CEASE-FIRE NEGOTIATORS IN KAESONG

The sixth session of armistice negotiations which convened at 09.58 this morning resulted in some additional progress being made toward the formation of a mutually accepted agenda on which to base the detailed discussion. Nevertheless, at least one major issue remained unsolved when the conference recessed for the day. Agreement on the key point is essential to the successful completion of the first phase of the negotiation.

In order to hasten the conferences to their ultimate goal, the United Nations senior delegate accepted two points presented by the Communists on the phraseology of agenda items, after placing on the record the United Nations' understanding of their basic intent.

Today's meeting moved rather ponderously, as had the previous meetings, due to language difficulties. Since three languages—Chinese, North Korean and English—are being used in the conference, it was necessary for each statement from either side to be translated twice.

Twice during today's talks recesses were requested. The first, a two-hour recess, was asked by the North Korean–Chinese delegates at 10.51 hours in order to study in detail a revised agenda which was presented by Admiral Joy at the conclusion of his opening statement of the morning.

At 12.55 the North Korean–Chinese delegation requested through their liaison officer an additional thirty-minute recess.

The afternoon session opened at 13.24 hours with a statement by the senior Communist delegate which was followed by a detailed exploration by both sides of the points of issue. At 14.37 the United Nations delegates requested a fifteen-minute recess.

Shortly after reconvening at 14.54, the two delegations found an area of mutual agreement on the phraseology of the second major point accepted during the day.

The conference adjourned at 15.24 hours (Seoul time) and will be resumed at 11.00 hours (Seoul time) tomorrow, 19 July 1951.

COMMUNIQUÉ ISSUED 19 JULY BY THE UNITED NATIONS COMMAND AFTER THE SEVENTH SESSION OF CEASE-FIRE NEGOTIATORS IN KAESONG

General Nam Il, North Korean–Chinese delegate, opened the seventh session of the armistice negotiations at 11.00 today by requesting the opinion of the United Nations senior delegate on the proposed North Korean–Chinese agenda.

Admiral Joy reiterated the United Nations stand that only matters of a military nature would be discussed. General Nam Il then replied with a statement obviously prepared in anticipation of the United Nations reply. The North Korean–Chinese senior delegate occupied the floor for approximately eighteen minutes and made it clear that their position was unchanged on the question under debate. About two-thirds of this time was spent in the translation of this statement into English and Chinese.

At the conclusion of General Nam Il's statement, Admiral Joy suggested a thirty-minute recess, to which the Communist delegation agreed.

After the recess the conference continued with discussions of the same subject. At 13.22 no progress had been made. It was agreed to adjourn until 10.00 (Seoul time), 20 July 1951.

COMMUNIQUÉ ISSUED 21 JULY BY THE UNITED NATIONS COMMAND AFTER THE EIGHTH SESSION OF CEASE-FIRE NEGOTIATORS IN KAESONG

At 11.38 hours today the North Korean and Chinese Communist senior delegates to the armistice negotiations requested a recess until 11.00 hours (Seoul time) on 25 July to enable both sides to study the proposals thus far presented.

The United Nations Command delegation agreed to this request although it sees no need for such a recess in view of the agreement reached thus far on points it considers necessary for an agenda.

The senior United Nations Command delegate requested that communications between the two delegations be maintained in order to facilitate a meeting at an earlier date than 25 July if at all possible.

[S/2266, 30 July 1951 Note transmitting texts of documents issued and received by UN Command relating to cease-fire negotiations at Kaesong]

COMMUNIQUÉ ISSUED 25 JULY BY THE UNITED NATIONS COMMAND AFTER THE NINTH SESSION OF CEASE-FIRE NEGOTIATORS IN KAESONG

The ninth meeting of the United Nations Command–Communist armistice negotiations today made considerable progress toward formulation of an agenda.

The general question of placing on the agenda the item of the withdrawal of military forces from Korea was discussed further, and the new proposal made by the Communist delegation was sufficiently interesting to cause the United Nations Command delegation at 15.13 to suggest an overnight recess to examine the matter in detail.

After General Nam Il's new proposal, the remainder of the afternoon was devoted to the exploration and clarification of both sides, with questions and replies flowing rapidly across the conference table.

The morning session was devoted to a statement by Vice-Admiral Joy, who expressed the

United Nations Command's views on the Communist agenda proposed at the last meeting. This was in response to the opening query by the senior Communist delegate in order that there be no misunderstanding on one of his more significant remarks.

Admiral Joy authorized a United Nations liaison officer to provide the Communist delegation with an extract in English of the statement in question.

The next conference is scheduled to be held tomorrow at 14.00 Seoul time.

GENERAL RIDGWAY'S ANNOUNCEMENT THAT CEASE-FIRE NEGOTIATIORS HAD AGREED ON AN AGENDA: 26 JULY

This afternoon the delegations representing the belligerent forces in Korea in the conference at Kaesong agreed upon an agenda for the regulation of the military armistice conference.

This agenda is as follows:

1. Adoption of the agenda.
2. Fixing a military demarcation line between both sides as as to establish a demilitarized zone as a basic condition for a cessation of hostilities in Korea.
3. Concrete arrangements for the realization of a cease-fire and an armistice in Korea, including the composition, authority and functions of a supervising organization for carrying out the terms of a cease-fire and armistice.
4. Arrangements relating to prisoners of war.
5. Recommendations to the governments of the countries concerned on both sides.

Having agreed upon an agenda, the way now is clear for the delegations to enter the area of really substantive discussion of the terms of a military armistice. Major problems remain to be solved in these discussions. It is much too early to predict either the success or the rate of progress to be obtained. Preliminary discussion began immediately after the agreement on the agenda in order that the potential for halting bloodshed in Korea may be realized as soon as possible.

It must be fully realized that mutual acceptance of an agenda is merely the initial step for the final goal of a military armistice and resultant cease-fire, which must be achieved under conditions giving every reasonable assurance against the resumption of hostilities.

There are numerous basic points within the framework of the agenda on which agreement must be reached and on which there is presently wide divergence of views.

COMMUNIQUÉ ISSUED 28 JULY BY THE UNITED NATIONS COMMAND AFTER THE TWELFTH SESSION OF CEASE-FIRE NEGOTIATORS IN KAESONG

Although the substantive discussions during today's armistice conference at Kaesong were in their entirety related directly or indirectly to item 2 of the agenda, little progress was made toward reaching an agreement in principle.

During both the morning and afternoon sessions, the viewpoints of the two delegations were stated in an atmosphere of cool military formality. The positions, restated today by the senior Communist delegate, had been first placed on the record by him during the conversation that preceded agreement on the agenda.

It was yesterday that the United Nations delegation expressed its views on agenda item 2, providing maps to the Communist delegation to supplement the statement.

At the end of today's session, recessed at 15.42, at the suggestion of the senior Communist delegate, the position of both delegations on the agenda item under discussion had not changed.

The thirteenth session will be held tomorrow morning at 11.00.

COMMUNIQUÉ ISSUED 29 JULY BY THE UNITED NATIONS COMMAND AFTER THE THIRTEENTH SESSION OF CEASE-FIRE NEGOTIATORS IN KAESONG

Discussions were continued today, at the thirteenth session of the military armistice conference, on item 2 of the agenda dealing with establishing a demilitarized zone between the opposing forces, with both delegations holding firm to their respective and previously-stated viewpoints.

In responding to the Communists' opening statement of the morning, Admiral Joy urged that the conference talks be limited to the immediate military problem faced by the negotiators. The Communists' opening statement had attempted to explore matters not germane to the current armistice negotiations.

The afternoon session was devoted largely to a series of brief statements by Admiral Joy in development and further clarification of the United Nations position.

Little tangible progress resulted from today's session, which adjourned for the day at 16.05 Seoul time.

The fourteenth session will meet tomorrow morning at 11.00, as suggested by the Communist delegation.

COMMUNIQUÉ issued 30 JULY BY THE UNITED NATIONS COMMAND AFTER THE FOURTEENTH SESSION OF CEASE-FIRE NEGOTIATORS IN KAESONG

The fourteenth and lengthiest single session of the Kaesong military armistice conferences today recessed after three hours and eight minutes with both sides holding firm to their views on item 2 of the agenda which deals with establishment of a demilitarized zone.

The United Nations senior delegate, Admiral Joy, in a series of prepared statements made a detailed analysis, both of the Communists' contentions as well as the United Nations poisition on the subject under discussion. He then once again invited comment by the Communists on the basic concept of the United Nations on the demilitarized zone 'so that the final solution to this item may reflect our mutual views'.

Shortly before noon, General Nam Il, senior Communist delegate, replying to an earlier clarifying statement by Admiral Joy, stated it was also his definite understanding that hostilities would continue during the current armistice negotiations.

The fifteenth session will meet tomorrow morning at 11.00. [*S/2275, 3 Aug. 1951, Note transmitting text of documents issued by UN Command relating to cease-fire negotiations at Kaesong.*]

Thus the major problems were quickly evident. General Nam Il, the leader of the Communist delegation, wanted the agenda to make specific reference to the 38th parallel as the demarcation line. The UN wished to establish a cease-fire line at the present military points of contact, and insisted that the re-establishment of the 38th parallel as a demarcation line would be a political question, which the UN delegation would not discuss.

It is understood, of course, that hostilities will continue in all areas except in those neutral zones agreed upon, until such time as there is an agreement on the terms governing the armistice, and until such time as an approved armistice commission is prepared to function.

The United Nations Command delegation is prepared to do its part in trying to work out an armistice agreement with representatives of the Communist forces in Korea for the cessation of hostilities in Korea under conditions which will assure against their resumption. This delegation is here for that sole purpose. It will discuss military matters in Korea relating to that subject.

This delegation will not discuss political or economic matters of any kind. This delegation will not discuss military matters unrelated to Korea. [*S/2277, 3 Aug. 1951, 25th Report of UN Command in Korea.*]

The presence of newspapermen was also a crucial difference between the position of the two delegations:

Within the limits of the conference room, although basic differences in view were revealed, an open and formal atmosphere and general harmony prevailed. However, in the area surrounding the conference room, Communist armed guards were constantly in evidence, and, acting obviously under orders of their superiors, presumed to question and restrict the movement of the United Nations Command delegates and couriers to and about the conference site.

At both the meetings Admiral Joy presented a proposal that international newsmen be admitted to the scene of the conference, emphasizing that they would not be admitted to the conference room. General Nam Il postponed answering. Admiral Joy informed him prior to the recessing of the second session that the Commander-in-Chief, United Nations Command, intended that twenty newsmen form an integral part of the United Nations Command delegation to all subsequent sessions of the armistice conferences.

On 12 July Communist armed guards denied the newsmen access to the conference area. The United Nations Command delegation was instructed to continue to recess until such representation as deemed proper by me was admitted to the conference area. Inasmuch as no change in the Communist attitude had been indicated by 13 July, I dispatched to the Communist commanders a review of the proposals that I or my representatives had made which would have produced in the conference area absolutely neutral conditions without restraints being imposed by either party. Though our proposals leading to these ends had been rejected or ignored, our delegation, in the interest of avoiding unnecessary bloodshed, had proceeded to the first two conferences. I informed the Communist commanders that the negotiations could proceed successfully only under conditions guaranteeing equality of treatment to the negotiators, removing the restrictions which had impeded the movement of United Nations delegates and couriers and removing armed personnel from the conference site. My recommended means for attaining these conditions was the establishment of a neutral zone around Kaesong free of armed personnel and the exclusion of armed personnel from routes to the zone.

To this latter recommendation the Communist leaders agreed on 14 July. The talks were resumed in a 2 to 4 o'clock meeting the afternoon of 15 July. [*Ibid.*]

At the eighteenth session of the negotiations each side was still restating its position with the Communists insisting that the cease-fire line must be along the 38th parallel, and the UN arguing for it to be at the point of contact, following terrain features. There now developed the pattern of charge and counter-charge which was to become all too familiar. Talks were broken off on 4 August when Admiral Joy complained of harassment by heavily-armed Chinese guards:

GENERAL RIDGWAY'S BROADCAST ON 5 AUGUST 1951

It has been officially verified by eye witnesses, confirmed with still and movie photography, that on or about 13.45 hours 4 August, armed military forces not belonging to the United Nations Command, were observed in Kaesong within approximately 100 yards of the conference house. These forces, approximating an infantry company, were proceeding in an easterly direction on foot and were armed with rifles, pistols, grenades, automatic weapons and mortars. . . .

I now invite your attention to this flagrant violation of the assurances which I required and which you promised. The United Nations Command delegation is prepared to continue conversations as soon as satisfactory explanation of this violation and assurances of non-recurrence are received. Meanwhile the United Nations Command delegation will remain within United Nations lines. I await your reply.

M. B. RIDGWAY
General, United States Army,
Commander in Chief, United Nations Command

UNOFFICIAL TEXT OF THE COMMUNIST REPLY, 6 AUGUST 1951

We have received your message.

On the matter concerning our Kaesong area guards entering the conference area armed with inappropriate weapons in violation of our agreement at 13.00 on 4 August, the chief delegate on our side ordered our liaison officer, Col. Chang Chun San at 09.30 on 5 August, to notify your delegation the details of the incident which was in violation of our agreement.

At the same time, the liaison officer was ordered to notify your delegation that our chief delegate has carefully reminded the Kaesong neutral area guards that they must not enter the vicinity of the Conference area, and that they have been ordered strictly to follow this order and see to it that such an incident will not recur.

In order that our conference will not be obstructed by such trivial accidental incidents, we have again ordered the guards of the Kaesong neutral zone to adhere strictly to the agreement of 14 July and to assure that such a violation of the agreement will not occur again.

We desire that you order your delegation to proceed to Kaesong to resume negotiations immediately upon receipt of this reply.

KIM IL SUNG
Supreme Commander, Korean People's Army
PENG TEH-HUAI
Commander, Chinese People's Volunteer Army
[S/2287, 8 Aug. 1951, Note transmitting text of documents issued by UN Command
relating to cease-fire negotiations at Kaesong.]

The meetings were resumed,[17] though the UN insisted that such incidents of harassment were far from trivial, especially when mortar and machine-gun squads were involved. However, the resumed meetings achieved little:

COMMUNIQUÉ ISSUED ON 10 AUGUST BY THE UNITED NATIONS COMMAND AFTER THE TWENTIETH SESSION OF CEASE-FIRE NEGOTIATORS IN KAESONG

The Communist delegation today refused adamantly to:

1. Discuss the battle line area as a possible location of the line of military demarcation.
2. Discuss any line other than the 38th parallel as a possible line of military demarcation.
3. Discuss any other item on the military armistice conference agenda other than item 2.

The blanket renunciation by the Communists came after a historical and unprecedented two-hour and eleven-minute period of silence on the part of General Nam Il, during which he failed to respond to Admiral Joy's reaffirmation of his 'complete willingness to discuss a demilitarized zone located generally in the area of the present battle line' and 'continued willingness to discuss possible adjustments of the proposed zone which thus far has been defined only in general terms'.

Admiral Joy completed this statement at 14.44 hours and from there until 16.55 there was utter silence on the part of the senior Communist delegate. When it was abundantly apparent that a deadlock was about to ensue, Admiral Joy, still in hope of finding possible areas of agreement, made a further proposal that the conference temporarily drop discussion on item 2, which deals with the establishment of a military demarcation line and demilitarized zone, and that the delegates proceed to substantive conversation on item 3 dealing with concrete arrangements for the realization of a military armistice and the resultant cease fire,

For the second time during the afternoon, General Nam Il, without equivocation, refused to discuss any point other than the 38th parallel and item 2.

The conference will resume tomorrow at 11.00 hours Seoul time.

COMMUNIQUÉ ISSUED ON 11 AUGUST BY THE UNITED NATIONS COMMAND AFTER THE TWENTY-FIRST SESSION OF CEASE-FIRE NEGOTIATORS IN KAESONG

Another United Nations Command effort to establish possible areas for productive dis-

[17] S/2304, 21 Aug. 1951, p. 3.

cussion was brusquely rebuffed today by the Communists in the twenty-first session of the military armistice conference at Kaesong.

General Nam Il brusquely rejected Admiral Joy's invitation during the morning session that the Communists indicate on a map their concept of a demilitarized zone based on the present battle line and the over-all military situation.

The remainder of today's session was devoted largely to another reiteration by General Nam Il of his single and inflexible proposal for solutions to item 2 of the agenda.

There was no progress made today toward the conclusion of a mutually acceptable military armistice. The twenty-second session will be held tomorrow at 11.00 hours. [*S/2304, 21 Aug. 1951, Note transmitting text of documents issued by UN Command relating to cease-fire negotiations at Kaesong.*]

The talks were broken off again when the Communists accused the UN Command of dropping a napalm bomb on the night of 22–23 August in the neutral conference area. The UNC insisted that the charges were ludicrous, and the Communist side then terminated negotiations. There followed in the next few weeks a series of charges by the Communists of violations of the neutral zone by the UNC, in three of which it admitted inadvertent violations but in the rest of which it totally rejected the evidence.

UNITED NATIONS COMMAND PRESS RELEASE, 23 AUGUST 1951, TOKYO

Further meetings of both the armistice delegations and the sub-committee were declared 'off from now on' at approximately 02.00 hours on 23 August by the Communists, on the basis of a charge of bombing the Kaesong area by United Nations forces.

Colonel Chang, the Communist liaison officer, speaking from written notes obviously prepared well in advance, made the above statements to Colonels A. J. Kinney and J. T. Murray, Jr., the United Nations liaison officers who had come to Kaesong at midnight at the request of the Communists to investigate the charges.

Colonel Kinney's report, based on investigation on the spot, but in darkness, clearly suggests the whole incident is a 'frame-up' staged from first to last.

The preliminary report from Admiral Joy follows:

'At 23.30 on 22 August the Communist liaison officer contacted the United Nations Command base camp by telephone. He stated the armistic conference site was bombed and strafed at 23.20. He requested the senior United Nations Command liaison officer to come immediately to make an investigation. I ordered United Nations Command liaison officers Colonels Kinney and Murray to investigate. They traveled by jeep to Kaesong, arriving there about 02.00 on 23 August.

'On arrival at the conference house in Kaesong, Col. Chang and Lieut. Col. Tsai, surrounded by the Communist Press corps, awaited the United Nations Command liaison officers.

'Col. Chang stated a United Nations Command aircraft had attached the Kaesong neutral zone at 23.20 on 22 August. The attack included strikes within the immediate conference area.

'Lieut. Col. Tsai then produced two marble-sized bits of metal which he alleged had hit the jeep of the senior Communist delegate.

'Col. Chang could not say whether one or more aircraft were involved. He stated he did not know how many bombs were dropped or how many passes the aircraft had made. He added that all present, including the Communist liaison officers, staff assistants, and Communist news reporters and photographers, had heard the aircraft. Cols. Kinney and Murray were then escorted to within 100 yards of the United Nations Command delegation house and there were shown a rumpled piece of rolled metal about 18 by 30 inches in size, covered with oil and lying on the road. Col. Chang asserted this was a napalm bomb. There was no bomb crater near and no scorched earth, but about 25 yards away there was a minor depression in the earth of about 24 inches in diameter and perhaps 6 inches deep.

'Col. Murray judges the depression a possible result of a buried explosive force about equal to a hand grenade. Col. Kinney is certain it is not a bomb crater.

'Near the residence of the Communist delegates three other pieces of metal were pointed out. Two of these appeared to be pieces of United Nations Command aircraft. Flush riveting was noticed on each piece, both of which were about 12 inches square. The third piece was the fin of a rocket.

'No craters or furrows were apparent in the vicinity. The pieces of metal were either lying on the ground or pushed in a few inches.

'On return to the Conference House Col. Kinney asserted the evidence plainly was not the result of a United Nations bombing. He pointed out there was no damage evident to any structure, person, or even to the crops.

'Speaking then from written notes, Col. Chang announced that there would be no further meetings.

'Col. Kinney inquired if Col. Chang meant sub delegation meetings as well as liaison meetings.

'Col. Chang replied all meetings "were off from this time". [*S/2311, 27 Aug. 1951, Note transmitting UN Command Press Release relating to cease-fire negotiations at Kaesong.*][18]

MESSAGE FROM GENERAL B. RIDGWAY TO GENERALS KIM IL SUNG AND PENG TEH-HUAI, 6 SEPTEMBER 1951

Your message to me, dated 1 September 1951 and received 2 September, is yet another of your false charges in which, without the slightest basis in fact, you have again impugned the good faith of the United Nations Forces. The charges you have levied in these alleged incidents are baseless and intentionally false. I have stated, and will again positively state, that our thorough investigations have indicated no instances where forces under my command have violated any of the agreements made by me or my representatives. Therefore, if the incidents did, in fact, occur, they were presumably initiated and perpetrated by your forces in order to provide spurious evidence for false and malevolent accusations against the United Nations Command.

I cannot provide you with guarantees against your own failure to exercise control in an area for which you are responsible. I cannot prevent the occurrence of incidents deliberately and maliciously manufactured by your forces in an area under your control. . . . [*S/2341, 12 Sept. 1951, text of document relating to cease-fire negotiations at Kaesong.*]

MESSAGE FROM GENERAL RIDGWAY TO GENERALS KIM IL SUNG AND PENG TEH-HUAI, TRANSMITTED THROUGH LIAISON OFFICERS AT PANMUNJOM, 23 SEPTEMBER 1951

Your message of 19 September, received 20 September 1951, has been noted.

Your suggestion therein that there are instances of alleged violations of the Kaesong neutral zone which remain unsettled is rejected. Each of the several cases wherein you reported an alleged violation was fully investigated. Where United Nations Command forces were responsible, that fact was reported. Where United Nations Command forces were not involved you were so advised and the cases closed. I have so instructed my representatives. I likewise reject the charges repeated in your letter that alleged violations of the neutral zone by United Nations Command forces made it impossible to continue the negotiations. The responsibility for the unnecessary interruption in the armistice conference is yours.

In your message you have dismissed the need to discuss conditions incident to the resumption of negotiations, in spite of the fact that the armistice discussions have been interrupted for prolonged periods because of incidents or alleged incidents. I have therefore given instructions to my liaison officers to insure that this vital subject receives careful attention in any future discussions with your liaison officers in order to minimize the likelihood of further interruptions.

Since you are now ready to terminate the suspension of armistice talks which you declared

[18] For further exchanges on the incident, see S/2326, 5 Sept. 1951.

on 23 August, my liaison officers will be at the bridge at Panmunjom at 10.00 hours on 24 September to meet your liaison officers and to discuss conditions mutually satisfactory for a resumption of armistice talks. [*S/2361, 2 Oct. 1951, Note transmitting text of documents relating to cease-fire negotiations at Kaesong.*]

The UN had shown that it was willing to accept responsibility on the few occasions where the evidence warranted it:

On 12 October 51, an unfortunate incident occurred. Investigation has established beyond reasonable doubt that United Nations Command jet aircraft made two ground strafing attacks (they dropped no bombs) in the Kaesong area about 17.30 hours on the afternoon of 12 October 1951, the same aircraft making both attacks. On 14 October 51 in a letter to Generals Kim Il Sung and Peng Teh Huai, I stated that these attacks had been made in violation of United Nations Command standing instructions which specifically direct all units and pilots to avoid attack or overflight of the Kaesong area, that beyond reasonable doubt United Nations jet aircraft had made the attacks, and that the United Nations Command, therefore, accepted responsibility. The United Nations Command will continue to make every effort to prevent any recurrence of incidents which violate previously made agreements. [*S/2432, 7 Dec. 1951, 31st Report on UN Command in Korea.*]

On 7 October the Communists formally proposed, and General Ridgway accepted, the transfer of the cease-fire talks to Panmunjom. Talks were resumed on 25 October 1951 on the basis of agreed conditions. After an initial round of reiterating the previously expressed views, some progress was made. The Communists now no longer insisted on the 38th parallel, and on 31 October agreed to basing the demarcation line on the firing line.

Some progress was made in negotiating a military armistice during the period. On 22 October 1951 liaison officers of the United Nations Command and Communist forces signed an agreement which specified terms of resumption of armistice negotiations. On this same date the senior delegate for the United Nations Command ratified the agreement by forwarding signed copies of it to the Communist delegation. On 23 October 1951 the Communist delegation in turn ratified the agreement. The text of the agreement and the mutually accepted understandings with respect to the agreement follow:

Text of the agreement:
   '1. The specific site at which the conference of the delegations will be resumed in the vicinity of Panmunjom is indicated on the attached map.
   '2. The conference site area is a circular area having a radius of 1,000 yards centred on the conference site as shown on the attached map.
   '3. No hostile acts of any kind shall be carried out by any armed force of either side, including all regular and irregular units and armed individuals of the ground, naval and air forces, against the conference site area as defined above.
   '4. Except for the military police provided for below, no armed personnel of either side shall be permitted in the conference site area. Designated officers of both sides shall be jointly responsible for the security and the preservation of order within the conference site area. Each side shall provide a military police detachment of two officers and fifteen men to assist in the performance of these duties while the delegation parties are present in the conference site area. During periods when the delegation parties are not present in the conference site area, one officer and five men of the military police from each side will be stationed in the conference site area. The military police shall carry only small arms, namely pistols, rifles and carbines.
   '5. Both delegations and their parties shall have free access to, and free movement within the Panmunjom conference site area. The composition of each delegation party shall be as determined by the senior delegate thereof.

'6. Physical facilities and communication and administrative arrangements with respect to the negotiations and the conference site area will be as agreed upon by the liaison officers of both sides. The delegation of the Korean People's Army and the Chinese People's Volunteers will be responsible for providing a suitable joint facility for use as a meeting place of the delegations and for the arrangements within the conference room. Except for this installation, each delegation will provide its own facilities.

'7. All armed forces of both sides, including all regular and irregular units and armed individuals of the ground, naval and air forces, shall refrain from hostile acts of any kind against the circular area having a radius of three miles centred on the traffic circle at Kaesong, against the camp area of the United Nations Command delegation contained within a circle having a radius of three miles centred as indicated on the attached map, and against the area of 200 metres to either side of the Kaesong–Panmunjom–Munsan road as indicated on the attached map.'

Text of mutually accepted understandings with respect to the agreement:
'1. The term "armed forces" as used in the agreement includes only the armed units and armed individuals under the control of or prompted either overtly or covertly by either side. When the factual findings of joint investigation prove beyond reasonable doubt that the persons responsible for an incident are under the control of or prompted either overtly or covertly by either side, that side shall not evade its responsibility for the incident.

'2. Investigation of reported violations of agreements shall be conducted as has been the practice of the liaison officers in the past.

'3. Agreements reached between the liaison officers on matters concerning the resumption of the armistice conference by the delegations will be the draft of the related part of the agreement of over-all arrangements to be stipulated by the delegations for the entire duration of the armistice negotiations.

'4. All previous security agreements and agreements regarding the Kaesong conference site area and neutral zone are superseded by the agreement of security arrangements for the entire duration of the armistice negotiations when the latter agreement is stipulated by the delegations of both sides.

'5. Except under weather and technical conditions beyond control, the military aircraft of both sides shall not fly over the conference site area at Panmunjom; the military aircraft of the United Nations Command shall not fly over the Kaesong area and the area of the road from there to the conference site area at Panmunjom; the military aircraft of the Korean People's Army and Chinese People's Volunteers shall not fly over the Munsan area and the area of the road from there to the conference site area at Panmunjom.' *[S/2469, 7 Jan. 1952, 32nd Report of UN Command in Korea.]*

In November the UNC introduced a new proposal—that the current contact line should constitute the demarcation line in the centre of the demilitarized zone and that only upon the armistice being signed within thirty days. This attempt to break the deadlock was not to prove successful,[19] because although

[19] Rees (pp. 300–1) comments: 'Whilst the new proposal apparently gave every incentive to reach an agreement quickly, it also stabilized the front for a month, for obviously neither side, and especially the UNC, would undertake offensive operations during the thirty-day period if territorial gains would have to be relinquished when an armistice was signed. The Communists thus gained a thirty-day *de facto* cease-fire on the ground, for . . . the plenary session, meeting for the first time since 25 October, ratified the agreement on 27 November. . . . Opening the way to this concession, [Admiral] Joy thought, was the failure to realize the use the Communists would make of the order of the agenda, with the subject of the demarcation line at its head. This meant that Nam Il and Hsieh Fang could reasonably insist that agreement on a cease-fire should be reached prior to the other substantive items. No general agreement was signed at Panmunjom by 27 December: in attempting to trade a temporary cease-fire for a quick armistice the Administration had lost its gamble.' See also C. T. Joy, *How Communists Negotiate* (1955), p. 129.

the proposal was accepted in principle, no agreement on the armistice was reached within the specified period. The war was now prolonged while the UN was subjected to continuing high casualties, and to charges of massacres of prisoners and of waging bacteriological warfare. The question of prisoners of war now began to assume an ever more important role in the negotiations:

Item 4 consists of 'arrangements pertaining to prisoners of war'. From 4 to 10 December the United Nations Command delegation daily urged that a separate sub-delegation be designated to discuss Item 4. This proposal was made by the United Nations Command delegation for the sole purpose of expediting the negotiations and in view of the humanitarian features of prisoner of war matters. Finally, on 11 December, after a week's time had been wasted, the Communists agreed to initiate discussions. At the outset of these discussions the United Nations Command made, and has made daily since then, two fundamental and logical proposals: namely, that information on prisoners of war be exchanged and that representatives of the International Committee of the Red Cross be permitted to visit prisoner of war camps. Both of these reasonable and humanitarian proposals, designed to alleviate the suffering of prisoners and their families, were callously and summarily rejected by the Communists. The United Nations Command long ago agreed to observe the Geneva Convention Relative to Prisoners of War, and has done so. Names of prisoners have been sent to the International Committee of the Red Cross. [*S/2514, 7 Feb. 1952, 35th Report of UN Command in Korea.*]

From mid-December 1951 until the signing of the armistice nearly twenty months later, the question of repatriation occupied a central place in the negotiations. As recounted elsewhere (pp. 184–7), the Communists insisted that all prisoners should be repatriated, whereas the UNC stood on the principle of voluntary repatriation. North Korea and China stated that Article 118 of the Geneva Convention on Prisoners of War constituted a clear duty to return all prisoners of war; the United States insisted that the purpose of this article was to protect the prisoners, and that she would not engage in the forcible repatriation of those who did not wish to return.[20] The UN's moral dilemma was acute, as the longer it held to the principle, the less likely was an armistice to be achieved, and the longer its own prisoners would remain in the North.

When the Communists released figures for the first time at the end of 1951, relations deteriorated yet further. In March 1951 the Communists had declared that they held 65,000 UN prisoners: they now listed only 11,500 prisoners—the massive discrepancy pointing to the inevitable conclusion that over 50,000 had died or been killed after capture.

By May 1952 agreement had been reached on other outstanding points. Argument had been revolving around (a) restrictions on the reconstruction of airfields, and (b) the composition of the proposed Neutral Nations Supervisory Committee. Nam Il, the North Korean delegate, now agreed to drop Russia's name from this Committee in exchange for the abandonment of aircraft rehabilitation. The big stumbling-block was therefore the question of repatriation of prisoners of war.

During the executive sessions and in the open sessions which preceded them, agreement had been reached on a number of matters relating to prisoners of war; but on the primary issues, the basis on which prisoners of war were to be exchanged, the positions of the Com-

[20] See above, p. 185.

munists and the United Nations Command were diametrically opposed. The Communists have been adamant in their demand for unconditional return of all prisoners of war held by each side; a demand absolutely unacceptable to the United Nations Command because it would almost certainly mean death or torture for the thousands of United Nations Command-held prisoners who signified their determination to resist return to communist control.

On two related issues the views of the Communists and the United Nations Command were violently opposed. The Communists attempted to lay claim to 37,000 South Korean civilian internees held by the United Nations Command who early in the war had largely been impressed into the North Korean army. At the same time the Communists refused to account for more than 50,000 persons admittedly captured by them but whose names were not on the prisoner lists submitted at the time such data were exchanged last December. Their only accounting for this group was the allegation that they had been released at the front, had died, or had been permitted to join their armed forces.

Discussions in the open sessions dragged on, sometimes under extremely trying circumstances. In an effort to create the most favourable possible atmosphere in which the detailed position of each side could be examined and discussed without the necessity for publicity to which the Communists appeared particularly sensitive, the United Nations Command proposed that executive, or secret, sessions be held.

On 25 March the first secret session was convened. The United Nations Command position on forced reparatiation was made unmistakably clear. The Communists indicated their willingness to negotiate but only on condition that the United Nations Command would provide an estimate of the total number of persons the Communists would expect to have returned to their side. The United Nations Command explained that since no poll of the individual preferences of prisoners had been taken, there was no basis for any realiable estimate of the number available for return. However, the United Nations Command guaranteed the return to the Communists of every North Korean and Chinese communist prisoner who desired to return to communist control. But in no case would the United Nations Command employ force to insure the return of any person who resisted repatriation. As a further indication of desire to effect the most equitable settlement of this issue, the United Nations Command agreed to permit any South Korean prisoner of war or civilian internee to transfer to the communist side if he so desired.

Continued insistence on the part of the Communists for a round number of persons to be returned to communist control compelled the United Nations Command to initiate a screening programme for all persons held in custody in the camps at Koje-do and Pusan.

The screening programme was designed to determine the number of North Korean and Chinese prisoners of war who could not be returned without the use of force to communist control and to give the nationals of the Republic of Korea held in custody by the United Nations Command, either as prisoners of war or civilian internees, freedom of choice to be returned to communist control or to remain in the Republic of Korea.

During a twenty-four hour period prior to the screening, North Korean and Chinese communist prisoners of war of each compound on Koje-do were carefully informed of the fact that they would be interviewed for the purpose of determining whether or not they would forcibly oppose repatriation. The prisoners were briefed not only on the importance of this decision, which was to be final, but on the fact that for their own safety they should not discus the matter with others or make known their decision before the individual interviews were held.

The interviews were conducted by unarmed United Nations Command personnel near the entrance to each compound. Each prisoner, carrying his personal possessions, was called forward individually and interviewed in private. Highly qualified personnel conducted the interrogations.

The series of questions used in the interview was designed to encourage a maximum number of prisoners to return to the Communists' side, not to oppose such return. The first question was designed to identify those who clearly desired to return. In the case of Chinese prisoners, the first question was: 'Would you like to return to China?' In the case of North Koreans, the first question was: 'Would you like to return to North Korea?' If the answer was in the affirmative, the prisoner was listed for repatriation without further questioning. Those who replied in the negative were subjected to additional questions designed to determine whether their opposition was nominal or whether they would violently oppose repatriation. The second question was: 'Would you forcibly resist repatriation?' If the answer was 'No' the prisoner of war was listed for repatriation. If the answer was 'Yes' the prisoner of war was asked four additional questions to determine fully his attitude. These were: 'Have you carefully considered the important effect of your decision upon your family?' 'Do you realize that you may stay in Koje-do for a long time, even after those who choose repatriation have already returned home?' 'Do you understand that the United Nations Command has never promised to send you to any certain place?' 'Do you still insist on forcibly resisting repatriation?' And then, perhaps the most important question: 'Despite your decision, if the United Nations Command should repatriate you, what would you do?' The prisoner was listed for repatriation unless during the questioning he mentioned suicide, fight to the death, braving death to escape, or similar intentions. As a result of these procedures all prisoners of war were included among those to be repatriated except those whose opposition to return was so strong that they would attempt to destroy themselves rather than return to communist control. A more humane, impartial and conscientious procedure could not be devised.

Prisoners of war and civilian internees in custody at the hospital compound in Pusan were screened under a similar procedure.

As a result of the screening, in which prisoners of war and civilian internees were interviewed to ascertain their decisions, approximately 70,000 prisoners of war and civilian internees will remain on Koje-do to await repatriation to the communist authorities following an armistice. [*S/2700, 14 July 1952, 44th Report of UN Command in Korea.*]

On 28 September 1952, the United Nations Command delegation reviewed past proposals that it had offered designed to solve the prisoner-of-war question and gain an armistice and presented three new ones, any one of which could solve the prisoner-of-war question if the Communists really wanted an armistice. The senior United Nations Command delegate's speech is quoted:

I have an important statement to make.

'For many weeks the prisoner-of-war issue has blocked the achievement of an armistice in Korea. On 1 July we suggested to you that a solution to the problem must be one that to a reasonable degree meets the requirements of both sides. You have admitted the soundness of that proposition.

'It must now be clear to you that one of the requirements of our side which cannot be compromised is that of no forced repatriation.

'Within this humanitarian principle the United Nations Command has made honest efforts to achieve an armistice. So that there can be no doubt of the objectivity and sincerity with which the United Nations Command delegation has attempted to find a solution to the prisoner-of-war question, I will restate the proposals which we have previously offered and which you have summarily rejected.

'We have previously proposed that joint teams of Red Cross teams with or without military observers of both sides be admitted to the prisoner-of-war camps of both sides to verify the fact that non-repatriates would forcibly resist return to the side from which they came. As an alternative we proposed that all the prisoners of war of both sides be delivered in groups of appropriate size to the demilitarized zone and be given the opportunity to express their preference on repatriation, the interview to be done by one or a combination of the following:

'A. International Committee of the Red Cross.

'B. Teams from impartial nations.

'C. Joint teams of military observers.

'D. Red Cross representatives from each side.

'Either one of these proposals, if accepted by your side, would have allayed any legitimate
10*

fears you might have had that the prisoners of war were being coerced into rejecting repatriation to your side and would have produced an armistice.

'I now present to you three additional alternative proposals, any one of which will lead
to an armistice if you truly desire one. I ask that you give careful consideration to them
because they represent the only remaining avenues of approach on which our side can
agree to an armistice. All of these proposals are based on the prior formal acceptance of an
armistice by both sides, with the disposition of prisoners of war to be determined thereafter
according to one of the following procedures.

'A. As soon as the Armistice Agreement goes into effect, all prisoners of war in the custody of each side shall be entitled to release and repatriation. Such release and repatriation
of prisoners of war shall begin in accordance with the provisions of article III of the Armistice Agreement. Both sides agree that the obligation to exchange and repatriate prisoners
of war shall be fulfilled by having them brought to an agreed exchange point in the demilitarized zone. The prisoner of war shall be identified and his name checked against the
agreed list of prisoners of war in the presence, if desired, of one or a combination of the
International Committee of the Red Cross, joint Red Cross teams, or joint military teams.
The prisoner of war shall thereupon be considered as fully repatriated for the purposes of
the agreement. Both sides agree, however, that any prisoner of war who at time of identification states that he wishes to return to the side by which he had been detained shall
immediately be allowed to do so. Such former prisoner of war shall thereupon go into the
custody of the side to which he wishes to go, which side shall provide him with transportation from the demilitarized zone to territory under its control in Korea. Such individual, of course, shall not be detained as a prisoner of war but shall assume civilian status,
and, in accordance with paragraph 52 of the Armistice Agreement, shall not again be
employed in acts of war in the Korean conflict.

'B. As soon as the Armistice Agreement goes into effect all prisoners of war who desire
repatriation will be exchanged expeditiously. All prisoners objecting to repatriation will
be delivered to the demilitarized zone in small groups where, at a mutually agreeable location, they will be freed from military control of both sides and interviewed by representatives of a mutually agreed country or countries whose forces are not participating in the
Korean hostilities, such persons being free to go to the side of their choice as indicated by
such interview. The foregoing procedure will be accomplished, if desired, with or without
military respresentation from each side and under the observation of one or a combination
of the following:

'(1) International Committee of the Red Cross;
'(2) Joint Red Cross teams;
'(3) Joint military teams.

'C. As soon as the armistice is signed and becomes effective all prisoners of war who
desire repatriation will be exchanged expeditiously. Concurrently, if logistical capability
permits, or as soon as possible thereafter, those prisoners of war who have previously
expressed their objections to repatriation will be delivered in groups of appropriate size to a
mutually agreed upon location in the demilitarized zone and there freed from the military
control of both sides. Without questioning, interview, or screening, each individual so
released will be free to go to the side of his choice. [*S/2897, 6 Jan. 1953, 54th Report of
UN Command in Korea.*]

These new proposals were rejected and the talks ran into deadlock. On
29 April 1952, the United States informed the UN that General Mark Clark
had been appointed to replace General Ridgway.[21] The deadlock during this
period had coincided with riots which occurred at the Koje camp in South
Korea, which the Communists were widely supposed to have organized. These
were the occasion for charges of atrocities against the UN. It was at this time

[21] S/2617, 29 Apr. 1952.

that the charges of bacteriological warfare began to be made against the UN, though the latter's offer for impartial investigation was refused.[22] Meanwhile, the war was continuing, with naval and air pressure against North Korea by the UNC, and Chinese probing attacks along the Korea Military Line of Resistance.[23]

The autumn of 1952 saw a presidential election in the United States, played out against a background of McCarthyism and general disillusion with politicians. The Democratic administration fell, and the Republican candidate, General Dwight D. Eisenhower, was elected President. On 2 October Eisenhower had urged that if there had to be a war in Korea, it should be one of Asians against Asians; and on 24 October he made his famous pledge that, if elected, he would go at once to Korea. As President-elect, he went to Korea from 2 to 5 December, and it became apparent that he was interested above all in seeking an honourable truce.[24]

In the UN the Indians had proposed a compromise resolution on prisoner-of-war repatriation, which the United States and the Assembly accepted as General Assembly resolution 610 (VII) on 3 December 1952. While it confirmed that the Geneva Convention could not permit the use of force either to prevent or compel the return of prisoners to their homelands, it proposed the setting up of a Neutral Nations Repatriation Commission. All released prisoners of war would be handled by this Commission. If at the end of ninety days following the armistice there still remained some non-repatriated prisoners, their status would be determined by a political conference to be held after the war. China and North Korea rejected the resolution, and major riots ensued in the prison camps of Pongam Island. The truce talks stood in recess.

Eisenhower and Dulles now believed that the only way to end the impasse was to threaten to widen the war; and in his State of Union message of 2 February 1953, Eisenhower cautiously heralded this new policy by stating that the Seventh Fleet would no longer deliberately stand between the Chinese mainland and an attack from Formosa. On 5 March Stalin died. Gradually some signs of movement became apparent. On 11 April an agreement was reached for the exchange of sick and wounded prisoners of war.[25] The Communists also gave ground on the principle of non-forcible repatriation. The ensuing document shows both the alteration of positions by the parties during this final phase—though the UNC did not give way on any of the main points of principle—and the text of the Armistice which was finally signed on 27 July 1953:

SPECIAL REPORT OF THE UNITED NATIONS COMMAND ON THE ARMISTICE IN KOREA

I. FOREWORD

The Government of the United States of America, as the United Nations Command, transmits herewith a special report on the United Nations action against aggression in Korea,

[22] See above, pp. 188–9.

[23] For details of the military campaign from June 1952 to April 1953, see Rees, pp. 364–420.

[24] See Mark Clark, *From the Danube to the Yalu* (1954), p. 221, who reports that Eisenhower was not interested in seeing the military estimates of how much it would take to win the war.

[25] S/3079, 7 Aug. 1953, p. 19.

together with a copy of the official text of the Armistice Agreement concluded by the Commander-in-Chief, United Nations Command, the Supreme Commander of the Korean People's Army, and the Commander of the Chinese People's Volunteers.

The agreement was signed by Lieutenant General William K. Harrison, senior delegate, United Nations Command delegation, and by General Nam Il, senior delegate, delegation of the Korean People's Army and Chinese People's Volunteers, at 10 am, 27 July 1953. It was subsequently signed by General Mark W. Clark, Commander-in-Chief, United Nations Command, by Peng Teh-Huai, Commander of the Chinese People's Volunteers, and by Marshal Kim Il Sung, Democratic People's Republic of Korea, Supreme Commander of the Korean People's Army. In accordance with the terms of the Armistice Agreement, hostilities ceased at 10 pm, 27 July 1953, and the Armistice Agreement became effective at that time.

The Armistice Agreement is a military agreement between military commanders. It is intended to make possible a final peaceful settlement and assumes that this end will, in good faith, be pursued. The authority of the United Nations Command under the resolutions of the Security Council of 27 June and 7 July 1950 to conduct military operations in Korea against aggression included also the authority to negotiate a military armistice to end the fighting on a basis consistent with United Nations objectives and principles. The authority of the United Nations Command to conclude an armistice and the desirability of an armistice generally along the lines finally incorporated in the Armistice Agreement of 27 July 1953 were in effect affirmed by the General Assembly in its resolution (*610 (VII)*) of 3 December 1952.

The Armistice Agreement has brought about a cessation of hostilities in Korea after more than thirty-seven months of bloodshed and destruction resulting from the Communist aggression. The armistice was signed more than twenty-five months after the first indications that, due to the achievements of United Nations forces in Korea and the determination of the United Nations to bring an honourable end to the fighting in Korea, the Communist aggressors were prepared to consider ending hostilities. During these twenty-five months, the representatives of the United Nations Command negotiated in good faith and made every effort to achieve an armistice. It was not until the spring of 1953 that the Communists appeared ready to settle the oustanding issues on an honourable basis. The intransigence of the aggressors was responsible for the continued loss of life and destruction, and for the long delay in bringing the armistice negotiations to a successful conclusion.

In negotiating this Armistice Agreement, the United Nations Command has been guided by the basic objectives of the United Nations military action in Korea—to repel the aggression against the Republic of Korea and to restore international peace and security in the area. The agreement leaves the forces of the Republic of Korea and of the United Nations in strong defensive positions and contains provisions offering reasonable assurances against renewal of the aggression.

As safeguards against resumption of hostilities, there are provisions for a demilitarized zone, with a Military Armistice Commission composed of representatives of both sides responsible for supervising the implementation of the armistice and for settling any violations of the agreement. There are also provisions prohibiting the introduction into Korea of reinforcing military personnel, combat aircraft, armoured vehicles, weapons and ammunition, together with arrangements for supervision and inspection to observe compliance with these prohibitions.

The armistice is in full accord with the humanitarian principles of the United Nations. A separate agreement, entered into on 8 June 1953, supplemented by an agreement of 27 July attached to and incorporated by reference in the Armistice Agreement, provides for the exchange of captured personnel on a basis consistent with the principles of the United Nations resolution 610 (VII) of 3 December 1952. It satisfies in particular the provision in that resolution that 'force shall not be used against prisoners of war to prevent or effect their return to their homelands . . .'

Attention is called to paragraph 60 of the Armistice Agreement, which recommends to the governments of the countries concerned on both sides that within three months after the signature of the armistice a political conference be held to settle through negotiation 'the questions of the withdrawal of all foreign forces from Korea, the peaceful settlement of the Korean question, etc.'. This recommendation has also been communicated to the governments of the other fifteen Members of the United Nations whose armed forces are participating in the Korean action and to the Government of the Republic of Korea.

The United Nations Command will do its utmost to ensure fulfilment of the terms of the Armistice Agreement. There can, of course, be no certain guarantee that the Communists will abide by its terms. The armistice, moreover, does not contain all the assurances against the renewal of aggression that might be desired. It became clear at the end of 1951 that it would not be possible to obtain all the arrangements behind enemy lines which the United Nations Command might have considered desirable. Moreover, while the safeguards achieved in the armistice are important, basically maximum assurance against the renewal of attack by the Communists lies in their knowledge that such unprovoked attack would meet with prompt reaction by the United Nations forces. The United Nations Command, therefore, agreed to waive certain safeguards (e.g., in regard to the construction and rehabilitation of military airfields in North Korea), but asked that the governments with forces under the Command should make clear in a declaration to be issued after the signature of an armistice that, if there was an unprovoked renewal of the armed attack by the Communists, the sixteen governments would again be united and prompt to resist. This arrangement was agreed upon in January 1952, by the sixteen Members of the United Nations whose armed forces were participating in the Korean action. The Declaration signed by representatives of the sixteen participating nations in Washington on 27 July 1953, shortly after the signature of the Armistice Agreement, provides:

'We, the United Nations Members whose military forces are participating in the Korean action, support the decision of the Commander-in-Chief of the United Nations Command to conclude an armistice agreement. We hereby affirm our determination fully and faithfully to carry out the terms of that armistice. We expect that the other parties to the agreement will likewise scrupulously observe its terms.

'The task ahead is not an easy one. We will support the efforts of the United Nations to bring about an equitable settlement in Korea based on the principles which have long been established by the United Nations, and which call for a united, independent and democratic Korea. We will support the United Nations in its efforts to assist the people of Korea in repairing the ravages of war.

'We declare again our faith in the principles and purposes of the United Nations, our consciousness of our continuing responsibilities in Korea, and our determination in good faith to seek a settlement of the Korean problem. We affirm, in the interests of world peace, that if there is a renewal of the armed attack, challenging again the principles of the United Nations, we should again be united and prompt to resist. The consequences of such a breach of the armistice would be so grave that, in all probability, it would not be possible to confine hostilities within the frontiers of Korea.

'Finally, we are of the opinion that the armistice must not result in jeopardizing the restoration or the safeguarding of peace in any other part of Asia.'

The achievement in Korea is a collective achievement. The people of Korea and the peoples of the world are indebted to the men of many countries, namely, Australia, Belgium, Colombia, Canada, Ethiopia, France, Greece, Luxembourg, the Philippines, the Netherlands, New Zealand, Thailand, Turkey, the Union of South Africa, the United Kingdom and the United States, who fought side by side with the forces of the Republic of Korea that aggression should not succeed. They were given assistance by the hospital units of Denmark, India, Italy, Norway and Sweden. Many other nations which made supporting contributions of other kinds also deserve the appreciation of the United Nations.

II. MILITARY ACTION

The course of military action during most of the fighting was described in the special report of the United Nations Command of 18 October 1952 (*A/2228*). The United Nations forces, after being compelled to withdraw southward by the intervention of massive Chinese Communist forces, took the initiative in early 1951 and by March had succeeded in advancing to a line across central Korea. The Communist armies were compelled by consistent pressure from United Nations forces to withdraw slowly northward, and by June 1951 United Nations forces had occupied positions generally north of the 38th parallel.

After the opening of armistice negotiations, neither the United Nations forces nor the Communists undertook sustained offensive action. There was, however, consistent and often heavy military contact, resulting in serious personnel casualties. During the last stages of negotiations, the Communists, on the night of 13–14 July, launched their heaviest offensive in over two years, resulting in limited advances by the Communist forces and heavy casualties to the United Nations forces, as well as appalling losses for the Communist attackers.

The operations of the United Nations Command were conducted solely for the purpose of achieving the military objective of the United Nations in Korea, i.e., repelling the aggression and restoring peace and security in Korea. For its part, the United Nations Command has sought in every way to minimize loss of life, and to conduct the action with the maximum respect for humanitarian considerations. The United Nations Command has never, as falsely charged in Communist propaganda, attacked any territory outside Korea or used bacteriological weapons or poison gas. It has always been prepared for, and has been willing to accept, inspection to verify these facts.

The forces of the United Nations Command suffered many casualties during the thirty-seven months of fighting. The number of killed, wounded and missing from the armed forces of the Republic of Korea exceeded 300,000. The total casualties of the United States Armed Forces were approximately 141,000, and of the armed forces of the other fifteen Members of the United Nations approximately 14,000. At the same time, United Nations forces inflicted on the enemy a far greater number of casualities. Enemy casualties are estimated at between 1,500,000 to 2 million. It is impossible to estimate the number of civilians who lost their lives or were injured, or the damage to property as a result of hostilities. Millions of Koreans were forced by hostilities to leave their homes, and there was a mass movement of refugees constantly southward towards the areas beyond Communist control.

III. ARMISTICE NEGOTIATIONS

A. *General*

The history of the continuing efforts of the United Nations Command and of the United Nations at all times to bring an end to the fighting in Korea on an honourable basis is set forth in various documents of the United Nations. The Command took numerous steps to this end on its own initiative and co-operated fully with proposals of others for bringing about peace on a basis consistent with United Nations objectives in Korea.

In July 1951, it appeared from statements made by Communist spokesmen that the aggressor forces were willing to cease hostilities. However, the hopes of the United Nations Command for quickly concluding an agreement that would stop the fighting soon proved illusory. Time after time the Communists stalled, injected extraneous issues, endeavoured to use the negotiations for propaganda purposes, and otherwise indicated a lack of good faith. Despite these obstacles, the United Nations negotiators consistently evinced a willingness to reach agreement.

The United Nations Command was determined that the armistice agreement must contribute to the achievement of the basic purposes of the United Nations military action in Korea—to repel the aggression against the Republic of Korea and to restore peace and security in the area. The United Nations Command therefore insisted on the following requirements:

(1) A line of demarcation based upon military realities and affording defensible positions for the opposing forces, consistent with the United Nations objective of repelling aggression;

(2) Other provisions offering maximum reasonable assurance against a renewal of the aggression;

(3) Appropriate arrangements for an exchange of prisoners of war on a basis that would ensure the return of United Nations Command prisoners of war and the disposition of prisoners safeguarding the right of asylum, consistent with international law, the Geneva Convention and humanitarian principles.

So long as the Communists refused to agree to an armistice on this basis, the United Nations Command was compelled to insist on the continuation of the fighting in accordance with the resolutions of the Security Council and the General Assembly, so as to compel the enemy to accept an honourable end to the fighting.

B. *Early obstacles to agreement*

(1) *Agenda and conference site*

At the very beginning of the negotiations, the Communists raised issues calculated to delay them. They sought the adoption of an agenda that would prejudice in their favour the substance of the items to be discussed. They sought, for example, to obtain agreement on language in the agenda recognizing the 38th parallel as the line of demarcation for the cease-fire. They also proposed an agenda item on the withdrawal of foreign forces from Korea. The United Nations Command insisted on an objective agenda, and one was finally adopted. The question of the withdrawal of foreign troops was rejected as beyond the scope of military negotiations.

Delay was also occasioned by Communist violations of the neutrality of the conference area and failure to provide equal treatment to both delegations as originally promised. Fabricated charges by the Communists that the United Nations Command had violated the neutrality of the conference area led to suspension of the talks for two months from August to October 1951.

(2) *Arrangements for implementing the armistice*

The armistice, of course, had to contain provisions for putting an end to the fighting. The United Nations Command delegation also sought arrangements which would make renewal of the hostilities less likely. The negotiations on these matters were extended and painstaking. The United Nations Command delegation wanted the broadest possible access to all parts of Korea for a supervisory body to ensure against violations of the armistice. It was quite willing to have such inspection behind its own lines. The Communists, however, for some time resisted all proposals for inspection and finally agreed to it only on a limited scale. At one point, the United Nations Command proposed inspection of the implementation of the armistice by joint teams to operate throughout Korea. Following Communist rejection of this proposal, agreement was reached on arrangements for inspection by observers drawn from countries not participating in the Korean action and acceptable to both sides. But the Communists further delayed the negotiations by nominating the Soviet Union as a 'neutral'; this was of course unacceptable to the United Nations Command.

The United Nations Command proposed a ban, applicable to both sides, on the construction of new military airfields and a ceiling on the number of civilian airfields that could be rehabilitated. Such a prohibition would have made resumption of the aggression more difficult and less likely. The Communists adamantly refused to agree to such a limitation.

(3) *Prisoners of war*

The issue that, in appearance at least, contributed most to the delay in achieving an armistice concerned the repatriation of prisoners of war. From the outset, the United Nations Command made it clear that, while it was prepared to repatriate all the prisoners of war in its custody, it would not agree to use force against prisoners resisting return to the Communists. The Communists stubbornly insisted, however, that all prisoners of war must be returned, by force if necessary.

In an extraordinary effort to break the long continuing deadlock on this issue, the United Nations Command, on 28 April 1952, offered a 'package proposal' providing that there should be no forced repatriation of prisoners of war; that the United Nations Command would not insist on prohibiting the reconstruction and rehabilitation of airfields; and that the United Nations Command would agree to accept Poland and Czechoslovakia as members of the Neutral Nations Supervisory Commission if the Communists agreed to accept Sweden and Switzerland (thus withdrawing their demand for the inclusion of the Soviet Union).

The United Nations Command made it clear that that proposal must be accepted as a unit. The Communists, however, purported to accept the second and third points only, remaining adamant on prisoners of war. As a result of their rejection, the armistice was delayed and the fighting continued for fifteen additional months. They persisted in this inhumane attitude for many months, contrary to international law and in the face of preponderant world opinion, even after the principle of non-forcible repatriation had been approved by the fifty-four Members of the United Nations which supported the resolution adopted by the General Assembly on 3 December 1952. Communist intransigence and Communist failure to bargain in good faith on this issue compelled the United Nations Command to recess the plenary negotiations on 8 October 1952. They were not resumed until 26 April 1953, when the Communists finally indicated that they were prepared to consider a solution for the prisoner-of-war question consistent with humanitarian principles and the principles of the General Assembly resolution.

C. *Agreements finally reached*

All the agreements between the United Nations Command delegation and the Communist delegation are set forth in the attached Armistice Agreement and the Prisoner-of-War Agreement, with the Supplementary Agreement of 27 July attached to it. In some cases, as the record of the negotiations indicates, the United Nations Command recorded its understanding as to the meaning of phrases in the Armistice Agreement that might otherwise be ambiguous.

(1) *Military demarcation line*

The Communists delayed negotiations for some time by insisting that the demarcation line between both sides should be the 38th parallel. Finally, however, they recognized the merit of the United Nations Command position that the line should be determined strictly on military grounds and should correspond to the actual line of contact between the opposing forces. The objective of the United Nations Command in insisting on such a line was to provide maximum defensive safeguards against a possible renewal of the aggression.

The line of demarcation was first marked out on 27 November 1951, on the basis of the line of contact at that time. It was then agreed that this should be the final demarcation line, provided an armistice was achieved within thirty days; otherwise the line should be redrawn on the basis of the line of contact at the time of the armistice. In fact, tentative agreement was reached on a new line in June 1953, when it seemed that an armistice could be signed within a very few days, but the Communists insisted that it be redrawn again to take account of the results of the offensive they launched on 13–14 July 1953. The demarcation line was finally agreed upon on the basis indicated in the map attached to the Armistice Agreement. The demilitarized zone was established in accordance with the agreement, each side withdrawing its forces 2 kilometres north and south of the demarcation line respectively.

(2) *Arrangements for implementing the armistice*

With the exception of the continuing disagreement on the rehabilitation of airfields, the arrangements for implementing the armistice were virtually completed by March 1952. The United Nations Command finally gave up its insistence on the limitation of airfields when it signed the armistice. The agreements on this subject may be summarized as follows:

(*a*) There will be a cease-fire within twelve hours of the signing of an armistice.

(*b*) Both sides will withdraw their forces from the demilitarized zone within seventy-two hours after the signing of an armistice.

(c) All military forces will be withdrawn from rear areas and the coastal islands and water of Korea within five days after the signing of an armistice.

(d) Both sides shall cease the introduction into Korea of reinforcing military personnel. However, the rotation of 35,000 military personnel a month shall be permitted. Rotated personnel shall enter Korea only through designated ports of entry, under the supervision and inspection of the teams of the Neutral Nations Supervisory Commission.

(e) Both sides shall cease the introduction into Korea of reinforcing combat aircraft, armoured vehicles, weapons and ammunition. However, the replacement of destroyed, damaged, worn-out or used up equipment on the basis of piece-for-piece of the same effectiveness and the same type is permitted. Such replacement shall take place only through designated ports of entry, under the supervision and inspection of teams of the Neutral Nations Supervisory Commission.

(f) A Military Armistice Commission, with headquarters at Panmunjom, composed of military officers of the United Nations Command and the Communist forces and aided by joint observer teams will:

(i) Supervise the implementation of the Armistice Agreement;

(ii) Deal with alleged armistice violations and settle through negotiations any such violations;

(iii) Report all violations of the Armistice Agreement to the Commanders of the opposing sides.

(g) A Neutral Nations Supervisory Commission, with headquarters in proximity to those of the Military Armistice Commission, composed of four senior officers, two of whom shall be appointed by neutral nations nominated by the United Nations Command and two of whom shall be appointed by neutral nations nominated jointly by the Supreme Commander of the Korean People's Army and the Commander of the Chinese People's Volunteers, will supervise, observe, inspect, and investigate adherence to the terms of the armistice agreement relative to the introduction into Korea of reinforcing military personnel and equipment. At the request of the Military Armistice Commission or senior member of either side, it can conduct special observation and inspection at places outside the demilitarized zone where violations have been reported. Twenty inspection teams, ten of which will be located at the designated ports of entry, five in North Korea and five in South Korea, with ten mobile teams in reserve, will assist the Commission.

(3) Political conference following an armistice

In order to counter the constant efforts of the Communists to inject political questions into the Korean armistice negotiations, and to prevent such extraneous issues from delaying armistice negotiations, the United Nations Command agreed to dispose of political questions by recommending their consideration at a political conference following an armistice. The United Nations Command delegation accepted a revised Communist proposal, now contained in article 60 of the Armistice Agreement, which provides:

'In order to ensure the peaceful settlement of the Korean question, the military Commanders of both sides hereby recommend to the governments of the countries concerned on both sides that, within three months after the Armistice Agreement is signed and becomes effective, a political conference of a higher level of both sides be held by representatives appointed respectively to settle through negotiation the questions of the withdrawal of all foreign forces from Korea, the peaceful settlement of the Korean question, etc.'

(4) Prisoners of war

The background of this question, and the position of the United Nations Command, were outlined in the special report of the United Nations Command of 18 October 1952 (A/2228). As indicated at that time, the only issue preventing agreement was Communist insistence that all prisoners of war must be repatriated, even if the use of force should be necessary to effect their return, and United Nations Command refusal to use force against such unwilling prisoners. When the Communists insisted that there were in fact no prisoners who refused to be repatriated, but that the United Nations Command was detaining them against their will, the United Nations Command made numerous proposals for an impartial determination of the true attitudes of the prisoners of war. The Communists refused to submit this question to the test and thus further delayed the achievement of an armistice.

On 8 October 1952, the United Nations Command delegation recessed the negotiations. In doing so, it made it clear that the numerous proposals which it had made for an honourable solution of the prisoner question remained open. Whenever the Communists were prepared to negotiate in good faith, to accept any one of the United Nations Command proposals, or to make a constructive proposal of their own on the prisoner issue, the United Nations Command delegation would be prepared to meet again.

At that juncture, the Korean question came before the General Assembly, and the United States Government, as the United Nations Command, reported on the state of the negotiations. It urged the Assembly to approve the principle of non-forcible repatriation and to call upon the Communists to accept an armistice on that basis. A definite plan for the solution of the prisoner-of-war question was proposed by India and discussed in the hope of gaining Communist approval. and on 3 December 1952, by a majority of 54 votes in favour, with only the Soviet bloc in opposition, the General Assembly adopted resolution 610 (VII). That resolution specified that force should not be used against prisoners to prevent or effect their return, and it set forth a detailed series of proposals which the Assembly believed would form a just and reasonable basis for an agreement on the prisoner issue. The Communists rejected that plan, and hopes for an armistice in the foreseeable future appeared dim.

Nevertheless, the United Nations Command continued to examine every possibility for solving the prisoner question. Seizing the opportunity offered by a resolution adopted by the Executive Committee of the League of Red Cross Societies on 13 December 1952, which appealed to the parties, as a gesture of good will, to implement the humanitarian principles of the Geneva Convention by repatriating sick and wounded prisoners of war, the Commander-in-Chief of the United Nations Command, on 22 February 1953, addressed a letter to the Communist commanders stating that the United Nations Command still remained ready to implement, immediately, the repatriation of the sick and wounded, and asking if the Communists were prepared to proceed with the repatriation of sick and wounded prisoners in their custody. The United Nations Command had made this same proposal to the Communists on a number of previous occasions during the armistice negotiations, but had met with no response. It was hoped that the Communists would at last agree to such an exchange, which would bring about the return of at least some of the United Nations Command prisoners of war, and that that first step might pave the way for the solution of the prisoner issue as a whole. The hopes of the United Nations Command in that regard proved not unwarranted. On 28 March, the Communists agreed to the principle of the exchange of sick and wounded, which, they stated, 'should be made to lead to the smooth settlement of the entire question of prisoners of war', and arrangements for the exchange were initiated through the respective liaison officers on 6 April.

The Communist acceptance was followed on 30 March by a statement by Mr. Chou En-lai, Foreign Minister of the Communist Central People's Government of the People's Republic of China, subsequently endorsed by the Prime Minister of the North Korean régime, indicating a desire to resume negotiations on the entire prisoner question and a readiness to take a more constructive and humane attitude on the question of forcible repatriation.

Sick and wounded prisoners of war were in fact exchanged between 20 April and 3 May 1953 pursuant to an agreement reached on 11 April 1953.

Negotiations by the plenary armistice delegations on the prisoner-of-war question as a whole were resumed on 26 April. At the outset, the Communists submitted a proposal for sending all prisoners not directly repatriated to an agreed neutral State, where for six months after their arrival representatives of the States to which they belonged would 'explain' to them matters related to their return; if after that period any non-repatriates remained, their disposition would be referred to the political conference. Discussion subsequently centred upon the questions of what neutral State should be nominated, of whether non-repatriates should be removed from Korea, and how long the non-repatriates would remain in neutral custody.

On 7 May, the Communists put forward a new proposal, providing for the establishment of a Neutral Nations Repatriation Commission to be composed of the four States already nominated for membership on the Neutral Nations Supervisory Commission, namely, Czechoslovakia, Poland, Sweden and Switzerland, and India as agreed upon by both sides. That Commission was to take custody of the prisoners in Korea. The United Nations Command on 13 May presented a counter-proposal shortening the period of time in which the non-repatriates would remain in neutral custody, providing for release of Korean non-repatriates immediately after the armistice, and proposing that only Indian forces take actual custody of the non-repatriates. The Communists rejected that proposal.

On 25 May, the United Nations Command, in another effort to obtain Communist agreement on an equitable solution of the prisoner issue, submitted a new proposal providing for the transfer of both Korean and Chinese non-repatriates to neutral custody and for consideration of the disposition of any remaining non-repatriates by the political conference for a limited period, after which they might either be released to civilian status or the question of their disposition referred to the General Assembly.

On 4 June, the Communists offered a counter-proposal in effect based upon the mechanics of General Assembly resolution 610 (VII), also closely paralleling the United Nations Command proposal of 25 May, but vague on the basic principle of non-forcible repatriation. The United Nations Command succeeded in reaching agreement with the Communists on the elaboration of the Neutral Nations Repatriation Commission's terms of reference, to ensure that there would be no abuse and that the principle approved by the General Assembly—that force should not be used to compel or to prevent repatriation of any prisoner of war—would be fully observed.

On 8 June, the senior delegates for the United Nations Command and for the Communists signed the Prisoner-of-War Agreement which is attached to and incorporated by reference in the Armistice Agreement. The delegations then proceeded to the final arrangements looking towards an early signature of the armistice.

As a result of discussions with the Republic of Korea, described in the succeeding section, a Supplementary Agreement on Prisoners of War was signed on 27 July 1953, which permits the United Nations Command, and the Communists if applicable, to transport the non-repatriates to the demilitarized zone, where the Neutral Nations Repatriation Commission will take custody of them.

D. *Attitude of the Republic of Korea*

On 18 June, an incident occurred which further delayed the achievement of an armistice at a time when the conclusion of hostilities seemed imminent. On that date, officials of the Republic of Korea brought about a break-out from prisoner-of-war camps of some 27,000 Korean prisoners of war who had previously indicated they would resist repatriation to North Korea. That action by the Republic of Korea was inconsistent with the Agreement on Prisoners of War of 8 June which the United Nations Command had entered into on behalf of all the forces under its command. The United Nations Command at once protested the action of the Republic of Korea Government. It immediately informed the Communists of the event and told them that, while efforts would be made to recover as many of the escapees as possible, there was not much hope that many of these could be recaptured since they had melted into the South Korean population.

That incident led to immediate discussions with the Republic of Korea by representatives of the United Nations. After prolonged conversations, the Republic of Korea gave assurance that it would not obstruct the implementation of the terms of the Armistice Agreement.

The incident, however, gave the Communists an excuse for delaying still further the conclusion of the armistice. They demanded assurances that the United Nations Command would live up to the Armistice Agreement, that the Republic of Korea and its forces would also abide by it, and that the released prisoners would be recaptured. The United Nations Command reply to the Communists stressed that the armistice was a military agreement between military commanders and that it was being entered into by the United Nations Command, as commander of all the forces under its command, including those of the Republic of Korea. The United Nations Command delegation also told the Communists that, as they had already been informed, it would be impossible to recover the released prisoners of war; it assured them, however, that the remaining non-repatriate prisoners would be turned over to the Neutral Nations Repatriation Commission, as provided in the agreement on prisoners of war. The Communists were assured that the United Nations Command forces, including those of the Republic of Korea, would observe the armistice. The United Nations Command informed the Communists, however, that it would not undertake to use force against the Republic of Korea forces to ensure compliance with the armistice by the Republic of Korea.

Despite these comprehensive assurances by the United Nations Command, the Communists continued to delay negotiations, and in the meanwhile launched the biggest offensive in more than two years, an offensive which obviously had taken much planning and preparation and caused heavy casualties. Finally, however, on 19 July, the Communists stated their readiness to proceed with the final work on the Armistice Agreement leading to its signature.

The Armistice was finally signed on 27 July 1953, at 10 a.m. Korean time.

IV. CONCLUSION

The fighting and bloodshed in Korea have been halted. After causing millions of casualties, untold civilian suffering and death, economic devastation and destruction of property, the Communist aggressors have been driven back to and beyond the point from which they started their initial attack. The heavy price of their aggression is evident.

As a result of the prompt and sustained collective action of the United Nations against aggression, an armistice has been effected on a basis that promises to maintain the integrity of the Republic of Korea against further aggression and that constitutes a major step towards the establishment of peace and security for that war-torn country. These achievements have been made possible by the heroic sacrifices of the troops of the United Nations and of the Republic of Korea.

The United States stands ready to participate and co-operate fully in political discussions leading to an enduring solution of the Korean problem on the basis of the objectives of the United Nations—the achievement by peaceful means of a unified, independent and democratic Korea. If the Communists abide by the armistice and negotiate in good faith, a true and lasting peace may yet come to the brave and long-suffering people of Korea.

APPENDIX A

AGREEMENT BETWEEN THE COMMANDER-IN-CHIEF, UNITED NATIONS COMMAND, ON THE ONE HAND, AND THE SUPREME COMMANDER OF THE KOREAN PEOPLE'S ARMY AND THE COMMANDER OF THE CHINESE PEOPLE'S VOLUNTEERS, ON THE OTHER HAND, CONCERNING A MILITARY ARMISTICE IN KOREA

PREAMBLE

The undersigned, the Commander-in-Chief, United Nations Command, on the one hand, and the Supreme Commander of the Korean People's Army and the Commander of the Chinese People's Volunteers, on the other hand, in the interest of stopping the Korean conflict, with its great roll of suffering and bloodshed on both sides, and with the objective of establishing an armistice which will insure a complete cessation of hostilities and of all acts of armed force in Korea until a final peaceful settlement is achieved, do individually, collectively, and mutually agree to accept and to be bound and governed by the conditions and terms of armistice set forth in the following articles and paragraphs, which said conditions and terms are intended to be purely military in character and to pertain solely to the belligerents in Korea.

Article I

MILITARY DEMARCATION LINE AND DEMILITARIZED ZONE

1. A Military Demarcation Line shall be fixed and both sides shall withdraw two (2) kilometers from this line so as to establish a Demilitarized Zone between the opposing forces. A Demilitarized Zone shall be established as a buffer zone to prevent the occurrence of incidents which might lead to a resumption of hostilities.

2. The Military Demarcation Line is located as indicated on the attached map (map 1).

3. The Demilitarized Zone is defined by a northern and a southern boundary as indicated on the attached map (map 1).

4. The Military Demarcation Line shall be plainly marked as directed by the Military Armistice Commission hereinafter established. The Commanders of the opposing sides shall have suitable markers erected along the boundary between the Demilitarized Zone and their respective areas. The Military Armistice Commission shall supervise the erection of all markers placed along the Military Demarcation Line and along the boundaries of the Demilitarized Zone.

5. The waters of the Han River Estuary shall be open to civil shipping of both side wherever one bank is controlled by one side and the other bank is controlled by the other side. The Military Armistice Commission shall prescribe rules for the shipping in that part of the Han River Estuary indicated on the attached map (map 2). Civil shipping of each side shall have unrestricted access to the land under the military control of that side.

6. Neither side shall execute any hostile act within, from, or against the Demilitarized Zone.

7. No person, military or civilian, shall be permitted to cross the Military Demarcation Line unless specifically authorized to do so by the Military Armistic Commission.

8. No person, military or civilian, in the Demilitarized Zone shall be permitted to enter the territory under the military control of either side unless specifically authorized to do so by the Commander into whose territory entry is sought.

9. No person, military or civilian, shall be permitted to enter the Demilitarized Zone except persons concerned with the conduct of civil administration and relief and persons specifically authorized to enter by the Military Armistice Commission.

10. Civil administration and relief in that part of the Demilitarized Zone which is south of the Military Demarcation Line shall be the responsibility of the Commander-in-Chief, United Nations Command; and civil administration and relief in that part of the Demilitarized Zone which is north of the Military Demarcation Line shall be the joint responsibility of the Supreme Commander of the Korean People's Army and the Commander of the Chinese People's Volunteers. The number of persons, military or civilian, from each side who are permitted to enter the Demilitarized Zone for the conduct of civil administration and relief shall be as determined by the respective Commander, but in no case shall the total number authorized by either side exceed one thousand (1,000) persons at any one time. The number of civil police and the arms to be carried by them shall be as prescribed by the Military Armistice Commission. Other personnel shall not carry arms unless specifically authorized to do so by the Military Armistice Commission.

11. Nothing contained in this article shall be construed to prevent the complete freedom of movement to, from, and within the Demilitarized Zone by the Military Armistice Commission, its assistants, its Joint Observer Teams with their assistants, the Neutral Nations Supervisory Commission hereinafter established, its assistants, its Neutral Nations Inspection Teams with their assistants, and of any other persons, materials, and equipment specifically authorized to enter the Demilitarized Zone by the Military Armistice Commission. Convenience of movement shall be permitted through the territory under the military control of either side over any route necessary to move between points within the Demilitarized Zone

where such points are not connected by roads lying completely within the Demilitarized Zone.

Article II

CONCRETE ARRANGEMENTS FOR CEASE-FIRE AND ARMISTICE

A. *General*

12. The Commanders of the opposing sides shall order and enforce a complete cessation of all hostilities in Korea by all armed forces under their control, including all units and personnel of the ground, naval, and air forces, effective twelve (12) hours after this Armistice Agreement is signed. (See paragraph 63 hereof for effective date and hour of the remaining provisions of this Armistice Agreement.)

13. In order to insure the stability of the Military Armistice so as to facilitate the attainment of a peaceful settlement through the holding by both sides of a political conference of a higher level, the Commanders of the opposing sides shall:

(*a*) Within seventy-two (72) hours after this Armistice Agreement becomes effective, withdraw all of their military forces, supplies, and equipment from the Demilitarized Zone except as otherwise provided herein. All demolitions, minefields, wire entanglements, and other hazards to the safe movement of personnel of the Military Armistice Commission or its Joint Observer Teams, known to exist within the Demilitarized Zone after the withdrawal of military forces therefrom, together with lanes known to be free of all such hazards, shall be reported to the Military Armistice Commission by the Commander of the side whose forces emplaced such hazards. Subsequently, additional safe lanes shall be cleared; and eventually, within forty-five (45) days after the termination of the seventy-two (72) hour period, all such hazards shall be removed from the Demilitarized Zone as directed by and under the supervision of the Military Armistice Commission. At the termination of the seventy-two (72) hour period, except for unarmed troops authorized a forty-five (45) day period to complete salvage operations under Military Armistice Commission supervision, such units of a police nature as may be specifically requested by the Military Armistice Commission and agreed to by the Commanders of the opposing sides, and personnel authorized under paragraphs 10 and 11 hereof, no personnel of either side shall be permitted to enter the Demilitarized Zone.

(*b*) Within ten (10) days after this Armistice Agreement becomes effective, withdraw all of their military forces, supplies, and equipment from the rear and the coastal islands and waters of Korea on the other side. If such military forces are not withdrawn within the stated time limit, and there is no mutually agreed and valid reason for the delay, the other side shall have the right to take any action which it deems necessary for the maintenance of security and order. The term 'coastal islands', as used above, refers to those islands which, though occupied by one side at the time when this Armistice Agreement becomes effective, were controlled by the other side on 24 June 1950; provided, however, that all the islands lying to the north and west of the provincial boundary line between Hwanghae-do and Kyonggi-do shall be under the military control of the Supreme Commander of the Korean People's Army and the Commander of the Chinese People's Volunteers, except the island groups of Paengyong-do (37° 58′ N, 124° 40′ E), Taechong-do (37° 50′ N, 124° 42′ E), Sochong-do (37° 46′ N, 124° 46′ E), Yonpyong-do (37° 38′ N, 125° 40′ E), and U-do (37° 36′ N, 125° 58′ E), which shall remain under the military control of the Commander-in-Chief, United Nations Command. All the islands on the west coast of Korea lying south of the above-mentioned boundary line shall remain under the military control of the Commander-in-Chief, United Nations Command. (See map 3.)

(*c*) Cease the introduction into Korea of reinforcing military personnel; provided, however, that the rotation of units and personnel, the arrival in Korea of personnel on a temporary duty basis, and the return to Korea of personnel after short periods of leave or temporary duty outside of Korea shall be permitted within the scope prescribed below. 'Rotation' is defined as the replacement of units or personnel by other units or personnel who are commencing a tour of duty in Korea. Rotation personnel shall be introduced into and evacuated from Korea only through the ports of entry enumerated in paragraph 43 hereof. Rotation shall be conducted on a man–for–man basis; provided, however, that no more than thirty-five thousand (35,000) persons in the military service shall be admitted into Korea by either side in any calendar month under the rotation policy. No military personnel of either side shall be introduced into Korea if the introduction of such personnel will cause the aggregate of the military personnel of that side admitted into Korea since the effective date of this Armistice Agreement to exceed the cumulative total of the military personnel of that side who have departed from Korea since that date. Reports concerning arrivals in and departures from Korea of military personnel shall be made daily to the Military Armistice Commission and the Neutral Nations Supervisory Commission; such reports shall include places of arrival and departure and the number of persons arriving at or departing from each such place. The Neutral Nations Supervisory Commission, through its Neutral Nations Inspection Teams, shall conduct supervision and inspection of the rotation of units and personnel authorized above, at the ports of entry enumerated in paragraph 43 hereof.

(*d*) Cease the introduction into Korea of reinforcing combat aircraft, armoured vehicles, weapons, and ammunition; provided, however, that combat aircraft, armoured vehicles, weapons, and ammuniton which are destroyed, damaged, worn out, or used up during the period of the armistice may be replaced on the basis of piece-for-piece of the same effectiveness and the same type. Such combat aircraft, armoured vehicles, weapons, and ammunition shall be introduced into Korea only through the ports of entry enumerated in paragraph 43 hereof. In order to justify the requirement for combat aircraft, armoured vehicles, weapons, and ammunition to be introduced into Korea for replacement purposes, reports concerning every incoming shipment of these items shall be made to the Military Armistice Commission and the Neutral Nations Supervisory Commission; such reports shall include statements regarding the disposition of the items being replaced. Items to be replaced which are removed from Korea shall be removed only through the ports of entry enumerated in paragraph 43 hereof. The Neutral Nations Supervisory Commission, though its Neutral Nations Inspection Teams, shall conduct supervision and inspection of the replacement of combat aircraft, armoured vehicles, weapons, and ammunition authorized above, at the ports of entry enumerated in paragraph 43 hereof.

(*e*) Ensure that personnel of their respective commands who violate any of the provisions of this Armistice Agreement are adequately punished.

(*f*) In those cases where places of burial are a matter of record and graves are actually found to exist, permit graves registration personnel of the other side to enter, within a definite time limit after this Armistice Agreement becomes effective, the territory of Korea under their military control, for the purpose of proceeding to such graves to recover and evacuate the bodies of the deceased military personnel of that side, including deceased prisoners of war. The specific procedures and the time limit for the performance of the above task shall be determined by the Military Armistice Commission. The Commanders of the opposing sides shall furnish to the other side all available information pertaining to the places of burial of the deceased military personnel of the other side.

(*g*) Afford full protection and all possible assistance and co-operation to the Military Armistice Commission, its Joint Observer Teams, the Neutral Nations Supervisory Commission, and its Neutral Nations Inspection Teams, in the carrying out of their functions and responsibilites hereinafter assigned; and accord to the Neutral Nations Supervisory Commission, and to its Neutral Nations Inspection Teams, full convenience of movement between the headquarters of the Neutral Nations Supervisory Commission and the ports of entry enumerated in paragraph 43 hereof over main lines of communication agreed upon by both sides (see map 4), and between the headquarters of the Neutral Nations Supervisory Commission and the places where violations of this Armistice Agreement have been reported to have occurred. In order to prevent unnecessary delays, the use of alternate routes and means of transportation will be permitted whenever the main lines of communication are closed or impassable.

(*h*) Provide such logistic support, including communications and transportation facilities, as may be required by the Military Armistice Commission and the Neutral Nations Supervisory Commission and their teams.

(*i*) Each construct, operate, and maintain a suitable airfield in their respective parts of the Demilitarized Zone in the vicinity of the headquarters of the Military Armistice Commission, for such uses as the Commission may determine.

(*j*) Insure that all members and other personnel of the Neutral Nations Supervisory Commission and of the Neutral Nations Reparatiation Commission hereinafter established shall enjoy the freedom and facilities necessary for the proper exercise of their functions, including privileges, treatment, and immunities equivalent to those ordinarily enjoyed by accredited diplomatic personnel under international usage.

14. This Armistice Agreement shall apply to all opposing ground forces under the military control of either side, which ground forces shall respect the Demilitarized Zone and the area of Korea under the military control of the opposing side.

15. This Armistice Agreement shall apply to all opposing naval forces, which naval forces shall respect the waters contiguous to the Demilitarized Zone and to the land area of Korea under the military control of the opposing side, and shall not engage in blockade of any kind of Korea.

16. This Armistice Agreement shall apply to all opposing air forces, which air forces shall respect the air space over the Demilitarized Zone and over the area of Korea under the military control of the opposing side, and over the waters contiguous to both.

17. Responsibility for compliance with and enforcement of the terms and provisions of this Armistice Agreement is that of the signatories hereto and their successors in command. The Commanders of the opposing sides shall establish within their respective commands all measures and procedures necessary to insure complete compliance with all of the provisions hereof by all elements of their commands. They shall actively co-operate with one another and with the Military Armistice Commission and the Neutral Nations Supervisory Commission and the Neutral Nations Supervisory Commission in requiring observance of both the letter and the spirit of all of the provisions of this Armistice Agreement.

18. The costs of the operations of the Military Armistice Commission and of the Neutral Nations Supervisory Commission and of their Teams shall be shared equally by the two opposing sides.

B. *Military Armistice Commission*

1. Composition

19. A Military Armistice Commission is hereby established.

20. The Military Armistice Commission shall be composed of ten (10) senior officers, five (5) of whom shall be appointed by the Commander-in-Chief, United Nations Command, and five (5) of whom shall be appointed jointly by the Supreme Commander of the Korean People's Army and the Commander of the Chinese People's Volunteers. Of the ten members, three (3) from each side shall be of general or flag rank. The two (2) remaining members on each side may be major generals, brigadier generals, or their equivalents.

21. Members of the Military Armistice Commission shall be permitted to use staff assistants as required.

22. The Military Armistice Commission shall be provided with the necessary administrative personnel to establish a secretariat charged with assisting the Commission by performing record-keeping, secretarial, interpreting, and such other functions as the Commission may assign to it. Each side shall appoint to the secretariat a secretary and an assistant secretary and such clerical and specialized personnel as required by the secretariat. Records shall be kept in English, Korean, and Chinese, all of which shall be equally authentic.

23. (*a*) The Military Armistice Commission shall be initially provided with and assisted by ten (10) Joint Observer Teams, which number may be reduced by agreement of the senior members of both sides on the Military Armistice Commission.

(*b*) Each Joint Observer Team shall be composed of not less than four (4) nor more than six (6) officers of field grade, half of whom shall be appointed by the Commander-in-Chief, United Nations Command, and half of whom shall be appointed jointly by the Supreme Commander of the Korean People's Army and the Commander of the Chinese People's Volunteers. Additional personnel such as drivers, clerks, and interpreters shall be furnished by each side as required for the functioning of the Joint Observer Teams.

2. Functions and authority

24. The general mission of the Military Armistice Commission shall be to supervise the implementation of this Armistice Agreement and to settle through negotiations any violations of this Armistice Agreement.

25. The Military Armistice Commission shall:

(*a*) Locate its headquarters in the vicinity of Panmunjom (37° 57′ 29″ N, 126° 40′ 00″ E). The Military Armistice Commission may re-locate its headquarters at another point within the Demilitarized Zone by agreement of the senior members of both sides on the Commission.

(*b*) Operate as a joint organization without a chairman.

(*c*) Adopt such rules of procedure as it may, from time to time, deem necessary.

(*d*) Supervise the carrying out of the provisions of this Armistice Agreement pertaining to the Demilitarized Zone and to the Han River Estuary.

(*e*) Direct the operations of the Joint Observer Teams.

(*f*) Settle through negotiations any violations of this Armistice Agreement.

(*g*) Transmit immediately to the Commanders of the opposing sides all reports of investigations of violations of this Armistice Agreement and all other reports and records of proceedings received from the Neutral Nations Supervisory Commission.

(*h*) Give general supervision and direction to the activities of the Committee for Repatriation of Prisoners of War and the Committee for Assisting the Return of Displaced Civilians, hereinafter established.

(*i*) Act as an intermediary in transmitting communications between the Commanders of the opposing sides; provided, however, that the foregoing shall not be construed to preclude the Commanders of both sides from communicating with each other by any other means which they may desire to employ.

(*j*) Provide credentials and distinctive insignia for its staff and its Joint Observer Teams, and a distinctive marking for all vehicles, aircraft, and vessels, used in the performance of its mission.

26. The mission of the Joint Observer Teams shall be to assist the Military Armistice Commission in supervising the carrying out of the provisions of this Armistice Agreement pertaining to the Demilitarized Zone and to the Han River Estuary.

27. The Military Armistice Commission, or the senior member of either side thereof, is authorized to dispatch Joint Observer Teams to investigate violations of this Armistice Agreement reported to have occurred in the Demilitarized Zone or in the Han River Estuary; provided, however, that not more than one half of the Joint Observer Teams which have not been dispatched by the Military Armistice Commission may be dispatched at any one time by the senior member of either side on the Commission.

28. The Military Armistice Commission, or the senior member of either side thereof, is authorized to request the Neutral Nations Supervisory Commission to conduct special observations and inspections at places outside the Demilitarized Zone where violations of this Armistice Agreement have been reported to have occurred.

29. When the Military Armistice Commission determines that a violation of this Armistice Agreement has occurred, it shall immediately report such violation to the Commanders of the opposing sides.

30. When the Military Armistice Commission determines that a violation of this Armistice Agreement has been corrected to its satisfaction, it shall so report to the Commanders of the opposing sides.

3. General

31. The Military Armistice Commission shall meet daily. Recesses of not to exceed seven (7) days may be agreed upon by the senior members of both sides; provided, that such recesses may be terminated on twenty-four (24) hour notice by the senior member of either side.

32. Copies of the record of the proceedings of all meetings of the Military Armistice Commission shall be forwarded to the Commanders of the opposing sides as soon as possible after each meeting.

33. The Joint Observer Teams shall make periodic reports to the Military Armistice Commission as required by the Commission and, in addition, shall make such special report as may be deemed necessary by them, or as may be required by the Commission.

34. The Military Armistice Commission shall maintain duplicate files of the reports and records of proceedings required by this Armistice Agreement. The Commission is authorized to maintain duplicate files of such other reports, records, etc., as may be necessary in the conduct of its business. Upon eventual dissolution of the Commission, one set of the above files shall be turned over to each side.

35. The Military Armistice Commission may make recommendations to the Commanders of the opposing sides with respect to amendments or additions to this Armistice Agreement. Such recommended changes should generally be those designed to ensure a more effective armistice.

C. *Neutral Nations Supervisory Commission*

1. Composition

36. A Neutral Nations Supervisory Commission is hereby established.

37. The Neutral Nations Supervisory Commission shall be composed of four (4) senior officers, two (2) of whom shall be appointed by neutral nations nominated by the Commander-in-Chief, United Nations Command, namely, Sweden and Switzerland, and two (2) of whom shall be appointed by neutral nations nominated jointly by the Supreme Commander of the Korean People's Army and the Commander of the Chinese People's Volunteers, namely, Poland and Czechoslovakia. The term 'neutral nations' as herein used is defined as those nations whose combatant forces have not participated in the hostilities in Korea. Members appointed to the Commission may be from the armed forces of the appointing nations. Each member shall designate an alternate member to attend those meetings which for any reason the principal member is unable to attend. Such alternate members shall be of the same nationality as their principles. The Neutral Nations Supervisory Commission may take action whenever the number of members present from the neutral nations nominated by one side is equal to the number of members present from the neutral nations nominated by the other side.

38. Members of the Neutral Nations Supervisory Commission shall be permitted to use staff assistants furnished by the neutral nations as required. These staff assistants may be appointed as alternate members of the Commission.

39. The neutral nations shall be requested to furnish the Neutral Nations Supervisory Commission with the necessary administrative personnel to establish a secretariat charged with assisting the Commission by performing necessary record-keeping, secretarial, interpreting, and such other functions as the Commission may assign to it.

40. (*a*) The Neutral Nations Supervisory Commission shall be initially provided with, and assisted by, twenty (20) Neutral Nations Inspection Teams, which number may be reduced by agreement of the senior members of both sides on the Military Armistice Commission. The Neutral Nations Inspection Teams shall be responsible to, shall report to, and shall be subject to the direction of, the Neutral Nations Supervisory Commission only.

(*b*) Each Neutral Nations Inspection Team shall be composed of not less than four (4) officers, preferably of field grade, half of whom shall be from the neutral nations nominated by the Commander-in-Chief, United Nations Command, and half of whom shall be from the neutral nations nominated jointly by the Supreme Commander of the Korean People's Army and the Commander of the Chinese People's Volunteers. Members appointed to the

Neutral Nations Inspection Teams may be from the armed forces of the appointing nations. In order to facilitate the functioning of the Teams, sub-teams composed of not less than two (2) members, one of whom shall be from a neutral nation nominated by the Commander-in-Chief, United Nations Command, and one of whom shall be from a neutral nation nominated jointly by the Supreme Commander of the Korean People's Army and the Commander of the Chinese People's Volunteers, may be formed as circumstances require. Additional personnel such as drivers, clerks, interpreters, and communications personnel, and such equipment as may be required by the Teams to perform their missions, shall be furnished by the Commander of each side, as required, in the Demilitarized Zone and in the territory under his military control. The Neutral Nations Supervisory Commission may provide itself and the Neutral Nations Inspection Teams with such of the above personnel and equipment of its own as it may desire; provided, however, that such personnel shall be personnel of the same neutral nations of which the Neutral Nations Supervisory Commission is composed.

2. Functions and authority

41. The mission of the Neutral Nations Supervisory Commission shall be to carry out the functions of supervision, observation, inspection, and investigation, as stipulated in sub-paragraphs 13(*c*) and 13(*d*) and paragraph 28 hereof, and to report the results of such supervision, observation, inspection, and investigation to the Military Armistice Commission.

42. The Neutral Nations Supervisory Commission shall:

(*a*) Locate its headquarters in proximity to the headquarters of the Military Armistice Commission.

(*b*) Adopt such rules of procedure as it may, from time to time, deem necessary.

(*c*) Conduct, through its members and its Neutral Nations Inspection Teams, the supervision and inspection provided for in sub-paragraphs 13(*c*) and 13(*d*) of this Armistice Agreement at the ports of entry enumerated in paragraph 43 hereof, and the special observations and inspections provided for in paragraph 28 hereof at those places where violations of this Armistice Agreement have been reported to have occurred. The inspection of combat aircraft, armoured vehicles, weapons, and ammunition by the Neutral Nations Inspection Teams shall be such as to enable them to properly insure that reinforcing combat aircraft, armoured vehicles, weapons and ammunition are not being introduced into Korea; but this shall not be construed as authorizing inspections or examinations of any secret designs or characteristics of any combat aircraft, armoured vehicle, weapon, or ammunition.

(*d*) Direct and supervise the operations of the Neutral Nations Inspector Teams.

(*e*) Station five (5) Neutral Nations Inspection Teams at the ports of entry enumerated in paragraph 43 hereof located in the territory under the military control of the Commander-in-Chief, United Nations Command; and five (5) Neutral Nations Inspection Teams at the ports of entry enumerated in paragraph 43 hereof located in the territory under the military control of the Supreme Commander of the Korean People's Army and the Commander of the Chinese People's Volunteers; and establish initially ten (10) mobile Neutral Nations Inspection Teams in reserve, stationed in the general vicinity of the headquarters of the Neutral Nations Supervisory Commission, which number may be reduced by agreement of the senior members of both sides on the Military Armistice Commission. Not more than half of the mobile Neutral Nations Inspection Teams shall be dispatched at any one time in accordance with requests of the senior member of either side on the Military Armistice Commission.

(*f*) Subject to the provisions of the preceding sub-paragraph, conduct without delay investigations of reported violations of this Armistice Agreement, including such investigations of reported violations of this Armistice Agreement as may be requested by the Military Armistice Commission or by the senior member of either side of the Commission.

(*g*) Provide credentials and distinctive insignia for its staff and its Neutral Nations Inspection Teams, and a distinctive marking for all vehicles, aircraft, and vessels, used in the performance of its mission.

43. Neutral Nations Inspection Teams shall be stationed at the following ports of entry:

Territory under the military control of the United Nations Command			*Territory under the military control of the Korean People's Army and the Chinese People's Volunteers*		
Inchon	(37° 28′ N,	126° 38′ E)	Sinuiju	(40° 06′ N,	124° 24′ E)
Taegu	(35° 52′ N,	128° 36′ E)	Chongjin	(41° 46′ N,	129° 49′ E)
Pusan	(35° 06′ N,	129° 02′ E)	Hungnam	(39° 50′ N,	127° 37′ E)
Kangnung	(37° 45′ N,	128° 54′ E)	Manpo	(41° 09′ N,	126° 18′ E)
Kunsan	(35° 59′ N,	126° 43′ E)	Sinanju	(39° 36′ N,	125° 36′ E)

These Neutral Nations Inspection Teams shall be accorded full convenience of movement within the areas and over the routes of communication set forth on the attached map (map 5).

3. General

44. The Neutral Nations Supervisory Commission shall meet daily. Recesses of not to exceed seven (7) days may be agreed upon by the members of the Neutral Nations Supervisory Commission; provided that such recesses may be terminated on twenty-four (24) hour notice by any member.

45. Copies of the record of the proceedings of all meetings of the Neutral Nations Supervisory Commission shall be forwarded to the Military Armistice Commission as soon as possible after each meeting. Records shall be kept in English, Korean, and Chinese.

46. The Neutral Nations Inspection Teams shall make periodic reports concerning the results of their supervision, observations, inspections, and investigations to the Neutral Nations Supervisory Commission as required by the Commission and, in addition, shall make such special reports as may be deemed necessary by them, or as may be required by the Commission. Reports shall be submitted by a Team as a whole, but may also be submitted by one or more individual members thereof; provided, that the reports submitted by one or more individual members thereof shall be considered as informational only.

47. Copies of the reports made by the Neutral Nations Inspection Teams shall be forwarded to the Military Armistice Commission by the Neutral Nations Supervisory Commission without delay and in the language in which received. They shall not be delayed by the process of translation or evaluation. The Neutral Nations Supervisory Commission shall evaluate such reports at the earliest practicable time and shall forward their findings to the Military Armistice Commission as a matter of priority. The Military Armistice Commission shall not take final action with regard to any such report until the evaluation thereof has been received from the Neutral Nations Supervisory Commission. Members of the Neutral Nations Supervisory Commission and of its Teams shall be subject to appearance before the Military Armistice Commission, at the request of the senior member of either side on the Military Armistice Commission, for clarification of any report submitted.

48. The Neutral Nations Supervisory Commission shall maintain duplicate files of the reports and records of proceedings required by this Armistice Agreement. The Commission is authorized to maintain duplicate files of such other reports, records, etc., as may be necessary in the conduct of its business. Upon eventual dissolution of the Commission, one set of the above files shall be turned over to each side.

49. The Neutral Nations Supervisory Commission may make recommendations to the Military Armistice Commission with respect to amendments or additions to this Armistice Agreement. Such recommended changes should generally be those designed to insure a more effective armistice.

50. The Neutral Nations Supervisory Commission, or any member thereof, shall be authorized to communicate with any member of the Military Armistice Commission.

Article III

ARRANGEMENTS RELATING TO PRISONERS OF WAR

51. The release and repatriation of all prisoners of war held in the custody of each side at the time this Armistice Agreement becomes effective shall be effected in conformity with the

following provisions agreed upon by both sides prior to the signing of this Armistice Agreement.

(*a*) Within sixty (60) days after this Armistice Agreement becomes effective, each side shall, without offering any hindrance, directly repatriate and hand over in groups all those prisoners of war in its custody who insist on repatriation to the side to which they belonged at the time of capture. Repatriation shall be accomplished in accordance with the related provisions of this article. In order to expedite the repatriation process of such personnel, each side shall, prior to the signing of the Armistice Agreement, exchange the total numbers, by nationalities, of personnel to be directly repatriated. Each group of prisoners of war delivered to the other side shall be accompanied by rosters, prepared by nationality, to include name, rank (if any) and internment or military serial number.

(*b*) Each side shall release all those remaining prisoners of war, who are not directly repatriated, from its military control and from its custody and hand them over to the Neutral Nations Repatriation Commission for disposition in accordance with the provisions in the annex hereto: 'Terms of Reference for Neutral Nations Repatriation Commission.'

(*c*) So that there may be no misunderstanding owing to the equal use of three languages, the act of delivery for a prisoner of war by one side to the other side shall, for the purposes of this Armistice Agreement, be called 'repatriation' in English, *Song Hwan* in Korean, and *Ch'ien Fan* in Chinese, notwithstanding the nationality or place of residence of such prisoner of war.

52. Each side ensures that it will not employ in acts of war in the Korean conflict any prisoner of war released and repatriated incident to the coming into effect of this Armistice Agreement.

53. All the sick and injured prisoners of war who insist upon repatriation shall be repatriated with priority. In so far as possible, there shall be captured medical personnel repatriated concurrently with the sick and injured prisoners of war, so as to provide medical care and attendance *en route*.

54. The repatriation of all of the prisoners of war required by sub-paragraph 51(*a*) hereof shall be completed within a time limit of sixty (60) days after this Armistice Agreement becomes effective. Within this time limit each side undertakes to complete the repatriation of the above-mentioned prisoners of war in its custody at the earliest practicable time.

55. Panmunjom is designated as the place where prisoners of war will be delivered and received by both sides. Additional place(s) of delivery and reception of prisoners of war in the Demilitarized Zone may be designated, if necessary, by the Committee for Repatriation of Prisoners of War.

56. (*a*) A Committee for Repatriation of Prisoners of War is hereby established. It shall be composed of six (6) officers of field grade, three (3) of whom shall be appointed by the Commander-in-Chief, United Nations Command, and three (3) of whom shall be appointed jointly by the Supreme Commander of the Korean People's Army and the Commander of the Chinese People's Volunteers. This Committee shall, under the general supervision and direction of the Military Armistice Commission, be responsible for co-ordinating the specific plans of both sides for the repatriation of prisoners of war and for supervising the execution by both sides of all of the provisions of this Armistice Agreement relating to the repatriation of prisoners of war. It shall be the duty of this Committee to co-ordinate the timing of the arrival of prisoners of war at the place(s) of delivery and reception of prisoners of war from the prisoner of war camps of both sides; to make, when necessary, such special arrangement as may be required with regard to the transportation and welfare of sick and injured prisoners of war; to co-ordinate the work of the joint Red Cross teams, established in paragraph 57 hereof, in assisting in the repatriation of prisoners of war; to supervise the implementation of the arrangements for the actual repatriation of prisoners of war stipulated in paragraphs 53 and 54 hereof; to select, when necessary, additional place(s) of delivery and reception of prisoners of war; to arrange for security at the place(s) of delivery and reception of prisoners of war; and to carry out such other related functions as are required for the repatriation of prisoners of war.

(*b*) When unable to reach agreement on any matter relating to its responsibilities, the Committee for Repatriation of Prisoners of War shall immediately refer such matter to the Military Armistice Commission for decision. The Committee for Repatriation of Prisoners of War shall maintain its headquarters in proximity to the headquarters of the Military Armistice Commission.

(*c*) The Committee for Repatriation of Prisoners of War shall be dissolved by the Military Armistice Commission upon completion of the program of repatriation of prisoners of war.

57. (*a*) Immediately after this Armistice Agreement becomes effective, joint Red Cross teams composed of representatives of the national Red Cross Societies of the countries contributing forces to the United Nations Command on the one hand, and representatives of the Red Cross Society of the Democratic People's Republic of Korea and representatives of the Red Cross Society of the People's Republic of China on the other hand, shall be established. The joint Red Cross teams shall assist in the execution by both sides of those provisions of this Armistice Agreement relating to the repatriation of all the prisoners of war specified in sub-paragraph 51(*a*) hereof, who insist upon repatriation, by the performance of such humanitarian services as are necessary and desirable for the welfare of the prisoners of war. To accomplish this task, the joint Red Cross teams shall provide assistance in the delivering and receiving of prisoners of war by both sides at the place(s) of delivery and reception of prisoners of war, and shall visit the prisoner of war camps of both sides to comfort the prisoners of war and to bring in and distribute gift articles for the comfort and welfare of the prisoners of war. The joint Red Cross teams may provide services to prisoners of war while *en route* from prisoner of war camps to the place(s) of delivery and reception of prisoners of war.

(*b*) The joint Red Cross teams shall be organized as set forth below:

(1) One team shall be composed of twenty (20) members, namely, ten (10) representatives from the national Red Cross Societies of each side, to assist in the delivering and receiving of prisoners of war by both sides at the place(s) of delivery and reception of prisoners of war. The chairmanship of this team shall alternate daily between representatives from the Red Cross Societies of the two sides. The work and services of this team shall be co-ordinated by the Committee for Repatriation of Prisoners of War.

(2) One team shall be composed of sixty (60) members, namely, thirty (30) representatives from the national Red Cross Societies of each side, to visit the prisoner of war camps under the administration of the Korean People's Army and the Chinese People's Volunteers. This team may provide services to prisoners of war while *en route* from the prisoner of war camps to the place(s) of delivery and reception of prisoners of war. A representative of the Red Cross Society of the Democratic People's Republic of Korea or of the Red Cross Society of the People's Republic of China shall serve as chairman of this team.

(3) One team shall be composed of sixty (60) members, namely, thirty (30) representatives from the national Red Cross Societies of each side, to visit the prisoner of war camps under the administration of the United Nations Command. This team may provide services to prisoners of war while *en route* from the prisoner of war camps to the place(s) of delivery and reception of prisoners of war. A representative of a Red Cross Society of a nation contributing forces to the United Nations Command shall serve as chairman of this team.

(4) In order to facilitate the functioning of each joint Red Cross team, sub-teams composed of not less than two (2) members from the team, with an equal number of representatives from each side, may be formed as circumstances require.

(5) Additional personnel such as drivers, clerks, and interpreters, and such equipment as may be required by the joint Red Cross teams to perform their missions, shall be furnished by the Commander of each side to the team operating in the territory under his military control.

(6) Whenever jointly agreed upon by the representatives of both sides on any joint Red Cross team, the size of such team may be increased or decreased, subject to confirmation by the Committee for Repatriation of Prisoners of War.

(*c*) The Commander of each side shall co-operate fully with the joint Red Cross teams in the performance of their functions, and undertakes to ensure the security of the personnel of the joint Red Cross team in the area under his military control. The Commander of each side shall provide such logistic, administrative, and communications facilities as may be required by the team operating in the territory under his military control.

(*d*) The joint Red Cross teams shall be dissolved upon completion of the programme of repatriation of all the prisoners of war specified in sub-paragraph 51(*a*) hereof, who insist upon repatriation.

58. (*a*) The Commander of each side shall furnish to the Commander of the other side as soon as practicable, but not later than ten (10) days after this Armistice Agreement becomes effective, the following information concerning prisoners of war:

(1) Complete data pertaining to the prisoners of war who escaped since the effective date of the data last exchanged.

(2) In so far as practicable, information regarding name, nationality, rank and other identi-fication data, date and cause of death, and place of burial, of those prisoners of war who died while in his custody.

(*b*) If any prisoners of war escape or die after the effective date of the supplementary infor-nation specified above, the detaining side shall furnish to the other side, through the Committee for Repatriation of Prisoners of War, the data pertaining thereto in accordance with the pro-visions of sub-paragraph 58(*a*) hereof. Such data shall be furnished at ten-day intervals until the completion of the programme of delivery and reception of prisoners of war.

(*c*) Any escaped prisoner of war who returns to the custody of the detaining side after the completion of the progamme of delivery and reception of prisoners of war shall be delivered to the Military Armistice Commission for disposition.

59. (*a*) All civilians who, at the time this Armistice Agreement becomes effective, are in territory under the military control of the Commander-in-Chief, United Nations Command, and who, on 24 June 1950, resided north of the Military Demarcation Line established in this Armistice Agreement shall, if they desire to return home, be permitted and assisted by the Commander-in-Chief, United Nations Command, to return to the area north of the Military Demarcation Line; and all civilians who, at the time this Armistice Agreement becomes effective, are in territory under the military control of the Supreme Commander of the Korean People's Army and the Commander of the Chinese People's Volunteers, and who, on 24 June 1950, resided south of the Military Demarcation Line established in this Armistice Agreement shall, if they desire to return home, be permitted and assisted by the Supreme Commander of the Korean People's Army and the Commander of the Chinese People's Volunteers to return to the area south of the Military Demarcation Line. The Com-mander of each side shall be responsible for publicizing widely throughout territory under his military control the contents of the provisions of this sub-paragraph, and for calling upon the appropriate civil authorities to give necessary guidance and assistance to all such civilians who desire to return home.

(*b*) All civilians of foreign nationality who, at the time this Armistice Agreement becomes effective, are in territory under the military control of the Supreme Commander of the Korean People's Army and the Commander of the Chinese People's Volunteers shall, if they desire to proceed to territory under the military control of the Commander-in-Chief, United Nations Command, be permitted and assisted to do so; all civilians of foreign nationality who, at the time when this Armistice Agreement becomes effective, are in territory under the military control of the Commander-in-Chief, United Nations Command, shall, if they desire to proceed to territory under the military control of the Supreme Commander of the Korean People's Army and the Commander of the Chinese People's Volunteers, be permitted and assisted to do so. The Commander of each side shall be responsible for publicizing widely throughout the territory under his military control the contents of the provisions of this sub-paragraph, and for calling upon the appropriate civil authorities to give necessary guidance and assistance to all such civilians of foreign nationality who desire to proceed to territory under the military control of the Commander of the other side.

(*c*) Measures to assist in the return of civilians provided for in sub-paragraph 59(*a*) hereof and the movement of civilians provided for in sub-paragraph 59(*b*) hereof shall be commenced by both sides as soon as possible after this Armistice Agreement becomes effective.

(*d*) (1) A Committee for Assisting the Return of Displaced Civilians is hereby established. It shall be composed of four (4) officers of field grade, two (2) of whom shall be appointed by the Commander-in-Chief, United Nations Command, and two (2) of whom shall be appointed jointly by the Supreme Commander of the Korean People's Army and the Commander of the Chinese People's Volunteers. This Committee shall, under the general supervision and direction of the Military Armistice Commission, be responsible for co-ordinating the specific plans of both sides for assistance to the return of the above-mentioned civilians, and for supervising the execution by both sides of all of the provisions of this Armistice Agreement relating to the return of the above-mentioned civilians. It shall be the duty of this Committee to make necessary arrangements, including those of transportation, for expediting and co-ordinating the movement of the above-mentioned civilians; to select the crossing point(s) through which the above-mentioned civilians will cross the Military Demarcation Line; to arrange for security at the crossing point(s); and to carry out such other functions as are required to accomplish the return of the above-mentioned civilians.

(2) When unable to reach agreement on any matter relating to its responsibilities, the Committee for Assisting the Return of Displaced Civilians shall immediately refer such matter to the Military Armistice Commission for decision. The Committee for Assisting the Return of Displaced Civilians shall maintain its headquarters in proximity to the headquarters of the Military Armistice Commission.

(3) The Committee for Assisting the Return of Displaced Civilians shall be dissolved by the Military Armistice Commission upon fulfilment of its mission.

Article IV

RECOMMENDATION TO THE GOVERNMENTS CONCERNED ON BOTH SIDES

60. In order to ensure the peaceful settlement of the Korea question, the military Commanders of both sides hereby recommend to the governments of the countries concerned on both sides that, within three (3) months after the Armistice Agreement is signed and becomes effective, a political conference of a higher level of both sides be held by representatives appointed respectively to settle through negotiation the questions of the withdrawal of all foreign forces from Korea, the peaceful settlement of the Korean question, etc.

Article V

MISCELLANEOUS

61. Amendments and additions to this Armistice Agreement must be mutually agreed to by the Commanders of the opposing sides.

62. The articles and paragraphs of this Armistice Agreement shall remain in effect until expressly superseded either by mutually acceptable amendments and additions or by provision in an appropriate agreement for a peaceful settlement at a political level between both sides.

63. All of the provisions of this Armistice Agreement, other than paragraph 12, shall become effective at 22.00 hours on 27 July 1953.

Done at Panmunjom, Korea, at 10.00 hours on the 27th day of July, 1953, in English, Korean, and Chinese, all texts being equally authentic.

KIM IL SUNG
*Marshal Democratic
 People's Republic of Korea
Supreme Commander
 Korean People's Army*

PENG TEH-HUAI
*Commander,
 Chinese People's Volunteers*

Mark W. CLARK
*General, United States Army,
Commander-in-Chief,
 United Nations Command*

Present:

NAM IL   William K. HARRISON, Jr.
General, Korean People's Army   *Lieutenant General, United States Army*
Senior Delegate, Delegation of the   *Senior Delegate, United Nations Command*
  Korean People's Army and the   *Delegation*
  Chinese People's Volunteers

ANNEX
TERMS OF REFERENCE FOR NEUTRAL NATIONS REPATRIATION COMMISSION

I

General

1. In order to ensure that all prisoners of war have the opportunity to exercise their right to be repatriated following an armistice, Sweden, Switzerland, Poland, Czechoslovakia and India shall each be requested by both sides to appoint a member to a Neutral Nations Repatriation Commission which shall be established to take custody in Korea of those prisoners of war who, while in the custody of the detaining powers, have not exercised their right to be repatriated. The Neutral Nations Repatriation Commission shall establish its headquarters within the Demilitarized Zone in the vicinity of Panmunjom, and shall station subordinate bodies of the same composition as the Neutral Nations Repatriation Commission at those locations at which the Repatriation Commission assumes custody of prisoners of war. Representatives of both sides shall be permitted to observe the operations of the Repatriation Commission and its subordinate bodies to include explanations and interviews.

2. Sufficient armed forces and any other operating personnel required to assist the Neutral Nations Repatriation Commission in carrying out its functions and responsibilities shall be provided exclusively by India, whose representative shall be the umpire in accordance with the provisions of article 132 of the Geneva Convention, and shall also be chairman and executive agent of the Neutral Nations Repatriation Commission. Representatives from each of the other four powers shall be allowed staff assistants in equal number not to exceed fifty (50) each. When any of the representatives of the neutral nations is absent for some reason, that representative shall designate an alternate representative of his own nationality to exercise his functions and authority. The arms of all personnel provided for in this paragraph shall be limited to military police type small arms.

3. No force or threat of force shall be used against the prisoners of war specified in paragraph 1 above to prevent or effect their repatriation, and no violence to their persons or affront to their dignity or self-respect shall be permitted in any manner for any purpose whatsoever (but see paragraph 7 below). This duty is enjoined on and entrusted to the Neutral Nations Repatriation Commission. This Commission shall ensure that prisoners of war shall at all times be treated humanely in accordance with the specific provisions of the Geneva Convention, and with the general spirit of that Convention.

II

Custody of prisoners of war

4. All prisoners of war who have not exercised their right of repatriation following the effective date of the Armistice Agreement shall be released from the military control and from the custody of the detaining side as soon as practicable, and, in all cases, within sixty (60) days subsequent to the effective date of the Armistice Agreement to the Neutral Nations Repatriation Commission at locations in Korea to be designated by the detaining side.

5. At the time the Neutral Nations Repatriation Commission assumes control of the prisoner of war installation, the military forces of the detaining side shall be withdrawn therefrom, so that the locations specified in the preceding paragraph shall be taken over completely by the armed forces of India.

11

6. Notwithstanding the provisions of paragraph 5 above, the detaining side shall have the responsibility for maintaining and ensuring security and order in the areas round the locations where the prisoners of war are in custody and for preventing and restraining any armed forces (including irregular armed forces) in the area under its control from any acts of disturbance and intrusion against the locations where the prisoners of war are in custody.

7. Notwithstanding the provisions of paragraph 3 above, nothing in this agreement shall be construed as derogating from the authority of the Neutral Nations Repatriation Commission to exercise its legitimate functions and responsibilities for the control of the prisoners of war under its temporary jurisdiction.

III

Explanation

8. The Neutral Nations Repatriation Commission, after having received and taken into custody all those prisoners of war who have not exercised their right to be repatriated, shall immediately make arrangements so that within ninety (90) days after the Neutral Nations Repatriation Commission takes over the custody, the nations to which the prisoners of war belong shall have freedom and facilities to send representatives to the locations where such prisoners of war are in custody to explain to all the prisoners of war depending upon these nations their rights and to inform them of any matters relating to their return to their homelands, particularly of their full freedom to return home to lead a peaceful life, under the following provisions:

(*a*) The number of such explaining representatives shall not exceed seven (7) per thousand prisoners of war held in custody by the Neutral Nations Repatriation Commission; and the minimum authorized shall not be less than a total of five (5);

(*b*) The hours during which the explaining representatives shall have access to the prisoners shall be as determined by the Neutral Nations Repatriation Commission, and generally in accord with article 53 of the Geneva Convention Relative to the Treatment of Prisoners of War;

(*c*) All explanations and interviews shall be conducted in the presence of a representative of each member nation of the Neutral Nations Repatriation Commission and a representative from the detaining side;

(*d*) Additional provisions governing the explanation work shall be prescribed by the Neutral Nations Repatriation Commission, and will be designed to employ the principles enumerated in paragraph 3 above and in this paragraph;

(*e*) The explaining representatives, while engaging in their work, shall be allowed to bring with them necessary facilities and personnel for wireless communications. The number of communications personnel shall be limited to one team per location at which explaining representatives are in residence, except in the event all prisoners of war are concentrated in one location, in which case, two (2) teams shall be permitted. Each team shall consist of not more than six (6) communications personnel.

9. Prisoners of war in its custody shall have freedom and facilities to make representations and communications to the Neutral Nations Repatriation Commission and to representatives and subordinate bodies of the Neutral Nations Repatriation Commission and to inform them of their desires on any matter concerning the prisoners of war themselves, in accordance with arrangements made for the purpose by the Neutral Nations Repatriation Commission.

IV

Disposition of prisoners of war

10. Any prisoner of war who, while in the custody of the Neutral Nations Repatriation Commission, decides to exercise the right of repatriation, shall make an application requesting repatriation to a body consisting of a representative of each member nation of the Neutral Nations Repatriation Commission. Once such an application is made, it shall be considered

immediately by the Neutral Nations Repatriation Commission or one of its subordinate bodies so as to determine immediately by majority vote the validity of such application. Once such an application is made to and validated by the Commission or one of its subordinate bodies, the prisoner of war concerned shall immediately be transferred to and accommodated in the tents set up for those who are ready to be repatriated. Thereafter, he shall, while still in the custody of the Neutral Nations Repatriation Commission, be delivered forthwit h tothe prisoner of war exchange point at Panmunjom for repatriation under the procedure prescribed in the Armistice Agreement.

11. At the expiration of ninety (90) days after the transfer of custody of the prisoners of war to the Neutral Nations Repatriation Commission, access of representatives to captured personnel as provided for in paragraph 8 above, shall terminate, and the question of disposition of the prisoners of war who have not exercised their right to be repatriated shall be submitted to the Political Conference recommended to be convened in paragraph 60, Draft Armistice Agreement, which shall endeavour to settle this question within thirty (30) days, during which period the Neutral Nations Repatriation Commission shall continue to retain custody of those prisoners of war. The Neutral Nations Repatriation Commission shall declare the relief from the prisoner of war status to civilian status of any prisoners of war who have not exercised their right to be repatriated and for whom no other disposition has been agreed to by the Political Conference within one hundred and twenty (120) days after the Neutral Nations Repatriation Commission has assumed their custody. Thereafter, according to the application of each individual, those who choose to go to neutral nations shall be assisted by the Neutral Nations Repatriation Commission and the Red Cross Society of India. This operation shall be completed within thirty (30) days, and upon its completion, the Neutral Nations Repatriation Commission shall immediately cease its functions and declare its dissolution. After the dissolution of the Neutral Nations Repatriation Commission, whenever and wherever any of those above-mentioned civilians who have been relieved from the prisoner of war status desire to return to their fatherlands, the authorities of the localities where they are shall be responsible for assisting them in returning to their fatherlands.

V

Red Cross visitation

12. Essential Red Cross service for prisoners of war in custody of the Neutral Nations Repatriation Commission shall be provided by India in accordance with regulations issued by the Neutral Nations Repatriation Commission.

VI

Press coverage

13. The Neutral Nations Repatriation Commission shall insure freedom of the press and other news media in observing the entire operation as enumerated herein, in accordance with procedures to be established by the Neutral Nations Repatriation Commission.

VII

Logistical support for prisoners of war

14. Each side shall provide logistical support from the prisoners of war in the area under its military control, delivering required support to the Neutral Nations Repatriation Commission at an agreed delivery point in the vicinity of each prisoner of war installation.

15. The cost of repatriating prisoners of war to the exchange point at Panmunjom shall be borne by the detaining side and the cost from the exchange point by the side on which said prisoners depend, in accordance with article 118 of the Geneva Convention.

16. The Red Cross Society of India shall be responsible for providing such general service personnel in the prisoner of war installations as required by the Neutral Nations Repatriation Commission.

17. The Neutral Nations Repatriation Commission shall provide medical support for the prisoners of war as may be practicable. The detaining side shall provide medical support as practicable upon the request of the Neutral Nations Repatriation Commission and specifically for those cases requiring extensive treatment or hospitalization. The Neutral Nations Repatriation Commission shall maintain custody of prisoners of war during such hospitalization. The detaining side shall facilitate such custody. Upon completion of treatment, prisoners of war shall be returned to a prisoner of war installation as specified in paragraph 4 above.

18. The Neutral Nations Repatriation Commission is entitled to obtain from both sides such legitimate assistance as it may require in carrying out its duties and tasks, but both sides shall not under any name and in any form interfere or exert influence.

VIII

Logistical support for the Neutral Nations Repatriation Commission

19. Each side shall be responsible for providing logistical support for the personnel of the Neutral Nations Repatriation Commission stationed in the area under its military control, and both sides shall contribute on an equal basis to such support within the Demilitarized Zone. The precise arrangements shall be subject to determination between the Neutral Nations Repatriation Commission and the detaining side in each case.

20. Each of the detaining sides shall be responsible for protecting the explaining representatives from the other side while in transit over lines of communication within its area, as set forth in paragraph 23 for the Neutral Nations Repatriation Commission, to a place of residence and while in residence in the vicinity of but not within each of the locations where the prisoners of war are in custody. The Neutral Nations Repatriation Commission shall be responsible for the security of such representatives within the actual limits of the locations where the prisoners of war are in custody.

21. Each of the detaining sides shall provide transportation, housing, communication, and other agreed logistical support to the explaining representatives of the other side while they are in the area under its military control. Such services shall be provided on a reimbursable basis.

IX

Publication

22. After the Armistice Agreement becomes effective, the terms of this agreement shall be made known to all prisoners of war who, while in the custody of the detaining side, have not exercised their right to be repatriated.

X

Movement

23. The movement of the personnel of the Neutral Nations Repatriation Commission and repatriated prisoners of war shall be over lines of communication as determined by the command(s) of the opposing side and the Neutral Nations Repatriation Commission. A map showing these lines of communication shall be furnished the command of the opposing side and the Neutral Nations Repatriation Commission. Movement of such personnel, except within locations as designated in paragraph 4 above, shall be under the control of, and escorted by, personnel of the side in whose area the travel is being undertaken; however, such movement shall not be subject to any obstruction and coercion.

XI

Procedural Matters

24. The interpretation of this agreement shall rest with the Neutral Nations Repatriation

Commission. The Neutral Nations Repatriation Commission, and/or any subordinate bodies to which functions are delegated or assigned by the Neutral Nations Repatriation Commission, shall operate on the basis of majority vote.

25. The Neutral Nations Repatriation Commission shall submit a weekly report to the opposing Commanders on the status of prisoners of war in its custody, indicating the numbers repatriated and remaining at the end of each week.

26. When this agreement has been acceded to by both sides and by the five powers named herein, it shall become effective upon the date the Armistice becomes effective.

Done at Panmunjom, Korea, at 14.00 hours on the 8th day of June 1953, in English, Korean, and Chinese, all texts being equally authentic.

(*Signed*) NAM IL   (*Signed*) William K. HARRISON, Jr.

APPENDIX B

TEMPORARY AGREEMENT SUPPLEMENTARY TO THE ARMISTICE AGREEMENT

In order to meet the requirements of the disposition of the prisoners of war not for direct repatriation in accordance with the provisions of the Terms of Reference for Neutral Nations Repatriation Commission, the Commander-in-Chief, United Nations Command, on the one hand, and the Supreme Commander of the Korean People's Army and the Commander of the Chinese People's Volunteers, on the other hand, in pursuance of the provisions in paragraph 61, article V of the Agreement concerning a military Armistice in Korea, agree to conclude the following Temporary Agreement supplementary to the Armistice Agreement:

1. Under the provisions of paragraphs 4 and 5, article II of the Terms of Reference for Neutral Nations Repatriation Commission, the United Nations Command has the right to designate the area between the Military Demarcation Line and the eastern and southern boundaries of the Demilitarized Zone between the Imjin River on the south and the road leading south from Okum-ni on the northeast (the main road leading southeast from Panmunjom not included), as the area within which the United Nations Command will turn over the prisoners of war, who are not directly repatriated and whom the United Nations Command has the responsibility for keeping under its custody, to the Neutral Nations Repatriation Commission and the armed forces of India for custody. The United Nations Command shall, prior to the signing of the Armistice Agreement, inform the side of the Korean People's Army and the Chinese People's Volunteers of the approximate figures by nationality of such prisoners of war held in its custody.

2. If there are prisoners of war under their custody who request not to be directly repatriated, the Korean People's Army and the Chinese People's Volunteers have the right to designate the area in the vicinity of Panmunjom between the Military Demarcation Line and the western and northern boundaries of the Demilitarized Zone, as the area within which such prisoners of war will be turned over to the Neutral Nations Repatriation Commission and the armed forces of India for custody. After knowing that there are prisoners of war under their custody who request not to be directly repatriated, the Korean People's Army and the Chinese People's Volunteers shall inform the United Nations Command side of the approximate figures by nationality of such prisoners of war.

3. In accordance with paragraphs 8, 9 and 10, article I of the Armistice Agreement, the following paragraphs are hereby provided:

(*a*) After the cease-fire comes into effect, unarmed personnel of each side shall be specifically authorized by the Military Armistice Commission to enter the above-mentioned area designated by their own side to perform necessary construction operations. None of such personnel shall remain in the above-mentioned areas upon the completion of the construction operations.

(*b*) A definite number of prisoners of war as decided upon by both sides, who are in the respective custody of both sides and who are not directly repatriated, shall be specifically authorized by the Military Armistice Commission to be escorted respectively by a certain

number of armed forces of the detaining sides to the above-mentioned areas of custody designated respectively by both sides to be turned over to the Neutral Nations Repatriation
Commission and the armed forces of India for custody. After the prisoners of war have been
taken over, the armed forces of the detaining sides shall be withdrawn immediately from
the areas of custody to the area under the control of their own side.

(*c*) The personnel of the Neutral Nations Repatriation Commission and its subordinate
bodies, the armed forces of India, the Red Cross Society of India, the explaining representatives and observation representatives of both sides, as well as the required material and
equipment, for exercising the functions provided for in the Terms of Reference for Neutral
Nations Repatriation Commission shall be specifically authorized by the Military Armistice
Commission to have complete freedom of movement to, from, and within the above-mentioned
areas designated respectively by both sides for the custody of prisoners of war.

4. The provisions of sub-paragraph 3(*c*) of this Agreement shall not be construed as derogating from the privileges enjoyed by those personnel mentioned above under paragraph 11,
article I of the Armistice Agreement.

5. This Agreement shall be abrogated upon the completion of the mission provided for in
the Terms of Reference for Neutral Nations Repatriation Commission.

Done at Panmunjom, Korea, at 10.00 hours on the 27th day of July, 1953, in English,
Korean and Chinese, all texts being equally authentic.

KIM IL SUNG   PENG TEH-HUAI   Mark W. CLARK

Present:

NAM IL   William K. HARRISON, Jr.

[*S/3079, 7 Aug. 1953.*]

It will be seen that the agreement on the repatriation of prisoners of war,
though made in advance of the Armistice, formed an integral part of the final
Armistice Agreement.

In so far as the UN enforcement action had sought to provide a unified
command under which the nations of the world could repel the invasion of
South Korea, it had thus succeeded. It had also held fast to its principle of
non-forcible repatriation, but had gone beyond the *status quo* in respect of the
fact that the 38th parallel was no longer the recognized demarcation line. But
this had been achieved at a vast cost in human terms, and with the realization
that the UN military instrument could not, in the event, be used to secure a
united Korea.

13

ANNEXES

A. *Checklist of Documents*

GENERAL ASSEMBLY

Resolutions

377 (V)	3 Nov. 1950	⎱
384 (V)	14 Dec. 1950	⎬ 5th sess., suppl. 20
498 (V)	1 Feb. 1951	⎰
500 (V)	18 May 1951	5th sess., suppl. 20A
610 (VII)	3 Dec. 1952	⎱
705 (VII)	18 Apr. 1953	⎬ 7th sess., suppl. 20
711 (VII)	28 Aug. 1953	⎰

SECURITY COUNCIL

1. RESOLUTIONS

S/1501	25 June 1950	⎱
S/1511	27 June 1950	⎬ *Resolutions and Decisions of the Security Council*, 5th yr.
S/1588	7 July 1950	⎰

2. COMMUNICATIONS CONCERNING INITIATION OF HOSTILITIES BY NORTH KOREA

S/1495 ⎱	
S/1496 ⎰	25 June 1950
S/1518	29 June 1950

3. MAJOR COMMUNICATIONS AND STATEMENTS OF NORTH KOREA AND CHINA

S/1554	3 July 1950	S/2671	20 June 1952
S/1583	6 July 1950	S/2707	16 July 1952
S/1722	28 Aug. 1950		

4. MAJOR COMMUNICATIONS AND STATEMENTS OF USSR

S/1517	29 June 1950	S/1603	14 July 1950
S/1596/Rev. 1	12 July 1950	S/2684	30 June 1952

5. REPORTS OF THE UN COMMAND

1st	S/1626		11th	S/1996	31 Jan.	1951
2nd	S/1694	17 Aug. 1950	12th, 13th, 14th	S/2021	24 Feb.	1951
3rd	S/1756	2 Sept. 1950	15th, 16th	S/2053	26 Mar.	1951
4th	S/1829	1 Oct. 1950	17th	S/2096	18 Apr.	1951
5th	S/1834	5 Oct. 1950	18th	S/2107	26 Apr.	1951
6th	S/1860	21 Oct. 1950	19th	S/2156	18 May	1951
7th	S/1883	3 Nov. 1950	20th	S/2170	25 May	1951
8th	S/1885	6 Nov. 1950	21st	S/2204	19 June	1951
9th & 10th	S/1953	28 Dec. 1950	22nd	S/2217	28 June	1951

23rd	S/2246	16 July 1951	52nd	S/2837	5 Nov. 1952
24th	S/2265	28 July 1951	53rd	S/2875 & Corr. 1	
25th	S/2277	3 Aug. 1951			19 Dec. 1952
26th	S/2333	10 Sept. 1951	54th	S/2897	6 Jan. 1953
27th	S/2377	16 Oct. 1951	55th	S/2898	6 Jan. 1953
28th	S/2408	13 Nov. 1951	56th	S/2920	30 Jan. 1953
29th	S/2410	29 Nov. 1951	57th	S/2970	30 Mar. 1953
30th	S/2412	15 Nov. 1951	58th	S/2971	30 Mar. 1953
31st	S/2432	7 Dec. 1951	59th	S/2972	30 Mar. 1953
32nd	S/2469	7 Jan. 1952	60th	S/2982	3 Apr. 1953
33rd, 34th	S/2507	31 Jan. 1952	61st	S/2991	16 Apr. 1953
35th	S/2514	7 Feb. 1952	62nd	S/2999	27 Apr. 1953
36th	S/2541	27 Feb. 1952	63rd	S/3017	22 May 1953
37th	S/2550	6 Mar. 1952	64th	S/3037 & Corr. 1.	
38th	S/2593	10 Apr. 1952			18 June 1953
39th	S/2605	16 Apr. 1952	65th	S/3038	18 June
40th	S/2619	30 Apr. 1952	66th	S/3070	24 July 1953
41st	S/2629	9 May 1952	67th	S/3084	20 Aug. 1953
42nd, 43rd	S/2662	13 June 1952	68th	S/3090	1 Sept. 1953
44th	S/2700	14 July 1952	69th	S/3091	1 Sept. 1953
45th	S/2715	23 July 1952	70th	S/3096	11 Sept. 1953
46th	S/2768	9 Sept. 1952	71st	S/3117	19 Oct. 1953
47th	S/2774	15 Sept. 1952	72nd	S/3132	30 Oct. 1953
48th	S/2789	25 Sept. 1952	73rd	S/3133	30 Oct. 1953
49th	S/2805	9 Oct. 1952	74th	S/3143	23 Nov. 1953
50th	S/2835	4 Nov. 1952	75th	S/3148	3 Dec. 1953
51st	S/2836	5 Nov. 1952			

6. REPORTS ON CEASE-FIRE NEGOTIATIONS

S/2266	30 July 1951	S/2326	4 Sept. 1951
S/2275	3 Aug. 1951	S/2341	12 Sept. 1951
S/2287	8 Aug. 1951	S/2361	2 Oct. 1951
S/2304	21 Aug. 1951	S/3079	7 Aug. 1953
S/2311	27 Aug. 1951		

7. OTHER DOCUMENTS

S/1522	29 June 1950	S/1617	21 July 1950
S/1543	30 June 1950	S/1618	21 July 1950
S/1545	30 June 1950	S/1619	21 July 1950
S/1562	3 July 1950	S/1622	24 July 1950
S/1570	5 July 1950	S/1676	8 Aug. 1950
S/1580	6 July 1950	S/1626	25 Aug. 1950
S/1591	8 July 1950	S/2617	29 Apr. 1952
S/1593	9 July 1950	S/2633	14 May 1952
S/1598	12 July 1950	S/2846	13 Nov. 1952
S/1601	12 July 1950	S/2605, Ann. 1,	
S/1602	12 July 1950		16 Apr. 1952
S/1611	21 July 1950	S/2975	31 Mar. 1952
S/1612	21 July 1950	S/3079	7 Aug. 1953
S/1613	21 July 1950		

B. *Bibliography*

Attia, G. *Les forces armées des Nations Unies en Corée et au Moyen Orient.* Geneva, 1963.

Bailey, S. *The Korean Crisis.* London, 1950.

Bowett, D. W. *United Nations Forces.* London, 1964.

Brugière, P. F. *La règle de l'unanimité des membres permanents au Conseil de Securité*; 'Droit de Veto'. Paris, 1952.

Clark, Mark. *From the Danube to the Yalu.* New York, 1954.

Epstein, Leon. *Britain—Uneasy Ally.* Chicago, 1954.

Day, G. *The droit de veto dans l'organisation des Nations Unies.* Paris, 1952.

Frankenstein, M. *L'organisations des Nations Unies devant le conflit coréen.* Paris, 1952.

Goodrich, Leland. *Korea: a Study of US Policy in the United Nations.* New York, 1956.

Green, L. C. Korea and the United Nations. *World Affairs* (1950).

Gross, L. Voting in the Security Council. *60 Yale Law Journal* (1951).

Gunther, John. *The Riddle of MacArthur.* New York, 1951.

Higgins, Trumbull. *Korea and the Fall of MacArthur.* New York, 1960.

Huntington, Samuel. *The Soldier and the State.* Camb., Mass., 1957.

International Red Cross, Geneva. *Le comité international de la Croix Rouge et le conflit de Corée*; Recueil de documents. 1952.

Joy, C. T. *How Communists Negotiate.* New York, 1955.

Kelsen, H. *Recent Trends in the Law of the United Nations.* London, 1951. (Suppl. to *The Law of the United Nations.* 1950.)

Korea Ten Years After. *Army*, June 1950. (Special number devoted to the Korean war.)

Leckie, Robert. *Conflict; the History of the Korean War, 1950–3.* New York, 1962.

McCune, G. M. *Korea Today.* Camb., Mass., 1950.

—— The Korean Situation. *Far Eastern Survey*, 18 Sept. 1948.

McDougal, M. and R. Gardner. The Veto and the Charter: an Interpretation for Survival. *60 Yale Law Journal* (1951).

Osgood, Robert. *Limited War.* Chicago, 1957.

Potter, P. Legal Aspects of the Situation in Korea. 44 *AJIL* (1950).

Rees, David. *Korea: the Limited War.* London, 1964.

RIIA, *Survey of International Affairs, 1947–8, 1949–50, 1951, 1952, 1953.*

Ridgway, Matthew. *Soldier.* 1956.

Rovere, Richard H. and A. M. Schlesinger. *The General and the President.* London, 1952.

Seyersted, F. *United Nations Forces in the Law of War and Peace.* Leyden, 1966.

Spanier, John W. *The Truman–MacArthur Controversy and the Korean War.* Camb., Mass., 1959.

Stone, J. *Aggression and World Order.* London, 1958.

—— *Legal Controls of International Conflict.* London, 1954.

Truman, Harry S. *Memoirs*, ii: *Years of Trial and Hope.* New York, 1956.

US Senate, Cttee on Foreign Relations. *The United States and the Korean Problem: Documents, 1943–53.* Washington, 1953.

Vatcher, William. *Panmunjom.* London, 1958.

Whiting, A. S. *China Crosses the Yalu.* New York, 1960.

Whitney, Courtney, *MacArthur: His Rendezvous with History.* New York, 1956.

Part 4

THE UNITED NATIONS MILITARY OBSERVER GROUP IN INDIA AND PAKISTAN (UNMOGIP), 1949–

9. RELATIONS WITH HOST STATES (p. 361)

Attitudes of India and Pakistan to nationalities represented on UNMOGIP; control of civilians within cease-fire lines; co-operation with UN during hostilities of 1965; attitudes towards Special Representative General Marambio; exchanges between Secretary-General and India about proper role of UNMOGIP and UNIPOM.

10. RELATIONS WITH OTHER STATES INVOLVED (p. 370)

Unimportance of this factor in the operation of UNMOGIP.

11. FINANCE (p. 370)

Figures, and explanations thereof, for UNMOGIP expenses and financing from 1949–66.

12. IMPLEMENTATION (p. 373)

The demise of UNCIP; the appointment of a Special Representative; mediation by General McNaughton; appointment of Sir Owen Dixon in 1950, and his replacement by Dr Frank Graham in 1957; resumption of bilateral talks; renewal of tension in 1957; Gunnar Jarring sent to India and Pakistan; UNMOGIP's role in achieving effective implementation of the cease-fire from 1949–65; reports of Chief Observer General Nimmo during this period; deterioration in 1964 and the breakdown of the cease-fire in 1965; the Secretary-General's initiatives; the implementation of the new cease-fire—the roles of UNMOGIP and UNIPOM; the work of the Security Council and Secretary-General; the diplomatic activity of the Soviet Union culminating in the Tashkent Agreement; withdrawal behind the cease-fire lines; UNMOGIP's contribution.

13. ANNEXES

I

INTRODUCTION

ON 1 January 1948 India complained to the Security Council of a situation the continuation of which was likely to endanger international peace and security. India claimed that Pakistan was giving aid to invaders who were mounting incursions into the State of Jammu and Kashmir.

The history of the India–Pakistan struggle for Kashmir considerably ante-dates the formation of India and Pakistan as separate sovereign states, for the seeds were sown well before that time.[1] On 20 February 1947 the British government announced its intention to transfer power in India not later than June 1948. Lord Mountbatten was appointed Viceroy and encharged with the task of effecting a peaceful transfer of administration either to a government of a united India, or to two governments of India and Pakistan. Mountbatten rapidly decided that it was impossible to create a united government, and on 3 June 1947 the British government published its plan for the partition of India. On 18 July the Indian Independence Act was passed, providing that on 15 August India and Pakistan were to become independent Dominions. India was to comprise the predominantly Hindu provinces, Pakistan the pre-dominantly Muslim provinces.[2] The question of the status of the princely states was an explosive one. The Indian National Congress refused to recognize the independence of any of the states, maintaining that they must accede to either Dominion, but this was opposed by the Muslim League. There were some 584 princely states, with a population of 99 million people. 'Some Princes repre-sented real power, such as the Nizam of Hyderabad, which had almost 17 million inhabitants and was about the size of Germany. Other Princely States were small in size and population. The overwhelming majority of them were Hindu; only half a dozen were Muslim.'[3]

The British Cabinet Mission had earlier advised, on 16 May 1946, that so far as the princely states were concerned, 'There should be a Union of India, em-bracing both British India and the States, which should deal with the following subjects: foreign affairs, defence, and communications'. In other matters 'the

[1] See, e.g., E. M. D. Sufi, *Kashmir, being a History of Kashmir* (1948); Josef Korbel, *Danger in Kashmir*, rev. ed. (1966), esp. pp. 1–44; Lord Birdwood, *Two Nations and Kashmir* (1956), esp. pp. 1–66; Sisir Gupta, *Kashmir, a Study in India–Pakistan Relations* (1966); J. B. Das Gupta, *Indo-Pakistan Relations* (1959); Alastair Lamb, *Crisis in Kashmir* (1966); Granville Austin, *Report on Kashmir* (1965).
[2] For the details of the negotiations preceding the Mountbatten proposals, see Korbel, pp. 44–65; Sisir Gupta, pp. 94–111.
[3] Korbel, p. 46.

States will retain all subjects and powers other than those ceded to the Union'.[4] Although the overall proposal of the Cabinet Mission was rejected, Mountbatten accepted—as did the June 1947 decision for partition—this basis for settlement so far as the princely states were concerned. Mountbatten confirmed that the Independence Act would mean the legal and technical independence of the princely states, but he also urged them to take note of the economic and geographical realities, and to decide as soon as possible whether to join with Pakistan or India. By Independence Day, 15 August 1947, only three states had not made this choice: Hyderabad, Junagadh,[5] and Kashmir. The Muslim Nizam of Hyderabad sought to remain independent, ruling over a largely Hindu population. India invaded Hyderabad in 1948 and absorbed it into the Union. Junagadh also was predominantly Hindu, ruled by a Muslim Nawab: in September 1947 he sought to accede to Pakistan, but the Indian army entered the country and ordered a plebiscite; the population voted to join India. There remained Kashmir, which, unlike Junagadh and Hyderabad, had an international frontier which approached the USSR and met the boundaries of Tibet, Afghanistan, Pakistan and India. Moreover, Muslim Kashmir was ruled by the Hindu Maharaja Sir Hari Singh. Thus the conditions existed for Kashmir to become a battlefield. The Maharaja made no move to join either India or Pakistan.[6]

In August 1947, when Kashmir state troops entered Poonch to suppress a revolt, the Muslim soldiers of the Ruler organized the Azad (Free) Kashmir movement,[7] and on 22 October, after a period of mounting tension, North-West Frontier Province tribesmen, inflamed by tales of Muslim suppression by the Maharaja, invaded Kashmir at the strategic outpost of Domel. There followed widespread destruction, pillage, and looting, with appalling loss of life.[8] India believed that Pakistan had planned the invasion; Pakistan, while denying this, certainly gave support to it.

The Maharaja decided to call on India for military help, and such aid could only come after accession.[9] On 24 October 1947 he signed an Instrument of Accession to India, and in a covering letter promised to set up a more popularly-based government under the leadership of Sheikh Abdullah. Sheikh Abdullah had been imprisoned in 1946 for his political activities against the

---

[4] Cmd 6821.

[5] For a detailed account of the problems of Hyderabad and Junagadh, see V. P. Menon, *The Story of the Integration of the Indian States* (1956).

[6] Pakistanis generally are convinced that Mountbatten was acting as an instrument of Delhi, urging the Maharaja either to accede to India or to remain independent. In fact, most scholars feel that the evidence does not support this view; rather, it would seem, Mountbatten urged the importance of joining one Dominion or the other, and of ascertaining the wishes of the people (A. Campbell-Johnson, *Mission with Mountbatten* (1951), pp. 117–21; Korbel, pp. 56–7).

[7] Alastair Lamb (p. 67) writes: 'The actual link between Azad Kashmir and Pakistan has, since early 1949, been under the supreme command of the Pakistan general staff; but there does appear to be a real distinction between Azad troops and Pakistani regulars.'

[8] For details of the savage and indiscriminate nature of the fighting, see Sisir Gupta, pp. 110–15, and Korbel, pp. 75–8.

[9] Korbel (p. 79), however, questions whether Mountbatten's view that military aid must be preceded by accession, even if only conditional accession, was legally correct.

Maharaja, and upon his release urged a 'free' Kashmir, based on Sikh–Muslim–Hindu co-operation. He opposed union with Pakistan, however. It seems likely that he was released from prison at the instigation of the Prime Minister, Nehru. Lord Mountbatten, now the Governor-General of India, accepted the Instrument of Accession, but indicated that he would like the Maharaja's decision to be ratified, when peace was restored, by the people of Kashmir. Military aid was dispatched by India to Srinagar on 27 October. It was now the turn of the Pakistanis to claim that this military intervention had been pre-arranged. Initially, the Governor-General of Pakistan, Mohammed Ali Jinnah, ordered the dispatch of troops to Kashmir, but was persuaded by Field-Marshal Sir Claude Auchinleck[10] to withdraw the order, and instead to invite Mountbatten to Lahore. Jinnah proposed a cease-fire, mutual withdrawal of 'alien' troops, and a jointly-organized plebiscite. Mountbatten, whose constitutional powers were more limited than Jinnah's, could not himself accept, but promised to present the proposal before his government. It was rejected by India. Mountbatten now proposed a UN-organized plebiscite, but this was at this stage rejected by Jinnah. Nehru insisted that the restoration of peace must come first, but that then 'the people of Kashmir should decide the question of accession by plebiscite or referendum under international auspices such as those of the United Nations. . . . By this declaration I stand.'[11] Yet Nehru rejected a proposal of Pakistan's Prime Minister, Liaqat Ali Khan, to take the case to the UN, saying that a UN role arose only when peace and order would have been restored in Kashmir. Subsequently, on 12 December, Nehru slightly modified his position by saying that India was prepared to invite UN observers to come and advise on the proposed plebiscite. He did not at this juncture accept the idea of a more direct role in the dispute. Although the fighting in Kashmir had slowed down,[12] it was still continuing, with a large death-roll of civilians and an enormous trek of refugees. By the turn of the year, however, India had decided to put the broader issue before the UN as a threat to international peace;[13] and thus it was that in January 1948 the UN was seized of the Kashmir dispute.

Pakistan rapidly submitted counter-charges,[14] and the Security Council invited both countries to participate in its debates. Pakistan's charges were presented in a lengthy document, divided into three parts; and supported by a five-hour-long speech by the Minister of Foreign Affairs, Sir Zafrullah Khan. Pakistan placed priority upon the withdrawal of all 'alien' elements at once: 'Sikh bands, *Rashtriya Sewak Sangh* volunteers, other people who have gone in, tribesmen, and any other people who may have gone in from the Muslim side, and men from Pakistan, Muslims who are Indian nationals and who were refugees in Pakistan—everybody'.[15] Pakistan believed that a plebiscite should

[10] Supreme Commander in charge of administering partition of the Indian Army.
[11] India, *White Paper on Jammu and Kashmir* (1948), pp. 61–7.
[12] For the military details of this phase, see Birdwood, pp. 67–71.
[13] S/628, 2 Jan. 1948.
[14] S/646 & Corr. 1, 15 Jan. 1948.
[15] *SCOR*, 3rd yr, nos 1–15, p. 36.

then be held under a neutral UN administration, to see if Kashmir wished to accede to Pakistan or to India. India, on the other hand, insisted that accession had already been completed, and that she had a duty to give military protection to Kashmir against Pakistani aggression. After order had been restored, a plebiscite could take place—under Sheikh Abdullah's administration—to see if the people wished to ratify the accession to India.[16] The Security Council passed a holding resolution (by 9 to nil, with the Ukraine and USSR abstaining), and agreed that the President should invite the representatives of India and Pakistan to have direct talks under his guidance:

> *The Security Council,*
> *Having heard* statements on the situation in Kashmir from representatives of the Governments of India and Pakistan,
> *Recognizing* the urgency of the situation,
> *Taking note* of the telegram addressed on 6 January 1948 by its President to each of the parties and of their replies thereto, in which they affirmed their intention to conform to the Charter of the United Nations.
> 1. *Calls upon* both the Government of India and the Government of Pakistan to take immediately all measures within their power (including public appeals to their people) calculated to improve the situation, and to refrain from making any statements and from doing or causing to be done or permitting any acts which might aggravate the situation;
> 2. *Further requests* each of those Governments to inform the Council immediately of any material change in the situation which occurs or appears to either of them to be about to occur while the matter is under consideration by the Council, and consult with the Council thereon. [*SC res. S/651, 17 Jan. 1948.*]

Although all the major divergences which existed between the parties emerged during the talks, agreement was reached on the idea of establishing a three-member Commission on India and Pakistan (UNCIP) to go to Kashmir to investigate the facts and exercise a mediatory influence. At this moment, at least, it looked as if real progress could be made towards a settlement. The agreement was adopted (again by 9 to nil, with the Ukraine and the Soviet Union abstaining) as UN resolution S/654 on 20 January 1948. The text is given on p. 330 below.

This resolution avoided any mention of certain of the major controversial issues—the withdrawal of tribesmen, Pakistani support, the Indian army, or the holding of a plebiscite. For reasons that are not revealed by the UN documents,[17] a delay of some three months occurred in actually sending this Commission out to the region. By this time Gandhi had been assassinated by a Hindu fanatic, and the snows had melted in Kashmir, permitting a renewed outbreak of massive hostilities. There was no realization in January that such a further deterioration of conditions might have occurred by the time UNCIP reached the subcontinent.

The consensus of 20 January rapidly disintegrated, to be replaced by bitter

---

[16] For detailed comments on the differing attitudes of India and Pakistan, and the various proposals considered by them, see (from an Indian standpoint, but comprehensively researched and well presented) Sisir Gupta, pp. 140–74; and Korbel, pp. 97–118.

[17] Or by any of the authors here relied upon; indeed, Korbel, p. 104, declares himself equally perplexed.

mutual accusations. The proposals of India and Pakistan grew farther apart: Pakistan clearly felt that no impartial plebiscite could take place under Sheikh Abdullah's government; whereas India, while conceding the possibility of a National Assembly being elected, clearly thought it should be done while Abdullah was still leader. This in turn led to disagreement on the UN's role, Pakistan wishing it to have temporary administrative authority, and India believing it should have an advising and observing capacity. Above all, India regarded accession as complete, and resented the view of many Security Council members that Lord Mountbatten's letter regarding accession was an integral part of the terms of accession.

In the initial phase at least, though there was a genuine attempt by the Security Council to find an acceptable solution, the majority of members inclined more to the Pakistani case. The United States' attitude was regarded as unfriendly to India, and there was much talk of the necessity of relying upon a veto of the Soviet Union. (Ironically, Pakistan too regarded Western support of the position as inadequate, and at this time opened diplomatic relations with the Soviet Union.) Canada, Belgium, Syria, Argentina, and Colombia all showed some sympathy for Pakistan's case. The United Kingdom was above all concerned to remain impartial as between two Commonwealth countries. The major exception was China, which gave support in the Council to the Indian case. There was considerable criticism in India of the failure to acquire the support of the Security Council, and this generated further bitterness. There was also in India a widespread feeling that the Pakistani delegation had put its case more successfully.

The debate continued, and on 5 February Sheikh Abdullah spoke at the Security Council, insisting forcefully that there could be no question of changing the administration in Kashmir before a plebiscite. A further round of private talks was held between India and Pakistan, under the guidance of the President of the Security Council—then General McNaughton of Canada. On 8 February, in the wake of great press criticism in India at the way in which the Kashmir affair was drifting, the Indian representative asked for adjournment, so that he could return to Delhi for consultations.

This request was greatly criticized by the Security Council, most members of which found a request for adjournment incompatible with the agreed seriousness of the situation. India, for her part, felt that 'the trend of opinion in the Security Council on fundamentals was such that, if it had then been allowed to crystallize itself into a resolution, the result would have been an impasse'.[18]

On 10 March the Indian delegation returned, and discussion was resumed. After other proposals failed to command the support of both the parties, the Security Council for the first time decided, on 21 April, to act despite the opposition of both Pakistan and Canada. It adopted a six-Power resolution sponsored by Belgium, Canada, China, Colombia, the United Kingdom, and the United States. Under this resolution, the membership of the Commission

[18] Per the India representative, Ayyangar, SCOR, 3rd yr, 285th mtg.

established by the resolution of 20 January would be enlarged to five, and would proceed at once to the sub-continent to place its good offices at the disposal of the two governments, to secure the restoration of peace and the holding of a plebiscite.

The Security Council,

Having considered the complaint of the Government of India concerning the dispute over the State of Jammu and Kashmir,

Having heard the representative of India in support of that complaint and the reply and counter-complaints of the representative of Pakistan,

Being strongly of the opinion that the early restoration of peace and order in Jammu and Kashmir is essential and that India and Pakistan should do their utmost to bring about a cessation of all fighting,

Noting with satisfaction that both India and Pakistan desire that the question of the accession of Jammu and Kashmir to India or Pakistan should be decided through the democratic method of a free and impartial plebiscite,

Considering that the continuation of the dispute is likely to endanger international peace and security,

Reaffirms its resolution 38 (1948) of 17 January 1948:

Resolves that the membership of the Commission established by its resolution 39 (1948) of 20 January 1948 shall be increased to five and shall include, in addition to the membership mentioned in that resolution, representatives of . . . and . . . , and that if the membership of the Commission has not been completed within ten days from the date of the adoption of this resolution the President of the Council may designate such other Member or Members of the United Nations as are required to complete the membership of five;

Instructs the Commission to proceed at once to the Indian subcontinent and there place its good offices and mediation at the disposal of the Governments of India and Pakistan with a view to facilitating the taking of the necessary measures, both with respect to the restoration of peace and order and to the holding of a plebiscite, by the two Governments, acting in co-operation with one another and with the Commission, and further instructs the Commission to keep the Council informed of the action taken under the resolution; and, to this end,

Recommends to the Governments of India and Pakistan the following measures as those which in the opinion of the Council are appropriate to bring about a cessation of the fighting and to create proper conditions for a free and impartial plesbiscite to decide whether the State of Jammu and Kashmir is to accede to India or Pakistan:

A. *Restoration of peace and order*

1. The Government of Pakistan should undertake to use its best endeavours:

(*a*) To secure the withdrawal from the State of Jammu and Kashmir of tribesmen and Pakistani nationals not normally resident therein who have entered the State for the purpose of fighting, and to prevent any intrusion into the State of such elements and any furnishing of material aid to those fighting in the State;

(*b*) To make known to all concerned that the measures indicated in this and the following paragraphs provide full freedom to all subjects of the State, regardless of creed, caste, or party, to express their views and to vote on the question of the accession of the State, and that therefore they should co-operate in the maintenance of peace and order.

2. The Government of India should:

(*a*) When it is established to the satisfaction of the Commission set up in accordance with the Council's resolution 39 (1948) that the tribesmen are withdrawing and that arrangements for the cessation of the fighting have become effective, put into operation in consultation with the Commission a plan for withdrawing their own forces from Jammu and Kashmir and reducing them progressively to the minimum strength required for the support of the civil power in the maintenance of law and order;

(*b*) Make known that the withdrawal is taking place in stages and announce the completion of each stage;

(*c*) When the Indian forces have been reduced to the minimum strength mentioned in (*a*) above, arrange in consultation with the Commission for the stationing of the remaining forces to be carried out in accordance with the following principles:

(i) That the presence of troops should not afford any intimidation or appearance of intimidation to the inhabitants of the State;

(ii) That as small a number as possible should be retained in forward areas;

(iii) That any reserve of troops which may be included in the total strength should be located within their present base area.

3. The Government of India should agree that until such time as the Plebiscite Administration referred to below finds it necessary to exercise the powers of direction and supervision over the State forces and police provided for in paragraph 8, they will be held in areas to be agreed upon with the Plebiscite Administrator.

4. After the plan referred to in paragraph 2 (*a*) above has been put into operation, personnel recruited locally in each district should so far as possible be utilized for the re-establishment and maintenance of law and order with due regard to protection of minorities, subject to such additional requirements as may be specified by the Plebiscite Administration referred to in paragraph 7.

5. If these local forces should be found to be inadequate, the Commission, subject to the agreement of both the Government of India and the Government of Pakistan, should arrange for the use of such forces of either Dominion as it deems effective for the purpose of pacification.

B. *Plebiscite*

6. The Government of India should undertake to ensure that the Government of the State invite the major political groups to designate responsible representatives to share equitably and fully in the conduct of the administration at the ministerial level while the plebiscite is being prepared and carried out.

7. The Government of India should undertake that there will be established in Jammu and Kashmir a Plebiscite Administration to hold a plebiscite as soon as possible on the question of the accession of the State to India or Pakistan.

8. The Government of India should undertake that there will be delegated by the State to the Plebiscite Administration such powers as the latter considers necessary for holding a fair and impartial plebiscite including, for that purpose only, the direction and supervision of the State forces and police.

9. The Government of India should, at the request of the Plebiscite Administration, make available from the Indian forces such assistance as the Plebiscite Administration may require for the performance of its functions.

10. (*a*) The Government of India should agree that a nominee of the Secretary-General of the United Nations will be appointed to be the Plebiscite Administrator.

(*b*) The Plebiscite Administrator, acting as an officer of the State of Jammu and Kashmir, should have authority to nominate his assistants and other subordinates and to draft regulations governing the plebiscite. Such nominees should be formally appointed and such draft regulations should be formally promulgated by the State of Jammu and Kashmir.

(*c*) The Government of India should undertake that the Government of Jammu and Kashmir will appoint fully qualified persons nominated by the Plebiscite Administrator to act as special magistrates within the State judicial system to hear cases which in the opinion of the Plebiscite Administrator have a serious bearing on the preparation for and the conduct of a free and impartial plebiscite.

(*d*) The terms of service of the Administrator should form the subject of a separate negotiation between the Secretary-General of the United Nations and the Government of India. The Administrator should fix the terms of service for his assistants and subordinates.

(*e*) The Administrator should have the right to communicate directly with the Government of the State and with the Commission of the Security Council and, through the Commission, with the Security Council, with the Governments of India and Pakistan and with their representatives with the Commission. It would be his duty to bring to the notice of any or all of the foregoing (as he in his discretion may decide) any circumstances arising which may tend, in his opinion, to interfere with the freedom of the plebiscite.

11. The Government of India should undertake to prevent, and to give full support to the Administrator and his staff in preventing, any threat, coercion or intimidation, bribery or other undue influence on the voters in the plebiscite, and the Government of India should publicly announce and should cause the Government of the State to announce this undertaking as an international obligation binding on all public authorities and officials in Jammu and Kashmir.

12. The Government of India should themselves and through the Government of the State declare and make known that all subjects of the State of Jammu and Kashmir, regardless of creed, caste or party, will be safe and free in expressing their views and in voting on the question of the accession of the State and that there will be freedom of the press, speech and assembly and freedom of travel in the State, including freedom of lawful entry and exit.

13. The Government of India should use and should ensure that the Government of the State also use their best endeavours to effect the withdrawal from the State of all Indian nationals other than those who are normally resident therein or who on or since 15 August 1947 have entered it for a lawful purpose.

14. The Government of India should ensure that the Government of the State releases all political prisoners and take all possible steps so that:

(a) All citizens of the State who have left it on account of disturbances are invited, and are free, to return to their homes and to exercise their rights as such citizens;

(b) There is no victimization;

(c) Minorities in all parts of the State are accorded adequate protection.

15. The Commission of the Security Council should at the end of the plebiscite certify to the Council whether the plebiscite has or has not been really free and impartial .

C. *General provisions*

16. The Governments of India and Pakistan should each be invited to nominate a representative to be attached to the Commission for such assistance as it may require in the performance of its task.

17. The Commission should establish in Jammu and Kashmir such observers as it may require of any of the proceedings in pursuance of the measures indicated in the foregoing paragraphs.

18. The Security Council Commission should carry out the tasks assigned to it herein. [*SC res. S/726, 21 Apr. 1948.*]

It will be noted that paragraph 17 provides the first mention of, and the initial legal authority for, the establishment of UN observers in Kashmir.

Initially the Indian government was very hostile to the resolution, and declared many parts of it unacceptable. India believed that the resolution did not sufficiently spell out Pakistan's obligations, much less condemn Pakistan. India had been put in the position of a 'co-accused'. Nor did the resolution take account of Kashmir's accession to India, and India's duty to defend Kashmir against external aggression. A coalition government would see the collapse of the administration in Kashmir. And finally, India objected to the wide powers being given to the Plebiscite Administration. Nor was Pakistan wholly pleased with the resolution, for she felt that earlier ground had been lost by a British and American desire to 'redress the balance'. Pakistani newspapers urged a closer collaboration with the Soviet Union.

India did, however, agree in May to receive the Commission. UNCIP was composed of representatives of Czechoslovakia (nominated by India on 10 February 1948); Belgium and Colombia (appointed by the Security Council, as additional members, on 23 April 1948); Argentina (nominated by Pakistan on 30 April 1948); and the United States (designated by the President of the Council on 7 May 1948, in the absence of agreement between Argentina and Czechoslovakia on the member to be designated by them).

Pakistan requested that UNCIP be charged also with remaining matters raised in its original charges to the Security Council, and going beyond the Kashmir dispute. The only one of those that remained a real issue was the question of the fulfilment of an India–Pakistan agreement on military stores. On 3 June, in the face of Indian objections to enlarging UNCIP's mandate, the Security Council adopted a resolution by eight votes to none, with China, the Soviet Union, and the Ukraine SSR abstaining:

The Security Council,
Reaffirms its resolutions of 17 January 1948, 20 January 1948 and 21 April 1948;
Directs the Commission of Mediation to proceed without delay to the areas of dispute with a view to accomplishing in priority the duties assigned to it by the resolution of 21 April 1948; and
Directs the Commission further to study and report to the Security Council when it considers it appropriate on the matters raised in the letter of the Foreign Minister of Pakistan, dated 15 January 1948, in the order outlined in Paragraph D of the resolution of the Council dated 20 January 1948. [*SC res. S/819.*]

UNCIP arrived on the Indian sub-continent on 7 July 1948, and immediately embarked upon consultations in Karachi and New Delhi. It adopted, on 13 August 1948, a resolution submitting to the two parties a cease-fire and truce agreement. This took into account the entire situation, especially the presence of Pakistani troops in Kashmir.[19] This resolution was accepted in its entirety by India and, subject to certain conditions especially concerning the holding of a free plebiscite, by Pakistan.

THE UNITED NATIONS COMMISSION FOR INDIA AND PAKISTAN

Having given careful consideration to the points of view expressed by the Representatives of India and Pakistan regarding the situation in the State of Jammu and Kashmir, and

Being of the opinion that the prompt cessation of hostilities and the correction of conditions the continuance of which is likely to endanger international peace and security are essential to implementation of its endeavours to assist the Governments of India and Pakistan in effecting a final settlement of the situation,

Resolves to submit simultaneously to the Governments of India and Pakistan the following proposal:

[19] Korbel, the Czechoslovak member of UNCIP, and its Chairman, explains that the news that there had been three Pakistani brigades in Kashmir since then—which news was given to UNCIP by Sir Zafrullah Khan when the Commission arrived in Karachi—came as a 'bombshell': UNCIP appeared equally dismayed at other aspects of its reception in Karachi, which seemed to indicate uncertainty by the Pakistani government as to its policy towards the Commission. See Korbel, pp. 121–2 and pages following, for an invaluable personal account. (By February 1949 Korbel, who had been appointed by Mazaryk, had been replaced by the new communist government in Czechoslovakia, for political reasons, by a more 'reliable Communist' delegate.)

PART I

Cease-fire order

A. The Governments of India and Pakistan agree that their respective High Commands will issue separately and simultaneously a cease-fire order to apply to all forces under their control in the State of Jammu and Kashmir as of the earliest practicable date or dates to be mutually agreed upon within four days after these proposals have been accepted by both Governments.

B. The High Commands of the Indian and Pakistan forces agree to refrain from taking any measures that might augment the military potential of the forces under their control in the State of Jammu and Kashmir.

(For the purpose of these proposals 'forces under their control' shall be considered to include all forces, organised and unorganised, fighting or participating in hostilities on their respective sides.)

C. The Commanders-in-Chief of the forces of India and Pakistan shall promptly confer regarding any necessary local changes in present dispositions which may facilitate the cease-fire.

D. In its discretion and as the Commission may find practicable, the Commission will appoint military observers who under the authority of the Commission and with the co-operation of both Commands will supervise the observance of the cease-fire order.

E. The Government of India and the Government of Pakistan agree to appeal to their respective peoples to assist in creating and maintaining an atmosphere favourable to the promotion of further negotiations.

PART II

Truce agreement

Simultaneously with the acceptance of the proposal for the immediate cessation of hostilities as outlined in Part I, both Governments accept the following principles as a basis for the formulation of a truce agreement, the details of which shall be worked out in discussion between their Representatives and the Commission.

A.

1. As the presence of troops of Pakistan in the territory of the State of Jammu and Kashmir constitutes a material change in the situation since it was represented by the Government of Pakistan before the Security Council, the Government of Pakistan agrees to withdraw its troops from that State.

2. The Government of Pakistan will use its best endeavour to secure the withdrawal from the State of Jammu and Kashmir of tribesmen and Pakistan nationals not normally resident therein who have entered the State for the purpose of fighting.

3. Pending a final solution, the territory evacuated by the Pakistan troops will be administered by the local authorities under the surveillance of the Commission.

B.

1. When the Commission shall have notified the Government of India that the tribesmen and Pakistan nationals referred to in Part II A 2 thereof have withdrawn, thereby terminating the situation which was represented by the Government of India to the Security Council as having occasioned the presence of Indian forces in the State of Jammu and Kashmir, and further, that the Pakistan forces are being withdrawn from the State of Jammu and Kashmir, the Government of India agrees to begin to withdraw the bulk of their forces from that State in stages to be agreed upon with the Commission.

2. Pending the acceptance of the conditions for a final settlement of the situation in the State of Jammu and Kashmir, the Indian Government will maintain within the lines existing at the moment of the cease-fire the minimum strength of its forces which in agreement with the Commission are considered necessary to assist local authorities in the observance of law and order. The Commission will have observers stationed where it deems necessary.

3. The Government of India will undertake to ensure that the Government of the State of Jammu and Kashmir will take all measures within their power to make it publicly known

that peace, law and order will be safeguarded and that all human and political rights will be guaranteed.

C.

1. Upon signature, the full text of the Truce Agreement or a communiqué containing the principles thereof as agreed upon between the two Governments and the Commission, will be made public.

PART III

The Government of India and the Government of Pakistan reaffirm their wish that the future status of the State of Jammu and Kashmir shall be determined in accordance with the will of the people and to that end, upon acceptance of the Truce Agreement both Governments agree to enter into consultations with the Commission to determine fair and equitable conditions whereby such free expression will be assured.' [S/AC.12/MA/1.]

Two days before, the Chairman of UNCIP had cabled the President of the Security Council, informing him that the Secretary-General had been requested to take steps to appoint, at short notice, military observers for the supervision of the cease-fire.[20]

On 22 November 1948 there was submitted to the Security Council an interim report by UNCIP on its activities for the period 15 June 1948—22 September 1948, when it had left the sub-continent for Geneva. (The Security Council was at that time in session in Paris.) The Security Council examined the report (S/1100), listened to a summary by the rapporteur, and agreed upon a statement by the President that it wished (1) to confirm to the Commission the full support of the Security Council in its work for the purpose of arriving at a peaceful solution, and (2) to bring to the attention of both parties the need for refraining from any action which might aggravate the military or political situation, and thus prejudice the negotiations being carried out. In spite of their reservations, the parties now ordered a cease-fire—the first in fourteen months —to become effective on 1 January 1949. On 5 January UNCIP adopted a new resolution, pointing the way to a phase of demilitarization, to be the last measure preceding the actual act of plebiscite.

COMMISSION'S PLEBISCITE PROPOSALS
AS APPROVED ON 11 DECEMBER 1948 AND
EMBODIED IN THE COMMISSION'S RESOLUTION OF 5 JANUARY 1949

A. The Commission reaffirms its resolution of 13 August 1948.
B. The Governments of India and Pakistan simultaneously accept supplementary to this resolution the following principles:

1. The question of the accession of the State of Jammu and Kashmir to India or Pakistan will be decided through the democratic method of a free and impartial plebiscite.
2. A plebiscite will be held when it shall be found by the Commission that the cease-fire and truce arrangements set forth in Parts I and II of the Commission's resolution of 13 August 1948 have been carried out and arrangements for the plebiscite have been completed.
3. (a) The Secretary-General of the United Nations will, in agreement with the Commission, nominate a Plebiscite Administrator who shall be a personality of high

---

[20] See below, p. 350.

international standing and commanding general confidence. He will be formally appointed to office by the Government of Jammu and Kashmir.

(*b*) The Plebiscite Administrator shall derive from the State of Jammu and Kashmir the powers he considers necessary for organizing and conducting the plebiscite and for ensuring the freedom and impartiality of the plebiscite.

(*c*) The Plebiscite Administrator shall have authority to appoint such staff of assistants and observers as he may require.

4. (*a*) After implementation of Parts I and II of the Commission's resolution of 13 August 1948, and when the Commission is satisfied that peaceful conditions have been restored in the State, the Commission and the Plebiscite Administrator will determine, in consultation with the Government of India, the final disposal of Indian and State armed forces, such disposal to be with due regard to the security of the State and the freedom of the plebiscite.

(*b*) As regards the territory referred to in A.2 of Part II of the resolution of 13 August, final disposal of the armed forces in that territory will be determined by the Commission and the Plebiscite Administrator in consultation with the local authorities.

5. All civil and military authorities within the State and the principal political elements of the State will be required to co-operate with the Plebiscite Administrator in the preparation for and the holding of the plebiscite.

6. (*a*) All citizens of the State who have left it on account of the disturbances will be invited and be free to return and to exercise all their rights as such citizens. For the purpose of facilitating repatriation there shall be appointed two Commissions, one composed of nominees of India and the other of nominees of Pakistan. The Commissions shall operate under the direction of the Plebiscite Administrator. The Governments of India and Pakistan and all authorities within the State of Jammu and Kashmir will collaborate with the Plebiscite Administrator in putting this provision into effect.

(*b*) All persons (other than citizens of the State) who on or since 15 August 1947 have entered it for other than lawful purpose, shall be required to leave the State.

7. All authorities within the State of Jammu and Kashmir will undertake to ensure, in collaboration with the Plebiscite Administrator, that:

(*a*) There is no threat, coercion or intimidation, bribery or other undue influence on the voters in the plebiscite;

(*b*) No restrictions are placed on legitimate political activity throughout the State. All subjects of the State, regardless of creed, caste or party, shall be safe and free in expressing their views and in voting on the question of the accession of the State to India or Pakistan. There shall be freedom of the Press, speech and assembly and freedom of travel in the State, including freedom of lawful entry and exit;

(*c*) All political prisoners are released;

(*d*) Minorities in all parts of the State are accorded adequate protection; and

(*e*) There is no victimization.

8. The Plebiscite Administrator may refer to the United Nations Commission for India and Pakistan problems on which he may require assistance, and the Commission may in its discretion call upon the Plebiscite Administrator to carry out on its behalf any of the responsibilities with which it has been entrusted.

9. At the conclusion of the plebiscite, the Plebiscite Administrator shall report the result thereof to the Commission and to the Government of Jammu and Kashmir. The Commission shall then certify to the Security Council whether the plebiscite has or has not been free and impartial.

10. Upon the signature of the truce agreement the details of the foregoing proposals will be elaborated in the consultations envisaged in Part III of the Commission's resolution of 13 August 1948. The Plebiscite Administrator will be fully associated in these consultations.

C. Part I and Part II of the Commission's resolution of 13 August 1948 will be put into effect without delay. [*S/AC. 12/MA/1*, pp. 24–6.]

The resolution was not accepted by India, who declared that UNCIP had the duty to see that the well-organized Azad forces were disbanded, and that this must come ahead of any demilitarization. It was also during January that the first UN observers arrived in Kashmir.

On 10 January 1949 UNCIP submitted a second interim report (S/1196), which was noted by the Security Council which now asked it to return to the sub-continent at its earliest convenience. This second interim report mentioned (para. 7) that UNCIP had acquired the services of a Belgian officer, Lt-General Maurice Delvoie, as Military Adviser. Negotiations had been progressing. UNCIP arrived back on the sub-continent on 4 February 1949, and started to work on the implementation of the agreed principles. A general truce line was agreed upon.

On 28 April 1949 UNCIP submitted to both governments detailed truce proposals, requesting unreserved acceptance. This was not forthcoming. Meanwhile, Admiral Nimitz had been nominated as Plebiscite Administrator by the Secretary-General, in consultation with the two governments and with UNCIP.

It had been decided to see if talks direct between the military of each side could succeed where their political masters had failed—namely, in the actual demarcation of the cease-fire agreed upon in January. It was hoped that as a result of such a conference it would be possible for the two Commanders-in-Chief to submit mutually-agreed recommendations in respect of Part II (of UNCIP resolution of 13 August 1948) to their respective governments.

2. *Decisions reached by the Conference*

A. *In respect of part I of UNCIP resolution*
   (i) It was agreed that the cease-fire in Jammu and Kashmir should be advanced from an informal to a formal basis.
   (ii) It was agreed that the following action should be taken in order to further the satisfactory implementation of the cease-fire:—
   (a) The local commanders in the area *Chhota Qasinag, Richmargali* and *Marol* were authorized to make any slight adjustments in their dispositions to which they might mutually agree in order to avoid minor incidents. If the local commanders did not consider adjustment necessary, or were unable to reach agreement, they would remain in their present positions.
   (b) Pakistan Army required the use of the road *Mirpur–Jhangar–Kotli* for the maintenance of their troops. Similarly, Indian Army required the use of the road *Poonch–Uri* for the same purpose. It was agreed that the local commanders should confer for the purpose of reaching mutual agreement on a satisfactory method of achieving these two objects.

B. *In respect of part II of UNCIP resolution*
   It was agreed that the following proposals for the implementation of part II of the UNCIP resolution should be referred by the Commanders-in-Chief for approval to their respective Governments:
   (i) In order to create an atmosphere in which it will be possible for UNCIP to proceed with part III of their resolution, the suggested plan is that:
   (a) All raiders should be withdrawn as soon as possible from the state of Jammu and Kashmir.

(*b*) The *Azad* Kashmir forces should be relieved in the forward areas by Pakistan regular forces and concentrated in the rear areas. Pakistan nationals in the *Azad* Kashmir forces would then be withdrawn from the State of Jammu and Kashmir. At the same time Pakistan Army would adjust their dispositions so that only the barest minimum of regular troops were left on the existing cease-fire line, the bulk being withdrawn.

(*c*) It was agreed that both the Indian and Pakistan armies would give all facilities to the UNCIP required for the establishment of observer teams in the area of Jammu and Kashmir. It was suggested that observer groups should be formed consisting of neutral observers appointed by UNCIP, each with one Indian and one Pakistani officer.

(*d*) Regarding withdrawal of Pakistan Army, see UNCIP resolution part II, paragraph B 1.

3. Commander-in-Chief Pakistan Army strongly recommended that, in order to ensure without question that the spirit of the UNCIP resolution part II is carried out, the following should also be agreed to by the Indian Government:

(*a*) From those members of the present *Azad* forces who were nationals of Jammu and Kashmir State a Civil Armed Force should be formed as directed by the UNCIP for the purpose of maintaining law and order in the area at present occupied by Pakistan troops and *Azad* Kashmir forces; the Civil Armed Force to be under the control of the UNCIP, and that a small Pakistan Army nucleus should be appointed to supervise the training and organization of this Force and to ensure compliance with the orders of UNCIP. This nucleus of regular Pakistan Army personnel should be withdrawn when UNCIP was satisfied with the organization of the Civil Armed Force.

(*b*) That when the Civil Armed Force has been satisfactorily organized this force would be stationed as directed by the UNCIP for the purpose of maintaining law and order. When this Force was ready to assume its duties the Pakistan screen of regular troops mentioned in paragraph B (i) (*b*) above would be withdrawn.

C-in-C Indian Army undertook to bring this recommendation to the notice of the Government of India.

4. *Communication of decisions to Lieutenant-General Delvoie*

Lieutenant-General M. Delvoie then entered the conference and Commander-in-Chief, Indian Army, explained the decisions and recommendations which had been agreed. He emphasized that this information was being communicated to General Delvoie at this stage for information only. General Delvoie thanked the Conference for informing him of their decisions and recommendations and communicated his satisfaction at the agreements which had been reached.

5. *Exchange of Prisoners*

It was decided that all prisoners of war should be exchanged as soon as it was possible. Commander-in-Chief, Pakistan Army, will exchange regular and State Force troops man for man for similar Pakistan troops and *Azad* forces in Indian Army hands. When all raiders and Pathans who were at present in civil custody in India were ready to be exchanged, the remainder of the Indian Regular and State Force troops in Attock camp will be exchanged for them. *There will be no question of man for man in this last exchange.* DMO Pakistan pointed out that owing to climatic conditions it would not be possible at this juncture to repatriate prisoners of war at present in *Gilgit* and *Skardu*. Pakistan Army, however, undertook to make the best arrangements it could to make these prisoners comfortable until it was possible to repatriate them to India.

6. *Return of abducted women*

Commander-in-Chief, Indian Army, raised the question of the return of abducted women (of service personnel) and said that already eight or ten had been sent back by the Indian Army to Pakistan. Commander-in-Chief, Pakistan Army, said that orders had been issued and he would inform Commander-in-Chief, Indian Army, of progress. He asked Commander-in-Chief, Indian Army, to let him have details of individual cases. DMO Pakistan pointed out the difficulty of obtaining the return of women who had been abducted by tribesmen and asked Commander-in-Chief, Indian Army, to bear this in mind.

7. *Maintenance of detachments in the Kishenganga area*
The Indian Army agreed to permit the maintenance of *Azad* element in the Kishenganga Valley (*Gurais* sector) by air because of the detachments being cut off by snow.

8. *Reported cases of burning of villages in Jammu and Kashmir*
India agreed to make arrangements for Pakistan observers to fly in light aircraft over areas where the burning of villages was alleged in order to see for themselves the true state of affairs.

(*Signed*)	A. J. WILSON	(*Signed*)	S. P. KAPILA
	Lieutenant-Colonel		*Lieutenant-Colonel*
	GSO I(C-in-C. and COS Sectt)		*Military Assistant to*
	GHQ Pakistan		*C-in-C Indian Army*
	15th January 1949		15th January 1949

[*S/1430, ann. 47, 3rd Interim Report of UNCIP*, p. 170 (*SCOR, 4th yr, spec. suppl. 7*).]

In July 1949 these renewed efforts of UNCIP bore fruit, and following joint military meetings held in Karachi on 18–27 July, the Karachi Agreement was signed. The text of this agreement is given below (p. 334). Section I provided that UNCIP 'will station Observers where it deems necessary', thus confirming the potential of Security Council resolution S/726 of 21 April 1948, section 17.[21] Thus UNMOGIP was now firmly authorized and was stationed either side of the newly-agreed cease-fire line.[22] It has been there ever since.

The ensuing pages focus on UNMOGIP's role in the search for peace in Kashmir, while in Section 12 a summary is given of the major political developments which provided the framework within which UNMOGIP operated after its establishment.

At the time of the Karachi Agreement the following observations were included in the confidential briefing and instructions given to the observers:

Civil Administration
(*a*) The area controlled by the Indian Army consists of the Districts of Jammu, Kathua, Udhampur, Riasi, Baramulla, Anantnag, Chenani Jagir (a jagir is a territory whose jagirdar or rajah has certain independent rights of taxation and jurisdiction) and parts of Astore and Ladakh.

Under the Maharajah of Jammu and Kashmir, who declared the accession of his State to the Dominion of India in October 1947, there is a Ministry, headed by a Prime Minister, Sheikh Abdullah.

The Ministry governs through civil officers, namely a Governor in each Province, and a Wazir Wazarat (or District Magistrate) in each District. The Districts are subdivided for administrative and revenue purposes into Tehsils, each in the charge of a Tehsildar.

(*b*) The area controlled by the Pakistan Army consists of Mirpur, Poonch, Muzaffarabad, Gilgit, Gilgit Agency and parts of Ladakh and Astore.

In Mirpur, Poonch and Muzaffarabad, there is an 'Azad Kashmir Government', in revolt against the Maharajah. Its President is Sirdar Ibrahim, and its principal officers are 'District Magistrates' in each of the Districts.

[21] See below, pp. 331–3.
[22] For details of its positioning, see below, pp. 354–7.

Gilgit, Gilgit Agency and those parts of Ladakh and Astore which are controlled by the Pakistan Army are governed by a Political Agent of Pakistan with headquarters at Gilgit.

The States of Hunza and Nagir to the north of Gilgit are also in direct relationship with Pakistan. [*S/AC.12/MA/1*, p. 10.]

2

ENABLING RESOLUTIONS AND VOTING

ON 20 January 1948 the Security Council adopted the following resolution which had been drawn up as a result of the talks.

The Security Council,

Considering that it may investigate any dispute or any situation which might, by its continuance, endanger the maintenance of international peace and security and that, in the existing state of affairs between India and Pakistan, such an investigation is a matter of urgency,

Adopts the following resolution:

A. A Commission of the Security Council is hereby established, composed of representatives of three Members of the United Nations, one to be selected by India, one to be selected by Pakistan, and the third to be designated by the two so selected. Each representative on the Commission shall be entitled to select his alternates and assistants.

B. The Commission shall proceed to the spot as quickly as possible. It shall act under the authority of the Security Council and in accordance with the directions it may receive from it. It shall keep the Security Council currently informed of its activities and of the development of the situation. It shall report to the Security Council regularly, submitting its conclusions and proposals.

C. The Commission is invested with a dual function: (1) to investigate the facts pursuant to Article 34 of the Charter of the United Nations; (2) to exercise, without interrupting the work of the Security Council, any mediatory influence likely to smooth away difficulties; to carry out the directions given to it by the Security Council; and to report how far the advice and directions, if any, of the Security Council have been carried out.

D. The Commission shall perform the functions described in clause C: (1) in regard to the situation in the Jammu and Kashmir State set out in the letter of the representative of India addressed to the President of the Security Council, dated 1 January 1948, and in the letter from the Minister of Foreign Affairs of Pakistan addressed to the Secretary-General, dated 15 January 1948, when the Security Council so directs.

E. The Commission shall take its decision by majority vote. It shall determine its own procedure. It may allocate among its members, alternate members, their assistants, and its personnel such duties as may have to be fulfilled for the realization of its mission and the reaching of its conclusions.

F. The Commission, its members, alternate members, their assistants, and its personnel shall be entitled to journey, separately or together, wherever the necessities of their tasks may require, and, in particular, within those territories which are the theatre of the events of which the Security Council is seized.

G. The Secretary-General shall furnish the Commission with such personnel and assistance as it may consider necessary. [*SC res. S/654.*]

VOTING: 9–0–2.

For: Argentina, Belgium, Canada, China, Colombia, France, Syria, UK, USA.

Against: None.
Abstaining: Ukrainian SSR, USSR.

The Soviet Union abstained because she did not approve of the principle governing the establishment of the Commission. At the 230th meeting the Russian delegate explained that UNCIP should consist of, and represent, those states represented in the Security Council. He did not accept the view of the United Kingdom delegate that it was sufficient that Clause B kept the Security Council informed.

It was not until the detailed resolution of 21 April that authorization was given to UNCIP to use observers:

The Security Council,

Having considered the complaint of the Government of India concerning the dispute over the State of Jammu and Kashmir, having heard the representative of India in support of that complaint and the reply and counter complaints of the representative of Pakistan;

Being strongly of the opinion that the early restoration of peace and order in Jammu and Kashmir is essential and that India and Pakistan should do their utmost to bring about a cessation of all fighting;

Noting with satisfaction that both India and Pakistan desire that the question of the accession of Jammu and Kashmir to India or Pakistan should be decided through the democratic method of a free and impartial plebiscite;

Considering that the continuation of the dispute is likely to endanger international peace and security,

Reaffirms the Council's resolution of 17 January;

Resolves that the membership of the Commission established by the resolution of the Council of 20 January 1948 shall be increased to five and shall include, in addition to the membership mentioned in that resolution, representatives of . . . and . . . , and that if the membership of the Commission has not been completed within ten days from the date of the adoption of this resolution the President of the Council may designate such other Member or Members of the United Nations as are required to complete the membership of five;

Instructs the Commission to proceed at once to the Indian sub-continent and there place its good offices and mediation at the disposal of the Governments of India and Pakistan with a view to facilitating the taking of the necessary measures, both with respect to the restoration of peace and order and to the holding of a plebiscite by the two Governments, acting in co-operation with one another and with the Commission, and further instructs the Commission to keep the Council informed of the action taken under the resolution, and to this end;

Recommends to the Governments of India and Pakistan the following measures as those which in the opinion of the Council are appropriate to bring about a cessation of the fighting and to create proper conditions for a free and impartial plebiscite to decide whether the State of Jammu and Kashmir is to accede to India or Pakistan.

A. *Restoration of Peace and Order*

1. The Government of Pakistan should undertake to use its best endeavours:

(*a*) To secure the withdrawal from the State of Jammu and Kashmir of tribesmen and Pakistani nationals not normally resident therein who have entered the State for the purposes of fighting, and to prevent any intrusion into the State of such elements and any furnishing of material aid to those fighting in the State.

(*b*) To make known to all concerned that the measures indicated in this and the following paragraphs provide full freedom to all subjects of the State, regardless of creed, caste, or party, to express their views and to vote on the question of the accession of the State, and that therefore they should co-operate in the maintenance of peace and order.

2. The Government of India should:

(a) When it is established to the satisfaction of the Commission set up in accordance with the Council's resolution of 20 January that the tribesmen are withdrawing and that arrangements for the cessation of the fighting have become effective, put into operation in consultation with the Commission a plan for withdrawing their own forces from Jammu and Kashmir and reducing them progressively to the minimum strength required for the support of the civil power in the maintenance of law and order;

(b) Make known that the withdrawal is taking place in stages and announce the completion of each stage;

(c) When the Indian forces shall have been reduced to the minimum strength mentioned in (a) above, arrange in consultation with the Commission for the stationing of the remaining forces to be carried out in accordance with the following principles:

(i) That the presence of troops should not afford any intimidation or appearance of intimidation to the inhabitants of the State,

(ii) That as small a number as possible should be retained in forward areas,

(iii) That any reserve of troops which may be included in the total strength should be located within their present base area.

3. The Government of India should agree that, until such time as the Plebiscite Administration referred to below finds it necessary to exercise the powers of direction and supervision over the State forces and police provided for in Paragraph 8, they will be held in areas to be agreed upon with the Plebiscite Administrator.

4. After the plan referred to in paragraph 2 (a) above has been put into operation, personnel recruited locally in each district should so far as possible be utilized for the re-establishment and maintenance of law and order with due regard to protection of minorities, subject to such additional requirements as may be specified by the Plebiscite Administration referred to in paragraph 7.

5. If these local forces should be found to be inadequate, the Commission, subject to the agreement of both the Government of India and the Government of Pakistan, should arrange for the use of such forces of either Dominion as it deems effective for the purpose of pacification.

B. *Plebiscite*

6. The Government of India should undertake to ensure that the Government of the State invite the major political groups to designate responsible representatives to share equitably and fully in the conduct of the administration at the Ministerial level, while the plebiscite is being prepared and carried out.

7. The Government of India should undertake that there will be established in Jammu and Kashmir a Plebiscite Administration to hold a plebiscite as soon as possible on the question of the accession of the State to India or Pakistan.

8. The Government of India should undertake that there will be delegated by the State to the Plebiscite Administration such powers as the latter considers necessary for holding a fair and impartial plebiscite, including, for that purpose only, the direction and supervision of the State forces and police.

9. The Government of India should at the request of the Plebiscite Administration make available from the Indian forces such assistance as the Plebiscite Administration may require for the performance of its functions.

10. (a) The Government of India should agree that a nominee of the Secretary-General of the United Nations will be appointed to be the Plebiscite Administrator.

(b) The Plebiscite Administrator, acting as an officer of the State of Jammu and Kashmir should have authority to nominate his assistants and other subordinates and to draft regulations governing the plebiscite. Such nominees should be formally appointed and such draft regulations should be formally promulgated by the State of Jammu and Kashmir.

(c) The Government of India should undertake that the Government of Jammu and Kashmir will appoint fully qualified persons nominated by the Plebiscite Administrator to act as special magistrates within the State judicial system to hear cases which in the opinion of the Plebiscite Administrator have a serious bearing on the preparation for and the conduct of a free and impartial plebiscite.

(*d*) The terms of service of the Administrator should form the subject of a separate negotiation between the Secretary-General of the United Nations and the Government of India. The Administrator should fix the terms of service for his assistants and subordinates.

(*e*) The Administrator should have the right to communicate direct with the Government of the State and with the Commission of the Security Council and, through the Commission, with the Security Council, with the Governments of India and Pakistan and with their representatives with the Commission. It would be his duty to bring to the notice of any or all of the foregoing (as he in his discretion may decide) any circumstances arising which may tend, in his opinion, to interfere with the freedom of the plebiscite.

11. The Government of India should undertake to prevent and to give full support to the Administrator and his staff in preventing any threat, coercion or intimidation, bribery or other undue influence on the voters in the plebiscite, and the Government of India should publicly announce and should cause the Government of the State to announce this undertaking as an international obligation binding on all public authorities and officials in Jammu and Kashmir.

12. The Government of India should themselves and through the Government of the State declare and make known that all subjects of the State of Jammu and Kashmir, regardless of creed, caste or party, will be safe and free in expressing their views and in voting on the question of the accession of the State and that there will be freedom of the Press, speech and assembly and freedom of travel in the State, including freedom of lawful entry and exit.

13. The Government of India should use and should ensure that the Government of the State also use their best endeavours to effect the withdrawal from the State of all Indian nationals other than those who are normally resident therein or who on or since 15 August 1947 have entered it for a lawful purpose.

14. The Government of India should ensure that the Government of the State release all political prisoners and take all possible steps so that:

(*a*) All citizens of the State who have left it on account of disturbances are invited and are free, to return to their homes and to exercise their rights as such citizens;

(*b*) There is no victimization;

(*c*) Minorities in all parts of the State are accorded adequate protection.

15. The Commission of the Security Council should, at the end of the plebiscite, certify to the Council whether the plebiscite has or has not been really free and impartial.

C. *General Provisions*

16. The Governments of India and Pakistan should each be invited to nominate a representative to be attached to the Commission for such assistance as it may require in the performance of its task.

17. The Commission should establish in Jammu and Kashmir such observers as it may require of any of the proceedings in pursuance of the measures indicated in the foregoing paragraphs.

18. The Security Council Commission should carry out the tasks assigned to it herein.

[*SC res. S/726, 21 Apr. 1948.*]

VOTING: The resolution was voted on paragraph by paragraph.

Decisions: *At the 286th meeting, on 21 April 1948, the Council adopted the draft resolution (S/726) paragraph by paragraph. The last paragraph of the preamble, and paragraphs A 1 (a), A 1 (b) A 2 (a), A 3, A 6, A 7, A 9, and A 10 were adopted by eight votes, with three abstentions (Syria, Ukrainian SSR and the USSR). On the main part of paragraph A 5, (excluding the clause beginning with 'subject' and ending with 'Pakistan'), the vote was the same, with China, the Ukrainian SSR and the USSR abstaining. Paragraph A 2 (c) was adopted by seven votes, with four abstentions (France, Syria, the Ukrainian SSR and the USSR). Paragraph A 5 (from 'subject'* to *'Pakistan'*) *was adopted by seven votes, with four abstentions (Argentina, Syria, the Ukrainian SSR and the USSR). The rest of the text was adopted by nine votes, with two abstentions (Ukrainian SSR and the USSR). At the 287th meeting, on 23 April, Belgium and Colombia were added to the Commission by seven votes in favour to none against, with four abstentions. At the 289th meeting, on 7 May 1948, the President designated the United States as the third member of the Commission, in view of the failure of Argentina (selected by Pakistan) and Czechoslovakia (selected by India), to agree upon a third member. [A/620, Report of Security Council to General Assembly, GAOR, 3rd sess., p. 70.]*

The Syrian representative had indicated that he would feel obliged to abstain on a resolution which did not have the support of both parties. The Ukraine and the Soviet Union again abstained on the ground that UNCIP should be composed of Security Council nations.

When on 21 August 1948 the Security Council received a cable from the Chairman of UNCIP (S/987) asking for the appointment of twenty military observers, the general feeling of the Security Council was that the Chairman already had authority for this, and it was not necessary for the Security Council to inscribe the matter upon its agenda and act further.[1] The USSR dissented from this proposition, believing that someone had to select, appoint, and train the observers, and that the Secretary-General could not himself do this. The Security Council was 'in duty bound to consider the question and to decide how and on what principle these military observers are to be selected, and which countries are to send them'.[2] This view did not prevail, and it was the Secretary-General who carried out these tasks. At no stage, however, did the Soviet Union object to the use of observers as such.

The observers were finally established in Kashmir upon the signing on 27 July of the Karachi Agreement on a cease-fire. This was a direct bilateral agreement between India and Pakistan, and was not voted on by the Security Council.

I. INTRODUCTION

A. The military representatives of India and Pakistan met together in Karachi from 18 July to 27 July 1949 under the auspices of the Truce Sub-committee of the United Nations Commission for India and Pakistan.

B. The members of the Indian delegation were: Lieutenant General S. M. Shrinagesh, Major General K. S. Thimayya, Brigadier S. H. F. J. Manekshaw. As observers: Mr H. M. Patel, Mr. V. Sahay.

C. The members of the Pakistan delegation were: Major General W. J. Cawthorn, Major General Nazir Ahmad, Brigadier M. Sher Khan. As observers: Mr M. Ayub, Mr A. A. Khan.

D. The members of the Truce Sub-committee of the United Nations Commission for India and Pakistan were: Mr Hernando Samper (Colombia), Chairman; Mr William L. S. Williams (United States); Lieutenant General Maurice Delvoie, Military Adviser; Mr Miguel A. Marín, Legal Adviser.

II. AGREEMENT

A. *Considering:*

1. That the United Nations Commission for India and Pakistan, in its letter dated 2 July

---

[1] See below, p. 350.
[2] *SCOR*, 3rd yr, 356th mtg, p. 6.

1949 (annex 25), invited the Governments of India and Pakistan to send fully authorized military representatives to meet jointly in Karachi under the auspices of the Commission's Truce Sub-committee to establish a cease-fire line in the State of Jammu and Kashmir mutually agreed upon by the Governments of India and Pakistan;

2. That the United Nations Commission for India and Pakistan in its letter stated that 'The meetings will be for military purposes; political issues will not be considered,' and that 'They will be conducted without prejudice to negotiations concerning the truce agreement';

3. That in the same letter the United Nations Commission for India and Pakistan further stated that: 'The cease-fire line is a complement of the suspension of hostilities, which falls within the provisions of part I of the resolution of 13 August 1948, and can be considered separately from the questions relating to part II of the same resolution';

4. That the Governments of India and Pakistan, in their letters dated 7 July 1949 to the Chairman of the Commission, accepted the Commission's invitation to the military conference in Karachi;

B. *The delegations of India and Pakistan, duly authorized, have reached the following agreement:*

1. Under the provisions of part I of the resolution of 13 August 1948, and as a complement of the suspension of hostilities in the State of Jammu and Kashmir on 1 January 1949, a cease-fire line is established.

2. The cease-fire line runs from *Manawar* in the south, north to *Keran* and from *Keran* east to the glacier area, as follows:[3]

(*a*) The line from *Manawar* to the south bank of the *Jhelum* River at *Urusa* (inclusive to India) is the line now defined by the factual positions about which there is agreement between both parties. Where there has hitherto not been agreement, the line shall be as follows:

(i) In *Patrana* area: *Kohel* (inclusive to Pakistan) north along the *Khuwala Kas* Nullah up to Point 2276 (inclusive to India), thence to *Kirni* (inclusive to India).

(ii) *Khambha, Pir Satwan,* Point 3150 and Point 3606 are inclusive to India, thence the line runs to the factual position at *Bagla Gala,* thence to the factual position at Point 3300.

(iii) In the area south of *Uri* the positions of *Pir Kanthi* and *Ledi Gali* are inclusive to Pakistan.

(*b*) From the north bank of the *Jhelum* River the line runs from a point opposite the village of *Urusa* (NL 972109), thence north following the *Ballaseth Da Nar* Nullah (inclusive to Pakistan), up to NL 973140, thence northeast to *Chhota Qazinag* (Point 10657, incl usive to India), thence to NM 010180, thence to NM 037210, thence to Point 11825 (NM 025354, inclusive to Pakistan), thence to *Tutmari Gali* (to be shared by both sides, posts to be established 500 yards, on either side of the *Gali*), thence to the northwest through the first 'R' of *Burji Nar* to north of *Gadori,* thence straight west to just north of Point 9870, thence along the black line north of *Bijidhar* to north of *Batarasi,* thence to just south of *Sudpura,* thence due north to the *Kathaqazinag* Nullah, thence along the Nullah to its junction with the *Grangnar* Nullah, thence along the latter Nullah to *Kajnwala Pathra* (inclusive to India), thence across the *Danna* ridge (following the factual positions) to *Richmar Gali* (inclusive to India), thence north to *Thanda Katha* Nullah, thence north to the *Kishanganga* River. The line then follows the *Kishanganga* River up to a point situated between *Jargi* and *Tarban,* thence (all inclusive to Pakistan) to *Bankoran,* thence northeast to *Khori,* thence to the hill feature 8930 (in Square 9053), thence straight north to Point 10164 (in Square 9057), thence to Point 10323 (in Square 9161), thence northeast straight to *Guthur,* thence to *Bhutpathra,* thence to NL 980707, thence following the *Bugina* Nullah to the junction with the *Kishanganga* River at Point 4739. Thereafter the line follows the *Kishanganga* River to *Keran* and onwards to Point 4996 (NL 975818).

(*c*) From Point 4996 the line follows (all inclusive to Pakistan) the *Jamgar* Nullah eastward to Point 12124, to *Katware,* to Point 6678, then to the northeast to *Sarian* (Point 11279), to Point 11837, to Point 13090, to Point 12641, thence east again to Point 11142, thence to

---

[3] The detailed map relevant to para. 2 above is to be found in S/1430/Add. 2, 12 Dec. 1949.

12

Dhakki, thence to Point 11415, thence to Point 10301, thence to Point 7507, thence to Point 10685, thence to Point 8388, thence south-east to Point 11812. Thence the line runs (all inclusive to India) to Point 13220, thence across the River to the east to Point 13449 (*Durmat*), thence to Point 14586 (*Anzbari*), thence to Point 13554, thence to Milestone 45 on the *Burzil* Nullah, thence to the east to *Ziankal* (Point 12909), thence to the southeast to Point 11114, thence to Point 12216, thence to Point 12867, thence to the east to Point 11264, thence to *Karo* (Point 14985), thence to Point 14014, thence to Point 12089, thence following the track to Point 12879. From there the line runs to Point 13647 (*Karobal Gali*, to be shared by both sides). The cease-fire line runs thence through *Retagah Chhish* (Point 15316), thence through Point 15889, thence through Point 17392, thence through Point 16458, thence to *Marpo La* (to be shared by both sides), thence through Point 17561, thence through Point 17352, thence through Point 18400, thence through Point 16760, thence to (inclusive to India), *Dalunang*.

(*d*) From *Dalunang* eastwards the cease-fire line will follow the general line Point 15495, *Ishmam, Manus, Gangam, Gunderman*, Point 13620, *Junkar* (Point 17628), *Marmak, Natsara, Shangruti* (Point 17531), *Chorbat La* (Point 16700), *Chalunka* (on the *Shyok* River), *Khor*, thence north to the glaciers. This portion of the cease-fire line shall be demarcated in detail on the basis of the factual position as of 27 July 1949 by the local commanders, assisted by United Nations Military Observers.

C. The cease-fire line described above shall be drawn on a one-inch map (where available) and then be verified mutually on the ground by local commanders on each side with the assistance of the United Nations Military Observers, so as to eliminate any no-man's land. In the event that the local commanders are unable to reach agreement, the matter shall be referred to the Commission's Military Adviser, whose decision shall be final. After this verification, the Military Adviser will issue to each High Command a map on which will be marked the definitive cease-fire line.

D. No troops shall be stationed or operate in the area of the *Burzil* Nullah from south of *Minimarg* to the cease-fire line. This area is bounded on the west by the ridge leading northeast from *Dudgaikal* to Point 13071, to Point 9447, to Point 13466, to Point 13463, and on the east by the ridge running from Point 12470, to Point 11608, to Point 13004, to Point 13976, to Point 13450. Pakistan may, however, post troops on the western of the above ridges to cover the approaches to *Kamri Bal* Pass.

E. In any dispositions that may be adopted in consequence of the present agreement troops will remain at least 500 yards from the cease-fire line except where the *Kishanganga* River constitutes the line. Points which have been shown as inclusive to one party may be occupied by that party, but the troops of the other party shall remain at a distance of 500 yards.

F. Both sides shall be free to adjust their defensive positions behind the cease-fire line as determined in paragraphs A through E, inclusive, subject to no wire or mines being used when new bunkers and defences are constructed. There shall be no increase of forces or strengthening of defences in areas where no major adjustments are involved by the determination of the cease-fire line.

G. The action permitted by paragraph F above shall not be accompanied or accomplished by the introduction of additional military potential by either side into the State of Jammu and Kashmir.

H. Except as modified by paragraphs A to G, inclusive, above, the military agreements between the two High Commands relating to the cease-fire of 1 January 1949 shall continue to remain operative.

I. The United Nations Commission for India and Pakistan will station Observers where it deems necessary.

J. The delegations shall refer this agreement to their respective Governments for ratification. The documents of ratification shall be deposited with the United Nations Commission for India and Pakistan not later than 31 July 1949.

K. A period of thirty days from the date of ratification shall be allowed to each side to vacate the areas at present occupied by them beyond the cease-fire line as now determined.

Before the expiration of this thirty-day period there shall be no forward movement into areas to be taken over by either side pursuant to this agreement, except by mutual agreement between local commanders.

In faith whereof the undersigned sign this document in three original copies

Done in Karachi on 27 July 1949.

For the Government of India:

(*Signed*) S. M. SHRINAGESH

For the Government of Pakistan:

(*Signed*) J. CAWTHORN
Major General

For the United Nations Commission for India and Pakistan:

(*Signed*) Hernando SAMPER
M. DELVOIE

[*S/1430/Add. 1, 29 July 1949, ann. 26, Agreement between military representatives of India and Pakistan regarding the establishment of a cease-fire line in the State of Jammu and Kashmir.*]

3

FUNCTIONS AND MANDATE

UNMOGIP's functions are generally agreed to be those stemming from the so-called Karachi Agreement between India and Pakistan of 27 July 1949. However, the nucleus of UNMOGIP was already in existence.

On 21 April 1948 the Security Council gave instructions to UNCIP, which it had established on 20 January 1948 by resolution S/654. UNCIP was instructed to proceed to the sub-continent to lend its good offices to attempts to restore peace and order, and to hold a plebiscite in the area. In paragraph 17 of this long and detailed resolution, it was provided: '17. The Commission should establish in Jammu and Kashmir such observers as it may require of any of the proceedings in pursuance of the measures indicated in the foregoing paragraphs.'[1]

On 13 August 1948 UNCIP had proposed to the parties that they should agree to a cease-fire, make arrangements for troop withdrawals, and meet to prepare a plebiscite. In partial fulfilment, on 1 January 1949 a cease-fire was announced. No further progress was made, in spite of UNCIP's efforts, in proceeding to a mutual withdrawal of troops and a plebiscite. UNCIP therefore decided, in July 1949, to proceed on the military plane alone, and called together the military representatives of India and Pakistan, in Karachi, to define a demarcation line. It was agreed that this should be without prejudice to

[1] S/726, 21 Apr. 1948.

political issues. Agreement was reached on 27 July 1949 and the Karachi Agreement stipulated in detail the cease-fire line. In paragraph I it provided that 'The United Nations Commission for India and Pakistan will station observers where it deems necessary.'

In paragraph B2 (*d*) the Agreement had stated:

From *Dalunang* eastwards the cease-fire line will follow the general line Point 15495, *Ishmam, Manus, Gangam, Gunderman*, Point 13620, *Junkar* (Point 17628), *Marmak, Natsara, Shangruti* (Point 17531), *Chorbat La* (Point 16700), *Chalunka* (on the *Shyok* River), *Khor*, thence north to the glaciers. This portion of the cease-fire line shall be demarcated in detail on the basis of the factual position as of 27 July 1949 by the local commanders, assisted by United Nations Military Observers.

Paragraph C continued:

The cease-fire line described above shall be drawn on a one-inch map (where available) and then be verified mutually on the ground by local commanders on each side with the assistance of the United Nations Military Observers, so as to eliminate any no-man's land. In the event that the local commanders are unable to reach agreement, the matter shall be referred to the Commission's Military Adviser, whose decision shall be final. After this verification, the Military Adviser will issue to each High Command a map on which will be marked the definitive cease-fire line. [*S/1430/Add. 1, 29 July, 1949, ann. 26.*]

After this a cease-fire was ordered in January 1949, but before the detailed demarcation of the Karachi Agreement of July 1949, Lt-General Maurice Delvoie of Belgium had been appointed Military Adviser of UNCIP. He was given the task—among others—of organizing a team of UN military observers (as already authorized under resolution S/726) who would control and check the cease-fire agreement as soon as it could be made operational.[2] The first military observers arrived on the sub-continent on 24 January 1949; and six weeks after the cease-fire observers were operating on both sides of the cease-fire line. The Military Adviser was thus both chief of the observers and adviser to UNCIP on tactical and demilitarization problems.

Early in February 1949 the Military Adviser provided the Chairman of UNCIP with the following information:

From low-flying planes, as well as by car and by jeep, I have inspected both the Pakistan and Indian fronts.

Observations common to both fronts:

(1) They are sited on very difficult mountains.

(2) They are very long.

(3) The communications to the rear and flanks, are very awkward, and supplies must sometimes be dropped by planes to isolated garrisons.

(4) There are no continuous lines, and this allows infiltrations and manœuvres by surprise. Each party endeavours to hold the summits of the ranges, which provide outstanding observation posts, to control the movements in the valleys.

(5) The conditions of life of the troops are very bad owing to the climate, the lack of shelter as well as of local resources.

---

[2] This information is derived from the excellent article of Sylvain Lourié, 'The United Nations Military Observer Group in India and Pakistan', *Int. Org.* (1955), pp. 19–31. M. Lourié was on the staff of the UN Commission for Pakistan, and has drawn on both personal experience and on matters contained in the documentary series S/AC.12/MA/1, p. 13.

To allow for easier supplies for both armies, it is desirable that:
(1) The blown-up bridges should be rebuilt.
(2) The first line should be rectified so as to give to each party a better use of the road-net. . . . [*S/AC.12/MA/2*, pp. 1–2.]

Further tasks devolved upon the Military Adviser following the talks at Commander-in-Chief level which were held on 11 February 1949.

On 14 March 1950 the Security Council replaced UNCIP with a UN Representative (S/1469). It was also decided to split the functions performed by the Military Adviser. Henceforth the observer group and its Chief were to be separated from the political work of the UN Representative. A new Chief Military Observer was thus appointed (Brigadier Angle of Canada) who had no duties towards the UN Representative.[3] The UN Representative was assigned Lt-General Courtney Hodges as his personal Military Adviser.

NOTES BY THE MILITARY ADVISER ON THE MEETING OF THE TWO COMMANDERS-IN-CHIEF ON 15 JANUARY 1949

Today, January the 15th, after their meeting, the two Commanders-in-Chief called me to impart to me the conditions they had agreed upon.

They divided their task into:
(1) A first part, entirely in their competence, which could be immediately achieved.
(2) A second part, for which the agreement of their respective Governments would be needed. This part being secret, none of its details have been communicated to the press.

Part One
Three main points must be dealt with:
(1) The areas occupied by the Armies have each been divided into three sectors. The opposing sector-commanders are requested to settle all incidents between themselves and to refer to higher authorities in case of disagreement only.
(2) Roads, held by detachments of one Army, but controlled by detachments of the over-looking ranges, must become the object of particular agreements in order to avoid all incidents.
(3) When one of the Armies needs to use the whole of a road, part of which is held by the other Army, to supply its troops, it will be allowed to do so. On my request, both Commanders-in-Chief agreed to restore the communications by road between Srinagar and Rawalpindi, and to rebuild the necessary bridges. In addition, telephonic liaisons between these two localities will be restored.

Part Two
It is understood that the tribesmen will be completely withdrawn from the Pakistani-held Kashmir area. In that area only the Azads who are Kashmir citizens will be kept, all the others being withdrawn.

Pakistan shall also withdraw its regular troops, leaving only a minimum of them with the task of controlling armed civilian elements, so as to prevent the latter creating incidents similar to those which arose when fires, probably caused by peasants burning herbs for manure in their fields, were mistaken for unfriendly acts. The Commanders-in-Chief consider there must be a police force strong enough to maintain law and order in the parts of Kashmir occupied by both Armies.

The Commanders-in-Chief suggest that in the Pakistani-occupied areas some civilians should be armed and enlisted in an organization to be called 'Civil Armed Force'. This force

---

[3] Lourié, *Int. Org.*, 1955, pp. 24–5.

would be composed of Kashmir citizens and would be under the leadership of the Pakistan Army. The strength of that force would be determined by the Military Adviser of the Commission and in agreement with the Commission. It is understood that the remainder of the Azads would be discharged. A few battalions, with a core of regular soldiers entrusted with the maintenance of discipline, would remain in the part of Kashmir at present held by Pakistan. As soon as the 'Civil Armed Force' would give sufficient guarantees of discipline, those regulars would be withdrawn. While Pakistan carries on the withdrawal of its forces, India would thin out its own. The strength of the Indian forces to remain in Kashmir should be decided by the Commission. When the withdrawal of troops will take place, observers will be sited at compulsory check points, so as to control the departure of the troops. Observers will stay at those points so as to control the ulterior movements of the troops, and to make sure that any movement from the rear to the front is justified by a relief and is not a process of reinforcement. Already now, both Commanders-in-Chief agree upon a total exchange of prisoners, including women. The Commander-in-Chief of the Pakistan Army insisted that the tribesmen should be liberated as well as the regulars, so as to prevent any difficulty between Pakistan and the tribes. The Commander-in-Chief of the Indian Army agreed upon this. Some Indian soldiers who are prisoners in the very high mountains—and who are at present well treated and supplied by the Pakistan Army—will probably not be released before the end of the winter as it would be very dangerous to undertake earlier the journey in those snowbound parts. [*S/AC.12/MA/4*, pp. 1-3.]

The procedure for implementing UNMOGIP's functions was gradually established.

4. Investigation of the breaches of cease-fire

A. General:

It was agreed upon by both High Commands that from 1 January 1949, troops would not advance or patrol beyond their forward positions, and that neither side would try to increase its military potential by bringing more troops or war-like stores into the territory of the state or by improving defensive positions.

B. Procedure:

When military observers were informed by a local commander in the field that the opposing troops had infringed this agreement, they contacted their opposite number. Together they interviewed the responsible commander and proceeded to the location of the alleged incident to conduct an investigation. They reported their findings, along with their recommendations, to Control Headquarters. . . .

The Military Adviser submitted to the two Armies a procedure for reporting alleged violations by local Commanders. This proposal was accepted, and helped to eliminate numerous incidents. Further, on June 7, after observers had complained that Commanders failed to provide them with sufficient information on which they could base their investigations, the Military Adviser suggested to both Commanders-in-Chief that local commanders reporting a complaint of cease-fire violations be considered personally responsible for its foundation in fact.

At the beginning of September, the Military Adviser obtained the agreement of the two Armies on the following precise definition of a breach of the cease-fire:

1. Crossing of the cease-fire line;

2. Firing and use of explosives within five miles of the cease-fire line without prior warning to the military observers;

3. New wiring or mining of positions;

4. Reinforcing of existing defensive positions with men or war-like stores;

5. Forward movement from outside into the state of Jammu and Kashmir of any warlike stores, equipment and personnel other than reliefs and maintenance;

6. Flying of aircraft over the other side's territory. . . .

5. *Activities of the Military Adviser with the Truce Sub-Committee*

Many problems relating to discussions on implementation of Part II of the Resolution of 13 August 1948 had a military significance. Two of the principal problems were disbandment of the Azad Kashmir forces and withdrawal of the Pakistan army and the bulk of the Indian troops.

a. *Disposal of the Azad Kashmir forces*

At the meeting of 15 January 1949 (Docs. S/AC.12/MA/3 and MA/4) the two Commanders-in-Chief agreed to present to their Governments proposals for the formation, under the supervision of the Commission, of a civil armed force composed of members of the Azad Kashmir Forces who were nationals of Jammu and Kashmir.

On 8 February, Pakistan accepted these proposals, but on 12 February the Government of India informed the Commission that they could not adhere to them (S/AC.12/MA/5).

In an effort to meet the opposing points of view, the Military Adviser contacted on 25 February Gen. Sir Douglas Gracey, C-in-C Pakistan Army, and suggested that the civil armed force be put under operational control of a senior UN military observer. Gen. Gracey agreed in principle, but insisted that the disbanding of the Azad Kashmir forces could not be considered.

At the meeting of the Truce Sub-Committee on 9 March, the Pakistan representative presented a plan for the reorganization of these forces. In its memorandum dated 28 March (S/AC.12/166) the Government of India repeated its opposition to the scheme.

b. *Withdrawal of the Pakistan Forces and of the Bulk of the Indian Forces*

The main difficulties facing the Military Adviser under this problem were:

(i) To determine what constituted the 'bulk' of the Indian forces, at the same time taking into account the wish of the Government of India to maintain after the truce sufficient forces in Jammu and Kashmir to protect the State against external aggression. (Part 3, Para. 2, Indian reply to Comm. Resolution dated 20 August 1949.)

(ii) To synchronize the withdrawals of the two armies in conformity with Para. 10 of Appendix I of the letter of the Commission dated 27 August 1948 to the Government of Pakistan (S/AC.12/55).

After consultations with the two High Commands, the Military Adviser presented a definite plan (Annex 4) for the implementation of points A.1, B.1, and B.2 of the Resolution of 13 August 1948. This plan was incorporated in the truce terms presented by the Commission to the two Governments on 15 April, and, with some alterations, in the proposals of 28 April.

At the request of the Chairman of the Commission, the Military Adviser personally assured the C-in-C Pakistan Army of the fairness of these proposals before they were submitted to the Governments.

When on 17 June, the Government of India informed the Commission of its position in the question of the withdrawal of the bulk of its forces (S/AC.12/214) the Military Adviser submitted a statement (S/AC.12/MA.8) in which he showed that the troops India proposed to withdraw did not, in his opinion, constitute the bulk of its forces.

On 27 June, the Military Adviser discussed at length this problem with Maj. Gen. Kalwant Singh, Chief of General Staff, Indian Army, but could not reach a compromise, as the Indian High Command considered that the situation existing on 13 August 1948 had been altered. (S/AC.12/MA.9).

6. *Demarcation of the Cease-fire Line*

The Cease-fire Agreement in January provided that troops of the two armies would remain on the positions they occupied on 1 January 1949. However, precise information on these positions was lacking, mainly in the northern areas where communications were hampered by snow and terrain. The principal dispute here concerned the Burzil Pass area (S/AC.12/MA.7).

In most sectors a wide no-man's land separating the troops was a constant source of friction and alleged incidents. On 17 February, the Military Adviser recommended to the Commission the establishment of a truce-line eliminating all no-man's land (S/AC.12/124).

At the meetings of the Truce-Sub-Committee on 9 and 12 March, (S/AC.12/TC/SR.1 and 2) the military representatives of India and Pakistan reached an agreement on a cease-fire line, except in the following sectors:

(1) the vicinity of Patrana,
(2) the vicinity of Aniwas,
(3) between Chakhoti and Tithwal,
(4) between Keran and the eastern Tilel valley.

These gaps and the inaccuracy of the map on which the line agreed upon was drawn resulted in numerous difficulties and disputes.

Having discussed the problems on 3 May with Gen. Thimmaya, commanding the Northern Indian front, and on 13 May with Gen. Gracey, C-in-C Pakistan Army, the Military Adviser concluded that the establishment on purely military grounds, of a precise cease-fire line easily recognizable on the ground was an urgent necessity. Such a line should be demarcated, even if no agreement was reached on implementation of the Truce.

On 2 July, the Commission invited the two Governments to send military representatives to Karachi to discuss the demarcation of a cease-fire line for the entire State of Jammu and Kashmir.

As a basis for discussions, the Military Adviser drew a compromise line, taking into account the point of view of Pakistan as outlined in the map submitted at the meeting of the Truce Sub-committee on 12 March, and the point of view of India which the C-in-C Indian Army had developed to him during an informal meeting on 8 July. (S/AC.12/MA.10).

The joint military meetings were held in Karachi from 18 to 27 July 1949, and full agreement establishing a cease-fire line was signed (S/AC.12/RC.4). It was also decided at Karachi that this line would be drawn on a one-inch map and then verified on the ground by local commanders of either side with the assistance of the military observers; further, that whenever local commanders could not reach agreement, the Military Adviser would give a final decision.

The Military Adviser immediately issued instructions to the military observers, giving top priority to this task.

The line, covering more than 500 miles was divided into eight sectors covering the areas of Manawar, Kotli, Poonch, Uri, Tithwal, Keran, Gurais and Kargil. The observers in charge of each sector called meetings of the opposing commanders and surveyed with them the line on the ground, making a written description of the natural boundaries and establishing signs such as marks on trees or stone cairns.

The military observers then supervised the forward movement or the withdrawal of the troops adjusting to the new line.

The Military Adviser was called upon to give his decision in the areas of Kambah, Hajira-Kotli, Uri, Tutmari-Gali, Gurais, Marpola, Kargil and Khor. Because of these differences, and of the extremely difficult terrain, the movement of troops was completed on 31 October, instead of 31 August as had been planned.

By 1 November 1949, a cease-fire line for the entire state of Jammu and Kashmir had been demarcated on the ground. [*S/AC.12/MA/13*, pp. 8–14.]

By September 1950 Sir Owen Dixon (the UN Representative) noted in his report:

10. The United Nations had established a corps of officers provided by various countries to act as observers and assist in maintaining the cease-fire along the line and to secure compliance by the parties with the terms of the armistice. Incidents in which the troops on one side fired on troops on the other or upon a civilian or civilians occurred frequently at some point or another on the line; but the incidents nearly all proved of small importance relatively and

none threatened a general outbreak of hostilities. [*S/1791, 15 Sept. 1950, Report to Security Council of Sir Owen Dixon, UN Representative for India and Pakistan.*]

In March 1951 the Security Council confirmed in its resolution S/2017/rev. 1 that 'the Military Observer Group shall continue to supervise the cease-fire in the State' (para. 7).

In the negotiations for the demilitarization of Kashmir, various roles were suggested for UNMOGIP. Pakistan, for example, proposed that 'the United Nations military observers should ensure that the withdrawal of forces on both sides proceeds according to the detailed plan'[4] and that UNMOGIP should also supervise the second stage of demilitarization envisaged in paragraph 4 of the resolution of 5 January 1959.[5] The Military Adviser to the UN Representative prepared a plan of demilitarization (S/2485) under which UNMOGIP would have been greatly increased 'to assure that there is no violation of the ceasefire agreements and to assist in demobilization of forces and give stability and backing to local governments in maintaining order'.[6] The subsequent UN representative, Frank Graham, addressed questionnaires to India and Pakistan to see if they would be willing to accept the stationing of observers in sufficient numbers for the purpose of demilitarization.[7] However, the demilitarization plans were never implemented and UNMOGIP was not called upon to undertake duties in this regard.

UNMOGIP's duties included not only observation of the cease-fire line, but also 'the competence to decide whether or not there is a violation of the Cease-Fire Agreement by either side'.[8] This adjudicative function has been carried out discreetly and with a minimum of publicity. It has not been customary to publish the awards of the Chief Military Observer, and in this way an attempt has been made to keep military facts distinct from political propaganda. In 1964–5, however, when the situation began rapidly to deteriorate, the parties themselves took to referring, in statements or letters to the Security Council, to awards given by the Chief Observer of UNMOGIP. These statements provide some illustration of this particular UNMOGIP function:

51. The Council will remember that during the period before Pakistan called for the last meeting of the Council on 16 January, Pakistan had taken every opportunity of creating difficulties and bringing about an atmosphere of crisis in Kashmir. In his letter of 1 November 1963 (S/5450), the representative of Pakistan had alleged military preparations by India of the cease-fire line and disturbances of the peace in the area of Chaknot. This Pakistani allegation was investigated by the United Nations Chief Military Observer who came to the conclusion that India had concentrated no troops in or in the vicinity of Chaknot, but that, on the contrary, Pakistani troops had been reinforced in the area contrary to the Cease-fire Agreement. Accordingly, he gave an award of 'no violation' against India and an award of 'violation' against Pakistan (S/5503). [*Per the representative of India, SCOR, 19th yr, 1104th mtg, 17 Mar. 1964.*]

India had published the terms of the findings on Chaknot of the Chief Military Observer, General R. H. Nimmo:

4 S/1791, App., para. 9 (vii).   5 Ibid. para. 13 (v).
6 S/2485, para. B.2 (a).   7 S/2448, ann. III.
                    8 S/5450, 1 Nov. 1963, para. 5.

12*

I am requested by my Government to enclose a copy of a communication received from the United Nations Chief Military Observer, giving his awards on cease-fire violation complaints lodged by India and Pakistan in regard to Chaknot. It will be seen that this communication from the Chief Military Observer vindicates the position which my Government took in my letter of 27 November 1963.

It is requested that this communication be brought to the notice of the members of the Security Council.

(*Signed*) B. N. CHAKRAVARTY
Permanent Representative of India to the United Nations

LETTER DATED 29 NOVEMBER 1963 FROM LT-GEN. R. H. NIMMO TO LT.-GEN. MOTI SAGAR, CHIEF OF THE GENERAL STAFF OF THE INDIAN ARMY

The following ACFVs (awarded cease-fire violations) were received on 21 October 1963 and 19 October 1963 respectively:

1. *Tangdhar 97*
'Pakistani troops in the area south-east of Kel have been reinforced.'
Investigation by United Nations Observers disclosed that troops had in fact reinforced the area contrary to the Karachi Agreement, and I am therefore obliged to award a Violation by Pakistan.
It would appear that the troops were moved on account of reports of Indian concentrations on the opposite side of the cease-fire line, which were unfounded. The troops have since been returned to base.

2. *Skardu 29*
'Indian troops have concentrated near cease-fire line in the Chaknot area at Danna and Tsuntwar.'
United Nations Observers were unable to find any trace of troop concentrations, and a decision of No Violation is given in this case.

(*Signed*) R. H. NIMMO

[*S/5503, Letter dated 3 Jan. 1964 from representative of India to President of Security Council.*]

In April 1964 the Indian representative referred to Pakistan newspaper reports on certain incidents on the Kel sector of the cease-fire line, and stated:

The version . . . has been proved to be a fabrication by no less an authority than the United Nations Military Observer Group in India and Pakistan, which investigated the incident . . . The award given by the Chief Military Observer states (*vide* Letter No. F. 326–60, dated 26 March 1964):

'. . . Extensive investigations were carried out by United Nations Observers in the area. These were started whilst physical evidence was still discernible in the snow and on the rocks by the river. There is no doubt that the Indian platoon, moving northwards towards Bor, was ambushed by Pakistan troops on the Indian side of the cease-fire line in the vicinity mentioned in the complaint. Fire was also directed from across the Kishenganga River. Two Indians escaped; nine were captured; and the remainder are missing, believed killed. The bodies have not been located by United Nations Observers.'

Violation by Pakistan for crossing the cease-fire line.
Violation by Pakistan for firing. [*S/5668, 24 Apr. 1964, Letter from representative of India to President of Security Council*, para. 4.]

The Chief Observer also had authority to make recommendations to the parties for the better observance of the cease-fire:

. . . As far back as 1957, the Indian military authorities reported the illegal activities of Pakistan armed civilians to the United Nations Chief Military Observer, who not only took up the matter with the Pakistan military authorities but also obtained an assurance of good conduct from them. In his letter No. CMO/92, dated 25 June 1958, the Chief Military Observer stated:

> 'I have drawn the attention of GHQ Pakistan to the advisability of exercising stricter control over the activities of civilians close to the cease-fire line, particularly in relation to the use of explosives.'

Again, in his letter No. CMO/115 dated 23 July 1958, the Chief Military Observer informed India as follows:

> 'I have had assurances from the Chief of Staff, Pakistan Army, that immediate steps will be taken to control the civilians in this area on the Pakistan side of the cease-fire line'.

[S/5911, *21 Aug. 1964, Letter from representative of India to President of Security Council*, para. 3.]

Thus it will be seen that the broad function of supervising the implementation of the Karachi Agreement and so contributing to its effectiveness, entails the investigation of complaints, adjudication upon them, and the making of recommendations where necessary.[9] If the matter is not settled satisfactorily in accordance with his recommendations to military observers in the field, the Chief Military Observer may take up the issue with army headquarters in Delhi or Rawalpindi. Although the control of civilians within a 500-yard zone along the cease-fire line is carried out by the local civil police, UNMOGIP becomes involved when civilian incidents take on a military flavour.[10]

UNMOGIP's functions also entail recording the identity and disposition of units of the two armies as well as any general troop information which might be covered by the provisions of the Karachi Agreement. The Indian and Pakistani armies submit a periodic report of their units to the Chief Military Observer. All such information is treated by UN observers as 'Top Secret'.[11]

Like all UN Forces and observer groups, UNMOGIP had developed a detailed practice over the years for fulfilling its broad mandate as specified in the Karachi Agreement:

[9] Further details are provided in Lourié (*Int. Org.*, 1955, p. 28): 'As soon as a complaint of alleged cease-fire violations or border incidents is registered, it is promptly and thoroughly investigated by the United Nations team which either through its frequent visits and inspection tours detected it or to which such report was dispatched either by Control Headquarters or by the "opposing number", that is the opposite Field Observer team on the ground. . . . On receipt of the complaint, an examination is made by the team to determine whether an actual violation of the Cease-Fire Agreement has occurred. First it checks to be sure that the local commander has confirmed the facts. The next step is to investigate on the spot the alleged violations and obtain all relevant details. . . . In order to check all accounts and substantiate the complaint, the United Nations team may call on witnesses provided their interview retains an informal character and no oath be administered. As soon as it has completed its investigation, the observer team reports to United Nations Control Headquarters setting out in three distinct chapters its factual findings, its conclusions and finally, its recommendations concerning the action to be taken by either army or by the Chief Military Observer.'

[10] '. . . there are some military encounters (over civilians) between representatives of the two armies who take it upon themselves to police the civilian territory. Observers are therefore enjoined to encourage the military commanders on both sides to desist from using their troops for that purpose . . . (In any event) the observers must ensure that such troops not be permitted to enter the 500 yard zone on either side of the line' (ibid. p. 30).

[11] Ibid. p. 29.

4. By subsequent agreed interpretations of the Agreement, a number of points were clarified, including six categories of activity constituting breaches of the cease-fire, viz.:

(*a*) Crossing of the cease-fire line, or infringement of the provision of the Karachi Agreement concerning the 500-yard zone. . . .[12]

(*b*) Firing and use of explosives within 5 miles of the cease-fire line without advising the United Nations observers well in advance.

(*c*) New wiring or mining of any positions.

(*d*) Reinforcing of existing forward defended localities with men or warlike stores, or strengthening of defences in areas where no major adjustments are involved by the determination of the cease-fire line.

(*e*) Forward movement, from outside the State of Jammu and Kashmir of any warlike stores, equipment and personnel, other than reliefs and maintenance.

(*f*) Flying of aircraft over the other side's territory.

5. The Chief Military Observer of UNMOGIP directs his observers to undertake an impartial investigation of every alleged breach of the Karachi Agreement and, after consideration of the verified facts, submits the finding to the two armies in order that, with their co-operation, the conditions of the cease-fire agreement may be safeguarded. In short, UNMOGIP functions on the basis of a detailed cease-fire agreement, subsequently clarified by a series of agreed interpretations, with which it has had more than fifteen years of working experience. [*S/6888, 9 Nov. 1965, Report by Secretary-General relating to an aspect of the procedures employed in observing and reporting on the cease-fire.*]

The outbreak of major hostilities in 1965 made it necessary for the Secretary-General publicly to remind UN members of UNMOGIP's functions, and the area to which they related:

3. The United Nations maintains UNMOGIP with its 45 observers along the CFL of almost 500 miles, about half of which is in high mountains and is very difficult of access. UNMOGIP exercises the quite limited function of observing and reporting, investigating complaints from either party of violations of the CFL and the cease-fire and submitting the resultant findings on those investigations to each party and to the Secretary-General, and keeping the Secretary-General informed in general on the way in which the cease-fire agreement is being kept. Because the role of UNMOGIP appears frequently to be misunderstood, it bears emphasis that the operation has no authority or function entitling it to enforce or prevent anything or to try to ensure that the cease-fire is respected. [*S/6651, 3 Sept. 1965, Report of Secretary-General on situation in Kashmir.*]

In 1965 these basic duties along the cease-fire line were directed to the particular needs of the new situation. By resolution 209 of 4 September 1965 the Security Council ordered a new cease-fire, and called upon the two governments to respect the existing cease-fire line and to withdraw to their own side of it. India and Pakistan were called upon 'to co-operate fully with the United Nations Military Observer Group in India and Pakistan . . . in its task of supervising the observance of the cease-fire'.[13] By resolution 211 on 20 September 1965 the Council had demanded that 'both Governments [should] issue orders for a cease-fire . . . and a subsequent withdrawal of all armed personnel to the positions held by them before 5 August 1965' (para. 2). Although the 1965

---

[12] The Karachi Agreement (see pp. 334–7) provided that troops would normally remain at least 500 yards from the cease-fire line, and that there should be no increase of forces or strengthening of defences.

[13] Security Council Res. 209, 4 Sept. 1965, para. 3.

cease-fire could be regarded as parallel with the one under the Karachi Agreement of 1949, two major differences existed: the first was that a detailed series of agreed interpretations had by now evolved on the supervising of the Karachi Agreement, whereas for the new one 'there is no agreed list of activities which are regarded as constituting breaches of the cease-fire and, especially, there is as of now, no agreed definition and demarcation of the actual over-all cease-fire line itself' (S/6888). The second major difference was that the Karachi Agreement was limited to the cease-fire line in Kashmir, whereas the 1965 fighting had taken place on a much wider front.

The Secretary-General regarded it as necessary to separate the supervision of the cease-fire and withdrawals along the Kashmir cease-fire line from the supervision of the cease-fire and withdrawals outside of Kashmir: UNMOGIP only had authority for the former task. In other words:

> The UNMOGIP is thus limited in its terms of reference and function to the cease-fire line in Kashmir, and the Secretary-General assumes no authority on his part to extend the scope of UNMOGIP's function beyond the CFL. Unfortunately, the conflict between India and Pakistan has extended beyond the Kashmir CFL to the borders of the two countries. Therefore, in the absence of any Security Council resolution expanding the scope and authority of UNMOGIP, it was necessary to set up a new operation in order to carry out fully the directive of the Security Council in paragraph 2 of its resolution 211 (1965) of 20 September. The new operation for this purpose, called the United Nations India–Pakistan Observation Mission (UNIPOM), with its broader scope, is based, therefore, on the Security Council resolution of 20 September. In the message of 23 September (S/6699/Add. 2), it may be pointed out, the Secretary-General stated that the two operations, UNMOGIP and UNIPOM, will be 'closely co-ordinated, administratively and operationally. [S/6738, 2 Oct. 1965, aide-mémoire of 25 Sept. 1965 from Secretary-General to representative of India.]

The Government of India was initially very unenthusiastic about the establishment of UNIPOM[14] and the Secretary-General's interpretation of the limits of UNMOGIP's authority, though it came to accept the situation. Pakistan, by contrast, approved of the Secretary-General's views from the outset.[15] India contended that there was already legal authority for a role for UNMOGIP beyond the Kashmir cease-fire line:

> . . . At one time the scope and functions of the UNMOGIP were expanded by agreement between the Chief Military Observer, on the one hand, and the local army commanders of India and Pakistan on the other, without reference to the Security Council, to include investigation of border incidents eastward from the south end of the cease-fire line at Manawar in a sector of the border between India and Pakistan in Jammu. [S/6735, 1 Oct. 1965, Letter of 30 Sept. 1965 from representative of India to Secretary-General.]

The Secretary-General replied:

> Speaking for myself only, I would say without hesitation that if, with regard to the observance of the cease-fire and withdrawals called for by the Security Council resolutions, there were to be agreement between the Chief Military Observer on the one hand and the local army commanders of India and Pakistan on the other, or agreement between India and Pakistan directly, that the scope of UNMOGIP should extend beyond Kashmir and the Kashmir CFL and

---

[14] For a detailed study of UNIPOM see below, Part 5.
[15] See below, p. 444.

cover the entire border between India and Pakistan, I could readily agree that a single operation would suffice. I do not and cannot, of course, speak for the Security Council on this, although I have no doubt that such an agreement would carry great weight in any consideration of the matter by the Council. To my regret, I am bound to add that the possibility of such an agreement in the prevailing circumstances would appear rather remote. [*S/6738*, p. 146.]

Pakistan emphasized that the agreement referred to by India showed not that authority existed for extending UNMOGIP's role, but rather the reverse:

In his letter of 30 September 1965 (S/6735) the Permanent Representative of India has adduced the instance of an agreement between the local army commanders of India and Pakistan and the Chief Military Observer in Kashmir to justify his request for the expansion of the scope and function of the UNMOGIP beyond Kashmir. This instance itself shows that any extension of the scope and function of UNMOGIP requires the consent of both parties.
5. Moreover, the agreement mentioned by the Indian Representative did not in any way extend the function of the UNMOGIP to the international frontier between India and Pakistan. When the Indian Representative talks of the 'border between India and Pakistan in Jammu', he talks of something which does not exist. The province of Jammu in the State of Jammu and Kashmir borders, for the great part, on Pakistan and, for the smaller part, on India; there is and can be no border between India and Pakistan in Jammu. [*S/6751, 5 Oct. 1965, Letter from representative of Pakistan to Secretary-General.*]

On 4 October 1965 the Secretary-General reported to the Security Council that although UNMOGIP and UNIPOM had different functions, General Nimmo was being asked to extend a general overseeing function with regard to both operations.[16] The Pakistan government let it be known that it

would appreciate a clarification as to the precise nature of the overseeing function assigned to General Nimmo in his personal capacity. In requesting you for this clarification, I have been instructed to reaffirm that irrespective of the question of General Nimmo's personal knowledge and experience of the area, the Government of Pakistan cannot acquiesce in any arrangements which tend, directly or indirectly, to extend the scope of UNMOGIP beyond the cease-fire line in Kashmir. [*S/6757, 7 Oct, 1965, Letter from representative of Pakistan to Secretary-General*, p. 2.]

The Secretary-General informed the government of Pakistan that 'no question of extending the scope of UNMOGIP beyond the cease-fire line in Kashmir is involved or contemplated' and that 'the arrangement in question is an informal one designed solely to take advantage of General Nimmo's rich experience'.[17]

Finally, one may note that both UNMOGIP and UNIPOM played a role in the withdrawals agreed upon at Tashkent and required under Security Council resolutions 211 and 215. The Tashkent Declaration of 10 January 1966 did not specifically mention functions for the UN observers, but it fell to the Secretary-General's Special Representative, Brigadier-General Tulio Marambio, to arrange joint meetings of the military representatives of India and Pakistan on 3, 6, 15, 25, and 29 January 1966. On 25 January the parties agreed upon ground rules for the implementation of the disengagement and withdrawal

[16] S/6699/Add. 7.
[17] S/6782, 13 Oct. 1965, Letter of 11 Oct. 1965 from Secretary-General to representative of Pakistan.

specified in the Tashkent Declaration. UNMOGIP and UNIPOM were to lend their good offices[18] to ensuring the initial disengagement of troops, in Phase I of the withdrawal. This they did.[19] UNIPOM was withdrawn fairly soon after its tasks had been fulfilled, while UNMOGIP continues to carry out its functions along the Kashmir cease-fire line.

[18] For details, see below, p. 406.   [19] S/6719/Add. 5, 17 Feb. 1966.

4

CONSTITUTIONAL BASIS

ON 20 January 1948 the Security Council adopted a resolution establishing UNCIP. The Security Council, after declaring that

it may investigate any dispute or any situation which might, by its continuance, endanger the maintenance of international peace and security and that, in the existing state of affairs between India and Pakistan, such an investigation is a matter of urgency

went on to state that UNCIP

is invested with a dual function: (1) to investigate the facts pursuant to Article 34 of the Charter of the United Nations; (2) to exercise, without interrupting the work of the Security Council, any mediatory influence likely to smooth away difficulties; to carry out the directions given to it by the Security Council; and to report how far the advice and directions, if any, of the Security Council have been carried out.   [*SC res. S/654, 20 Jan. 1948.*]

It thus seems clear that UNCIP was established under Chapter VI of the Charter and, at least so far as the investigatory powers were concerned, specifically under Article 34.[1] No reference was made in this resolution to observers, but rather to 'members, alternate members, their assistants, and its personnel' who could be assigned duties to facilitate the carrying out of UNCIP's mandate. UNCIP did in fact appoint a Military Adviser, and later he was to be UNMOGIP's first Chief Observer.[2]

In April 1948 the Security Council passed a resolution[3] which was clearly directed to achieving a cessation of the fighting in Kashmir, and which laid down certain detailed recommendations to that end. The resolution also provided that: 'The Commission should establish in Jammu and Kashmir such observers as it may require of any of the proceedings in pursuance of the measures indicated in the foregoing paragraphs'.[4]

[1] See D. W. Bowett, *United Nations Forces* (1964), p. 63.
[2] Below, p. 360. However, very shortly afterwards the functions of Military Adviser to UNCIP, and Chief Military Observer of UNMOGIP, were separated, pp. 338–9.
[3] For text, see p. 320.   [4] S/726, 21 Apr. 1948, para. 17.

This resolution would seem clearly to fall within the terms of Article 40 of the Charter,[5] even though that Article was not specifically mentioned. The authority for establishing UNMOGIP thus stemmed from Chapter VII rather than Chapter VI. This authority was not utilized until August 1948, when the Chairman of UNCIP sent a cable to New York: 'Chairman of UNCIP informs President of the Security Council that Secretariat was instructed to request Secretary-General to take steps to appoint at short notice military observers for supervision ceasefire in Kashmir'.[6] The Security Council clearly thought— and rightly—that this request was a work of supererogation so far as its own role was concerned.

the President of the Council has before him a message from the Chairman of the United Nations Commission for India and Pakistan (S/987) in which the Chairman of the Commission asks the Secretary-General to take immediate steps to appoint twenty observers. I do not see why this message should call for a discussion in the Council, given the fact that under the terms of our resolution of 21 April (S/726) the appointment of observers is a function of the Commission itself. [*Per the Belgian representative, SCOR, 3rd yr, pt 3, 356th mtg*, p. 3.]

The representatives of the United States (p. 4) and the United Kingdom (p. 5) held the same view, as did the representative of Syria (p. 8). The Soviet Union, however, dissented:

The Security Council has no right to sidetrack this request; it is in duty bound to consider the question and to decide how and on what principle these military observers are to be selected, and which countries are to send them. The Secretary-General cannot decide these questions alone. Only the Mediator for Palestine has dared to take upon himself the responsibility for such arbitrary decisions. [*Ibid.* p. 6.]

On a vote, only the Soviet Union and Ukraine voted for the matter to receive the attention of the Security Council. The seven other members abstained. The Security Council thus issued no instructions, and the question of composition was left to the Secretary-General.

These observers in fact only became operational upon the implementation of the Karachi Agreement of 29 July 1949 which demarcated the cease-fire ordered by the Security Council, and provided that 'the United Nations Commission for India and Pakistan will station observers where it deems necessary'.[7]

When UNCIP was replaced by a UN Representative in Kashmir, UNMOGIP continued to operate as before. On 30 March 1951 the Security Council passed a resolution accepting the resignation of Sir Owen Dixon as UN Representative in Kashmir; it also: '*Decides* that the Military Observer Group shall continue

---

[5] Art. 40 provides: 'In order to prevent an aggravation of the situation, the Security Council may, before making the recommendations or deciding upon the measures provided for in Article 39, call upon the parties concerned to comply with such provisional measures as it deems necessary or desirable. Such provisional measures shall be without prejudice to the rights, claims, or position of the parties concerned. The Security Council shall duly take account of failure to comply with such provisional measures'.

[6] S/987, 21 Aug. 1948, transmitting message from President of Security Council.

[7] S/1430, ann. 26.

to supervise the cease-fire in the state.'[8] The authority for UNMOGIP was thus confirmed.

The constitutional authority for UNMOGIP—as well as the scope of its functions—became a matter of some significance again in the autumn of 1965. After major hostilities had broken out between India and Pakistan, the Secretary-General made known his reasons for believing that UNMOGIP would need to be assisted, in supervising the new cease-fire, by a second UN observer corps, UNIPOM.[9] Among these was the view that:

The difference in the origin of the two operations [UNMOGIP and UNIPOM] is clear and a matter of history. The origin of UNMOGIP is found in the resolution of United Nations Commission for India and Pakistan of 13 August 1948, part 1, section D. . . . The further basis for UNMOGIP is the 'Agreement between the military representatives of India and Pakistan regarding the establishment of a cease-fire line in the State of Jammu and Kashmir', signed on 27 July 1949, commonly called the 'Karachi Agreement'. Security Council resolution 210 (1965), of 6 September, adopted prior to the cease-fire agreement, requests the Secretary-General 'to take all measures possible to strengthen the United Nations Military Observer Group in India and Pakistan' but the scope of UNMOGIP obviously continued to be the Kashmir cease-fire line. The UNMOGIP is thus limited in its terms of reference and function to the cease-fire line in Kashmir, and the Secretary-General assumes no authority on his part to extend the scope of UNMOGIP's function beyond the cease-fire line. [*S/6738*, *2 Oct. 1965*, aide-mémoire *of the Secretary-General, 25 Sept. 1965*.]

The Pakistani view was that a distinction between the two operations was necessary because:

The two operations . . . differ in nature, in origin and in the legal authority behind each. Like the remaining provisions of the UNCIP resolutions of 13 August 1948, the UNMOGIP derives its authority from that resolution as accepted by both India and Pakistan. Its origin is the cessation of hostilities effected in Jammu and Kashmir upon the acceptance of that resolution. It follows that it bears no relation, beyond that of the administrative co-ordination dictated by practical necessities, to the UNIPOM which is based on Security Council resolution 211 (1965) of 20 September 1965 . . . [*S/6751, 5 Oct. 1965, Letter from representative of Pakistan to Secretary-General*.]

two parallel cease-fire exist, namely, one based on the Karachi Agreement between India and Pakistan of July 1949, relating only to Kashmir, and the other being the over-all cease-fire applying to the entire area of conflict, which is based on the acceptance by India and Pakistan on 22 September 1965 of the cease-fire called for by the Security Council in its resolution 211 (1965). [*S/6888, 9 Nov. 1965, Report by Secretary-General relating to an aspect of the procedures employed in observing and reporting on the cease-fire*.]

[8] S/2017, 30 Mar. 1951, para. 7.
[9] For other and more major reasons, see below, pp. 446–7. See also Part 5 below.

5

POLITICAL CONTROL

At a very early stage it was arranged that the channel of responsibility should run from the Chief Military Observer to the Secretary-General, who in turn was responsible to the Security Council. To a degree even greater than usual, the Security Council has in effect delegated its authority to the Secretary-General. No periodic reports from the Chief Observer are laid before it (and here one may contrast the practice of the UN Truce Supervision Organization in Palestine) nor is it presented with an annual progress report by the Secretary-General (and here one may contrast the practice of UNEF). Though in 1965 the Security Council instructed the Secretary-General to enlarge UNMOGIP to meet the new situation caused by the outbreak of major hostilities, it was the Secretary-General who decided—as he had done from the outset[1]—what was the appropriate size and composition of UNMOGIP.

UNMOGIP exercises the quite limited function of observing and reporting, investigating complaints from either party of violations of the CFL and the cease-fire and submitting the resultant findings on those investigations to each party and to the Secretary-General, and keeping the Secretary-General informed in general on the way in which the cease-fire agreement is being kept . . . The Secretary-General exercises responsibility for the supervision and administrative control of the UNMOGIP operation. . . .

[Since 5 August 1955] Lt-Gen. Robert H. Nimmo, the Chief Military Observer of UNMOGIP, has been sending the United Nations Headquarters daily telegrams on the incidents that have been occurring as reported to him, together with as much confirmed information as possible on the basis of the investigations of specific incidents by United Nations military observers. . . .

On 23 August I asked General Nimmo to come promptly to United Nations Headquarters for consultation with me about the situation in Kashmir. . . .

The procedure that has been followed is for General Nimmo to submit the reports of the investigations of each incident and the observers' findings fixing blame, to each party, confidentially, and to send copies to me, without any public disclosure. [*S/6651, 3 Sept. 1965, Report of Secretary-General on situation in Kashmir.*]

The appointment of the Chief Observer is also a matter for the Secretary-General.

[1] Though originally it was the Chairman of UNCIP who had suggested the figure of 20—and then 40—observers.

6

ADMINISTRATIVE AND MILITARY CONTROL

THE overall administrative responsibility for UNMOGIP lies with the Secretary-General: 'The Secretary-General exercises responsibility for the supervision and administrative control of the UNMOGIP operation'.[1] It was for the Secretary-General to ensure proper administrative co-ordination with UNIPOM, when that body was established in 1965,[2] and it was in fulfilment of this that the Secretary-General ordered

General Nimmo, in an informal way, to exercise a general overseeing function with regard to both UNMOGIP and UNIPOM. Thus, the arrangement in question is an informal one designed solely to take advantage of General Nimmo's rich experience over many years with cease-fire observation through the United Nations Cease-Fire Operation in Kashmir, which clearly could be very helpful to General Macdonald[3] as a newcomer in the area. Moreover, this purely personal arrangement serves to facilitate that close administrative and operational co-ordination which I have from the beginning assured the Council will exist in the supervision of the observance of the cease-fire and of the required withdrawals. . . . [*S/6782, Letter of 11 Oct. 1965 from Secretary-General to representative of Pakistan.*]

Detailed instructions were issued, from the outset, to UNMOGIP observers:

1. INSTRUCTIONS FOR THE OBSERVERS

(1) The layout of the observers will be parallel to the layout of the armies, and is thus liable to be subsequently altered with it.

Organization
    (*a*) The observers will work in teams of two: one senior and one junior officer. The final organization in teams may be delayed until all observers have arrived.
    (*b*) The observers will be divided into two groups, one on each side.
    (*c*) The observer in charge of each group will stay with the Commander of the operations theatre of his side.
    (*d*) Each group will be divided into sections, each of one or more teams.
    (*e*) The observers in charge of a section will stay with the authorities directly subordinated to the Commander of the operations theatre. . . .
(2) The Commanders-in-Chief have agreed that the observers will be allowed to use the telephone and radio nets for the purpose of their duties. Transport and accommodation will also be provided to the observers by the unit to which they are attached.
(3) All observers must make a thorough reconnaissance of the area of the unit to which they are attached so as to become perfectly acquainted with the part of the front they are working on.

---

[1] S/6651, para. 3.   [2] See below, pp. 426–7.
[3] The Chief of Staff of UNIPOM. See below, Part 5.

(4) The tendency in each Army is to settle all incidents between the opposing sector or sub-sector commanders, and to refer to higher instance only when that procedure should fail.

(5) At the time of the cease-fire, both parties issued orders so as to:

  (*a*) hold the lines of forward defended localities as they were at that time.

  (*b*) ensure that no further advance was made from these positions.

  (*c*) ensure that there was no patrolling forward of the forward defended localities.

  (*d*) carry out reliefs as ordered before.

  (*e*) help local refugees to settle again in their homes.

(6) When breaches of those orders occur or when important incidents take place in the area of the unit to which they are attached, it is the duty of the observers

  (*a*) to accompany the local authorities in their investigations.

  (*b*) to gather as much information as possible.

  (*c*) to report as completely, accurately and impartially as possible to the observer in charge of the section or group to which they belong.

It must be understood that any direct intervention from the observers between the opposing parties or any interference in the orders must be avoided.

(7) It is requested that the observers refrain from taking part in any political discussion.

(8) Instructions concerning the leaves and reliefs of the observers will be issued later.

[s] Maurice DELVOIE,
Lieutenant-General

[*S/AC.12/MA/1*, pp. 1–2.]

On 15 January 1949 the Military Adviser had presented the following plan:

1. division of the observers into two groups, one attached to each army;
2. establishment by the senior officer of each group of a 'Control Headquarters' under direct command of the Military Adviser and in close liaison with the commander of the operations theatre on his side;
3. division of each group into teams of two observers, attached to the tactical formations in the field and directly responsible to the Control Headquarters.

On 3 February, this plan was put into effect on the Pakistan side, and on 10 February on the Indian side.

The following schedule was arranged:

Pakistan side		Indian side	
Control Hqrs—Rawalpindi		Control Hqrs—Jammu	
Teams at	Kazibakar	Teams at	Jammu
	Kotla		Naushera
	Hajira		Pooch
	Domel		Srinagar

Accommodation and transport facilities were placed at the disposal of the observers by the two armies. Use of military radio and telephone nets was also extended to them.

As more observers arrived and as the weather permitted access to the mountainous areas in the north, additional teams were established on the Pakistan side at Sialkot, Kamri and Dhanni; and on the Indian side at Uri, Gurais and Akhnur.

At the end of March, Control Headquarters on the Indian side moved from Jammu to Srinagar, and the team in Srinagar was subsequently abolished. In the first days of October, at the request of the Indian Army Hqrs, who had always showed concern about possible activities in the northern areas, orders were issued by the Military Adviser to Control Headquarters in Pakistan to establish a permanent team in Gilgit.

On 19 October, the Military Adviser issued orders (Annex 2) for the distribution of observers during the winter months, as the problem of communications and of living conditions during the cold season would not allow maintenance of teams in certain areas:

Pakistan side		Indian side	
Control Hq.	Rawalpindi	Control Hq.	Jammu
Teams with Div. Hq.	Jhelum	Teams with Div. Hq.	Jammu
	Rawalpindi		Naushera
	Batrasi		Srinagar
Additional teams	Hajira	Additional teams	Poonch
at important	Domel	at important	Uri
points	Gilgit	points	

[*S/AC.12/MA/13*, pp. 2–3.]

Further detailed arrangements were subsequently made for the administration and organization of the observers during the winter months:

1. The office of the Military Adviser will be alternately in Rawalpindi and Delhi.
2. Control Headquarters with the Pakistan Army will remain in Rawalpindi.
3. Control Headquarters with the Indian Army will move to Jammu between the 15th and 31st November.
4. Teams of three or more observers will be located with each Division Headquarters (and L.O.C. area HQ on the Indian side).
5. Teams of two observers will be located:—
   (*a*) On the Indian side at Poonch and Uri.
   (*b*) On the Pakistan side at Hajira, Domel and Gilgit.
6. A colonel or lieutenant-colonel will be in charge of each team.
7. It is the responsibility of the Control Headquarters to:—
   (*a*) Maintain liaison between the military authorities of Jammu and Rawalpindi respectively and the Military Adviser.
   (*b*) Inspect the various teams to control and co-ordinate their activies, and to improve their working and living conditions wherever possible.
   (*c*) To order investigations and transmit their results with recommendations to the Military Adviser.
   (*d*) To handle all administrative matters relating to observers (leave, per diem, mail, etc.).
8. It is the responsibility of the teams located with the Division Headquarters (or L.O.C. headquarters) to:
   (*a*) Maintain liaison with Div. headquarters and with Control Headquarters.
   (*b*) To carry out investigations.
   (*c*) To study and verify on the ground the disposition of the troops (including artillery and armoured units), the improvements made to the defensive positions, to the lines of communications, etc.
9. The responsibility of the other teams is similar except that they maintain liaison between brigade headquarters and control headquarters. Control headquarters will determine the areas and the responsibilities of these teams.
10. The team at Gilgit will discreetly check the amount of supplies and war-like stores brought by air into Gilgit.
11. All observers should be fully aware of the importance of obtaining and transmitting quickly all relative information.
12. The new organization will be effective immediately, however the observers still engaged in the demarcation of the cease-fire line or in the control of the subsequent movement of troops will carry out these duties before they join their new stations.
13. Control headquarters will transmit to this office a copy of the orders issued in compliance with this directive.
14. Control headquarters with the Indian army will transfer two colonels (or lieutenant-colonels) to the Pakistan side effective immediately. [*Ibid.*, pp. 18–19.]

These documents thus show the following administrative arrangements: division into two groups, one attached to the Indian army, one to the Pakistani army; establishment by the senior officers of each group of a Control Head-quarters under the direct command of UNCIP's Military Adviser and in close liaison with the commander of operations theatre on his side; and division of each group into teams of two observers, attached to the tactical formations in the field and directly responsible to Control Headquarters.[4]

A UN Military Control Headquarters was established on each side of the line—in Rawalpindi (Pakistan) and Jammu. With the advent of more clement weather in March 1949, the Control Headquarters on the Indian side moved from Jammu to Srinagar, and the observer team in Srinagar moved to Jammu.[5] The practice now is for the UNMOGIP staff to spend half the year at Srinagar.

The Chief Military Observer is assisted by a Chief of Military Staff who is responsible for liaison with the staff and co-ordination of the activities of the headquarters staff, and by an Operations Officer. It falls to the latter to recom-mend the location of the Field Observation Teams. An Intelligence Officer keeps records of the identity and disposition of the military units on whichever side of the line the Control Headquarters happens to be located. For the opposing army the record is kept by the Staff Officer placed on the other side of the cease-fire line. The Chief Military Observer is also assisted at Control Headquarters by an Administrative Officer (who is a UN staff member) who has responsibility for overall expenditure of UN funds and for administrative control over his own UN civilian staff and radio operations. He is responsible to the Chief Military Observer, but also maintains direct contacts with the Secretary-General.[6]

UNMOGIP staff and liaison officers are attached to various military and civilian centres to assist Control Headquarters. They deal with staff matters (liaison with army headquarters of India and Pakistan, and keeping records of all changes of troop strength and location) and administrative matters (trans-portation facilities, leave of observers, etc.).[7] Such offices exist in Delhi, Rawal-pindi (when the HQ is located in Srinigar), Srinigar (when the HQ is located in Rawalpindi), and Karachi.[8]

[4] S/AC.12/MA/13, p. 2. I have in this summary drawn heavily, and at times almost verbatim, upon Lourié, *Int. Org.* 1955, p. 23.
[5] Ibid.   [6] Ibid. p. 26.   [7] Ibid. p. 27.
[8] A Finnish military observer has provided the following chart:

See Reino Saarinnen, 'Views of a Military Observer of UN activities regarding the Kashmir Crisis' *Military R,* Jan. 1966.

The observers operate in teams of two or more military observers and one radio operator. Both armies provide them with a jeep and driver, to ensure freedom of movement. The number of field stations varies according to needs, and they are at different distances back from the cease-fire line. The observers maintain radio contact with the headquarters staff, and the UNMOGIP staff is also in radio contact with the UN offices in Karachi.[9] The senior Military Observer in any team is considered the officer in charge, though in matters relating to the Karachi Agreement, the professional military opinion of each observer is given equal weight. The observers work under the direction of, and are responsible to, the Chief Military Observer. The teams are rotated periodically from side to side of the cease-fire line in order to avoid a spirit of partisanship.[10]

[9] Ibid. I am grateful to Mr James Knott, Director of the International Peace-Keeping Organization, for making Capt. Saarinnen's paper available to me.
[10] Lourié, *Int. Org.*, 1955, p. 26.

7

COMPOSITION AND SIZE

I T is customary with UN forces or observer groups that, although the parties agree to their presence, they do not specify their size. The appropriate strength has been a matter for the determination of the Secretary-General, often upon the advice of his representative on the spot.

Chairman of United Nations Commission for India and Pakistan informs President of Security Council that Secretariat was instructed to request Secretary-General to take steps to appoint at short notice military observers for supervision cease-fire in Kashmir.

Note: on 11 August 1948, the Secretary-General received from his personal representative with the United Nations Commission for India and Pakistan a cable elaborating this request, the relevant part of which is as follows:

'I have been instructed by the Chairman of UNCIP to request you to take immediate steps to appoint at short notice pending UNCIP final decision twenty military observers in view of possible achievement of cease-fire agreement in nearest future. Observers required good knowledge English. Number given is preliminary estimate. Observers should consist of active officers fit for field duty. [*S/987, 21 Aug. 1948, Cable of 21 Aug. 1948 from Chairman of UNCIP to Secretary-General.*][1]

In December of the same year the Military Adviser suggested to UNCIP that the request might appropriately be for forty observers.[2] In fact, the overall

[1] For Security Council debate on this request, see above, p. 350.
[2] S/AC.12/MA/13, p. 1.

size of UNMOGIP has been very modest. The total UNMOGIP staff has rarely gone much over 100 (save during the major outbreak of fighting in 1965, when UNMOGIP was strengthened) and the number of military observers has been even more modest:

Year	No. of Military Observers
1957	32
1958	32
1959	32
1960	32
1961	29
1962	29
1963	36
1964	36
1965	43
1966	44

Note: Compiled by the Editor from official sources. Not an official document.
The military observers have been supplemented by a small aircrew, usually of about four persons

Though there were 43 military observers at the time of the adoption of Security Council resolution 210 (1965), an additional 59 were provided by those countries already contributing, bringing the total at the height of the crisis in September–October 1965 to 102. Of this total 13 were detailed to UNIPOM, leaving 89 actually on duty with UNMOGIP.[3] The following breakdown, showing the strength of UNMOGIP as of 6 July 1966, indicates the composition of this small band of observers:[4]

Australia	6	Italy	3
Belgium	2	New Zealand	4
Canada	9	Norway	4
Chile*	2	Sweden	5
Denmark	5	Uruguay	1
Finland	3		—
			44

* Including Gen. Tassara Gonzalez (Chief Military Observer).

This total of 44 was supplemented by an air crew of 8, making an overall total of 52.

As of 11 October 1965 these 89 observers were deployed in the UNMOGIP area of operations, which extends on both sides of the cease-fire line in Kashmir (nearly 500 miles long and of the stretch between Pakistan and Jammu (about 120 miles long) as follows:

[3] See S/6699/Add. 9, quoted below.
[4] The supporting staff of UNMOGIP has been drawn from a wider range of nationalities, and has included civilian officials from France, Greece, Honduras, Italy, Japan, Netherlands, Philippines, Spain, Thailand, and the UK.

		No. of HQ staff and observers
On the India side		
Headquarters:	Srinagar	4
Stations:	Kargil	2
	Baramula	9
	Punch	6
	Galuthi	7
	Naoshera	7
	Jammu	8
	Akhnur	4
Liaison office:	New Delhi	1
	Total	48

		No. of HQ staff and observers
On the Pakistan side		
Headquarters:	Rawalpindi	–
Stations:	Skardu	2
	Domel	7
	Rawalakot	8
	Kotli	9
	Bhimbar	7
	Sialkot	6
Liaison Office:	Rawalpindi	2
	Total	41

[*S/6699/Add. 9, 14 Oct. 1965*, para. 5.]

During UNMOGIP's long existence other nations have also contributed, including the United States and Mexico. The very first group of observers sent to Kashmir in 1950 consisted of nationals from Belgium, Canada, Norway, Mexico, and the United States.[5]

It was only during the major hostilities of 1965 that it was felt necessary or desirable to enlarge UNMOGIP:

10. Since the Security Council resolution of 6 September also requested me to take all possible measures to strengthen the United Nations Military Observer Group in India and Pakistan (UNMOGIP), I wish to inform the Council that, as a matter of course, I had consultations with Lt.-Gen. R. H. Nimmo, the Chief Military Observer, during my mission. While in the present situation the role of UNMOGIP is obviously even more difficult than usual, I have benefited much from the knowledge and experience of General Nimmo. I have taken immediate steps to obtain extra transport and communications equipment to facilitate UNMOGIP in its task. I have also made provisional arrangements to increase the number of military observers in UNMOGIP at a short notice should developments make this increase necessary. [*S/6686, 16 Sept. 1965, 2nd Report of Secretary-General on his mission to India and Pakistan.*]

On 21 September the Secretary-General reported: 'I have already made specific approaches to the Governments providing military observers to make

[5] S/AC.12/MA/13, pp. 15–16.

available additional observers so that the overall strength of the Group can be very substantially increased.'⁶ A favourable response was soon received:

6. In response to my approaches, the Governments of Canada, Denmark, Italy and Norway have each placed 10 observers at my disposal and the Governments of Finland and Sweden 5 observers each. These observers will proceed to the Mission area from their respective centres in the immediate future.

7. Additional observers may well be forthcoming from Finland and Sweden as well as from Uruguay and other Governments providing military observers to UNMOGIP. [*S/6699/Add. 3, 23 Sept. 1965.*]

6. In response to my request, the Government of New Zealand has agreed to provide 5 additional military observers for service with UNMOGIP. [*S/6699/Add. 4, 24 Sept. 1965.*]

4. As of 27 September, 42 additional observers had arrived in the area to strengthen UNMOGIP.

5. In addition, 9 observers were in transit to the area and 15 more observers for UNMOGIP were preparing to depart from their home countries. [*S/6699/Add. 5. 27 Sept. 1965.*]

The first Chief Military Observer⁷ of UNMOGIP was Brigadier H. Angle of Canada, who served until his tragic death in an air crash in July 1950. He was replaced by Major-General R. H. Nimmo of Australia, who served for the extraordinarily long period of November 1950–January 1966. General Nimmo died on 4 January 1966. From January to July 1966 Colonel J. H. Gauthier of Canada was Acting Chief Military Observer. In July 1966 the first non-Commonwealth national was appointed to the post—Major-General Luis Tassara Gonzalez of Chile.

⁶ S/6699, 21 Sept. 1965, Report by Secretary-General on his efforts to give effect to Security Council res. 211 (1965).
⁷ UNCIP had originally had its own Military Adviser (Gen. Delvoie), who also has the task of preparing the formation of observer teams in readiness for the moment when the parties would agree to them becoming operational. Thereafter, the task of Chief Military Observer of UNMOGIP was separated from that of Military Adviser to UNCIP (and later, to the UN's Special Representative). See Lourié, *Int. Org.*, 1955, p. 24.

8

RELATIONS WITH CONTRIBUTING STATES

RELATIONS between the UN and the nations contributing to UNMOGIP gave rise to no difficulties. As may be seen from the preceding section on the composition and size of UNMOGIP, participation in UNMOGIP has extended to countries not represented in the original group of observers.

No formal agreement was entered into by the UN and the countries concerned in respect of the service of the latter's nationals.

The observers receive their salaries from their respective national armies, but are paid a subsistence allowance of $100 for personal field clothing and equipment. The UN assumes responsibility for total disability or death of observers, and India and Pakistan provide hospitalization and other medical expenses in case of temporary disability.[1]

[1] Lourié, *Int. Org.*, 1955, p. 27.

9

RELATIONS WITH HOST STATES

ALTHOUGH UNCIP was authorized to appoint observers wherever it thought necessary, this authorization was given in respect of duties agreed upon by India and Pakistan (S/726). They had, of course, agreed also to permit UNCIP (and later the UN Representative for India and Pakistan) to operate in Kashmir. The UN observers did not, however, become operational until the conclusion of the Karachi Agreement in 1949 (S/1430). Their presence in Kashmir may thus be seen as contingent (albeit indirectly) upon the consent of India and Pakistan.

It is, of course, the very question of sovereignty in Kashmir which is in dispute, and the UN has thus at all times treated both India and Pakistan as 'host' nations. The UN military observers operate on either side of the cease-fire line demarcated by the Karachi Agreement, dealing with India on one side, with Pakistan on the other, and with both on overall administrative and political questions.[1]

UNMOGIP is an observer corps rather than a peace force, and no status-of-forces agreement exists between the UN and India, or the UN and Pakistan. None the less, relations between UNMOGIP and the host states have always been excellent. Neither India nor Pakistan raised objections to any of the nationalities represented on UNMOGIP.[2] However, after Pakistan was promised military assistance by the United States in February 1954, the Prime Minister of India, Nehru, said of the eighteen Americans then serving on UNMOGIP that they 'can no longer be treated by us as neutrals in this dispute and hence their presence appears to us as improper'.[3] The response of the State Department was to indicate that this was a matter between the UN and India. Secretary-General Hammarskjöld, anxious on the one hand to avoid bad relations with India, and on the other hand to retain the UN's right to designate its own personnel, evolved a compromise formula by which it was privately agreed between the UN and India that the US officers should serve out their

[1] See above, pp. 355–6.   [2] For listing, see above, p. 358.
[3] Indian Embassy in Washington DC., Indiagram 403, 3 Mar. 1954.

present term of duty, but would not then be replaced.[4] At this period of time the Communist Party of India was militantly opposed to the UN presence. When Kashmiris had demonstrated in August 1953 in Srinagar and Bakshi, the Communists claimed that the demonstration had been encouraged and supported by UNMOGIP observers. On 30 August 1953 the Communist Party of India called for the expulsion of the UN from Kashmir, and this demand was repeated in January 1954.[5] None the less, Indian government policy has remained fully co-operative with UNMOGIP, as has that of Pakistan.

Undoubtedly, minor incidents have occurred to mar this relationship, but because of the confidential nature of the Chief Military Observer's reports they are not readily documented. As has been observed in other contexts, the only breakdown in this system of confidential reporting occurred in the period 1964–5, marked by rapidly deteriorating relations between India and Pakistan, when India apparently decided, for political reasons, to make public matters relating to UNMOGIP:

According to our reports, Pakistan rejected a request by the Military Observer Group for an assurance of the safety of the personnel of the United Nations Observer Group who had to be sent to the affected area. India, on the other hand, offered all facilities and co-operation to these personnel. [*Per the representative of India, SCOR, 19th yr, 1104th mtg*, para. 52.]

89. In October 1963, the Chief Military Observer proposed to treat the activities of armed civilians and armed police within 500 yards on either side of the cease-fire line as a breach of the cease-fire agreement. On 24 June 1964, the Chief Military Observer proposed a meeting between the military representatives of India and Pakistan to work out agreed principles for the control of civilians in the area of the cease-fire line. While India accepted the suggestion, so far Pakistan has not done so. On 8 March 1965, the Chief Military Observer again proposed a meeting between military representatives of India and Pakistan in order to work out agreed principles for controlling the activities of civilians in the area. On 26 March 1965, India agreed to the proposal. On 5 April, India was informed by the Chief Military Observer that a meeting would not be possible, since Pakistan was not agreeable to it. [*Per the representative if India, SCOR, 20th yr, 1237th mtg.*]

With the grave deterioration of the situation in August and September 1965, the Secretary-General himself now approached India and Pakistan 'to avert further deterioration of that situation and to restore normal conditions in the area'.[6]

4. There has been a disturbing increase in the number of incidents involving violations of the CFL since the beginning of 1965. In mid-June 1965, for example, General Nimmo reported that during the previous five months, a total of 2,231 complaints from both sides charging violation of the cease-fire had been submitted to UNMOGIP. Most of these involved firing across the CFL, although some concerned crossings of the line by armed men. As of that date, 377 violations in all categories had been confirmed by investigations of the observers, 218 of which were committed by Pakistan and 159 by India. Some of these violations took the form of 'heavy and prolonged firing' from weapons up to the calibre of field artillery. Among the most serious of the violations was one that occurred in May of this year, when Indian troops in battalion strength attacked and captured Pakistan positions in the

---

[4] This information comes from Korbel, pp. 163–4.   [5] Ibid.
[6] S/6651, 3 Sept. 1965, para. 1.

Kargil area of Kashmir and remained in occupation of them. In the interest of preserving the CFL, I appealed to the Government of India to withdraw its troops from the Pakistan side of the line. On assurance from me that United Nations observers would henceforth be stationed on both sides of the line in that area, which India considered strategically vital to the security of the Srinagar-Leh road, the Government of India agreed to do so and in due course the Indian troops were withdrawn, thus closing the matter and making unnecessary any further consideration of a report on it to the Security Council. Subsequently, there were some military attacks on the road by armed elements from the Pakistan side. . . .

EFFORTS OF THE SECRETARY-GENERAL

9. On the morning of 9 August 1965, a telegram was received from General Nimmo warning that the situation was deteriorating along the CFL. On the basis of this report, I saw the representative of Pakistan at 12.30 hours on that day, and asked him to convey to his Government my very serious concern about the situation that was developing in Kashmir, involving the crossing of the CFL from the Pakistan side by numbers of armed men and their attacks on Indian military positions on the Indian side of the line, and also my strong appeal that the CFL be observed. That same afternoon I saw the representative of India, told him of the information I had received from General Nimmo and of the *démarche* I had made to the Government of Pakistan, and asked him to convey to his Government my urgent appeal for restraint as regards any retaliatory action from their side. In subsequent days, I repeated these appeals orally for transmission to the two Governments, asking also that all personnel of either party still remaining on the wrong side of the line be withdrawn to its own side. I have not obtained from the Government of Pakistan any assurance that the cease-fire and the CFL will be respected henceforth or that efforts would be exerted to restore conditions to normal along that line. I did receive assurance from the Government of India, conveyed orally by its representative to the United Nations, that India would act with restraint with regard to any retaliatory acts and will respect the cease-fire agreement and the CFL if Pakistan does likewise. In the meantime, reports from UNMOGIP as of 2 September indicate a continuation of violations of the cease-fire and the CFL from both sides.

10. In view of the continuing deterioration in the situation as of 16 August I gave consideration to a further step in the form of a draft statement about the cease-fire violations which was designed for public release. The draft was handed to the two representatives to be transmitted for the information of their Governments. Both Governments reacted promptly. The Government of India had no objection to the release of the statement but at first wished certain modifications which in part at least I regarded as unacceptable. The Government of Pakistan was strongly negative about the statement in general on the grounds that it favoured India in that it dealt only with the current cease-fire situation without presenting the political background of the broad issue and thus was lacking in balance since a cease-fire alone supports the *status quo* to India's benefit.

11. Weighing carefully all considerations I came to the conclusion that a public statement by the Secretary-General at that time would serve no constructive purpose and might well do more harm than good. My first and primary objective had to be to see the fighting end rather than indicting or denouncing any party for starting and continuing it. I thought it might be helpful to make another quiet effort toward achieving observance of the cease-fire through a new approach to the two Governments. Consequently I gave thought to the possibility of sending urgently to the area a Personal Representative of the Secretary-General for the purpose of meeting and talking with appropriate authorities of the two Governments and with General Nimmo; conveying to the Governments my very serious concern about the situation; and exploring with them ways and means of preventing any further deterioration in that situation and regaining quiet along the CFL. If such a mission had materialized, I had it in mind to ask Mr Ralph J. Bunche, Under-Secretary for Special Political Affairs, to undertake it. The idea was broached by me informally to the two parties on 20 August. The subsequent responses of the Governments, while not negative, involved in each case conditions which,

in my view, would make the mission not feasible at that time and therefore I abandoned it.
[*S/6651, 3 Sept. 1965, Report of Secretary-General on situation in Kashmir.*]

The Secretary-General had also issued appeals on 1 September to both India
and Pakistan (S/6647). It is interesting that in his listing of pre-conditions
for the restoration of the cease-fire[7] he includes '(*e*) allowing full freedom of
movement and access to the United Nations Observers by both parties on both
sides of the line'.

On 4 September 1965 the Security Council adopted resolution 209 calling
for an immediate cease-fire:

(*a*) To General Nimmo's 'official protest and urgent request' for the withdrawal of Pakistan
troops from the Chhamb sector which was lodged on 3 September, the Chief of Staff, Pakistan
gave the following reply:

'We are aware of your genuine efforts to make the Indians vacate their aggression. But
having seen the hopelessness of these efforts we were forced to take action to stop the
Indians from annexing Azad Kashmir. Our action was taken after repeated requests to you
to convey to Indians that their failure to vacate positions on our side of the CFL will have
very serious consequences. The Indians apparently refused to heed our warning. They are
maintaining their occupation of posts on our side of the CFL in the Kargil, Tithwal and
Uri-Punch sectors and have now crossed the CFL in yet another sector. Under those circumstances how can you expect us to unilaterally halt our purely defensive operations which are
designed to forestall Indian aggressions?' [*S/6661, 6 Sept. 1965, Report of Secretary-
General on situation in Kashmir, para. 4.*]

Pakistan let it be known that she was ill pleased with the suggestion that her
entry into Kashmir on 5 August marked the abrogation of the 1949 cease-fire
agreement:

. . . I am constrained to express my surprise and regret that, though the United Nations
Military Observer Group has admitted that, in most cases, the actual identity of those engaging
in the armed attacks on the Indian side of the line and the actual crossing of it could not be
verified by direct observation and evidence, yet the Group should have thought it fit to conclude that the uprising in Jammu and Kashmir resulted from the crossing of the cease-fire
line from the Pakistan side by armed men for the purpose of armed action on the Indian side.
[*S/6666, 7 Sept. 1965, Telegram from President of Pakistan to Secretary-General.*]

The Secretary-General communicated to India and Pakistan the terms of
the Security Council's resolutions of 4 and 6 September. Both agreed to a
cease-fire, but upon conditions.[8] The President of Pakistan emphasized the
necessity of a long-term solution, for in his view a cease-fire 'followed immediately by withdrawal of all armed Pakistan personnel to the Pakistan side
of the cease-fire line and the consolidation of the cease-fire line through the
strengthening of the United Nations Military Observer Group would result in
restoring India's military grip over Kashmir'.[9]

At around the same time, General Nimmo reported that UNMOGIP was
receiving less than full co-operation from Pakistan:

(*f*) After Sialkot became an area of hostilities, the United Nations observer team there
found it extremely difficult to keep in contact with the Pakistan local command which appeared

[7] S/6651, para. 15.   [8] See below, p. 393.

[9] S/6683, 16 Sept. 1965, Preliminary Report of Secretary-General on his mission to India and
Pakistan, para. 9.

reluctant to keep the team informed of the situation and gave the impression that they had no further requirements for the United Nations observers. In the absence of General Nimmo, who had left for New Delhi to report to the Secretary-General, the Acting Chief Military Observer addressed a message to the Chief of the General Staff of Pakistan, on 11 September, to bring the matter to his attention and to call on him to rectify this state of affairs. In his reply, which was received by the Acting Chief Military Observer on 13 September, the Chief of the General Staff recalled that the function of the United Nations observer teams was to supervise the cease-fire in Jammu and Kashmir and that the observer team at Sialkot had been stationed there at Pakistan's specific request. Since, he continued, India and Pakistan were now at war, the United Nations team could no longer perform its duties until this war ended. Due to Indian attacks, he further stated, Sialkot now was in an operational zone and Pakistan could no longer guarantee the safety of the team. Therefore he requested the Acting Chief Military Observer immediately to withdraw the team from Sialkot. In view of this reply, the Acting Chief Military Observer instructed the Sialkot team to proceed to Bhimber, which is the closest United Nations observers' station to Sialkot on the Pakistan side and to operate temporarily from there.

(g) On 14 September the Sialkot team, which was proceeding from its temporary base of Bhimber toward Sialkot, was stopped by Pakistan military police at approximately 13 miles east of the latter city and prevented from going further. They did not hear any shelling from the place where they were stopped and could not obtain any information on the battle situation in the Sialkot area [*S/6687, 16 Sept. 1965, Report of Secretary-General on the military situation in the area of conflict between India and Pakistan*, para. 9.]

On 20 September the Secretary-General informed India and Pakistan of the adoption of Security Council resolution 211, demanding a cease-fire to take effect on 22 September. The Secretary-General indicated to both parties that

I am proceeding on the assumption that the governments of both countries will accede to the Security Council's demand, and therefore,

(1) I request you to inform me as quickly as possible that orders have been or will be issued for the cease-fire;
(2) I request your plan and schedule for the indicated withdrawal of your troops;
(3) I have taken steps to determine the availability of a number of military observers to ensure the supervision of the cease-fire and the subsequent withdrawals, and have alerted them to be prepared for early departure;
(4) I have set in motion the necessary logistical arrangements for the maintenance of a team of observers in the field. [*S/6699, 21 Sept. 1965, Report of Secretary-General on his efforts to give effect to Security Council Res. 211 (1965)*, para. 3.]

It is interesting to note that under paragraph (3) above, the Secretary-General felt no need to secure the consent of India and Pakistan for an enlargement of the number of observers, or their participation in securing the new cease-fire.

India indicated that she would cease hostilities if Pakistan did so[10] and Pakistan, though considering the Security Council resolution as 'unsatisfactory', agreed to call a cease-fire.[11]

On 22 October 1965, with the cease-fire now in effect, U Thant communicated with the new Prime Minister, Lal Bahadur Shastri, on the question of withdrawal of troops, and the UN role therein.

With regard to your Excellency's suggestion that the local Commanders in particular areas should first meet under the auspices of the observers and enter into discussions with a view to reaching agreement on the stabilization of the cease-fire, I may inform you that efforts to this effect are already under way and it is my hope that they will meet with success.

[10] S/6699, para. 5.   [11] Ibid. Add. 1.

I particularly welcome your expressed willingness, at a suitable time, to accept an arrangement under which appropriate representatives of India and Pakistan would meet in the area to consider the question of withdrawals. I note that you would wish such a meeting to be with the Chief Military Observer of UNMOGIP. I appreciate the high regard you have for General Nimmo, which I share, and certainly by his long experience in the area he is very well qualified for such an assignment. I cannot, however, consider such an arrangement feasible. The task of supervising the observance of the cease-fire is an extremely difficult and demanding one and with an enlarged corps of observers, General Nimmo is more than fully occupied with this highly responsible and vital work. I take it for granted that the assignment in connexion with the withdrawals will be difficult, complex and prolonged and will require the full time of the United Nations official assigned to it. Moreover, as pointed out in the penultimate paragraph of my letter of 12 October to the Permanent Representative of India (SG 6782, sect. II), I agreed with the position taken in item 4 of the letter from the Permanent Representative of India to me of 8 October (S/6761), that there should be no telescoping of the cease-fire and withdrawals into a single operation. I am quite convinced that it would be impossible for any one person to undertake responsibility for both of these efforts. This applies, of course, to General Macdonald as well as to General Nimmo.

In these circumstances, therefore, I have it in mind to designate a thoroughly experienced senior officer in the United Nations family to be my representative on the matter of withdrawals, to go to the area at an early date, to visit both capitals and to arrange for representatives of India and Pakistan to meet at some mutually agreed place, possibly near the front lines, to seek agreement on a plan and schedule for the withdrawals by both parties. For this highly important assignment I would name Maj.-Gen. Syseno Sarmento of Brazil, Commander of the United Nations Emergency Force in Gaza and Sinai. General Sarmento serves the United Nations with distinction as Commander of the United Nations Emergency Force. [*S/6719/Add. 3, Letter of 22 Oct. 1965 from Secretary-General to representative of India conveying message to Prime Minister of India.*]

In the event, the Secretary-General was obliged to appoint a different Representative:

2. I am now able to report that after helpful consultations with both parties, I have appointed as my representative Brig.-Gen. Tulio Marambio of Chile, who is to meet with representatives of India and Pakistan for the purpose of formulating an agreed plan and schedule for the withdrawals, as envisaged in paragraph 3 of resolution 215 (1965). I am advised by both parties that they will receive and co-operate with General Marambio.

3. General Marambio, who is 54 years of age, is Director of the War Academy in Chile.

4. General Marambio will be proceeding to the two capitals shortly with the objective of arranging an early meeting at a mutually agreed place with the representatives to be designated by India and Pakistan in order to formulate an agreed plan and schedule for the mutual withdrawals, within an agreed time-limit.

5. Members of the Council will recall that prior to the adoption of Security Council resolution 215 (1965) I had addressed messages to the two parties on 22 October in which I had offered a suggestion that Maj.-Gen. Syseno Sarmento, Commander of the United Nations Emergency Force in Gaza and Sinai, might be designated as my representative on the matter of withdrawals and had expressed my hope for a favourable reaction to this suggestion by both (see 6719/Add. 3). A favourable reply by letter was promptly received from the Government of Pakistan (S/6825). No similar reply, however, had been received from the Government of India at the time of the adoption of resolution 215 (1965) on 5 November. . . . [*S/6719/Add. 4, 25 Nov. 1965, Report by Secretary-General on compliance with Security Council res. 211 (1965).*]

A difficulty arose between the UN and India over the use of the term 'troops' and 'positions' in the directives used to India and Pakistan:

. . . I note your assurance that the use of the word 'troops' in the identical communications that you sent to me and to the Permanent Representative of Pakistan on 20 September connotes no restriction on the meaning and purpose of the Security Council resolution which relates to the withdrawal of 'all armed personnel'. As noted in paragraph 6 of your report of 3 September (S/6651), '. . . the series of violations that began on 5 August were to a considerable extent in subsequent days in the form of armed men, generally not in uniform, crossing the cease-fire line from the Pakistan side for the purpose of armed action on the Indian side'. It will be recalled that throughout the recent discussions in the Security Council and your discussions with the Prime Minister of India in New Delhi, the greatest emphasis has been placed by us on the withdrawal of these armed men coming from Pakistan. The Security Council resolution itself, by naming 5 August as the date in connexion with withdrawal to previous positions has, undoubtedly, recognized the fact that armed infiltrators from Pakistan, to which reference has been made in your report, must be withdrawn. In your *aide-mémoire* it had been stated that in the expression 'withdrawal of all armed personnel to the positions held by them before 5 August 1965', the word 'positions' 'must connote identifiable military positions of some nature which prior to 5 August 1965 have presumably been occupied by some kind of armed personnel under Government control and/or direction'. The Government of India is unable to accept this restrictive interpretation of the Security Council resolution. In fact, such an interpretation is not warranted by the Security Council resolutions, and the Secretary-General's report to the Security Council of 3 September, and the discussions in the Council. In paragraph 15, sub-paragraph (b) of that document, it will be recalled that it was proposed that one of the conditions under which restoration of the cease-fire and return to normal conditions along the cease-fire line could be achieved was 'readiness on the part of the Government of Pakistan to take effective steps to prevent crossings of the CFL from the Pakistan side by armed men, whether or not in uniform'. It has always been the understanding of the Government of India that the withdrawal of all 'armed personnel' contemplated in the three resolutions of the Security Council (209 (1965), 210 (1965) and 211 (1965)) must include the withdrawal of such personnel not in uniform who have crossed the cease-fire line from Pakistan since 5 August. Any schedule or plan of withdrawal of Indian troops has, therefore, necessarily to be related to and co-ordinated and synchronized with the withdrawal of Pakistan regular forces as well as armed men not in uniform who have crossed the cease-fire line and the international border between Jammu and Kashmir and West Pakistan, for all of whom Pakistan must undertake full responsibility. [*S/6720, 28 Sept. 1965, Letter from representative of India to Secretary-General.*]

2. I have been instructed to inform you that the Government of India is unable to accept as a practical assumption for the guidance of the military observers the restrictive interpretation given by you of the word 'positions' used in the Security Council resolutions. As already stated in my letter of 28 September (*S/6720*), it has always been the understanding of the Government of India that the withdrawals of all 'armed personnel' contemplated in the resolutions of the Council must include the withdrawals of such personnel 'not in uniform' who crossed the cease-fire line from Pakistan since 5 August 1965. Whether the personnel 'not in uniform' did or did not hold 'identifiable military positions' prior to 5 August does not affect their obligation to withdraw in terms of the Security Council resolutions.

3. The above understanding of the Government of India is fully in accord with the Security Council resolutions and represents the position of my Government.

4. I shall be grateful if this letter is circulated as a Security Council document. [*S/6756, 7 Oct. 1965, Letter from representative of India to Secretary-General.*]

The Secretary-General replied that he had 'carefully noted' these views, and that he 'need only reiterate here that it is only the Council itself which can make authoritative interpretations of its resolutions' (S/6782). A further correspondence ensued on related matters:

13

I have the honour to acknowledge receipt of your letter of 8 October 1965, bringing to my attention certain comments of the Government of India on my report to the Security Council of 27 September 1965 (S/6719).

With regard to section (1) of your letter, I am happy to be in full agreement with your statement that what is relevant is 'the military positions held by each party at 22.00 hours GMT on 22 September'. The United Nations observers, throughout the area, have sought to establish the exact location of those positions, although with great difficulty in some places.

I also agree entirely that under the cease-fire there should be no 'fluidity' about the military positions, since they were supposed to become frozen at the time the cease-fire went into effect. In the report to which you refer it was stated that the list of military positions held by each party on the opposite side of the line in the entire area of conflict, as of 24 September, does not purport to be exhaustive or complete'. The following sentences explained this by pointing out that the 'military situation throughout the area of conflict continues to be fluid', and the military observers had reported that complaints about positions on the wrong side of the line were 'continuous' and were coming from both parties. It was further stated that these complaints were being investigated by the observers and, as confirmed, would necessitate corrections in the list, that is, indicating either forward movements which would be in violation of the cease-fire, or withdrawals. Thus, what I stated in my report was only a statement of the unhappy fact that there was a certain 'fluidity' because, despite the efforts of the observers who are unarmed and have no means of actual enforcement, there was some forward movement at various places along the line and from both sides of it, with the apparent purpose of tactical improvement of military positions (for reported instances, see S/6710/Add. 3, paragraphs 8–9, 12–16, 23, 24, 26 and 27).

There was, most emphatically, no question of United Nations observers condoning any such movement or any change in the cease-fire line at any place. To the contrary, the observers, to the fullest extent that their resources have permitted, have protested every forward movement and 'inching' advance since the cease-fire came into effect. They have demanded, although with a minimum of effect, withdrawals to the positions held at the effective hour of the cease-fire.

I assure you that all of the United Nations observers on duty in India and Pakistan are thoroughly informed of their duty to ensure, to the fullest extent they can, the observance of the cease-fire throughout the entire area of conflict and along the entirety of the line as it existed at 22.00 hours GMT on 22 September 1965. They protest and report every violation of the cease-fire and the cease-fire line that they can observe or confirm.

As to section (2) of your letter, your statements concerning the activities of Pakistan forces and of their asserted claim about certain areas they have occupied in Rajasthan, have been carefully noted.

With respect to section (3) of your letter, I may point out that paragraph 4 of my report of 27 September merely sought to delineate the situation as it was reported to be by the observers. Their reports, I must add, would not substantiate a contention that there had been movement forward into new positions since the effective date of the cease-fire from one side of the line only.

Full note is taken of the views of the Government of India about paragraph 5 of my report as set forth in section (4) of your letter. In that paragraph, which presents only a view offered by General Nimmo, the reference is exclusively to withdrawals. General Nimmo considered it inadvisable to try to define positions from which each side should withdraw, preferring that there be withdrawals by each party everywhere to its own side of the line.

I may assure you, therefore, that there is no idea in that paragraph, direct or implied, of 'telescoping cease-fire and withdrawals into a single operation'. In this regard, may I point out that the concern of this particular report, as made clear by its title, is compliance with the withdrawal and not the cease-fire provisions of the Council's resolution 211 (1965) of 20 September. . . . [*S/6782, 13 Oct. 1965, Letter of 12 Oct. 1965 from Secretary-General to representative of India.*]

Pakistan also had some complaints about the identification of 'positions held' from which she would be required to withdraw.

I have the honour to acknowledge receipt of your letter of 26 October 1965 (S/6839), in which you refer to my reports to the Security Council of 27 September and 5 October on the compliance with the withdrawal provision of Security Council resolution 211 (1965) of 20 September (S/6719 and Add. 1).

In the first paragraph of your letter, the view is expressed that in the above-mentioned reports the limits of the areas held by Pakistan troops at the time of the cease-fire have not been described accurately and you draw my attention to the areas in the Bhimber-Akhnur sector and in the Kasur-Khem Karan and Sulaimanke-Fazilka sectors which you affirm were then occupied by Pakistan troops. I note also your request that the limits of the areas under the occupation of Pakistan troops in these two sectors be included in an addendum to one of my reports to the Security Council.

In this connexion, may I point out, at the outset, that my reports to which reference is made did not undertake to present a precise description of the positions held by the opposing forces at the time of the cease-fire; they attempted only to afford to the members of the Security Council 'some indication of the dimensions of the problem of withdrawals' (S/6719, para. 1). In this regard, it may be recalled that I indicated in my report of 27 September that the list of military positions held by each party on the opposite side of the line as of 24 September, as given in that report, 'does not purport to be exhaustive or complete' (*ibid.* para. 3) and that complaints about positions on the wrong side of the line were being investigated by United Nations military observers and, as confirmed, would necessitate corrections in the list. I further indicated in the same document that it was in many cases very difficult to define accurately the exact position held by each party on the wrong side of the line, especially in the southern part of the cease-fire line. In a later report on the observance of the cease-fire, I referred again to this question and pointed out that 'in places where observers were not deployed at the time of the cease-fire—and there are many—the observers often find it very difficult to verify the exact positions held just before the cease-fire' (S/6710/Add. 4, para. 8).

Military observers are still attempting, in certain areas, to verify the positions assertedly under the military control of each side at the time of the cease-fire. The results of these efforts will be reported to the Security Council in due course.

In the first paragraph of your letter, it was stated that immediately after the cease-fire, Pakistan Army authorities informed UNIPOM about the limits of the Indian territory under their control in various sectors at the time of the cease-fire.

The Chief Officer of UNIPOM reported this to me at the time. As you know, however, UNIPOM and UNMOGIP have also received from Indian Army authorities information on the positions held by the respective armies at the time of the cease-fire, which is considerably at variance with that given by Pakistan. United Nations observers, therefore, have no alternative but to consider the information received from each side as a claim by one of the parties, until, where possible, it can be verified by the observers. This verification process continues. . . . [*S/6878, 4 Nov. 1965, Letter from Secretary-General to representative of Pakistan.*]

It has been noted elsewhere[12] that there was initial disagreement between India and the Secretary-General on the establishment of UNIPOM as a separate entity from UNMOGIP. India had wished UNMOGIP to operate not only on the 1949 Kashmir cease-fire line, but on the new cease-fire lines of the 1965 fighting; and had advanced reasons as to why she thought this legally possible, as well as administratively desirable (S/6735).[13] The Secretary-General, however, took the view that UNMOGIP had authority to act only

---

[12] Full details, above, pp. 442–7.
[13] See also S/6742, S/6782.

along the 1949 cease-fire line, and that a new unit was needed unless both parties were willing to extend UNMOGIP's authority. Pakistan was not willing, stating that 'any attempted merging of the two operations, UNMOGIP and UNIPOM, will be illegal, arbitrary, and lacking consent' (S/6751); thus the Secretary-General's view prevailed, and came to be accepted by India.

It will be seen that the positions taken by India and Pakistan *vis-à-vis* the UN, and UNMOGIP in particular, were merely expressions of the normal problems of disengagement from hostilities. At all times both India and Pakistan have accepted a UN role in the Kashmir question, and have welcomed the presence of UNMOGIP as an impartial agent. While UNIPOM has now withdrawn from the Indian sub-continent, upon the completion of its tasks, UNMOGIP remains, maintaining its eighteen-year-old cordial relationship with India and Pakistan.

10

RELATIONS WITH OTHER STATES INVOLVED

NO MAJOR interests of other Powers intruded upon the UN's relations with India and Pakistan in respect of UNMOGIP. The 'Commonwealth' interest and position of the United Kingdom is dealt with in Section 1 (pp. 315–18 above); and the role of the Soviet Union in the Tashkent Agreement in Section 12 (pp. 411–13 below).

11

FINANCE

UNMOGIP is among those UN peacekeeping operations which have been raised on the regular budget, without major controversy, under the heading of 'Special Missions and Inquiries'.[1]

1. In 1949 and 1950 UNMOGIP did not appear in the Budget as a separate item: instead, UNCIP includes an item for 'travel and subsistence of observers'. The figure for 1949 was $226,937, and for 1950 $276,173.

2. From 1951–4 UNMOGIP was included as a separate listing in the Budgetary Estimates, with a complete breakdown appearing in the Detailed Schedule.

[1] For general observations on this budgetary procedure, see vol. I of this work, *The Middle East* p. 133 n. 1.

(*US dollars*)

	1951	1952	1953	1954
Temporary assistance	88,720	52,019	25,509	19,907
Travel and subsistence of military observers	264,648	371,656	286,044	185,216
Travel and subsistence of staff	151,838	207,000	136,914	94,631
Communications services	4,871	2,945	2,413	1,788
Rental of premises	8,745	8,108	7,968	11,075
Stationery and office supplies	3,816	7,882	2,716	2,334
Local transport	81,533	58,106	3,464	3,119
Operation and maintenance of transport equipment		3,593	38,794	27,136
Freight, cartage, and express	3,556	20,326	11,452	10,543
Rental of aircraft				79,805
Insurance	5,725	10,600	10,780	4,241
Miscellaneous supplies and services	14,383	21,264	16,081	11,708
Contractual support services			46,592	
Transportation equipment	1,645	6,871	14,925	17,912
Miscellaneous equipment	7,088	10,086	8,188	3,276
Hospitality	684	36	11	
Consultants	539			
TOTAL	$637,791	$780,492	$611,851	$472,691
Documentary source:	A/2125	A/2383	A/2647	A/2904

Note: The official records for the 11th session of the Assembly give no details of allocations for individual 'Special Missions', nor details of expenditures for the previous year. Only a total figure is given for the entire item 'Special Mission', together with a breakdown for the UN Advisory Council for Somaliland under Italian Administration. The Editor has therefore been unable to provide the figures for 1955.

3. After the eleventh session, the Budget Estimates no longer contained a Detailed Schedule, and an alteration thus occurred in the method of presenting UNMOGIP estimates and expenditures:

(US dollars)

	1956	*1957*	*1958*
Salaries and wages	25,602	39,122	32,009
Travel and subsistence of military observers	145,683	153,638	146,338
Travel and subsistence of staff	82,988	82,283	59,887
Transportation equipment	8,745		
Miscellaneous equipment	163,061	131,332	108,951
Miscellaneous supplies and services			
Permanent equipment		24,475	15,347
TOTAL	431,965	430,850	362,532
Documentary source:	A/3600	A/3825	A/4110

4. At the fifteenth session a further change occurred in the method of presenting budgetary figures for 'Special Missions and Related Activities'.

(US dollars)

	1959	*1960*	*1961*	*1962*	*1963*	*1964*	*1965*	*1966*
Common staff costs	—	—	—	—	—	—	—	107,244
Salaries of staff	30,330	23,092	39,431	45,094	45,714	53,011	56,727	285,851
Subsistence and travel of staff	60,521	55,796	60,582	62,358	62,667	82,114	124,501	188,442
Subsistence and travel of military observers	161,252	167,956	197,095	197,409	191,094	232,069	431,475	374,497
Maintenance and rental of premises and equipment	25,003	15,363	17,382	18,192	21,123	18,763	45,299	81,695
Maintenance of vehicles	22,337	22,826	15,301	16,011	17,472	24,120	25,288	62,815
Communications, freight, supplies, services	41,936	44,000	50,200	54,175	54,121	58,416	118,279	99,873

	1959	1960	1961	1962	1963	1964	1965	1966
Rental of aircraft	69,183	67,657	45,000	42,000	25,795	38,219	176,765	126,262
Purchase of furniture and fixtures	11,997	15,499	12,930	12,178	15,104	2,703	133,422	165,717
Purchase of vehicles	12,480	9,726	8,415	8,905	4,870	9,277	113,753	6,410
TOTAL	435,039	421,915	446,336	456,332	437,960	518,692	1,225,509	1,498,806
Documentary source:	A/4370	A/4770	A/5205	A/5505	A/5805	A/6005	A/6305	A/6705

The increases in the expenditures for 1965 were due to the emergency strengthening of UNMOGIP under Security Council res. 210 (1965) of 6 Sept. 1965 (see above, pp. 392–3).

I 2

IMPLEMENTATION

I T will be recalled that UNMOGIP's tasks were to help in the demarcation of the cease-fire line, to observe any breaches of the cease-fire, and by its very presence to encourage observation of the cease-fire: it later was also required to assist the supervision of the 1965 cease-fire in so far as that related to the original Kashmir cease-fire line and to participate in securing the withdrawal of troops back to their own side of the line. It may fairly be said that UNMOGIP has very effectively carried out these tasks. The outbreak of major hostilities in 1965 was due to no inefficiency or inadequacy on UNMOGIP's part, but rather to the failure over the years of any progress to a political solution. It was never part of UNMOGIP's task either to achieve a political solution to Kashmir, or to enforce the peace. The Security Council established first UNCIP, and then a series of UN Special Representatives, to seek a political solution: but long before 1965 an impasse had been reached.

A résumé of the major political events up to UNMOGIP's effective formation in mid-1949 has been given in Section 1 (pp. 315–30). In December 1949, with UNMOGIP now operational, UNCIP submitted its third interim report (S/1430). It reported considerable progress with the truce, and said that its investigative function was now complete. So far as mediation was concerned, UNCIP believed that it had exhausted all the possibilities. It thought that any further attempts at negotiations would be better carried out by an individual UN representative. (A minority report was appended by the Czechoslovakian delegate,[1] criticizing certain aspects of the Commission's work, and notably the fact that the Commission was not composed of all the members of the Security Council. Such a Commission would be appropriate for carrying on the task of mediation.) However, both the majority and minority reports agreed that broader terms of reference were needed. The Security Council now agreed (with the abstention of Russia and the Ukraine) that its President (General McNaughton of Canada) should endeavour to mediate between the parties. The President submitted his report and proposals (S/1453). These were summarized in the Council's report to the Assembly:

> The principal considerations underlying that proposal were that the future of the State should be determined by a free and impartial plebiscite, to take place as early as possible; that agreements already reached between the parties should be preserved; and that discussion of disputed issues of the past should be avoided. The demilitarization should include the withdrawal of the regular forces of Pakistan; the withdrawal of the regular forces of India not required for the security of the maintenance of law and order on the Indian side of the cease-fire line; and also the reduction of local forces including, on the one side, the armed forces and militia of the State, and, on the other side, the *Azad* forces. The administration of the northern area should, subject to United Nations supervision, be continued by the existing local authorities. The Government of Pakistan should give unconditional assurance to the Government of India that it would deal effectively within its own borders with any possibility of tribal incursions into the State and should undertake to keep the Senior United Nations Military Observer informed and to satisfy him that the arrangements to this end were, and continued to be, adequate. The Governments of India and Pakistan should confirm the inviolability of the cease-fire line. Agreement should be reached between the Governments of India and Pakistan on the basic principles of demilitarization; on the minimum forces required for the maintenance of security and of local law and order and on their general disposition; on a date by which the reduction of forces was to be accomplished and on the progressive steps to be taken in reducing and redistributing the forces to a level sufficiently low so as not to constitute a restriction on the free expression of opinion for the purpose of the plebiscite. The two Governments should further agree that a United Nations representative be appointed by the Secretary-General to supervise the progressive steps of the demilitarization programme and to interpret the agreements between the parties on the follow-matters: demilitarization, minimum forces and their general disposition; the date of reduction of forces; and the progressive steps in reducing and redistributing the forces. When this programme had been accomplished to the satisfaction of the United Nations representative, the Plebiscite Administrator should proceed to exercise the functions assigned to him by the Commission's resolution of 5 January 1949. The United Nations representative should be authorized to make any suggestions to the parties, which, in his opinion, would be likely to contribute to the expeditious and enduring solution of the dispute and to place his good offices at their disposal. [*A/1361*, *Report of Security Council to General Assembly*, p. 8 (*GAOR*, 5th sess., Suppl. 2).]

General McNaughton continued to act as a channel between the parties after the expiry of his term as President. However, it became apparent that fundamental differences still existed between the parties. India charged the UN with failing to secure the withdrawal of the Pakistani troops which had entered Kashmir after October 1948, before UNCIP actually arrived. India reiterated that her acceptance of UNCIP's proposals had been conditional upon the sovereignty of Sheikh Abdullah's government not being brought into question;

---

[1] No longer Josef Korbel, who had been withdrawn.

upon no recognition being afforded to the Azad Kashmir government; and upon the disbanding of the Azad Kashmir forces. Pakistan, on the other hand, insisted that, as minimum conditions, all foreign troops should withdraw, that a non-partisan administration should be established in Kashmir, and that a plebiscite should be organized and conducted by the UN.

On 14 March 1950 the Security Council adopted the following resolution (by 8 votes, with India and Yugoslavia abstaining, and with the Soviet Union absent):

The Security Council,

Having received and noted the reports of the United Nations Commission for India and Pakistan, established by the resolutions of 20 January and 21 April 1948

Having also received and noted the report of General A. G. L. McNaughton on the outcome of his discussion with the representatives of India and Pakistan which were initiated in pursuance of the decision taken by the Security Council on 17 December 1949

Commending the Governments of India and Pakistan for their statesmanlike action in reaching the agreements embodied in the United Nations Commission's resolutions of 13 August 1948 and 5 January 1949 for a cease-fire, for the demilitarization of the State of Jammu and Kashmir and for the determination of its final disposition in accordance with the will of the people through the democratic method of a free and impartial plebiscite and commending the parties in particular for their action in partially implementing these resolutions by

(1) The cessation of hostilities effected 1 January 1949;

(2) The establishment of a cease-fire line on 27 July 1949, and

(3) The agreement that Fleet Admiral Chester W. Nimitz shall be Plebiscite Administrator,

Considering that the resolution of the oustanding difficulties should be based upon the substantial measure of agreement on fundamental principles already reached, and that steps should be taken forthwith for the demilitarization of the State and for the expeditious determination of its future in accordance with the freely expressed will of the inhabitants,

1. *Calls upon* the Governments of India and Pakistan to make immediate arrangements without prejudice to their rights or claims and with due regard to the requirements of law and order, to prepare and execute within a period of five months from the date of this resolution a programme of demilitarization on the basis of the principles of paragraph 2 of General McNaughton's proposal or of such modifications of those principles as may be mutually agreed;

2. *Decides* to appoint a United Nations Representative for the following purposes who shall have authority to perform his functions in such place or places as he may deem appropriate:

(*a*) To assist in the preparation and to supervise the implementation of the programme of demilitarization referred to above and to interpret the agreements reached by the parties for demilitarization,

(*b*) To place himself at the disposal of the Governments of India and Pakistan and to place before these Governments or the Security Council any suggestions which, in his opinion, are likely to contribute to the expeditious and enduring solution of the dispute which has arisen between the two Governments in regard to the State of Jammu and Kashmir,

(*c*) To exercise all of the powers and responsibilities devolving upon the United Nations Commission by reason of existing resolutions of the Security Council and by reason of the agreement of the parties embodied in the resolutions of the United Nations Commission of 13 August 1948 and 5 January 1949,

(*d*) To arrange at the appropriate stage of demilitarization for the assumption by the Plebiscite Administrator of the functions assigned to the latter under agreements made between the parties,

13*

(e) To report to the Security Council as he may consider necessary submitting his conclusions and any recommendations which he may desire to make;

3. *Requests* the two Governments to take all necessary precautions to ensure that their agreements regarding the cease-fire shall continue to be faithfully observed, and *calls upon* them to take all possible measures to ensure the creation and maintenance of an atmosphere favourable to the promotion of further negotiations;

4. *Extends* its best thanks to the members of the United Nations Commission for India and Pakistan and to General A. G. L. McNaughton for their arduous and fruitful labours;

5. *Agrees* that the United Nations Commission for India and Pakistan shall be terminated, and decides that this shall take place one month after both parties have informed the United Nations Representative of their acceptance of the transfer to him of the powers and responsibilities of the United Nations Commission referred to in paragraph 2 (*c*) above.   [*SC res. S/1469, 14 Mar. 1950.*]

On 12 April 1950 the Council appointed Sir Owen Dixon of Australia as UN Representative for India and Pakistan[2] (by 8 votes to nil, with India and Yugoslavia abstaining, and the USSR absent).[3] On 15 September 1950 he submitted his first report to the Security Council (S/1791). He reported that the parties had done nothing to agree upon the details necessary for the carrying out of the plebiscite, and that his various proposals had all been rejected by India, or more infrequently, by Pakistan. The concluding part of his report clearly reveals that he felt the situation hopeless, and that the UN would have to resign itself to a *de facto* division of Kashmir.

A Commonwealth attempt to mediate in early 1951 was no more successful. Pakistan accepted all the proposals made by the Commonwealth Prime Ministers' Conference, but India felt unable to accept any of them.

The Security Council passed yet another resolution (S/2017) appointing a UN Representative to effect, after consultation with India and Pakistan, the demilitarization of Kashmir within three points, and to itemize points of difference arising over interpretations of the UNCIP resolutions[4] which the parties had accepted. The resolution also contained a clause for arbitration, in case of failure. This caused India to reject it. In April 1951 Dr Frank Graham was appointed UN Representative none the less. He was accorded a hostile reception on the Indian sub-continent. Tension between India and Pakistan was again very great,[5] and in the summer of 1951 war appeared imminent. With a remarkable resilience Dr Graham persevered long enough, in extraordinarily difficult circumstances, to produce five reports to the Security Council.[6] He sought to identify the differences and to overcome them one by one. Much progress was made, but agreement could not be reached on the scaling of the phases of demilitarization, or the time at which Admiral Nimitz, the Plebiscite Administrator, should enter into the area.

In 1953 India and Pakistan resumed bilateral talks, removing the matter from

[2] S/INF/5/rev. 1, p. 3.

[3] The Korean war had now broken out, at a period when Russia was absenting herself from the Council.

[4] See above, pp. 323–9.

[5] This period is well described in Korbel, pp. 178 ff.

[6] S/2375, 18 Oct. 1951; S/2448, 19 Dec. 1951; S/2611, 22 Apr. 1952; S/2783, 19 Sept. 1952; S/2967, 27 Mar. 1953.

the UN for the first time in six years. Relations between the two countries became more conciliatory. However, on 9 August Sheikh Abdullah was suddenly dismissed from office[7] and Ghulam Mohammed Bakshi was nominated Prime Minister of Kashmir. New violence against Muslims broke out in Kashmir. Immediate Pakistani–Indian consultations were held, and a joint communiqué of 20 August 1953 confirmed that the issue should be resolved by plebiscite. It indicated that the demilitarization problem should be dealt with directly between them, and that a plebiscite administration should be appointed by the end of April 1954. This, too, came to nothing (partly because of disagreement as to whether Nimitz should remain Plebiscite Administrator, which Pakistan wanted and India did not, and partly because both governments were under tremendous domestic pressure not to give ground. It did, however, mark a certain turning-point in the Kashmir affair, in that the UN peaceful-settlement role has never again been as sustained as it was before August 1953. Since the communiqué the UN has concentrated on keeping the peace in Kashmir, and has resigned itself to the fact that only direct agreement can settle the dispute. From 1953 to 1956 the matter did not appear on the Security Council agenda. In February 1957 the Security Council, faced with renewed major tensions, decided to send its President, Gunnar Jarring of Sweden (a country which had not hitherto had occasion to commit itself on Kashmir), to hold talks with the governments of India and Pakistan. (At this time Dr Graham was still UN Representative for India and Pakistan.) Jarring, faced with the old argument that India would not permit a plebiscite because Pakistan had not carried out her part of the agreement, i.e. withdrawal, suggested arbitration on whether implementation by either of the parties of their agreement to the UNCIP resolution of August 1948 was indeed still lacking. Jarring emphasized that what he had in mind was not traditional arbitration, but rather fact-finding, from which they could move forward. After hesitation, Pakistan agreed; but India refused.

Henceforth there were sporadic references to the UN of complaints, by India or Pakistan; but now the UN's main role lay in keeping the peace, through UNMOGIP. And it is to its effectiveness in that area that we now turn.

(a) 1950–65

The success of UNMOGIP in containing breaches of the cease-fire is beyond dispute. In 1950 Sir Owen Dixon, making his report to the Security Council, noted:

10. The United Nations had established a corps of officers provided by various countries to act as observers and assist in maintaining the cease-fire along the line and to secure compliance by the parties with the terms of the armistice. Incidents in which the troops on one side fired on troops on the other or upon a civilian or civilians occurred frequently at some point or another on the line, but the incidents nearly all proved of small importance relatively and none threatened a general outbreak of hostilities. [S/1791, 15 Sept. 1950, Report to Security Council of UN Representative for India and Pakistan.]

[7] See Korbel, pp. 240–50; and Lamb, pp. 70–85.

His successor, Frank Graham, pertinently observed a year later:

In the state of Jammu and Kashmir itself the United Nations organization for the supervision, by means of the Military Observer Group, of the cease-fire line, was working effectively and, despite incidents, was continuing its successful assistance to the two Governments
in their will to fulfil their commitments under the cease-fire arrangements.

Finally, the United Nations Representative should like to emphasize the importance of the
task of the United Nations Military Observer Group on the sub-continent in supervising the
cease-fire in the State of Jammu and Kashmir. [*S/2375, 15 Oct. 1951, Report to Security
Council of UN Representative for India and Pakistan.*]

At the same time minor incidents continued to occur across the cease-fire
line, over which India and Pakistan exchanged accusations:

I am instructed to transmit to you the following communication dated 29 June 1951 from
the Prime Minister and Foreign Minister of India:

'1. The Government of India desires to invite the attention of the Security Council to
the series of violations by Pakistan, which have occurred during the last fortnight, of the
cease-fire line and of the agreement between India and Pakistan. Of these, the Government
of India would draw prominent attention to three incidents. One of these occurred in
Jammu Province inside Indian territory and 800 yards from the border. Two of our troops
were ambushed by Pakistan armed forces and killed. The bodies were dragged into Pakistan
territory and after considerable delay were recovered from Pakistan by one of the United
Nations observers and handed back to our troops. Another incident quickly followed, also
within our territory in the same area. Our patrols were fired at from the border by Pakistan
armed forces and one of our men was killed and three wounded. A third incident occurred
in the Tithwal area, also within our territory. When our troops were patrolling along the
border, Pakistan troops fired at them from the other side, wounded three, and kidnapped
one of the wounded to their territory. The kidnapped man, after the intervention of the
United Nations observers, was returned to us four days later. Pakistan troops further
opened fire on two other occasions on our troops patrolling the area near Uri. . . .'
[*S/2225, 30 June 1951, Letter from representative of India to President of Security Council.*]

1. On 25 June 1951 at Uri, a platoon of Pakistan troops and fifty civilians raided three
villages 1,000 yards within Indian territory, flogged the male inhabitants and looted 4,000
rupees' worth of ornaments and took away 186 goats or sheep.

2. On 25 June 1951, seven Pakistan Border Police laid ambush eight and one-half miles
south west of Ranbirsinghpura, and drove away all cattle from a village within Indian
territory.

3. On 26 June 1951 at Samba, Pakistan Border Police opened fire on a patrol within Indian
territory killing one and wounding four, and

4. On 30 June 1951 also at Samba, Pakistan Border Police fired 2,000 rounds at an Indian
patrol within Indian territory.

I am further to inform you that the first and third incidents reported in my letter of 30
June 1951, forwarding a communication from the Prime Minister and Minister for Foreign
Affairs of India, occurred on 23 June 1951 and the second incident reported therein on 26
June 1951. All of these incidents were duly reported to the United Nations observers.
[*S/2233, 5 July 1951, Letter from representative of India to President of Security Council.*]

The military situation remained fairly constant from 1951 to 1963: minor
violations, reported and investigated by UNMOGIP, and virtually no progress
on a political solution. In 1963 a particular dispute arose between India and
Pakistan over the village of Chaknot (Changar); and over the status of
UNMOGIP in relation thereto:

1. I am instructed by the Government of Pakistan to draw the attention of the Security Council to certain unmistakably hostile military activities on the part of Indian authorities which have resulted in a grave situation along the cease-fire line in Kashmir.

2. The background of this situation consists of measures taken by the Government of India, for sometime past, to evict the Muslim population residing on the Indian side of the cease-fire line from its homes and push it into Azad Kashmir. Protests in this regard were lodged with the Government of India on 19 November 1960, 10 December 1960 and 25 February 1961. Though the Government of India denied the basis of these reports, yet the eviction of the Muslim population continued spasmodically. By June 1961 some 2,000 Muslims from Indian-occupied Kashmir had crossed over to Azad Kashmir and by March 1963, 503 families consisting of 2,787 members had been forced to flee their homes and take refuge in Azad Kashmir.

3. Recently, there have been indications that Indian forces are planning to step up these operations. In particular, Indian armed patrols have been paying increasing attention to Chaknot village (also called Changnar on certain maps) which, though lying on the Indian side of the cease-fire line, has been under the administrative control of the Azad Kashmir authorities ever since the conclusion of the Agreement regarding the establishment of a cease-fire line in 1949. The position of this village is not unique: there are a number of such areas in Kashmir which, being difficult of access from the Indian side, did not suffer the intrusion of the Indian army, as was the case with the rest of Indian-occupied Kashmir, and have, therefore, remained under the political and administrative control of the Azad Kashmir Government. Now, in an apparent attempt to wrest Chaknot and its adjoining hamlets by force from Azad Kashmir, Indian troops and armed police have employed the criminal means of murder and assault; consequently, a number of families were forced to leave their homes in Ring Bela and move into Azad Kashmir on 8 August 1963. Recently, the Indian army has constructed a mule track from Ring Pain to Long Ridge, overlooking Chaknot, and has been seen to be in the process of establishing an armed post on Long Ridge, preparatory to the moving of its troops into the village.

4. The Government of Pakistan addressed a note on 16 October 1963 to the Government of India, through their High Commissioner in Pakistan, strongly protesting against these moves and asking the Government of India to desist from proceeding with any plans aimed at the forcible seizure of Chaknot or other such areas in Kashmir. The note stated that 'if the Government of India tried to go forward with the plan, Azad Kashmir forces would be compelled to take whatever steps would be necessary to defend themselves'.

5. Normally, complaints of hostile activities on the cease-fire line in Kashmir fall within the purview of the United Nations Military Observer Group in India and Pakistan and it is within their competence to decide whether or not there is a violation of the Cease-Fire Agreement by either side. The present situation, as described above, however, is of far greater significance than a mere breach of the Cease-Fire Agreement inasmuch as it is the result of an attempt to upset by violence the political and administrative status of an area which is under the control of Azad Kashmir. It is relevant to mention here that the people of the area concerned have been paying land revenue to the Azad Kashmir Government and receiving *taccavi* loans from it. The Indian authorities made attempts on 5 and 8 August 1962 to force these people to pay those dues to them and, having failed, are now making military preparations to occupy the area. They are thus trying to wrest the area by the use, or threat, of force from Azad Kashmir. Evidently, this conduct is in total negation of the spirit of the international agreement which governs the status of Jammu and Kashmir.

6. It appears from reports that, for their hostile activities, the Government of India are putting forward the excuse that the village of Chaknot, like some other such areas, lies on the Indian side of the cease-fire line. My Government is confident that this excuse will be found unacceptable by the United Nations, because it is based upon a wilful misrepresentation of the legal and human realities surrounding the cease-fire line. This line was established, in the language of the Agreement of 27 July 1949, 'as a complement of the suspension of hostilities'. As such, it was meant to denote only the separation of troops on the two sides. It could not,

and does not, in any way determine the political or administrative status of any area whatsoever in the State of Jammu and Kashmir nor does it govern the movement or activities of civilians on either side. That a party should use, or threaten to use, force to secure its position on a line which itself represented the cessation of the use of force, is a position that cannot be justified on any grounds whatsoever. [*S/5450, 1 Nov. 1963, Letter from representative of Pakistan to President of Security Council.*]

India made the following points in reply:

4. The Government of India has built no mule track leading to the village of Chaknot or Changnar, nor set up any armed post in the village or on any ridge overlooking the village. No Indian troops have been concentrated in this area. On the contrary, Pakistan troops have been recently deployed in the Kel area, in the vicinity of this village, and Pakistan aircraft have been seen flying over this area. The Government of India has already denied the Pakistan allegations of the so-called 'spasmodic eviction of Muslims'. It is absurd to suggest that Muslims are being ejected from Kashmir, when Kashmir is a State where the Muslims form a proud majority. The United Nations observers are stationed along the cease-fire line and the Government of India has already brought Pakistan's violations of the Cease-Fire Agreement to their notice and they have full confidence that the United Nations observers will duly ascertain the facts.

5. The Pakistan Government has taken great pains to argue that Pakistan's violations of the cease-fire line and its attempts at disturbing the normal life of villages on the Indian side of the cease-fire line should be treated as falling outside the scope of the Cease-Fire Agreement and the tasks assigned to the United Nations observers under the Agreement. This is a further attempt by the aggressor to wriggle out of his solemn commitments and prepare the ground for further aggression. All this can deceive no one, particularly when the world at large is aware that India has categorically stated that it will not use force across the cease-fire line, but defend itself, if attacked. Pakistan could have referred its allegations of Indian troop concentrations along the cease-fire line to the United Nations observers who are there to look into complaints of this nature. Instead Pakistan is deliberately adopting this alternative of writing letters to the Security Council with the sole object of maligning India and misleading the Security Council. [*S/5467, 27 Nov. 1963, Letter from representative of India to President of Security Council.*]

The Chief Military Observer found in this particular case in favour of India, and gave an award of 'violation' against Pakistan (S/5503).

The year 1964 marked a period of rapid deterioration in India–Pakistan relations. The number and seriousness of incidents greatly increased:

On the instructions of my Government, I have the honour to transmit a copy of a note containing the protest lodged by the Government of India with the Government of Pakistan against a dastardly attack by the Pakistan Armed Forces on an Indian police patrol on 21 February 1964. In consequence of this grave violation by Pakistan of the cease-fire line and the Cease-fire Agreement, proven by the findings of the United Nations Military Observers Group in India and Pakistan, fourteen valuable lives were lost and nine members of the patrol captured and unlawfully detained.

This is the second serious incident in which the United Nations Chief Military Observer has had to give an award against Pakistan in recent months. The first was in the case of Chaknot on which I had the honour to address two letters to you on 27 November 1963 and on 3 January 1964.

It is quite clear that the Government of Pakistan are deliberately trying to create tension and conflict across the cease-fire line, in utter disregard of the provisions of the Cease-fire Agreement.

It is requested that this communication be brought to the notice of the members of the Security Council.

(*Signed*) B. N. CHAKRAVARTY
Permanent Representative of India to the United Nations

NOTE DATED 11 APRIL 1964 FROM THE MINISTRY FOR EXTERNAL AFAIRS OF THE GOVERNMENT OF INDIA TO THE HIGH COMMISSION FOR PAKISTAN IN INDIA

1. The Ministry for External Affairs, Government of India, presents its compliments to the High Commission for Pakistan in India, and has the honour to bring to its notice a grave violation of the Cease-fire Agreement by the Pakistan Armed Forces.

2. On 21 February 1964, an Indian armed constabulary patrol was ambushed on the Indian side of the cease-fire line near Keran by Pakistan troops. Fire was also opened on the patrol from across the Kishenganga River. Only two members of the patrol managed to return.

3. Admission of this attack on the Indian patrol, which was on routine duty, was given great prominence in the Pakistan Press on 23 February 1964. The *Khyber Mail* of 23 February 1964 reported with bold headlines: 'Heavy casualties were inflicted on the Indian soldiers who intruded into "Azad" Kashmir territory today, it was officially stated here tonight. The engagement took place near Bor village on the Kel sector of the cease-fire line, it was stated. . . . An official source said the "Azad" forces opened fire on the Indian intruders in self-defence.' The same newspaper, in its issue of 29 February 1964, reported a statement by Mr K. H. Khurshid, the so-called ' "Azad" Kashmir' President, in the following words:

'All Indian intruders were either killed or captured by "Azad" Kashmir troops along with their arms and ammunition. Mr. Khurshid said that intrusion into "Azad" Kashmir territory on Friday was a deliberate and well-planned act on the part of Indian rulers, as that was the day when the Chinese Prime Minister, Mr. Chou En-lai, had arrived in Rawalpindi. The Indians, by precipitating a situation in Kashmir, wanted to mar the atmosphere of goodwill and amity that had been created by Mr. Chou En-lai's visit and thus to force the attention of the Western Powers on Kashmir to the disadvantage of Pakistan. This sinister move of Indian rulers, Mr. Khurshid said, however, proved very expensive for India. Friday's incident on the cease-fire line, the "Azad" Kashmir President said, was the biggest one since the termination of hostilities in Kashmir in 1949 in view of the number of casualties, prisoners taken and arms captured.'

4. The version of the event as given out in these reports widely published in Pakistan newspapers, has been proved to be a fabrication by no less an authority than the United Nations Military Observers Group in India and Pakistan, which investigated the incident following an Indian complaint of cease-fire line violation against Pakistan Armed Forces. The award given by the Chief Military Observer states (*vide* letter No. F.326–60, dated 26 March 1964):

'*Tangdhar No. 101*—(Bor area). One (Indian) patrol, strength one platoon of the Armed Constabulary on way from Keran to Bor on 21 February 1964 was ambushed at approximately 11.00 hrs. by Pakistanis in area Nullah-Track junction NL 969802. One head constable and one constable have returned to Keran. There is no news of remaining twenty-three police troops.

'Extensive investigations were carried out by United Nations Observers in the area. These were started whilst physical evidence was still discernible in the snow and on the rocks by the river. There is no doubt that the Indian platoon, moving northwards towards Bor, was ambushed by Pakistan troops on the Indian side of the cease-fire line in the vicinity mentioned in the complaint. Fire was also directed from across the Kishenganga River. Two Indians escaped; nine were captured; and the remainder are missing, believed killed. The bodies have not been located by United Nations Observers.

'*Violation by Pakistan* for crossing the cease-fire line.

'*Violation by Pakistan* for firing.

'It is requested that the captives should be returned to India at an early date, and that their names and numbers should be communicated to Indian Army Headquarters. It is also requested that armed forces of any kind avoid the section of Bor village situated south of the cease-fire line and within 500 yards of it. The villagers would be delighted if they did.'

5. The Government of India strongly protest against this deliberate and carefully planned violation by Pakistan of the cease-fire line and the Cease-fire Agreement, the result of which has been a heavy loss of valuable Indian lives. The Government of India take the most serious view of this incident. They call upon the Government of Pakistan to honour the terms of the Karachi Agreement and hope there will be no repetition of such incidents in the future. The Government of India also demand an immediate return of the nine Indian constables captured by the Pakistan Armed Forces.

6. The Government of India demand of the Government of Pakistan full compensation for the relatives of fourteen members of the patrol who lost their lives as a result of the illegal and aggressive action by the Pakistan Armed Forces in violation of the Cease-fire Agreement.

[*S/5668, 24 Apr. 1964, Letter from representative of India to President of Security Council.*]

1. I am instructed by my Government to draw the attention of the Security Council to certain grave violations by India of the cease-fire line in Jammu and Kashmir and of the Agreement pertaining to it. As can be seen below these violations have consisted of callous and cold-blooded acts of attacking, kidnapping and murdering unarmed civilians by the Indian armed forces.

2. I set out below a description of these incidents, along with the verdict given in each case by the United Nations Chief Military Observer:

(*a*) At 11.00 hours on 26 February 1964, in sector Domel No. 108 (Lubgiran area) two companies of armed Indian soldiers occupied ring contour 8338 on the Pakistan side of the cease-fire line and started firing on Lubiran 8437. Simultaneously, one Indian army patrol crossed the cease-fire line in area 8438 and moved towards the north-west of Lubgiran. The incident was thoroughly investigated by the United Nations Military Observer Group in India and Pakistan who gave a verdict of cease-fire violations against India.

The award given by the United Nations Chief Military Observer stated:

'The investigation disclosed that the Indians crossed the cease-fire line in two places, kidnapped five civilians, two of whom were later released and three killed, and fired on a Pakistani post. (Violation by India for crossing cease-fire line; violation by India for firing.)'

(*b*) On the night of 23–24 March 1964, one company of Indian troops crossed the cease-fire line, raided the village of Bara (0602) at 05.00 hours, killed three civilians, wounded a woman, kidnapped eight civilians, burnt a house and killed nine head of cattle and returned to the Indian-occupied area at 07.00 hours. The dead body of one civilian was also carried away by the Indian troops to the Indian-occupied area.

'Decision: Violation by Indian troops for crossing cease-fire line; violation by Indian troops for firing and use of explosives, 2″ mortars and 3·5 rockets, killing at least five villagers, wounding at least three others and capturing ten civilian prisoners.'

(*c*) On 24 March 1964, India lodged a complaint with the United Nations Military Observer Group regarding an incident on the same date, according to which, at about 00.35 hours (Indian standard time), armed personnel, presumably Razakars, crossed into the Indian side of the cease-fire line and when challenged by the Indian ambush party at NM 146053 (43J/4) opened fire and, in the encounter that followed, twenty-four men from the Pakistan side were killed, and six rifles, three muzzle-loaders, one bayonet and five grenades, and some small arms ammunition were recovered. The complaint was thoroughly investigated by the United Nations Military Observer Group and the award given by the Chief Military Observer was:

'*Decision:* Violation by Indian troops for firing and use of an explosive within five miles of the cease-fire line thereby killing twenty-four civilians without justification.'

(*d*) On 18 May 1964, at about 05.30 hours, an Indian army unit took position in area 9254 and 9354 (map sheet 43F/15) and one company opened fire with mortars and machine-guns in area 9254 aimed at the civilian labourers working there, and another company raided and killed four, and wounded three of them.

The incident was investigated by the United Nations Chief Military Observer who gave an award of:

'Violation by India for firing within five miles of the cease-fire line.'

(*e*) On 20 May 1964, an Indian patrol, with a strength of six, armed with light machine-guns and rifles, crossed the cease-fire line, came to area grid reference 263816 and fired four light machine-gun bursts at 17.30 hours. The fire was directed towards area grid reference 263824 where civilians were grazing their cattle. As a result of the shooting, one woman named Shahjehan, wife of Alaf Din, of the village of Mantahar was killed.

This violation was investigated by the United Nations Chief Military Observer whose award stated:

'Investigation disclosed that an armed party from the Indian side crossed the cease-fire line to a ridge and fired further into the territory of the Pakistan side. A woman was killed by a bullet in the head . . . (Violation by India for firing.)'

3. These are the more serious violations by India of the cease-fire line which have taken place recently. A list of other incidents, though not fatal, but clearly provocative, is given in the appendix. It is regretted that some other incidents have also taken place more recently. These are still under investigation and are not, therefore, included in this list.

4. It is pertinent here to describe the facts about an incident which was the subject of a protest by the Government of India to the Government of Pakistan. On 21 February 1964, an Indian patrol came well within 500 yards of the cease-fire line and kidnapped two men of the Northern Scouts from the Pakistan side of the cease-fire line. On hearing the screams and shouts of these men, Pakistan troops from the neighbourhood attempted to rescue them. This precipitated a clash between the Indian patrol and the Pakistan troops and it was in the heat of the chase, necessitated by sheer reason of self-defence, that the Pakistan troops were eft with no choice but to cross the cease-fire line.

The background of this incident is as follows: Bor village in Keran sector is split into two by the cease-fire line. Under the cease-fire line Agreement, the cease-fire line in this area is inclusive to Pakistan, therefore, under the Agreement, Pakistan has the right to patrol right up to the cease-fire line. This facility is, however, not admissible to India.

In December 1963, it was noticed that the Indian patrols were carrying out aggressive patrolling and violating the Agreement by intruding into Bor village. These dangerous moves, in violation of the Agreement, were brought to the notice of the Chief Military Observer. On 9 January 1964 the Chief Military Observer ruled that under the Agreement 'Pakistan may patrol up to the cease-fire line in that sector, and Indian troops shall remain at a distance of 500 yards of the cease-fire line'. It is a matter of great regret that in spite of the clear decision by the Chief Military Observer, the Government of India ignored this ruling, reinforced its positions in this sector with additional troops and continued to indulge in provocative and aggressive acts. In fact during the period December 1963–February 1964, Indian patrols violated the Agreement on no less than eight occasions, before the patrol clash complained of by the Government of India took place.

It is thus evident that the incident was provoked deliberately by the Indian patrols who, in defiance of the decision of the Chief Military Observer, persistently indulged in aggressive patrolling in the Keran sector. The responsibility for this incident, therefore, clearly rested on the Government of India.

5. It must be added here that the Government of Pakistan has lodged strong protests with the Government of India on these deliberate violations of the cease-fire line by India and has

expressed its grave concern at the wanton attacks by the Indian armed forces. [*S/5836, 27 July 1964, Letter from representative of Pakistan to President of Security Council.*]

India repudiated these charges, and referred to a deliberate policy by the Pakistan government of creating tension along the cease-fire line. India listed awards given by the Chief Observer against Pakistan.[8]

It is noteworthy that six of these awards against Pakistan were given in respect of incidents in June alone. Pakistan newspapers are now openly admitting that the so-called 'Azad Kashmir Mujahids' (irregulars trained in guerilla tactics), not the so-called 'Azad Kashmir civilians'—a term employed in the Acting Permanent Representative's letter—are clashing with the Indian Army.

8. Faced with this violence deliberately unleashed by the Pakistan authorities and a planned and continued threat to the cease-fire line, the Government of India cannot abdicate their responsibility for ensuring the security of their population or their right of self-defence. The Indian military authorities exercise every care in reducing the number of such occasions to a minumum and in employing the least amount of force to repel the raids and attacks from Pakistan on Indian piquets, posts and patrols. The quickest and the most effective way of preventing such defensive action by India, which sometimes results in Pakistan casualties, lies in Pakistan's own hands. One order from them to their armed forces, to respect the provisions of the cease-fire Agreement and the cease-fire line, as indeed they are honour bound to do, would put a stop to these incidents and restore peace and tranquillity so desired by everyone in the area.

9. The Security Council will no doubt recall the Pakistan Government's allegations in regard to the alleged incidents in the area of village Chaknot (S/5450). The United Nations Chief Military Observer's award against Pakistan and in favour of India (S/5467 and S/5503) exposed the falseness of the Pakistan allegations.

10. Among the instances mentioned by the Acting Permanent Representative of Pakistan in his letter under reference (S/5836) there are those in which the Chief Military Observer has either given 'violation' awards against Pakistan or 'no-violation' awards against India. As was to be expected, the Government of Pakistan promptly suppressed these inconvenient facts. To give a few examples:

(i) *Sub-para.* (d) *of para. 2:* The Acting Representative of Pakistan has suppressed the fact that in this incident, the Chief Military Observer also awarded violation against Pakistan in the following words:

Tangdhar Case 104
'Violation by Pakistan for troops crossing the cease-fire line.'
'Violation by Pakistan for constructing new defences in an area contrary to the Karachi Agreement.'

(ii) *Para. 3:* The Acting Permanent Representative of Pakistan has suppressed the facts in six out of nine cases mentioned in the appendix to his letter. In at least three cases (Nos. 3, 8 and 9), the Chief Military Observer, in corresponding complaints filed by India, awarded violations against Pakistan (Naushera Case 138, Poonch Case 265 and Poonch Case 264). In regard to item 4, the Acting Permanent Representative has chosen to give only part of the award, suppressing the portion unfavourable to Pakistan. The full text of the awards is:

'The evidence reveals that both sides fired.
'Violation by India for firing across the cease-fire line.
'Violation by Pakistan for firing across the cease-fire line.'

He should have also informed the Security Council that the alleged violation mentioned in item No. 5 in the appendix was dismissed by the Chief Military Observer (Rawalakot Case 210B). Further, the date and details of the incident as alleged by the Government of Pakistan

---

[8] Pakistan had circulated comparable awards against India (S/8804, app.).

in item 7 of the appendix pertain to a complaint (Rawalakot Case 227) which was, in fact, dismissed by the Chief Military Observer. There are other misrepresentations in the appendix to which I need not refer.

(iii) *Para. 4:* Even here the acting Permanent Representative of Pakistan has not been able to resist the temptation of withholding vital information from the Security Council. Details of this grave violation of the cease-fire Agreement by Pakistan resulting in the death of fourteen Indian policemen and the arrest and detention of nine others, and the Chief Military Observer's award against Pakistan, were given in my letter of 24 April 1964 (S/5668). He has now sought to justify Pakistan's dastardly attack on the Indian patrol in the first sub-paragraph of paragraph 4 of his letter, suppressing the fact that his Government had lodged a complaint against India with the Chief Military Observer, who rejected it by awarding No Violation against India as detailed below:

Domel Case 107 (Bor area)
   'One Indian patrol of approximately thirty strong fired at our Bor post SQ 9881 at 09.15 hours on 21 February 1964 and carried away two men of Armed Constabulary who were at that time cutting wood outside.
   CMO's Decision: 'No Violation.'

It is noteworthy that the Acting Permanent Representative of Pakistan admits that the Pakistan troops did cross the cease-fire line.

In the same paragraph, he has alleged that between December 1963 and February 1964, Indian patrols violated the cease-fire Agreement on no less than eight occasions in this sector, before the Indian patrol was ambushed. The facts are that Pakistan lodged two complaints covering seven alleged incidents in this sector with the Chief Military Observer. One of these complaints covering six incidents (Domel Case 105) was dismissed by the Chief Military Observer. In another (Domel Case 107) he awarded No Violation against India. Details of the eighth alleged incident are not available to the Government of India.

11. I should like to add that the Government of India have already lodged this year twenty-nine protests with the Government of Pakistan against grave violations of the cease-fire Agreement, demanding compensation in some cases. These protests are based on the Chief Military Observer's awards of Violations by Pakistan. More protests are being lodged.

12. Unlike Pakistan, India is anxious to maintain the integrity of the cease-fire line and the cease-fire Agreement. India is also anxious to avoid incidents across or in the vicinity of the cease-fire line which create tension and worsen the atmosphere for talks, negotiations and conciliation between the two countries. The Government of India are prepared to concert with the Government of Pakistan in considering ways and means of completely eliminating such incidents and in ensuring the inviolability of the cease-fire line to mutual advantage. Further, the Government of India are prepared to do all this in co-operation with the United Nations Military Observers Group for India and Pakistan (UNMOGIP). Let the Government of Pakistan accept a gentlemen's agreement for avoiding incidents and for full co-operation with the Government of India and the UNMOGIP in making the cease-fire Agreement fully effective in this regard.

13. It is requested that this communication be brought to the notice of the members of the Security Council. (*S/5911, 21 Aug. 1964, Letter from representative of India to President of Security Council.*]

The Security Council discussed the situation at fifteen meetings held between 3 February and 18 May 1964.[9] During the course of these Pakistan asserted[10] that the tense situation arose from the continued imprisonment of Sheikh Abdullah, and India's declared intention to 'integrate' Kashmir into Indian Union territory. Pakistan pointed to the Indian Prime Minister's statement on

[9] See A/5802, Report of Security Council to General Assembly, *GAOR*, 19th sess., pp. 85–92.
[10] Ibid. pp. 85–87.

27 November 1963 that Article 370 of the Indian constitution, which gave Kashmir a special status, would be subject to a process of 'gradual erosion'. Pakistan regarded this as destroying the basis of agreement on Kashmir, and as violative of Security Council resolutions of 30 March 1951 and 24 January 1957.[11]

India replied that the whole of Kashmir had become an integral part of India when the ruler of Jammu and Kashmir had executed the Instrument of Accession to India and the then Governor-General had accepted the Instrument. The Instrument was not conditional upon the people being consulted. It was in this context that the UNCIP resolutions of 1948 and 1949 had to be understood: the very foundation of those resolutions was that the presence of Pakistan in parts of Kashmir was illegal, and that Pakistan must withdraw her troops. Only when that was done, could a plebiscite be held. India's agreement to a plebiscite had only been given in that context. Moreover, its purpose had been to ascertain the wishes of the people. Since then, Kashmir had had three general elections with universal adult franchise, and these had returned to power a party supporting integration with India. The UNCIP resolutions were therefore absolute and no longer binding on India.[12]

Pakistan retorted that the obligation to withdraw her troops was not a unilateral one, but was to have been part of a synchronized withdrawal, leading to the demilitarization of the state. India had refused to co-operate in arriving at an agreement to this end.[13] In spite of long and detailed discussion, no resolution was advanced by the Security Council, which instead entrusted its President to draw up agreed conclusions to the debate. These were:

I. (a) The members of the Council noted that the debate of the last week followed the discussions which had taken place in February and March of this year on the question of Jammu and Kashmir. They recalled that, especially during the month of February, they had already expressed the views of their Governments on the basic facts pertaining to the problem, including the pertinent resolutions of the United Nations, the question of the juridical status of Jammu and Kashmir, and the principles of the Charter applicable to the case. They confirmed that the statements which they had made at that time were still valid.

(b) The members of the Council expressed their concern regarding two great countries which should have good relations one with the other and the opinion that the present differences between them—particularly the question of Jammu and Kashmir—should be settled amicably in the interests of world peace.

(c) The members of the Council expressed their feeling that recent developments might lead to a softening of the positions adopted, to better mutual understanding and, therefore, to a situation in which the conversations between the parties concerned would have a better chance of leading to a settlement.

(d) The members of the Council expressed their conviction that everything possible should be done to consolidate these favourable elements and to avoid jeopardizing these advantages, which would require on the part of the parties concerned an attitude of conciliation and moderation and, on the part of the United Nations, an attitude of prudence, as well as of careful and vigilant attention.

(e) The members of the Council expressed the hope that the two parties would abstain from any act that might aggravate the situation and that they would take such measures

---

[11] See above, pp. 376–7.   [12] A/5802, p. 85.   [13] Ibid. p. 90.

as would re-establish an atmosphere of moderation between the two countries and also peace and harmony among the communities.

(*f*) The members of the Council expressed the hope that, in the light of the debate, the two countries would resume their contacts as soon as possible in order to resolve their differences by negotiation, in particular their differences related to Jammu and Kashmir.

II. A number of members of the Council had expressed the view that the Secretary-General of the United Nations might eventually give useful assistance to the parties to facilitate the resumption of negotiations on the question of Jammu and Kashmir or to assist them in carrying out those negotiations if they should meet with any difficulties. Other members of the Council, on the other hand, had expressed the view that the negotiations between India and Pakistan might be complicated by the intervention of any outside elements, and that the parties should be left to come to agreement on the very principle of turning to the Secretary-General.

III. The India–Pakistan question remained on the agenda of the Security Council. [*A/5802, Report of Security Council, 16 July 1963–15 July 1964, to General Assembly (GAOR, 19th sess., suppl. 2, p. 101).*]

The year 1965 marked a complete breakdown of the cease-fire agreement of 29 July 1949. In the early part of the year fighting had broken out over the Rann of Kutch.[14] The United Kingdom had played a considerable part in mediation on this dispute, and by 30 June 1965 India and Pakistan had agreed to call for an immediate cease-fire in the Rann of Kutch and the restoration of the *status quo ante*. The agreement[15] provided that the two governments would seek to determine the border, but that if they had not succeeded within two months, they would have recourse to a tribunal of three persons, none of whom would be an Indian or Pakistani. On 14 December 1965 the Secretary-General, at the request of the two governments, nominated Judge Lagergren of Sweden as chairman, and the tribunal began its hearings on 18 February 1966. On 19 February 1968 the tribunal awarded 10 per cent of the disputed territory to Pakistan and the remainder to India.[16]

In June 1965 Pakistan charged that an Indian military build-up was taking place in Kashmir; and that two separate attacks had been made on posts on the Pakistani side of the cease-fire line. The situation rapidly deteriorated, and the Secretary-General, referring to 'recent extensive disregard for the cease-fire agreement and the cease-fire line',[17] submitted a report to the Security Council. He stated that '2. There can be little doubt that the Kashmir problem has again become acute and is now dangerously serious' (para. 2) and indicated that the Karachi cease-fire agreement of 27 July 1949, realizing the objective of the Security Council resolution of 21 April 1948, had collapsed. Throughout the years UNMOGIP's

very presence in the area, of course, had acted to some extent as a deterrent, but this is not the case at present . . .

INCREASE IN VIOLATIONS OF THE CEASE-FIRE

4. There has been a disturbing increase in the number of incidents involving violations of

---

[14] *YBUN, 1965*, pp. 159–60.   [15] 548 UNTS 277.

[16] For details see Higgins, 'Findings on the Rann of Kutch', *World Today*, Apr. 1968.

[17] S/6651, para. 1.

the CFL since the beginning of 1965. In mid-June 1965, for example, General Nimmo reported that during the previous five months, a total of 2,231 complaints from both sides charging violation of the cease-fire had been submitted to UNMOGIP. Most of these involved firing across the CFL, although some concerned crossings of the line by armed men. As of that date, 377 violations in all categories had been confirmed by investigations of the observers, 218 of which were committed by Pakistan and 159 by India. Some of these violations took the form of 'heavy and prolonged firing' from weapons up to the calibre of field artillery. Among the most serious of the violations was one that occurred in May of this year, when Indian troops in battalion strength attacked and captured Pakistan positions in the Kargil area of Kashmir and remained in occupation of them. In the interest of preserving the CFL, I appealed to the Government of India to withdraw its troops from the Pakistan side of the line. On assurance from me that United Nations observers would henceforth by stationed on both sides of the line in that area, which India considered strategically vital to the security of the Srinagar–Leh road, the Government of India agreed to do so and in due course the Indian troops were withdrawn, thus closing the matter and making unnecessary any further consideration of a report on it to the Security Council. Subsequently, there were some military attacks on the road by armed elements from the Pakistan side.

EVENTS SINCE 5 AUGUST 1965

5. The current serious trouble affecting the cease-fire and the CFL in Kashmir dated from 5 August 1965, and consists of a large number of violations of the CFL by crossings of the Line, by firing across it with artillery pieces, and by the occupation of positions on the wrong side of the Line. Lt.-Gen. Robert H. Nimmo, the Chief Military Observer of UNMOGIP, has been sending the United Nations Headquarters daily telegrams on the incidents that have been occurring as reported to him, together with as much confirmed information as possible on the basis of the investigations of specific incidents by United Nations military observers. The investigations, being conducted on the spot, require time, of course, particularly since some of the places are very difficult of access, fighting is going on and the roads are sometimes closed by military order. UNMOGIP has never before been called upon to cope with such a great number of simultaneous violations of the CFL. The adequacy of the present number of observers and of their functions may well be reappraised in the light of experiences since 5 August.

6. General Nimmo has indicated to me that the series of violations that began on 5 August were to a considerable extent in subsequent days in the form of armed men, generally not in uniform, crossing the cease-fire line from the Pakistan side for the purpose of armed action on the Indian side. This is a conclusion reached by General Nimmo on the basis of investigations by the United Nations observers, in the light of the extensiveness and character of the raiding activities and their proximity to the CFL, even though in most cases the actual identity of those engaging in the armed attacks on the Indian side of the line and their actual crossing of it could not be verified by direct observation or evidence. As regards violations by artillery, there was heavy and prolonged artillery fire across the CFL from the Pakistan side in the Chhamb–Bhimber area on 15 and 16 August, and on 19 and 26 August the town of Punch was shelled from the Pakistan side, some of the shells hitting the building occupied by United Nations military observers. Pakistan artillery again shelled the town of Punch on 28 August. There was an exchange of artillery fire between the Uri sector on the Indian side and the Chakothi sector on the Pakistan side on 14 August. Also, it has been confirmed and reported on 25 August that Indian artillery shelled the village of Awan, in Pakistan, 5 miles from the CFL in the Bhimber sector. It is likewise confirmed that as of 24 August armed elements from Pakistan were still occupying Indian positions (pickets) north of Mandi in the Punch sector of the CFL. On the other hand, it is confirmed by both United Nations observers and official Indian sources that on 15 August, Indian Army troops reoccupied the Pakistan positions in the Kargil area and have remained there; Indian Army troops supported by artillery on 24 August occupied Pakistan positions in the Tangdhar–Nauseri (Tithwal) area and still

hold them, while on 27 and 28 August, Indian artillery shelled the area north of Punch on the Pakistan side and Indian troops crossed the CFL in the Uri-Bedori area. It has been confirmed that Indian troops have reached the Haji Pir Pass, which is 5 miles on the Pakistan side of the CFL on the Uri–Punch road. Each instance of violation is protested by the United Nations observers who demand that troops on the wrong side of the line be withdrawn.

7. The United Nations Military Observer Group received an Indian complaint of Pakistan shelling, on 1 September, of pickets and a battalion headquarters in the Chhamb area of the Jammu–Bhimber sector of the cease-fire line. The complaint stated that at 02.30 hours on that day one and a half Pakistan tank squadrons supported by artillery, crossed the cease-fire line in this area. Pakistan artillery was also said to have fired on a battalion headquarters near Punch from 16.30 hours on 1 September and on an Indian battalion headquarters in the Jangar area. The substance of these complaints was subsequently confirmed by United Nations military observers. A Pakistan complaint reported that Indian soldiers had crossed the CFL in strength in the Kargil, Tithwal and Uri-Punch sectors, as reported above. Pakistan, in this complaint also affirmed the crossing of the CFL by Pakistan troops in the Bhimber area on 1 September, as a defensive measure to forestall Indian action, asserting also that in this sector the Indian Air Force had taken offensive action against Pakistan troops. Also on 1 September armed infiltrators ambushed an Indian convoy at Gund, north-east of Srinagar on the Leh road, and both sides sustained casualties. On 2 September the Jammu team of UNMOGIP received an Indian complaint that Pakistan aircraft had attacked the road between Chhamb and Jaurian during the morning of 2 September and that Jaurian village was in flames. The air attack on Jaurian was confirmed by United Nations military observers. The complaint also alleged that Pakistan troops had crossed the border with approximately 90 tanks and were moving from the Chhamb sector toward the east. Pakistan artillery fired in the Punch area during the night of 1–2 September and in the afternoon of 2 September.

8. An annotated list of complaints of incidents of violation that have been investigated thus far by the observers, as reported to me by General Nimmo, is presented in part II of this report. A map of Jammu and Kashmir showing the approximate location of the CFL is contained in an annex.

EFFORTS OF THE SECRETARY-GENERAL

9. On the morning of 9 August 1965, a telegram was received from General Nimmo warning that the situation was deteriorating along the CFL. On the basis of this report, I saw the representative of Pakistan at 12.30 hours on that day, and asked him to convey to his Government my very serious concern about the situation that was developing in Kashmir, involving the crossing of the CFL from the Pakistan side by numbers of armed men and their attacks on India military positions on the Indian side of the line, and also my strong appeal that the CFL be observed. That same afternoon I saw the representative of India, told him of the information I had received from General Nimmo and of the *démarche* I had made to the Government of Pakistan, and asked him to convey to his Government my urgent appeal for restraint as regards any retaliatory action from their side. In subsequent days, I repeated these appeals orally for transmission to the two Governments, asking also that all personnel of either party still remaining on the wrong side of the line be withdrawn to its own side. I have not obtained from the Government of Pakistan any assurance that the cease-fire and the CFL will be respected henceforth or that efforts would be exerted to restore conditions to normal along that line. I did receive assurance from the Government of India, conveyed orally by its representative to the United Nations, that India would act with restraint with regard to any retaliatory acts and will respect the cease-fire agreement and the CFL if Pakistan does likewise. In the meantime, reports from UNMOGIP as of 2 September indicate a continuation of violations of the cease-fire and the CFL from both sides.

10. In view of the continuing deterioration in the situation as of 16 August I gave consideration to a further step in the form of a draft statement about the cease-fire violations which was designed for public release. The draft was handed to the two representatives to be transmitted for the information of their Governments. Both Governments reacted promptly.

The Government of India had no objection to the release of the statement but at first wished certain modifications which in part at least I regarded as unacceptable. The Government of Pakistan was strongly negative about the statement in general on the grounds that it favoured India in that it dealt only with the current cease-fire situation without presenting the political background of the broad issue and thus was lacking in balance since a cease-fire alone supports the *status quo* to India's benefit.

11. Weighing carefully all considerations I came to the conclusion that a public statement by the Secretary-General at that time would serve no constructive purpose and might well do more harm than good. My first and primary objective had to be to see the fighting end rather than indicting or denouncing any party for starting and continuing it. I thought it might be helpful to make another quiet effort toward achieving observance of the cease-fire through a new approach to the two Governments. Consequently I gave thought to the possibility of sending urgently to the area a Personal Representative of the Secretary-General for the purpose of meeting and talking with approrpriate authorities of the two Governments and with General Nimmo; conveying to the Governments my very serious concern about the situation; and exploring with them ways and means of preventing any further deterioration in that situation and regaining quiet along the CFL. If such a mission had materialized, I had it in mind to ask Mr Ralph J. Bunche, Under-Secretary for Special Political Affairs, to undertake it. The idea was broached by me informally to the two parties on 20 August. The subsequent responses of the Governments, while not negative, involved in each case conditions which, in my view, would make the mission not feasible at that time and therefore I abandoned it.

12. As a further and immediate step, however, on 23 August I asked General Nimmo to come promptly to the United Nations Headquarters for consultation with me about the situation in Kashmir, and he arrived in New York from Srinagar on 26 August. Consideration of other efforts that I might make was then undertaken in the light of the discussion with General Nimmo.

13. General Nimmo's reports on incidents continue to be received as the military observers carry out their investigations of specific actions. The procedure that has been followed is for General Nimmo to submit the reports of the investigations of each incident and the observers' findings fixing blame, to each party, confidentially, and to send copies to me, without any public disclosure. This procedure, which has been found to be in the best interest of the effective functioning of UNMOGIP is being continued.

14. In view of alarming reports indicating a steady escalation of the fighting in the air and on the ground, involving regular army forces on both sides, I addressed on 1 September an appeal to the Prime Minister of India and the President of Pakistan which was circulated to the Council (S/6647).

CONDITIONS FOR A RESTORATION OF THE CEASE-FIRE

15. Restoration of the cease-fire and a return to normal conditions along the CFL can be achieved only under the following conditions:

(*a*) A willingness of both parties to respect the agreement they have entered into;

(*b*) A readiness on the part of the Government of Pakistan to take effective steps to prevent crossings of the CFL from the Pakistan side by armed men, whether or not in uniform;

(*c*) Evacuation by each party of positions of the other party now occupied and withdrawal of all armed personnel of each party to its own side of the line, which would include the withdrawal once more of Indian troops from Pakistan positions in the Kargil area;

(*d*) A halt by both parties to the firing across the CFL that has been occurring from both sides in some sectors with artillery and smaller guns;

(*e*) Allowing full freedom of movement and access to the United Nations observers by both parties on both sides of the line. [*S/6651, 3 Sept. 1965, Report of Secretary-General on situation in Kashmir*, paras 4–15.][18]

[18] S. 2, which contained an itemized list of incidents across the cease-fire line occurring between 5 Aug. and 3 Sept. 1965, has not been included. It reveals major breaches by both countries.

(b) 1965-6

i. Implementing the Cease-Fire

On 4 September 1965 the Security Council met to consider the situation, with the representatives of India and Pakistan participating without the right of vote. India insisted that on 5 August 5,000 regular Pakistani soldiers, disguised as civilians, had crossed the cease-fire line. Pakistan denied the allegation, and pointed to India's crossing of the cease-fire line in May and June, and the shelling of a Pakistani town, which had escalated the conflict. The Security Council unanimously adopted the following resolution:

The Security Council,
Noting the report of the Secretary-General of 3 September 1965,
Having heard the statements of the representatives of India and Pakistan,
Concerned at the deteriorating situation along the cease-fire line in Kashmir,
1. *Calls upon* the Governments of India and Pakistan to take forthwith all steps for an immediate cease-fire;
2. *Calls upon* the two Governments to respect the cease-fire line and have all armed personnel of each party withdrawn to its own side of the line;
3. *Calls upon* the two Governments to co-operate fully with the United Nations Military Observer Group in India and Pakistan (UNMOGIP) in its task of supervising the observance of the cease-fire;
4. *Requests* the Secretary-General to report to the Council within three days on the implementation of the present resolution. [*SC res. 209 (1965), 4 Sept. 1965.*]

The Security Council met again on 6 September, and had before it a new report of the Secretary-General:

1. This report is submitted urgently so that members of the Council may be informed of new and serious developments in the conflict between India and Pakistan over Kashmir since the adoption by the Security Council on 4 September 1965 of resolution 209 (1965) calling for an immediate cease-fire.
2. The Council's resolution was transmitted to the Governments of India and Pakistan immediately after its adoption. No official response to this call for a cease-fire has been received from either Government.
3. Reports received from the United Nations Chief Military Observer in Kashmir, Lt-Gen. R. H. Nimmo, on 5 and 6 September indicate that the fighting continues on both sides of the cease-fire line (CFL). Indeed, it is clear that the conflict between India and Pakistan is broadening and intensifying.
4. General Nimmo has reported the incidents of fighting listed below, as breaches of the cease-fire, since 4 September.
(a) To General Nimmo's 'official protest and urgent request' for the withdrawal of Pakistan troops from the Chhamb sector which was lodged on 3 September, the Chief of Staff, Pakistan gave the following reply:

'We are aware of your genuine efforts to make the Indians vacate their aggression. But having seen the hopelessness of these efforts we were forced to take action to stop the Indians from annexing Azad Kashmir. Our action was taken after repeated requests to you to convey to Indians that their failure to vacate positions on our side of the CFL will have very serious consequences. The Indians apparently refused to heed our warning. They are maintaining their occupation of posts on our side of the CFL in the Kargil, Tithwal and Uri-Punch sectors and have now crossed the CFL in yet another sector. Under those circumstances how can you expect us to unilaterally halt our purely defensive operations which are designed to forestall Indian aggressions?'

(*b*) Observers in the Jammu sector in the morning of 5 September observed two Pakistan jet fighters in the sector which were engaged by Indian anti-aircraft.

(*c*) The following information concerning the Haji Pir area has been confirmed: An Indian infantry brigade, supported by two field artillery batteries (25-pounders) and one medium gun, is operating on that front. The brigade is deployed on a 12-mile front. The Indian command informed the military observers that the action in the Haji Pir Pass area was necessary in self-defence to cut off infiltrators.

(*d*) A captain captured at the Haji Pir Pass was interviewed by a United Nations observer and stated that he belonged to the 6th Azad Kashmir Battalion and was in charge of 100 *mujahids* whose task was to harass Indian troops covering Uri.

(*e*) The Indian local commander in the Baramula sector confirmed to United Nations observers that his troops had crossed the CFL in Sunjoi (3 miles north of Tangdhar) and had captured some hill features with the aim of cutting the supply line to Pakistan infiltrators in the north of the Tangdhar area, specifically a Pakistan company group located 5 miles north of Sunjoi and 1·5 miles on the Indian side of the CFL. On 5 September, at 18.07 hours, the Pakistan local command at Domel complained that Indian troops had occupied Sunjoi East (NL 8952) after heavy shelling on the night of 3–4 September.

(*f*) As regards the Jammu/Bhimber sector of the cease-fire line, United Nations observers at Jammu were informed by the Indian local command on 5 September, at 12.00 hours, that 'Pakistan troops attacked along the Jaurian–Akhnur road with two armoured regiments and along the Kalit–Akhnur road with one armoured regiment and were approximately 14 miles on the Indian side of the cease-fire line'. They also stated that the attack was being supported by three medium artillery regiments, two self-propelled 155 mm. artillery regiments and one 208 mm. battery. The military observers had not confirmed this information at the time it was despatched but stated, however, that Radio Pakistan on 5 September, at 20.30 hours, had broadcast that 'Azad Kashmir' and Pakistan troops on 5 September, at 08.00 hours, had reached Jaurian which is 14 miles on the Indian side of the CFL. This corresponds with the statement attributed to a Pakistan spokesman that Pakistan forces had advanced to within a a few miles of Akhnur. The military observers also reported that the Indian Radio had broadcast on 5 September, at 21.00 hours, that heavy fighting had taken place in the Jaurian area on 5 September.

(*g*) General Nimmo reported in the early morning of 6 September that the following information had just been received from the 'C.G.S., Pakistan command: "At 5 hours on 6 September 1965, Indian troops attacked across the West Pakistan border from Jassar bridge (Pathankot area and south to Sulamainke). Major attacks on Lahore and Sialkot from Jassar and on Kasur from Ferozepore (all in Pakistan). Estimated strength whole Indian Army less four divisions." ' General Nimmo also stated that in this regard the United Nations military observers stationed in Sialkot had just reported hearing shelling east of their location which was coming from the border between Kashmir and Pakistan in the Jammu–Sialkot sector.
[*S/6661, 6 Sept. 1965, Report of Secretary-General on development of situation in Kashmir since adoption of Security Council res. 209.*]

The fighting had extended beyond the cease-fire line, and across the international boundary.

After a debate the Security Council unanimously adopted the following resolution:

The Security Council,
Noting the report of the Secretary-General. . . .
Noting with deep concern the extension of the fighting which adds immeasurably to the seriousness of the situation,

1. *Calls upon* the parties to cease hostilities in the entire area of conflict immediately, and promptly withdraw all armed personnel to the positions held by them before 5 August 1965;

2. *Requests* the Secretary-General to exert every possible effort to give effect to the present

resolution and to resolution 209 (1965), to take all measures possible to strengthen the United Nations Military Observer Group in India and Pakistan,[19] and to keep the Council promptly and currently informed on the implementation of the resolutions and on the situation in the area;

3. *Decides* to keep this issue under urgent and continuous review so that the Council may determine what further steps may be necessary to secure peace and security in the area. [*SC res. 210 (1965), 6 Sept. 1965.*]

In fulfilment of the mandate given to him, the Secretary-General left for the sub-continent the next day. He saw the Prime Ministers of the two countries and addressed to them identical appeals for an unconditional cease-fire to take effect on 14 September:

The Indian Prime Minister's reply of 14 September accepted the Secretary-General's proposal with effect from 06.30 hours Indian Standard Time on 16 September, provided the Secretary-General confirmed that Pakistan was agreeable also. However, until Pakistan withdraws its armed infiltrators, Indian security forces would have to deal with them. Moreover, India would not agree to leaving the door open for further infiltrations and was resolved to maintain its sovereignty over the State of Jammu and Kashmir.

The reply of the President of Pakistan, also received on 14 September, said that Pakistan would welcome a cease-fire which would provide a self-executing arrangement for a final settlement of the Kashmir dispute. Implementing the Council's resolution of 6 September would merely result in restoring the Indian military grip over Kashmir, thus rewarding the aggressor. To resolve the real cause of the conflict the cease-fire should be followed by a complete withdrawal of Indian and Pakistan forces from Jammu and Kashmir; then a United Nations sponsored Afro-Asian force should be sent to maintain order and a plebiscite should be held in the State within three months.

Later on 14 September the Secretary-General had sent a second message to the President of Pakistan and the Prime Minister of India expressing his appreciation of their positive attitude towards the cease-fire, but noting that both had added conditions and qualifications which the Secretary-General could only refer to the Security Council. Pending consideration by the Council, the Secretary-General again asked both parties to agree to order a cease-fire in the whole area of conflict as of 06.30 IST on 16 September.

The Indian Prime Minister replied on 15 September reaffirming his willingness to order a simple cease-fire as soon as it was confirmed that the Government of Pakistan had agreed to do likewise.

While awaiting the reply of the President of Pakistan, the Secretary-General had sent a third message to the Prime Minister and the President imploring them to stop the fighting which, in existing circumstances, could solve nothing and lead only to disaster. While desiring a cease-fire, each side had posed conditions unacceptable to the other. Recalling the joint statement of the Heads of the two Governments of 29 November 1962, the Secretary-General suggested that urgent consideration be given to a meeting between them, either with or without the Secretary-General's presence. He assured them that he remained at their disposal for any assistance toward stopping the fighting and taking the first steps to mutual accommodation, and noted that certain offers had been made by world leaders indicating that they were available for conciliatory assistance. On 16 September the Secretary-General submitted to the Council a further report on his mission. He noted that both sides had expressed their desire for a cessation of hostilities. Despite this, he reported, he had not yet succeeded in securing an effective practical measure of compliance. . . . The Council might take a number of steps; it might first order the two Governments concerned, pursuant to Article 40 of the Charter, to desist from further hostile military action and declare that failure to comply with this order would demonstrate the existence of a breach of the peace within the meaning of Article 39 of the Charter. The Council might also consider what assistance it could provide in ensuring the observance of the cease-fire and the withdrawal of all armed personnel by the

[19] For action taken under this instruction, see above, pp. 359–60.

two sides. It could also request the two Heads of Government to meet in a country friendly to both in order to discuss the current situation and the problems underlying it, as a first step in resolving the outstanding differences between their two countries. In conclusion, the Secretary-General's report referred to measures being taken to strengthen the United Nations Military Observer Group.

The Secretary-General submitted a separate report on the military situation. A sizeable number of infiltrators continued to operate on the Indian side of the cease-fire line and tribesmen from the North-West Frontier were arriving at the front. The report listed Indian crossings of the cease-fire line, of the Jammu border and of the India-Pakistan border, as well as Pakistan crossings of the cease-fire line, and noted that there had been a considerable use of air forces by both sides.

Also submitted to the Council was the text of messages sent on 4 September by the Chairman of the Council of Ministers of the USSR to the Prime Minister of India and the President of Pakistan, expressing the USSR's concern over the conflict, calling for an immediate cessation of hostilities and withdrawal of troops and offering its good offices should both parties consider them useful. The Chairman had added that military action could not lead to the solution of disputes, including the Kashmir question.

At the meeting of the Security Council held on 17 September the representative of India emphasized his country's desire for peace and said that every step it had taken in the present conflict had been in self-defence. Moreover, it was now becoming evident that Pakistan had launched its attack on India in the expectation that the People's Republic of China would support it. India had nevertheless agreed to accept an unconditional cease-fire, as its Prime Minister had made clear in his letters of 14 and 15 September; it was Pakistan alone which had posed conditions. The Security Council should accordingly determine, under Article 39 of the Charter, the existence of an act of aggression by Pakistan and call upon it to desist from hostilities.

At the next meeting of the Council, on 18 September, the representative of Pakistan referred to his Government's suggestions to the Secretary-General during his visit to Pakistan, concerning ways in which a cease-fire could be achieved and the steps which should follow it. He denied the charge made by India that members of the Pakistan Army had crossed the cease-fire line and entered Indian-occupied Kashmir on 5 August. The hue and cry about infiltrators raised by India was intended to give it a pretext for a new campaign of terror against the people of Kashmir, who had risen against India's military occupation. Pakistan shared the Secretary-General's disappointment that his efforts in the cause of peace had not met with success. That was due partly to his restricted terms of reference and partly to the negative attitude of India. The Prime Minister of India, in his letter of 14 September, had clearly imposed the condition that the cease-fire not be linked to the Kashmir dispute, which was the cause of the war. The Indian allegation that Pakistan was conspiring with the People's Republic of China to destroy India was a baseless attempt to impress public opinion.

At the following meeting, on the afternoon of 18 September, the Indian representative informed the Council that Chinese troops were massing on the Indian border. That was an extension of the India-Pakistan conflict, he said; the People's Republic of China was fighting India through Pakistan. [*A/6301*, *Annual Report of Secretary-General, 1955–6* (*GAOR, 21st sess., suppl. 1*, p. 12).]

The fighting nevertheless continued,[20] though the end was now in sight.[21]

On 20 September the Security Council adopted a further resolution (for text see p. 424) demanding a cease-fire and subsequent withdrawal of armed personnel, and providing the Secretary-General with the necessary assistance

[20] For the Secretary-General's report on the military situation, see S/6687, 16 Sept. 1965.

[21] There was a widespread feeling that China issued her warning to India in order to achieve a diplomatic victory in Pakistan, but that she refrained from doing so until it was clear that the fighting was in any event about to stop.

to supervise this. This resolution was adopted by 10 votes to none, with Jordan abstaining. The text of it was transmitted to the parties by the Secretary-General, who told them that he wished to receive confirmation that a cease-fire had been ordered, and plans and schedules for troop withdrawals.[22] He also indicated that

(3) I have taken steps to determine the availability of a number of military observers to ensure the supervision of the cease-fire and the subsequent withdrawals, and have alerted them to be prepared for early departure;
(4) I have set in motion the necessary logistical arrangements for the maintenance of a team of observers in the field.
I should much appreciate it if this message would be given most urgent consideration.
[S/6699, 21 Sept. 1965, Report of Secretary-General on his efforts to give effect to Security Council res. 211 (1965).]

India and Pakistan now both agreed to the unequivocal demand for a cease-fire.[23] Pakistan emphasized that if the UN did not now address itself to securing an honourable settlement of the underlying problem, she would have to leave the Organization.

The Secretary-General proceeded with steps to implement the Security Council resolutions. He decided to separate the supervision of the cease-fire and withdrawals in areas outside of Kashmir from the existing UNMOGIP machinery along the 1949 cease-fire line.[24] The team of observers operating outside Kashmir would be known as the UN India–Pakistan Observation Mission.[25] UNIPOM and the strengthened UNMOGIP would be closely co-ordinated:

... I have been taking steps to provide the necessary assistance to ensure the supervision of the cease-fire and the withdrawal behind the lines of all armed personnel. In this connexion, I have despatched a number of military observers to the area, and more will soon be coming, to provide the necessary assistance in the discharge of this supervisory function. . . Because of the difference in origin of the two operations, I am separating the supervision of the cease-fire and the withdrawals in areas outside of Kashmir from United Nations Military Observer Group in India and Pakistan (UNMOGIP), the existing cease-fire operation in Kashmir. The team of observers operating outside of Kashmir will be known as the United Nations India–Pakistan Observation Mission and will be directed by an officer of appropriate rank and experience. Pending the appointment of such an officer, the new operation will be under the direction of Lt-Gen. Robert H. Nimmo, the Chief Military Observer of UNMOGIP. The two operations, however, will be closely co-ordinated, administratively and operationally.
[S/6699/Add.2, 23 Sept. 1965.]

UNMOGIP and UNIPOM were to play an indispensable role in the slow process of securing a cease-fire and the eventual withdrawal of troops.

INCIDENTS OF FIGHTING

1. According to the latest information on 26 September 1965 from United Nations observers in the Lahore sector the 'situation has further deteriorated in the whole Lahore sector and especially in the area of the Bambanwala–Ravi–Bedian link canal which is just north of Lahore City'.
2. It is confirmed by United Nations observers that Indian forces began an artillery

[22] S/6699, para. 3.
[23] S/6699/Add. 1.
[24] For details on the Indian and Pakistan response to this decision as well as the legal reasons in favour of it, see above, pp. 442–7.
[25] See below Part 5.

barrage and attacks in the general area of Burki (grid reference 759972) on 24 September, at 17.30 hours. As a result of this action the local Pakistan command claims to have suffered a number of casualties in killed, wounded and missing. The United Nations military observers saw two prisoners taken in this action and interviewed one of them on the Indian side, Burki is located approximately 6 miles east-south-east of Lahore.

3. Military observers stationed in the Lahore sector stated that they have detected thus far no further movements of troops there.

4. Colonel Gauthier, who is in charge of a team of observers in the Lahore area, states that observers of UNIPOM have been deployed on both the Indian and Pakistan sides of the line. Colonel Gauthier has submitted the following report on one of his efforts to stop fighting:

'I personally went to the area of the cease-fire line with one observer in the afternoon of 24 September to investigate complaints received from local headquarters that Indian troops were edging forward of the positions they held at the time of the cease-fire. The situation started shortly after first light on 23 September. Efforts were made by us to contact the Indian Battalion Commander but to no avail. Shelling started at 17.15 hours on 24 September from the Indian side with medium and field artillery, recoilless rifle, tank and small-arms fire. From where we were standing, all fire seemed to be falling 600 to 1,000 yards away in the general area of a canal which is at present the dividing line between the two opposing forces. This heavy firing went on for half an hour, forcing us to take cover. On returning to Lahore I immediately asked UNMOGIP to pass a strong protest to the Vice-Chief of Staff of the Indian Army, which was done. I then visited the local command who assured me that no Pakistan artillery had fired. It is difficult to state categorically if Pakistan artillery did retaliate, but the considered opinion is that the Indians started the firing, and I believe some shots were returned. I consider this situation explosive and I am experiencing great difficulty in preventing the Pakistan side from retaliating.'

5. In the Lahore sector, particularly, the cease-fire is not holding as of 26 September.

WITHDRAWALS

6. Following is a report from General Nimmo concerning communications with Indian and Pakistan military authorities, respectively, on the subject of withdrawals.

'On 25 September I sent the following message to the Commander-in-Chief, Western Command, Indian Army, in reply to his complaint of Pakistan advances in the Sulaimboke area:

"OPS/496. Your complaint regarding message 0-2006 of 25 September has been received, and I have taken action with the Chief of the General Staff, Pakistan. At the same time, I request you to order the withdrawal of all Indian troops now on the Pakistan side of the international border to the Indian side."

'On 25 September I also sent the following message to the Vice-Chief of Army Staff, India:

"The Indian local command at Baramula has confirmed to military observers that his troops occupy hill features at points NL 831389 and NL 836394 on the Pakistan side of the cease-fire line (CFL) (in the Domel sector). This is contrary to the cease-fire agreement, and I request that these troops be withdrawn to the Indian side of the CFL."

'Replies have not been received yet to either of these requests, and there has been no indication of withdrawals anywhere. In my message OPS/498, of 25 September, to the CGS. of the Pakistan Army, referring to his complaints regarding Indian attacks in the Sulaimanke area of southern Rajasthan, east of Hyderabad, I stated as follows:

"All commanders should everywhere respect the cease-fire order, of which they are well aware. You will appreciate that it is not possible to remind them of this in detail in respect of a variety of separate places. I have asked the Vice-Chief of Army Staff, India, to order the troops to cease firing and stop any other offensive operations in area under reference. May I also ask that your troops should withdraw to their own side of the border in that area."

'In his reply dated 25 September the CGS, Pakistan, stated as follows:

"Our Government has not yet accepted withdrawal of troops to own side of border. Agreement thus far is only on cease-fire. In view of this you are requested to concentrate on implementation of cease-fire. We will accept your instructions regarding withdrawal of troops after an agreement on the subject is reached. Please intimate reaction of the Vice-Chief of Army Staff, India, to your request."

'Message OPS/493 from the Chief Military Observer to the CGS, Pakistan:

"It is confirmed by joint investigation of military observers that Pakistan troops have established themselves from point NR 152118 to NR 153117 and at NR 166116 across the CFL (in Naushera sector). This is contrary to the cease-fire agreement, and I request that these troops be withdrawn to the Pakistan side of the CFL."

'In his reply the CGS, Pakistan, stated the following:

"Your OPS/493 of 25 September received. In this connexion your attention is invited to my message of 24 September. Request Indian authorities be made to observe cease-fire agreement. Our troops will withdraw to own side of the CFL, when an agreement about general withdrawal from territories under other side's control before the outbreak of hostilities is reached between the two governments."'

7. Observance of the cease-fire and withdrawals are closely linked. [*S/6710/Add. 1, 26 Sept. 1965.*]

1. Information on observance of the cease-fire which has been received from the United Nations military observers on 26 September 1965 since that set forth in document S/6710/ Add. 1 is presented in this report.

2. Military observers at Domel received on 26 September, at 07.35 hours, a Pakistan complaint alleging that Indian troops in company strength had overrun a Pakistan standing patrol in the area of Shahkot bridge, 2·5 miles on the Pakistan side of the cease-fire line (CFL) during the night of 25–26 September. The complaint also alleged that Indian troops had fired with artillery and medium machine-guns into Shahkot village and were also attacking in the direction of Bugina, which is approximately 3 miles north of Shahkot.

3. A cease-fire proposed by the military observers for 09.45 hours, West Pakistan time (WPT), was not accepted by the Pakistan local commander who stated that unless the United Nations guaranteed total Indian withdrawal in this area he would commence full offensive operations. He stated that he had approval of his higher headquarters for these operations, as the bridges over the Kishenganga are considered vital. At 10.30 hours WPT the Pakistan commander stated that his offensive would begin immediately. At 11.00 hours he stated again that the Indians had so far fired approximately 110 rounds of 3·7-inch howitzer and/or 3-inch mortar shells into Shahkot village but that his higher headquarters had requested him to contact the United Nations once again.

4. The General Headquarters of Pakistan reported later that they had directed their local command to exercise restraint and added they however could not allow the Indians to occupy territory under their control and requested the Indians vacate these positions as soon as possible.

5. The Indian local commander confirmed to the military observers at Baramula that there had been an exchange of fire in that area in the early hours of 26 September 1965 but claimed that it had been initiated by Pakistan forces and that his troops had been in possession of the whole area between the CFL and the Kishenganga.

6. The occupation of this area by Indian troops, however, has never been reported to the military observers. They have requested that the Indian troops in that sector be withdrawn to their side of the CFL.

7. The military observers at Domel and Baramula are trying to arrange a meeting of the local commanders. [*S/6710/Add. 2, 26 Sept. 1965.*]

Throughout the remainder of the year each side complained of violation by the other.[26] However, in spite of these many small incidents, the cease-fire became effective, and the work of UNMOGIP and UNIPOM contributed to this end:

1. A summary of information on the observance of the cease-fire that has been received from the United Nations military observers from 7 October 1965, the date of my last report on the subject (S/6710/Add.3), through 17 October, is set forth below.

2. In my report of 7 October, I noted that the most recent reports from the field had indicated in general an over-all tendency toward improvement in the observance of the cease-fire. The situation has not improved and may have worsened during the period under review, when there have been numerous confirmed breaches of the cease-fire of varying seriousness, a great many complaints about alleged violations of it have been submitted by each party, and tension is reported to remain high in most sectors. The observance of the cease-fire, therefore, still leaves much to be desired. Though the extent of heavy fighting has decreased considerably, the existence of the cease-fire must be considered precarious.

3. Experience gained thus far in the supervision of the cease-fire reveals some of the major difficulties in maintaining it. India and Pakistan have accepted the cease-fire and there is no reason to doubt the earnestness of either party in desiring to honour this agreement. But this attitude is not always reflected accurately at the front. There it has been found that both sides in various localities attempt to improve their positions by such actions as digging, wiring and mining in the forward areas, or by edging forward for tactical purposes. Such actions inevitably provoke reactions from the opposing side which are made all the more dangerous when the respective forward positions, as often is the case, are already very close to each other.

4. Another problem is that of the positions occupied by the two forces at the time the cease-fire came into effect. Each side claims that the other side has occupied new positions after the cease-fire, and local commanders threaten to retake such positions by force. This cause of friction can be completely eliminated only when both sides agree to withdraw their armed personnel, as demanded by the Security Council, back to the positions held by them before 5 August 1965. Thus, while the cease-fire is the necessary first stage, subsequent withdrawals are essential to its continuing effectiveness. Efforts to this end are being continued. Meanwhile, local agreements are being sought, as indicated in an earlier report, for tactical readjustments or short pull-backs in certain areas by both sides in order to reduce tension and avoid accidental incidents.

5. The flights of observation type aircraft over or near areas occupied by the opposing side also lead to tension and, in a number of instances, have provoked shooting incidents. Negotiations are underway in the field toward achieving agreement of the two sides to stop such activities.

5. The employment of civilians in defence works in the forward areas and even their presence in those areas for such purposes as gathering crops may also cause trouble. In sectors where Indian troops occupy positions in Pakistan territory, the Indian command has charged that Pakistan civilians working in forward areas are being used as 'spies'. The problem arising from the role of civilians is compounded by the fear, felt by both sides, of infiltrators and infiltrations.

7. The observers indicate that any firing near the front, such as weapon testing, increases tension among the nervous civilian population and may induce panic. They are seeking agreement of both sides to eliminate such firing near the front lines.

8. Specific incidents relating to the cease-fire which have been reported by the observers during the period under review are outlined in the following sections. These reports of the observers are unavoidably piecemeal, incomplete and not infrequently inconclusive. This is due to a number of factors. Until quite recently, owing to communications inadequacies, much less information has been coming in from observers on the Indian side of the line, and

[26] For listing of accusations and counter-accusations, see checklist, pp. 415-16.

coming in more slowly, than from those on the Pakistan side. Thus, this report unavoidably sets forth more information concerning military activities by Indian than by Pakistan forces, since more such information has become available and sooner. On a cease-fire line extending for almost 1,500 miles, and given the limited number of observers and the limited transportation and communication facilities available to UNMOGIP and UNIPOM, the observers cannot possibly hope to be on the scene of all breaches or alleged breaches of the cease-fire. In many cases, and for obvious reasons, completely different versions of the same occurrence are given to observers on each side of the line. The observers, unless they happen to be physically on the spot during the actual events, find it extremely difficult to arrive at a firm assessment of blame for a particular incident. Furthermore, it is not unusual for one side to complain that the other has moved its positions forward from the line held at the time of the cease-fire, and that, therefore, action taken to recover ground allegedly lost since 23 September 1965 should not be regarded as a violation. In places where observers were not deployed at the time of the cease-fire—and there are many—the observers often find it very difficult to verify the exact positions held just before the cease-fire.

9. All complaints of violations of the cease-fire received by the Secretary-General are immediately transmitted to the observers, but in many cases the time-lag is so considerable that effective investigation by military observers is not possible. Investigation, of course, is facilitated when complaints are submitted direct to the observers in the different sectors by the military headquarters in which they originate. . . . [*S/6710/Add. 4, 18 Oct. 1965, Report of Secretary-General on observance of cease-fire.*]

It was, of course, impossible for UNMOGIP and UNIPOM to function identically in respect of their cease-fire duties, for each stemmed from a different constitutional authority,[27] with a different history:

1. Reports received by the Secretary-General from United Nations military observers on the observance of the cease-fire called for by the Security Council in its resolution 211 (1965), of 20 September 1965, indicate that the observers encounter some special problems in connexion with the procedures of cease-fire observation and reporting. These arise from the fact that two parallel cease-fire exist, namely, one based on the Karachi Agreement between India and Pakistan of July 1949, relating only to Kashmir, and the other being the over-all cease-fire applying to the entire area of conflict, which is based on the acceptance by India and Pakistan on 22 September 1965 of the cease-fire called for by the Security Council in its resolution 211 (1965). The sole purpose of this report is to acquaint members of the Council with this aspect of the cease-fire situation which, perhaps, is less obvious than others.

2. On 13 August 1948, the United Nations Commission for India and Pakistan (UNCIP), resolved to submit immediately to the Governments of India and Pakistan a proposal for an immediate cease-fire, and suggested the appointment of military observers to supervise the observance of the cease-fire. The cease-fire came into effect on 1 January 1949, but the formal basis for the activities of the United Nations Military Observer Group in India and Pakistan (UNMOGIP) is the Agreement between the military representatives of India and Pakistan regarding the establishment of a cease-fire line in the State of Jammu and Kashmir, signed in Karachi on 27 July 1949, known as the Karachi Agreement, which established the Kashmir cease-fire line.

3. The cease-fire line, as described in the Karachi Agreement and by the terms of that Agreement, was to be verified on the ground by local commanders on each side assisted by United Nations military observers, and thereafter was to be regarded as the definitive cease-fire line. The Agreement provided, *inter alia*, that in general troops would remain at least 500 yards from the cease-fire line and that there should be no increase of forces or strengthening of defences. Under the Agreement, UNCIP would station observers where it would be deemed necessary.

[27] For further documentation on the distinctions between UNMOGIP and UNIPOM see S/6738 and S/6782.

14

4. By subsequent agreed interpretations of the Agreement, a number of points were clarified, including six categories of activity constituting breaches of the cease-fire, viz.:

(*a*) Crossing of the cease-fire line, or infringement of the provision of the Karachi Agreement concerning the 500-yard zone referred to in paragraph 3 above as interpreted by mutual agreement;

(*b*) Firing and use of explosives within five miles of the cease-fire line without advising the United Nations observers well in advance;

(*c*) New wiring or mining of any positions;

(*d*) Reinforcing of existing forward defended localities with men or warlike stores, or strengthening of defences in areas where no major adjustments are involved by the determination of the cease-fire line;

(*e*) Forward movement, from outside the State of Jammu and Kashmir of any warlike stores, equipment and personnel, other than reliefs and maintenance;

(*f*) Flying of aircraft over the other side's territory.

5. The Chief Military Observer of UNMOGIP directs his observers to undertake an impartial investigation of every alleged breach of the Karachi Agreement and, after consideration of the verified facts, submits the finding to each of the two armies in order that with their co-operation, the conditions of the cease-fire agreement may be safeguarded. In short, UNMOGIP functions on the basis of a detailed cease-fire agreement, subsequently clarified by a series of agreed interpretations, with which it has had more than fifteen years of working experience.

6. On the other hand, the sole basis for the supervision of the over-all cease-fire called for by the Security Council resolution, which applies to Kashmir as well as to the areas outside of Kashmir, is the very general mandate given in the Security Council's resolution 211 (1965) 'to ensure supervision of the cease-fire and the withdrawal of all armed personnel', i.e. to the positions held by them before 5 August 1965. Thus, for the cease-fire of 22 September 1965, there is no agreed list of activities which are regarded as constituting breaches of the cease-fire and, especially, there is as of now, no agreed definition and demarcation of the actual over-all cease-fire line itself. In short, the observers outside of Kashmir are supervising a simple cease-fire in general terms without detailed and agreed definitions of a line or of violations and with no agreed system of operations procedure and relationships with the two opposing armies.

7. These differences of history and of terms of reference find unavoidable reflection in the present observation operation along the original Kashmir cease-fire line and beyond it, and also in the reporting on the observance of the cease-fire in Kashmir and beyond it. United Nations observers find, for example, that local Indian and Pakistan commanders in the field, many of whom have had experience with cease-fire procedures under the Karachi Agreement, often expect those procedures to be followed under the 22 September cease-fire beyond the Kashmir cease-fire line as well as along it.

8. The Secretary-General, in any case, reports to the Council on the basis of information received from the military observers on the observance of the cease-fire throughout the entire area of conflict. [*S/6888, 9 Nov. 1965, Report by Secretary-General relating to an aspect of procedures employed in observing and reporting on cease-fire.*]

In December a relapse in the situation made it necessary to seek a new military agreement to cease all firing unless actually under attack:

6. As indicated in paragraph 20 below, a firing incident took place in the Kotli–Naoshera sector on the morning of 27 December, the responsibility for which was attributed by the observers in the area to the Indian side. In connexion with this breach of cease-fire, which took place after 17.00 hours on 26 December, the Acting Chief Military Observer of UNMOGIP addressed a message to the Vice-Chief of Army Staff of the Indian Army, expressing regret at this contravention of the newly reached agreement and requesting assurance that other such incidents would not be tolerated by the Indian Command.

7. On 29 December the Vice-Chief of the Indian Army Staff stated that since the Pakistan Chief of General Staff had confirmed his agreement to issue no-firing orders, he agreed to take similar action and would confirm it in writing on the return of the Chief of Army Staff, who was away on a tour.

8. On 29 December observers on the Indian side reported that no-firing orders had been received by the respective formations. [*S/6710/Add.14, 30 Dec. 1965.*]

This proved a useful and significant move: 'Recent reports from observers show that since no-firing agreement at the military level was reached at the end of December 1965, there has been a general relaxation of tension along the front line and a marked decrease in the number of incidents.'

UNMOGIP and UNIPOM also took a diplomatic initiative in negotiating an agreement to limit air activity, which proved a further contribution to peace in the area:

3. On 14 December, the Chief Military Observer of the United Nations Military Observer Group for India and Pakistan (UNMOGIP) and the Chief Officer of the United Nations India–Pakistan Observation Mission (UNIPOM) jointly addressed identical messages to the Indian Chief of Army Staff and the Pakistan Chief of General Staff, setting forth the terms of the agreement as reached in principle during the discussions with both parties and requesting them to confirm them. The terms of the agreement, which were applicable to the entire area of conflict, were as follows:

(*a*) Both sides agree that their light aircraft should not fly within 1,600 metres of their respective lines of control.

(*b*) Both sides agree that their high performance aircraft should not fly within 10,000 metres of their respective lines of control.

(*c*) Observance of the agreement is to be supervised by United Nations military observers.

4. On 18 December, the Indian Command notified its acceptance of the terms of the agreement.

5. On 4 January 1966, the Acting Chief of General Staff, Pakistan, notified acceptance of the agreement by Pakistan, while reserving its right 'to use own air' should the Indian side violate the cease-fire agreement and attack the Pakistan positions. [*S/6710/Add. 15, 7 Jan. 1966.*]

By mid-January 1966 the situation was well under control.[28]

ii. Implementing the Order to Withdraw Troops

The implementation of the Security Council's order for withdrawal followed —necessarily—a parallel course with the success in achieving a reliable cease-fire. Here, too, UNMOGIP had a part to play:

1. This report is submitted for the purpose of affording the members of the Security Council some indication of the dimensions of the problem of withdrawals. Security Council resolution 211 (1965), of 20 September, in its operative paragraph 1, demands that after cease-fire orders have been issued by both Governments, 'a subsequent withdrawal of all personnel to the positions held by them before 5 August 1965' shall take place. In its operative paragraph 2, the resolution requests the Secretary-General 'to provide the necessary assistance to ensure supervision of the cease-fire and withdrawal of all armed personnel'.

2. I have informed the two parties that I am prepared to provide this assistance, and I have twice requested them to advise me of their plans and schedules for their respective withdrawals (S/6699, para. 3 and S/6699/Add.2, sect. II). The reply of Pakistan to my cabled message of

[28] S/6710/Add. 17, 23 Jan. 1966

20 September on this subject is set forth in document S/6715. No reply has been received from India as of the date of this report.

3. Military positions held by each party on the opposite side of the line in the entire area of conflict, as of 24 September, are indicated in the list below. It must be emphasized, however, that this list does not purport to be exhaustive or complete. The military situation throughout the area of conflict continues to be fluid, and revisions of the list may be necessary from day to day or even hour to hour. Complaints about positions on the wrong side of the line are reported by United Nations military observers to be 'continuous', and they emanate from both sides. These complaints are being investigated by military observers and, as confirmed, will necessitate corrections in the list. The list of the positions held by the armed forces of each party on the other party's side is as follows:

Cease-fire line (cfl)

(1) Kargil–Skardu sector: Indian troops occupy hill 13620 and some positions on ridge running north-east. This feature is on the Pakistan side of the CFL.

(2) Domel–Tangdhar sector:

(*a*) Sunjoi area: Indian troops occupy hill features in grid squares NL 8753, 8851, 8852, 8853, 8854 and 8954 and a ridge in NL 8450, 8550 and 8650.

(*b*) Tithwal area: Indian troops occupy Pakistan positions and hill features outlined as follows: from the River Kishenganga at point NL 770430 southwards to points NL 760420, 755410, 760400, 720390, 780380, 780370, 790370 to the CFL at 805378.

(*c*) Induspura area: Indian troops occupy a ridge in grid squares NL 8438 and 8538, and positions at NL 831839 and 836394.

(3) Rawalakot–Uri–Punch sector: Indian troops occupy the portion of the Bedori bulge on the Pakistan side of the CFL mainly east of the Uri–Haji Pir Pass–Punch road and a few positions west of the road on hill features in grid squares NL 1282, 1283 and 1277.

(4) Bhimber–Akhnur sector: Pakistan troops occupy Indian positions and territory on the Indian side of the CFL roughly limited by northing 70 and easting 78.

(5) Pakistan military-para-military forces are occupying some pockets of resistance on the Indian side of the CFL in Kashmir. One example of this is the pocket situated 3 miles north-east of Galuthi.

Border

(6) Sialkot–Jammu border: Indian troops are on the Pakistan side of the border. The exact extent of their advance in that sector is unknown to the military observers.

(7) India/West Pakistan border: Indian troops are on the Pakistan side of the border in the Narowal–Lahore–Kasur sector, and in southern Rajasthan.

(8) The CGS of Pakistan reported that Pakistan troops occupy some areas of the Indian State of Rajasthan. The area they are said to occupy is bounded by Raichandwala (LM 62), Buili Kalan (IM 60), Sachu (WE 39), Achri Toba (LM 02), Sadhewala (LM 10), Longanewala Tar (LQ 81), Gotharu (LQ 76), Shangarh (LQ 54), Pochina (LY 94), Miajlar (LW 03), Rasliani (QB 19), track junction (QB 0869), Kelnor (QB 42), Bijliar (QB 53), Dota Katal (QB 63), But (QB 62) and Binjasar (QB 51).

4. It is reported from the field that apparently some occupations of new positions or territory are being made under orders of local commanders, or by units not fully under control, especially in cases where para-military or 'irregular' elements are involved.

5. General Nimmo has advised that in view of the difficulty of defining accurately the exact positions held by each party on the wrong side of the line, it would be preferable that the troops of each side withdraw to their well-known respective sides of the line in the entire area of conflict, rather than try to define the precise positions from which they must withdraw. [*S/6719, 27 Sept. 1965, Report of Secretary-General on compliance with Security Council res. 211 (1965).*]

A little over two weeks later the Secretary-General submitted another report on this matter:

1. Additional information relating to the question of withdrawal of armed personnel which has been received since the circulation on 5 October 1965 of the last report on this subject (S/6719/Add. 1), is set forth below.

2. The withdrawals of all armed personnel foreseen in the Security Council resolutions 211 (1965) of 20 September, and 214 (1965), of 27 September, have not taken place and there is no present indication that they are likely to take place any time soon under present circumstances, unless some new effort is made.

3. Replies of Pakistan and India to the two requests of the Secretary-General for an indication of their plans and schedules for the withdrawal of their respective forces to the positions held by them before 5 August 1965, were conditional and have been circulated to the Council (S6715 and S/6720).

4. On 13 October I addressed the following third message on the subject of withdrawal to the Prime Minister of India and the President of Pakistan:

'I have the honour to communicate with Your Excellency further on the question of the withdrawal of all armed personnel to the positions held by them before 5 August 1965, as called for in paragraph 1 of Security Council resolution 211 (1965), of 20 September. In this regard, I would also call to your attention the last paragraph of resolution 214 (1965), of 27 September on this subject. Your Excellency will, no doubt, recall my messages to your Government of 20 and 23 September requesting from you the plan and schedule for the withdrawals required. I am, of course, mindful of your Government's reply as set forth in the letter of your Permanent Representative to the United Nations (S/6715 and S/6720 respectively). Nevertheless, it is a matter of great concern to me and, I believe, to the members of the Security Council, that as of the date of this message, the withdrawals foreseen in the Security Council resolutions have not taken place.

'The Security Council resolution 211 (1965) of 20 September, in its paragraph 1, demanded that "a cease-fire should take effect on Wednesday, 22 September 1965, at 07.00 hours GMT and called for a subsequent withdrawal of all armed personnel to the positions held by them before 5 August 1965". Security Council resolution 214 (1965), of 27 September in its last paragraph "calls upon the parties promptly to withdraw all armed personnel as necessary steps in the full implementation of the resolution of 20 September". United Nations military observers with the function of ensuring supervision of the cease-fire and the withdrawal of all armed personnel are now stationed throughout the area of conflict, and the cease-fire which was accepted by both parties is becoming increasingly effective. I now therefore would like to renew my appeal to you to take the necessary steps to bring about the withdrawals called for by the Security Council resolutions.

'I would hope that each party might find it possible to formulate its own plan and schedule of withdrawal and that the respective time schedules might be co-ordinated with the assistance of United Nations military observers. If, however, this should not be considered feasible I would suggest that appropriate military representatives of each side be brought together by and with an acceptable representative to be designated by me to meet either in the area or at United Nations Headquarters for the purpose of formulating an agreed withdrawal plan.

'I hope for an early reply to this message. In view of Security Council concern with this matter, I am circulating this message to the Council for the information of its members.'

5. Approaches from the field have been made to appropriate authorities on both sides with a view to securing tactical readjustments along the line for the purpose of avoiding incidents resulting from the close proximity of opposing forces which might unintentionally lead to a resumption of fighting. Replies to these suggestions are awaited from both sides. The proposed tactical readjustments, of course, would be only a temporary measure pending the full implementation of the withdrawal provisions of the Security Council resolutions. [*S/6719/Add. 2, 14 Oct. 1965.*]

   U Thant agreed to a Pakistani suggestion that UNMOGIP and UNIPOM needed to be assisted, in the question of withdrawals, by a special Representative of the Secretary-General. The matter was one of urgency, as by now a full month had elapsed since the cease-fire came into effect, but no withdrawals had yet taken place.

   I have noted the reiteration of your view that 'no withdrawal could take place until it had been jointly agreed to by the representatives of the armed forces of India and Pakistan and a mutually accepted programme of withdrawal had been drawn up'. I note also your doubt about the feasibility of the suggestion in my message of 13 October that India and Pakistan might formulate their own plans and schedule of withdrawal, with the respective time schedules being co-ordinated with the assistance of United Nations military observers. In place of this you consider to be more practical my other suggestion that appropriate military representatives of each side should meet in the area to formulate an agreed plan with the assistance of representatives of sufficiently high rank to be designated by me.
   I welcome this favourable response and I propose to proceed on that basis. Accordingly, I have it in mind to designate a thoroughly experienced senior officer in the United Nations family for this purpose. It would be my idea that he should go to the area at an early date to visit both capitals and to arrange for representatives of India and Pakistan to meet at some mutually agreed place, possibly near the front lines, to seek agreement on a plan and schedule for the withdrawals by both parties. For this highly important assignment I would name Maj.-Gen. Syseno Sarmento of Brazil, Commander of the United Nations Emergency Force in Gaza and Sinai. General Sarmento serves the United Nations with distinction as Commander of the United Nations Emergency Force. . . . [*S/6719/Add. 3, 22 Oct. 1965.*]

In the event, General Sarmento was not to prove acceptable to both the parties, and an alternative Representative, General Marambio, was named by the Secretary-General.[29]

   The arrangement was confirmed by the Security Council:

The Security Council,
   Regretting the delay in the full achievement of a complete and effective cease-fire and a prompt withdrawal of armed personnel to the positions held by them before 5 August 1965, as called for in its resolutions 209 (1965) of 4 September, 210 (1965) of 6 September, 211 (1965) of 20 September and 214 (1965) of 27 September 1965,
   1. *Reaffirms* its resolution 211 (1965) in all its parts;
   2. *Requests* the Governments of India and Pakistan to co-operate towards a full implementation of paragraph 1 of resolution 211 (1965); calls upon them to instruct their armed personnel to co-operate with the United Nations and cease all military activity; and insists that there be an end to violations of the cease-fire;
   3. *Demands* the prompt and unconditional execution of the proposal already agreed to in principle by the Governments of India and Pakistan that their representatives meet with a suitable representative of the Secretary-General, to be appointed without delay after consultation with both parties, for the purpose of formulating an agreed plan and schedule for the withdrawals by both parties; urges that such a meeting take place as soon as possible and that such a plan contain a time-limit on its implementation; and requests the Secretary-General to report on the progress achieved in this respect within three weeks of the adoption of the present resolution;
   4. *Requests* the Secretary-General to submit for its consideration as soon as possible a report on compliance with the present resolution. [*SC res. 215 (1965), 5 Nov. 1965.*]

[29] See above, p. 366.

Jordan and the Soviet Union abstained on this resolution.[30]

General Marambio, acting with UNIPOM and UNMOGIP, succeeded in his mission, and the details of the withdrawal procedures agreed upon (and UNMOGIP's role therein) are sufficiently interesting to merit reproduction *in toto*. The manner in which military observers can perform a good offices function in certain circumstances is particularly instructive.

1. In my report of 25 November 1965 (S/6719/Add. 4) on compliance with the withdrawal provisions of Security Council resolutions 211 (1965) of 20 September and 215 (1965) of 5 November 1965, I informed the Council of the appointment of General Tulio Marambio as my Representative, to meet with representatives of India and Pakistan for the purpose of formulating an agreed plan and schedule for the withdrawal of all armed personnel to the positions held by them before 5 August 1965.

2. After a week of consultations at United Nations Headquarters, General Marambio departed on 5 December 1965 for the sub-continent, where he arrived on 6 December. Following a number of separate informal consultations with each side, as well as with the Chief Military Observer of the United Nations Military Observer Group for India and Pakistan (UNMOGIP) and the Chief Officer of the United Nations India-Pakistan Observation Mission (UNIPOM), General Marambio succeeded in arranging for joint meetings of the military representatives of India and Pakistan to be convened under his auspices.

3. The joint meetings took place on 3, 6, 15, 25 and 29 January 1966. India was represented at those meetings by Lieutenant-General Harbakhsh Singh and Lieutenant-Colonel T. S. Padde, and Pakistan by Lieutenant-General Bakhtiar Rana and Brigadier-General Hassan Khan. The joint meetings were held at United Nations operational headquarters in Lahore (Pakistan) and Amritsar (India) alternately. In accordance with arrangements proposed by General Marambio and agreed to by the parties, a United Nations aircraft with the customary identification markings was made available to the military representatives of both parties for their transportation between Lahore and Amritsar, and United Nations vehicles were provided to them for transportation between the airport and the United Nations headquarters in both cities. Responsibility for security at the meetings was assumed by the United Nations.

4. In their joint declaration of 10 January 1966 at Tashkent the Prime Minister of India and the President of Pakistan agreed that all armed personnel of their countries should be withdrawn not later than 25 February to the positions held by them before 5 August 1965. The implementation of this declaration would, of course, also fulfil the withdrawal provisions of the Security Council resolutions (209 (1965), 210 (1965), 211 (1965), 214 (1965) and 215 (1965)). A meeting between the Chief of Army Staff, India, and the Commander-in-Chief, Pakistan Army, was scheduled for 22 January to discuss military problems of mutual concern, including the question of withdrawal.

5. At the joint meeting on 15 January, the parties agreed on the principles of a plan and schedule for withdrawal for submission to the two military leaders at their meeting scheduled for 22 January. These principles were as follows;

(*a*) *First stage:* seven days for reducing tensions and bringing about amity and peace;

(*b*) *Second stage:* a five-day period for disengagement; in the plains and also in the mountainous areas where the troops are too close they would withdraw 1,000 yards on each side;

(*c*) *Third stage:* a twenty-one day period for lifting of mines, dismantling of defensive and field works by unarmed personnel in uniform; ground rules for procedure to be made at the next joint meeting; and

(*d*) *Fourth and final stage:* seven days, or balance of days before 25 February, for pulling

---

[30] The Security Council had on 27 September adopted Res. 214 by which it had expressed its concern that the cease-fire was not holding, calling upon the parties to fulfil their obligations, and 'to withdraw all armed personnel as necessary steps in the full implementation of resolution 211 (1965).'

troops back to their respective 'territories'. The role to be assumed by United Nations observers in the withdrawal plan was also discussed during this meeting.

6. On 22 January, the COAS, India, and the C-in-C, Pakistan Army, met in New Delhi and agreed on a plan for disengagement and withdrawal of their troops. This agreement, the text of which was communicated to General Marambio by the COAS, India, on 23 January at a meeting at New Delhi, provided that ground rules to implement the withdrawal in the western sector (along the cease-fire line in Kashmir and the border between India and Western Pakistan) were to be formulated by Lt-General Bakhtiar Rana and Lt-General Harbaksh Singh, under the chairmanship of General Marambio.

7. At the joint meeting of 25 January, the parties discussed and agreed upon the ground rules for the implementation of the disengagement and withdrawal plan. A draft of a document embodying the relevant parts of the agreement reached by the two military leaders on 22 January, as well as the ground rules for implementing the withdrawals, was introduced by General Marambio for discussion by the parties with their respective Governments before its final approval at the next meeting, projected for 29 January in Lahore. At the meeting of 25 January, the parties also agreed that the implementation of phase I of the disengagement and withdrawal plan should begin immediately, that is, on 25 January.

8. At the joint meeting of 29 January, the draft mentioned above was given final approval by the parties. The text of the agreement thus concluded, which was signed by Lt-General Harbakhsh Singh for India, by Lt-General Bakhtiar Rana for Pakistan, and by General Marambio as the Representative of the Secretary-General of the United Nations, is appended to this report.

9. In essence, the agreement reached provided for the disengagement and withdrawal of armed personnel. It was in two parts, as follows:

(a) *Part I: Disengagement of troops and reduction of tension*
This part is divided in two phases:
In phase I, both forces would withdraw to a distance up to 1,000 yards from the line of actual control in specified areas where their respective positions were too close to each other. The period for completing this phase would be five days.

In phase II, both sides would remove and nullify all defences, including the lifting of mines and the dismantling of all other defence works. This phase would commence immediately after the five-day period assigned for the completion of phase I and would be completed within twenty-one days.

The existing agreement regarding restriction of flights of aircraft would continue to apply. The good offices of UNMOGIP and UNIPOM would be requested to ensure that the action agreed to in part I was fully implemented. In the event of disagreement between the parties, the decision of UNMOGIP and UNIPOM would be final and binding on both sides.

(b) *Part II: Withdrawal of troops from occupied areas*
After dismantling of defences had taken place, all troops, para-military forces and armed police who were on the other side of the international border and the cease-fire line would be withdrawn. This withdrawal would be completed by 25 February 1966. For immediate settlement of any points of dispute that might arise, sector commanders not below the rank of major-general would be designated by both sides, who would meet to settle any differences. Any matter on which there was disagreement would be referred to the C-in-C, Pakistan Army, and the COAS, India, for their joint decision. If the issue could not be solved by them, the good offices of General Marambio would be requested and his decision would be final and binding on both sides. It was agreed that General Marambio's functions in this regard would cease no later than 28 February 1966.

10. On 31 January 1966, UNMOGIP and UNIPOM reported that phase I of part I of the disengagement and withdrawal plan had been completed without incident or difficulty in all sectors concerned. Later reports from them indicate that phase II has been progressing favourably although the removal of defences has been hampered by severe weather conditions

in a few areas in Kashmir. Meetings of Indian and Pakistan army representatives at various levels have been held regularly in accordance with the agreement. There have been no confirmed incidents involving breaches of the cease-fire since my last report on the observance of the cease-fire (S/6710/Add. 17, 28 January 1966). United Nations observers have reported a few cases of looting and destruction of civilian property in occupied areas by both sides. These cases were brought to the attention of the local commanders concerned and corrective action was promised.

11. United Nations observers have also reported that since the agreement came into effect three exchanges of prisoners have taken place with the assistance of the representative of the International Committee of the Red Cross and United Nations Observers. On 2 February, an exchange of nineteen Pakistan and seventeen Indian disabled officers took place at Lahore, while 583 Pakistan and 552 Indian prisoners were exchanged at Hussainwala. On 8 February, a third exchange, involving 175 Indian and 162 Pakistan prisoners, took place at Hussainwala.

12. In general, it may be said that since 25 February the withdrawal programme has been implemented according to plan and without any hitches at all. The completion of the withdrawals operation will be promptly reported to the Council.

ANNEX

Agreement between the military representatives of India and Pakistan regarding the withdrawals of their armed personnel in pursuance of the Security Council resolutions of 20 September 1965 and 5 November 1965

1. The military representatives of India and Pakistan met together on 3, 6, 15, 25 and 29 January 1966 in Amritsar and Lahore under the auspices of General Tulio Marambio, Representative of the Secretary-General of the United Nations, who was assisted by Mr Miguel A. Marín, Principal Secretary;

2. The representatives of India were: Lieutenant-General Harbakhsh Singh, GOC-in-C, Western Army Command, assisted by Lieutenant-Colonel T. S. Padde, Staff Officer, Western Command;

3. The representatives of Pakistan were: Lieutenant-General Bakhtiar Rana, Commander, One Corps, assisted by Brigadier Gul Hassan Khan, Director of Military Operations;

4. Considering that the Security Council in its resolution of 20 September 1965 calls for withdrawal of all armed personnel back to the positions held by them before 5 August 1965;

5. Considering that the Security Council, on 5 November 1965, adopted a resolution which, *inter alia*, demands the prompt and unconditional execution of the proposal already agreed to in principle by the Governments of India and Pakistan, that their representatives meet with a suitable representative of the Secretary-General for the purpose of formulating an agreed plan and shedule for the withdrawal by both parties, and urges that such a meeting shall take place as soon as possible and that such a plan contain a time-limit on its implementation;

6. Considering that the Prime Minister of India and the President of Pakistan, in their joint declaration on 10 January 1966 at Tashkent, agreed that all armed personnel of the two countries shall be withdrawn not later than 25 February 1966 to the positions they held before 5 August 1965;

7. Considering that on 15 January 1966, at the joint meeting held in Lahore, the parties agreed on the principles of a plan and schedule of withdrawal of armed personnel to be submitted to the then forthcoming meeting of the Chief of the Indian Army Staff and the Commander-in-Chief of the Pakistan Army;

8. Considering that, on 22 January 1966, the Chief of the Indian Army Staff and the Commander-in-Chief of the Pakistan Army agreed and formulated a plan for 'disengagement and withdrawal of troops';

9. Considering that, in paragraph 26 of the above-mentioned agreement, it was stated that ground rules to implement the withdrawal in the Western Sector will be formulated by Lt-

14*

Gen. Bakhtiar Rana (Pakistan) and Lt-Gen. Harbakhsh Singh (India) under the chairmanship of General Tulio Marambio as early as possible;

10. The parties to the present agreement, duly authorized, have agreed to incorporate in
the present document the relevant parts of the above-mentioned plan and, as an annex, the
ground rules formulated accordingly:

(1) This agreement is in two parts:

PART I—Procedure concerning the immediate disengagement of troops and reduction of
tension;

PART II—Procedure concerning the withdrawal of troops from the occupied areas.

PART I

DISENGAGEMENT OF TROOPS AND REDUCTION OF TENSION

Phase I

(2) Both forces will withdraw 1,000 yards from the line of actual control in sectors as
specified below:

(a) Rajasthan/Sind

(b) Amritsar/Lahore

(c) Jammu/Sialkot

(d) Akhnur/Chhamb (from River Chenab NW 8061 to Mawa Wali Khad NW 7770). In
all other sectors including sectors divided by the 1949 cease-fire line, troops will continue to
hold their respective picquets as by so doing they will be automatically separated from each
other. The only exception to this will be where, in hilly terrain, opposing forces are at present
considered to be too close to each other, each side will withdraw to a distance to be mutually
agreed upon by the local commanders not below the rank of Brigadier.

(*Note:* In the Amritsar–Lahore sector, this 1,000 yards withdrawal will be modified so
that Pakistani troops who are actually on the west bank of the Bambanwala–Ravi–Bedian
Canal (BRB) and Indian troops who are on the east bank of the BRB Canal facing each other
will withdraw all armed personnel off the embankment to a distance of 200 yards on each side.
Unarmed personnel may, however, live, move and work in this area. The same principle will
apply in Sulaimanki–Fazilka sector, Hussainwala sector and Khem Karan sector.)

(3) After the withdrawal in this phase no new defences of any kind will be prepared in
occupied territory.

(4) There will be no movement of armed military, para-military or police personnel either
armed or unarmed within the demilitarized zone and no civilian personnel will be permitted
within it by either side.

(5) The period for completion of this phase will be five days.

Phase II

(6) In this phase both sides will remove and nullify all defences which will include the

(a) Lifting of mines, and

(b) Dismantling of all other defence works, less permanent defence structures constructed
of steel and cement.

The period for completing this phase will be twenty-one days which will commence
immediately after the five-day period mentioned in paragraph (5).

(7) Working parties for this purpose will be found by unarmed military personnel in uniform. No civilian or civil labour will be used for these tasks.

(8) While every effort will be made to dismantle all defence works within the specified
period, where, owing to weather and other conditions, it is not possible to complete this, the
uncleared areas so left will be clearly marked and a sketch of these given to the other side.

(9) There will be no firing of weapons or use of explosives within 10,000 metres of the line
of actual control. Where explosives have to be used to dismantle defence works, this will only
be done under supervision as specified later and after due intimation to the other side.

(10) The present agreement affecting restriction on flights of aircraft will continue to apply.

(11) To ensure that the action agreed to in part I above is being implemented in letter and in spirit, the good offices of UNMOGIP and UNIPOM will be requested. In the event of a disagreement, their decision will be final and binding to both sides.

PART II
WITHDRAWAL OF TROOPS FROM OCCUPIED AREAS

(12) After the dismantling of defences has taken place, all troops, para-military forces and armed police who are now on the other side of the international border and cease-fire line, will be withdrawn. This withdrawal will be completed by 25 February 1966. If, in any particular sector or part of a sector, the dismantling of defences has been completed earlier than the last date specified, withdrawal may be sectorwise if mutually agreed to.

(13) During this withdrawal, there will be no follow-up by civilians, armed military, para-military or police personnel until 25 February 1966. Only unarmed military personnel at a strength mutually agreed upon at the sector level may move into these unoccupied areas for normal police duties (see para. (16) below).

(14) After troops of both sides have crossed into their own territory, the procedure which was being followed by Pakistan and India before 5 August 1965, for the security of the international border and the cease-fire line, will apply. Attention is drawn to Ground Rules 1961 for West Pakistan/Punjab, Rajasthan and Gujerat (India).

(15) It is essential that under all circumstances troops must move out of occupied areas by 25 February 1966, even if the dismantling of defences and lifting of mines have not been completed.

(16) For immediate settlement of any points of dispute that may arise, sector commanders not below the rank of Major-General will be designated by name and appointment both by India and Pakistan who will meet to settle the differences. Telephone or R/T communication will be established between these designated sector commanders and will be permanently manned.

(17) Any matter on which there is disagreement will be referred to the C-in-C Pakistan Army and COAS India for their joint decision. If the issue is still not resolved by them, the good offices of General Tulio Marambio will be requested and his decision will be final and binding on both sides.

11. At the joint meeting in Amritsar on 25 January 1966, it was agreed that General Marambio's functions in regard to paragraph (17) above will cease no later than 28 February 1966.

12. In faith whereof the undersigned sign this document in three original copies. Done in Lahore on 29 January 1966.

India   *Pakistan*
(*Signed*) Lt-Gen. Harbakhsh SINGH   (*Signed*) Lt-Gen. Bakhtiar RANA

Representative of the Secretary-General of the United Nations
(*Signed*) General Tulio MARAMBIO

ANNEX
GROUND RULES OF PROCEDURE
General

1. The ground rules of procedure given in the succeeding paragraphs are in amplification of the terms of agreement between COAS India and C-in-C Pakistan Army for disengagement and withdrawal of troops and will be read in conjunction with it. The ground rules of procedure will come into force with effect from 06.00 hours (IST)/05.30 hours (WPT) 25 January 1966.

Phase I

2. Taking the average depth of the minefields and other obstacles on either side of the line of actual control as approximately 300 yards, troops will pull back only 700 yards from the line of forward posts in areas where the stipulation of a 1,000 yards withdrawal is applicable. The 200 yards rule as amplified in the note to paragraph 2 of the agreement will be applicable only to the areas specified therein.

3. After evacuation unarmed observation posts, sentries and guards in uniform may be left in the present forward posts wherever necessary. The strength of such personnel will be the barest minimum as mutually agreed to by local commanders.

4. Although no defence works are permitted in the new positions, living shelters may be dug down or constructed above the ground (including tentage) avoiding areas/features of tactical importance.

5. In hilly terrain where it is mutually agreed that the present positions are too close and may thus interfere with the removal of mines and the dismantling of defences, the withdrawal of the opposing garrisons from such posts, up to a distance to be mutually agreed upon between the local commanders, should be considered adequate.

Phase II

Mines

6. Before work on the lifting of mines and dismantling of defences is started, opposing commanders will meet each other at a mutually agreed place and time, and explain their respective work plans. This procedure will be followed every day. Apart from these daily meetings or any other meetings between commanders there will be no fraternization between opposing forces. The level of liaison for discussing daily work plans will not be below battalion commanders, accompanied by United Nations representatives.

7. Working parties will, under no circumstances, proceed beyond the Line of Actual Control. Working parties will function within areas to be demarcated by white flags.

8. Before a mine is exploded for the purpose of its destruction, intimation will be given to the opposing commander. All mines will be exploded between 15.00 hours to 17.00 hours (IST)/14.30 to 16.30 hours (WPT).

9. Where it has not been possible to lift mines either for want of time or on account of weather conditions, the area will be marked by flags planted every fifty yards or part thereof. Flags will be red in colour and mounted on flag poles three clear feet above ground level. The dimensions of the flag will be $2\frac{1}{2}' \times 2'$. A sketch of such areas (scale $1'' = 100$ yards) will be handed over to opposing sides on completion of phase II.

10. After removal, mines will be evacuated to respective sides of the international border/cease-fire line, at the end of the day. No local mine dumps will be permitted.

Defence works

11. Where the dismantling and destruction of defence works involves damage to civilian/government property including bridges/culverts and waterways (canals, flood drains and so on) these will be left intact, marked and intimated to opposing commanders.

12. Local material used on the construction of defence works will be left *in situ*.

13. No construction material will be removed from existing civilian/government property under the guise of defence stores. There will be no destruction of civil/government property with immediate effect.

14. Defence stores will be evacuated to respective sides of the international border/cease-fire line after dismantling, at the end of the day. No local defence store dumps will be permitted.

15. All defence works including trenches, ditches and so on, will be nullified by dismantling and filling up. Built-up positions will be levelled to the ground.

16. Where explosives are to be used for dismantling of works this will be done between 15.00 to 17.00 hours (IST)/14.30 to 16.30 hours (WPT) after due intimation to the opposing side and under supervision of United Nations observers.

17. Salvage lying between opposing forward posts will be collected only by the side which originally owned it. This will include the following:
(a) *Pakistan*
Two tanks lying in area Bhaini Bridge;
One tank in Khem Karan sector.
(v) *India*
One tank near Chander (Sialkot sector).
One tank in Khem Karan sector.
This equipment will not be interfered with or damaged by opposing side and will be evacuated by the respective side through mutual agreement by sector commanders.

18. In areas of difficult terrain where it is physically impracticable to evacuate defence stores and mines at the end of the day, temporary dumps will be permitted for periods not lasting more than three days at a time after mutual agreement between sector commanders.

Air flights
19. Reference paragraph 10 of the agreement—exceptions will be made for evacuation of serious casualties requiring urgent medical attention. Each such mission will be carried out after prior intimation to the opposing commanders and the local United Nations observers.

Phase III

20. In modification of paragraphs 12 and 13 of the agreement it has been decided that:
(*a*) Evacuation of occupied territories will be completed by 18.00 hours (IST)/17.30 hours (WPT), 25 February 1966;
(*b*) No armed or unarmed personnel of opposing sides will be permitted to come into evacuated areas before 06.00 hours (IST)/05.30 hours (WPT), 26 February 1966.

21. The good offices of UNMOGIP and UNIPOM will also be requested for part II of the agreement.

Miscellaneous

22. Throughout the above phases there will be no activity between 19.00 hours (IST)/ 18.30 hours (WPT) and 05.00 hours (IST)/04.30 hours (WPT) in the evacuated areas.

23. The first meeting between the sector commanders will be at 10.00 hours (IST)/09.30 hours (WPT), on 27 January 1966. For details see appendix A attached.

24. Establishment of signal communications between opposing sector commanders will be finalized during their first meeting on 27 January 1966.

25. When a meeting between opposing commanders is desired the liaising parties will carry flags as follows:
India: Yellow ($2\frac{1}{2}' \times 2'$);
Pakistan: Navy blue ($2\frac{1}{2}' \times 2'$).

(*Signed*) Lt-General Harbakhsh SINGH   (*Signed*) Lt-General Bakhtiar RANA
     GOC-in-C, Western Army Command   *Commander, One Corps*

(*Signed*) General Tulio MARAMBIO
Representative of the Secretary-General of the United Nations

[*S/6719/Add. 5, 17 Feb. 1966, Report of Secretary-General on compliance with Security Council res. 211 (1965)*.]

On 8 December 1966 it had been announced that both India and Pakistan had accepted a Russian invitation to go to Tashkent in January to discuss the problems of their two countries. The good offices of the Soviet Union were to prove extremely valuable. On 10 January 1967 India and Pakistan signed the Tashkent Declaration:

TASHKENT DECLARATION

The Prime Minister of India and the President of Pakistan having met at Tashkent and having discussed the existing relations between India and Pakistan, hereby declare their firm resolve to restore normal and peaceful relations between their countries and to promote understanding and friendly relations between their peoples. They consider the attainment of these objectives of vital importance for the welfare of the 600 million people of India and Pakistan.

I

The Prime Minister of India and the President of Pakistan agree that both sides will exert all efforts to create good neighbourly relations between India and Pakistan in accordance with the United Nations Charter. They reaffirm their obligation under the Charter not to have recourse to force and to settle their disputes through peaceful means. They considered that the interests of peace in their region and particularly in the Indo-Pakistan Sub-Continent and, indeed, the interests of the peoples of India and Pakistan were not served by the continuance of tension between the two countries. It was against this background that Jammu and Kashmir was discussed, and each of the sides set forth its respective position.

II

The Prime Minister of India and the President of Pakistan have agreed that all armed personnel of the two countries shall be withdrawn not later than 25 February 1966 to the postions they held prior to 5 August 1965, and both sides shall observe the cease-fire terms on the cease-fire line.

III

The Prime Minister of India and the President of Pakistan have agreed that relations between India and Pakistan shall be based on the principle of non-interference in the internal affairs of each other.

IV

The Prime Minister of India and the President of Pakistan have agreed that both sides will discourage any propaganda directed atainst the other country, and will encourage propaganda which promotes the development of friendly relations between the two countries.

V

The Prime Minister of India and the President of Pakistan have agreed that the High Commissioner of India to Pakistan and the High Commissioner of Pakistan to India will return to their posts and that the normal functioning of diplomatic missions of both countries will be restored. Both Governments shall observe the Vienna Convention of 1961 on Diplomatic Intercourse.

VI

The Prime Minister of India and the President of Pakistan have agreed to consider measures towards the restoration of economic and trade relations, communications, as well as cultural exchanges between India and Pakistan, and to take measures to implement the existing agreements between India and Pakistan.

VII

The Prime Minister of India and the President of Pakistan have agreed that they give instructions to their respective authorities to carry out the repatriation of the prisoners of war.

VIII

The Prime Minister of India and the President of Pakistan have agreed that the sides will continue the discussion of questions relating to the problems of refugees and evictions/illegal immigrations. They also agreed that both sides will create conditions which will prevent the exodus of people. They further agreed to discuss the return of the property and assets taken over by either side in connexion with the conflict.

IX

The Prime Minister of India and the President of Pakistan have agreed that the sides will continue meetings both at the highest and at other levels on matters of direct concern to both countries. Both sides have recognized the need to set up joint Indian–Pakistani bodies which will report to their Governments in order to decide what further steps should be taken. . . .
[*S/7221, 25 Mar. 1966*, ann.]

While no one will wish to deny the invaluable role played by the Soviet Union at this stage of India–Pakistan relations, the contribution of UNMOGIP and UNIPOM to providing the military conditions which made the Russian initiative possible should not be forgotten. UNIPOM, having fulfilled its mandate to help secure a cease-fire and troop withdrawals along the international frontier, withdrew in March 1966. UNMOGIP, whose 1965 duties were superimposed upon its duties under the Karachi Agreement of 1949, at the time of writing, remains on the Kashmir cease-fire line. With political progress on Kashmir still in stalemate, it is likely to remain there for the foreseeable future.

13

ANNEXES

A. *Checklist of Documents*

SECURITY COUNCIL

I. RESOLUTIONS

S/654	20 June 1948	⎫
S/726	21 Apr. 1948	⎬ *Resolutions and Decisions of the Security Council,* 3rd yr.
S/819	3 June 1948	⎭
S/1469	14 Mar. 1950	ibid. 5th yr.
S/2017/Rev.1	30 Mar. 1951	⎫ ibid. 6th yr.
S/2392	10 Nov. 1951	⎭
S/2883	23 Dec. 1952	ibid. 7th yr.
S/3779	24 Jan. 1957	⎫
S/3792	21 Feb. 1957	⎬ ibid. 12th yr.
S/3922	2 Dec. 1957	⎭

SC res. 209 (1965) 4 Sept.
SC res. 210 (1965) 6 Sept.
SC res. 211 (1965) 20 Sept. }ibid. 20th yr.
SC res. 214 (1965) 27 Sept.
SC res. 215 (1965) 5 Nov.

2. CEASE-FIRE AGREEMENT SIGNED 29–30 JULY 1949
S/1430, ann. 26   5 Dec. 1949

3. REPORTS OF THE UN COMMISSION FOR INDIA AND PAKISTAN
S/995   13 Aug. 1948   S/1196   5 Jan. 1949
S/1100   9 Nov. 1948   S/1430/Rev. 1   5 Dec. 1949

4. MILITARY ADVISER'S PLAN FOR DEMILITARIZATION
S/2485   21 Jan. 1952

5. REPORT OF GUNNAR JARRING
S/3821   29 Apr. 1957

6. REPORTS OF THE UN REPRESENTATIVE
S/1453   6 Feb. 1950   S/2727   31 July 1952
S/1791   15 Sept. 1950   S/2783   19 Sept. 1952
S/2375   15 Oct. 1951   S/2910   23 Jan. 1953
S/2248 & Ann. 19 Dec. 1951   S/2967   27 Mar. 1953
S/2611   24 Apr. 1952   S/3984   28 Mar. 1958
S/2619   29 May 1952

7. MAIN STATEMENTS BY INDIA AND PAKISTAN ON THEIR POSITION OVER KASHMIR
S/1942   14 Dec. 1950   S/2225   30 June 1951
S/2119   4 May 1951   S/2233   6 July 1951
S/2207   21 June 1951

8. EXCHANGE OF CLAIMS OF BREACH OF THE 1949 AGREEMENT OVER KASHMIR
(a) Claims by India
S/3999   1 May 1958   S/4273   2 Mar. 1960
S/3994 24 Apr. 1958   S/4317   20 May 1960
S/4042   6 July 1958   S/4327   27 May 1960
S/4046 14 July 1958   S/5435   7 Oct. 1963
S/4086 18 Aug. 1958   S/5450   1 Nov. 1963
S/4088 19 Aug. 1958   S/5467   27 Nov. 1963
S/4095 10 Sept 1958   S/5503   3 Jan. 1964
S/4107 24 Oct. 1958   S/5522   24 Jan. 1964
S/4138 17 Dec. 1958   S/5612   19 Mar. 1964
S/4177 31 Mar. 1959   S/5673   30 Apr. 1964
S/4202   8 Aug. 1959   S/5668   24 Apr. 1964
S/4228 12 Oct. 1959   S/5911   21 Aug. 1964
S/4234 29 Oct. 1959   S/6125   26 Dec. 1964
S/4238 12 Nov. 1959   S/6218   5 Mar. 1965
S/4249 22 Dec. 1959   S/6303   27 Apr. 1965

(b) Claims by Pakistan
S/3981 28 Mar. 1958   S/4292   29 Mar. 1960
S/3985   2 Apr. 1958   S/4556   1 Nov. 1960
S/4003   6 May 1958   S/5058   11 Jan. 1962

S/4032	19 June 1958	S/5068	29 Jan. 1962
S/4036	25 June 1958	S/5437	9 Oct. 1963
S/4048	15 July 1958	S/5467	27 Nov. 1963
S/4070	31 July 1958	S/5504	3 Jan. 1964
S/4092	28 Aug. 1958	S/5517	16 Jan. 1964
S/4110	10 Nov. 1958	S/5576	4 Mar. 1964
S/4139	19 Dec. 1958	S/5657	14 Apr. 1964
S/4152	28 Jan. 1959	S/5836	27 July 1964
S/4157	6 Feb. 1959	S/6114	17 Dec. 1964
S/4185	7 May 1959	S/6292	20 Apr. 1965
S/4217	9 Sept. 1959	S/6305	27 Apr. 1965
S/4219	11 Sept. 1959	S/6360	17 May 1965
S/4242	3 Dec. 1959	S/6367	18 May 1965
S/4259	22 Jan. 1960	S/6458	18 June 1965
S/4278	24 Mar. 1960	S/6481	28 June 1965

9. THE RANN OF KUTCH DISPUTE

S/6281	11 April 1965	S/6340	7 May 1965
S/6291	19 April 1965	S/6389	28 May 1965
S/6308	27 April 1965	S/6423	7 June 1965
S/6321	3 May 1965	S/6466	22 June 1965
S/6322	3 May 1965	S/6507	6 July 1965

10. COMMUNICATIONS OF SECRETARY–GENERAL TO INDIA AND PAKISTAN CONCERNING HOSTILITIES OF 1965

S/6647	1 Sept. 1965	S/6878	5 Nov. 1965
S/6782	13 Oct. 1965		

11. COMMUNICATIONS FROM INDIA AND PAKISTAN TO SECRETARY–GENERAL CONCERNING HOSTILITIES OF 1965

S/6666	7 Sept. 1965	S/6753	6 Oct. 1965
S/6715	20 Sept. 1965	S/6754	6 Oct. 1965
S/6720	28 Sept. 1965	S/6756	7 Oct. 1965
S/6735	1 Oct. 1965	S/6762	11 Oct. 1965
S/6742	4 Oct. 1965	S/6825	25 Oct. 1965
S/6751	5 Oct. 1965	S/6558	1 Nov. 1965
		S/6920	12 Nov. 1965

12. REPORTS OF SECRETARY–GENERAL CONCERNING THE HOSTILITIES OF 1965

S/6651	3 Sept. 1965
S/6661	6 Sept. 1965
S/6683	16 Sept. 1965
S/6686	16 Sept. 1965
S/6687	16 Sept. 1965
S/6699 & Adds. 1–12	20 Sept. 1965–15 Dec. 1965
S/6710 & Adds. 1–17	25 Sept. 1965–28 Jan. 1966
S/6719 & Adds. 1–4	27 Sept. 1965
S/6888	9 Nov. 1965

13. CLAIMS BY INDIA AND PAKISTAN OF BREACHES OF THE CEASE–FIRE OF SEPTEMBER 1965

(a) *Claims by India*

S/6711	25 Sept. 1965	S/6848	29 Oct. 1965
S/6725	29 Sept. 1965	S/6862	2 Nov. 1965
S/6744	4 Oct. 1965	S/6867	3 Nov. 1965

S/6746	5 Oct. 1965		S/6884	5 Nov. 1968
S/6752	6 Oct. 1965		S/6889	9 Nov. 1965
S/6755	7 Oct. 1965		S/6890	9 Nov. 1965
S/6764	8 Oct. 1965		S/6895	10 Nov. 1965
S/6768	11 Oct. 1965		S/6925	12 Nov. 1965
S/6772	11 Oct. 1965		S/6926	12 Nov. 1965
S/6773	11 Oct. 1965		S/6927	12 Nov. 1965
S/6777	12 Oct. 1965		S/6939	16 Nov. 1965
S/6778	12 Oct. 1965		S/6945	17 Nov. 1965
S/6781	13 Oct. 1965		S/6952	18 Nov. 1965
S/6790	14 Oct. 1965		S/6968	23 Nov. 1965
S/6788	14 Oct. 1965		S/6977	29 Nov. 1965
S/6808	19 Oct. 1965		S/6982	30 Nov. 1965
S/6810	19 Oct. 1965		S/6984	2 Dec. 1965
S/6812	20 Oct. 1965		S/7004	9 Dec. 1965
S/6813	21 Oct. 1965		S/7009	13 Dec. 1965
S/6819	22 Oct. 1965		S/7018	16 Dec. 1965
S/6826	25 Oct. 1965		S/7033	20 Dec. 1965
S/6832	26 Oct. 1965		S/7050	21 Dec. 1965
S/6836	27 Oct. 1965		S/7040	27 Dec. 1965
S/6840	27 Oct. 1965		S/7060	3 Jan. 1966
S/6841	28 Oct. 1965		S/7070	7 Jan. 1966
S/6842	28 Oct. 1965			

(b) *Claims by Pakistan*

S/6712	25 Sept. 1965		S/6811	20 Oct. 1965
S/6713	26 Sept. 1965		S/6815	21 Oct. 1965
S/6714	26 Sept. 1965		S/6816	21 Oct. 1965
S/6726	29 Sept. 1965		S/6821	22 Oct. 1965
S/6727	29 Sept. 1965		S/6839	27 Oct. 1965
S/6745	4 Oct. 1965		S/6849	31 Oct. 1965
S/6750	5 Oct. 1965		S/6850	31 Oct. 1965
S/6753	6 Oct. 1965		S/6869	4 Nov. 1965
S/6754	6 Oct. 1965		S/6870	4 Nov. 1965
S/6759	8 Oct. 1965		S/6879	5 Nov. 1965
S/6760	8 Oct. 1965		S/6894	10 Nov. 1965
S/6765	9 Oct. 1965		S/6901	11 Nov. 1965
S/6766	11 Oct. 1965		S/6947	17 Nov. 1965
S/6770	11 Oct. 1965		S/6948	17 Nov. 1965
S/6771	11 Oct. 1965		S/6950	18 Nov. 1965
S/6779	12 Oct. 1965		S/6960	19 Nov. 1965
S/6784	14 Oct. 1965		S/6988	3 Dec. 1965
S/6785	14 Oct. 1965		S/6992	4 Dec. 1965
S/6789	14 Oct. 1965		S/6995	7 Dec. 1965
S/6792	15 Oct. 1965		S/7017	18 Dec. 1965
S/6793	15 Oct. 1965		S/7035	21 Dec. 1965
S/6794	15 Oct. 1965		S/7036	21 Dec. 1965
S/6795	16 Oct. 1965		S/7045	28 Dec. 1965
S/6796	16 Oct. 1965		S/7061	3 Jan. 1966
S/6799	18 Oct. 1965		S/7251	12 Apr. 1966
S/6800	18 Oct. 1965		S/7310	19 May 1966

14. DEBATES IN THE SECURITY COUNCIL
 SCOR, 3rd yr, mtgs 229–30, 382
 SCOR, 4th yr, mtgs 399, 457–8
 SCOR, 5th yr, mtgs 463–71, 503
 SCOR, 6th yr, mtgs 532–40, 543, 548, 564, 566
 SCOR, 7th yr, mtgs 540–2, 605–11
 SCOR, 11th yr, mtgs 761–5, 791, 795–805, 807, 808
 SCOR, 17th yr, mtgs 990, 1007–16
 SCOR, 19th yr, mtgs 1007–16, 1104–15, 1112–17
 SCOR, 20th yr, mtgs 1237–42, 1244, 1245, 1247–9, 1251

15. TASHKENT AGREEMENT
 S/7221   25 Mar. 1966

B. *Bibliography*

Abdullah, Sheikh Muhammed. Kashmir, India and Pakistan. *Foreign Affairs*,
 Apr. 1965.
Austin, Granville. *History Past and History Present*; *Report on Kashmir*. New
 York, 1965, mimeo.
Birdwood, C. B. *Two Nations and Kashmir*. London, 1956.
Brecher, Michael. Kashmir: a Case Study in United Nations Mediation.
 Pacific Affairs, 1963.
Campbell-Johnson, A. *Mission with Mountbatten*. London, 1951.
Das Gupta, J. B. *Indo-Pakistan Relations, 1947–55*. Amsterdam, 1959.
Gupta, Sisir. *Kashmir; a Study in India–Pakistan Relations*. Bombay, 1966.
Korbel, Josef. *Danger in Kashmir*. Rev. ed. Princeton, 1966.
—— The Kashmir Dispute after Six Years. *International Organization*, 1953.
Lamb, Alastair. *Crisis in Kashmir, 1947–66*. London, 1966.
Lourié, Sylvain. The United Nations Military Observer Group in India and
 Pakistan. *International Organization*, 1955.
Menon, V. P. *The Story of the Integration of the Indian States*. Bombay, 1956.
Millar, T. B. Kashmir, the Commonwealth and the United Nations. *Australian
 Outlook*, 1963.
Saarinnen, Reino. Views of a Military Observer of UN Activities regarding the
 Kashmir Crisis. *Military Review*, Jan. 1966.
Sen, D. K. The Security Council and the Kashmir Dispute. 6 *Indian Law
 Review* (1952).
Sufi, Ghulam Muhyi'd Din. *Kashmir, being a History of Kashmir from Earliest
 to Our Own Times*. Lahore, 1948.
Tinker, Hugh. *India and Pakistan: a Political Analysis*. 2nd ed. London, 1962.
—— India's Relations with Pakistan. *International Studies*, spec. ed., July–Oct.
 1966.

Part 5

THE UNITED NATIONS
INDIA–PAKISTAN OBSERVATION MISSION
(UNIPOM), 1965-6

the order to withdraw; difficulties relating to opposing Indian and Pakistani views on scope of the Security Council's jurisdiction under resolutions of 4, 6, and 20 September 1965.

10. RELATIONS WITH OTHER STATES INVOLVED (p. 455)
Absence of major difficulties.

11. FINANCE (p. 455)
Initial estimates; revised lower figures; the financing of UNIPOM beyond the initial three-month period; appointment among UN membership; reactions of India, Pakistan, France, and Soviet Union.

12. IMPLEMENTATION (p. 459)
UNIPOM'S contribution to achieving the cease-fire; delays in implementation; UNIPOM initiatives and local commander agreements; need for further cease-fire orders by Chiefs of Staff in December 1965; UNIPOM'S contribution to securing the withdrawal of armed personnel; Secretary-General nominates Brigadier-General Marambio as his personal representative in the matter of withdrawals; diplomatic activity by the Soviet Union leads to the Declaration of Tashkent; UNIPOM assists in implementing Tashkent understandings.

13. ANNEXES

I

INTRODUCTION

THE background to the formation of the UN India–Pakistan Observation Mission (UNIPOM) lies quite clearly in the breakdown, in August 1965, of the Karachi Agreement on a cease-fire of July 1949. The establishment of a cease-fire line under that Agreement, and the observer and other functions of the UN Military Observer Group (UNMOGIP), have been fully recounted in the preceding Part. Detailed reference has also been made to the sharp deterioration which occurred in 1965 in Indo-Pakistani relations (pp. 387–9). Not only had fighting occurred in the early part of the year over the Rann of Kutch,[1] but UNMOGIP reported a marked increase in violations of the Kashmir cease-fire line. Large-scale hostilities occurred from 5 August onwards and, being fully reported in the preceding Part (see especially pp. 389–40) need no repetition here. The factual situation, and the attribution of blame, can briefly be summarized in the following report by the Secretary-General on information received by him from UNMOGIP:

6. General Nimmo has indicated to me that the series of violations that began on 5 August were to a considerable extent in subsequent days in the form of armed men, generally not in uniform, crossing the cease-fire line from the Pakistan side for the purpose of armed action on the Indian side. This is a conclusion reached by General Nimmo on the basis of investigations by the United Nations observers, in the light of the extensiveness and character of the raiding activities and their proximity to the CFL, even though in most cases the actual identity of those engaging in the armed attacks on the Indian side of the line and their actual crossing of it could not be verified by direct observation or evidence. As regards violations by artillery, there was heavy and prolonged artillery fire across the CFL from the Pakistan side in the Chhamb–Bhimber area on 15 and 16 August, and on 19 and 26 August the town of Punch was shelled from the Pakistan side, some of the shells hitting the building occupied by United Nations military observers. Pakistan artillery again shelled the town of Punch on 28 August. There was an exchange of artillery fire between the Uri sector on the Indian side and the Chakothi sector on the Pakistan side on 14 August. Also, it has been confirmed and reported on 25 August that Indian artillery shelled the village of Awan, in Pakistan, 5 miles from the CFL in the Bhimber sector. It is likewise confirmed that as of 24 August armed elements from Pakistan were still occupying Indian positions (pickets) north of Mandi in the Punch sector of the CFL. On the other hand, it is confirmed by both United Nations observers and official Indian sources that on 15 August, Indian Army troops reoccupied the Pakistan positions in the Kargil area and have remained there; Indian Army troops supported by artillery on 24 August occupied Pakistan positions in the Tangdhar–Nauseri (Tithwal) area and still hold them, while on 27 and 28 August, Indian artillery shelled the area north of Punch on the Pakistan side and Indian troops crossed the CFL in the Uri–Bedori area. It has

[1] For the outcome of this particular issue, see R. Higgins, 'Findings on the Rann of Kutch', *World Today*, Apr. 1968, pp. 134–6.

been confirmed that Indian troops have reached the Haji Pir Pass, which is 5 miles on the Pakistan side of the CFL on the Uri–Punch road. Each instance of violation is protested by the United Nations observers who demand that troops on the wrong side of the line be withdrawn.

7. The United Nations Military Observer Group received an Indian complaint of Pakistan shelling, on 1 September, of pickets and a battalion headquarters in the Chhamb area of the Jammu–Bhimber sector of the cease-fire line. The complaint stated that at 02.30 hours on that day one and a half Pakistan tank squadrons supported by artillery, crossed the cease-fire line in this area. Pakistan artillery was also said to have fired on a battalion headquarters near Punch from 16.30 hours on 1 September and on an Indian battalion headquarters in the Jangar area. The substance of these complaints was subsequently confirmed by United Nations military observers. A Pakistan complaint reported that Indian soldiers had crossed the CFL in strength in the Kargil, Tithwal and Uri–Punch sectors, as reported above. Pakistan, in this complaint, also affirmed the crossing of the CFL by Pakistan troops in the Bhimber area on 1 September, as a defensive measure to forestall Indian action, asserting also that in this sector the Indian Air Force had taken offensive action against Pakistan troops. Also on 1 September armed infiltrators ambushed an Indian convoy at Gund, north-east of Srinagar on the Leh road, and both sides sustained casualities. On 2 September the Jammu team of UNMOGIP received an Indian complaint that Pakistan aircraft had attacked the road between Chhamb and Jaurian during the morning of 2 September and that Jaurian village was in flames. The air attack on Jaurian was confirmed by United Nations military observers. The complaint also alleged that Pakistan troops had crossed the border with approximately 90 tanks and were moving from the Chhamb sector toward the east. Pakistan artillery fired in the Punch area during the night of 1–2 September and in the afternoon of 2 September. [*S/6651, 3 Sept. 1965, Report of Secretary-General on situation in Kashmir.*]

On 4 September the Security Council had adopted resolution 209 calling for an immediate cease-fire, and requiring India and Pakistan to co-operate with UNMOGIP 'in its task of supervising the observance of the cease-fire'.[2] Fighting continued, however, and after examining a further report of the Secretary-General[3] the Security Council adopted resolution 210.[4] This resolution, in addition to repeating the call for a cease-fire, urged the Secretary-General to take all possible measures to strengthen UNMOGIP, and this he did. A further resolution was adopted on 20 September 1965[5] giving a specific time for the cease-fire to become operative, and asking the Secretary-General 'to provide the necessary assistance to ensure supervision of the cease-fire and the withdrawal of all armed personnel'.

It was against this background[6] that UNIPOM came into existence.

---

[2] For text, see Part 4, p. 391.   [3] S/6661, 6 Sept. 1965.   [4] For text, see below, p. 423.
[5] Security Council res. 211; for text, see below, p. 424.
[6] Full documentation on the period 5–30 Sept. 1965 is provided in Part 4 above. See especially S/6687, S/6683, & S/6686.

2

ENABLING RESOLUTIONS AND VOTING

WHILE resolution 211 is the most directly relevant to UNIPOM, the events which necessitated its establishment are reflected in other, related resolutions, and it has been thought appropriate to reproduce each of them here.

The Security Council,

Noting the report of the Secretary-General of 3 September 1965,

Concerned at the deteriorating situation along the cease-fire line in Kashmir,

1. *Calls upon* the Governments of India and Pakistan to take forthwith all steps for an immediate cease-fire;

2. *Calls upon* the two Governments to respect the cease-fire line and have all armed personnel of each party withdrawn to its own side of the line;

3. *Calls upon* the two Governments to co-operate fully with the United Nations Military Observer Group in India and Pakistan (UNMOGIP) in its task of supervising the observance of the cease-fire;

4. *Requests* the Secretary-General to report to the Council within three days on the implementation of the present resolution.   [*SC res. 209, 4 Sept. 1965.*]

VOTING: 11–0.

In favour: Bolivia, China, France, Ivory Coast, Jordan, Malaysia, Netherlands, USSR, UK, USA, Uruguay.

The Security Council,

Noting the report of the Secretary-General on developments in the situation in Kashmir since the adoption of Security Council resolution 209 (1965) of 4 September 1965 calling for a cease-fire,

Noting with deep concern the extension of the fighting which adds immeasurably to the seriousness of the situation,

1. *Calls upon* the parties to cease hostilities in the entire area of conflict immediately, and promptly withdraw all armed personnel to the positions held by them before 5 August 1965;

2. *Requests* the Secretary-General to exert every possible effort to give effect to the present resolution and to resolution 209 (1965), to take all measures possible to strengthen the United Nations Military Observer Group in India and Pakistan, and to keep the Council promptly and currently informed on the implementation of the resolutions and on the situation in the area;

3. *Decides* to keep this issue under urgent and continuous review so that the Council may determine what further steps may be necessary to secure peace and security in the area. [*SC res. 210, 6 Sept. 1965.*]

VOTING: 11–0.

In favour: Bolivia, China, France, Ivory Coast, Jordan, Malaysia, Netherlands, USSR, UK, USA, Uruguay.

The Security Council,

Having considered the reports of the Secretary-General on his consultation with the Governments of India and Pakistan,

Commending the Secretary-General for his unrelenting efforts in furtherance of the objectives of Security Council resolutions 209 (1965) and 210 (1965) of 4 and 6 September 1965,

Having heard the statements of the representatives of India and Pakistan,

Noting the differing replies by the parties to an appeal for a cease-fire as set out in the report of the Secretary-General, but noting further with concern that no cease-fire has yet come into being,

Convinced that an early cessation of hostilities is essential as a first step towards a peaceful settlement of the oustanding differences between the two countries on Kashmir and other related matters,

1. *Demands* that a cease-fire should take effect on Wednesday, 22 September 1965, at 07.00 hours GMT, and calls upon both Governments to issue orders for a cease-fire at that moment and a subsequent withdrawal of all armed personnel to the positions held by them before 5 August 1965;

2. *Requests* the Secretary-General to provide the necessary assistance to ensure supervision of the cease-fire and the withdrawal of all armed personnel;

3. *Calls on* all States to refrain from any action which might aggravate the situation in the area;

4. *Decides* to consider, as soon as paragraph 1 of Council resolution 210 (1965) has been implemented, what steps could be taken to assist towards a settlement of the political problem underlying the present conflict, and in the meantime calls on the two Governments to utilize all peaceful means, including those listed in Article 33 of the Charter of the United Nations, to this end;

5. *Requests* the Secretary-General to exert every possible effort to give effect to the present resolution, to seek a peaceful solution, and to report to the Security Council thereon. [*SC res. 211, 20 Sept. 1965.*]

VOTING: 10–0, with 1 abstention.

In favour: Bolivia, China, France, Ivory Coast, Malaysia, Netherlands, USSR, UK, USA, Uruguay.

Against: None.

Abstaining: Jordan.

The Jordan representative availed himself of the right to explain his vote. He reminded the Security Council that his delegation had supported resolutions 209 and 210, but they had failed:

. . . Both have proved inadequate to bring about even the most immediate goal of the Security Council. War between India and Pakistan nevertheless went on and is still going on. What is needed is something basically different. What is lacking is an analysis and a resolution that deal face to face with the issues involved. My delegation most emphatically submits that a reaffirmation of Security Council resolution 47[1] (1948) of 21 April 1948 and the two resolutions of the United Nations Commission for India and Pakistan of 13 August 1948 and 5 January 1949 is a 'must'. Today's resolution makes no reference whatsoever to the said basic resolutions, and I ask: are we on the threshold of burying also the relevant and pertinent resolutions?

77. In addition, the reference to the need for peaceful settlement, of outstanding differences between India and Pakistan deserves more attention and emphasis than it is accorded in the

[1] The Jordan representative is here employing the new, renumbered reference to the resolution We have employed the new reference since its inception, but have not retrospectively renumbered earlier resolutions which did not at the time follow this system. The resolution to which he refers is S/726, and is reproduced, under this designation, at pp. 320–2 above.

resolution. My delegation would like to see the parties undertake such peaceful discussions within a reasonable time, lest we face another outbreak of hostilities in the future between India and Pakistan.

78. My delegation would also like the Security Council to demand that such peaceful settlement be conducted on the basis of the previous resolutions to which I referred earlier. The mere call for discussions without mention of the basics of any such discussions is, in the opinion of my delegation, fruitless. We know it is fruitless from experience and it is fruitless for lack of coherence and realism. Therefore my delegation abstained in the voting. [*SCOR, 20th yr, 1242nd mtg.*]

A quite different view was advanced by the Malaysian government who, explaining that his government regarded the resolution as 'like the curate's egg —good in parts and not so good in other parts', said:

86. With reference to operative paragraph 4 of the resolution, . . . we should have liked not to have this resolution cluttered up with a reference to the political settlement. . . . Therefore, had my friend from the Netherlands not objected to the resolutions being put to the vote in separate parts, we would not have voted in favour of operative paragraph 4. . . .

87. My Government is undoubtedly just as anxious as anyone else at this table that there should be a cease-fire and that it should arrive as soon as possible; with the reservations I have just stated, and because we are so anxious, we voted in favour of this resolution. [*Ibid.*]

Both France and the Ivory Coast explained that they saw the two aspects—the cease-fire and progress to a political solution—as essentially intertwined, each relying on the other.[2]

On 27 September a further resolution was adopted:

The Security Council,
Noting the reports of the Secretary-General,
Reaffirming its resolutions 209 (1965) of 4 September, 210 (1965) of 6 September and 211 (1965) of 20 September 1965,
Expressing its grave concern that the cease-fire agreed to unconditionally by the Governments of India and Pakistan is not holding,
Recalling that the cease-fire demand in the Council's resolutions was unanimously endorsed by the Council and agreed to by the Governments of both India and Pakistan,
Demands that the parties urgently honour their commitments to the Council to observe the cease-fire, and further calls upon the parties promptly to withdraw all armed personnel as necessary steps in the full implementation of resolution 211 (1965). [*SC res. 214, 27 Sept. 1965.*]

VOTING: This resolution was adopted without vote.

Yet one more resolution on the India–Pakistan situation was adopted in 1965.

The Security Council,
Regretting the delay in the full achievement of a complete and effective cease-fire and a prompt withdrawal of armed personnel to the positions held by them before 5 August 1965, as called for in its resolutions 209 (1965) of 4 September, 210 (1965) of 6 September, 211 (1965) of 20 September and 214 (1965) of 27 September 1965,
    1. *Reaffirms* its resolution 211 (1965) in all its parts;
    2. *Requests* the Governments of India and Pakistan to co-operate towards a full implementation of paragraph 1 of resolution 211 (1965); calls upon them to instruct their armed personnel to co-operate with the United Nations and cease all military activity; and insists that there be an end to violations of the cease-fire;

[2] *SCOR*, 20th yr, 1242nd mtg, paras. 88, 90–94.

3. *Demands* the prompt and unconditional execution of the proposal already agreed to in principle by the Governments of India and Pakistan that their representatives meet with a suitable representative of the Secretary-General, to be appointed without delay after consultation with both parties, for the purpose of formulating an agreed plan and schedule for the withdrawals by both parties; urges that such a meeting take place as soon as possible and that such a plan contain a time-limit on its implementation; and requests the Secretary-General to report on the progress achieved in this respect within three weeks of the adoption of the present resolution;

4. *Requests* the Secretary-General to submit for its consideration as soon as possible a report on compliance with the present problem.   [*SC res. 215, 5 Nov. 1965.*]

VOTING: 9–0, with 2 abstentions.
In favour: Bolivia, China, France, Ivory Coast, Malaysia, Netherlands, UK, USA, Uruguay.
Against: None.
Abstaining: Jordan and USSR.

Jordan explained that she rested on her earlier position:

We all have rightly concentrated on the cease-fire and withdrawal. This is important, but we know that after a cease-fire and withdrawal we shall again come face to face with the basic problem, the problem which led to the unfortunate hostilities. To concentrate only on the cease-fire and withdrawal will bring us no nearer a solution, and for this reason we believe that we should benefit from our own experience. . . . Withdrawal and solution are two sides of the same coin. . . .   [*SCOR, 20th yr, 1251st mtg,* paras 63, 65.]

France stated that her approval of the resolution was 'subject to the reservations which I made at the 1247th meeting[3] on the principles which, in our opinion, should guide the Security Council in the application of its decision'.[4] The Soviet Union categorically stated that it was necessary to abstain because

only the Security Council was competent to take the necessary decisions on all specific matters connected with the United Nations military observers.

84. It is the Council that must decide such questions as the functions of military observers, their number, their command, their terms of reference, the financing of their activities, and so on. We have drawn particular attention to the fact that the Security Council set a definite time-limit for the stay of the United Nations observers in India and Pakistan, which should in no case exceed three months.   [*Ibid.* paras 83–84.]

---

[3] See below, pp. 434–5.
[4] *SCOR,* 20th yr, 1251st mtg, para. 71.

3

FUNCTIONS AND MANDATE

SECURITY COUNCIL resolution 211 of 20 September 1965 requested the Secretary-General 'to provide the necessary assistance to ensure supervision of the cease-fire and the withdrawal of all armed personnel'. UNIPOM's functions were thus to provide, by observer duties, assistance in these two matters in the area outside of Kashmir.[1] Moreover,

. . . In view of the difference in origin and function between the United Nations Military Observer Group in India and Pakistan (UNMOGIP) and the new group of observers, I have decided to organize the observers whose function it is to supervise the cease-fire and withdrawals as an organization separate from UNMOGIP, entitled United Nations India–Pakistan Observation Mission (UNIPOM). Obviously, the operations of UNIPOM and UNMOGIP will be closely co-ordinated, both administratively and operationally, but I have thought it advisable, in view of their separate functions, to maintain them as two separate entities. [*S/6699/Add. 3, 23 Sept. 1965*, para. 2.]

Although the two organizations were separate, the functions of cease-fire observation and assistance in troop withdrawals were acknowledged by the Secretary-General as being closely interwoven: '. . . The cease-fire and withdrawal provisions of the resolutions of the Council are being dealt with as a whole and in the area as a whole. . . .'[2] At the same time he reassured the Indian representative that these functions would not be 'telescoped into . . . a single operation'.[3]

Both India and Pakistan accepted that UN observers had an indispensable task to play in cease-fire observance and troop movements, but there was none the less a profound difference of opinion between them as to whether these functions should be carried out by one observer group or two. U Thant decided that two observer groups were needed, because UNMOGIP had duties specifically in relation to the 1949 Karachi Agreement, and the Kashmir cease-fire line, which antedated the assistance requested of UN observers by the Security Council in 1965. Moreover, UNMOGIP's agreed authority was limited to Kashmir, and the 1965 fighting had occurred along the international frontier as well as across the Kashmir cease-fire line. India thought that UNMOGIP should be the sole agent for assistance in the tasks of cease-fire observation and troop withdrawal, and that the proper course would be for India and Pakistan to agree to extend its authority beyond the confines of Kashmir. Pakistan, however, insisted that there should be two, separate, operations, and was suspicious even of arrangements made by the Secretary-General for necessary administrative co-ordination between them. This dispute—which related not so much to UNIPOM's functions, but to whether UNIPOM or UNMOGIP should be entrusted with the duties in resolution 211—is fully recounted below.[4]

On 4 October there were published the instructions which the Secretary-General had issued to Major-General Bruce F. Macdonald, the Chief Officer. These provide a useful illustration of UNIPOM's duties in the field:

[1] S/6699/Add. 2, 23 Sept. 1965. UNMOGIP was limited in its terms of reference and function to the cease-fire line in Kashmir (see above pp. 346–8). For divergent Indian and Pakistani views as to whether UNIPOM could operate along the entire 1965 cease-fire line, see above, pp. 369–70.

[2] S/6699/Add. 6, para. 2, 1 Oct. 1965.

[3] S/6782, 13 Oct. 1965.

[4] See also S/6742, S/6751, S/6757, S/6761, S/6762, S/6782. The origins and functions of UNMOGIP, and the established practice which had developed in respect thereof, were laid out in S/6888; and are reproduced in Part 4 above, pp. 399–400.

(*a*) The function of UNIPOM is based on Security Council resolution 211 (1965) of 20 September 1965. In operative paragraph 2 of that resolution the Secretary-General is requested 'to provide the necessary assistance to ensure supervision of the cease-fire and the withdrawal of all armed personnel';

(*b*) The scope of UNIPOM is the area of conflict between India and Pakistan outside of Kashmir and beyond the Kashmir cease-fire line;

(*c*) UNIPOM is an observation mission with the primary duty of observing and reporting;

(*d*) The reports submitted by the observers should be thoroughly objective and as accurate and complete as possible;

(*e*) The reports are to be submitted in the name of the Chief Officer directly to the Secretary-General;

(*f*) The observers in the field, in supervising the observance of the cease-fire, shall do all that they reasonably can to persuade local commanders to restore and observe the cease-fire in cases where firing occurs. Observers, however, have no power or authority to order or command an end to firing. Where their persuasive efforts fail, their recourse is to report fully to the Chief Officer on the circumstances leading to the breach of the cease-fire, on their efforts and on the results;

(*g*) The problem of achieving the withdrawals called for by the Security Council resolutions is difficult and complicated. Specific instructions for observers on this aspect of their functions will be communicated at the appropriate time;

(*h*) The observers must enjoy freedom of access and movement in the areas of their operation and the usual immunities of United Nations personnel. Agreements on these matters are being negotiated with the two Governments;

(*i*) The observers are to serve as individuals and never as national teams. They are assimilated to United Nations Secretariat status while on UNIPOM duty;

(*j*) The observers are subject to the direct orders of the Chief Officer of the Mission and must take no orders, instructions or advice from their Governments or their national military authorities on the performance of their United Nations duties;

(*k*) The observers shall wear their national uniforms with the United Nations headgear and insignia;

(*l*) The observers shall carry no arms;

(*m*) The observers should be deployed in approximately equal numbers on each side of the line;

(*n*) The observers should be deployed as close to the line as possible and particularly in the sensitive areas. They should, as a general rule, not be stationed in population centres;

(*o*) The operation of UNIPOM should be conducted as unobtrusively as possible, with a minimum of contact with the people of the country;

(*p*) On the other hand, the closest possible co-operation should be developed with the local military commands on both sides of the line;

(*q*) Any intrusion or intervention in the internal affairs of the country should be scrupulously avoided;

(*r*) Firm instructions should be given to the observers to refrain from any public utterances about any aspect of the conflict between India and Pakistan or of the United Nations operation. Moreover, they should be instructed to be extremely careful about what they say on these matters in their private conversations, in their messages and correspondence;

(*s*) The observers should be instructed firmly to give no interviews to the Press and to make no statements for publication;

(*t*) The observers must not communicate any information concerning the mission to their Governments and should be so instructed;

(*u*) I have assured both the Security Council and the Governments of India and Pakistan that there will be close co-operation and co-ordination between UNMOGIP and UNIPOM both administratively and operationally, and therefore I have asked the Chief Officer of UNIPOM to establish and maintain the closest possible direct links with Lt-Gen. Robert H. Nimmo and UNMOGIP. . . . [*S/6699/Add. 7, 4 Oct. 1965.*]

From the outset, General Macdonald interpreted these instructions as a mandate authorizing him to take the initiative in arranging meetings with either side, or in suggesting practical arrangements to assist in the cease-fire or withdrawals.[5]

Both UNIPOM and UNMOGIP were given additional tasks under the detailed agreement reached, in January 1966, between India and Pakistan for disengagement and withdrawal. The text of this agreement is reproduced above (pp. 407–11) but here we may note that in the first phase, during which withdrawal up to 1,000 yards from the line of control and nullification of all defences was to take place, 'the good offices of UNMOGIP and UNIPOM would be requested to ensure that the actions agreed to in part I was fully implemented. In the event of disagreement between the parties, the decision of UNMOGIP and UNIPOM would be final and binding on both sides.'[6]

[5] See e.g. S/6710/Add. 3, paras. 30–1; and also other examples in s. 12 below, pp. 459ff.
[6] S/6719/Add. 5, para. 9, 17 Feb. 1965.

4

CONSTITUTIONAL BASIS

THE constitutional basis for UNIPOM is not identified with precision in any of the relevant Security Council resolutions. UNIPOM was established so that the Secretary-General should be able to carry out the Security Council's request, in resolution 211, to provide all necessary assistance in observing the cease-fire and facilitating troop withdrawals. The cease-fire and withdrawal had been demanded by the Security Council in categorical terms. It is thus possible to regard the establishment of UNIPOM as falling under Article 40 of the Charter—a provisional measure for dealing with a breach of the peace— or as falling, like most purely observer functions, under Chapter VI.

Although it was the Security Council which, in broad terms, asked for this assistance, it was none the less the Secretary-General who established UNIPOM. The establishment of UNIPOM, as such, was not foreseen by the Security Council. That organ had, in resolution 210 of 6 September 1965, asked for the strengthening of UNMOGIP; and the call for the provision by the Secretary-General of 'all necessary assistance' presumably envisaged assistance through an enlarged UNMOGIP. The Secretary-General found that, for historical, legal, and practical reasons,[1] it was not possible for UNMOGIP to carry out these tasks beyond the Kashmir cease-fire line. He set up UNIPOM to meet the Security Council request in respect of the international frontier outside Kashmir. Although the Security Council was informed of the

[1] See below, pp. 442–7.

Secretary-General's reasons for establishing UNIPOM as a unit separate from UNMOGIP, no formal authorization by that organ occurred. However, the opportunity for protest was at all times present, for the Council was kept fully informed of developments. Protest as to the formation of a separate unit was in fact voiced by India. The exchange of views between India and the Secretary-General are reproduced below (pp. 442–4). India fortified her arguments by insisting that the relevant resolutions only authorized one operation:

These operations, and the cease-fire which brought an end to them, can only be treated as one whole, and the supervision of the cease-fire has, therefore, necessarily to be a single operation to be carried out by a single group of observers under one command. . . .
   It may also be noted that the Security Council's resolution of 6 September [resolution 210 (1965)] called upon the parties to cease hostilities in the entire area of conflict and requested you to take all measures possible to strengthen the United Nations Military Group in India and Pakistan. Obviously, even at that stage the Security Council contemplated one group to supervise the cease-fire. . . . [*S/6735, 1 Oct. 1965, Letter of 30 Sept. 1965 from representative of India to Secretary-General.*]

The Secretary-General replied that it was not within his authority to extend UNMOGIP's functions in the manner desired by India:

The Security Council in its resolution 211 (1965), operative paragraph 2, 'requests the Secretary-General to provide the necessary assistance to ensure supervision of the cease-fire and the withdrawal of all armed personnel'. In the discharge of this function, the Secretary-General, as he had informed the two parties and the Council, is convinced that he can most effectively render this assistance by the creation of a new *ad hoc* operation in addition to UNMOGIP. The difference in the origin of the two operations is clear and a matter of history. The origin of UNMOGIP is found in the resolution of the United Nations Commission for India and Pakistan of 13 August 1948, part I, section D, of which states: 'In its discretion and as the Commission may find practicable, the Commission will appoint military observers who, under the authority of the Commission and with the co-operation of both Commands, will supervise the observance of the cease-fire order'. The further basis for UNMOGIP is the [Karachi Agreement, signed on 27 July 1947]. Security Council resolution 219 (1965), of 6 September, adopted prior to the cease-fire agreement, requests the Secretary-General 'to take all measures possible to strengthen the United Nations Military Observer Group in India and Pakistan', but the scope of UNMOGIP obviously continued to be the Kashmir cease-fire line.
   The UNMOGIP is thus limited in its terms of reference and function to the cease-fire line in Kashmir, and the Secretary-General assumes no authority on his part to extend the scope of UNMOGIP's functions beyond the CFL. Unfortunately, the conflict between India and Pakistan has extended beyond the Kashmir CFL to the borders of the two countries. Therefore, in the absence of any Security Council resolution expanding the scope and authority of UNMOGIP, it was necessary to set up a new operation in order to carry out fully the directive of the Security Council in paragraph 2 of its resolution 211 (1965), of 20 September. . . . [UNIPOM] is based, therefore, on the Security Council resolution of 20 September. . . . [*S/6738, 2 Oct. 1965*, aide-mémoire *from Secretary-General to representative of India.*]

While this position commended itself to Pakistan (indeed, Pakistan was anxious lest administrative co-operation succeeded in fusing UNMOGIP with UNIPOM),[2] India continued to assert that there should be one observer group only. Referring to India's letter of 8 October (S/6762), the Secretary-General said:

[2] See below, pp. 444–5.

Most careful note is again taken of the position of the Government of India on this question, which is that 'the supervision of the cease-fire should be a single operation to be carried out by a single group of observers under one command'. In this regard, may I say that what alone is at issue, as I see it, is the question of my authority to initiate action to extend the scope of UNMOGIP beyond Kashmir and the cease-fire line. . . . You will appreciate, I am sure, that I cannot be induced to take any action that I am firmly convinced I lack authority to take. [*S/6782, 13 Oct. 1965.*]

Although the Secretary-General viewed the decision to establish UNIPOM as flowing, in part, from the need not to usurp the Security Council's authority, the Soviet Union nevertheless felt that the Council's authority was being invaded. These misgivings related not so much to the establishment of UNIPOM as a unit separate from UNMOGIP, but to such matters as the composition of UNIPOM and the methods by which it was to be financed, and to the general scope of the Secretary-General's discretion. Russia's arguments were part of her wider views on constitutional authority for all UN peacekeeping operations.[3]

The Soviet Union, as everyone will recall, has always supported the resolutions adopted by the Security Council on the subject of the armed conflict between India and Pakistan. . . . [Nonetheless] we have a question in our minds which is of significance in terms of principle. The Soviet delegation deems it essential to draw the attention of the Security Council to the fact that the actions undertaken by the Secretary-General in the question of the United Nations observers in India and Pakistan, which came after the adoption by the Security Council of the resolutions of 6 and 20 September of this year, depart from the provisions of the United Nations Charter, in accordance with which only the Security Council is competent to adopt appropriate measures on concrete questions connected with observers of the United Nations, namely, with their functions, their numbers, the command, the method of financing their activities, and so on. And yet, all of these matters in actual fact are being decided upon apart from the Security Council whose members are merely informed of measures already adopted. [*S/PV. 1247*, p. 122.]

N. T. Fedorenko also added later, during the same meeting:

What is in fact being provided in the Security Council resolutions of 6 and 20 September of this year? In the first of these resolutions (S/RES/210, 1965) reference is made to measures to strengthen a group of military observers in India and Pakistan. We weigh our words and we draw attention to the formula involving strengthening the group.

In the resolution of the Council of 20 September (S/RES/211, 1965), it is proposed that the Secretary-General provide the necessary assistance to ensure supervision of the cease-fire and withdrawal of all armed personnel. These are the provisions of the resolutions of the Security Council which, as we see it, are sufficiently clear. These decisions of the Security Council contain nothing else.

What is taking place in actual fact? It is well known to all that in fact actions and steps are being taken not towards strengthening the group of military observers of the United Nations in India and Pakistan, but towards a substantial expansion of the group. This is a substantially new feature. Further, we see that a new organ is being created altogether: a mission of the United Nations military observers. But is there anything at all of this kind contained in the resolutions adopted by us? There is no mention of this kind at all in them. The decisions of the Security Council do not refer to them at all. If the Council truly did have in mind the creation

---

[3] For a detailed exposition of Soviet views on constitutional aspects of UN peacekeeping, see Higgins, 'UN Peace-keeping: Political and Financial Problems', *World Today*, Aug. 1965.

of this new group then, clearly, on that score it is certain that a clean-cut decision would have to be adopted providing for it.

With due regard to the strengthening of the new group of military observers, a special provision in the Security Council decision was formulated. How can it be possible then to depart or to diverge so much from adopted decisions in their implementation? Thus a rather large number of military observers is being sent to India, and Pakistan—and, we must note, four times more than the initial number in the existing group. A new group of military observers is created. The command posts are being occupied essentially by the NATO general staff. Substantial expenditures are earmarked for the maintenance of these military observers. . . . All this is done in circumvention of the Security Council.

However the representative of the United States might try to interpret the resolutions of the Security Council, this cannot alter the obvious fact that the above-mentioned resolutions of the Security Council do not give any basis for the actions that were taken in their implementation. . . .

That is why we venture again to note the need for the strictest compliance with the provisions of the Charter of our Organization, the need not to depart from them, and the need also to show respect for the competence of the Security Council which is called upon to pass on such matters. [*Per USSR*, pp. 141–2, 146.]

A different argument was advanced by Arthur Goldberg, the United States ambassador. Referring to resolution 210 of 6 September, he noted that it had called upon the Secretary-General to strengthen UNMOGIP and to keep the Council fully informed of the implementation of the cease-fire and the situation in the area:

Our Secretary-General did exactly that. He filed a steady stream of reports indicating the steps that he was taking pursuant to this resolution in order to give effect to what this Council had decided. And he frankly shared his thoughts, his views, his recommendations and his actions with the members of the Council. On 16 September—I shall not read all his reports as they are too voluminous and the hour is late—in his report, the Secretary-General said this:

"I have taken immediate steps to obtain extra transport and communications equipment to facilitate UNMOGIP in its task. I have also made provisional arrangements to increase the number of Military Observers in UNMOGIP at short notice, should developments make this increase necessary'. (*S/6686*, para. 10.)

We were on notice of this when we met on 20 September to consider the deteriorating situation which had developed in connexion with this dispute. Being on notice of this, this Security Council again adopted a resolution which, in this respect, was agreed to by all parties. This Council requested in this resolution:

. . . the Secretary-General to provide the necessary assistance to ensure supervision of the cease-fire and withdrawal of all armed personnel;'. (*S/RES/211 (1965)*.)

In another paragraph we requested:

. . . the Secretary-General to exert every possible effort to give effect to this resolution . . .' (Ibid.)

The next day the Secretary-General supplied us with another of his many reports. In this report the Secretary-General pointed out what had transpired during this period. The original cease-fire line was a cease-fire line of a little less than 500 miles. The Secretary-General reported that there were crossings of the border, the international boundary between the two countries, and then he went on to say:

'The border between Indian and West Pakistan, where fighting has been taking place between India and Pakistan armed forces, extends for a distance of over 1,000 miles from the Arabian Sea to the foothills of the Himalayas on the southern edge of the State of Jammu and Kashmir'. (*S/6699*, para. 10.)

Then he went on to point out specifically in detail that because of this situation:

'In the supervision of the cease-fire and of the withdrawals, it is the intention to deploy, at least initially, a team of approximately 100 military Observers with the necessary logistical and staff support'. (Ibid., para 11.)

He was not talking at that point about UNMOGIP; he was talking about recruiting a team of military observers for the international boundary, as we all necessarily understood. The Secretary-General continued:

'It is the purpose to have those Observers in the area at the earliest possible date after the cease-fire becomes effective. According to tentative plans, the locations outside of Kashmir where Observers might be most usefully stationed would be the following:'. (Ibid.)

Then there are specified in detail the headquarters on the Indian side and on the Pakistan side for this group of Observers. Then the Secretary-General went on in a separate paragraph to talk about what he intended with respect to UNMOGIP. He stated:

'Security Council resolution 210 of 6 September 1965 calls upon the Secretary-General "to take all measures possible to strengthen UNMOGIP". To this end, I have already made specific approaches to the Governments providing military observers to UNMOGIP to make available additional observers so that the over-all strength of UNMOGIP can be very substantially increased. As stated in my second report to the Council on my mission to India and Pakistan (*S/6686*), I have also taken urgent steps to provide extra transport and communications equipment for UNMOGIP'. (Ibid. para. 16.)

This Council met on 27 September and noted the reports of the Secretary-General. There was not a voice raised in this Council at the time, although we were fully apprised of every step that the Secretary-General had taken, that the Secretary-General in any sense was deviating from the mandate that this Council had given him in carrying out the task and heavy responsibility we had entrusted to him.

And the Secretary-General did not leave us in the dark as to what he was doing. Quite the contrary; on 1 October 1965 he told us in specific detail what observers he was recruiting for both these forces: 'As of 30 September, a total of ninety Observers has been provided for UNIPOM'. Then he goes into it in detail. Then, 'As of 30 September, a total of fifty-nine additional Observers have been provided for UNMOGIP'.

Now, it seems to my Government and to my delegation that the Secretary-General has proceeded exactly in accordance with the resolutions that this Council has unanimously adopted and that he has advised the members of the Security Council, step by step, of every step he has taken in order to execute the Council's resolutions. There would have been time at any point during these proceedings to raise the question of whether the Secretary-General was proceeding improperly, and that was not done. That was not done although the facts were known and were laid before us.

My Government wishes to commend the Secretary-General for the steps taken by him to carry out what we agreed upon here. And in regard to the status of the cease-fire, it is a plain and simple fact of life that we owe much to the patient efforts of the United Nations Observers who have promptly gone to work thanks to the Secretary-General's expeditious action in response to the Council's mandate to him on 20 September 'to provide the necessary assistance to ensure supervision of the cease-fire and withdrawal of all armed personnel' (*S/6694*, para 2), as well as the mandate of 6 September 'to strengthen the UNMOGIP' (*S/6662*, para. 2). Had the Secretary-General not acted rapidly and firmly, with our authorization, and had he not received the prompt co-operation of the Governments to which he turned for observer personnel and equipment, it is highly likely, in my view, that we should be meeting today not to call for the implementation of withdrawal, but to call anew for the cessation of hostilities. There have been violations, regretfully, of the cease-fire, and complaints from both sides have been confirmed by the Observers on the spot; but it is nevertheless true, and it is apparent from the reports of the Secretary-General, that the Observers are there, and the fact that they are there and that they arrived very promptly had much to do with the fact that the situation is not worse.

I wish to make it clear that my Government emphatically rejects the suggestion that the Secretary-General acted beyond his mandate or that he should have consulted the Council in advance on the details of the actions he took under that mandate. In our view, his actions were entirely reasonable, well within the limits that could be envisaged in view of the seriousness of the problem. If forty-three Observers were appropriate, as has been long recognized by this Council, to observe a cease-fire under peaceful conditions and in a cease-fire line of less than 500 miles, then 200 Observers are obviously reasonable for supervising a cease-fire line that now extends 1,500 miles under the grave and troubled conditions that now exist between India and Pakistan.

I think I for one understood what the Council was mandating in our discussion. We made it very clear that we asked and requested and directed the Secretary-General to take steps to strengthen the force, and also to take steps to see to it that there was appropriate supervision of what we had demanded that India and Pakistan should do. Therefore it seemed to me that there can be no question about this. . . . [*Per the United States, S/PV. 1247*, pp. 127–32.]

The United Kingdom representative indicated that his government was 'satisfied that the Secretary-General has throughout acted in complete accord with the clear mandates given to him by the Security Council in its resolutions of 4, 6, 20, and 27 September'.[4] The representative of France made what was in effect a speech on France's position on principles of UN peacekeeping; he avoided relating these principles to the specific case of UNIPOM:

. . . the French delegation considers it necessary to recall briefly the principles which, each time the Security Council decides to set up a peace-keeping operation—even if it is limited to the sending of an observer mission or a control mission—must guide our action. Without challenging the urgent measures which the Secretary-General may be called upon to take, we believe that it is for the Security Council, taking into account the information submitted to it by the Secretary-General, to pronounce itself upon the importance, the high command and the main characteristics of the mission or the force that it has set up. The Security Council should not become lost in a discussion of details, which would cause it to be paralysed, but has rather to make sure that the proposed means are in keeping, at all stages, with the political aspects of the problem as they are found to exist by the Council itself. We believe that within this context the action of the Secretary-General would avoid the difficulties which doubtless would occur if his mandate were, on the other hand, defined too vaguely, thus giving rise to deep differences of interpretation by the members of the Council.

The Council should certainly not be disinterested in the financial aspects of the operation which it decides to undertake. It should set a ceiling for the expenditures on the basis of the proposals of the Secretary-General and should decide on the method of financing, whether it be of a voluntary or compulsory nature. Whatever method is decided upon, it should invite the General Assembly to allocate these funds from the regular budget of the Organization.

I do not intend here to open a discussion on a matter which the Committee on Peace-Keeping Operations has dealt with and will probably deal with in the future, but I wish once again to stress the fact that we cannot ask the Security Council to take simple decisions of principle, leaving it to other organs to implement them. In the same way, the French delegation considers that it is for the Security Council to decide in its resolutions on the duration of the decisions that it adopts. Such a rule, which must be interpreted with the necessary flexibility, does give the Council the means of acting, periodically if necessary, and of carrying out a reassessment of the functions allocated to the Secretary-General, and also of weighing the

[5] S/PV. 1247, p. 136.

political objectives on which the members of the Council agreed. These are the comments that my delegation wished to make concerning the matters of principle raised, as we see them, by the implementation of the resolutions of the Security Council in the field of peace-keeping. [*Ibid.*, pp. 136–7.]

The statement made by the representative of the Ivory Coast made it clear that the Secretary-General had African support for the way in which he had handled matters:

. . . the Council must demand an effective cease-fire and reiterate its request for the withdrawal of all armed personnel back to the positions held by them before 5 August 1965, as stated in operative paragraph 1 of resolution 211 (1965).

55. The Secretary-General has taken steps to that end and we must encourage him to continue his efforts and to ensure that India and Pakistan co-operate with him and with the United Nations observers. But we should perhaps also ask our colleagues in the Security Council to co-operate with the Secretary-General. You cannot give with one hand and take away with the other, as the saying goes. The Council requested the Secretary-General to provide the necessary assistance to ensure supervision of the cease-fire and the withdrawal of all armed personnel. What is necessary depends on the length of the frontiers and the kind of warfare the parties are engaged in. We believe that the Secretary-General, in acceding to our request and in taking steps which, perhaps because of their inadequacy, have not yet been successful, has not so far exceeded his mandate. Accordingly, we shall not criticize him prematurely.

56. In any event, the Council had the opportunity of knowing the financial implications of the resolution it had adopted; all it had to do was to ask the Secretary-General for a preliminary report. . . .

57. The Council could also have specified the number of United Nations observers in Kashmir. . . . It may, however, have thought that the situation called for prompt action and that it was best to leave that decision to the Secretary-General. The Council was right to do so, and it was right for the Secretary-General to act as he did. [*SCOR, 20th yr, 1248th mtg.*]

The representative of China also supported the Secretary-General,[5] and the representative of Malaysia said:

22. The representative of the Soviet Union . . . referred to the matter in two aspects. First, he said that the Secretary-General did not have the specific authority of the Security Council to take the steps he had taken, pursuant to its resolutions in the instant matter and second, that he had acted in breach of the provisions of the Charter. . . .

23. With regard to the first criticism, it is only fair to point out that, since resolution 211 (1965) of 20 September, the Secretary-General has supplied us with no less than ten successive reports as of today on his efforts to give effect to resolution 211 (1965). On 27 September, even before the Council met again, the reports had added up to no less than six.

24. In the very first of those reports, that of 21 September (S/6699), the Secretary-General not only gave us a very detailed report, running to several closely typed pages, of how he was proceeding with the organization of observers into two groups but also gave us reasonably precise particulars of their number, their staff and their logistical support—both on the cease-fire line and on the international boundary. In that very first report he estimated the cost for a three-month period in the sum of $1,645,000. That figure alone demonstrates that a detailed compilation of cost had been made, and that he was not merely guessing.

25. In the third report, dated 23 September (S/6699/Add. 2), the Secretary-General circulated copies of his telegrams to the Prime Minister of India and the President of Pakistan, in which he explained why he felt it necessary to regard the two operations as separate exercises—in his own words, 'because of the difference in origin of the two operations'—and stated that

[5] *SCOR*, 20th yr, 1249th mtg, para. 13.

the United Nations Military Observer Group in India and Pakistan would continue to supervise the cease-fire line and the new group of observers would be organized as the United Nations India–Pakistan Observation Mission.

26. In his fourth report, dated 23 September (S/6699/Add. 3), he dealt with the two operations under separate heads and again explained the need to differentiate between them. He also gave information regarding the countries to which he had applied for assistance in providing military observers for the new group.

27. In his report dated 24 September (S/6699/Add. 4), he indicated his designation of General Macdonald of Canada as the Chief Officer of the United Nations India–Pakistan Observation Mission.

28. In his next report (S6699/Add. 5), circulated on 27 September just before the 1245th meeting of the Council, he indicated particulars of transport and other logistical support he had been endeavouring to obtain and stated that he was airlifting it to the subcontinent.

29. For our part, we cannot help but feel that the Secretary-General has been diligently and efficiently carrying out the precise duties cast upon him by this Council and has been keeping this Council informed of what he has been doing almost from day to day. If—I repeat: if—he was acting in excess of the authority given him by the Security Council in its resolutions, surely it was open to any one of us who felt doubts about the extent of the authority he was exercising in any particular matter to bring them immediately to the notice of the Secretary-General, and if necessary to the Security Council, if a more particularized and precisely delimited authority appeared to be required. And all of us, in any event, had that opportunity during the lengthy gathering we held on 27 September. [*Per the representative of Malaysia, ibid., 1249th mtg.*]

The Netherlands delegation also contributed its views to the debate on these constitutional points:

25. In doing so, I should like above all to emphasize that my delegation can find no fault with the manner in which the Secretary-General has acquitted himself of the heavy and very difficult task imposed upon him by the Council. As has been proved here in the statements, supported by quotations, made by several speakers in the debate, the resolutions of the Council gave him a clear mandate to carry those resolutions into effect, and he did so expeditiously. Furthermore, in doing so he reported regularly and elaborately to the Council, in no less than ten reports, on all the steps he had taken. If the Council had been of the opinion that in some way the Secretary-General had gone too far, it could have expressed that view in connexion with any one of his reports—but it did not do so. . . .

28. Let me first try to summarize briefly the different viewpoints which have been defended here. They are, roughly speaking, three. In the first place, there are those countries that hold that the basic resolutions of the Security Council contain sufficient authority for the Secretary-General to take executive measures for their implementation. Those countries believe that the Secretary-General, in doing so, should have a reasonable margin of authority and that it is sufficient if the Secretary-General regularly reports to the Security Council on his executive measures, to which the Council can then raise objections if it so wishes.

29. The second school of thought holds that the Security Council should be entitled, if not obliged, to pronounce itself upon the main characteristics of a particular operation initiated in the execution of its resolutions. Those directives should, according to the countries holding that view, deal with such aspects as the strength, the composition, the command, the duration and the financing of peace-keeping forces.

30. With regard to the financing, the Council should, in that view, indicate a ceiling for the expenditures on the basis of the Secretary-General's proposals and indicate a method of financing. Within the context of the directives of the Security Council, the Secretary-General should then have freedom of action to take the necessary steps for the implementation of Security Council resolutions.

31. Different variations of flexibility of this point of view are possible. The reasoning

behind this attitude is that under the present system extensive commitments are being made on behalf of the United Nations before the Security Council knows it, commitments which could afterwards not be rejected even if the Council should wish to do so. So much for the second school of thought.

32. There is a third school of thought, which goes even further and holds that decisions concerning all aspects of peace-keeping forces should emanate exclusively from the Security Council.

33. My delegation believes that if the aim is to guarantee a certain degree of control by the Security Council over the execution of its own resolutions, it is possible to achieve that by steering a middle course, based on a few general considerations. A first, and in our view self-evident, consideration is that the Security Council should always be entitled to interpret its own resolutions. Consequently, and in addition, it would be helpful if the Council would from time to time, whenever it deemed that desirable, give broad directives—I emphasize the word 'broad'—for the execution of those resolutions. A second principle is that the ultimate approval of the financial aspects and the apportioning of the expenses rests with the General Assembly, in accordance with the provisions of Article 17 of the United Nations Charter. A third principle to which we believe one should adhere is that the Secretary-General, as principal administrative officer of the Organization, should have sufficient freedom of movement to carry out the resolutions of the Security Council without having to ask the authorization of the Council for every step in detail. If the Secretary-General should have to ask such authorization for each separate step, once the task of the implementation of a resolution had been entrusted to him, his work would, we fear, become practically impossible and the implementation of the Council's resolution would become fictitious.

34. A practical system based on those three principles implies that the Secretary-General should continue to report formally and regularly on the steps taken, as he has always done, but also that it might be helpful in the future, perhaps more than heretofore, The Secretary-General and his staff would consult informally with members of the Security Council about any intended steps.

35. With regard to financing, it means that the Secretary-General should, as soon as possible after the adoption of a Security Council resolution of this nature, make an estimate of the expenses so that the Security Council could give a directive on the general level of expenses, but that the final approval and the apportioning of these expenses should be left to the General Assembly.

36. These are only the rough outlines for a procedure which we could try to apply in cases such as the India–Pakistan conflict. We believe that such a procedure would go a long way in meeting the desire, which we understand, of those members who hold that the Security Council should exercise greater control over the execution of its own decisions; at the same time this procedure would, we believe, be flexible enough to leave the Secretary-General the necessary leeway in order not to be hamstrung in the exercise of his important and heavy executive functions. [*Per the Netherlands, ibid. 1251st mtg.*]

5

POLITICAL CONTROL

THE broad purposes for which UNIPOM's assistance was required were laid down in resolutions of the Security Council. To that extent, therefore, political control of the observers lay with the Security Council. The Secretary-General was acting under the Council's orders in providing assistance for observing the cease-fire and withdrawals. The establishment of UNIPOM, as such, was not formally requested by the Security Council. However, the Secretary-General kept the Council informed of his actions and the reasons therefor. It was he who decided which nations to approach to contribute personnel; the number of personnel needed; and the command arrangements. UNIPOM was established initially for a three-month period, but the Secretary-General informed the Council that he proposed to accede to India and Pakistan's request that UNIPOM stay for a further three months. No formal vote was taken on this extension. Instructions to General Macdonald, for the observers, were issued by the Secretary-General.

Undoubtedly, the ultimate responsibility was the Security Council's—indeed, in his correspondence with India and Pakistan on a wide range of issues, the Secretary-General was at pains to emphasize that he could not, and would not, encroach upon the Security Council's authority. None the less, the Soviet Union thought that U Thant had overstepped his powers in setting up UNIPOM without specific authorization, and in failing to refer matters relating to composition, size, instructions, etc., to the Council. Most countries, however, took the view that, given the fact that the Security Council could, if it had wished, issue detailed instructions on these matters and had not done so, the Secretary-General was entitled to assume this responsibility; and that he had at all times kept the Security Council fully informed. Details on the argument over political control exercised by the Secretary-General and the Security Council are reproduced above (pp. 352 and 426).

It was the Secretary-General who appointed General Macdonald; and who asked General Nimmo to exercise a general overseeing function. Day-to-day political control was undoubtedly exercised by the Secretary-General, and although the Security Council was kept fully informed, it would have required positive action on the Council's part effectively to assert its ultimate and undoubted authority.

6

ADMINISTRATIVE AND MILITARY CONTROL

MAJOR-GENERAL B. F. Macdonald, of Canada, was designated Chief Officer of UNIPOM. He was in charge of UNIPOM's activities, and was responsible to the Secretary-General. Pending his arrival, while he was being briefed for a few days in New York, UNIPOM was under the command of Lt-General Nimmo, the Chief Military Observer of UNMOGIP. General Macdonald arrived in the mission area on 28 September.[1]

[1] S/6699/Add. 6, para. 5.

All military observers acted under the same instructions in respect of their duties under Security Council resolution 211 of 20 September 1965. These instructions—issued by the Secretary-General, but for the carrying out of which General Macdonald was responsible—have been reproduced above (p. 428). The observers 'report to various designated centres for purposes of operational and administrative efficiency. All of the observers, incidentally, of whatever rank and position, are under the full control and orders of the Secretary-General.'[2] Reports from observers were to be 'submitted in the name of the Chief Officer directly to the Secretary-General'.[3] Observers were required, wherever they saw a breach of the cease-fire, to report fully to the Chief Officer on the circumstances leading to the breach of the cease-fire, on their efforts and on the results'.[4] The observers were subject to the direct orders of the Chief Officer, and were to take no orders from, and pass no information to, their own national authorities.[5]

Obviously, the closest co-ordination was needed between UNIPOM and UNMOGIP, both administratively and operationally. The Secretary-General asked General Macdonald to establish direct links with General Nimmo, and: 'In view of his long experience and extended service in the area, I have asked General Nimmo to exercise overseeing function with regard to both operations.'[6] Pakistan required some reassurance on this point, for the government of that country had been anxious to establish the principle that UNIPOM and UNMOGIP were to be two separate units, even if engaged on the same operation.

. . . Your letter[7] seeks a clarification from me 'as to the precise nature of the overseeing function assigned to General Nimmo in his personal capacity'. . . .

For the purpose of clarification I may inform you that on 28 September I advised Lieutenant-General Nimmo and Major-General Macdonald that because of his long experience in the area, I would expect General Nimmo, in an informal way, to exercise a general overseeing function with regard to both UNMOGIP and UNIPOM. Thus, the arrangement in question is an informal one designed solely to take advantage of General Nimmo's rich experience over many years with cease-fire observation through the United Nations Cease-fire Operation in Kashmir, which clearly could be very helpful to General Macdonald as a newcomer in the area. Moreover, this purely personal arrangement serves to facilitate that close administrative and operational co-ordination which I have from the beginning assured the Council will exist in the supervision of the observance of the cease-fire and of the required withdrawals. . . .

[S/6782, 13 Oct. 1965, Letter from the Secretary-General to the representative of Pakistan, 11 Oct. 1965.]

[2] S/6782, 13 Oct. 1965.   [3] S/6699/Add. 7, para. 2(e).   [4] Ibid. para. 2(f).
[5] Ibid. para. 2 (i).   [6] Ibid. para. 3.   [7] S/6757, 7 Oct. 1965.

15*

7

COMPOSITION AND SIZE

THE Secretary-General, in referring to the cease-fire line outside of Kashmir—UNIPOM's area of operation—suggested at the outset a team of approximately 100 military observers with the necessary logistical and staff support. He estimated that approximately 60 supporting civilian personnel would be required for the cease-fire and withdrawal operation outside Kashmir.[1]

Subsequently, the Secretary-General reported to the Council that a total of ninety observers had been provided for the Observation Mission and that the observer strength of the Military Observer Group had been increased to 102. The observers of the Mission were provided by Brazil, Burma, Canada, Ceylon, Ethiopia, Ireland, Nepal, Netherlands, Nigeria and Venezuela and those of the Military Observer Group came from Australia, Belgium, Canada, Chile, Denmark, Finland, Italy, New Zealand, Norway, Sweden and Uruguay. [*A/6301, Annual Report of Secretary-General, 1965–6 (GAOR, 21st sess., Suppl. 1, p. 14).*]

On 24 September Major-General B. F. Macdonald, of Canada, was appointed Chief Officer of UNIPOM. He came to UNIPOM from service with the UN Force in Cyprus.[2] He took up his duties on 28 September. By 27 September some 22 observers had arrived within UNIPOM's area of operation. In addition, 13 observers from UNMOGIP were temporarily deployed in this area pending the arrival of an adequate number of UNIPOM observers.[3] A further 15 observers were loaned by the UN Truce Supervision Organization.[4] UNIPOM also had, by early October, two Caribou aircraft of the Royal Canadian Air Force, and six Otter aircraft, which were organized into an air transport unit. By 30 September UNIPOM was at its full final complement of 90 observers. The Secretary-General felt that no additional number could be supported with ground transport and communications equipment.[5]

As of 14 October 1965 82 observers were actually deployed in the UNIPOM area of operations.

		No. of headquarters staff and observers
On the Pakistan side:		
Headquarters:	Lahore	8
Stations:	Pasrur	6
	Lahore (separate from headquarters)	6
	Rukhanwala	6
	Sulaimanke	6
	Rahim Yar Khan	5
	Chor	5
	Total	42

[1] S/6699, 21 Sept. 1965.   [2] S/6699/Add. 4, 24 Sept. 1965.   [3] S/6699, Add. 5, 27 Sept. 1965.
[4] S/6699/Add. 9, 13 Nov. 1965. For UNTSO see vol. 1 of this work, *The Middle East.*
[5] S/6699/Add. 6, para. 3.

		No. of headquarters staff and observers
On the Indian side:		
Headquarters:	Amritsar	9
Stations:	Dera Nanak	2
	Khasa	4
	Narla	5
	Bopa Rai	5
	Fazilka	7
	Barmer	7
Liaison office:	Sinwa (Indian Western Army Command)	1
	Total	40

[S/6699/Add. 9, 14 Oct. 1965.][6]

[6] It seems that by 22 Oct. 1965 the number had increased, and minor alterations occurred. Mr H. S. Vahali, of the Indian High Commission in London, informs me that UNIPOM gave the following information to New Delhi in a letter of 22 Oct.:

On the Pakistan side:		*On the Indian side:*	
Pasrur	7	Amritsar	8
Lahore	7	Narla	7
Rukhanwala	8	Bopa Rai	7
Sulaimanke	9	Fazilka	5
Rahim Yarkhan	9	Ferozepore	3
Khokhropar	7	Jaisalmer	9
		Gadra	7
Total	—		
	47	Total	46

(Letter to the editor, 5 June 1968.)

8

RELATIONS WITH CONTRIBUTING STATES

THE following nations contributed observers to UNIPOM: Brazil, Burma, Canada, Ceylon, Ethiopia, Ireland, Nepal, the Netherlands, Nigeria and Venezuela. However, these observers served as individuals and not as nationals. No formal agreements were concluded between the UN, on the one hand, and those nations on the other. The contributing governments were aware, of course, of the requirement that

(*i*) The observers are to serve as individuals and never as national teams. They are assimilated to United Nations Secretariat status while on UNIPOM duty;

(*j*) The observers are subject to the direct orders of the Chief Officer of the Mission and must take no orders, instructions or advice from their Governments or their national military authorities on the performance of their United Nations duties. [S/6699/Add. 7, p. 4.]

No problems are believed to have arisen between the UN and the states contributing observers.

9

RELATIONS WITH THE HOST STATES

IN the instructions to observers issued by the Secretary-General[1] reference is made to the fact that negotiations were being held with India and Pakistan for agreements to cover freedom of movement and the usual immunities. However, it was not found necessary to pursue the matter and no formal agreements were negotiated. UNIPOM successfully asserted, from the outset, the right of complete freedom of movement on the grounds that this was implied in, and necessary for, the implementation of paragraph 2 of Security Council resolution 211 (1965). This view was fully accepted by both parties, and virtually no problems arose in this regard until UNIPOM was terminated in spring 1966.

An examination of the relations between the UN, on the one hand, and Pakistan and India on the other, can conveniently be organized under several headings.

(a) The establishment of UNIPOM

The Secretary-General experienced considerable difficulty in persuading India that the establishment of UNIPOM, as an operation distinct from UNMOGIP, was legally and constitutionally[2] necessary. Pakistan, on the other hand, made it clear that she would not give the necessary consent for the functions and geographical scope of UNMOGIP's role to be extended, but instead wanted the establishment of UNIPOM as an organization separate from UNMOGIP.

Replying to the Secretary-General's aide-mémoire on the division of the supervision of the cease-fire between two groups of observers,[3] the Indian representative stated:

The operations in the Kashmir sector cannot be separated from the operations by the two countries in the Punjab and other sectors. It should be recalled that Pakistan not only sent a large number of armed infiltrators across the cease-fire line into the Indian State of Jammu and Kashmir, it also launched a massive invasion across the international frontier in the Chhamb–Jaurian sector. It was this latter attack which necessitated the limited defensive action by the Indian armed forces across other sectors of the Indo–Pakistan frontier. Your own report to the Security Council (S/6651) clearly shows that the massive armed infiltrations from Pakistan were the starting point of the sequence of happenings. These operations, and the cease-fire which brought an end to them, can only be treated as one whole, and the supervision of the cease-fire has, therefore, necessarily to be a single operation to be carried out by a single group of observers under one command.

---

[1] S/6699/Add. 7, para. 2 (h).
[2] For the constitutional points at issue, see s. 4 above, pp. 429–37.
[3] S/6738 (above, p. 351).

You have yourself stated in the aide-mémoire of 25 September that it is not to be assumed that in the administrative action contemplated by you to divide supervisory functions between two groups there is any suggestion of treating the conflict between India and Pakistan and the supervision of the cease-fire in different sectors otherwise than as a whole. The Government of India, therefore, all the more does not see the necessity of supervision of the cease-fire in different sectors by different groups under different commands. The supervision of the cease-fire by two groups separately in different sectors is bound to cause confusion, and the Government of India fears that it will not be possible to achieve the close co-ordination, administrative and operational, which you consider essential to the proper implementation of the cease-fire.

It may also be noted that the Security Council's resolution of 6 September (resolution 210 (1965)) called upon the parties to cease hostilities in the entire area of conflict and requested you to take all measures possible to strengthen the United Nations Military Group in India and Pakistan. Obviously, even at that stage the Security Council contemplated one group to supervise the cease-fire.

While it is clear from the foregoing that there should be only one group of observers under one command to supervise the cease-fire in the entire area of conflict, the question is whether this group should be the United Nations Military Observer Group in India and Pakistan (UNMOGIP) or the United Nations India–Pakistan Observation Mission (UNIPOM), which you have now constituted. In justification of the establishment of UNIPOM, it is stated that UNMOGIP is limited in its terms of reference and functions to the cease-fire line in Kashmir and that you are unable to assume authority to extend the scope of its functions beyond the line. I should like to point out that at one time the scope and functions of the UNMOGIP were expanded by agreement between the Chief Military Observer, on the one hand, and the local army commanders of India and Pakistan on the other, without reference to the Security Council, to include investigation of border incidents eastward from the south end of the cease-fire line at Manawar in a sector of the border between India and Pakistan in Jammu. On the other hand, if you would prefer the UNIPOM to the UNMOGIP for the supervision of the cease-fire along the entire border my Government would have no objection to it.

The Government of India is of the view that the supervision of the present cease-fire in the entire area of conflict should be ensured through a single observer organization under a single command. They are convinced of the necessity and the desirability of this and hope that you will see your way to give effect to this important consideration. [S/6735, 1 Oct. 1965.]

The Secretary-General now addressed himself to these points:

. . . Speaking for myself only, I would say without hesitation that if, with regard to the observance of the cease-fire and withdrawals called for by the Security Council resolutions, there were to be agreement between the Chief Military Observer on the one hand and the local army commanders of India and Pakistan on the other, or agreement between India and Pakistan directly, that the scope of UNMOGIP should extend beyond Kashmir and the Kashmir CFL and cover the entire border between India and Pakistan, I could readily agree that a single operation would suffice. I do not and cannot, of course, speak for the Security Council on this, although I have no doubt that such an agreement would carry great weight in any consideration of the matter by the Council. To my regret, I am bound to add that the possibility of such an agreement in the prevailing circumstances would appear rather remote. Therefore, I would like to repeat what I said in my aide-mémoire of 25 September, namely that 'the Secretary-General assumes no authority on his part to extend the scope of UNMOGIP's function beyond the CFL' and that therefore 'in the absence of any Security Council resolution expanding the scope and authority of UNMOGIP, it was necessary to set up a new operation in order to carry out fully the directive of the Security Council in paragraph 2 of its resolution 211 (1965), of 20 September'.

As to the fear of the Government of India that 'it will not be possible to achieve the close co-ordination, administrative and operational' which I may consider essential to the proper implementation of the cease-fire, I hasten to give to the Government of India fullest assurance that this close co-ordination will exist and that the supervision of the cease-fire as a whole in the entire area of conflict will be carried out efficiently and objectively.

As regards paragraph 4 of your letter, I note your views but would point out, as you are aware, that I have kept the Security Council fully informed of my actions. . . . [*S/6738, 2 Oct. 1965, Letter from Secretary-General to representative of India.*]

The Indian reply was unenthusiastic:

. . . While the Government of India does not attach significance to any administrative arrangements which the Secretary-General might make, it is not clear as to the difference in the origin of the two operations. The Security Council resolution 210 (1965), of 6 September, speaks of the cessation of hostilities in the 'entire area of conflict'. Neither that resolution of the Council nor any other provides any warrant for treating the conflict and the operation otherwise than as a whole. . . . [*S/6742, 4 Oct. 1965*, aide-mémoire *from Government of India to Secretary-General.*]

Pakistan now made her position clear. After quoting the Secretary-General's explanation in his aide-mémoire of 25 September 1965[4] of the difference in origin between UNMOGIP and UNIPOM, the Pakistan representative added:

. . . The separation of the two operations, UNMOGIP and UNIPOM, is not a matter solely of administrative necessity. On the contrary, it reflects the distinction between the two operations which differ in nature, in origin and in the legal authority behind each. Like the remaining provisions of the UNCIP resolutions of 13 August 1948, the UNMOGIP derives its authority from that resolution as accepted by both India and Pakistan. Its origin is the cessation of hostilities effected in Jammu and Kashmir upon the acceptance of that resolution. It follows that it bears no relation, beyond that of the administrative co-ordination dictated by practical necessities, to the UNIPOM which is based on Security Council resolution 211 (1965) of 20 September 1965, adopted after the invasion of Pakistan by India on 6 September 1965.

In his letter of 30 September 1965 (S/6735) the Permanent Representative of India has adduced the instance of an agreement between the local army commanders of India and Pakistan and the Chief Military Observer in Kashmir to justify his request for the expansion of the scope and function of the UNMOGIP beyond Kashmir. This instance itself shows that any extension of the scope and function of UNMOGIP requires the consent of both parties.

Moreover, the agreement mentioned by the Indian Representative did not in any way extend the function of the UNMOGIP to the international frontier between India and Pakistan. When the Indian Representative talks of the 'border between India and Pakistan in Jammu', he talks of something which does not exist. The province of Jammu in the State of Jammu and Kashmir borders, for the greater part, on Pakistan and, for the smaller part, on India; there is and can be no border between India and Pakistan in Jammu.

In view of these elementary considerations, my Government would like it to be clearly understood that any attempted merging of the two operations, UNMOGIP and the UNIPOM, will be illegal, arbitrary and, lacking consent, will give rise to consequences of a nature which, I am confident, both you and the Security Council would like to avert. . . . [*S/6751, 5 Oct. 1965, Letter from representative of Pakistan to Secretary-General.*]

Nor was Pakistan content to let the matter rest there. The Secretary-General found himself under pressure on this matter, in different directions, from both Pakistan and India:

[4] For text, see above, p. 351.

In your report to the Security Council on the implementation of resolution 211 (1965) of 20 September 1965 (S/6699/Add. 7), the scope of UNMOGIP has been clearly defined as 'the area of the conflict between India and Pakistan outside of Kashmir and beyond the Kashmir cease-fire line'. However, in the last paragraph of that report it is stated that you have asked General Nimmo,[5] in view of his long experience and extended service in the area, to exercise a general overseeing function with regard to both operations. The degree of co-operation between the two operations which may be considered necessary from the administrative point of view is a matter which lies within your competence . . . [but] the Government of Pakistan would appreciate a clarification as to the precise nature of the overseeing function assigned to General Nimmo in his personal capacity. In requesting from you this clarification, I have been instructed to reaffirm that, irrespective of the question of General Nimmo's personal knowledge and experience of the area, the Government of Pakistan cannot acquiesce in any arrangements which tend, directly or indirectly, to extend the scope of UNMOGIP beyond the cease-fire line in Kashmir. . . . [S/6757, 7 Oct. 1965, Letter from representative of Pakistan to Secretary-General.]

The Secretary-General replied:

. . . the arrangement in question is an informal one designed solely to take advantage of General Nimmo's rich experience over many years with cease-fire observation through the United Nations Cease-Fire Operation in Kashmir, which clearly could be very helpful to General MacDonald as a newcomer in the area . . . I may assure you that no question of extending the scope of UNMOGIP beyond the Cease-Fire Line in Kashmir is involved or contemplated in the arrangement since, as I have stated on several occasions, I have no authority to take any such action. [S/6782, 13 Oct. 1965, Letter from Secretary-General to representative of Pakistan.]

The government of India, on the other hand, reiterated that:

. . . The supervision of the cease-fire should be a single operation to be carried out by a single group of observers under one command. As stated earlier, the hostilities between India and Pakistan in the entire area of conflict were but one operation. There could be and is only one cease-fire, and it must, therefore, be observed and maintained as one single operation by a single group of observers under a single command.

You may recall that in its resolution 210 (1965), of 6 September 1965, the Security Council called upon the parties 'to cease hostilities in the entire area of conflict'. This same resolution went on to request you to take all measures possible to strengthen the UNMOGIP. 'The necessary assistance to ensure supervision of the cease-fire' requested of you by the Council in paragraph 2 of its resolution of 211 (1965), of 20 September 1965, could only be viewed in the context of the Council's earlier request for the strengthening of UNMOGIP. That is why the Government of India suggested for your consideration that the entire operation of cease-fire observation and maintenance should be entrusted to one single group, which could be UNMOGIP.

In your letter of 2 October, you have stated that if there were to be an agreement between the Chief Military Observer on the one hand and the local army commanders of India and Pakistan on the other, or an agreement between India and Pakistan directly that the scope of UNMOGIP should extend beyond the Kashmir cease-fire line and cover the entire border between India and Pakistan, you could readily agree that a single operation would suffice. The Government of India is not aware whether you had at any time consulted the Government of Pakistan in this matter. The Government of India wishes to make it clear it was not consulted in this matter at any time and regrets that it cannot agree with the suggestion that two or more operations are called for, a suggestion which is in contradiction with what had been stated in your aide-mémoire of 25 September 1965 (see S/6738), viz. that the supervision

[5] The Chief Observer of UNMOGIP (see above, pp. 352, 360).

of the cease-fire cannot be otherwise than as a whole. I am further desired to point out that the lack of agreement about an extension of the scope and functions of UNMOGIP could hardly be interpreted as sufficient reason to create another group of observers without consultation with, or agreement of, the Government of India.

I need hardly reiterate the assurance of the Government of India's co-operation with you in the observation and maintenance of the cease-fire. The Government of India, however, hopes that in instituting the machinery, it will be consulted at every stage and that no effort will be made to impose decisions on it on grounds of administrative or other requirements which are not warranted by the resolutions of the Council and to which it feels unable to subscribe. The Indian Government has instructed me to urge you once again to immediately unify the cease-fire observation operation under a single command. So far as the Government of India is concerned, it will continue to treat the operation as a whole. . . . [S 6762, 8 Oct. 1965, Letter from representative of India to Secretary-General.]

To this the Secretary-General responded:

Most careful note is again taken of the position of the Government of India on this question, which is that 'the supervision of the cease-fire should be a single operation to be carried out by a single group of observers under one command'. In this regard, may I say that what is at issue, as I see it, is the question of my authority to initiate action to extend the scope of UNMOGIP beyond Kashmir and the cease-fire line. My position on this question has been clearly stated in my communications to you of 25 September and 2 October 1965 (S/6738). You will appreciate, I am sure, that I cannot be induced to take any action that I am firmly convinced I lack authority to take.

I fully agree with the statement in the first paragraph of your letter that there is 'only one cease-fire'. That cease-fire, naturally, is the one called for by Security Council resolution 211 (1965) of 20 September, and it came into effect at 22.00 hours GMT on 22 September 1965. That cease-fire, I may also assure you, in pursuance of paragraph 2 of the resolution of 20 September, is being supervised by United Nations military observers deployed along the entire India–Pakistan line, including the Kashmir cease-fire line. All of these observers act under the same instructions and have the same duties with regard to the cease-fire; they report to various designated centres for purposes of operational and administrative efficiency. All of the observers, incidentally, of whatever rank and position, are under the full control and orders of the Secretary-General.

With regard to the second paragraph of your letter, I have stated above in this letter and in previous communications to you my position on my inability to extend the scope of UNMOGIP. You will recall, also, that in earlier communications I have stressed the point that only the Security Council itself can make authoritative interpretations of its resolutions. Consequently, I pass no judgement on the interpretation presented in your second paragraph. I have nothing to add on these points.

I note that in the third paragraph of your letter you raise the question as to whether I had consulted the Government of Pakistan about a possible agreement on their part to an extension of the scope of UNMOGIP, pointing out at the same time that India had not been consulted. The answer is, of course, that no approach about extending the scope of UNMOGIP was made by me to either Government. The cease-fire and the cease-fire line, which were based upon the Karachi Agreement between India and Pakistan, were being extensively violated at the time. Indeed, on the date the cease-fire came into being the two parties—to quote an expression used at the 1244th meeting—were 'locked in battle', a situation reflected in the public exchanges of their high officials at the United Nations and elsewhere.

Clearly, this was not a propitious time to raise with the two Governments so sensitive a question as the extension of the scope of a voluntary agreement between them which was already being widely disregarded. To be frank, in the prevailing circumstances, I could not regard such a step as realistic. Your letter, I observe, does not suggest that such an agreement could have been possible then, or since.

Note is taken of the assertion in the third paragraph of your letter that there is a 'contradiction' between the two statements in my aide-mémoire of 25 September that 'the supervision of the cease-fire cannot be treated otherwise than as a whole' and 'the suggestion that two or more operations are called for'. May I point out, for the sake of accuracy, that what I actually said in the eighth paragraph of my aide-mémoire of 25 September was the following: 'it is not to be assumed that in this purely administrative action there is any suggestion of treating the conflict between India and Pakistan and the supervision of the cease-fire and the withdrawals otherwise than as a whole'. Moreover, there has never been any suggestion by me of 'two or more operations'. I have thoroughly explained why, if the cease-fire outside of Kashmir were to be supervised by observers designated by me, there was no alternative for me but to make a new arrangement. But at the same time, I gave firm assurance that the cease-fire would be supervised as a whole. There is, obviously, not the least contradiction between the two statements; the cease-fire is being supervised and observed as a whole, through the co-ordinated functioning of the two observation operations.

I am happy to note and I welcome the reiteration in the fourth paragraph of your letter of the assurance of the Government of India's co-operation with me in the operation and maintenance of the cease-fire. The Government of India may rest assured that the cease-fire will be supervised as one cease-fire throughout the area of conflict. Your Government may also be confident of my strong desire to maintain a helpful consultative relationship with both parties and of my intention to keep the two Governments as well as the Security Council fully informed. Your Government may be certain further of my determination always to act only in accordance with the wishes and intentions of the Security Council as expressed in its resolutions.

May I take this opportunity to express to the Government of India my very great appreciation of the co-operation and assistance accorded to the United Nations observers by the military authorities of India and by your military officers in the field. [*S/6782, 13 Oct. 1965, Letter from Secretary-General to representative of India.*]

(*b*) The demarcation of the cease-fire line and the scope of the order to withdraw

In its resolution 211 of 20 September 1965, the Security Council demanded a cease-fire and called for 'a subsequent withdrawal of all armed personnel to the positions held by them before 5 August 1965'. The Secretary-General was required to give the necessary assistance to ensure supervision of the cease-fire and the withdrawal of all armed personnel. Two related problems arose almost immediately: the first was that UN observers were faced by charges emanating from one side that the armed personnel of the other had moved into particular positions—where they now claimed the cease-fire line should be drawn—only after the final time given for the cease-fire order; the other was a dispute as to whether resolution 211 required the withdrawal of armed civilians, or irregulars, as well as regular troops and whether positions held by these could constitute points on the new cease-fire line.

On the morning of 23 September Pakistan armed troops in khaki uniforms intruded into Indian territory in the Jhangar sector and started digging into the area. The local United Nations team in Naushera was informed by the Indian authorities of this intrusion, which is not only completely illegal, but is likely seriously to jeopardize the present cease-fire agreement. Our authorities have asked the United Nations team to visit the site, and have also indicated that the intrusion should be vacated within twenty-four hours, whereafter we may be compelled to take necessary measures for the eviction of the Pakistan troops who have illegally entered our territory.

The United Nations team at Naushera referred the matter to the United Nations team at

Kotli, which made enquiries from the local Pakistan commander. The Pakistan commander's view was that the troops had been in position prior to the present cease-fire. This statement is baseless and we do not accept it. The Indian authorities are awaiting a further communication from the United Nations team. . . .

In the area south of Burki, Pakistan troops started intruding into Indian-held territory at two places on 24 September. In one case the intrusion began with Pakistan troops trickling in, one by one or in pairs, building up to company strength. In another case the intrusion was committed by two companies of Pakistan troops. These intrusions have led to firing in the area.

Pakistan must accept the fact that there can be no forward movement from the positions held by Pakistan troops at the time of cease-fire. Any attempt by Pakistan forces to move forward is bound to affect the situation, and the responsibility for any consequences flowing from this will lie squarely with Pakistan. . . . [S/6711, 25 Sept. 1965, Letter from representative of India to Secretary-General.]

The Secretary-General pointed to the difficulties in establishing a precise list of cease-fire positions, and mentioned the particular problem of movements made by 'irregular' units. General Nimmo made proposals for dealing with this difficulty:

3. Military positions held by each party on the opposite side of the line in the entire area of conflict, as of 24 September, are indicated in the list below. It must be emphasized, however, that this list does not purport to be exhaustive or complete. The military situation throughout the area of conflict continues to be fluid, and revisions of the list may be necessary from day to day, or even hour to hour. Complaints about positions on the wrong side of the line are reported by United Nations military observers to be 'continuous', and they emanate from both sides. These complaints are being investigated by the military observers and, as confirmed, will necessitate corrections in the list. The list of the positions held by the armed forces of each party on the other party's side is as follows:

Cease-fire line (CFL)

(1) Kargil–Skardu sector: Indian troops occupy hill 13620 and some positions on a ridge running north-east. This feature is on the Pakistan side of the CFL.

(2) Domel–Tangdhar sector:

(a) Sunjoi area: Indian troops occupy hill features in grid squares NL 8753, 8851, 8852, 8853, 8854, and 8954 and a ridge in NL 8450, 8550 and 8650.

(b) Tithwal area: Indian troops occupy Pakistan positions and hill features outlined as follows: from the river Kishenganga at point NL 770430 southwards to points NL 760420, 755410, 760400, 720390, 780380, 780370 and 790370 to the CFL at 805378.

(c) Induspura area; Indian troops occupy a ridge in grid squares NL 8438 and 8538, and positions at NL 831839 and 836394.

(3) Rawalakot–Uri–Punch sector: Indian troops occupy the portion of the Bedori bulge on the Pakistan side of the CFL mainly east of the Uri–Haji Pir Pass–Punch road and a few positions west of the road on hill features in grid squares NL 1282, 1283 and 1277.

(4) Bhimber–Akhnur sector: Pakistan troops occupy Indian positions and territory on the Indian side of the CFL roughly limited by northing 70 and easting 78.

(5) Pakistan military-para-military forces are occupying some pockets of resistance on the Indian side of the CFL in Kashmir. One example of this is the pocket situated 3 miles north-east of Galuthi.

Border

(6) Sialkot–Jammu border: Indian troops are on the Pakistan side of the border. The exact extent of their advance in that sector is unknown to the military observers.

(7) India/West Pakistan border: Indian troops are on the Pakistan side of the border in the Narowal–Lahore–Kasur sector, and in southern Rajasthan.

(8) The C.G.S. of Pakistan reported that Pakistan troops occupy some areas of the Indian State of Rajasthan. The area they are said to occupy is bounded by Raichandwala (LM 62), Buili Kalan (LM 60), Sachu (WE 39), Achri Toba (LM 02), Sadhewala (LM 10), Longane-wala Tar (LQ 89), Ghotaru (LQ 76), Shangarh (LQ 54), Pochina (LV 94), Miajlar (LW 03), Rasliani (QB 19), track junction (QB 0869), Kelnor (QB 42), Bijliar (QB 53), Dota Katal (QB 63), But (QB 62) and Binjasar (QB 51).

4. It is reported from the field that apparently some occupations of new positions or territory are being made under orders of local commanders, or by units not fully under control, especially in cases where para-military or 'irregular' elements are involved.

5. General Nimmo has advised that in view of the difficulty of defining accurately the exact positions held by each party on the wrong side of the line, it would be preferable that the troops of each side withdraw to their well-known respective sides of the line in the entire area of conflict, rather than try to define the precise positions from which they must with-draw. [*S/6719, 27 Sept. 1965, Report of Secretary-General on compliance with Security Council res. 211 (1965).*]

India now showed anxiety lest the use of the term 'troops' by the Secretary-General in certain communications concerning withdrawals, be taken to mean that only withdrawals by regular units was demanded by the UN:

I note your assurance[6] that the use of the word 'troops' . . . connotes no restriction on the meaning and purpose of the Security Council resolution which relates to the withdrawal of 'all armed personnel'. As noted in paragraph 6 of your report of 3 September (S/6651), '. . . the series of violations that began in 5 August were to a considerable extent in sub-sequent days in the form of armed men, generally not in uniform, crossing the cease-fire line from the Pakistan side for the purpose of armed action on the Indian side'. It will be recalled that throughout the recent discussions in the Security Council and your discussions with the Prime Minister of India in New Delhi, the greatest emphasis has been placed by us on the withdrawal of those armed men coming from Pakistan. The Security Council resolution itself, by naming 5 August as the date in connexion with a withdrawal to previous positions has, undoubtedly, recognized the fact that armed infiltrators from Pakistan, to which reference has been made in your report, must be withdrawn. In your *aide-mémoire* it had been stated that in the expression 'withdrawal of all armed personnel to the positions held by them before 5 August 1965', the word 'positions' 'must connote identifiable military positions of some nature which prior to 5 August 1965 have presumably been occupied by some kind of armed personnel under Government control and/or direction'. The Government of India is unable to accept this restrictive interpretation of the Security Council resolution. In fact, such an inter-pretation is not warranted by the Security Council resolutions, and the Secretary-General's report to the Security Council of 3 September, and the discussions in the Council. In para-graph 15, sub-paragraph (*b*), of that document it will be recalled that it was proposed that one of the conditions under which restoration of the cease-fire and a return to normal conditions along the cease-fire line could be achieved was 'readiness on the part of the Government of Pakistan to take effective steps to prevent crossings of the CFL from the Pakistan side by armed men, whether or not in uniform'. It has always been the understanding of the Govern-ment of India that the withdrawal of all 'armed personnel' contemplated in the three reso-lutions of the Security Council (209 (1965), 210 (1965) and 211 (1965)) must include the withdrawal of such personnel not in uniform who have crossed the cease-fire line from Pakistan since 5 August. Any schedule or plan of withdrawal of Indian troops has, therefore, necessarily to be related to and co-ordinated and synchronized with the withdrawal of Pakistan regular forces as well as armed men not in uniform who have crossed the cease-fire line and the international border between Jammu and Kashmir and West Pakistan, for all of whom

---

[6] This was given in the Secretary-General's *aide-mémoire* of 25 Sept. 1965 (S/6738, p. 2).

Pakistan must undertake full responsibility. . . .   [*S/6720, 28 Sept. 1965, Letter from repre-sentative of India to Secretary-General.*]

India had previously complained in detail[7] about massive crossing of the cease-fire line since 5 August by thousands of armed Pakistani infiltrators. The Secretary-General responded:

It is noted particularly that the Government of India finds unacceptable the statemen, made in my aide-mémoire of 25 September to the effect that the word 'positions' employed in the Security Council resolutions in the context of withdrawal 'must connote identifiable military positions of some nature which prior to 5 August 1965 have presumably been occupied by some kind of armed personnel under Government control and/or direction'. As pointed out in my aide-mémoire, this was a practical assumption which I had to make in attempting to give guidance to the military observers seeking to 'ensure supervision of the cease-fire and the withdrawal of all armed personnel', as called for in the Council's resolution 211 (1965) of 20 September. I do not know what other meaning might be attributed to 'positions'. In this regard, however, I would especially call to your attention the statement in the second para-graph of my aide-mémoire to the effect that the clarifications that I sought to give in it 'are not to be construed in any sense as authoritative interpretations of the Security Council resolu-tions, since only the Security Council itself is capable of making such interpretations'. . . . [*S/6738, 2 Oct. 1965, Letter from Secretary-General to Government of India.*]

India continued to take every opportunity to emphasize the need for Pakistani withdrawal of irregular, as well as regular forces. Referring to the Secretary-General's communications to India concerning withdrawals,[8] the Indian government noted:

. . . identical communications have been sent to Pakistan requesting the President of Pakistan to submit a plan and schedule for the withdrawal of Pakistan troops. The Security Council resolutions speak of withdrawal of 'all armed personnel'. In the context of the rele-vant documentation, specially the Secretary-General's report of 3 September 1965 (S/6551), the term 'all armed personnel' clearly means both regular troops in uniform and armed per-sonnel not in uniform whom Pakistan has sent across the cease-fire line and the international border. It is, therefore, not clear why the Secretary-General has chosen to address India and Pakistan in identical terms. While in the case of India, withdrawal of troops only is involved, in the case of Pakistan there is the obligation of withdrawal of armed personnel not in uniform who would not strictly come in the category of 'troops'.   [*S/6742, 4 Oct. 1965, aide-mémoire from Government of India to Secretary-General.*]

General Nimmo had earlier advised (S/6719) that disputes would be inevi-table over the demarcation of the exact positions at the moment of cease-fire, and he was to prove correct:

Pakistan forces . . . have continuously endeavoured to improve their positions by occupying, openly or clandestinely, new positions east of the line held by them on 22 September at the time of the cease-fire, so as to present a *fait accompli* to the United Nations observers. The Government of India cannot permit such patent violations . . . [and] will not recognize any positions occupied by Pakistan forces since the time of the cease-fire on 22 September. Para-graph 3, item 8 of your report[9] mentions the claim of Pakistan to some areas under its occupa-tion in Rajasthan at the time of the cease-fire. This claim is totally incorrect. The only area in Rajasthan occupied by Pakistan at the time of the cease-fire coming into effect was the border

---

[7] S/6672, 8 Sept. 1965.   [8] S/6699 & S/6699/Add. 2.   [9] S/6719, 27 Sept. 1965.

outpost of Munabao. [*S/6761, 8 Oct. 1965, Letter from representative of India to Secretary-General.*]

The Secretary-General admitted the difficulties, without committing himself on specific locations:

. . . I also agree entirely that under the cease-fire there should be no 'fluidity' about the military positions, since they were supposed to become frozen at the time the cease-fire went into effect. In the report to which you refer, it was stated that the list of military positions held by each party on the opposite side of the line in the entire area of conflict, as of 24 September, 'does not purport to be exhaustive or complete'. The following sentences explained this by pointing out that the 'military situation, throughout the area of conflict continues to be fluid', and the military observers had reported that complaints about positions on the wrong side of the line were 'continuous' and were coming from both parties. It was further stated that these complaints were being investigated by the observers and, as confirmed, would necessitate corrections in the list, that is, indicating either forward movements which would be in violation of the cease-fire, or withdrawals. Thus, what I stated in my report was only a statement of the unhappy fact that there was a certain 'fluidity' because, despite the efforts of the observers who are unarmed and have no means of actual enforcement, there was some forward movement at various places along the line and from both sides of it, with the apparent purpose of tactical improvement of military positions (for reported instances, see S/6710/Add. 3, paragraphs 8, 9, 12–16, 23, 24, 26 and 27).

There was, most emphatically, no question of United Nations observers condoning any such movement or any change in the cease-fire line at any place . . . [*S/6782, 13 Oct. 1965, Letter from Secretary-General to representative of India.*]

As the Secretary-General pointed out, complaints about forward movements since 22 September—and consequently about the accuracy of the demarcation of the cease-fire line—were by no means limited to one side:

I have been instructed by my Government to refer to your reports dated 27 September and 5 October 1965 to the Security Council (S/6719 and Add. 1) on the compliance with the withdrawal provision of Security Council resolution 211 (1965) of 20 September 1965, and to comment as follows:

1. In both the above-mentioned reports the boundary of the areas held by Pakistan in Indian-held Kashmir as well as in Indian territory has not been described accurately. In particular the following discrepancies have been noted:

(*a*) In the Bhimbar–Akhnur sector, Pakistan troops were in occupation of the area up to the general line at northing NW 78 and touching northing NW 80 in certain areas, and not up to northing NW 70 as stated in your report of 27 September.

(*b*) While the boundary of the Indian territory in Rajasthan sector under the occupation of our troops at the time of the cease-fire was mentioned in your report of 27 September, the area under the occupation of our troops in the Kasur–Khem Karan and Sulaimanke–Fazilka sectors has not been described in either report.

Immediately after the cease-fire, our Army authorities had informed UNIPOM, about the boundary of the Indian territory under our control at the time of the cease-fire in these sectors. Copies of the Army's communications are attached.

2. Traces of areas of Indian territory which were under the control of our forces at the time of the cease-fire were also handed over to the UNIPOM observers in every sector. Furthermore, the line of control was shown to the observers on the ground. Later all these traces were compiled and a single trace map showing the areas of Indian and Indian-held Kashmir territory under our control and of Pakistan and Azad Kashmir territory under Indian control was prepared and handed over to the Chief Officer of UNIPOM. A copy of this map is also attached.

3. I have been directed by my Government to request you to kindly include information on

the boundary of the area under the occupation of our troops in the Kasur-Khem Karan and Sulaimanke–Fazilka sectors in an addendum to your report to the Security Council.

As regards the unfounded allegations of the Permanent Representative of India contained in his letter of 8 October (S/6761) that we are endeavouring to improve our positions and occupying fresh areas of Indian territory, I have been instructed to inform you that the actual position is quite the reverse.

While we have made no effort to enlarge the territory under our control, the Indians have been continuously on the offensive in the Rajasthan sector in an effort to regain lost territory. Since the cease-fire came into effect they have recaptured Sachu (WE 39), Raichandwala (LN 6529), Malesar (LN 6129), Kelnor (QB 4126), Mithrau (QB 4916), Binjasar (QB 5914), But (QB 6728), Ghotaru (LQ 7367) and Nawatala (QB 4926). They have also launched numerous attacks against other areas in this sector, all of which were repulsed by our troops. The truth of the above statement is amply borne out by the reports submitted by you to the Security Council on the observance of the cease-fire. In particular I invite your attention to paragraphs 66 to 71 of your report dated 18 October (S/6710/Add. 4) and paragraphs 1 to 15 of your report dated 23 October (S/6710/Add. 5). According to the latter, the Chief Officer of UNIPOM considers Rajasthan area 'to be probably the most potentially dangerous sector of the conflict between India and Pakistan'. It is amply evident from the report that, in spite of the best efforts of the Chief Officer of UNIPOM, the Indians have not given up their aggressive course of action. I must reiterate the firm position of my Government that if India proceeds with its evil intentions and launches an attack on our positions in Rajasthan, the armed forces of Pakistan will take whatever military action is deemed necessary in this and other sectors of the war front.

In a vain effort to justify the offensive action in the Rajasthan sector, which it has undertaken in complete defiance of the Security Council's resolutions and contrary to the assurances given to the United Nations observers by the local Indian commander, as reported in paragraph 31 of your report of 7 October (S/6710/Add. 3), India has been claiming that Pakistan held only the border outpost of Munabao in the Rajasthan sector when the cease-fire came into effect. This is a totally false assertion. As I have pointed out above, UNIPOM was informed of the boundary of the area under our occupation in this sector immediately after the coming into effect of the cease-fire. The Indian ruse to use their false assertion to launch offensive action against Pakistan positions has also been exposed in your reports of 18 and 23 October 1965. I refer to paragraphs 68 and 70 of your report of 18 October in which it has been clearly brought out that Malesar, Raichandwala, Ghotaru and Kelnor were definitely located in the area held by Pakistan, and to paragraph 71 of your report of 18 October and paragraph 8 of your report of 23 October in which it is stated that United Nations observers informed the Indians that the village of Nawatala seized by them 'had been definitely occupied by Pakistan troops'.

3. The Indian Army has also continued its offensive operations in the State of Jammu and Kashmir despite the cease-fire. Since 23 September, the Indians have captured 35 square miles of territory between the cease-fire line and Kishenganga river, as already reported in my letter of 18 October (S/6799). The captured operation order mentioned in my letter, a copy of which was attached to my letter of 25 October (S/6828), establishes beyond any doubt that the Indian offensive in this area was carried out in accordance with a deliberate and well-coordinated plan. I should also like you to take serious note of the fact that this offensive action was taken in total disregard of the interventions made by United Nations observers referred to in your report of 26 September (S/6710/Add. 2).

The Indians have also launched repeated attacks in the Bhimbar–Akhnur sector and have recaptured the area between northings NW 78 and NW 80. . . . [S/6839, 27 Oct. 1965, *Letter from representative of Pakistan to Secretary-General.*]

(c) The scope of the Security Council's jurisdiction under the resolutions of 4, 6, and 20 September 1965

In its relations with India and Pakistan the UN was faced with the further problem of a fundamental disagreement between the two parties as to the scope of the Security Council's jurisdiction. From the outset Pakistan made it clear that she did not believe that the Security Council's cease-fire and withdrawal orders could be taken in isolation. It was necessary to see them in the context of the history of the Kashmir dispute and particularly, in Pakistan's view, India's refusal to move forward to holding a plebiscite.

The current war is not of Pakistan's seeking. The records of the United Nations during the last seventeen years bear testimony to the fact that Pakistan has accepted every proposal of the United Nations or its mediators to settle the Kashmir dispute peacefully, while India has rejected every one of these proposals. The responsibility of unleashing the present war lies squarely with India which is seeking to perpetrate her stranglehold on the State of Jammu and Kashmir by means of a military decision. . . .

. . . [Though] we would welcome a cease-fire . . . it should provide for a self-executing arrangement for the final settlement of the Kashmir dispute which is the root cause of the India–Pakistan conflict.

While you propose a 'cease-fire without condition' you go on to add that the Security Council would, soon after the cease-fire, proceed to implement its resolutions of 6 September. The provisions of the Security Council resolutions of 4 September and 6 September that the cease-fire be followed immediately by withdrawal of all armed Pakistan personnel to the Pakistan side of the cease-fire line and the consolidation of the cease-fire line through the strengthening of the United Nations Military Observer Group would result in restoring India's military grip over Kashmir. We would thus merely revert to the same explosive position which triggered the present conflict. . . .

. . . The only honourable way to resolve this conflict over Kashmir is for both India and Pakistan, as well as the United Nations, to fulfil their pledge to the people of Kashmir contained in the resolutions of 13 August 1948 and 5 January 1949 of the United Nations Commission for India and Pakistan[10] and permit them, in exercise of their inherent right of self-determination, freely to decide whether their State should join India or Pakistan. This is the only way in which we can achieve enduring peace between Pakistan and India . . . [S/6683, 16 Sept. 1965, reply from President Ayub Khan of 13 Sept. contained in Secretary-General's preliminary report.]

Pakistan also gave warning that if this opportunity were not taken finally to resolve the Kashmir question, she would leave the UN. Although she did not in fact carry out this threat, it was taken seriously at the time. Indonesia had recently withdrawn from the UN, and there had been some talk of setting up, together with Mainland China, a 'rival UN'. On 22 October Pakistan sought to bring the broader Kashmir question before the Security Council:

. . . the Government of Pakistan is appalled at the reports of the grave political developments in Indian-occupied Kashmir as a result of the repressive measures adopted by the Indian army and police and the puppet government in Srinagar. The arrest of all popular leaders, and the daily use of violence by the Indian authorities in Kashmir, have created an unprecedented situation in Srinagar and throughout the Vale of Kashmir which is bound to have immediate repercussions on peace between India and Pakistan.

In view of all these considerations, my Government requests that a meeting of the Security Council should be called immediately to consider the deteriorating situation in Jammu and Kashmir and to take prompt action to implement Security Council resolution 211 (1965) of 20 September. [S/6821, 22 Oct. 1965, Letter from representative of Pakistan to President of Security Council.]

[10] For details, see Part 4, pp. 323–7.

The Indian government made it clear that if a meeting of the Security Council were held to consider issues relating to the cease-fire and withdrawal of armed personnel an Indian delegation would participate. However, if the Security Council sought to discuss other matters raised by Pakistan in respect of Kashmir

. . . we would be unable to participate in such discussions and deliberations, because the points raised by the Permanent Representative of Pakistan in those paragraphs related to matters which are solely within the domestic and sovereign jurisdiction of India and his reference to them was a gross interference in the internal affairs of India. [*S/6833, 26 Oct. 1965, Letter from Minister of External Affairs of India to President of Security Council.*]

At the Security Council meeting the President of the Council intervened during the speech of the Pakistan representative to say

I should like to point out that according to our agenda the subject for discussion today is the implementation of Security Council resolutions 211 (1965) and 214 (1965) of 20 and 27 September 1965 concerning the cease-fire and the withdrawal of troops and I would most respectfully and sincerely invite him to confine his comments to the subject which is the reason for the Council's meeting. [*SCOR, 20th yr, 1247th mtg.*]

The Indian government said it hoped that the Security Council would not permit Zulficar Ali Bhutto, the Foreign Minister of Pakistan, to use the forum of the Council 'to hurl' abuse at India and discuss 'the internal situation of a constituent unit of India, i.e. the State of Jammu and Kashmir', and declined to participate in the next scheduled meeting of the Council on 27 October.[11] From the Indian perspective, Pakistan was using this cease-fire as she had used the one ordered on 1 January 1949—not to reduce tensions and establish good relations with India, but to marshal 'all its diplomatic forces, in the world capitals and at the United Nations, in an effort to persuade the international community to overlook the real facts of the armed conflict which was begun by Pakistan and escalated at each stage by Pakistan'.[12] Further, at the meeting of the Security Council on 25 October,

A representative said that the Council had assumed jurisdiction in the question before it and the parties had accepted the authority of the Council and therefore the term 'domestic juris-diction' did not apply. I must make it quite clear to the Council that at no time did India surrender its sovereignty over the State of Jammu and Kashmir to anybody; no one except India—not even the Security Council—has assumed or could assume jurisdiction over the Indian State of Jammu and Kashmir. . . . If it is implied that, because India brought a complaint to the Council nearly eighteen years ago against Pakistan's aggression on the Indian State of Jammu and Kashmir, India thereby allowed the Security Council to assume juris-diction over this State, he is sadly mistaken. [*Ibid.*]

[11] S/6833, 26 Oct. 1965.   [12] S/6836, 27 Oct. 1965.

10

RELATIONS WITH OTHER STATES INVOLVED

THE UN experienced no major problems in respect of its relations with other nations having a direct interest in the operation of UNIPOM or the outcome of the fighting of 1965.

11

FINANCE

ON 21 September 1965 the Secretary-General reported on his efforts to give effect to the Security Council resolution 211 which had been passed the previous day. As we have seen above (p. 430), it was from this resolution that he regarded the constitutional basis of UNIPOM as flowing.

Although this first report did not spell out in detail the formation of a new observer group—UNIPOM—as a unit distinct from UNMOGIP, the implication was already present. He described the border between India and Pakistan, outside Kashmir, where fighting had occurred, and then stated:

12. It is estimated that approximately 60 supporting civilian personnel will be required for the cease-fire and withdrawal operation outside of Kashmir.

13. These observers will require communications both on the ground and in the air, and the necessary equipment will be procured for this purpose. Aircraft will also be required. A provisional requirement is foreseen for 2 Caribou and 6 Otter aircraft. Detailed tables of equipment, vehicles, etc., have been worked out.

14. The estimated total cost for a three-month period would be approximately $1,645,000. [*S/6699, 21 Sept. 1965, Report by Secretary-General.*]

This cost estimate was later confirmed on 1 October 1965.[1] It was also stated at this point that the cost for strengthening UNMOGIP would be $2 million for a period of one year. Revised—and lower—estimates were published on 14 October 1965, when the figure was given as $1,427,000:

[1] S/6699/Add. 6, para. 7.

Operation of UNIPOM for 3 months

Travel and allowances of military observers	$288,800
Aircraft	$362,000
Equipment (including vehicles, radio, office equipment, etc.)	$363,500
Personnel, premises, maintenance of vehicles, and other costs	$402,700
	$1,427,000

[*S/6699/Add. 9*, p. 8.]

In the event, India and Pakistan requested that UNIPOM stay beyond the initial three-month period, and, as the Secretary-General reported on 15 December 1965,[2] this raised the question of how UNIPOM would be financed:

7. It is my intention, in the circumstances to continue the United Nations activities relating to the cease-fire and withdrawal provisions of the Security Council resolutions in the area as a whole after 22 December, on the assumption, naturally, that the finances necessary for their support will become available. This would mean the continuation of UNIPOM for a second period of three months as from 22 December 1965. . . .

8. The estimated costs for [UNIPOM's] continuation for another three months beyond 22 December is $819,000. This latter estimate provides for the following additional requirements strongly requested by the Chief Officer of the Mission and which the Secretary-General deems necessary for full and effective discharge of the Security Council's mandate: 2 Otter aircraft, equipment for certain field stations, and 7 field service personnel. . . .

10. It is proposed that, in accordance with the normal budgetary arrangements as they have customarily applied to UNMOGIP, the additional requirements for its strengthening, as these have now been established, should be provided for as revised estimates under sections 16 and 17 of the United Nations budget for the financial years 1965 and 1966, respectively. On the assumption that necessary appropriation action with respect to UNMOGIP will be taken by the General Assembly during its twentieth session, it would be possible for the Secretary-General as an interim measure, to continue to finance the commitments in respect of UNIPOM and the withdrawal mission of General Marambio, under the provisions of the annual General Assembly resolutions relating to unforseen and extraordinary expenses. [*S/6699/Add. 11*, *15 Dec. 1965*.]

UNIPOM's expenses were thus to be apportioned among the general membership of the UN, and raised under the provision for unforeseen and extraordinary expenses. In the event, no appropriation action was taken by the General Assembly in respect of either the estimated cost of $1,427,000 for the first three months, or the estimated cost of $819,000 for the second three months. The amount actually spent in 1965 was $1,160,000; and not only was expenditure less than the estimated costs in 1965, but the estimate for January–March 1966 was reduced to $593,700.[3] There was also money available on surplus account in 1966, and it was thus possible to meet the 1966 costs for UNIPOM from these credits.

As indicated in United Nations accounts for the year ended 31 December 1965, an amount of $3,064,268 has become available on surplus account, consisting of $1,943,320, representing the excess of income over obligations incurred for the year ended 31 December 1965, and

[2] S/6699/Add. 11.
[3] A/6436, 23 Sept. 1966, suppl. estimates for 1966, *GAOR*, 21st sess., a.i. 73, ss. 16.15 & 16.16.

$1,120,948, representing savings effected in liquidating the prior year's obligations. In conformity with regulation 4.3 of the Financial Regulations of the United Nations, these amounts are now available for credit against the assessed contributions of Member States for 1967. The General Assembly might consider it appropriate to reduce the credit due in respect of 1965 by the amount of $1,160,000 spent on the UNIPOM operations in that year. The 1966 portion of these costs, amounting to $539,700, can be met from within the total credits currently available under section 16. [*A/6436, 23 Sept. 1966.*]

On 5 October 1965 the Indian representative had written to the Secretary-General on the matter of finance:

. . . I have been instructed by my Government to clarify its position in the matter of financing the expenses arising out of the establishment of the new observer corps on the borders between India and Pakistan, as well as the cease-fire line in the Indian State of Jammu and Kashmir:

(1) Resolution 1874 (S–IV) of the General Assembly, enumerating the principles to serve as guidelines for the sharing of costs of future peace-keeping operations, in its paragraph 1, sub-paragraph (*e*), affirms:

'Where circumstances warrant, the General Assembly should give special consideration to the situation of any Member States which are victims of, and those which are otherwise involved in, the events or actions leading to a peace-keeping operation'.

(2) This principle was based upon paragraph 10 of the memorandum (A/AC 113/18) submitted to the Working Group on the Examination of the Administrative and Budgetary Procedures of the United Nations by some African, Asian and Latin American countries, including India. This paragraph reads as follows:

'The situation of a Member State or Member States, victims of acts that led to a peace-keeping operation, should be taken into special consideration, including total exemption for them in the apportionment of the expenses.'

(3) Your own report to the Security Council dated 3 September 1965 (S/6651) . . . makes it clear that India was a victim of this aggression and that this was what resulted in the dispatch by you of the new corps of observers to India and Pakistan. . . .

The Government of India, therefore, considering that, as a victim of an aggression, in accordance with the spirit and letter of General Assembly resolution 1874 (S–IV), it cannot be expected to participate in the financing of the expenses arising out of the dispatch of this new corps of observers to the sub-continent, reserves its position in this behalf. . . . [*S/6747, 5 Oct. 1965.*]

This reservation was restated in the Fifth Committee on 26 October,[4] and the representative of India abstained from voting on the pertinent supplementary appropriations.[5] The sum of $47,545 was subsequently withheld by India from her overall budgetary contribution for 1966 in this respect.

The Pakistan government chose not to enter a discussion on the principle of collective financial responsibility for peacekeeping, but rather merely to deny that it had been the aggressor. In a document which concentrated on trying to show that overall, and long-term, responsibility for the fighting lay with India, the Pakistan government merely said:

The financing of peace-keeping operations has been the subject of a long controversy in the United Nations and, while Member States have yet to reach an agreement generally acceptable to all Members, including the principal Powers, it is a matter for satisfaction that the deadlock

---

[4] *GAOR*, 20th sess., 5th Cttee, 1076th mtg.
[5] Ibid. 1114th mtg; see also 118th mtg.

which prevented the effective functioning of the General Assembly last year has at last been broken. It is not my intention in this letter to enter into a discussion of the principles which should govern the sharing of the costs of observer missions in Kashmir and on the India–Pakistan border. At the appropriate time, the Government of Pakistan will make known its views on these matters, as well as on the specific question of the financing of the observation mission set up in pursuance of Security Council resolution 211 (1965) of 20 September 1665. . . . [S/6858, 1 Nov. 1965.]

In the event, this point was never pursued by Pakistan. In the Fifth Committee her representative voted for the supplementary appropriations[6] and expressed deep regret at the Indian position.

The constitutional authority for authorizing UNIPOM expenditures became a matter of controversy in the Security Council, where members sought to reiterate their established positions on all questions of UN peacekeeping[7] including finance. Thus the Soviet Union thought that 'only the Security Council is competent to adopt appropriate measures on . . . the method of financing their activities'.[8] Given both the general constitutional objections which the Soviet Union had expressed on a variety of matters relating to UNIPOM, and her views on the specific question of financial authority, a withholding of funds might have been expected. However, the Soviet Union did not withhold any funds in respect of UNIPOM from her contributions for 1965 and 1966. France indicated that

The Council should certainly not be disinterested [sic] in the financial aspects of the operation which it decides to undertake. It should set a ceiling for the expenditures on the basis of the proposals of the Secretary-General and should decide on the method of financing, whether it be of a voluntary or compulsory nature. Whatever method is decided upon, it should invite the General Assembly to allocate these funds from the regular budget of the Organization. [S/PV.1247, p. 137.]

Other nations, however, agreed with the view expressed by the Dutch representative that

35. With regard to financing, . . . the Secretary-General should, as soon as possible after the adoption of a Security Council resolution of this nature, make an estimate of the expenses so that the Security Council could give a directive on the general level of expenses, but that the final approval and the apportioning of those expenses should be left to the General Assembly. [SCOR, 20th yr, 1251st mtg.]

---

[6] Ibid. 113th mtg.

[7] For other constitutional aspects, see above, s. 4, pp. 429–37.

[8] S/PV. 1247, p. 122. The published version of this meeting is not yet available, and references are thus to the PV series.

12

IMPLEMENTATION

THE record of UN observers in fulfilling their mandate in Kashmir between 1950 and 1965 has been assessed in Part 4 (pp. 373–87 above). We have also recounted the events which led to a breakdown of the Karachi Agreement of 1950 for a cease-fire, and UNMOGIP's role in re-establishing the cease-fire, and supervising troops withdrawals, in Kashmir from 1965 onwards.

UNIPOM, by contrast, came into being only in September 1965 and, as indicated above (pp. 426–7), was engaged in tasks, under certain Security Council resolutions, concerning the cease-fire along the international frontier beyond Kashmir. UNIPOM's tasks were the same as those of the UN Observer Group in Lebanon[1] in the post-September 1965 period—namely, the implementation of the cease-fire and of the withdrawal orders of the Security Council. The difference lay in the origin and location of the two operations. Many matters relating to these two tasks were dealt with on a basis common to both UNMOGIP and UNIPOM. Where this was so, the relevant materials have been subsumed under section 12 of Part 4 (pp. 390–406 above). It is with this narrower picture that we are here concerned: the reader interested in the period 1951–65, or in Kashmir from 1965 to 1967, or in the broad background issues during and after the war of 1965, should turn to Part 4 above.

(a) Implementing the cease-fire

As soon as Security Council resolution 211 had been adopted, calling for a cease-fire to take effect at 07.00 hrs GMT on 22 September, the Secretary-General contacted both the Indian and the Pakistan governments:

I am proceeding on the assumption that the Governments of both countries will accede to the Security Council's demand, and therefore,

(1) I request you to inform me as quickly as possible that orders have been or will be issued for the cease-fire. . . . [*S/6699*, para. 3.]

A conditional affirmative reply was received from India:

The Secretary-General notes that the Prime Minister of India is 'willing to order a simple cease-fire and a cessation of hostilities on being informed of Pakistan's agreement to do likewise' and also his statement that to carry into effect the cease-fire at the time requested by the Security Council resolution it would be necessary for him to arrange for the issue of the necessary orders to the field commanders by 1200 hours GMT on 21 September.

As of 1000 hours EDT on 21 September no word had been received by the Secretary-

[1] See Vol. I of this work, *The Middle East*.

General from the Government of Pakistan concerning its intention with regard to the Security Council resolution 211 (1965) . . .

[But in order to meet the terms of that resolution] . . . each party should instruct its forces to cease fire as of 0700 hours GMT on 22 September without condition, although it would be understandable if in issuing these orders the troops were instructed to fire only if fired upon, that is, if there would be a breach of the cease-fire by the other side. [*Ibid.* para. 6.]

At 2.00 hours US Eastern Daily Time on 22 September Pakistan sent the following message to the Secretary-General:

Pakistan considers the Security Council resolution 211 (1965), of 20 September, as unsatisfactory. However, in the interest of international peace, and in order to enable the Security Council to evolve a self-executing procedure which will lead to an honourable settlement of the root cause of the present conflict, namely, the Jammu and Kashmir dispute, I have issued the following orders to the armed forces of Pakistan:

(1) They will stop fighting as from 1205 hours, West Pakistan time, today;

(2) As from that time they will not fire on enemy forces unless fired upon; provided the Indian Government issues similar orders to its armed forces. [*S/6699/Add. 1, 22 Sept. 1965.*]

The Security Council met again and agreed in the early hours of the morning of 22 September that, in order to give the governments the time to issue the necessary orders, the cease-fire should go into effect at 22.00 hrs GMT on 22 September. The cease-fire became effective at this time.[2]

The cease-fire started off very badly in the Lahore area, in spite of the fact that UNIPOM observers were stationed both sides of the cease-fire line.[3] As working contacts were established with local commanders there was a general improvement along the cease-fire line.[4] Most of the military observers assigned to UNIPOM were fully deployed by 6 October, but they were initially hampered from operating efficiently 'because of a serious lack of transport and communications equipment'.[5]

By 6 October the cease-fire was holding in the Lahore–Amritsar sector, with the two sides about 300 yards apart on average 'but along the Bambanwala–Ravi–Bedian (BRB) Canal, the distance narrowed to about 50 yards. . . . Dograi itself was under Indian control, and there was a 25 yards wide strip of no man's land between this locality and the east bank of the Canal. Attempts by Pakistan forces to run their vehicles through that strip between the northern and southern salients had given rise to tension. . . .'[6] In other sectors patrolled by UNIPOM sporadic shooting was also reported. In Sulaimanke, Pakistan troops were found to have moved forward since the cease-fire, and UNIPOM observers held a meeting on 3 October with Indian and Pakistani officers to discuss improvements needed in the Rajasthan sector.[7]

By 18 October, when the next report was issued, tension was still high in most sectors, and 'though the extent of heavy fighting had decreased considerably, the existence of the cease-fire must be considered precarious'.[8] The observers used considerable initiative in seeking ways of improving the situation, and

---

[2] S/6699/Add. 2.   [3] S/6710/Add. 1.   [4] S/6699/Add. 8.
[5] S/6710/Add. 3, para. 2.   [6] Ibid. para. 25.   [7] Ibid. paras. 26 & 30.
[8] S/6710/Add. 4. For details of the sorts of problems reported in this report see above, pp. 398–9.

frequently found themselves in the line of fire. Thus when there was firing in the Siphon area of the Lahore sector

The observers arranged for Indian troops to fill a trench and for Pakistan troops to destroy a bunker, whereupon both sides evacuated these positions which had caused the trouble.

49. On 15 October observers investigated and confirmed a Pakistan complaint that Indian forces were building new bunkers in the Siphon area. Four rounds were fired at the observers from the Pakistan side while they investigated the complaint. [*S/6710/Add. 4, 18 Oct. 1965.*]

The problems facing UNIPOM's Chief Officer and the qualities demanded of him, are well illustrated by the following report on the cease-fire in the Rajasthan area:

3. During his first visit to the desert area, from 10 to 14 October, General Macdonald regarded the situation there to be most disturbing. Indian troops had just launched a series of attacks against positions held by Pakistan forces on the Indian side of the international border and these attacks were continuing. Indian authorities contended that Pakistan had occupied those positions after the cease-fire came into effect. The Indian divisional commander at Jaisalmer informed General Macdonald that he had orders to push hard against the Pakistan infiltrators holding villages on the Indian side of the border, and General Macdonald was convinced that he would do so. On the other hand, the Pakistan command insisted that Pakistan troops had taken those villages before the time of the cease-fire and were determined to fight if necessary to hold them.

4. On 14 October General Macdonald flew to New Delhi and met with the Chief of the Army Staff (Indian Army). The COAS agreed to the following:

(*a*) If Pakistan would agree to withdraw its troops to its side of the international border in the desert area; Indian troops would be withdrawn to their side of the border;

(*b*) If Pakistan troops would withdraw to their side of the border, the COAS would ensure that Indian troops would not occupy the vacated villages on the Indian side;

(*c*) The COAS would order his troops to stop any offensive action until 19 October in order to enable General Macdonald to seek an agreement on tactical readjustment.

5. Later on the same day, General Macdonald flew to Rawalpindi and met there with the Pakistan Commander and Chief of General Staff. Generald Macdonald was given the Commander's written reply dated 12 October, to his letter of 8 October setting forth his proposals for tactical readjustment. General Musa agreed in principle to General Macdonald's proposals, but suggested that instead of asking both sides to step back, the burden of withdrawal in each instance should be on the force in occupation of territory belonging to the other side. An identical letter had been addressed to the Indian COAS, and the latter, in a reply dated 11 October, had also agreed in principle to the proposed tactical readjustment. During the meeting, General Macdonald proposed that in view of the current clashes in the Rajasthan area, negotiations for tactical readjustment should begin with that area. The Pakistan officers stated that they would prefer an over-all arrangement on tactical readjustment comprising the whole of the line supervised by UNIPOM observers. General Macdonald then proposed that agreements be negotiated sector by sector, beginning with the Rajasthan area, but that the implementation of such agreements be withheld until agreements were reached for all sectors. The Pakistan Commander stated that the Pakistan reply to this proposal would be given after General Macdonald had conveyed to the Indian side the Pakistan suggestion that the burden of readjustment should fall on troops on the wrong side of the border.

6. On 15 October observers in the Chor sector reported that during the past 48 hours Indian troops had continued their advances in the Rajasthan area, supposedly on orders from higher authorities.

7. On the same day General Macdonald sent an urgent message to the COAS of the Indian Army, (*a*) informing the latter that Pakistan had agreed in principle to tactical readjustment; (*b*) asking that the COAS instruct his armed forces to cease all offensive action and forward

movement as previously agreed; (c) asking that the Indian tactical commander be available in the Barmer area for discussing arrangements for tactical readjustment negotiations which would hopefully begin on 17 October; (d) suggesting that in addition to the criteria contained in his letter of 8 October, it may be anticipated that the main burden of tactical withdrawals will fall on the force which is in occupation of territory belonging to the other side; (e) recommending that discussions for tactical readjustment be held on an area-by-area basis starting with the Chor–Barmer sector, but that execution of the agreement should await general agreement for all sectors.

8. On 15 October, also, an observer in the Chor–Barmer sector who had proceeded to the village of Nawatala, reported that the village had been attacked on 14 October by Indian troops and occupied by them the next day. When the observer told the Indian major that the village previously had been definitely occupied by Pakistan troops, the Indian local commander replied that he had instructions to clear Pakistan infiltrators from Indian territory. The observer later received the same reply from the Indian battalion and brigade commanders. The report of the observer was brought to the attention of the Indian COAS by General Macdonald in a message dated 16 October.

9. On 16 October the Indian COAS replied to General Macdonald's message of 15 October on behalf of the COAS, who was away on tour. He confirmed that instructions had been issued to cease all offensive action and forward movement until 19 October and that a local tactical commander would meet General Macdonald at Barmer on 17 October. Regarding, however, the suggestions on tactical readjustment negotiations set forth in paragraph 6, sub-paragraphs (d) and (e), he stated that they would be put to the COAS and a reply to them would be forthcoming by 17 October.

10. Also on 16 October, the COAS, Pakistan, called General Macdonald on the telephone and asked whether the latter had received any reaction to the proposal concerning tactical readjustment. When informed of the Indian message referred to in paragraph 9 above, the CGS expressed disappointment [that] the Pakistan proposal had not been accepted by India. However, when General Macdonald urged the CGS to permit him to start negotiations on tactical readjustments on 17 October, as planned, the CGS agreed that General Macdonald could discuss the tactical readjustment proposals with his local commander, but he would not agree to any joint meetings with the Indian commander until a basis for negotiations had been established.

11. On 17 October observers at Chor reported that following the Indian advances in the Kelnor sector, the Pakistan local command had been planning retaliatory action. The observations made led them to believe that an attack by Pakistan forces on the Gadra front was imminent.

12. Early in the morning of 17 October General Macdonald left for the desert area where he stayed until the afternoon of the next day. In a meeting with two Pakistan brigadiers, General Macdonald established an agreed basis for negotiations, but the Pakistan officers would not agree to meet the Indian officers until the proposals in paragraph 7, sub-paragraph (d), and preferably also in sub-paragraph (e), had been agreed upon. The Indian divisional commander with whom General Macdonald met twice appeared to be agreeable in principle to the negotiations.

13. On 18 October General Macdonald received a message from the Pakistan CGS to the effect that reliable information indicated that Indian troops in Rajasthan were being reinforced by one fresh infantry division and that India was planning a major offensive to be launched on 19 October. During his visit to the desert area on 21 and 22 October, General Macdonald had received reports from the observers about a substantial build-up of Indian forces in the Jaisalmer sector. Observers on the Pakistan side report that Pakistan forces on that side have also built up their strength in this area.

14. On 19 October General Macdonald saw the Indian COAS in New Delhi. He stated that he believed he had established a workable basis for discussions leading to a tactical readjustment. However, the Pakistan command would not agree to any bilateral discussions until Indian agreement would be forthcoming to their formula that withdrawal should be confined

to the force which occupied the territory belonging to the other side. The COAS pointed out that any formula acceded to would inevitably be applied along the entire border, including Kashmir. Therefore, he would have to consult with his Minister. Despite General Macdonald's observation that the readjustments would be so small that political involvement would be minimal, the COAS insisted on the need to consult his Minister. However, he did agree that his undertaking to stop offensive action and forward movement would be extended for a further period and promised to notify General Macdonald of his decision by wire.

15. On 20 October General Macdonald addressed a message to the Pakistan CGS, (a) informing him that the Indian military authorities were considering the Pakistan counter-proposal regarding tactical readjustment and that this might take three or four days; and (b) expressing the hope that during this crucial period both sides would refrain from offensive or provocative actions. [*S/6710/Add. 5, 23 Oct. 1965, Report by Secretary-General on observance of cease-fire.*]

On 24 October General Macdonald was informed by the Director of Military Operations, Indian Army, that in view of the Secretary-General's intention to send a special Representative to the sub-continent (p. 404 above) on the withdrawal of armed personnel, the Chief of Army Staff felt that the whole matter of tactical readjustments should now await the arrival of the special Representative.[9] However, the Chief Officer did have some success in eliminating test-firing—in response to his approaches both sides agreed to ban test-firing within 10,000 yards of the front line.[10]

Although large-scale fighting had by now ceased, sporadic outbreaks of shooting continued to occur, especially in areas where there were 'conflicting views of the local commanders on both sides as to the positions occupied by the respective armies at the time of the cease-fire'.[11] In certain places—such as in the Sulaimanke–Fazilka sector—UNIPOM was successful in marking a 'no-patrolling' line, to keep local tensions down.[12] Originally this was limited to the firing of tank, anti-tank, and artillery pieces. The agreement was then extended to an arrangement that smaller weapons, including rifles and machine-guns, would not be fired without prior notification to the UN observers in the area.[13]

The Barbanwala–Ravi–Bedian Canal, in the Lahore–Amritsar sector,[14] continued to be particularly troublesome:

26. In early October agreement was reached that certain bunkers south of Dograi on the east bank of the BRB Canal would not be occupied by either party. This agreement was kept until approximately 14.00 hours West Pakistan time on 5 November, when Pakistan forces occupied the bunkers. This took place at a time when Indian forces had just rotated a battalion in the area. The Indian local command complained, and the observers attempted to persuade the Pakistan forces to move, but without success.

27. The Indian command agreed to refrain from action until 16.30 hours local time. At 15.20 hours the Lahore sector observer team arrived at the Canal. At 15.30 hours the Khasa observer team arrived at Dograi. They found small arms, mortar and anti-tank firing in progress. An Indian officer had been killed before their arrival. At 16.00 hours, whilst under fire, the Khasa team moved forward through Dograi, to the Canal, waved flags and shouted for the Lahore observer team. A temporary cease-fire was arranged to remove the Indian officer's body. At 17.05 hours the Pakistan forces opened fire, wounding an Indian soldier who was assisting in carrying the body. Despite the observers' strenuous efforts and the waving

[9] S/6710/Add. 6.   [10] Ibid. para. 3.   [11] S/6710/Add. 7, para. 6.
[12] Ibid. para. 22.   [13] S/6710/Add. 9, para. 2.   [14] See map, p. 478.
16

of blue flags, heavy firing then broke out, including tanks and artillery. The observer team was forced to take cover until about 17.30 hours, when they were able to withdraw.

28. At 18.15 hours UNIPOM headquarters negotiated by telephone a cease-fire on both sides as of 18.30 hours. Both sides agreed. At 18.30 Indian forces claimed they had ceased fire, and that Pakistan forces had not. UNIPOM headquarters in Lahore advised patience. By 18.45 hours both sides advised that firing had ceased. On 6 November, at 14.17 hours, the Khasa observer team advised that Pakistan forces had vacated the disputed bunkers. [S/6710/ Add. 8, 6 Nov. 1965.]

A gradual improvement in the holding of the cease-fire was thus attained, though on 4 December it was reported that UNIPOM had sent in disquieting reports about the desert area:

72. In appraising the situation in the desert area, the Chief Officer of UNIPOM considered that the present situation had arisen from the Indian determination to push Pakistan troops back to the international border and Pakistan's equally strong determination to retain the positions they had occupied. He concluded that effective cease-fire did not exist in this area and that military action would be likely to continue there. . . . [S/6710/Add. 11, 4 Dec. 1965.]

The situation deteriorated sufficiently for it to be necessary for General Macdonald to ask the two Chiefs of Staff to issue clear orders for the cessation of fire by all formations:

2. At a meeting in New Delhi on 15 December 1965, the Chief of Army Staff, Indian Army, informed the Chief Military Observer of UNMOGIP and the Chief Officer of UNIPOM of his intention to order a unilateral cessation of firing by all formations, effective 26 December at 17.00 hours, unless actually under attack.

3. On 22 December, the Chief of General Staff, Pakistan, agreed to take similar action. This was confirmed by a letter dated 24 December addressed to the Chief Officer of UNIPOM. In this letter the Chief of General Staff stated that Pakistan had had no intention in the past of disturbing the cease-fire except in self-defence and that, in view of the decision taken by the Chief of Indian Army Staff, he would issue fresh orders to his troops in order to re-emphasize his stand.

4. On the morning of 27 December the Chief Officer of UNIPOM sent messages to the Chief of Army Staff, Indian Army, and the Pakistan Chief of General Staff, respectively, to take note of the commitments made by both sides and to express confidence that the concurrent action taken by them would help to ensure observance of the cease-fire in the entire area of conflict, in keeping with the demand set forth in the Security Council resolutions 211 (1965), of 20 September and 214 (1965), of 5 November 1965.

5. However, reports received from observers in the UNIPOM area of operation indicated that as of 27 December Indian formations had not received the no-firing order. [S/6710/Add. 14, 30 Dec. 1965, Report of Secretary-General on observance of cease-fire.]

On 3 January the Indian Vice-Chief of Army Staff confirmed that Indian troops would not open fire unless actually attacked.[15]

The observers investigated not only complaints submitted to them, but also complaints transmitted to them for investigation by the Secretary-General. The Chief Officer made it clear, however, that in this latter function UNIPOM's effectiveness could only be very limited, because of the time-lag involved. The submission of complaints to the Secretary-General, with a request that they be circulated to the Security Council, was done largely for political purposes. But

[15] S/6710/Add. 15, para. 6.

if results in the field were desired, then 'investigation is much facilitated when complaints are submitted direct to the observers in the different sectors by the military headquarters in which they originated'.[16]

(b) Securing the withdrawal of armed personnel

The demand in resolution 211 for withdrawal of armed personnel was regarded by the Secretary-General as closely interwoven with, though distinct from, the achievement of a cease-fire. The difficulties which arose over whether the withdrawal order extended to irregular forces, and armed civilians, have been recounted above (pp. 449–50).

Pakistan sought to tie the question of withdrawals to the securing of a satisfactory long-term solution to the Kashmir problem. Accordingly, when the Secretary-General asked, on 21 September 1965, for plans and schedules for the troop withdrawals,[17] Pakistan replied:

You have asked for a plan and schedule for withdrawal of our troops from their present positions and you offer to send United Nations military observers to assist in the withdrawal. You would appreciate that no withdrawal can take place until it has been jointly agreed to by representatives of the two armed forces and a mutually accepted programme of withdrawal has been prepared. So long as such a programme has not been agreed to, withdrawal cannot start and so the United Nations observers cannot begin to perform their function of supervising the withdrawal.

In the meantime, I should like to state my Government's position on this question. You appear to be concentrating almost exclusively on making arrangements for withdrawal of troops and re-establishing the old cease-fire in Jammu and Kashmir. In our judgement, however, military disengagement should proceed concurrently with an honourable political settlement. In other words, it is imperative that we should evolve a self-executing arrangement and procedures that would ensure an honourable settlement of the Jammu and Kashmir dispute which is the basic cause of the present conflict. Without such an arrangement, it is hard to envisage an effective programme for the withdrawal of forces. [S/6715, Letter of 26 Sept. 1965 from representative of Pakistan to Secretary-General.]

To supervise the cease-fire and the withdrawals in the area outside Kashmir, UNIPOM observers were to be stationed at strategic points. The Secretary-General suggested:

According to tentative plans, the locations outside of Kashmir where observers might be most usefully stationed would be the following:

Indian side—headquarters: Jullundur; observer locations: Dehra Babananak, Dariwal, Amritsar, Ferozepore, Ganganagar, Bikaner, Gargariya.

Pakistan side—headquarters: Lahore; observer locations: Shakargarh, Narowal, Wahga, Kasur, Bahawalnagar, Bahalpur, Chor . . . [S/6699, para. 11.]

Pakistan and India were informed of the assistance available to them, and the Secretary-General also issued a detailed listing of the positions of both sides on the international border.[18]

However, on 14 October 1965 the Secretary-General had to report that

2. The withdrawals of all armed personnel foreseen in the Security Council resolutions 211 (1965) of 20 September and 214 (1965), of 27 September, have not taken place and there is no

[16] S/6710/Add. 16, para. 3.   [17] S/6699, para. 3.
[18] S/6719, paras. 6–8, & S/6719/Add. 1, para. 3.

present indication that they are likely to take place any time soon under present circumstances unless some new effort is made. . . .

4. On 13 October I addressed the following third message on the subject of withdrawal to the Prime Minister of India and the President of Pakistan . . . [in which I said]:

'Security Council resolution 211 (1965) of 20 September, in its paragraph 1, demanded that "a cease-fire should take effect on Wednesday, 22 September 1965, at 07.00 hours GMT" and called for a subsequent withdrawal of all armed personnel to the positions held by them before 5 August 1965'. Security Council resolution 214 (1965) of 27 September "in its last paragraph" calls upon the parties promptly to withdraw all armed personnel as necessary steps in the full implementation of the resolution of 20 September'. United Nations military observers with the function of ensuring supervision of the cease-fire and the withdrawal of all armed personnel are now stationed throughout the area of conflict, and the cease-fire which was accepted by both parties is becoming increasingly effective. I now therefore would like to renew my appeal to you to take the necessary steps to bring about the withdrawals called for by the Security Council resolutions.

'I would hope that each party might find it possible to formulate its own plan and schedule of withdrawal and that the respective time schedules might be co-ordinated with the assistance of United Nations military observers. If, however, this should not be considered feasible, I would suggest that appropriate military representatives of each side be brought together by and with an acceptable representative to be designated by me to meet either in the area or at United Nations Headquarters for the purpose of formulating an agreed withdrawal plan. . . .'
[S/6719/Add. 2, 14 Oct. 1965, Report by Secretary-General on compliance with Security Council res. 211 (1965).]

India accepted the suggestion contained in the last paragraph quoted above, but tied it to her preference for dealing with General Nimmo of UNMOGIP.[19] The Secretary-General replied:

. . . I appreciate the high regard you have for General Nimmo, which I share, and certainly by his long experience in the area he is very well qualified for such an assignment, I cannot, however, consider such an arrangemeht feasible. The task of supervising the observance of the cease-fire is an extremely difficult and demanding one and with an enlarged corps of observers, General Nimmo is more than fully occupied with this highly responsible and vital work. I take it for granted that the assignment in connexion with the withdrawals will be difficult, complex and prolonged and will require the full time of the United Nations official assigned to it. Moreover, . . . [we are agreed] that there should be no telescoping of the cease-fire and withdrawals into a single operation. I am quite convinced that it would be impossible for any one person to undertake responsibility for both of these efforts. This applies, of course, to General Macdonald as well as to General Nimmo.

In these circumstances, therefore, I have it in mind to designate a thoroughly experienced senior officer in the United Nations family to be my representative on the matter of withdrawals, to go to the area at an early date, to visit both capitals and to arrange for representatives of India and Pakistan to meet at some mutually agreed place, possibly near the front lines, to seek agreement on a plan and schedule for the withdrawals by both parties. . . .
[S/6719/Add. 3, 22 Oct. 1965.]

The Secretary-General named Major-General Sarmento of Brazil the Commander of UNEF; but as this did not prove acceptable to India, Brigadier-General Tulio Marambio was nominated instead. General Marambio held consultations with each side, and with the Chief Military Observer of UNMOGIP and the Chief Officer of UNIPOM.

[19] For India's views on the standing of UNIPOM, and her desire to extend UNMOGIP's activities, see above, pp. 445–6.

The increasing efficacy of the cease-fire facilitated his tasks, as did the adoption on 5 November of resolution 215 by the Security Council calling upon the parties to instruct their armed personnel to co-operate with the UN and cease all military activity. On 15 December the Secretary-General had notified the Security Council that the first three-month period of the cease-fire would elapse on 22 December, but that he proposed to accede to the Pakistani and Indian request that the UN observers should function beyond this period.

On 8 December it had been announced that the Prime Minister of India and the President of Pakistan had accepted the invitation of the government of the USSR to meet at Tashkent. On 10 January 1966, at Tashkent, an agreement was signed whereby all armed personnel of the two countries would be withdrawn not later than 25 February 1966 to the positions that they had held before 5 August 1965. General Marambio now acted on this foundation, and a series of joint military meetings was convened during January 1966 at UN operational headquarters in Lahore and Amritsar. On 29 January an agreement was signed by the two parties and by General Marambio. The text has been reproduced in Part 4 (pp. 334–337 above), as have the details of the ground procedures to be followed for disengagement and withdrawal. The text explains clearly UNIPOM's and UNMOGIP's role in this phase, during which both forces would withdraw to a distance of 1,000 yards from the line of actual control in specified areas, and within the next twenty-one days would remove and nullify all defences. All forces, paramilitary forces, and armed police who were on the wrong side of the international border and cease-fire line would then be withdrawn during a second phase, which was to be completed by 25 February 1966. Both phases were carried out on schedule.[20]

2. I may now report further that phase II of the withdrawals was completed on 20 February. I am informed that certificates of mine clearance and the dismantling of defence works have been exchanged at the sector and sub-sector levels and that sketches of unrecovered mines and unexploded bombs and shells were attached to the certificate. United Nations military observers are carrying out aerial and ground reconnaissance in order to confirm the conditions stated in the certificates. Whenever discrepancies are discovered, they are reported to the parties concerned.

3. Unless unforeseen delays occur owing to bad weather or other circumstances, the withdrawals are expected to be completed by the target date of 25 February 1966. At a meeting on 23 February with the military representatives of India and Pakistan, it was agreed that the main function of the United Nations India–Pakistan Observation Mission (UNIPOM) between 26 and 28 February, after the withdrawals are completed, will be to accompany teams of both armies working in 'recovered territory' to ensure that such areas shall be safe for re-occupation.

4. If expectations stated above are fulfilled, the responsibilities of General Tulio Marambio will come to an end on 28 February and his mission on withdrawals will be terminated on that date, as having been successfully completed.

5. On the same assumption, the task of UNIPOM along the International Frontier between India and West Pakistan also will have been successfully completed, and it will be possible to withdraw its personnel, close its headquarters, remove its installations and terminate the Mission. The Chief Officer of UNIPOM indicates that about one week will be required to bring in all observers and vehicles from outstations and that a further ten days would be

[20] See S/6719/Add. 5 & 12.

needed to repatriate observers and dismantle communications equipment. The air unit of UNIPOM will cease operations only after all observers have been brought in from outstations. It is my intention, therefore, provided the withdrawals are completed by 25 February, to have UNIPOM cease all functions as of 1 March 1966, and thereafter to disband it as quickly as possible, but in any event not later than 22 March. . . . [*S/6699/Add. 12, 23 Feb. 1966, Report by Secretary-General.*][21]

UNIPOM thus came to an end. It had successfully—though not without difficulties—helped achieve an effective cease-fire, and it played an indispensable role at the military level in bringing about the withdrawal of armed personnel to within their own borders. UNIPOM, like UNMOGIP, was not charged with finding a long-term solution to the problem of Kashmir[22]—this is a question which remains unresolved. It was assigned more immediate tasks and, under the direction of General Macdonald, carried them out with distinction.

[21] At the time of going to press only the mimeo. version of this document was available.

[22] For Pakistan's attempts to get the Security Council to deal with the broader question, and India's reaction thereto, see above.

13

ANNEXES

A. *Checklist of Documents*

SECURITY COUNCIL

1. RESOLUTIONS

209	4 Sept. 1965	
210	6 Sept. 1965	
211	20 Sept. 1965	*Resolutions and Decisions of the Security Council, 20th yr.*
214	27 Sept. 1965	
215	5 Nov. 1965	

2. REPORTS BY THE SECRETARY-GENERAL

S/6683	16 Sept. 1965	Prelim. Rep. on mission to India and Pakistan
S/6686	16 Sept. 1965	2nd Rep. on mission to India and Pakistan
S/6687	16 Sept. 1965	Rep. on military situation in area of conflict
S/6699/Add. 1–12	20 Sept.–15 Dec. 1965	
		Rep. on efforts to give effect to res. 210, 211, & 215.
S/6710/Add. 1–17	25 Sept. 1965–28 Jan. 1966	
		Rep. on observance of cease-fire under res. 211 of 20 Sept. 1965
S/6719/Add. 1–4	5 Oct.–25 Nov. 1965	
		Rep. on compliance with withdrawal provisions of res. 211 of 20 Sept. 1965
S/6888	9 Nov. 1965	Rep. on an aspect of procedures employed in observing and reporting on cease-fire

3. COMMUNICATIONS FROM PAKISTAN RELATING TO UNIPOM

S/6715	26 Sept. 1965	S/6839	27 Oct. 1965
S/6751	5 Oct. 1965	S/6845	29 Oct. 1965
S/6757	7 Oct. 1965	S/6858	1 Nov. 1965
S/6804	18 Oct. 1965	S/6878	5 Nov. 1965
S/6821	22 Oct. 1965	S/6920	12 Nov. 1965

4. COMMUNICATIONS FROM INDIA RELATING TO UNIPOM

S/6720	28 Sept. 1965	S/6761	8 Oct. 1965
S/6735	1 Oct. 1965	S/6762	8 Oct. 1965
S/6742	4 Oct. 1965	S/6810	19 Oct. 1965
S/6747	5 Oct. 1965	S/6833	26 Oct. 1965
S/6756	7 Oct. 1965		

5. COMMUNICATIONS FROM THE SECRETARY-GENERAL TO INDIA AND PAKISTAN RELATING TO UNIPOM

S/6738	2 Oct. 1965	S/6782	13 Oct. 1965

6. DEBATES IN SECURITY COUNCIL

SCOR, 20th yr, mtgs 1237–40, 1242, 1247–8, 1250–1

Note: For details of Indian and Pakistani claims of breaches of the cease-fire, see Part A, Annex A, above, p. 415–17.

B. *Bibliography*

Andronov, I. Kashmir Conflict: Some Antecedents. *New Times*, Oct. 1965.

Breaking the Rules. *Economist*, Sept. 1965.

Brockway, Fenner. Indo-Pakistani Clash. *Eastern World*, Oct. 1965.

Brumberg, Abraham. The Cold Wind from Moscow: Detente Illusions Die Hard. *Reporter*, Oct. 1965.

Harris, Richard. The Indo-Pakistan Conflict: The Communist Attitude. *Listener*, Sept. 1965.

How the United Nations Came Back to Life. *US News and World Report*, Oct. 1965.

International Studies, July–Oct. 1966. Special issue: India's Relations with Pakistan.

Martin, Kingsley. The Kashmir crisis: Heading for War? *New Statesman*, Sept. 1965.

Olver, A. S. B. India, Pakistan and Kashmir. *World Today*, Oct. 1965.

Pakistan: Why Ayub Did It. *Economist*, Sept. 1965.

Streiff, Eric. Fluctuating Tensions between India and Pakistan. *Swiss Review of World Affairs*, Jan. 1966.

Taylor, Edmund. Tortured Kashmir: The Smoke and the Fire. *Reporter*, Nov. 1965.

Thanks for Muffing It. *Economist*, Sept. 1965.

The Road to Peace. *Economist*, Sept. 1965.

U.N. Puts Its Weight behind Kashmir Truce. *Business Week*, Oct. 1965.

Weill-Tuckermann, Anne. Kashmir: The UN's Perilous Chance. *Nation*, Sept. 1965.

Wint, Guy. The Indo-Pakistan Conflict: British Feelings. *Listener*, Sept. 1965.

Woodcock, George. Kutch and Kashmir: How the War Started. *Commonwealth*, Oct. 1965.

MAPS

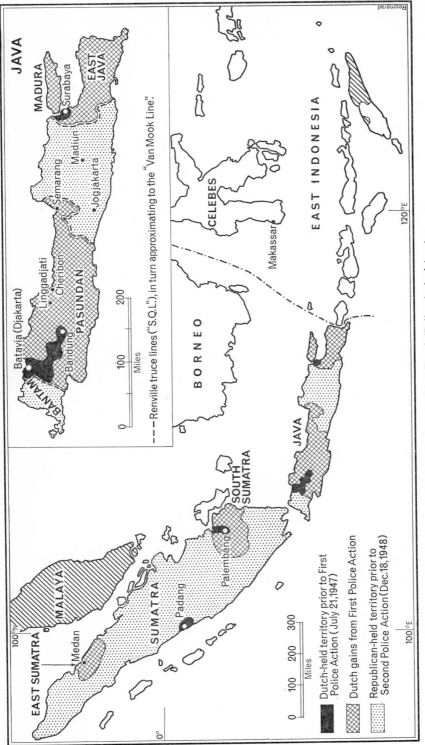

1. Indonesia after the First Dutch 'Police Action' (p. 3)
Based on the map appearing at p. 46 of Alastair Taylor's
Indonesian Independence and the United Nations (1960), published by Stevens & Sons

- - - Renville truce lines ("S.Q.L."), in turn approximating to the "Van Mook Line".

Dutch-held territory prior to First Police Action (July 21,1947)

Dutch gains from First Police Action

Republican-held territory prior to Second Police Action(Dec.18,1948)

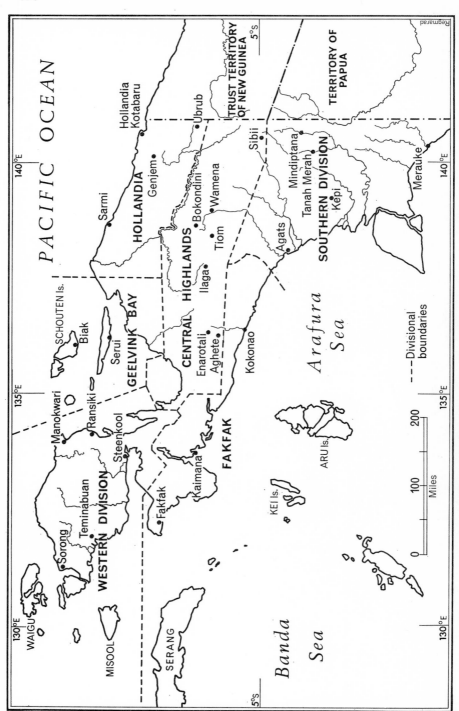

2. West Irian (West New Guinea) (p. 93)

Based on UN, *The United Nations in West New Guinea* (1962), pp. 16, 17

3. Korea: Provincial Boundaries in 1945 (p. 153)
Based on *YBUN, 1952*, p. 213

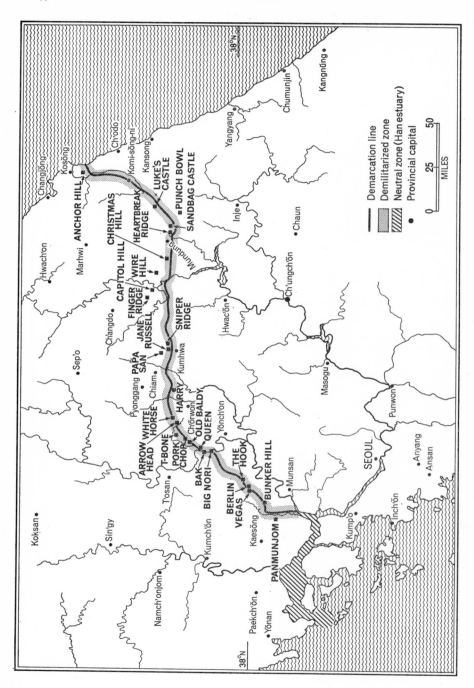

4. Korea: Detailed Area of Neutral Zone (p. 153)
Based on *YBUN, 1953*, p. 112

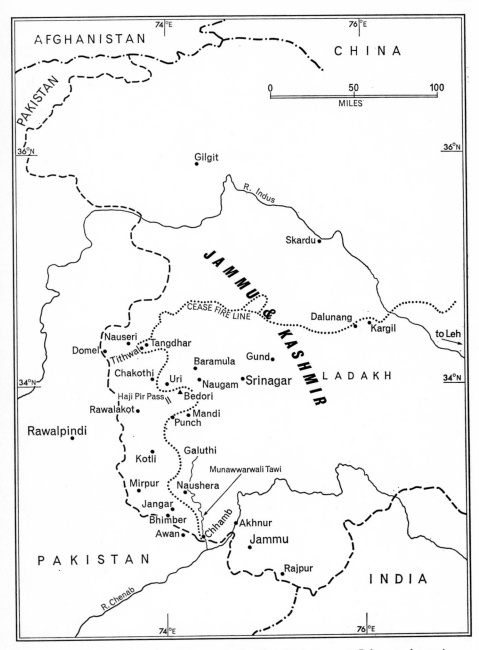

5. The Cease-Fire Line agreed upon in the Karachi Agreement, July 1949 (p. 315)
Based on *S/6651*, ann. (*SCOR*, 20th yr, suppl. June–Sept. 1965)

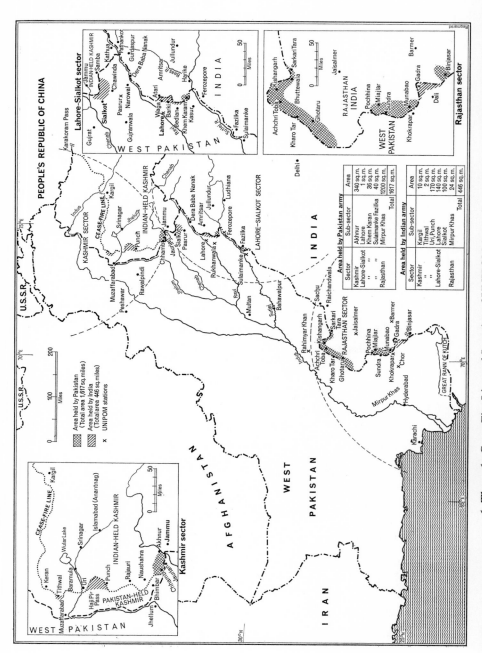

6. The 1965 Cease–Fire Line and Location of UNIPOM (p. 421)

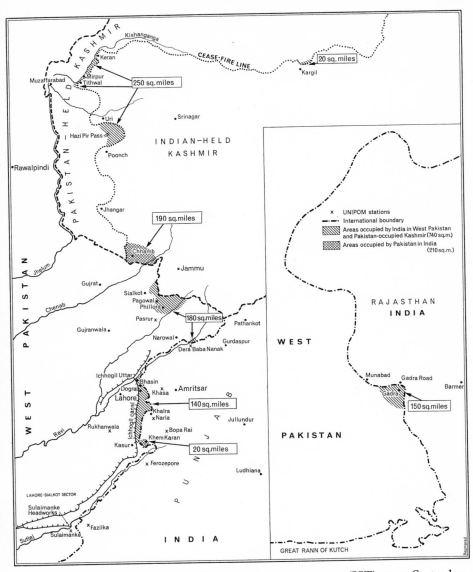

7. Areas Occupied by Indian and Pakistani armies as at 3.30 a.m. (IST) on 23 September
1965, and Location of UNIPOM (p. 421)
Based on Indian sources.

INDEX

Abdoh, Djalal, 123, 124, 126, 131, 132, 141; *see also* UN Administrator in West Irian

Abdullah, Sheikh, 316, 318, 374, 377, 385

Additional Measures Committee, for UN action in Korea, 168, 180

Afghanistan, 316

Amritsar, 460, 463, 467

Angle, Brig. H., 339, 360

Argentina, 323

Armistice, Korean, 290–308; negotiations, 169, 170–2, 183, 222, 265–90

Australia: position on Indonesian claims to independence, 8, 28; represented on Consular Commission, 35, 58; member of GOC, 20, 35; views on role of GOC and Consular Commission for Indonesia, 22; recognizes Indonesia *de facto*, 28; makes proposals on GOC with USA, 42; nominated to UNTCOK, 156, 157; agreement with South Korea, 206, 248–9; participates in UNMOGIP, 358

Azad Kashmir, 341

Bacteriological warfare, 170

Bakshi, Ghulam Mohammed, 377

Bambanwala–Ravi–Bedian Canal, 460, 463

Bandung Federal Conference, May 1948, 14, 43, 69–70

Batavia, 9, 10, 19, 34, 46, 47, 50, 55, 58, 60, 61, 62, 74; *see also* Djakarta

Beel, Louis, 5

Belgium: member of GOC, 20, 35; represented on Consular Commission, 35; agreement with USA re Korea, 205–6; represented on UNCIP, 323; participates in UNMOGIP, 358

Bevin, Ernest, 4

Borneo, 27, 34, 37, 87

Brazil: views on functions of GOC and Consular Commission for Indonesia, 20–1; provides military observers for UN in West Irian, 125

Bunche, Ralph, 363, 390

Bunker, Ellsworth, 99, 100

Byelorussian Soviet Socialist Republic, 156, 256

Cairo Conference, Nov. 1943, 153

Canada: provides supporting aircraft and aircrew for UNSF, 125; nominated to UNTCOK, 156, 157; participates in UNMOGIP, 358

Certain Expenses of the United Nations, 177, 178 n.12

Ceylon, provides military observers for UN in West Irian, 125

Chile, 358

China, Nationalist: position on Indonesian claims to independence, 8; represented on Consular Commission for Indonesia, 35, 58; approves Indonesia–Netherlands Agreement on West Irian, 113; joint statement on Korea after Cairo Conference, Nov. 1943, 153; nominated to UNTCOK, 156; right to sit on Security Council unchallenged, 164; applicability of laws of war, 194; offer of troops for Korea rejected, 197; participation in Korean war urged by MacArthur, 202, 260; supports Secretary-General's interpretation on UNIPOM, 435

China, People's Republic of: enters Korean war, 167, 180, 258–60; denounces US bombing, 180, 227–9; urges compulsory return of prisoners of war, 183–7; Korean Armistice negotiations, 183, 265–90; applicability of Geneva Conventions, 193; relations with UN, 224, 226–31; Korean Armistice text, 290–308

Christison, Lt.-Gen. Sir Philip, 4

Clark, Gen. Mark, 186, 196, 202, 280, 302, 308

Colombia, 323

Committee of Good Offices, *see* UN Committee of Good Offices in Indonesia (GOC)

Congo (Léopoldville), UN operation in, 113, 122, 123, 125, 128

Consular Commission, *see* UN Consular Commission in Indonesia (UNCC)

Critchley, T. K., 52, 55, 70

Curaçao, 6, 7

Czechoslovakia, 156, 256, 323

Delhi, 356, 359

Delvoie, Lt.-Gen. Maurice, 327, 328, 338, 354, 360

Demilitarized zones, *see* Zones, demilitarized

Denmark, 358

Dixon, Sir Owen, 342, 376, 377, 388; *see also* UN Representative for India and Pakistan

Djakarta, 3; *see also* Batavia

Drees, W., 5

duBois, C., 43, 70

Dulles, Alan, 155, 281

Egypt, 28, 161, 162–3, 164, 256

Eisenhower, Dwight, D., 281

El Salvador, 150

Entezam, N., 167, 181

Expenses Case, see *Certain Expenses of the United Nations*

Fawzi, Mahmoud, 162

Fedorenko, N. T., 431

Finland, 358